Reach For The Stars

Helping Yourself
with
Personal Astrology

Reach For The Stars

Helping Yourself with Personal Astrology

Kenneth Babbin

Walter Oleksy

Parker Publishing Company, Inc.
West Nyack, New York

Library of Congress Cataloging in Publication Data

Babbin, Kenneth
    Reach for the stars.

    Bibliography: p.
    1. Astrology. I. Oleksy, Walter G.
joint author. II. Title.
BF1708.1.B32   133.5   79-19644
ISBN 0-13-753251-2

Printed in the United States of America

Astrology—
Your Lifeline to
Success and Happiness

J.P. Morgan, one of the richest men in the world, said that millionaires do not use astrology, but *billionaires* do!

Many successful business men today use astrology to predict stock market trends and to guide them in making other very important financial decisions.

It stands to reason that the better you know yourself, and other people and influences on you, the better your chances will be of finding career and financial success, personal happiness, and achieving inner satisfaction and peace.

But *how* can you get to know yourself and others you live or work with? One *exceptionally accurate* and *proven method* which can help you to discover your qualities, strengths, weaknesses, and potential for success and happiness is astrology.

Following the simple guidelines in this book, you can *quickly* and *easily* learn how to construct a birth chart, for yourself and others—your boss, co-workers, employees, mate, friends, relatives, even your children.

Then you will learn how to analyze a chart, to draw a wealth of information out of the placements of the planets that will tell you more about yourself and others than you ever thought possible.

Astrology is a *science* and an *art* and does not conflict in any way with the beliefs of the world's major religions. It should be considered to be another useful tool for living which can help us to lead richer lives and understand ourselves better.

Even the dictionary describes astrology as an art or science, with no mention of religious beliefs involved. It should be remembered that some of the Catholic popes were enthusiastic followers of astrology. (More on this will be discussed in Chapter 1.)

Astrology can be a very complex subject, but not in this book, which is perhaps the most direct and easy-to-follow guide to a complete understanding of astrology ever written. The book shows you, step-by-step and in very simple language, all you need to know about astrology to make it work for you every day in your personal and professional life.

Another valuable tool this book provides is a comprehensive ephemeris, a table of where the planets were positioned in the heavens, covering 68 years from 1922 to 1990. By locating your planets in the ephemeris you can most accurately draw up a birth chart that can reveal many secrets and guidelines which can help you in your life and work. Few guides to astrology offer a self-contained ephemeris as this book does.

The knowledge astrology can bring you is almost as varied as the number of stars in the heavens. By knowing and analyzing your birth chart, you can learn, among other important things....

* *What careers you are best suited for* (see Chapters 5, 11, 12, and 13.)
* *Whether you have the qualities to go into business for yourself, or whether you would be happier and more successful working within an organization* (see Chapter 11.)
* *How you can choose the most compatible business or marriage partner* (see Chapters 4 and 13.)
* *How you can discover your social, business or sales talents* (see Chapters 8, 11, 12, and 13.)
* *Whether you are an idea person and a self-starter, or are stronger in following-through on others' programs* (see Chapter 5.)
* *How you can overcome shortcomings in your nature, or quirks in your personality* (see Chapters 12 and 13.)
* *How you can find what your real needs are, in order to become more content and happy* (see Chapter 13.)
* *Where your inner powers come from and how you can make them work to your best advantage* (see Chapters 11 and 12.)
* *How you can predict or anticipate coming trends or challenges in your life and prepare for them* (see Chapter 14.)

Regarding your career or work, there are several astrological indicators that tell you what your natural talents are. They suggest fields in which you are likely to be especially successful, lucky, and satisfied.

Astrology also can teach you a lot about yourself and other people. It can tell you why you get along better with some people than others, or how you can "tune in" better to people you want to influence.

By following the easy-to-understand system of learning astrology in this book, you will soon discover the fuller depths of your nature and abilities, your strengths and weaknesses—and those of others—which can guide you in making decisions dealing with other people.

You may have read general descriptions of your birth sign in daily newspaper horoscopes and found that they did not always fit you. It may have made you question the accuracy of astrology. But you birth sign is just one piece of the astrology puzzle that describes your character. Analyzing your whole birth chart can tell you a great deal more about yourself.

Astrology can reach deep into your personal life and help you to make decisions as to where and how to live that will bring *more harmony and satisfaction* into your everyday life. Your birth chart reveals what you are looking for in a close friend or lover, how you respond to people, and how other people see you.

Romantically, for example, Sagittarians are happy-go-lucky and love 'em and leave 'em. A Sagittarius can't stand being tied down, to one person or place, so he or she is a hard fish to catch. A Capricorn, on the other hand, falls hard for one person. He or she does not usually fall in love easily or quickly, but once in love, is very loyal to that person.

All of these birth sign qualities, regarding not only friendship and love, but also all the other aspects of life, are strongly modified by the condition of the chart as a whole. You have to learn about your complete birth chart if you really want to benefit from what astrology can offer you. The simplified system of building and analyzing a birth chart offered in this book will soon have you casting horoscopes and learning an infinite amount of information about yourself and others.

The planets are like magnets, having certain influences or "pull" over you. Every day the different interactions of the "magnetic" forces in the solar system affect us differently because the positions of the planets are always changing. Sometimes planets line up in a way that seems to create problems for us. At other times, the alignment of the planets is more favorable and helps to bring forth things we enjoy.

Following the daily movements of the planets, you can go *with* the flow of life instead of against it. Astrology can give you *an advance knowledge* or warning about things that are coming up, so you can become more aware of what is going on now and what tomorrow may bring. This mental knowledge opens up more possibilities to think about what is going on in your life from new and sometimes clearer points of view.

Though you were born with certain "magnetic" influences because of the positions of the planets at the time and place of your birth, you are not necessarily stuck with them. It is as if you were born with a hand of cards dealt to you. The cards you were dealt may stay with you for the rest of your life, and you can't change your hand, but you can learn how to play your cards much, much better.

Astrology can show you *how to work with your energies* so that you can turn a flaw into a virtue, a weakness into a strength, a downer into an upper.

Every "problem" that is shown in your birth chart, every weakness, can be turned into a strength if you recognize it, accept it, and learn how to use it properly. Astrology is especially good at doing this because it is an *extremely accurate* way of diagnosing personal traits.

When problems come up in your life, whether they involve a love affair, career indecision or dissatisfaction, or any number of other things including the blue blahs for no particular reason, astrology can be your best friend. It can tell you when and why different problem periods will be coming, how to get through them, and when they will end.

Even in good times, astrology can show you *how to have more fun and enjoy life more.* It also can tell you *how to take full advantage of opportunities.*

Let astrology into your life. See how much you learn about yourself. Learn from this book the simplest way to cast a *complete* birth chart, using *the same basic methods used by professional astrologers.*

REACH FOR THE STARS. They are up there in the sky and they are within you.

As you learn more about astrology, it will help you to bring the level of your life up out of the daily earthly grind and into *a higher perspective* where you can look down and have a clearer view of your life and the lives of the people around you.

Kenneth Babbin
Walter Oleksy

Contents

Living Under the Stars—Astrology's Past, Present, and Future

THE OLDEST SCIENCE

It is no accident that astrology is called "the oldest science." Its origin goes back to the dawn of time, to the creation of the Sun and Earth and the other planets.

Earliest man hunted for his food, sought a place of comfort and safety to live, looked up into a night sky full of stars and wondered. Soon he began to notice that there was a pattern to the heavens. For periods of time, stars could be found in about the same place each night. Then after more time, some of these "stars" (the planets) moved into different positions.

It wasn't long before man began to notice that the Sun and Moon seemed to have something to do with sunlight and darkness, warmth and cold, rain and snow. The more intelligent even noted that the shape of the Moon corresponded with their emotions and moods.

As man the hunter was joined by man the gatherer, primitive farmers began to depend on the regularity of the Sun to bring seasons when crops could grow best. The New Moon of Spring, they discovered, was the ideal time to plant seeds. The Full Moon of Autumn was found to be the right time to harvest the crops. Taking a tip from the animals around them, man learned that there also were ideal seasons for mating. (Even a young cave man's fancy turned to thoughts of love in Springtime.)

Long before he learned to write, man drew pictures to record his knowledge for his sons and daughters who would trod the Earth after him. He made crude carvings in caves that to him represented certain planets, each associated with some trait, such as a bringer of sunlight or rain.

Ancient civilizations unearthed around the globe over the centuries have revealed earlier man's use of astrology in astonishingly modern ways. Time-telling instruments carved in stone from the British Isles to Central and South America have left record that earlier civilizations studied the heavens in some form of astrology.

THE FIRST HOROSCOPE

The first known horoscope was cast in 2767 B.C. by Imhotep, an architect who designed some of the great pyramids in Egypt which many believe were built for mystical, if not astrological, reasons.

Some modern researchers suggest that astrology actually was brought to our planet eons ago by visitors from outer space. These visitors may have built, or shown others how to build, the pyramids and other marvels of centuries past which were used as observatories or calendar instruments to monitor the movements of the planets and stars.

Astrology is defined as "the ancient art or science of divining the fate and future of human beings from indications given by the positions of the stars and other heavenly bodies." It had its origin in the study of astronomy and is first found in a developed form among the ancient Babylonians.

Babylonian priests determined the will of the gods by two chief methods. One was inspection of the liver of a sacrificial animal, the other was astrology, basing predictions on a theory of a divine government of the world. They traced all of man's life, fortunes, and happiness, as well as the fertility of the soil, the light and warmth of the Sun, the havoc and damage from violent storms, all to the phenomena in the heavens. This led the Babylonians to conclude that the gods had their seats in the heavens.

Victories or defeats in war, bountiful harvests or crop failures, even the rise and fall of kings, were attached to the movements of the Moon, Sun, and planets. If an army was victorious under a New Moon on a cloudy day, the sign was looked upon as being a good omen and a favorable one in which to enter battle next time. On the other hand, a New Moon coming earlier than expected was considered to be a bad omen, warning of defeat in battle, since it was believed that anything premature would suggest an unfavorable outcome.

The Babylonians' astrology was limiting in at least one major way. In the movements and positions of the planets, astrologers were concerned only with the national welfare and the person of the king. It was believed that if the king stood in good favor with the gods, the fortunes of the kingdom and everyone in it would prosper. Personal astrology, to help or study individuals, did not come until much later.

GREEK ASTROLOGY

Astrology spread to Greece during the middle of the 4th Century B.C., where it became even more strongly linked with the gods. Plato maintained that the planets were twelve heavenly gods, and the traits attributed to them correspond remarkably to those assigned by modern astrology.

Under the Greeks, the scope of astrology spread into most of the known sciences: botany, chemistry, zoology, mineralogy, anatomy, and medicine. Through study of astrology as applied to the natural sciences, the Greeks sought to learn what the future had in store.

Astrology also led to assigning the days of the week to the planets. Sunday was named after the Sun's day, Monday after the Moon's day, Tuesday after Tiw the god of war, Wednesday after Mercury or the god Woden, Thursday after Jupiter or the god Thor, Friday after Venus or the love goddess Friga, and Saturday was Saturn's day.

Few men among the highly civilized Greeks held positions of greater esteem than the astrologers. Aristotle taught that the stars have a life force that rules all power on Earth. Astrology's influence on Greek daily life was so strong that it carried importantly into the medical practice of the day. Even Hippocrates, the father of medicine, practiced astrology in treating patients. (Some doctors in our present time are of the same opinion, that before conducting any surgery on a patient, his horoscope should be consulted.)

ROMAN ASTROLOGY

Alexander the Great's invasions helped spread Greek astrology over most of the known world. It reached Rome before the start of the Christian era. Scholars find many astrological references throughout the Bible, perhaps the most conspicuous being the apostle Matthew's recording that after the birth of Jesus, three astrologers from the East arrived to honor the Christ child. Many other Biblical passages tend to point out how strongly the early Christians believed that the heavenly bodies greatly influenced man.

Astrology reached a new height of practice among the Romans, led by their first emperor, Caesar Augustus, who began the Roman practice of having an astrologer assigned to each emperor. The monarch's personal astrologer was always a seer of great power and influence.

Through the centuries, astrology has gone through cycles of being enthusiastically supported by the different organized religions, depending on personal beliefs of the religious leaders, and whether they thought that a belief in astrology was a threat to their own influence.

Many of the popes had personal astrologers. Pope Urban VIII was himself an astrologer. Pope Paul III also was very interested in astrology.

Down through the ages, many faithful religious people, Catholics and Protestants, have been persecuted or executed for their belief in astrology, which they insisted did not conflict with their religious faith. This persecution persisted into our own country's early years, most notably in the Salem witch trials when those who practiced astrology were called sorcerers and burned at the stake.

A TOOL OF LIVING

Astrology today is officially disregarded or frowned upon as a superstition by much of organized religion, although many highly respected churchmen privately are believers in astrology. However, it has become more evident lately among learned church leaders and the religious of all faiths that astrology is not a threat to any religion. It need not be considered a religion in itself; it can be used as another tool of living that we can accept or reject, not interfering with our religious beliefs. Astrology can take its place among philosophy, psychology, yoga, and other guides and systems of thought to help us better understand ourselves and others.

Astronomers and other scientists—once among the strongest practitioners of astrology—began rejecting astrology in the 18th Century, claiming it was not founded in science. The argument continues to this day. Several modern studies are currently underway, using sophisticated computer techniques, in attempts to prove once and for all that astrology is valid. Whether the studies succeed or not, it is a fair bet that, at least among hardened skeptics, astrology still will not gain its deserved place as a respected science.

Ironically, modern Western society is perhaps the only major civilization since the dawn of history that has not officially recognized the accuracy of astrology. Despite this, astrology has played an important part in guiding the destinies of many nations and great men, as recently as the founding of our own country.

So strongly did Thomas Jefferson and Benjamin Franklin believe in astrology that they insisted that the Declaration of Independence giving birth to our nation be signed early on the morning of July 4, 1776. They calculated that to be the best astrological moment for a favorable future for America.

NEW RENAISSANCE IN ASTROLOGY

Currently, astrology is on the brink of what could be its greatest and widest acceptance. People of all ages, from all walks of life and countries, are now investigating astrology as a source for self-awareness. Its widespread popularity is very evident in the fact that most newspapers and many magazines publish regular columns on astrology, and daily horoscopes are often given over radio and television programs. Doctors, psychiatrists, lawyers, even stock brokers are known to consult astrology before making important decisions.

With the "dawning of the Age of Aquarius," the world leaves a 2,000 year period of achievement but of awesome wars and great injustices. We are entering an Aquarian era of brotherhood, concern for our fellow man, our world and our universe, when there will be justice and equality for everyone, men and women.

Uranus, the planet which rules Aquarius, is the planet of astrology, which forecasts a new and even more influential place for astrology in our lives.

Astrology at a Glance

*A quick look at what you need to know in
order to cast a horoscope, and to understand
what your birth chart is trying to tell you*

In this book, you will be introduced to all of the elements that make up the basic level of the "real" astrology—the kind of approach that professional astrologers use. In some cases, while you are learning how to cast the chart, you will be shown a simplified version of the techniques that astrologers use.

After you have mastered the simple versions of these techniques, you will be shown how to add the extra refinements that astrologers use in order to achieve greater accuracy.

In many cases, if you are doing charts just for fun, you may want to stick with the more simple methods, since they are easier to use.

The authors' experience has been that many would-be students of astrology are scared away from getting into casting charts because they are only shown the complicated "official method," which can look pretty scary to a novice. Then they are expected to "swallow it all in one gulp."

We have divided these techniques into two parts—the basic part and the advanced part.

This is sort of like learning to drive on a car with automatic transmission, then after you have mastered that, learning how to use a stick shift. That is easier than trying to learn "The Rules of the Road" and learn to drive stick shift all at the same time.

Stretching the comparison a little farther, the beginning driver can become quite good at basic driving before he decides that he wants to learn how to shift the gears himself, or that he wants to learn to drive the kind of vehicle that requires this extra ability.

The beginning astrologer can go pretty far in astrology using only the basics before he decides to look into the huge warehouse of advanced techniques that are used by experienced astrologers.

We recommend that you master the basics before you try to move on to the refinements. This book is an introduction to the "real" astrology of casting and reading a complete chart. Even if you know nothing about astrology now, by the time you finish this book, and cast a few charts just to get in practice, you will have learned the language of astrology.

You will be able to understand intermediate-level astrology classes and books. You will be able to speak the impressive-sounding jargon of houses, planets, signs, aspects, rulerships, and ascendants.

Perhaps best of all, you will be able to meet a member of the opposite sex at a party and invite her home so you can cast her chart, analyze her character, and tell her with whom she is romantically compatible.

Now let's take a look at the different factors that the astrologers use to figure out your character, learn your past, and predict your future.

Astrology Can "Work"

Since most of us were reared believing either in a conservative religion or a skeptical scientific attitude, we have to stretch our imaginations at first, in order to accept the possibility that astrology might "work."

If you open your mind long enough to give astrology a chance, you will see that it works with amazing accuracy. As you become more expert in astrology, you will be able to understand the inner motivations of yourself and your friends or business associates. You will be able to predict trends and events in your life and the lives of others. You will be able to get a pretty good idea of "what's on the menu," what's coming up for you, before it happens.

Be Prepared for Challenges

You will be able to predict when difficult periods are coming up, and you will know in which areas the problems will focus, and what you will have to do, what you will have to work on, if you want to confront the challenges in your life in the most direct and efficient way.

There is no way to avoid having problems and challenges in life, but astrology can show you where your own individual challenges really lie, and how you are equipped to meet them, as well as different areas in which you are probably fooling yourself about what you need or want, and how you are really equipped to go about getting it.

Have You Lived Before?

Most astrologers believe in reincarnation. They believe that the soul does not die when the body dies, but that the soul then leaves the body, travels in other realms, and later returns again to enter a new body and have new experiences on Earth.

They believe that the soul picks its own birth chart by deciding exactly when and where it will be reborn. They maintain that the soul picks the people (the souls) that it wants to have for parents in this lifetime, and that these are often people that the soul has known before, in other lifetimes. As impossible as it sounds, the soul that is now incarnated as your father may have been your son in your last life.

However, astrology can stand on its own as a science with or without a belief in reincarnation.

The Power of the Planets

The planets are like a big computer that spins out the different vibrations of energy that influence life on Earth. Everyone knows that the Moon influences the tides on Earth, and farmers have known for thousands of years that the phases of the Moon influence the growth and life of plants. The 28-day human menstrual cycle also corresponds to the 28-day cycle of the Moon. The motions of the planets even create such important things as the seasons on Earth, and the mating and migrating seasons of animals.

If the planets have such a strong effect on seasons, tides, and the lives of plants and animals, it seems logical that they might also have a strong effect on the lives of humans. Despite our spiritual and mental achievements, the bodies that we are equipped with are really the same kinds of bodies that animals have, and they respond to the forces of nature as all physical things do.

When You Truly Came to Life

Just as the soul supposedly picks its own parents, so it picks the moment of birth when the planets are "charging" the place of birth with the kind of energy that the soul wants to receive as it begins its new life on Earth. Astrologically, your first breath is considered to be your first act as a separate, independent being in this life.

This first breath is considered to be the moment when you, as an individual, "plugged into" the energy of the physical universe. That is why it is so important to know your exact time of birth. Some of the "wheels" in the computer of the solar system spin very quickly, and even the difference of a few minutes can sometimes mean the difference between a temperament that is fiery, extroverted, and enthusiastic (Aries on the ascendant), or one that is quiet, introverted, sympathetic, and solitary, like a monk (Pisces on the ascendant).

The Sun Sign

The first thing that most people think about in astrology (and for some people, it is the only thing) is the Sun sign. The Sun sign is what people refer to when they say "I am a Virgo" or "I am a Sagittarius."

Your Sun sign is determined by your date of birth. Astrologically, the year begins on the first day of Spring, around March 20. That is when the Sun leaves the last sign of the Zodiac, Pisces, and enters the first sign of the Zodiac, Aries.

The Sun enters Aries at a slightly different time each year. Sometimes the Sun enters Aries on March 20, sometimes on March 21.

In order to know the exact time when the Sun enters Aries, and when it enters the other signs, astrologers use an ephemeris, which is a book that lists exactly where the planets are or were in the Zodiac each day. Modern science has made it possible to buy an ephemeris which accurately predicts the planets' positions for many years into the future.

As a beginner, you will start by working with an ephemeris in this book that shows where the Sun, Moon, and other planets were in the Zodiac when you were born.

Now let's take a quick look at the rest of the book and see how it presents what you will need to know in order to unlock the secrets hidden within your chart.

What the Zodiac Is

One of the first things you will need to know is what the Zodiac is. Basically, the Zodiac is an imaginary belt in the sky around the Earth. As the planets travel around within this belt, we keep track of where they are by noticing which stars they are near.

We can do this because the stars do not move. Actually, they do move, but if you don't have a very sophisticated telescope, chances are that you could never detect much movement among the stars, even if you were to watch for a thousand years. The constellations of the Big Dipper, the Little Dipper, and Taurus the Bull look the same today from where you look at the star-filled sky as they did when Cleopatra gazed at them from her barge on the Nile. So you can see that the stars offer a fairly stable backdrop for keeping track of the wandering planets.

The 12 Signs of the Zodiac

The Zodiac is divided into 12 equal parts, and each of these parts is a sign and has its own special qualities. The Zodiac is described in more detail in Chapter 3.

The Groups of Signs

Chapter 4 explains the groups of signs in the Zodiac—how they are similar and different, and how they get along with each other. The ancient astrologers thought that everything on Earth was made up of four "elements"—Fire, Earth, Air, and Water.

Of the 12 signs of the Zodiac, three signs are ruled by each of the four elements. The three Fire signs, for instance, are Aries, Leo, and Sagittarius. People born under these three signs have fiery tempers, strong egos, and love action and excitement. People born under the three Earth signs—Taurus, Virgo, and Capricorn—on the other hand, want peace, prosperity, security, and practicality. They feel solid and stable, like the Earth we stand on.

Fire people feel forceful, hot, exciting, and excitable. They can spread their enthusiasm or their anger like the spark that starts a forest fire. Fire people tend to see Earth people as being a little bit on the dull side, like clumps of Earth that sort of sit there and don't do much.

Earth people tend to see Fire-sign people as being rowdy, volatile, over-exciteable troublemakers who rock the boat too much. For these reasons, Earth and Fire people are theoretically incompatible. That is a generality, of course, but people do tend to hang out with friends of compatible signs.

The other sign-grouping system is the "types" of signs—Cardinal, Fixed, and Mutable. The four Cardinal signs are the starters, the four Fixed signs are the finishers, and the four Mutable signs are the adjusters.

Whatever sign you are, you are either Cardinal, Fixed, or Mutable, and you are either Fire, Earth, Air, or Water. Aries, for instance, is Cardinal Fire. Taurus is Fixed Earth. Gemini is Mutable Air. (Don't worry if that doesn't make much sense to you yet. It will when you read Chapter 4.)

Qualities of the Signs

Chapter 5 outlines the qualities of the 12 signs. Look up your Sun sign in Chapter 5 and see how closely you fit the description of your Sun sign. Some people will fit the description to a tee, while others will not. If you don't fit the description of your Sun sign, that is because other factors in your chart modify the qualities of your Sun.

If your Sun, Moon, Mercury, and Mars are all in Virgo, for instance, then you will probably fit the description of Virgo pretty well. If your Sun is in Virgo but your Moon, Mercury, Mars, and Venus are in Sagittarius, then you might not be a very typical Virgo.

Character Traits

Chapter 5 explains the traits that you can expect to find in anyone born under each sign. Even if someone doesn't seem to show all of the qualities of their sign, those qualities are in there somewhere. Sometimes Sun sign qualities are easy to spot, and sometimes you have to look more closely at the chart.

The Chapter 5 description of Aries will apply to you if you have Sun in Aries or Ascendant in Aries. It will even apply, to some extent, if you have any group of planets in Aries. The descriptions in this chapter are especially written to describe the nature of the Sun in each sign, but they are also general descriptions of the natural qualities of each sign.

The Planets and Mythology

Chapter 6 introduces us to the planets. In astrology, we often call the Sun and the Moon "planets" because "planet" means "wanderer," and the Sun and Moon appear to wander around the sky just as the other planets do. The Sun and Moon are very important in astrology because they are the "luminaries" or "givers of light."

Each planet bears the name of one of the gods or goddesses of ancient mythology, and has the same qualities as that god or goddess. In fact, the ancients probably invented their gods in order to fit the qualities of the planets. Some of the ancient myths are probably romanticized versions of things that the planets did—eclipses, explosions, changes in orbit, falling into the Sun, etc.

The Planets and Human Energy

Each planet rules an aspect of human energy. Mars is the aggressive energy, Mercury the mental energy, Venus the artistic energy, etc.

The condition of each of the planets in your chart (by house, sign, and aspect) shows how that energy (aggressive, mental, artistic, or other) operates in you and in your life.

Positions of the Planets

Chapter 7 tells how to find out where the planets were (by sign, and by degree of Zodiacal longitude) when you were born, and how to place the planets in the houses of your chart.

The ephemeris at the end of this book lists where the planets were during the years 1922 to 1990, which should include the ages of most people reading this book. The ephemeris is the most basic tool of the astrologer and gets its name because it lists the "ephemeral" or "quickly changing" positions of the planets.

Character Analysis

Chapter 8 goes into detailed character analysis, based on the positions of your planets by sign.

What the "Houses" Tell You

Chapter 9 explains the houses of your chart. Your birth chart divides the sky around the Earth into 12 parts or "houses." The planets and signs fall into these houses in ever-changing patterns, depending on the revolution of the Earth and the movements of the planets.

The house pattern in your birth chart shows the relationship of heaven and Earth at the time and place of your birth. Each of the 12 houses in your chart shows the nature of some area, or "department" of your life. One house rules money, one rules lovers, one rules friends, one rules your reputation, etc.

By studying which signs and planets are in each house in your chart, you can learn what to expect in that area of your life, what to watch out for, what to hope for, how to develop the best use of your energies in that area of your life, and how to master problems in each area.

Your Ascendant

Chapter 10 shows how to find your Ascendant (also called the "rising sign" or "rising point"), and how to set up the house structure of your chart.

Planets in the Houses

Chapter 11 describes how the different areas of your life (love, money, health, career, friends, etc.) are affected by the planets that are located in each house of your chart.

What the "Aspects" Signify

Chapter 12 deals with the aspects, or angles, formed between the planets in the chart. For some reason that no one seems to know, certain angles create problems, tensions, and difficulties, while other angles create ease, good luck, talent, money, love, and other pleasant things.

Chapter 12 analyzes the effect of the aspects, or planetary angles, in your chart. It shows the often hidden dynamics that are happening in your body, your conscious and subconscious mind, and in the events of your life.

Putting It All Together

Chapter 13 shows how to put all the separate factors in your chart together into one understandable picture that does not contradict itself.

What's Coming in Your Life

Chapter 14 starts you on the road to becoming a practical "magician," by giving you the keys to begin predicting the future.

Tricks for Greater Accuracy

Chapter 15 tells how to add the extra accuracy that will make your charts as mathematically precise as those done by professional astrologers. You can get charts cast accurately and inexpensively if you don't wish to set up a chart yourself. You can still read and interpret the charts yourself.

You probably will find it useful throughout your reading to refer to the Glossary of astrology terms, Recommended Reading, and "Tricks of the Trade" at the end of this book, to increase or reinforce your knowledge of astrology while you are increasing both your accuracy and enjoyment.

The Complete Picture of Astrology

Don't be concerned if some or even all of the terms or concepts in this chapter went over your head. This has been a summary of everything that goes into astrology and has been meant as a helpful overview or thumbnail introduction to astrology.

As you progress chapter by chapter and complete this basic guide, the complete picture of astrology and how it can work in your life will become clear to you.

The Zodiac and the Signs in Your Chart

*What the Zodiac is and how it forms the
foundation of your birth chart*

Do you like to be touched? Do you fall in love with one person and stay in love with him or her, or do you fall in love with two people at once and soon go on to a third?

Are you a good salesman? Do you have great powers of persuasion? Are you better at starting new business ventures or catching the ball from someone else and having the persistence to complete a long and difficult project?

THE ZODIAC TELLS YOU ABOUT YOURSELF

These and other character traits, strengths and weaknesses, are some of the *insights* into yourself that you can gain by understanding the zodiac and where you fit into it.

In this chapter, you will learn what the Zodiac is, where it came from, and how you can apply it to many varied aspects of your life, helping you on your way to greater personal happiness and career success and wealth.

The Zodiac is the most basic tool of astrology. In order to fully understand how and why the Zodiac works in astrology, it is necessary to learn a little bit of history and astronomy.

HOW THE ANCIENTS FOLLOWED THE STARS

When ancient peoples studied the evening sky, they had a view of the stars that was sharp and clear. They saw thousands of stars against the backdrop of a pitch-black sky, for they had no air pollution, and their cities and towns were free of the glare of electric streetlights.

These people watched the sky closely and with great interest, for they used the stars for navigation, and they used the motions of the planets to predict the future.

They divided the sky into recognizable areas by picking out groups of stars, and they named each group after a figure or image that the stars seemed to suggest. These groups of stars are the constellations, such as the Big Dipper, Little Dipper, Aries the Ram, Taurus the bull, etc. So the constellations must have been devised as reference points for navigation and for keeping track of the movements of the planets.

THE HEAVENS TODAY

If you look up on a clear night today you will see the same stars as the ancients saw. The only difference today is that the constellations are no longer where they were when the ancients set up our system of astrology. Today our view of the heavens has shifted slightly so that the constellations are no longer where they are "supposed" to be.

There is no need to get technical about this, because for our astrology purposes, it is not necessary. In this chapter we will talk about the Zodiac as if we still viewed it the way they did 2,000 years ago.

Today as you look at the sky you may notice some of the planets, many of which are brighter than the stars. The planets do move against the backdrop of the constellations, but they do not wander all over the sky. They stay within, or almost within, a certain path around the Earth.

This path is 16 degrees wide and is called the Zodiac. In the center of the Zodiac is the ecliptic, which is the apparent yearly path of the Sun (eclipses always occur along the ecliptic).

"Zodiac" is Latin for "circle of animals." As you can see from the illustration, the Zodiac is like a belt around the Earth, divided into 12 equal sections.

The entire Zodiac is a circle containing 360 degrees (as circles always do in geometry). Therefore, each sign of the Zodiac contains 30 degrees, since there are 12 signs ($360 \div 12 = 30$). (These degrees are officially termed "degrees of Zodiacal longitude".)

"The Circle of Animals"

Each section (each sign) contains a constellation, and most of the constellations are seen in the form of animals.

All of the planets move around the circle of the Zodiac at different speeds. The Moon goes through all 12 signs every 27⅓ days; the Sun goes through the circle of the Zodiac every 365¼ days.

The planets that are farther away from the Earth and the Sun require more time to go through the signs. Uranus, Neptune, and Pluto require about 84, 165, and 250 years, respectively, to go once around the Zodiac.

The important point to remember is that even though your Sun sign is, for instance, Virgo (meaning that the Sun was in the Virgo area of the Zodiac when you were born), your Mercury could be in Libra, your Moon in Scorpio, etc., and each of these factors is important in your chart.

EXAMPLE OF A BIRTH CHART

Here is an example of how the Zodiac forms the foundation of your chart.

Congratulations! You have just become a father. Leaving the hospital, you take a walk alone out under the night sky full of stars. To your surprise, an astrologer approaches you.

"So, you have a new son," the astrologer says. "Maybe you would like to know more about him. The Zodiac can tell you this, if we study the planets as they appear in the sky at the moment he was born, in this place."

SUN SIGN

"I see that the Sun soon will be rising," says the astrologer. "Since Virgo is now on the horizon, and the Sun is just below the horizon, the Sun is in Libra. So your son's birth or Sun sign is in Libra.

"Librans are attractive, charming people who love beauty and harmony. Venus, the planet that rules Libra, gives them a love of the arts and of refinement. Your son will be very interested in other people and will do well in partnerships, because he prefers not to work alone.

"Librans are very diplomatic and like to see that everyone is treated equally and fairly. They are peace-loving and try to help other people solve their problems and disputes.

"Your son will probably like to start a lot of new projects, but may have difficulty finishing them.

"Librans' love of beauty and the arts means that your son could become successful as an artist, beautician, or tailor. His persuasiveness, tact, and diplomacy could make him rise in the world as a lawyer, politican, or diplomat. His strong desire for justice could make him go into social work or become a sociologist.

"But this is only a fraction of what astrology can tell you about your son's future. The positions of the planets at this moment tell us what kind of energy we are all receiving from the heavens.

"Your son, since he was born under these planets, will carry the influence of this heavenly configuration for the rest of his life. You and I were born years ago, under different heavenly configurations which continue to influence us.

"But we and others not born under these planets are nonetheless under their influence as they play upon the planets in our own birth charts. We are influenced by the changing positions of the planets just as we are influenced by the changing conditions of the weather."

PLANETS IN THE SIGNS

"Directly overhead," says the astrologer, "you see the constellation of Gemini, the Twins. Within the area of the sky covered by Gemini, you recognize Mars, the red planet.

"Since Gemini is the mental sign, the sign of thinking, speaking, and writing, and Mars is the planet of forceful, aggressive energy, this is a time when the planets are broadcasting a great deal of mental energy to the Earth.

"Therefore, it is an excellent time to begin any kind of project that requires a lot of mental energy, such as writing a book or beginning to read and study a new subject.

"For businessmen, this would be an especially good time to begin a sales campaign, because Mars, the planet of powerful energy, is in Gemini, the sign of clever persuasiveness. So sales, sales pitch, persuasion tactics, communication are all at our beck and call at this time.

"Since Mars is in Gemini, anyone born at this time will have a desire to put a great deal of energy into writing, thinking, and speaking all through his life, since his birth chart will have Mars in Gemini. He will have a desire to put the aggressive energy of Mars into Gemini's mental activities—talking, thinking, writing, and reading.

"Mars is the planet of war and fighting, so words (Gemini) will be your son's weapons. He is likely to argue and cut with sharp words rather than use his body to fight."

THE MIDHEAVEN

"Now notice that Venus and Mars are straight above us, in the very middle of the sky, in the middle of the heavens," the astrologer tells you.

"In the language of astrologers, Venus and Mars are now 'in the Midheaven,' in the 'point at the top of the sky,' where everyone can see them clearly.

"So it will be with Venus and Mars in the life of your son. Everyone will see his passionate, romantic nature, and his love of beauty. His love affairs will be well-publicized, for the Midheaven tells us what we will be known for by the world, what our reputation will be, and how people will see us publicly.

"So here allow me to give you some advice. Since your son will be known for his passionate love of beauty and his charming way with words, why not educate him so that he can become a poet or author? Or someone who can use communications professionally, such as an advertising or public relations man. Then he can put these gifts to use so that the whole world can benefit from them. With Gemini in his Midheaven, these careers are written for him in the stars!"

CONJUNCTION—AN ASPECT

"Notice," the astrologer continues, "that Venus also is in Gemini, and is quite close to Mars. This means that Venus, planet of love and harmony, and Mars, the aggressive planet, are so close together they are blending their energies, and the angry fire of Mars is soothed and pacified by the calming influence of Venus. In astrology, we call this aspect of two planets touching a conjunction.

"Therefore, in your son's life, the fiery force of Mars is more likely to be expressed in passionate love affairs, rather than in battles or fistfights. Your son will want to make love, not war.

"But Gemini is the sign of flirting and the roving eye. Your son will like variety and novelty in his love life. It will not be easy for him to choose a wife and settle down. Since Gemini is the sign of charming words, he will steal his lady's heart with words—clever compliments, poems, and love letters. He may be prone to stretch the truth with little white lies to his lover. This could extend into business practices, including writing bad checks or shoplifting, if Venus is badly aspected in his chart. He may feel that he can be marginally dishonest if he can get away with it, or if he feels it won't seriously hurt someone else.

"People with Venus in Gemini are very particular about whom they allow to touch them, and how they want to be touched or fondled. Their close contact with friends or lovers may more often be on an intellectual rather than a physical level. A Venus-in-Gemini daughter might prefer an evening of attending art films rather than acting them out on a couch.

She would be very particular about how you persuaded her into a more intimate evening, so her suitor would have to use charm and tact. A Venus-in-Gemini son will be good at this kind of persuasion."

THE ASCENDANT

"Now let us look at the Eastern horizon, which we call the ascendant," says the astrologer. "You see that the constellation of Virgo, the Virgin, is rising over the horizon.

"That means that your son's birth chart has Virgo rising, or Virgo on the ascendant.

"The ascendant tells us what qualities we will work on and develop. With Virgo, the sign of perfection, on the ascendant, your son will always be striving to make himself and his work perfect, down to the last tiny detail. What is good enough for others will not be good enough for him.

"Notice also that the planet Mercury can be seen there, just above the horizon, and that Mercury is in Virgo. Mercury is the mental planet. It rules both Gemini and Virgo, which are both mental signs (Virgo being more technical and Gemini more intellectual).

"Since Mercury is so close to the Eastern horizon, we would say that Mercury is conjunct the ascendant in your son's chart. Any planet conjuncting the ascendant at the time of birth is especially strong and will flavor the whole personality."

THE MENTAL SIGNS

"With all of this mental influence of Mercury, Gemini, and Virgo being emphasized by the heavens at the time of his birth, your son will be quite an intellectual," the astrologer assures you. "The best thing you can do for him is to provide him with an excellent education, so that he can use his mind to its best advantage.

"Here is another piece of advice. Precise Virgo is the sign of the craftsman. With Virgo rising and Mercury in Virgo, your son, if trained as a maker of fine furniture, could produce pieces of the very highest quality, because he would not consider the job done right until it was perfect.

"But I want to tell you one more thing... Your son would not be happy as a rough laborer or in any other coarse kind of work. He is too refined for that. His Gemini Midheaven means that he wants to use his intelligence in making his mark on the world, and Venus on the Midheaven indicates that he will want to express himself in the arts. So I hope you are not a farmer or a coal miner, expecting your son to follow in your footsteps.

"By knowing the planets' influences upon your son, you will be able to better understand him and how he is different from you. Using astrology, you can help him to live a successful, happy life."

SEASONS OF THE ZODIAC

Now let us leave our new father and his astrologer and see how the signs of the Zodiac fit into the seasons of the year. The quality of each sign corresponds to the time of year when the Sun is in that sign. It tells us what the qualities (influences) of the signs are in our life. You must study this in order to get a complete picture of what the Zodiac is.

ASTROLOGICAL "NEW YEAR"

Each year, on or about March 21, the Sun crosses the celestial equator to give Spring and Summer to the Northern Hemisphere. This event is known as the vernal equinox and is the beginning of Spring.

Traditionally, many cultures have celebrated this event as the beginning of nature's new year. The Persian calendar starts its new year with the vernal equinox, and the Sun enters the first sign of the Zodiac (Aries) at the vernal equinox, the first day of Spring.

During the first 30 days or so of Spring, while the Sun is in Aries, it sends to Earth Aries-type energy—forceful, fresh, fiery, impulsive, enthusiastic, and masculine.

Then, about 30 days after the vernal equinox, the Sun enters Taurus (around April 21) and floods the Earth with a different type of energy. When the Sun is in Taurus, we receive an energy that is quiet, feminine, calm, and pleasant. During the month of Taurus, people love to appreciate and enjoy the natural beauty of the Earth, since Taurus is the first of the Earth signs, of which you will learn more later. This is the time of year when we get "Spring fever" and run out to roll in the new grass and smell the fresh flowers, and want to play hooky from work.

After Taurus comes Gemini, then Cancer, Leo, Virgo, Libra, Scorpio, Sagittarius, Capricorn, Aquarius, and Pisces. Each sign has the qualities of its own season or time of year.

THE CARDINAL SIGNS

Four signs of the Zodiac begin the four seasons of the year. Spring begins at the vernal equinox when the Sun enters Aries, about March 21. Summer begins at the summer solstice, the longest day of the year, when the Sun enters Cancer, about June 22. Autumn begins with the autumnal equinox (day and night are again of equal length), as the Sun enters Libra, about September 23. Winter begins when the Sun enters Capricorn, at the winter solstice. This is the shortest day and longest night of the year, about December 22.

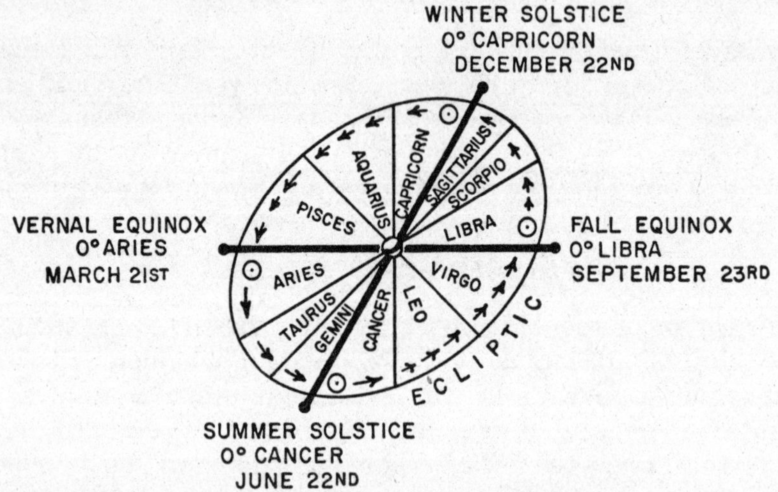

These four signs which begin the seasons are called the "cardinal" signs ("cardinal" means "fundamental" or "beginning" in Latin). People born with the Sun in a cardinal sign love to begin new projects and to be very active. They like to look ahead to the future and anticipate new developments.

When the Sun is in a cardinal sign, this is the ideal time for starting new plans and projects, and for getting new ideas off the ground.

The signs of the Zodiac are based on the cardinal points of the year—the equinoxes and the solstices. It is the equinoxes and solstices which establish where the signs begin and where they end.

THE FIXED SIGNS

After the cardinal signs come the "fixed" signs. These are the signs that occur in the middle of each season.

The cardinal sign Aries begins Spring, March 21. When the Sun is in Aries, Spring is bursting forth, pushing away winter. When the Sun leaves Aries, it enteres the fixed sign of Taurus. When the Sun is in Taurus, April 21-May 21, Spring reaches the height of its glory. Winter is gone and Summer is still to come.

The Sun in Taurus is the time of pure, concentrated springtime; not the beginning, not the end, but right in the middle. The fixed signs have great power and concentration because they represent pure energy—not a transition, not a half-way kind of thing, but a stable, *fixed*, single energy.

The four fixed signs are Taurus (Spring), Leo (Summer), Scorpio (Autumn), and Aquarius (Winter). When the Sun is in a fixed sign, this is the time to "gear up for the long haul" and settle down to tasks requiring patience, drive, and perseverance.

THE MUTABLE SIGNS

After the fixed signs come the mutable (which means "changeable") signs. These are the signs that end the seasons. The four mutable signs are Gemini (the end of Spring), Virgo (end of Summer), Sagittarius (end of Autumn), and Pisces (end of Winter).

When the sun leaves Taurus on May 22, it moves into Gemini and Spring begins to fade as Summer approaches. The times of the mutable signs are times of adjustment and changeability.

The season is ending and the Earth is getting ready for the coming of the new season. When the Sun is in a mutable sign, it is the best time to make alterations and adjustments of things that are already in progress. It is a good time to edit, modify, perfect, and add finishing touches on existing projects.

THE CUSPS

The dividing points between the signs are called "cusps." When a planet is located on a cusp it expresses an energy that is a blend or mix of the qualities of the two neighboring signs.

If you were born, for instance, on August 22 while the Sun was in the final degrees of Leo, and about to enter Virgo, then you would have strong qualities of both of these signs, because on August 22 the influence of Leo is fading and the influence of Virgo is beginning to be felt, even though the Sun might not actually enter Virgo until August 24.

For a few days before and after the Sun changes signs, the "blending" or "overlapping" influence of the cusp can be felt. If you were born "on a cusp," you are a rather complicated person, since the Sun in your chart is expressing a blend of two different kinds of energy.

THE KEY TO ASTROLOGY

This chapter has explained the structure of the Zodiac in a detailed way, so that you can understand not only how to use the Zodiac, but also what it really is and how it came into being.

It is important to have a complete knowledge of the Zodiac, because the Zodiac is the key to astrology, and the foundation of your birth chart.

In the next chapter, you will learn more about the structure of the Zodiac. You will see what qualities the different signs have in common, and why people of different signs get along (and sometimes don't get along) with each other.

"Types" and "Elements" of the Zodiac

Are you passionate, practical and conservative, intellectual or emotional? Are you a self-starter or a follower? Your Sun sign, by type and element, can tell you which you are and which signs you are compatible with.

What type of person are you? A patient worker or an impulsive starter?

What is your "element"—Fire, Earth, Air, or Water?—and what does that mean about you?

What signs are you likely to have harmonious and productive relationships with?

How can you find a partner who has (and can help you develop) the qualities that you lack?

Why do you get along well with people born under some signs, but not with others?

What is the basic, simple geometry of the Zodiac, and where do you fit into it?

STRUCTURE OF THE ZODIAC

The Zodiac is not just a group of signs placed around a circle. It is a simple, yet multi-dimensional geometric figure which reveals a wealth of abstract and practical information to anyone who will spend a short time learning to unlock its secrets.

Look at the relationships of the squares, triangles, and other simple geometric figures and angles that form in your birth chart. From them you can learn where you have natural talent and luck, where problem areas are, how to overcome them, and how you can evaluate the true compatibility potential of friends and associates.

ANGLES FORMED BETWEEN THE SIGNS

The first step in unlocking the Zodiac is understanding the angular relationships of the signs.

To do this, we will look at the "Natural Zodiac," which is simply a horoscope chart cast with all of the signs on the cusps of their "natural" houses (the houses that they rule).

In the Natural Zodiac, Aries, the first sign of the Zodiac, rules the cusp of the chart's first house (the "native house" of Aries). Taurus, the second sign, rules the second house, etc.

We will talk about "houses" more in Chapter 5. Basically, the houses are the pie-shaped sectors in the chart.

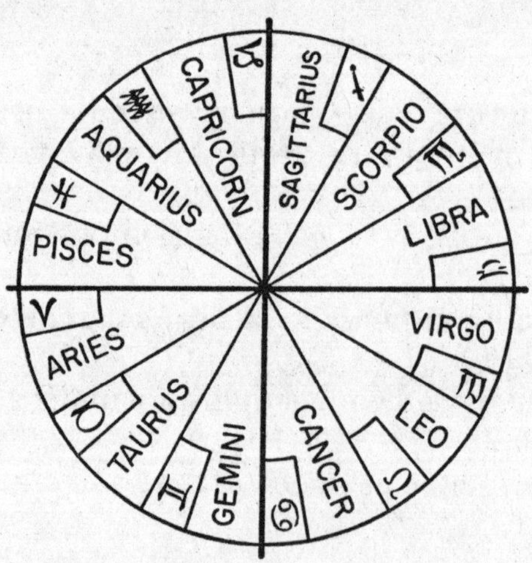

The Natural Zodiac

Notice that the horizontal axis and vertical axis divide the chart into four large sectors. Each sector in the Natural Zodiac represents a season.

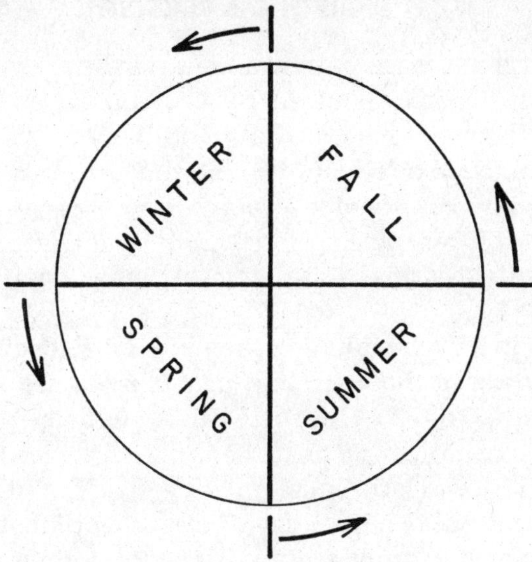

As was said in Chapter 3, Aries begins Spring, Cancer begins Summer, Libra begins Autumn, and Capricorn begins on the first day of Winter. These four signs are the "Cardinal" or "beginning" signs.

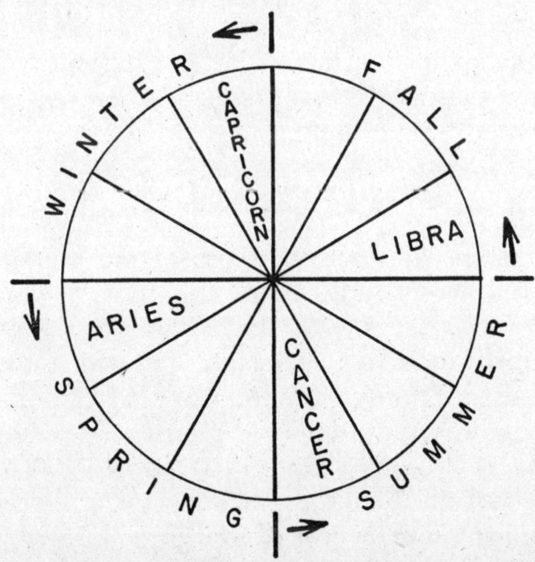

The Cardinal signs

THE CARDINAL PERSON

If you were born while the Sun was in a Cardinal sign, you probably like to plan for and think about the future. You are enthusiastic about starting new projects, but may run out of patience in the middle of them and wish that someone else would finish them for you.

The Cardinal person is basically active and energetic, someone who does not like to be restricted. You live in the present time, basing decisions on realistic, immediate factors... what has to be done *right now.*

If your Sun is in a Cardinal sign, then you partake of these qualities. Keep in mind, however, that astrology paints a picture of you that is not based on your Sun alone. All of the other planets (plus some other factors) paint the complete picture.

So, if your Sun is in a Cardinal sign, but you do not fit this description very closely, you probably have most of your other planets in the Fixed or Mutable signs. Do not draw any final conclusions about yourself or about astrology until you can look at and understand the complete chart.

If you do fit the Cardinal description very closely, then you probably have many planets in Cardinal signs. In that case, you are well-advised to find friends and associates born under the Fixed signs. These people have the qualities that you are short on, including patience, stability, and the ability to stick with long projects by doing them one step at a time.

Therefore, in choosing a partner, either in marriage or business, if you are born under a Cardinal sign, you could be very successful with someone born under a Fixed sign.

THE FIXED PERSON

The Fixed signs are Taurus, Leo, Scorpio, and Aquarius. They fall in the middle of the seasons, in the Natural Zodiac, as you can see by the chart.

If you were born under a Fixed sign, you are not only persistent, determined, and unstoppable, you probably are stubborn and somewhat reluctant to change your opinions and habits.

Basically, the Fixed signs have very strong egos. This explains the positive qualities of the Fixed signs: will power, self-confidence, an ability to fully enjoy the pleasures of life.

Negative qualities of the Fixed signs are also caused by strong egos, such as stubbornness, inflexibility, over self-confidence, selfishness, jealousy, fixed opinions, lack of diplomacy, and some difficulty in recognizing the other person's point of view.

While the Cardinal-sign person tends to race abot like a jack-rabbit, those born under a Fixed sign could best be compared to a freight train. They are hard to get moving in the beginning, but are productive and unstoppable once they are on a steady course. Fixed-sign people have a great deal of inertia.

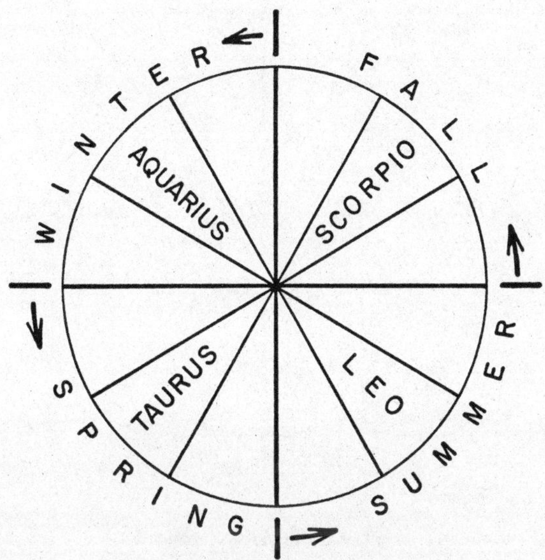

The Fixed Signs

If you have a lot of Fixed energy in your chart, you can bring more balance into your life by associating closely with, and learning from, Cardinal-type and Mutable-type people. Cardinal people can help you get out of grooves and ruts, and help you find new direction. Mutable people operate by flexibility and adaptability to change and to other people. These are the qualities that Fixed-sign people often need to develop.

THE MUTABLE PERSON

In Latin, the word "mutable" means "changeable." People born under the mutable signs of Gemini, Virgo, Sagittarius, and Pisces are capable of changing themselves or adapting to their environment like chameleons. They can fit in anywhere and handle any type of situation.

The Mutable signs are oriented toward mentality and intellect. They enjoy learning and study, and they like to examine, analyze, criticize, edit, and adjust. This is in keeping with the fact that the Mutable signs occur, in the Natural Zodiac, at the end of each season, when nature is, in effect, "editing," or putting the final touches on the events of the dying season. Nature is making small adjustments, changes, and adaptations for the coming season.

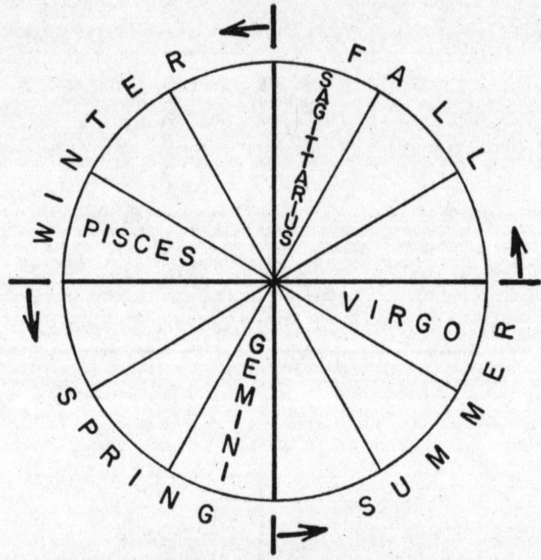

The Mutable signs

The three types—Cardinal, Fixed, and Mutable—could also be thought of, respectively, as the "starters," the "persisters," and the "adjusters."

HOW TO MAKE THE TYPES OF SIGNS
WORK FOR YOU

This concept can be illustrated with a business example. If you wanted to build and operate a hotel or shopping center, you would want to employ or work with the three different types of people for three different purposes.

For getting the deal started, the best people to choose would be people of the Cardinal types—as real estate agents, lawyers, etc.

For the long, step-by-step process of construction, people of the Fixed type would be ideal, since they have the patience, persistence, and strength to stick out a long haul and plow through heavy obstacles. Fixed-sign people tend to be blunt and undiplomatic, however. Therefore, once construction was completed, you would want Mutable-type people as desk clerks, salespeople, *maitre-de-hotel*, etc., since dealing with the public requires a flexible person who can see the other person's point of view.

This illustration is strictly theoretical, of course, since everyone is a mix of different astrological factors, and specific factors within the complete chart are often more important than the Sun-sign when it comes to looking at a specific area of your life, such as which career you are best suited for.

"MASCULINE" AND "FEMININE" SIGNS

The 12 signs of the Zodiac are divided into two groups—the "positive" or "masculine" signs, and the "negative" or "feminine" signs.

Do not get the impression, however, that the positive signs are "better" than the negative signs, or that men born under the "feminine" signs are not as manly as men born under the "masculine" signs. That is not the way it works in astrology. These terms simply refer to two different kinds of energy, like the positive and negative poles of a battery.

Balancing the Polarities

Here is an overview of how the two polarities work to balance each other in the "economy" of the Zodiac.

"Positive" signs	**"Negative" signs**
(These are the Fire and Air signs: Aries, Gemini, Leo, Libra, Sagittarius, and Aquarius)	(These are the Earth and Water signs: Taurus, Cancer, Virgo, Scorpio, Capricorn, Pisces)
—	—
Restless	Patient
Active	Reactive
Sociable, Gregarious, Outgoing, Partygoer	Seek more privacy, quiet
Like to "live for today"	Conserve resources for the future and security
Mental, Enthusiastic, Fiery	Earthly, Common Sense, Emotional
"Gad-about"	"Stick-in-the-Mud"
"Make it happen"	"Wait for the right time"
Aggressive, extroverted	Passive, introverted
"Masculine" (traditionally)	"Feminine" (traditionally)
Seek excitement, action	Seek peace, security, solidity

As you can see, the positive signs see life in a very different way than the negative signs do. Traditionally, astrology has advised us in most cases to choose people of our own "polarity" (positive or negative) as husbands, wives, intimate friends, and for other close associations. For business partnerships, you may prefer to work with someone who is of the same polarity, because you complement each other.

In general, you will probably find that most of your closest friends, if you are born under a negative sign, are friends of the negative signs. People usually choose friends, lovers, and business partners of the same polarity since their fundamental temperaments are similar. They generally understand each other better and work together harmoniously.

Polarities and Their Angles

Now let's see how the Natural Zodiac expresses this principle in its geometric structure.

Here are the positive and negative signs as they occur in the Zodiac.

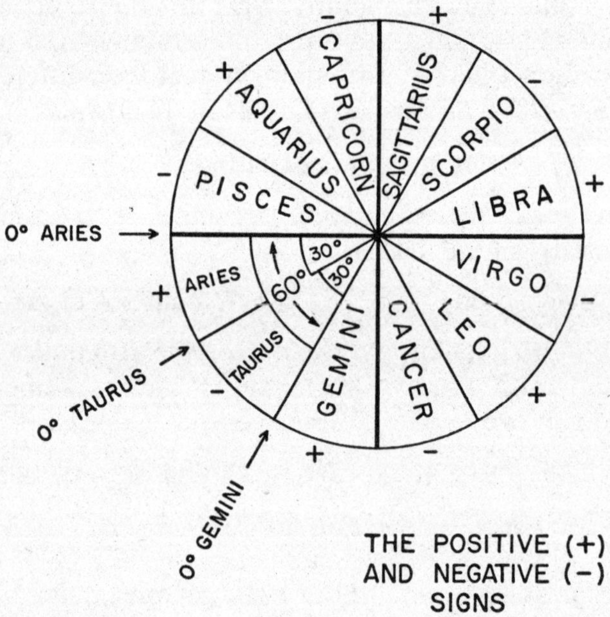

As you can see, the signs alternate—positive, negative, positive, etc. Since each sign represents 30 degrees of the circle, signs of the same polarity are always 60°, 120°, or 180° apart.

Beginning with Aries and going around the Zodiac, the next positive sign we come to is Gemini. If we count the number of degrees from 0° of Aries to 0° of Gemini, we find that these points are 60° apart, since Gemini is the second sign after Aries, and each sign contains 30 degrees.

The Positive Aspects

In astrology, a 60° angle is called a sextile aspect, and the experience of astrology indicates that the 60° angle creates a very harmonious flow of energy, bringing talents, abilities, good luck, etc.

Astrologers have found that the angles of the equilateral triangle and the hexagon (120° and 60°), when formed by signs, planets, or other factors in astrology, create strongly positive, harmonious energies.

The "Good" Aspects

(Easy, harmonious, "soft," "lucky")

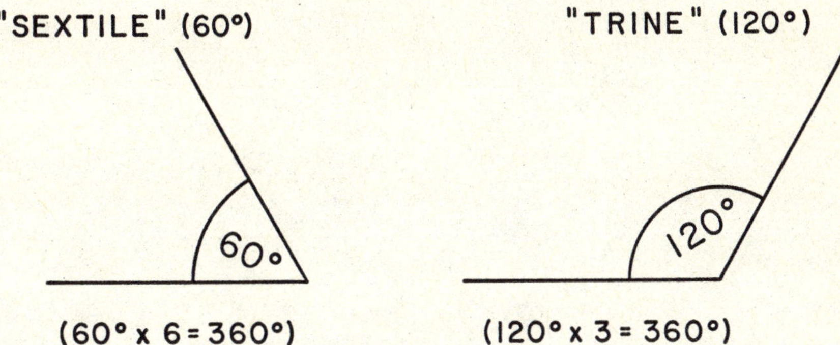

Signs of the same polarity are always either trine (120°) or sextile (60°) to each other, so their basic natures work well together.

THE FOUR ELEMENTS

In ancient times, the Greeks considered all things of heaven and Earth to be composed of four elements: fire, earth, air, and water.

People were thought to be a balance of these four elements, with some being of an especially fiery, excitable nature, while others seemed to be more earthy—calm, conservative, practical.

Modern science sees things differently than the ancient Greeks did, but the four "elements" are still useful as concepts, and you will find that people you know will always fit the nature of the balance of elements in their chart. As always, the Sun sign alone does not tell the whole story.

Fire

If you are born under a Fire sign, you are enthusiastic, active, excitable, sports-loving, and have a temper that flares up and dies down quickly.

Fire-sign people tend to look athletic and active, and their faces often have a reddish glow, from excitement, anger, or robust health.

The Fire signs are each 120° apart—a trine aspect—so they are basically compatible with each other.

Fire is the first element. The fire signs are:

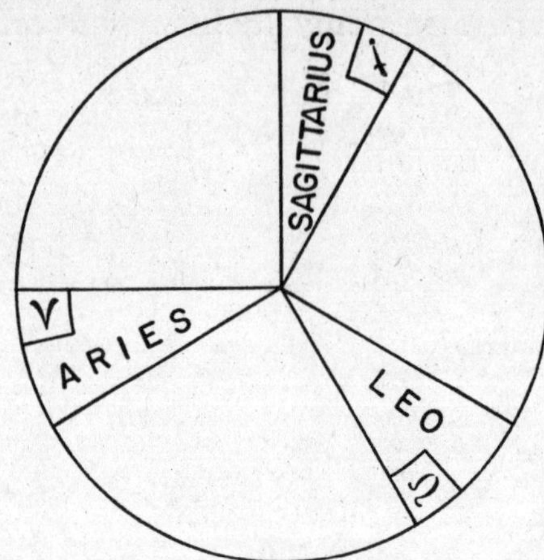

The Fire Signs

Earth

Next come the Earth signs. These are:

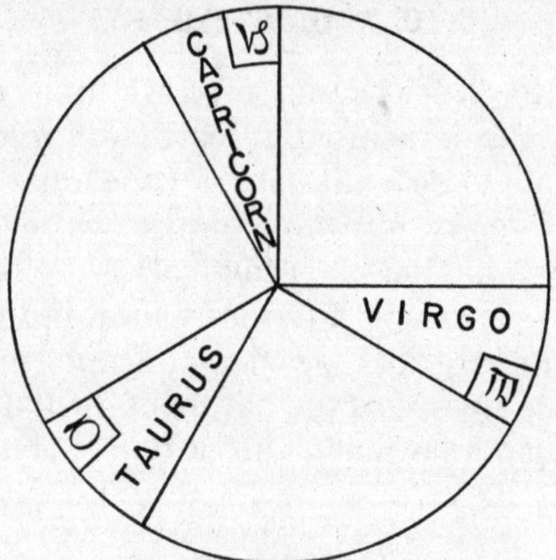

The Earth Signs

The qualities of Earth are exactly opposite those of Fire. Earth is practical, security-minded, slow to react, conservative, traditional, somewhat serious, solid, and dependable.

Earth-sign people tend to look solid and earthy, with a tendency to have dark skin, dark hair, and brown eyes.

People of the Earth signs have the qualities that are usually associated with people of the Earth... the type of person you would expect to find living in a small town or on a farm. They are sensible, conservative, practical, skeptical, thrifty, dependable.

Fire-sign people like the action and excitement of city life. They are naturally better-suited to a more fast-paced and dangerous life. They make good soldiers, adventurers, firemen, police officers, reporters, etc.

People of the Fire and Earth signs are theoretically incompatible. This is reflected in the geometry of the Zodiac, since no Fire sign ever forms a major harmonious aspect (60° or 120°) to any Earth sign.

Working with "Incompatible" Signs

For instance, if you are an Aries (Sun sign), you are theoretically incompatible with Virgo, an Earth sign. However, you may have a good friend who has Sun in Virgo. This could happen for one of three reasons:

1. Your chart may have some planets in Virgo—that would allow you to "tune in" to the Virgo vibration, even though your Sun is not very compatible with Virgo.

2. Your friend may have planets in Aries, near your Sun.

3. You and your Virgo-Sun friend may both have planets in the same spot somewhere else in the chart. For example, you may both have Moon and Mars in Pisces.

People who have nothing or next to nothing in common astrologically, such as a person who is mostly Fire and Air (positive signs), and a person who is mostly Earth and Water (negative signs), are unlikely to get involved in any kind of relationship. Since they are not "tuned into the same wave lengths," their being together is like two people trying to dance together while carrying radios tuned to different stations. If they do have, for instance, one planet in common somewhere in their chart, they will be able to communicate on that level, but not very well on the other levels.

If only their Mercuries are compatible (Mercury rules the mind), they will be able to communicate mentally, but not emotionally. If only their Moons are compatible (the Moon rules the emotions), then they will be sympathetic emotionally but may find it hard to communicate verbally.

The Ideal Partnership

In the best birth chart comparisons for long-term associations, the two charts (the two people) will have many compatible planets, so that they will be able to share and communicate on many different levels. With just a bit of practice, you will be able to predict—with amazing accuracy—how compatible any person is with you on any level, whether it is mental, emotional, sexual, romantic, financial, etc.

Air

The next element after Earth is Air. Here are the Air signs:

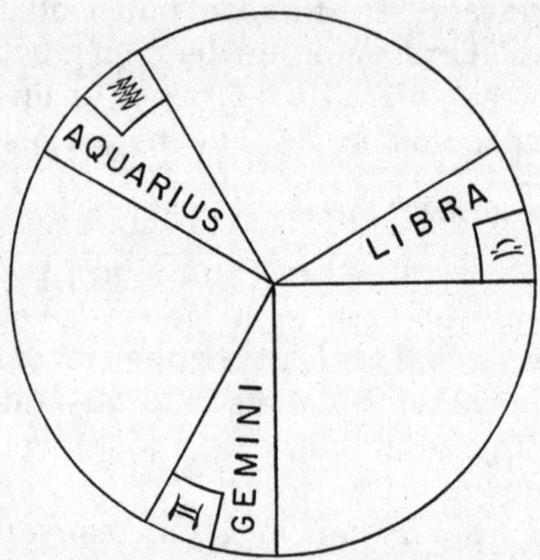

The Air Signs

The element of Air rules the intellect. Thoughts, communication, learning, culture, art, literature and abstract ideas are important to people born under the Air signs. These people have a natural ability to work in any field involving communications, writing, learning, etc. (any kind of mental work).

If one or more of the career indicators in your chart are in Air signs, you may be well-suited for this type of work, even though your Sun is not in Air.

Generally, the Air signs prefer to work with their minds rather than doing hard physical work. Air sign people tend to be thin, often tall, and to look somewhat intellectual.

The air signs are considered to be compatible with the Fire signs, since both Fire and Air are "positive" in polarity.

The air signs are theoretically incompatible with the Earth and Water signs, since Earth and Water are "negative" in polarity.

Water

The final element is Water. Here are the Water signs:

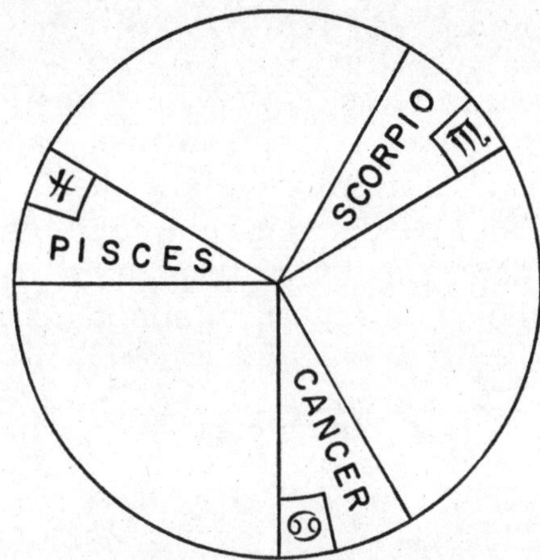

The Water Signs

Astrologically, Water rules the emotions, intuitions, and the subconscious mind. Water-sign people are very sensitive emotionally, and usually make their decisions based on their inner feelings and hunches rather than relying on logic alone. Their extra sensory perception potential is very strong and they can usually tell how you really feel about them regardless of what you say or pretend, since they are tuned-in directly to what your subsconscious is telling their subconscious.

The Water signs are the most fertile signs for planting and gardening, and these people tend to have "green thumbs" and love plants. Likewise, they are fertile for the conception of children.

Water and Earth signs (the "negative" or "feminine" signs) are almost always considered to be either "fertile" or "semi-fertile," while almost all of the Fire and Air signs (the "positive" or "masculine" signs) are classed as either "barren" or "semi-barren." These categories apply to gardening, farming, animal husbandry, and human fertility.

Farmers, gardeners, and animal breeders have found it helpful to follow the sign position of the Moon in order to take advantage of the best times for planting, pruning, harvesting, and breeding.

ASTROLOGICAL BIRTH CONTROL

Astrological measurements of fertility have proven so exact that an effective method of astrological birth control has been developed (see Recommended Reading). This technique has about the same success rate as the pill, the diaphragm, and other accepted methods of birth control, and is seriously recommended by doctors in the Soviet Union as another effective form of birth control.

THE BASIC DRIVES

You can understand the basic orientation of each of the signs by looking at its combination of type and element, using the technique of combining astrological "key words." This is a useful trick when considering the basic drives of people you know, and also in analyzing the importance of the different planets in your chart.

Let's use this method to discover, in simple terms, the most basic drives of some of the signs.

Key Words

Types
Cardinal—Begins
Fixed—Continues, steady effort
Mutable—Corrects, adjusts

Elements
Fire—Action, excitement
Earth—Practical, security
Air—Mental perfection, ideas, idealism
Water—Emotions, desires

Sign	*Type*	*Element*
Aries— Cardinal, Fire	*Begins* new things	Based on a desire for action, excitement (Fire)
Taurus— Fixed, Earth	*Continues,* steady effort	Based on desire for *practical* earthy *security* (Earth)
Gemini— Mutable, Air	*Corrects, adjusts*	Based on a desire for *mental* perfection, idealism (Air)
Cancer— Cardinal, Water	*Begins* new things	Based on a desire of the *emotions* (Water)
Leo— Fixed, Fire	*Continues,* steady effort	Based on a desire for *action, exitement* (Fire)
Virgo— Mutable, Earth	*Corrects, adjusts*	Based on a desire for *practical* earthy *security* (Earth)
Libra— Cardinal, Air	*Begins* new things	Based on a desire for *mental* perfection, *idealism* (Air)

Following this guide, you can work out the basic natures of the other six signs if you wish. To do a more comprehensive list, go beyond these four key words used above and draw upon all of the information in this chapter on types and elements. You may be amazed at how much you can analyze and sum up the character traits of people you know, according to their type and element.

Your Sun Sign and Rising Sign

*How they help you to know yourself better,
your strengths and weaknesses, your special
interests and abilities, your best job or career
potentials, ways of working with others, and
your romantic and emotional needs.*

Your Sun sign and Rising sign are both very strong factors in your birth chart. Basically, your Sun sign shows your will power, your basic inner nature, what things in life are most important to you, and what your general *modus operandi* is, relating to your career or work life, as well as your personal life.

HOW THIS WORKS

For instance, if your Sun is in Virgo, then practicality, cleanliness, order, and attention to detail are very important to you. Your basic inner nature would be to seek perfection in every area of your life, down to the smallest detail.

Your method of operating, if Virgo is your Sun sign, would be to do things in small steps, one step at a time, each step done as perfectly as possible (or more perfectly than most people would think possible). You would do this with each step until the whole project was done superbly, with each of its details in order.

This fits in with the nature of Virgo by type and element, as was said in Chapter 4—"Virgo corrects and adjusts, based on a desire for practical, earthy security."

SUN IN ARIES

A person born with Sun in Aries would have entirely different traits in these areas. The basic inner nature would be to lead, and to seek excitement and adventure.

Aries' method of operating would be to do things in a flamboyant manner, and quickly, on a large scale, assigning the details to someone else, whenever possible.

This is in keeping with Aries' element (Fire) and type (Cardinal), which indicate a person who primarily loves to "begin new things, based on a desire for action and excitement."

Your Sun sign basically shows *who you* are.

IMPORTANCE OF RISING SIGN

Your Rising sign is the sign that was on the Eastern horizon at the moment you were born. You will be able to calculate your Rising sign in Chapter 11.

Your Rising sign is, in a way, even more important than your Sun sign, because your Rising sign shows you who you are *striving to become*. It shows the qualities that you need and want to develop in yourself, to become successful and happy.

Putting It Together

For example, if your Sun is in Virgo and you are rising on Aries, then you already possess the qualities of patience, practicality, and attention to detail, since your Sun is in Virgo.

Virgoans, however, have a tendency to be shy and hide in the background, waiting for someone to tell them what to do. Aries rising indicates that one of your greatest goals in life is to overcome shyness and hesitation, and develop the Arian qualities of independence, self-motivation, courage, and decisive action.

A person with the opposite configuration—Aries Sun and Virgo rising—would have the opposite challenge. He would already know how to lead himself and others boldly and decisively (Aries Sun), but would be striving to learn patience, practicality, and attention to detail; and the value of unselfish service (Virgo rising).

INFLUENCES OF PAST LIVES

Most astrologers believe in reincarnation and feel that many of your present strengths, talents, and aptitudes show abilities that you have developed in past lives. At the same time, many of the problems, fears, and weaknesses you have in this life were created by traumatic experiences in past lives (just as psychologists feel that present phobias and problems were created by childhood traumas).

Whether you accept this theory or not, you will find that your Sun sign shows *who you are*, and your Rising sign shows who you are *striving to become.*

DISCOVER HIDDEN TRAITS WITHIN YOU

Here, then, are the qualities of the signs. If you look deeply enough into yourself, you will find that just about everything said about your Sun sign will apply to you to some extent. The extent depends on whether other factors in your birth chart work with or against each of your Sun-sign traits.

As you will see in Chapter 10, each of the twelve signs has some influence over one of the twelve areas of your life. But certain signs, such as your Sun sign and Rising sign, have a strong general influence in your chart and your life.

MAKE UP A LIST

Before you read the following delineations, you might want to make a list of everyone whose birthday or Sun sign you know—family, friends, work associates, or others. Keep them in mind as you read the descriptions and see how closely they fit their Sun signs. You might find that you recognize qualities in them that you never noticed before.

General character traits for each Sun sign are described, then specific attention is given to traits dealing with success in business and career, followed by a list of key words related to that sign. It is important to become familiar with the characteristics astrology has prescribed for each sign. With a little practice, soon you will be able to recognize the traits of a Cancer, a Leo, a Sagittarius, etc., which can be extremely important in dealing with people, from making friendships to closing big financial deals, or from going on your first date with someone to setting off on your honeymoon.

The "general" qualities listed in the key words that follow for each sign will apply to everyone born under or rising on a particular sign. The "positive" qualities refer to a person with that sign well-aspected in his chart, or one who is using the qualities of that sign constructively. The "negative" key words refer to qualities that will manifest if the sign is badly aspected (afflicted), or if the person is not using his sign qualities well.

ARIES (the Ram)

March 21 to April 20
Glyph: ♈

Type: Cardinal
Element: Fire
Planetary Ruler: Mars
Native House: First
Key phrase: "I am".

People born with Sun in Aries or who have Aries rising are energetic and on-the-go. They are the "gusto" people in the television commercials, who don't wait for life to come to them—they go out and grab all the life they can get.

Ariens like to meet new people and take on new things. Though they like to start new projects, they become bored easily and will drop a project, probably never returning to complete it.

They are very generous people, loyal to friends, and are courageous, independent, and adventurous. Physically, they have athletic, healthy bodies and enjoy being physically fit.

Negative aspects of Aries make Ariens somewhat selfish and conceited. They may have a quick temper and want things to go their way right away. This can make an Arien impatient and overbearing.

Business traits: Ariens make good leaders, seeking out opportunities of responsibility and command. They are ambitious, enthusiastic, confident, and "accomplishers."

Career directions: Ariens can be successful in engineering, working with metals and mechanics, exploration, the military, professional sports, and dangerous or challenging careers such as policeman or fireman.

Aries Key Words

General	*Positive*	*Negative*
A leader	Confident	Impatient
Action	Courageous	Argumentative
Energetic	Accomplisher	Tempermental
Resourceful	Enthusiastic	Overbearing
Initiative	Ambitious	Headstrong
Aggressive	Pioneer	Egotistical
Impulsive	Spontaneous	Jealous

TAURUS (the Bull)

April 21 to May 21
Glyph: ♉

Type: Fixed
Element: Earth
Planetary Ruler: Venus
Native House: Second
Key phrase: "I have"

Those born with Taurus Sun or with Taurus rising are "the salt of the earth." They are dependable, gentle and mild people, unless provoked.

Taureans love wealth and beautiful things. Material wealth is very important to them. Because they are ruled by Venus, Taureans are attractive people who love beauty in every form—in art, music, nature, and in other people.

Negatively, Taureans may be quite jealous, very possessive of those they love. A Taurean can turn on you very angrily if he feels you have taken advantage of him.

Physically, Taureans are built solidly and somehow look solid, even if they are not tall or muscular.

Business traits: Taureans are determined to succeed and endure. They are materialistic and practical, though generally conservative.

Career directions: Their love of beauty makes Taureans good candidates for careers in the arts, such as sculptor, model, art dealer, singer (Taurus rules the throat). With Earth as an element, businesses related to money-management are appropriate. Also carpenter and architect.

Taurus Key Words

General	*Positive*	*Negative*
Determined	Creative	Possessive
Endure	Patient	Jealous
Artistic	Affectionate	Indulgent
Materialistic	Industrious	Lazy
Practical	Persistent	Stubborn
Emotional	Generous	Sensual
Thorough	Stable	Rigid

GEMINI (the Twins)

May 22 to June 21
Glyph: ♊

Type: Mutable
Element: Air
Planetary Ruler: Mercury
Native House: Third
Key phrase: "I think"

Gemini people are rich in the blessings of youth—they always look younger than their age, they are enthusiastic, always eager to learn, and have a positive outlook on life.

Since Mercury rules Gemini, those born with Sun in Gemini or with Gemini rising are intelligent and quick-witted. They have excellent memories and are adept conversationalists.

Geminis love change and are easily adaptable to new situations. They enjoy having more than one thing to focus their attention on, whether in business or in love. They can handle two jobs and may have several love affairs going at the same time.

On the negative side, Geminis can change their mood or attitude abruptly, confusing other people. Generally, Geminis quickly change back to their normally friendly selves again.

Business traits: Geminis are very ambitious and have a strong inner drive to be successful. They can be very persuasive.

Career directions: Salespersons, travel agents, pilots, and careers in communications, including journalist, lecturer, teacher, writer, broadcaster, secretary.

Gemini Key Words

General	Positive	Negative
Changeable	Ambitious	Impatient
Adaptable	Persuasive	Indecisive
Literary	Resourceful	Talky
Sociable	Intelligent	Worrier
Practical	Quick-witted	Idle
Restless	Versatile	Lazy
Alert	Creative	Nervous

CANCER (the Crab)

June 22 to July 23
Glyph: ♋

Type: Cardinal
Element: Water
Planetary Ruler: the Moon
Native House: Fourth
Key phrase: "I feel"

Cancer is the first "Water" sign, and the water signs are all sensitive and emotional. Cancerians are warm, friendly people with strong needs for both material and emotional security. This is especially true since Cancer's natural position in the Fourth house rules the home and also is associated with the need for psychological security.

Cancerians are very loyal and hold on to friends and loved ones very strongly. They are very helpful to their friends and also generous.

They can be quite successful, but may first have to work hard and long for it. They like to do things their own way and usually have the ability to warrant this independence.

Cancerians are worriers, especially regarding their health. They can imagine and worry themselves into having a fatal illness when their malady is really quite minor.

Business traits: Cancerians are persistent and determined, willing to struggle a long time before they achieve success. Highly imaginative, they are adaptable to many careers.

Career directions: Cancerians' imagination makes them excellent writers, artists, musicians. Born collectors, they make good antique-dealers, museum curators, hobby shop owners. Loving children, they make good teachers and parents.

Cancer Key Words

General	*Positive*	*Negative*
Imaginative	Creative	Worrier
Romantic	Unselfish	Possessive
Artistic	Positive	Dreamer
Feeling	Intuitive	Stingy
Emotional	Protective	Touchy
Home-loving	Sympathetic	Self-contained
Sensitive	Dramatic	A putter-offer

LEO (the Lion)

July 24 to August 23
Glyph: ♌

Type: Fixed
Element: Fire
Planetary Ruler: the Sun
Native House: Fifth
Key phrase: "I will"

Leos love to be the centers of attention, a character trait derived from the fact that Leo is ruled by the Sun, the local star of our solar system.

Fortunately, Leo is native to the 5th house, which is the house of self-expression, and Leos are warm, generous, enthusiastic, and lion-hearted. They love adventure and are courageous. They love to be loved and may not understand why their love is not always returned.

Physically, Leos have a proud look, usually with a thin waist but a rather large upper body and head.

Leos' love of attention can turn some people off, especially if the Leo is overbearing or dictatorial.

Business traits: Leos love to lead. They also love to inspire confidence and enthusiasm in others.

Career directions: Leos' leadership qualities make them good bosses. Their flair for attention makes them good actors, dancers, masters of ceremonies, public relations persons, and they can be successful in radio, television, and advertising. Their love of young people makes them good teachers and youth workers.

Leo Key Words

General	Positive	Negative
Confident	Leader	Vain
Superior	Fearless	Overbearing
Aggressive	Dignified	Arrogant
Self-Approving	Commanding	Domineering
Want Recognition	Courageous	Dictatorial
Outspoken	Magnanimous	Closed-Minded
Ardent	Dynamic	Stubborn

VIRGO (the Virgin)

August 24 to September 22
Glyph: ♍

Type: Mutable
Element: Earth
Planetary Ruler: Mercury
Native House: Sixth
Key phrase: "I analyze"

Virgoans like their life, work, and world to be in perfect order. They are careful, neat, and fastidious people.

Virgo is native to the 6th house, the house of service and work, so Virgoans have a strong desire to be of service to others.

They have excellent memories and love to keep on learning. You may think a Virgo is cool and unemotional, but when you get to know them, they are actually very affectionate and sensitive, even quite passionate in love.

Physically, Virgo people are of medium height and build, with fine facial features.

Business traits: Virgoans are critical people, and make good critics of movies, television shows, plays, and books, as well as of other people. They are very good at finding even the smallest mistake or error, so they make good inspectors or proofreaders.

Career directions: Their desire for service to others and their interest in health and hygiene makes Virgoans ideally suited for careers in health, including nurses, doctors, dentists, health inspectors. Their logical minds make them successful as scientists, computer operators, accountants, and researchers.

Virgo Key Words

General	*Positive*	*Negative*
Mental	Meticulous	Critical
Cautious	Quick-learner	Indecisive
Practical	Self-sacrifice	Skeptical
Scientific	Dependable	Apathetic
Reserved	Orderly	Puritanical
Honest	Clean	Possessive
Precise	Studious	Worrier

LIBRA (the Scales)

September 23 to October 23
Glyph: ♎

Type: Cardinal
Element: Air
Planetary Ruler: Venus
Native House: Seventh
Key Phrase: "We balance"

Librans are charming people who love beauty and harmony. Because of Venus' influence, they also can be good-looking, and have a strong appreciation for the arts.

They are very diplomatic and interested in other people, because Libras' native house, the 7th, rules partnerships and other people. Librans like starting new projects, but prefer working with a partner rather than working alone.

Librans are peace-makers, willing to mediate with others to bring peaceful resolutions to arguments and fights. They want everyone to be treated equally and fairly.

Business traits: Librans' charm and persuasiveness are two of their strongest qualities, as well as their ability to mediate.

Career directions: Librans' love of beauty make them good artists, barbers, beauticians, tailors, dressmakers. Their charm and persuasiveness make them ideal lawyers or politicians. A strong desire to serve others suits them to be welfare workers or sociologists.

Libra Key Words

General	*Positive*	*Negative*
Refined	Considerate	Temperamental
Idealistic	Neat	Vain
Balanced	Sympathetic	Indecisive
Justice-seeker	Honest	Impatient
Partner	Creative	Extravagant
Peace-lover	Cooperative	Moody
Romantic	Expressive	Too precise

SCORPIO (the Scorpion)

October 24 to November 22
Glyph: ♏

Type: Fixed
Element: Water
Planetary Ruler: Pluto
Native House: Eighth
Key phrase: "I desire"

Scorpios are deep, intense, secretive, and passionate people, capable of doing just about anything they set their mind to. In fact, Scorpios can be so compulsive about pursuing their goals that they may even risk their lives in order to accomplish that which they have set out to do.

They are very curious about just about everything, including your innermost secrets, though they will seldom if ever reveal their own depths to you.

Scorpios both love and hate intensely. Though they are loyal in love, they may be very possessive and jealous of those they love. They also are fiercely independent people who will not allow others to dominate them.

Adventure and excitement are of paramount importance for Scorpios, who are not satisfied with a humdrum job or lifestyle. Physically, they are built strong and energetic and they may have an intense stare.

Business traits: Dogged tenacity in becoming successful in any pursuit makes Scorpios excellent prospects in any chosen field. Their imagination and curiosity add to their success characteristics.

Career directions: Scorpios' intensity and depth make them good doctors, surgeons, psychiatrists, occultists, and insurance agents. Their love for adventure suits them for military or police work.

Scorpio Key Words

General	*Positive*	*Negative*
Deep	Aggressive	Suspicious
Intense	Creative	Stubborn
Secretive	Tenacious	Excessive
Passionate	Courageous	Domineering
Curious	Determined	Jealous
Forceful	Devoted	Sarcastic
Emotional	Trustworthy	Violent

SAGITTARIUS (the Archer)

November 23 to December 21
Glyph:

Type: Mutable
Element: Fire
Planetary Ruler: Jupiter
Native House: Ninth
Key Phrase: "I perceive"

Sagittarius is the fun-loving free spirit of the Zodiac. Those with Sun in Sagittarius or with Sagittarius rising are happy-go-lucky, adventurous, warm, out-going, and optimistic.

They love the outdoors and life in general, spreading this vitality and love around them. Freedom and travel are very important to Sagittarians, who usually don't stay in one place very long and may leave a trail of broken hearts behind them when they go off on another adventure.

Sagittarians, above all, want to lead a happy, carefree, healthy life and enjoy all the good things life has to offer—nature, knowledge, love, and people. To them, this is "the good life," and though they can be successful in what they set out to do, they may not become rich, but they will be happy.

Physically, Sagittarians are handsome, healthy-looking specimens whether male or female. They typically look like the blond, tanned, outdoorsy All-American Boy or Girl.

Business traits: Sagittarians' enthusiasm and optimism are strong traits they can capitalize on in any occupation. They want to learn and do new things.

Career directions: Adventure-loving, Sagittarians make very good athletes, travel agents, flight attendants, tour guides. Their love of knowledge and learning suits them for careers in teaching, the ministry, and in books—as publishers, lecturers, book sellers, librarians. Love of abstract knowledge and mental challenges serve them well as lawyers or judges.

Sagittarius Key Words

General	*Positive*	*Negative*
Restless	Enthusiastic	Excessive
Fun-loving	Happy-go-Lucky	Lazy
Free Spirit	Honest	Uncontrolled

General	*Positive*	*Negative*
Active	Tolerant	Scattered
Optimistic	Cheerful	Gullible
Aspiring	Generous	Impractical
Loving	Loyal	Wanderer

CAPRICORN (the Goat)

December 22 to January 20
Glyph: ♑

Type: Cardinal
Element: Earth
Planetary Ruler: Saturn
Native House: Tenth
Key Phrase: "I utilize"

Capricorns are serious, purposeful people and hard workers. Conscientious, they always have a purpose in mind and are willing to overcome any obstacles in order to meet their duties and obligations.

A love of nature is strong in Capricorns, so they are happiest in the outdoors. They make good friends because they are generous and kind and often very helpful to others.

If Capricorn people seem distant and cool on first meeting, once you get to know them you will usually find they are really warm and loving.

Security-conscious, Capricorns also want to be famous and respected, so although they like money for the security it brings, they may choose instead to have respect and reputation over money.

Physically, Capricorns are dark, even sensuous-looking, and actually become more attractive as they grow older.

Business traits: Determination and a willingness to succeed despite obstacles and hard times mark Capricorns for success, as well as their desire to keep busy and not waste time.

Career directions: Capricorns are good at managing any kind of structure, so they make good architects, builders, carpenters, surveyors. Other careers for Capricorns are politician, teacher, scientist, dentist, farmer, or manager of a shop or factory.

Capricorn Key Words

General	*Positive*	*Negative*
Patient	Dependable	Secretive
Security-Minded	Trustworthy	Melancholy

General	Positive	Negative
Cautious	Conscientious	Fearful
Responsible	Helpful	Selfish
Systematic	Humble	Pessimistic
Practical	Efficient	Materialistic
Conservative	Self-Sacrificing	Unsympathetic

AQUARIUS (the Water Bearer)

January 21 to February 19
Glyph: ∿∿

Type: Fixed
Element: Air
Planetary Ruler: Uranus
Native House: Eleventh
Key Phrase: "I know"

Aquarians are idealistic by nature, though they have very strong likes and dislikes. They love freedom and independence almost as much as Sagittarians, but they are not as emotional.

Friendship and comradeship are very important to Aquarians, who make friends for life and are very loyal. Even though Aquarians may not demonstrate their friendship in an emotional way, they are always ready to help their friends.

Aquarians are efficient, steady workers but they do not blow their own horn. At times, you get the wrong idea about Aquarians and think they are lazy or slow, when in truth they are merely efficient, but in a quiet way.

They are down-to-earth people who hate hypocrisy and are bored by formality. They can fit in at any social level, because they can come up or down to anyone's level, but they prefer to be casual and "old shoe," especially around the house.

Aquarians love knowledge and intellectual pursuits, and they may prefer to relate to you on an intellectual level rather than an emotional level. Expressing their emotions can be difficult or almost impossible for Aquarians, though through many subtle expressions of help or interest they convey the fact that they care for those who love them.

Business traits: A quiet sort of competence is strong in Aquarians, who are up to just about any task, whether mental or physical. Ideas and mental stimulation are "toys" to Aquarians.

Career directions: An underlying drive for fair play makes Aquarians particularly suited for careers working with humanitarian organizations, especially in ecology and political reform, or with charity groups. Other careers include scientist, technician, electrician, inventor, radio and television performer or repairman, pilot, writer, public relations person, and sociologist.

Aquarius Key Words

General	*Positive*	*Negative*
Detached	Helpful	Reclusive
Mental	Friendship	Unsympathetic
Independent	Brotherhood	Impetuous
Universal	Intuitive	Rebellious
Reformer	Persistent	Eccentric
Student of Life	Humanitarian	Bohemian
Unconventional	Inventive	Exacting

PISCES (the Fish)

February 20 to March 20
Glyph: ♓

Type: Mutable
Element: Water
Planetary Ruler: Neptune
Native House: Twelfth
Key Phrase: "I believe"

Pisces people are deep, infinite, and mysterious, like Neptune's oceans. They have a very dual nature and seem to be swimming in two different directions at the same time.

Pisceans are able to tolerate a lot of adversity in their life, and suffer inwardly rather than show their pain or sorrow. They can be moved to tears, however, by witnessing or knowing about someone else's suffering.

Very sensitive to the feelings and thoughts of other people, Pisceans often have psychic abilities. Often they do good for others in such a quiet and unselfish way, their good works go unobserved and unrewarded.

Most Pisces people would rather "switch than fight," avoiding arguments and fights, and retreating from the pressures of the world. On the negative side, Pisceans may be indecisive, impractical, and lack self-confidence.

Business traits: Pisceans' intuitive nature and inspirational qualities suit them well in many occupations, and they are very sensitive to the feelings and needs of other people.

Career directions: Pisceans' sensitivity and intuition qualify them to do well in the arts, especially as writers, photographers, poets, artists, musicians, dancers. Tuned in to illusions and disguises, they make natural actors and magicians, while their sensitivity to the needs of others suits them for work as nurses, or in any aspect of medicine or health care.

Pisces Key Words

General	*Positive*	*Negative*
Sensitive	Sympathetic	Hypersensitive
Deep	Devoted	Secretive
Infinite	Self-sacrificing	Indecisive
All-suffering	Intuitive	Impractical
Psychic	Patient	Confused
Romantic	Spiritual	Lack Confidence
Non-aggressive	Philanthropic	Reclusive

The Planets

*Each planet rules one of the basic drives
within you, such as your physical desires,
your drive for status and reputation, your
need for love, your desire for wealth,
achievement, and property.*

Each of the planets of our solar system influences or "rules" a basic drive in us, such as the need or desire for wealth, success, reputation, ambition, power, security, love, knowledge, happiness, and peace of mind.

Mercury, for instance, rules your mind. It shows how you think as well as what kinds of things you like to think about. It indicates mental and literary ability, according to where it is placed in the chart, and what aspects it forms to the other planets.

Venus rules love, art, and beauty in your life, showing what kinds of people and things you find attractive. Venus also indicates talent in work related to art and beautification.

Jupiter in your chart shows the areas in which you are most likely to find luck on your side in achieving wealth and success. Jupiter shows optimism, a sense of humor, and other attributes that can add up to happiness in your life.

SUCCESS DRIVES

Mars and Saturn are both associated with the drive for success. Mars in your birth chart shows the pure, raw energy that you use to achieve your goals.

Saturn signifies your desire for reputation and security. Both Mars and Saturn show your ambition in life. A real drive for power is shown in the chart usually by a strong Pluto or Mars planetary configuration.

In this way, each planet rules one of the basic human drives, desires, or needs within you. We each have needs for security, excitement, pleasure, achievement, creative expression, etc. But each person satisfies these needs in different ways, and these individual ways are shown by the condition of the planets in your birth chart.

SIGN CHARACTERISTICS

Each planet also rules a sign, and that sign has the same characteristics as its ruling planet.

Gemini, for instance, is ruled by Mercury (the mental planet), and Geminians love to think, write, send letters, and start conversations. And they fit naturally into any field of work involving writing, speech, or communicating in any form.

Each planet-sign combination also rules a house of the chart, as we will see later. (Mercury and Gemini, for instance, rule the 3rd house, which rules thought, speech, and communications in your life.)

GODS AND GODDESSES

The ancient Greeks and Romans believed that each planet was a god or goddess that ruled over a part of our lives, and they built temples to each one and prayed to Mars for victory in War, Venus for success in love, etc.

They invented stories that illustrated the qualities of each of these "gods" or planets. Some of these stories may actually have been romanticized accounts of celestial events such as eclipses, comets, planets falling into the Sun, etc.

Of course, we no longer believe in these gods, but experience shows that the planets still influence our lives, just as the ancients thought they did.

SPEED OF THE PLANETS

The planets travel through the Zodiac at various rates of speed. The Moon goes once around the Zodiac every 27⅓ days, the Sun goes around the complete Zodiac once each year, Saturn once every 28 years, and Pluto every 250 years.

Therefore, we have in effect a huge computer with ten planets as variables (the Sun and Moon are included as "planets" for convenience in speaking and writing in astrology), 12 signs (with 30 degrees in each sign), and each planet moving at a different speed. The combinations are practically infinite, so you are astrologically unique, unless someone happened to be born within a few miles of your birth, and at exactly the same moment.

THE EPHEMERIS

All ten planets are in your chart, and only the Sun can be closely correlated, by day of year, to its position in the Zodiac. So the only way to find out what sign Mars was in when you were born is by looking it up in an "ephemeris." An ephemeris is a table listing the positions of the planets. The ephemeris at the back of the book contains the information you will need to set up your birth chart.

Mars rules aggression, physical activity, danger, fighting, anger, and the masculine half of the sexual drive within you.

If Mars was in a Fire sign when you were born, you are adventurous and sometimes enjoy risky situations, fast driving, and dangerous sports. You are well-suited to work in dangerous occupations, and your temper flares up quickly and dies quickly.

If Mars was in an Earth sign when you were born, you have a cautious, conservative attitude toward danger and risk. Where physical activity is concerned, you tend to put your energy into practical projects rather than athletics or dangerous activities.

HOUSE AND ASPECT INFLUENCES

The influence of each planet in your chart also depends on the planet's position by house (which area of your life it influences—home, work, romance, health, etc.—which you will learn about in Chapter 10). The planet's influence in your chart also is determined by what kinds of aspects it forms to the other planets in your chart, as you will see in Chapters 13 and 14.

"BENEFIC" AND "MALEFIC"

Astrology divides the planets of the Zodiac into two categories—the "benefics" which theoretically bring good fortune, the "neutrals," and the "malefics" which tend to bring danger and difficulties.

Depending on the aspects and sign placements, benefics—the "good luck" planets—can sometimes bring problems, and likewise, the "bad luck" planets can at times be fortunate.

Jupiter and Venus are the most fortunate planets and even their bad aspects seldom create serious problems. The Sun is often considered to be benefic, but it will bring great problems if it forms stressful aspects to the malefic planets.

Mars, Saturn, Uranus, and Pluto are to various degrees considered to be malefic, and create danger, difficulties, problems, and accidents.

The Moon, Mercury and Neptune are fairly neutral and will bring good or bad fortune depending on their condition in the chart.

SUN

The Sun is the center of the solar system, providing the light and energy for all the planets, and the Sun is perhaps the single most important influence in your birth chart. This is why astrology by Sun sign alone can be somewhat valid, even though your Sun's position by sign really shows only one part of your complex astrological nature.

If the Sun is prominently placed in your chart, you possess strong leadership abilities. You are full of vitality, strong-willed, and have the confidence and determination to get what you want—many of the requirements needed for success.

If the Sun is badly aspected in your chart, you will have difficulties dealing with authority figures, because of a poor relationship with your father early in life. An afflicted Sun can mean poor health, a lack of physical strength and insufficient will power and determination to succeed. It also could mean an over-bearing, domineering personality or an egotist.

The Sun in your chart shows relationships with your father and with men in your business and personal life, whether you are a man or a woman. What kind of men you will come in contact with and your attitude toward them will be revealed.

Each planet rules a part of the body. The Sun rules the back. If the sun is well-aspected in your chart, you will have a strong back. If badly-aspected, you may tend to have back troubles.

Since the Sun rules Leo, careers suitable for a strong Sun in your chart are virtually the same as for Leo. See Chapter 5 for Sun-sign career directions for Leo, basically involving careers requiring leadership and courage.

The "key words" that follow for the Sun, and at the end of our discussion for each of the other planets, are meant to be a quick and easy reference. The "general" qualities describe the general characteristics of each planet. "Positive" describes qualities that planet will express when it is well-aspected or well-placed in your chart or when it is used constructively. "Negative" key words describe the characteristics expressed by the planet when it is badly-aspected (afflicted) or poorly used.

Sun Key Words

General	*Positive*	*Negative*
Leader	Determined	Arrogant
Confident	Commanding	Ostentatious
Vitality	Self-confident	Rebellious
Strength	Loyal	Willful
Individual	Generous	Jealous
Ambitious	Stable	Vain

MOON

The Moon in your chart shows your emotions, personality, and your everyday way of responding to life. The Sun, Moon, and Ascendant generally are considered to be the three most important factors in the birth chart.

How people see you, on a superficial level, is largely an influence of the Moon in your chart. For instance, if your Moon is in Capricorn, the well-organized, businesslike sign, you may actually appear to others to be better organized than you really are. On the other hand, if your Moon is in Pisces, the dreamy, idealistic sign, you may appear to be day-dreaming or ineffectual, although you are actually very productive, but in a quiet sort of way.

The condition of the Moon in your chart shows your relationship with your mother and with women in your life. It shows what kinds of women you will become closely involved with, in your private and business life, as well as your attitude toward them.

The Moon rules the stomach and breasts. If the Moon is badly-aspected in your chart, you may have indigestion and stomach troubles.

The Moon rules Cancer, so for careers you should consider things requiring sensitivity, either work related to the public or occupations dealing with children or homes (see Cancer career directions in Chapter 5).

Moon Key Words

General	*Positive*	*Negative*
Maternal	Protective	Possessive
Sensitive	Flexible	Imitative
Changeable	Creative	Dreamer

General	*Positive*	*Negative*
Imaginative	Romantic	Worrier
Domestic	Sociable	Moody
Instinctive	Inspirational	Materialistic

MERCURY

Mercury rules the mind. In your chart, Mercury's condition by sign, house placement, and aspect shows how you think and what you like to think about.

Mercury well-aspected in your chart gives you intelligence, clear-thinking, speaking, and writing ability. You also will have good abilities for working with your hands, which are ruled by Mercury. The planet also rules the arms and lungs.

An afflicted Mercury tends to give problems in these areas of the body. It also can give problems in reading and writing, such as illegible handwriting, poor spelling or grammar, or reading perception problems. Afflicted Mercury can tend to make you glib and prone to manipulate the truth. In Roman times, Mercury was god of merchants and thieves. Mercury also rules shoplifting.

Mercury well-aspected is very beneficial for career success in work involving communications, such as radio and television, public relations, advertising, teaching, secretarial work, and personnel. More career directions for Mercury can be found in Chapter 5 for Gemini, which Mercury rules.

Mercury Key Words

General	*Positive*	*Negative*
Mental	Quck learner	Indecisive
Active	Aware	Skeptical
Adaptable	Versatile	Critical
Unemotional	Articulate	Nervous
Scientific	Resourceful	Restless
Reasoning	Efficient	Feel superior

VENUS

Venus rules love, art, and beauty. The condition of Venus in your chart shows romance, popularity, and artistic ability in your life. Venus is a benefic or fortunate planet and will generally dispense blessings to whatever part of the chart she finds herself in.

If Venus is strong in your chart, people find you to be attractive and charming, which can be very helpful in business, especially in occupations involving public contact. Also, Venus confers talent in the arts or in any work involving art or beautification, ranging from television commercial production to landscape architecture to the fine arts.

Negative aspects of Venus indicate problems in love and romance and difficulty achieving popularity, even though you may try very hard. You do not develop your looks or appearance to their full potential. These are tendencies shown in your chart, and being aware of them can help you in overcoming them. This is one of the greatest benefits of using astrology in improving your life.

Venus, through its rulership of Taurus, rules the neck and throat, which produce beautiful speaking and singing voices; and also the waist, hips, lower back, and kidneys, through its rulership of Libra. Afflictions to Venus or to planets in these signs indicate potential health problems in these areas.

Fields involving art, beauty, and creation of attractive environments are good career areas for Venus, ruler of Taurus and Libra. For more career directions see Taurus and Libra in Chapter 5.

Venus Key Words

General	*Positive*	*Negative*
Beauty	Attractive	Vain
Love	Creative	Indecisive
Art	Inspirational	Jealous
Gentle	Charming	Frivolous
Feminine	Considerate	Indulgent
Romantic	Responsible	Impractical

MARS

The ancients thought of Mars as the god of war. Mars in your chart signifies your aggressiveness, drive, impulsiveness, physical strength, and the masculine half of your sex drive.

Well-aspected Mars in your chart gives you many success potentials derived from a wealth of energy. You are forceful, enthusiastic, dynamic, and love action and excitement. You have the courage to plow through obstacles and endure until you win. A person with a strong Mars does not back down in a conflict with others. A well-aspected Mars also confers an ability to excel in sports.

If Mars is badly-aspected in your chart, you have destructive tendencies. You are rash, impulsive, and have a bad temper.

Mars, ruler of Aries, rules the head. People who have Sun in Aries or Aries rising always have a scar somewhere on their head from a childhood accident. Mars conjunct the ascendant or otherwise shown as extremely strong in the chart will also produce this scar.

Any career requiring a lot of energy, courage, or aggressiveness is indicated for those with a very strong Mars, such as police work, the military, sports. Mars, like the Sun, tends to give leadership abilities. See Aries in Chapter 5 for more Mars career directions.

Mars Key Words

General	*Positive*	*Negative*
Forceful	Enthusiastic	Destructive
Courageous	Dynamic	Rash
Active	Excitement-loving	Temperamental
Independent	Energetic	Impulsive
Venturesome	Aggressive	Egotistical
Impulsive	Determined	Obstinate

JUPITER

Jupiter, like Venus, is a benefic or "good luck" planet. Jupiter's name is a shortened version of "Jovis Pater," which the Romans used to call him, which literally meant "jovial father."

Wherever you find Jupiter in your chart, you find abundance, good luck, wealth, and what could be considered divine protection. It is wise to study the position and aspects of Jupiter in your chart, so that you can learn how to cash in on the good luck that this planet ungrudgingly provides.

The best single piece of career counseling advice for anyone except those with Jupiter extremely afflicted in their chart is to get involved in a field related in some way to the position of Jupiter in your chart by sign, house, aspect, or a combination of these. You will see how to do this in Chapters 9, 12 and 13. If you follow this advice, you will be happier and more prosperous.

Since Jupiter rules abundance, the only problems he usually brings are cases of "too much of a good thing"—too much food, drink, money, or easy luck, which can lead to being over-weight, over-indulgent, over-optimistic, etc.

Jupiter rules the thighs and buttocks, areas that prosper a little too much when we indulge in too much of a good thing.

Jupiter, which rules Sagittarius, also is associated with sports and sportsmanship, fair play, publishing, philosophic thought, travel, colleges and universities. Careers involving these fields are indicated (see Sagittarius in Chapter 5).

Jupiter Key Words

General	*Positive*	*Negative*
Abundance	Ambitious	Extravagant
Confident	Idealistic	Overconfident
Optimistic	Successful	Conceited
Jovial	Popular	Impractical
Generous	Understanding	Excessive
Benevolent	Philanthropic	Indulgent

SATURN

Saturn is sometimes considered to be the most malefic planet. It brings hard work, delays, obstacles, and disappointments. However, it also indicates success and reputation in the world, since these are usually achieved through patience and the ability to overcome difficulties.

If you have Saturn prominent in your chart, you have experienced your share of difficulty, disappointment, and depression. You are also serious, responsible, a loner, and a deep thinker.

If Saturn is well-aspected in your chart, you are a responsible person who knows the value of hard work, good organization, and fulfilling your promises and following through on your obligations.

On the positive side, Saturn's gifts to us are the strength, structure, and self-discipline that are developed by overcoming hardships.

Although people tend to be afraid of Saturn in their charts, the fact is that Saturn really brings perfect justice. If you have been living responsibly, fulfilling your obligations and treating other people fairly, there is no need to worry when Saturn approaches an important point in your chart.

On the other hand, people who have been dishonest or immoral in business or personal affairs will experience grave difficulties of all kinds when Saturn aspects key points in their chart. These difficulties could include bankruptcy, scandal, violent accident, sickness, and even death.

Saturn rules the hard structural parts of the body, the teeth and bones, particularly the knees. Badly-aspected, you could spend a lot of time at the dentist.

Relating to careers, if you have a strong Saturn, you are good at managing anything, such as a large organization or group of people, because you understand structure and efficiency. You are a good manager and know how to delegate responsibility well. Saturn rules Capricorn, so refer to Capricorn in Chapter 5 for more career direction.

Saturn Key Words

General	Positive	Negative
Sincere	Patient	Fearful
Restrained	Disciplined	Suppressive
Cautious	Enduring	Exacting
Justice	Dutiful	Rigid
Stable	Thrifty	Selfish
Conventional	Diplomatic	Pessimistic

URANUS

Uranus rules genius and originality in your chart. It also shows areas of your life in which you like to do things your way—a way that may be somewhat unusual or unconventional. Wherever Uranus shows up in your chart, you don't want someone else telling you how to do things.

Uranus also is almost always a factor in people becoming self-employed. You will see how this works later, in Chapter 13.

If Uranus is strong in your chart, you are original, inventive, intuitive, freedom-loving, and humanitarian. You may also have scientific, mathematic, or electronic abilities. You also may be somewhat unpredictable, but also ingenious and resourceful.

A badly-aspected Uranus would make you eccentric, Bohemian, rebellious, irresponsible, and the kind of person who will do anything just to be different or just for the sake of contradicting other people.

Uranus rules the ankles and calves. Badly-aspected, you should be careful with those parts of the body in order to avoid sprains.

Since Uranus rules change, careers indicated by a strong Uranus include fields involving new things—scientific invention, electronics, space, aviation, astronomy, and astrology. Uranus rules Aquarius, so refer to Aquarius career directions in Chapter 5.

Uranus Key Words

General	Positive	Negative
Original	Freedom-loving	Radical
Independent	Humanitarian	Eccentric
Inventive	Intuitive	Irresponsible
Idealistic	Progressive	Erratic
Friendly	Resourceful	Impractical
Restless	Strong-willed	Indiscreet

NEPTUNE

The ancients thought of Neptune as the god-ruler of the oceans. Neptune rules the sign of Pisces, which is symbolized by two fish swimming in opposite directions but tied together.

As you might imagine from this image, Neptune is a planet of complexities and contradictions. Specifically, it rules illusions, delusions, psychic experience, drugs, and alcohol.

On the positive side, Nepturn brings inspiration beyond the humdrum level of daily life. Theatre, music, films, and religious experience are all associated with Neptune.

A well-aspected Neptune indicates a person who lives his life by spiritual values and who can inspire other people.

An afflicted Neptune indicates a person who is dreamy, indecisive, disorganized, spaced-out, and lacking in self-confidence. These problems will manifest especially in the areas of the chart that Neptune influences by sign, house, and aspect.

Nepturn rules the feet, the unsung heroes of the body that humbly support us all day, while we hardly give them a thought.

Careers for Neptune people include film, theatre, dance, music, art, and religious and social service work such as nursing. Neptune rules Pisces, so see Pisces career directions in Chapter 5.

Neptune Key Words

General	*Positive*	*Negative*
Sensitive	Compassionate	Indecisive
Emotional	Imaginative	Dreamy
Psychic	Mystic	Disorganized
Abstract	Genius	Fearful
Idealistic	Spiritual	Self-indulgent
Metaphysical	Sympathetic	Immoral

PLUTO

When Pluto was discovered in 1930, the United States was plagued by the great Depression, racketeering, and a wave of kidnappings. In Europe, dictators were coming to power.

In mythology, Pluto ruled the underworld and was the first kidnapper. As you might expect from all this, Pluto is associated with deep, far-reaching struggles, terror, and violence. Pluto is closely linked to Mars. Mars co-rules Pluto's native sign of Scorpio, a very deep, powerful sign which often manifests violent tendencies.

A strong, well-aspected Pluto indicates tremendous will power, unshakeable courage, and an uncompromising sense of purpose. Pluto does nothing half-way, and a person with strong Pluto influences will live a full, complete life rather than settling for mediocrity.

Pluto people are very loyal and will risk their lives to protect a friend or loved one.

Pluto rules the sex organs. Well-aspected, Pluto gives you a very strong sexual appetite. People with this configuration should seek a mate with equally strong physical desires.

Those with a strong Pluto or Pluto in one of the career houses make good corporate executives, psychiatrists, detectives, psychics, undertakers, and spies. They are good at anything that taxes them to put out their total effort and which they feel is important, rather than something mundane or trivial. Pluto rules Scorpio, so see Scorpio career directions in Chapter 5.

Pluto Key Words

General	*Positive*	*Negative*
Courageous	Determined	Destructive
Forceful	Powerful	Fanatical
Purposeful	Spiritual	Reckless
Intense	Deep Thinker	Criminal
Loyal	Perceptive	Regimented
Will power	Psychic	Lawless

7

Finding Your Planets

***How to find the planets and place
them in your chart***

Each planet was in an exact degree of one of the twelve signs of the Zodiac at the moment when you were born, just as each planet is in an exact degree of one of the 12 signs right now.

The sign that the planet was in at the time of your birth determines what quality was "flavoring" or "coloring" that planet when you were born.

It is as if the planets were spotlights and each sign was a different colored filter or piece of glass. As the spotlights (planets) shone through different colored glasses, their light would pick up the coloration of the filter (sign) they were in at that time.

The sign position of each of your planets tells a great deal about you. For instance, if Mercury in your chart is in Gemini (Gemini rules the color yellow), then your mind (Mercury) is light, quick, cheerful, and bright like the color yellow.

If your Mercury is in Scorpio (the color of Scorpio is a deep, dark purplish red, like wine or blood), your thinking is passionate, powerful, emotional, sometimes angry. If your Mercury is in Capricorn (black), your mind is serious, steady, dark, and deep, with a tendency to be gloomy. You also may be shrewd and, quite possibly, have a love for "black humor."

Similarly, the other planets take on different colorations or influences as they go through the different signs.

As you consider the sign placements of each of your planets, you may find it helpful to consider the qualities of the colors that each sign rules.

You might also want to try wearing a color to stimulate a certain planet or sign in your chart. For instance, if your Venus is in Scorpio, wearing

80

dark red will tend to strengthen your powers of romantic attraction. If your Mercury is in Capricorn, wearing something black or very dark will help you to concentrate in your work. Wearing a black or deep blue tie could help you to make an important sale or achieve success in a business venture.

Here are the colors of the Zodiac, which can be very useful aids in remembering the qualities of the signs:

> *Aries:* Red
> *Taurus:* Pale blue, pink
> *Gemini:* Lemon yellow
> *Cancer:* White or silver
> *Leo:* Gold, orange
> *Virgo:* Brown (also navy blue, dark grey)
> *Libra:* Pale blue, pink, and pastels
> *Scorpio:* Wine, maroon, dark red
> *Sagittarius:* Royal blue, purple
> *Capricorn:* Black (also dark grey, forest green)
> *Aquarius:* Electric blue, plaids, bright combinations
> *Pisces:* Sea green, ocean blue, violet

Finding the positions of the planets in your birth chart is really simple. All you do is look up the date of your birth in the ephemeris in this book and make a list of which planets were where on that day.

In order to find out exactly where the planets were (which becomes important later, when you interpret your aspects), a few simple calculations are necessary.

1. Take a sheet of paper and label it "Planets' Positions:" and write your name.

2. Write your date, year, place, and time of birth.

3. In finding your planets, you will need to have your birth time in Standard Time (not Daylight Savings Time—D.S.T.). If you were born during D.S.T., simply subtract 1 hour from your birth time to find your birth time in Standard Time.

4. In constructing a birth chart, you must work with Greenwich Mean Time (G.M.T.), which is the world's time standard for astronomy and navigation. (The Royal Observatory in Greenwich, England marks the "prime meridian" or primary geographical and astronomical reference point of the world.)

This is how you find G.M.T.:
> E.S.T. (Eastern Standard Time) + 5 hours = G.M.T.
> C.S.T. (Central Standard Time) + 6 hours = G.M.T.

M.S.T. (Mountain Standard Time) + 7 hours = G.M.T.
P.S.T. (Pacific Standard Time) + 8 hours = G.M.T.

For example, Al Smith, born on July 5, 1960 at 7:00 p.m. E.S.T., we add 5 hours to find out what time it was in Greenwich when Al was born.

7:00 p.m. E.S.T. + 5 hours = 12:00 Midnight G.M.T.

Of course, 12:00 Midnight, July 5, can also be thought of as 12:00 a.m., or "zero hour," of July 6, since this is the exact moment when July 5 ends and July 6 begins. So Al was born at 12:00 a.m. ("zero hour") July 6, Greenwich Mean Time.

Therefore, all we have to do to find out where the planets were in the Zodiac when he was born is to look up July 6, 1960 in the ephemeris. We write down the positions listed there:

Sun: 14° Cancer	Saturn: 16° Capricorn
Mercury: 0° Leo	Uranus: 19° Leo
Venus: 18° Cancer	Neptune: 6° Scorpio
Mars: 11° Taurus	Pluto: 4° Virgo
Jupiter: 27° Sagittarius	North Node: 19° Virgo

(The Moon's nodes and their importance in the chart are explained in Chapter 11.)

5. If you did not happen to be born when it was zero hour in Greenwich on one of the days listed in the ephemeris, then it is necessary to go between the two closest listings to find your planets' positions.

For instance, if you were born on July 1, 1960 at 6:00 p.m. C.S.T., then it was 12:00 a.m. (zero hour) July 2 in Greenwich when you were born. Looking at the ephemeris for July 1960 we see that the Sun was at 9 Cancer on July 1, and at 14 Cancer on July 6, five days later. The Sun moved 1° each day. Therefore, add 1° to the Sun's position on July 1 (9° Cancer), and you have the Sun's position on July 2: 10° Cancer.

Basically, what you are doing is looking at the two listings closest to your birth day and time and estimating where each planet was at the time of your birth. You can see how this is done by the following example from an ephemeris:

	Sun	Mercury	Venus	Mars
January 1	11 Cp	27 Cp	16 Sg	14 Ar
6	16 Cp	25 Cp	22 Sg	17 Ar

If you were born January 3, halfway between January 1 and 6, your Mercury would be at 26° Capricorn, which is halfway between 27° Capricorn (January 1) and 25° Capricorn (January 6).

And so on. Use the same process to find the Moon's positions, which are listed in the ephemeris at the end of each year.

Since the Moon moves so quickly, it is helpful to consider the Moon's rate of travel when calculating her position. (The Moon moves about 12° per day, about 1° every two hours.)

Simply add or subtract the appropriate number of degrees from the closest listing, to find the position of the Moon in your birth chart.

For instance, if you were born when it was zero hour, G.M.T., July 6, 1960; you would subtract 12° (1 day's travel) from the July 7 listing of the Moon at 19° Sagittarius to find the position of your Moon.

19° Sagittarius
−   12° (one day's travel)
7° Sagittarius

So the Moon in your chart would be at 7° Sagittarius.

The slow-moving planets are listed once a month by their positions on the first of the month.

If you were born on May 15, look at Saturn's position on May 1 and June 1. Estimate halfway between these two positions, since you were born halfway through the month.

For example, if Saturn was at 25° Pisces on May 1, and at 27° Pisces on June 1, then put Saturn at 26° Pisces in your chart.

The method used here gives you the planet's positions to an accuracy of about 1° (a few degrees for the Moon).

In a case where a planet is on a cusp, read the delineations for both signs to see which fits you. The methods that are used by professional astrologers to obtain accuracy to the minute (1/60th of a degree) and even to the second (1/60th of 1/60th of a degree) are quite complex. If you want a super-accurate chart, see "Tricks of the Trade" for astrological computing services or instructions on how you can do it yourself.

Your Planets in the Signs

*How each planet influences you, depending
on which sign it was in when you were born*

*Each planet in your chart represents one of the basic human drives
within you.*

Saturn, for instance, shows the need for security and responsibility.
Venus shows the desire to create beauty. Mars indicates your drive for
physical satisfaction.

The Moon indicates imagination and your emotional nature and,
along with Saturn, shows areas or ways in which you seek security.
Jupiter shows good fortune, abundance, good humor, and philosophy in
your life.

Mercury in your chart shows how your mind functions. Uranus shows
originality, inventiveness, and independence. Neptune shows idealism
and inspiration or deception and illusions. Pluto shows either outstand-
ing ability and determination or a compulsion to dominate others.

The positive side of each planet will be expressed in your chart if the
planet is placed in a sign in which it is comfortable and/or if it forms
positive aspects to other planets, as we will see in Chapter 12.

The negative sides of the planets will cause trouble in your life if the
planets are placed in signs in which they are uncomfortable or do not
feel at home, and especially if they form negative aspects to other
planets. This also will be examined in Chapter 12.

The overall influence of a planet in your chart—good or bad—depends
on the combination of many factors. Its placement by sign is somewhat
good or bad, but mostly just gives the planet a different "flavor" in each
sign. "Good or bad" influences are for the most part shown by the
aspects, as we will see in Chapter 12.

Now let us see how the energy of each planet is affected by the flavor of each sign. You will notice that, as we go around the Zodiac, the character of the signs gets more complex. Aries is the easiest to understand, Pisces the most complicated. In each case, key words or phrases will be used.

THE MOON

The Moon in your chart tells you about your personality and senses, how popular you are with others, and what role women play in your life.

Moon in Aries: Energetic, aggressive, restless, adventurous, sports-minded.

Moon in Taurus: Sensual, love pleasure and food, need security.

Moon in Gemini: Clever, perceptive, logical, pleasant, sympathetic.

Moon in Cancer: Very imaginative, receptive to other's feelings.

Moon in Leo: You are a warm person with a great love of life.

Moon in Virgo: Analytic and work like a Swiss watch.

Moon in Libra: You give off harmonious, almost healing vibrations.

Moon in Scorpio: A power-seeker; emotional about what you want.

Moon in Sagittarius: Strong sense of humor; positive, optimistic.

Moon in Capricorn: Serious, deep, somewhat fearful.

Moon in Aquarius: Science-minded; unpredictable emotions.

Moon in Pisces: Talented, especially in art and music. Sensitive and sympathetic.

MERCURY

Mercury shows how your mind functions and makes decisions, and also tells what you like to think about most.

Mercury in Aries: You are restless, brash, and speak your mind.

Mercury in Taurus: Peace-loving, slow forming opinions.

Mercury in Gemini: Very perceptive and aware of opposites. Glib.

Mercury in Cancer: Emotionally sensitive to others' opinion of you.

Mercury in Leo: Exuberant and joyful; you may act too hastily.

Mercury in Virgo: Quick-minded and aware of details.

Mercury in Libra: Aloof and distant, cautious of physical affection.

Mercury in Scorpio: You see into others' minds and motives.

Mercury in Sagittarius: Optimistic, happy-go-lucky.

Mercury in Capricorn: Deep thinker; you may take things too seriously.

Mercury in Aquarius: An idea person who may not act on your ideas.

Mercury in Pisces: Imaginative and poetic; a complete romantic.

VENUS

Venus in your chart shows how you respond to beauty and what kind of things you enjoy, what people you are attracted to.

Venus in Aries: Passionate, usually in love and with several lovers.
Venus in Taurus: You love deeply and only one person at a time.
Venus in Gemini: You're fickle and like to flirt and play around.
Venus in Cancer: Romantic, sentimental, you *love* love.
Venus in Leo: Amorous and bold, a physical lover.
Venus in Virgo: Shy and reserved in love; not very physical.
Venus in Libra: You are delicate and like graceful situations.
Venus in Scorpio: Manipulative and subtle in getting what you want.
Venus in Sagittarius: Love is fun and you don't take it seriously.
Venus in Capricorn: Your love is deep but slow to express itself.
Venus in Aquarius: Unpredictable, flirtatious, sometimes zany.
Venus in Pisces: Very sensitive and romantic; you need protection.

MARS

The sign position of Mars in your chart shows how you express your physical energy, and also the masculine half of your sexual nature.

Mars in Aries: Very energetic and active at all times.
Mars in Taurus: Hard-working, good at long or major projects.
Mars in Gemini: You are combative, like to argue, and are rather fidgety.
Mars in Cancer: Sensuous, easily hurt, and touchy. You make a good lover.
Mars in Leo: Heroic, brave, bold. You love to take risks.
Mars in Virgo: Mechanically-minded, a builder and tinkerer.
Mars in Libra: Peace-loving, artistic, but slow to be motivated.
Mars in Scorpio: Passionate, but also very jealous.
Mars in Sagittarius: Positive and exhuberant; sports-loving.
Mars in Capricorn: Very efficient and get a lot done.
Mars in Aquarius: Scattered energies and totally unpredictable.
Mars in Pisces: Sentimental; very sensitive to others' feelings.

JUPITER

Jupiter concerns philosophy in life and shows your area of greatest enthusiasm.

Jupiter in Aries: Very enthusiastic, mostly about yourself.
Jupiter in Taurus: Enthusiastic about your possessions and values.
Jupiter in Gemini: Strong communicator (reading, writing, talking).

Jupiter in Cancer: Deep enthusiasm for love relationships.
Jupiter in Leo: A big thing in your life is to enjoy entertainment.
Jupiter in Virgo: You are very careful and cautious.
Jupiter in Libra: World peace is your main goal.
Jupiter in Scorpio: You want what you want, when you want it.
Jupiter in Sagittarius: You want to enjoy, especially adventure.
Jupiter in Capricorn: You love history and classical things.
Jupiter in Aquarius: New and untried things attract you.
Jupiter in Pisces: Most any experience excites you.

SATURN

Your sense of responsibility and discipline is shown by Saturn's sign position in your chart. It also tells you about the roles of work and security in your life, and your attitude toward authority.

Saturn in Aries: You are ambitious and want success.
Saturn in Taurus: Hard-working, though rather slow and methodical.
Saturn in Gemini: Your work and ideas are expressed in physical ways.
Saturn in Cancer: You may be fearful and have subconscious fears.
Saturn in Leo: Good manager and leader.
Saturn in Virgo: You can work out most any problem.
Saturn in Libra: A good social manager; you take responsibility seriously.
Saturn in Scorpio: Self-honesty is paramount to you.
Saturn in Sagittarius: You can make your dreams come true.
Saturn in Capricorn: Enduring, persistent, ambitious.
Saturn in Aquarius: Inventive, especially in scientific subjects.
Saturn in Pisces: Very sympathetic to others.

Note: The following planets move very slowly, so they only pass through a few signs during your lifetime.

URANUS

Uranus in your chart shows what parts freedom, individuality, new ideas, and surprises will play in your life.

Uranus in Aries: Independent, active, positive.
Uranus in Taurus: Headstrong, resourceful, disruptive.
Uranus in Gemini: Very aware of science and the universe.
Uranus in Cancer: Very romantic; emotions may be uncontrolled.
Uranus in Leo: A vibrant person who can stimulate others.
Uranus in Virgo: Oriented toward technological and ecological ends.

Uranus in Libra: Human relations, world peace are your goals.
Uranus in Scorpio: You can change and revitalize the world.
Uranus in Sagittarius: You are scientific, imaginative.
Uranus in Pisces: Very intuitive, emotional.

NEPTUNE

Neptune stays 10 to 15 years in each sign, so it will influence the spiritual and artistic attitude of a whole generation. Its sign placement shows how you and your generation relate to inspiration, sensitive emotions, psychic communication, and drugs.

Neptune in Leo: You are artistic and dramatic.

Neptune in Virgo: You are skeptical, and have trouble expressing inner feelings.

Neptune in Libra: Peace-loving, gentle, artistic, musically inclined.

Neptune in Scorpio: Intense, often psychic.

Neptune in Sagittarius: Blind optimist and big adventurer.

PLUTO

Pluto remains about 20 years in each sign, so its influence is more historical than personal. Its sign position shows where you and your generation will create social change.

Pluto in Cancer: Intense, need family structure, can create changes in family life.

Pluto in Leo: Tend toward excesses. Your revolution is in sex, love, self-expression, open enjoyment of life.

Pluto in Virgo: Cautious in the use of energy; also sexually careful. Focus energy on environmental change.

Pluto in Libra: Use energies to create peace and order; partnerships are important.

Pluto in Scorpio: People born during this period will be strongwilled and courageous. Many of them will have psychic gifts, especially talents for psychic healing.

The Houses in Your Chart

*How the Houses describe you as an
unique individual*

Astrology has divided the life of Man into 12 areas. Everything that has happened, is happening, or will happen to you is ruled by one of the 12 areas or "Houses" of your chart.

By studying the condition of each house of your chart, you can learn what kinds of natural tendencies influence each area of your life, and how you can cooperate with, and make the most of, these natural tendencies rather than fighting against them.

The houses of your chart reveal information about you that is much more specific and personal than the general information shown by your Sun-sign.

For instance, if Capricorn in your chart falls on your 7th house (the house of marriage and partnerships), then you will only be satisfied with a partner who fulfills, first and foremost, your needs for long-range emotional and financial security. This is because Capricorn values security above all else.

On the other hand, if one of the "flashier" or more "glamorous" signs—such as Leo or Libra—rule your 7th house cusp, then you are looking for a partner who is sociable, charming, and attractive. Security would be of secondary importance to you.

HOW TO FIND REAL SATISFACTION

In a similar but more detailed fashion, your chart points out what it is that will bring you true satisfaction in each area of your life—career, marriage, friendship, financial rewards, etc.

Your chart refers to you as *an unique individual.* It shows why you may be very happy in a job that your best friend would hate. It tells why he might enjoy a hobby of repairing old watches or tinkering with fine-precision gadgets, while you prefer to do something more simple like go fishing.

Truly, "one man's meat is another man's poison." Nothing illustrates this fact of life more clearly than your birth chart. It spells out your unique, individual talents, problems, needs, and desires in clear, definite, specific terms.

WHAT THE FUTURE HOLDS FOR YOU

Keep in mind that your chart shows not only *what you are*, but also *what you want and need to become.*

Some of the potentials in your chart have already been activated in your life. Others remain to be discovered and developed.

Astrology can help you discover and learn how to develop your individual potentials more effectively than any other tool, since your birth chart presents a complete and accurate picture of your drives—mental, emotional, social, financial, etc.—in each area of your life.

On page 91 are the 12 houses in the sky that contain the seeds of all events on earth.

The planet and sign located in each house in this chart are the "rulers" of that house.

Each combination (sign-planet-house) shares a similar character. For instance, Aries, Mars, and the 1st house are all aggressive, forceful, and sometimes selfish. Pisces, Neptune, and the 12th house are all inspirational, sensitive, elusive, and sometimes confusing or wishy-washy.

"OVERLAPPING AFFAIRS"

Certain areas of your life can be influenced by a combination of two or more houses. Your work, for instance, is influenced in different ways by your 2nd house (earned income), your 6th house (service and duty), and your 10th house (career and reputation).

Your love life is affected by your 5th house (love affairs), your 7th house (close partnerships), and your 8th house (sex and shared resources). These two areas will be discussed in detail in Chapter 13.

With a little practice, you will see how things tie together and what advice the houses of your chart give you about your life.

"RETURN TO A FLAT EARTH"

Now let's look at how the houses are formed by the earth and sky. The easiest way to visualize this is to imagine, as people did long ago, that the earth is flat and that the planets and stars revolve around it.

As you can see, the chart on page 92 shows the Sun in the 12th house, Mercury in the 12th, Venus and Jupiter in the 11th, etc.

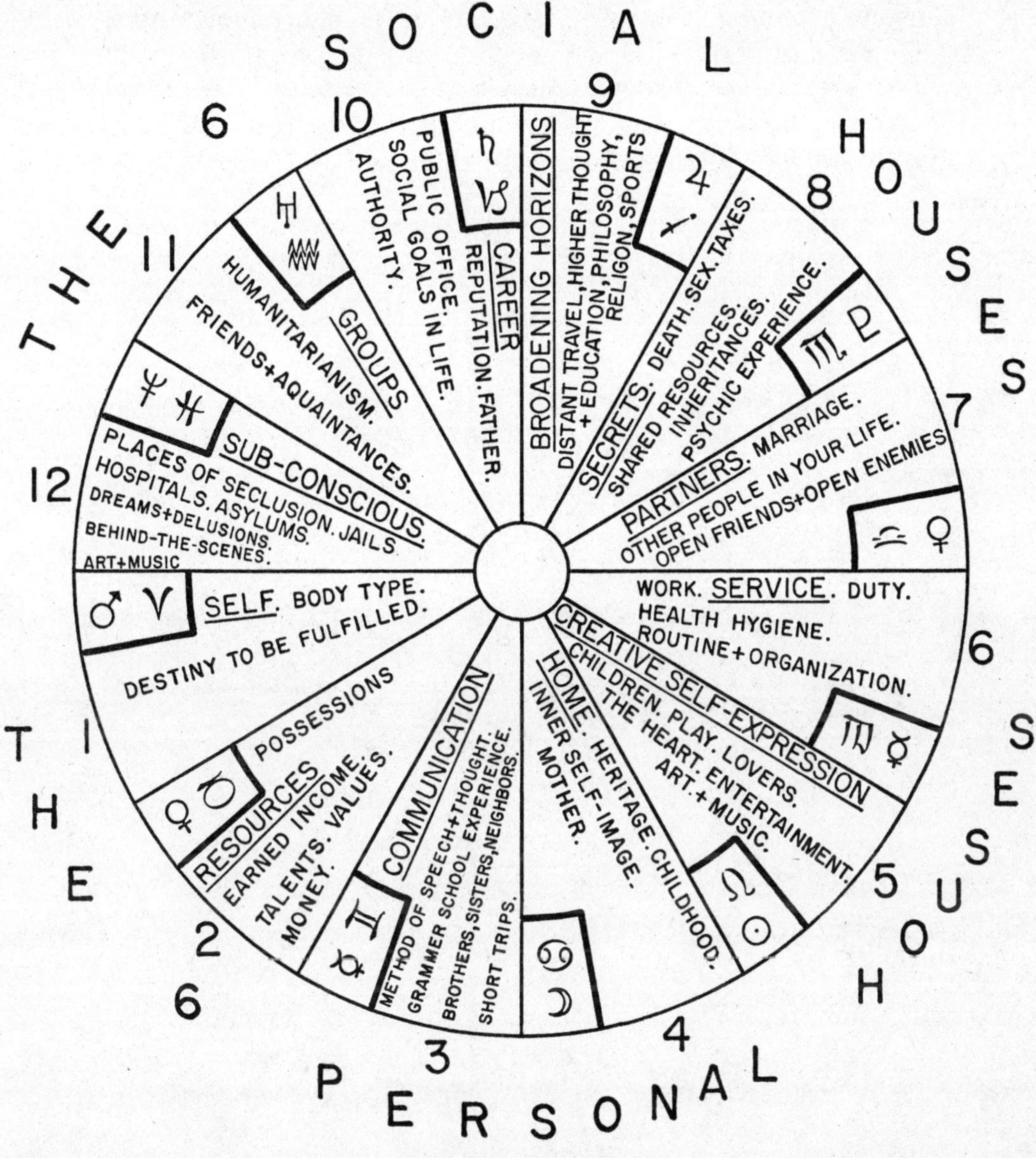

The Houses

"GOING BACKWARD" THROUGH THE HOUSES

The earth's rotation causes the Sun, Moon, and all of the planets to go once around the houses each day in a "backward" fashion: from 12th house to 11th to 10th to 9th, etc.

The Ascendant, as we said earlier, corresponds to the Eastern horizon.

Anyone born just after dawn, such as in the chart shown here, would have the Sun in their 12th house in their birth chart. Anyone born just before sunrise would have the Sun in their 1st house (under the horizon). Anyone born exactly at sunrise would have the Sun right on, or "conjunct to," their Ascendant.

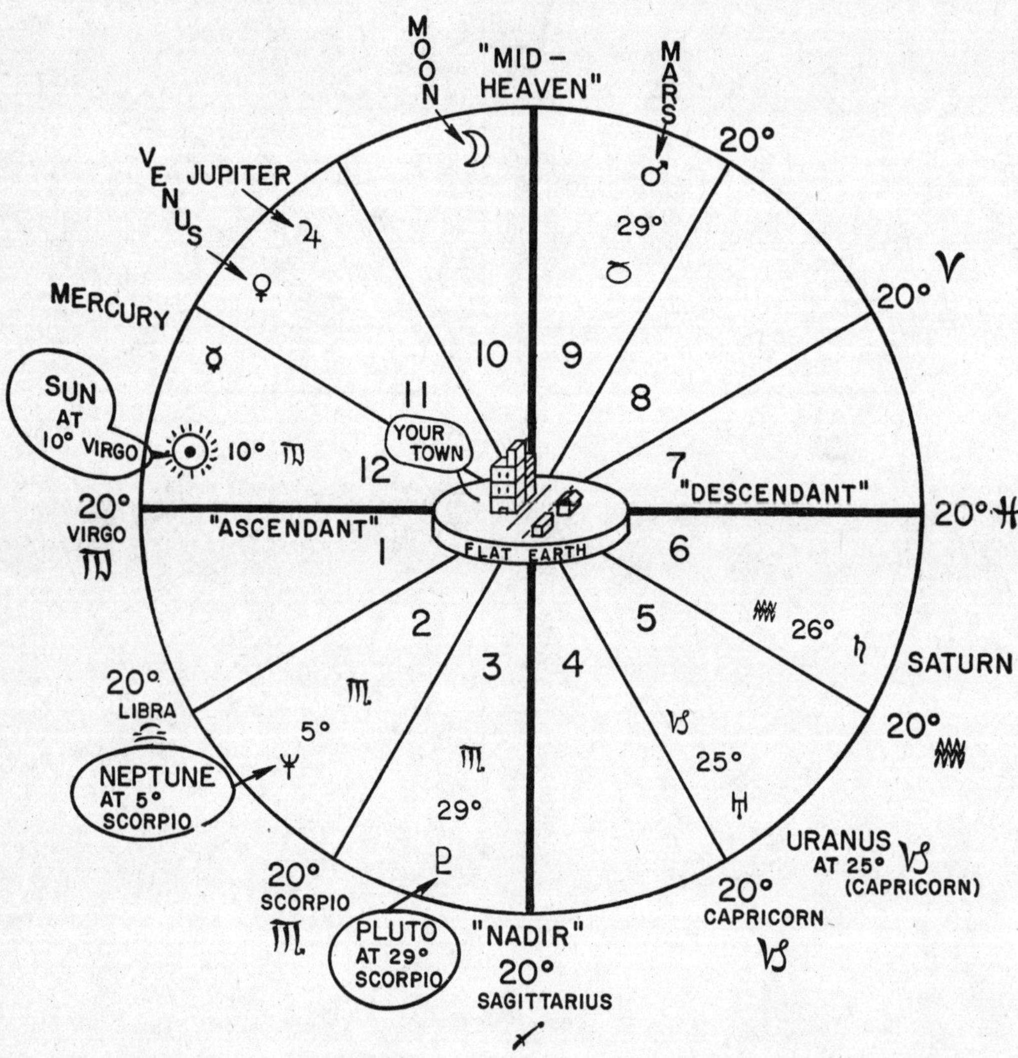

You can judge approximately where the Sun should be in your chart by the time of day that you were born. If you were born about noon, the Sun is near the top of your birth chart—near the Midheaven—in the 9th or 10th house. If born around sunset, the Sun is near your "Descendant" (6th or 7th house). If you were born during the evening, your Sun is in one of the lower houses—houses 1 through 6. A midnight birth would put the Sun near the Nadir—3rd or 4th house.

"THE PERSONAL HOUSES"

The first six houses of the chart—the houses that correspond to the dark side of the earth—are called the personal houses.

If you had all or most of your planets in the first six houses, the bottom half of the chart, your life would be mostly personal. You would enjoy your home, your privacy, your own activities, your family and a few close friends. You would tend to be what psychologists call an "introvert." You would have little interest in politics, big parties, corporate mergers, or social trends, except when they affect you in a personal way.

"THE SOCIAL HOUSES"

On the other hand, if you had all of your planets in the top half of your chart—the social half—you would have very little desire to lead such a private, quiet, personal life. Your great desire would be to be out in public—partying, organizing, leading, changing social trends, being precinct captain, mayor, president, boss—anything that got you out among people, anything social. You would tend to be what psychologists call an "extrovert."

OPPOSING HOUSES

There are two more important points to learn about houses. First is the principle of "opposing" or "complementary" houses.

Each personal house is matched by a social house that is directly opposite to it in the chart, and that deals with a similar issue, but in a social rather than an individual way.

For instance, the 1st house is the house of your self. The 7th house (opposite to the 1st in your chart) is the house of other people in your life—partners, husband or wife, close friends, etc.

The 2nd house is your house of your own income and resources. The 8th (opposite the 2nd) rules resources that mesh with the resources of others—taxes, inheritances, insurance, shared resources in a partnership, etc.

Your 3rd house rules your own thinking and communication—how you think and speak, what you like to think and talk about. The 9th house rules social thought in your life. This is where you learn the thoughts of others and see how your ideas and their ideas fit together, such as college, travel, philosophy, religion, etc.

Your 4th house is your home, your roots of heritage and family, your physical and psychological places of shelter from the world. The 10th house is where you go out into the world, to make your mark, your contribution, and to be seen by the world.

Your 5th house is your own personal creativity, self-expression, and enjoyment. The 11th is where you join with others to accomplish things together with others, where you enjoy being together, or do both at the same time. This would involve clubs, groups, organizations, etc.

Your 6th house is where you fulfill your own personal responsibilities and take care of yourself. The 12th house is where you help to fulfill society's responsibilities and either help to take care of others, or are taken care of by others. This would involve hospitals, convents, monasteries, homes for the aged or sick, prisons, etc., places where people serve society or are served by society.

THE CYCLE OF LIFE

The order of the houses also represents the cycle of human life in a symbolic form.

In the 1st house (the self), the child is born and is aware mostly of itself and its own body. In the 2nd house (resources), the child learns to handle toys and other things outside itself. In the 3rd house (communication), the child learns to speak and to think logically. In the 4th house, the child learns about home and family, and establishes his relationship with his mother.

In the 5th house, he goes to school and learns how to do things. In the 6th, he learns to take care of all his own affairs properly so that he can meet with others in the 7th house.

In the 8th house, he learns to share with others and do things with them. In the 9th he learns to share his thinking with others and exchange ideas in a social forum. In the 10th he builds a social "home" for himself in the world—an office, an official way he is known by the world (not necessarily how he makes his income, but how he is known by the world).

In the 11th house he joins with others for social action, social expression, and finally, in the 12th house, he serves the community or retires to rest, contemplate, and let go of concerns that have bound him to this world.

HOW TO USE THIS INFORMATION

A close study of where the planets and signs are in your chart, by house, can reveal an amazing amount of information about yourself—your drives, desires, ambitions, needs—and about how you can achieve success and happiness. If you really want to let astrology work for you in your life, you will make the best use of this information and apply it to your daily living and to your future efforts and plans.

Finding Your Ascendant and Building Your Houses

How to set up a basic birth chart

In this chapter you will learn to calculate the sign and degree of your ascendant and other house cusps, which lays the framework for the complete birth chart.

The method you will use is a simplified version of the one used by professional astrologers. It is much easier and faster, but not quite as accurate as the full professional technique.

FINDING YOUR ASCENDANT

1. Label a sheet of paper "Ascendant" and write your name.

2. Write down your time of birth in Standard Time. (If you were born during Daylight Savings Time, subtract one hour from your birth time to find your birth time in Standard Time.)

3. "Sidereal Time" is a time measure of the earth's daily motion in relation to the stars (the Zodiac). It is an astronomical time reference system also used in constructing a birth chart.

Find your birthday in the following chart "Sidereal Times at Noon". If your birthday is not listed, use the closest date that is listed, or estimate between the two closest dates.

Let's use an example of someone born at 1:30 p.m. on January 9 of any year. Find the Sidereal Time at noon on January 9, which is 19' 10" (19 hours, 10 minutes), from the table published here.

Sidereal Times at Noon

	1	3	6	9	12	15	18	21	24	27	30
Jan	18'40"	18'50"	19'00"	19'10"	19'25"	19'35"	19'50"	20'00"	20'10"	20'25"	20'35"
Feb	20'40"	20'50"	21'00"	21'15"	21'25"	21'40"	21'50"	22'00"	22'10"	22'25"	
Mar	22'40"	22'45"	22'55"	23'10"	23'20"	23'30"	23'45"	23'55"	0'10"	0'20"	0'30"
Apr	0'40"	0'50"	0'60"	1'10"	1'22"	1'35"	1'45"	1'60"	2'10"	2'20"	2'30"
May	2'40"	2'45"	2'60"	3'10"	3'20"	3'30"	3'45"	3'55"	4'10"	4'20"	4'30"
Jun	4'40"	4'50"	4'60"	5'10"	5'20"	5'35"	5'45"	5'60"	6'10"	6'20"	6'35"
Jul	6'40"	6'45"	6'60"	7'10"	7'20"	7'30"	7'45"	7'55"	8'10"	8'20"	8'30"
Aug	8'40"	8'50"	9'0"	9'10"	9'20"	9'35"	9'50"	10'00"	10'10"	10'20"	10'35"
Sep	10'40"	10'50"	11'00"	11'15"	11'25"	11'40"	11'50"	12'00"	12'10"	12'25"	12'40"
Oct	12'41"	12'50"	13'00"	13'10"	13'25"	13'35"	13'50"	13'60"	14'10"	14'25"	14'35"
Nov	14'40"	14'50"	15'00"	15'15"	15'25"	15'40"	15'50"	16'00"	16'10"	16'25"	16'40"
Dec	16'41"	16'50"	17'00"	17'10"	17'25"	17'35"	17'50"	18'00"	18'10"	18'35"	18'35"

4. Write down the Sidereal Time (S.T.) at noon:

	hours	minutes
S.T. at noon:	19'	10"
Then add *Birth Time Past noon:*	1'	30" (1:30 p.m.)
and you have the *Total Sidereal Time:*	20'	40"

5. "Birth Time Past Noon": If you have a p.m. birth, like the one shown here, simply write in the hour and minute of birth in Standard Time. Add it to the "S.T. at Noon" to find the "Total Sidereal Time" (which you will use to find your Ascendant.)

If you have an a.m. birth, add 12 hours to it before you write it in as the "Birth Time Past Noon."

For instance, 1:00 a.m. would be 13 hours (13'10") past noon. 6:30 a.m. would be 18 hours, 30 minutes (18'30") past noon, etc.

6. In your "Total Sidereal Time," if your "minutes" figure is 60 or more, it will have to be converted into hours.

Example:

Total Sidereal Time:	5'	75"
equals:	6'	15"

7. If your "Total Sidereal Time" is greater than 24 hours, subtract 24 hours from it.

Example:

Total Sidereal Time:	25'	10"
	−24'	00"
equals:	1'	10"

8. Once you have your "Total Sidereal Time", you find your Ascendant and house cusps by looking up your "Total Sidereal Time" in a Table of Houses.

If your exact Sidereal Time is not listed in the Table of Houses, estimate or calculate between the two closest listings. Make a note of the sign and degree of your Ascendant and house cusps.

Table of Houses
For the United States and Canada

Side- real Time	1st (Ascen)	2nd	3rd	4th	5th	6th
			House Cusps			
0'0"	19 Ce	9 Lo	1 Vr	0 Lb	6 Sc	15 Sg
0'15"	22 Ce	12 Lo	5 Vr	4 Lb	11 Sc	19 Sg
0'35"	26 Ce	15 Lo	9 Vr	9 Lb	16 Sc	23 Sg
0'51"	29 Ce	19 Lo	13 Vr	14 Lb	21 Sc	28 Sg
1'10"	3 Lo	23 Lo	18 Vr	19 Lb	26 Sc	2 Cp
1'30"	7 Lo	27 Lo	22 Vr	24 Lb	1 Sg	6 Cp
1'50"	11 Lo	2 Vr	28 Vr	29 Lb	6 Sg	11 Cp
2'6"	14 Lo	5 Vr	2 Lb	4 Sc	10 Sg	15 Cp
2'26"	18 Lo	10 Vr	6 Lb	9 Sc	15 Sg	19 Cp
2'46"	22 Lo	14 Vr	11 Lb	14 Sc	19 Sg	23 Cp
3'6"	26 Lo	18 Vr	16 Lb	19 Sc	24 Sg	27 Cp
3'27"	29 Lo	23 Vr	21 Lb	24 Sc	29 Sg	1 Aq
3'50"	4 Vr	28 Vr	27 Lb	30 Sc	5 Cp	7 Aq
4'8"	8 Vr	2 Lb	1 Sc	4 Sg	8 Cp	10 Aq
4'30"	12 Vr	6 Lb	6 Sc	9 Sg	13 Cp	15 Aq
4'50"	16 Vr	11 Lb	11 Sc	14 Sg	18 Cp	19 Aq
5'12"	20 Vr	16 Lb	16 Sc	19 Sg	23 Cp	24 Aq
5'30"	25 Vr	20 Lb	21 Sc	24 Sg	28 Cp	28 Aq
6'0"	29 Vr	26 Lb	26 Sc	29 Sg	4 Aq	4 Ps
6'17"	3 Lb	0 Sc	0 Sg	4 Cp	7 Aq	9 Ps
6'40"	8 Lb	4 Sc	5 Sg	9 Cp	12 Aq	13 Ps

Side-real Time	1st (Ascen)	2nd	3rd	4th	5th	6th
			House Cusps			
7'00"	12 Lb	9 Sc	10 Sg	14 Cp	17 Aq	17 Ps
7'22"	16 Lb	14 Sc	15 Sg	19 Cp	22 Aq	22 Ps
7'44"	21 Lb	18 Sc	18 Sg	24 Cp	27 Aq	26 Ps
8'8"	25 Lb	23 Sc	25 Sg	30 Cp	3 Ps	2 Ar
8'25"	29 Lb	27 Sc	29 Sg	4 Aq	7 Ps	6 Ar
8'46"	3 Sc	1 Sg	4 Cp	9 Aq	12 Ps	10 Ar
9'6"	7 Sc	5 Sg	9 Cp	14 Aq	17 Ps	14 Ar
9'25"	11 Sc	10 Sg	13 Cp	19 Aq	22 Ps	19 Ar
9'45"	14 Sc	14 Sg	18 Cp	24 Aq	26 Ps	23 Ar
10'8"	19 Sc	19 Sg	24 Cp	29 Aq	2 Ar	28 Ar
10'24"	22 Sc	22 Sg	28 Cp	4 Ps	6 Ar	1 Tr
10'42"	26 Sc	26 Sg	2 Aq	9 Ps	10 Ar	5 Tr
11'1"	29 Sc	1 Cp	7 Aq	14 Ps	15 Ar	9 Tr
11'20"	3 Sg	5 Cp	12 Aq	19 Ps	19 Ar	13 Tr
11'38"	7 Sg	9 Cp	17 Aq	24 Ps	23 Ar	17 Tr
12'0"	11 Sg	15 Cp	24 Aq	29 Ps	29 Ar	21 Tr
12'15"	14 Sg	18 Cp	28 Aq	4 Ar	2 Tr	25 Tr
12'33"	18 Sg	23 Cp	3 Ps	9 Ar	6 Tr	28 Tr
12'52"	22 Sg	28 Cp	9 Ps	14 Ar	11 Tr	2 Gm
13'10"	26 Sg	3 Aq	15 Ps	19 Ar	15 Tr	7 Gm
13'29"	0 Cp	9 Aq	20 Ps	24 Ar	19 Tr	10 Gm
13'50"	6 Cp	16 Aq	27 Ps	29 Ar	25 Tr	15 Gm
14'7"	9 Cp	21 Aq	2 Ar	4 Tr	28 Tr	18 Gm
14'26"	14 Cp	27 Aq	8 Ar	9 Tr	2 Gm	23 Gm
14'46"	20 Cp	4 Ps	14 Ar	14 Tr	7 Gm	27 Gm
15'6"	25 Cp	11 Ps	20 Ar	19 Tr	11 Gm	2 Ce
15'27"	1 Aq	18 Ps	26 Ar	24 Tr	16 Gm	6 Ce
15'51"	9 Aq	27 Ps	4 Tr	29 Tr	21 Gm	13 Ce
16'8"	15 Aq	3 Ar	9 Tr	4 Gm	25 Gm	17 Ce
16'29"	23 Aq	11 Ar	15 Tr	9 Gm	0 Ce	22 Ce
16'51"	1 Ps	18 Ar	20 Tr	14 Gm	5 Ce	28 Ce
17'12"	9 Ps	26 Ar	26 Tr	19 Gm	10 Ce	4 Lo

Side-real Time	1st (Ascen)	2nd	3rd	4th	5th	6th
			House Cusps			
17'34"	19 Ps	3 Tr	2 Gm	24 Gm	15 Ce	10 Lo
18'00"	29 Ps	12 Tr	9 Gm	29 Gm	22 Ce	18 Lo
18'17"	8 Ar	17 Tr	13 Gm	4 Ce	26 Ce	24 Lo
18'39"	17 Ar	23 Tr	18 Gm	9 Ce	2 Lo	1 Vr
19'01"	26 Ar	0 Gm	23 Gm	14 Ce	7 Lo	9 Vr
19'22"	4 Tr	6 Gm	28 Gm	19 Ce	13 Lo	16 Vr
19'44"	12 Tr	11 Gm	3 Ce	24 Ce	19 Lo	24 Vr
20'9"	21 Tr	17 Gm	9 Ce	29 Ce	26 Lo	3 Lb
20'25"	26 Tr	21 Gm	12 Ce	4 Lo	1 Vr	9 Lb
20'46"	2 Gm	26 Gm	17 Ce	9 Lo	7 Vr	16 Lb
21'5"	8 Gm	1 Ce	21 Ce	14 Lo	13 Vr	24 Lb
21'26"	14 Gm	6 Ce	26 Ce	19 Lo	19 Vr	0 Sc
21'45"	19 Gm	10 Ce	0 Lo	24 Lo	25 Vr	7 Sc
22'8"	24 Gm	15 Ce	5 Lo	29 Lo	3 Lb	14 Sc
22'24"	28 Gm	18 Ce	9 Lo	4 Vr	7 Lb	19 Sc
22'42"	2 Ce	22 Ce	13 Lo	9 Vr	13 Lb	24 Sc
23'1"	6 Ce	26 Ce	17 Lo	14 Vr	19 Lb	0 Sg
23'20"	10 Ce	0 Lo	22 Lo	19 Vr	24 Lb	5 Sg
23'38"	14 Ce	4 Lo	26 Lo	24 Vr	0 Sc	10 Sg
24'00"	19 Ce	9 Lo	1 Vr	0 Lb	6 Sc	15 Sg

Professional astrologers use books which contain a separate table of houses for each of the world's major cities. In this book, we have published a more general table of houses for the United States and Canada.

This is really a table of houses for 41° North Latitude. If you were born about as far north as New York City, Chicago, Denver, Salt Lake City, or northern California, this table of houses is very accurate for your chart.

If you were born north of 41° North Latitude, subtract 1° from the sign positions listed in the table for your "Total Sidereal Time" for every 2 degrees north of 41° North.

If you were born south of 41° North Latitude, add 1° to the sign positions for every 2 degrees South of 41° North.

9. Now draw a blank chart, like this:

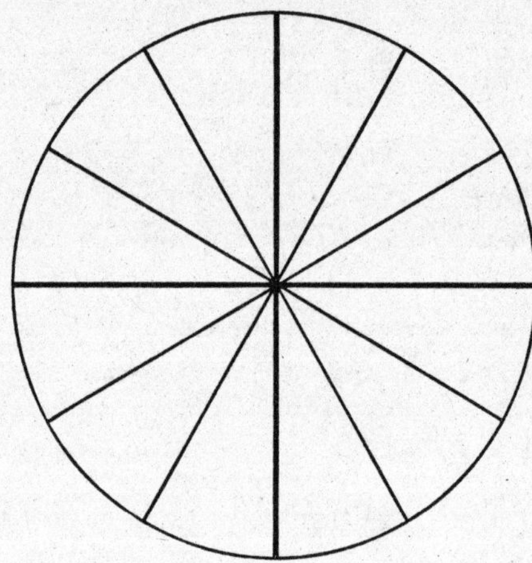

10. Fill in the sign and degree of your Ascendant (which is your 1st house cusp) and your 2nd, 3rd, 4th, 5th, and 6th house cusps. Here is an example based on the first listing in the table of houses (0'00" Sidereal Time).

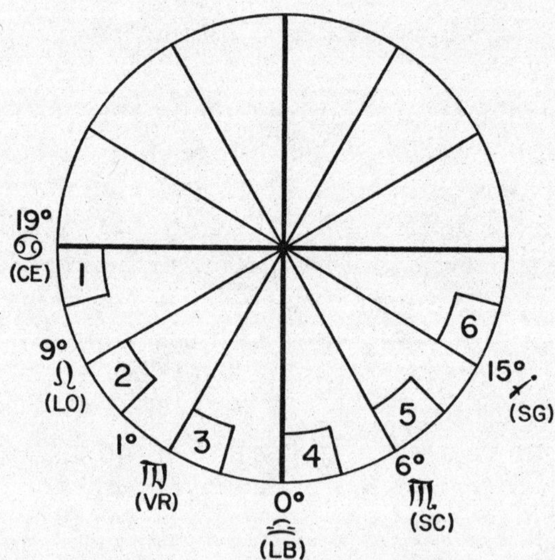

11. Now fill in the opposite signs on the opposite houses, but put the same degree number on the opposite houses, like this:

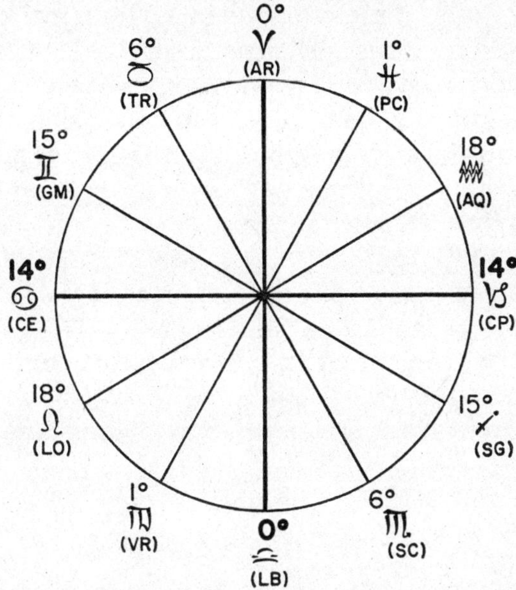

12. If you have one sign on two different house cusps, as in the example below, then you have an "intercepted" sign also somewhere in your chart.

An intercepted sign is a sign that is "stuck in the middle" of a house—a sign that does not rule a cusp. An intercepted sign shows an energy that usually has difficulty in expressing itself in your life. Other people will expect you to express the quality of the sign that is on the *cusp* of the house. Your challenge here is to learn to express the quality of the sign that is intercepted (the one in the middle of the house).

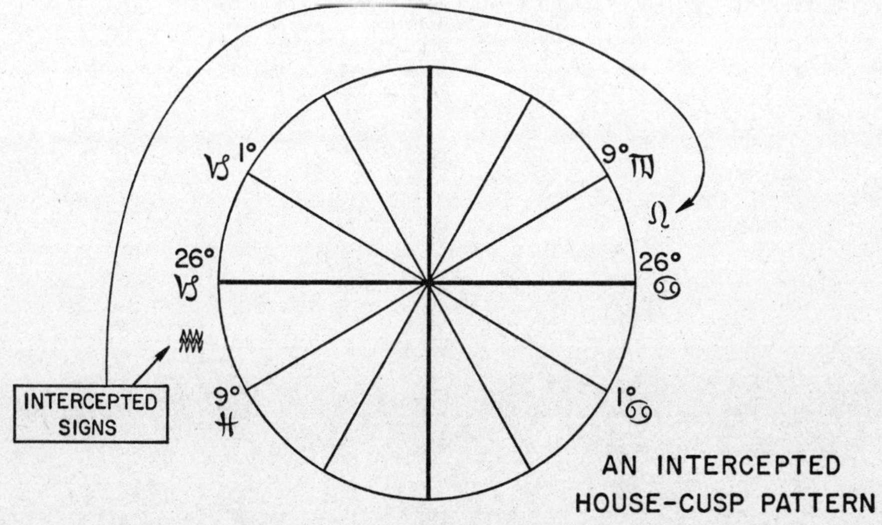

13. If you find that you are rising on one of the final degrees (27°, 28°, or 29°) of a sign, or one of the earliest degrees (0°, 1°, or 2°) of a sign, then you are "rising on a cusp," and your Ascendant will be strongly influenced by the neighboring sign. There will be a blend of the qualities of the two signs, with the sign that the Ascendant is actually in being the more powerful of the two influences. This principle applies to any house cusps or planets that fall near a cusp.

14. Now take your list of planets' positions (from Chapter 7) and use it to place your planets into their proper houses in your chart.

Try to place the planets as accurately as possible, and plan it out before you start writing them in, in order to avoid any last-minute crowding.

Here is an example of a complete chart, with the planets in the houses:

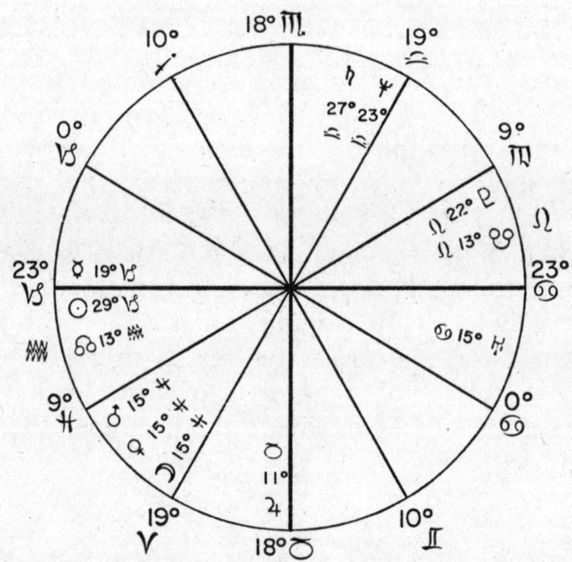

The Planets in Your Houses

How to find new insights into your life

Every planet represents a basic drive or function in your life. The sign that the planet is in, in your birth chart, describes the basic flavor of that influence in your life.

The house that the planet is in describes where in your life that drive will operate.

So all three factors—planet, sign, and house—work together to influence a part of your life.

For instance, Mercury in the 1st house indicates a person who is always thinking—a mental person who spends a lot of time thinking about himself (the 1st is the house of the self and of the image you project). This person also spends a great deal of time projecting his personality verbally.

Mercury in the 2nd house indicates someone who is usually thinking about money and how to make more of it. This person is often busy thinking of how to improve his resources. He could earn money (2nd house) by mental agility: writing, communications, broadcasting, bargaining, salesmanship, and quick thinking.

Along with the house placement of each planet in your chart, consider the planet's position by sign.

For instance, Mercury in the 2nd house in a fire sign would belong to a person that could use his mind to make money by way of forceful, positive, exciting ways such as communications or sales. This person likes to think on a grand scale and leave the details to others.

Mercury in the 2nd house in Capricorn or Virgo indicates a person who would earn money through mentality or communications in a more patient, disciplined, detailed way, such as an accountant, banker, secretary, statistician, researcher, etc. This is a person whose mind is more formal, reserved, and introverted; someone who doesn't mind detail and would prefer to leave the salesmanship to someone else.

Here, then, are brief descriptions of what the planets in the houses of your chart indicate. As you read them, spend some time thinking about each one, and about how each of your planets is influenced by its sign-and-house combination.

You may want to review the nature of each sign involved (see Chapters 5 and 8) and each house involved (Chapter 9) in order to synthesize a more detailed picture of what that planet says about you and your life.

Even professional astrologers, after years of studying their own charts, continue to find new insights into their lives just by looking at their own charts with a mind that is open to seeing things there that they have never noticed before.

Never assume that you have exhausted all of the information that your chart can tell you. There is always more, if you are willing to look a little deeper.

The following section tells the influences of the planets in the different houses, which can give you a great deal of knowledge about yourself and your dealings with others. While you will learn a lot about a wide variety of subjects in this section, you also can benefit greatly by consulting similiar information in other books describing the planet influences in the houses.

Often you may be amazed at how accurately astrology paints a picture of you and even reveals your innermost secrets about yourself, your way of doing or looking at things, and your basic drives. Even those who do not believe in astrology often marvel at the accuracy of the information they obtain from studying the planets in the houses.

PLANETS IN THE HOUSE

1st house—Planets in the 1st house influence your public personality—how you see the world, and reveal your basic potential or tendencies.

Sun in 1st house: You have a great deal of self-confidence and identity with and acceptance of yourself. You want to be recognized and appreciated by others and to be well-known. Your health and endurance will be excellent for both work and romance.

Moon in 1st house: You are keenly tuned in to things and people around you. You are full of enthusiasm. Romantically, you are sensitive to your partner.

Mercury in 1st house: Intellectual, mental things stimulate you, such as books and talking. You may be restless, even nervous, which can influence your career and romance pursuits.

Venus in 1st house: This placement gives beauty or good looks and charm. You are very love-directed and may be a flirt. Others are attracted to you because you give off positive vibrations.

Mars in 1st house: You have a high level of energy. Others either see you as a hero or perhaps as an overly aggressive type. You are a person of courage and great pride, with a strong positive attitude that can serve you well in career and romance.

Jupiter in 1st house: You are cheerful and open-minded, with great ability to impress influential people who can help you in many ways. Life generally holds great good fortune for you.

Saturn in 1st house: A strong ambition is coupled with a tenacious nature so you finish what you start. However, inhibition may restrict you, and needs controlling. Overcome timidity in romance and also don't be too serious.

Uranus in 1st house: Your nature is unconventional and you do things in eccentric or unexpected ways. You may be regarded as being unstable to others, and they will resent your efforts to dominate them.

Neptune in 1st house: You are good at changing identities and creating illusions and moods. If properly used, these traits can be helpful in career and romance. Others may think you are deceiving them.

Pluto in 1st house: A strong sense of power makes you want to dominate people or things. Romantically, you want lots of experience, so the placement is not good for marriage.

2nd house—Planets in your 2nd house are related to money matters and material security in your life.

Sun in 2nd house: Making money and acquiring possessions dominate you. You may be over-possessive, with things and people. Romantically, you will be successful because of your generosity.

Moon in 2nd house: You are shrewd in business and have a strong drive to save. A strong need for security makes you want to have familiar things around you. Money may influence your choice in marriage.

Mercury in 2nd house: You have good powers to bargain and to be an aggressive salesperson. Intellectual pursuits will bring you financial rewards, but your fortune will tend to fluctuate. Impatience in financial matters can interfere with your love life.

Venus in 2nd house: You can make money in the arts, from nature, or land. Obtaining possessions may dominate your drives. You may become financially lucky in love, such as marrying someone wealthy.

Mars in 2nd house: You are ambitious and can make big money but also may become a big spender. You may have to fight for what you get in life, but you usually will get what you want, in career and in a life partner.

Jupiter in 2nd house: You will have a great deal of business ability and expansive energy, having good luck in money and real estate matters. You will get gifts of money and be generous with it to others. Romantically, you are kind and sympathetic but probably underappreciated.

Saturn in 2nd house: You have a great deal of ambition and are willing to work hard for financial rewards, material possessions, and the status career success can bring. You have strong concentrative energy. You may allow money matters to dominate your romantic life.

Uranus in 2nd house: For you, money will be "easy come, easy go." You will earn money in unconventional ways, but lose it, then make more, and lose it. Be careful of impractical business ventures.

Neptune in 2nd house: You are idealistic about the use of money and have a spiritual energy. Your fortune could be made in fields related to the sea, from oils, perfumes, or music. Carelessness regarding money matters can interfere with romantic happiness.

Pluto in 2nd house: You have a great desire for money and material things, and have strong regenerative energy. Happiness can be achieved by putting your financial motives on a higher, altruistic plane. This is a good aspect for bankers or stock brokers. Romantically, you may be emotionally hard for your mate to reach.

3rd house—Planets in the 3rd house influence the way you communicate with others. Sun, Moon, or other planets in this house indicate success in writing, speaking, reading.

Sun in 3rd house: You have a strong desire to achieve success and status through intellectual pursuits. You are eager to learn new things, especially scientific, and to express what you learn and know. You also love to travel. Romantically, you have an ability to make very good contacts, especially on your travels.

Moon in 3rd house: Your thinking and communication is strongly influenced by your imagination and you may tend toward daydreaming and fantasy. Trivial things may preoccupy you. Writing and teaching are ideal occupations for you. Romantically, you should mix and assert yourself, not allowing your mate to dominate you.

Mercury in 3rd house: You have superior intellectual abilities, and are an original thinker. Writing, television, radio are very important to you. Reason will tend to guide you in romantic matters.

Venus in 3rd house: You are interested in artistic and cultural matters, especially literature and poetry. You are very friendly and can communicate harmoniously with others. Romantically, you are always agreeable to compromise and are therefore easy to love and live with.

Mars in 3rd house: You are aggressive and have an alert mind; a quick-thinker in emergencies. But you may tend to jump to conclusions, communicate too abruptly, or lack tact. Careers may be in communications, machinery or automotive fields. Your mate may not appreciate your short temper and abruptness.

Jupiter in 3rd house: You are optimistic, philosophic, and spiritual. You love to learn and could be successful in education, publishing, philosophy, religion, or communications. You also love to travel and communicate with people of other cultures.

Saturn in 3rd house: You are very practical and concentrate on useful ideas. Your thinking is methodical and you could do well in mathematic or scientific fields. Your communication is of a precise nature. You travel more for business than for pleasure. Relatives, especially in-laws, can interfere with romantic harmony.

Uranus in 3rd house: You are free-thinking and intuitive, basing your conclusions on experience or fact. Inventors and scientists often have this placement. You communicate by way of theories, inspiration, and vision. Your unconventional nature may make it hard for the opposite sex to understand you.

Neptune in 3rd house: You are quite intuitive and receive ideas from images that come to your mind. You probably are gifted with mental telepathy. Your psychic powers could turn off the opposite sex. Be careful entering into contracts.

Pluto in 3rd house: You have a probing mind able to understand many of life's basic meanings. Your original ideas will make you attractive to business partners. Good careers are science and other mental fields. You will be a student all your life. Your wit will add to your romantic desirability.

4th house—Planets in the 4th house describe your experience in the family, both that in which you were born and that which you will create.

Sun in 4th house: You want a secure home and family life. You are proud of your heritage and have a strong feeling and need for home, land, ecology, and natural resources. You may not attain money and security until later in life. Romantically, you want a comfortable home life that will last all your life.

Moon in 4th house: A strong emotional tie to home and family as a young person makes it imperative that you establish a strong home-family relationship in maturity. Careers related to the home, such as real estate, cooking, home products, are indicated. You have a strong parental instinct and want very much to have children.

Mercury in 4th house: Your home life will be full of mental and educational energy. You may even work at home. Careers may be in real estate, farming, geology, and ecology. Your quest for new and exciting adventures may cause many changes in your love life.

Venus in 4th house: You are emotionally attached to the home and most likely will have good relationships with your family. You enjoy entertaining friends and lovers at home. You are close to your parents and may inherit money or property from them. You love the land and enjoy gardening. Your childhood home life may have been so pleasant, you may not establish a home and family of your own until later in life.

Mars in 4th house: You are an active person who will be restless at home and has to keep busy there. You will enjoy improving your home environment, especially in do-it-yourself projects. Your married home life may not be peaceful.

Jupiter in 4th house: Comfort, security, and safety in the home are of major interest to you. This aspect indicates inheritance of property from the parents. Much happiness will come to you in and through the home and family relationships. Good fortune in real estate dealings is indicated.

Saturn in 4th house: Heavy responsibilities are placed upon you through home and family ties. Your parents may be strict and conservative. You may feel restricted or limited at home. A negative outlook regarding home life may interfere with your romantic life.

Uranus in 4th house: You want freedom at home, to come and go as you please. One of your parents may be exceptional in some way, making life difficult for you. You may move a lot. Your best friends will be like part of your family. You need things around the home to keep you from becoming anxious or restless.

Neptune in 4th house: Strong subconscious ties bind you to the home and family. One parent may be psychic. You are a dreamer at home and can create a very pleasant environment. You have a strong need to live by or with water. Your idealism regarding the home may make it hard for you to achieve your dream home situation.

Pluto in 4th house: You want to be master of your home. Such a dominating nature may create problems with other family members. You may have an almost mystic love of nature and will be very involved in ecology or conservation. You will be restless at home and want freedom and adventure. Careers in archaeology and real estate are indicated. You may move a lot.

5th house—Planets here show what you love most to do, and also how you express the feelings in your heart.

Sun in 5th house: You have a great love of life and a strong drive to express yourself in creative ways. You love pleasure and want others to notice and appreciate you. Happy-go-lucky, you will have lots of friends. You give and receive love very well. Careers in the arts or sports are favored.

Moon in 5th house: Your imagination and emotional needs strongly influence your romantic and recreational pursuits. You have a strong need to give and receive love, and also to enjoy life. If your Moon is afflicted, beware of impulsive or speculative money dealings or of gambling.

Mercury in 5th house: You are artistic and creative, perhaps suited to be a playwright or other writer, even a critic. You express yourself forcefully in writing or speaking and want others to admire you for your intellect. A good placement for stock brokers. Romantically, you want to communicate with those whom you love.

Venus in 5th house: You have a great love for pleasure and for nature in a romantic way. You have a bright, positive outlook on life and romance is very important to you. You are very successful in giving and receiving love and affection. You get along very well with young people and could be successful as a teacher or child psychiatrist. You'll make a great parent.

Mars in 5th house: You keep yourself busy pursuing love and pleasure. You have a strong sexual need to find a satisfactory sex partner. The placement is good for artists who work with tools, especially sculptors. You are cheerful, out-going, masculine.

Jupiter in 5th house: You are optimistic in love matters. You also are an adventurer and could enjoy group love situations. Careers indicated are in the arts, sports, and education, primarily involving children. Also the stock market and investments.

Saturn in 5th house: You need a lot of affection and may have difficulty expressing love and your inner feelings. You may have considerable responsibilities involving children. You are conservative but could do well as an investor or broker. Your need for self-expression could serve you well in politics or business management.

Uranus in 5th house: You like unusual people and they like you. Your romantic relationships may be unpredictable, even rather zany. Your activity in the stock market could bring you sudden changes of wealth. Careers in movies, radio, television, and recording are favored.

Neptune in 5th house: You are in love with love and tend to look at the world through rose-colored glasses. You can easily be deceived by those you love. Your ability to play roles suits you well for an acting career. Gifts of intuition may serve you for success concerning investments and speculations.

Pluto in 5th house: You have a great deal of creative power which can express itself in many ways. You may be greatly gifted in the arts. Your love relationships will be creative and intense. Sex and love are merged for you and are both very important to you. If your Pluto is afflicted, beware of financial losses through speculation.

6th house—This house describes what jobs or careers you are best suited for, your attitude toward work, and how you want to be of service to others.

Sun in 6th house: You have a strong need to become recognized for your work and service to others. Careers in social work or health occupations where you can make use of your creative expression are indicated. You are a good worker and take pride in your work, but you also want recognition for your efforts. You may have rather delicate health, but if you take proper care of yourself you can achieve your most challenging goals.

Moon in 6th house: Your health, largely affected by your emotions, will play an important part in your work life and how you get along with employer or fellow employees. You may tend to change jobs often. Careers working with small animals, in hospitals, or service organizations are favored.

Mercury in 6th house: You are skilled working with figures, details, or intellectual matters. Keeping up with the latest trends, techniques, and research in your field is important to you. Careers in medicine, science, engineering are favored. You may tend to overwork or be a perfectionist.

Venus in 6th house: Artistic or social work is indicated. You will love your work and get along well with others in your work life. You may very well meet your future mate through your work. Your love of beautiful clothing suits you for careers in dressmaking and designing. You also love small animals and could do well working for pet shops or zoos.

Mars in 6th house: You have a lot of energy regarding work and also a strong need to serve others. Careers indicated involve work with powerful machinery or sharp tools, such as machinist, mechanic, heavy-equipment operator or builder, steelworker, mechanical engineer. You may be argumentative or feisty on the job.

Jupiter in 6th house: You are strongly interested in both service work and work that is constructive. You want to be of very practical benefit to others. Strong interest in the body and mind suit you for work in healing, religion, massage, homeopathy and other types of natural medicine. The position indicates an advocate of the Christian Science religion or similar philosophy.

Saturn in 6th house: You will be a hard and efficient worker, since you take your work very seriously. Your work or service will bring you heavy responsibility. Careers in medicine, diet, food processing, science, engineering are indicated. Because of health reasons or low vitality, be careful of overwork and worry.

Uranus in 6th house: Unusual types of healing and of diet are of great interest to you. Careers indicated include homepathy, audio therapy, spiritual healing, diet planning. A similar interest in advanced technology suggests careers in electronic engineering or computer programming. Your need to serve yourself above others may make it hard for you to keep a steady job. You may be more successful working for yourself.

Neptune in 6th house: Your work or service will be performed in a spiritual way. Your work may be either very confusing or very relaxing. You are strongly tuned in to the feelings of others. You love animals and may be able to communicate psychically with them. Careers indicated include spiritual healing, homeopathy, health foods.

Pluto in 6th house: You will be very powerful in your work and could have jobs that are physically demanding or grueling. You have an ability to improve the methods of the work you choose. Positive thinking and good diet planning can help you overcome health problems.

7th house—This house shows the type of person you will marry and also indicates your most stable partnerships including business partners.

Sun in 7th house: You have an ability to attract strong, capable, loyal friends. You will probably marry someone with a strong sense of identity, or a brave or creative person. Marriage is of very high importance in your life. Since you deal well with people, you could be successful in public relations, sales, or promotion.

Moon in 7th house: You will marry for emotional reasons and your need for domestic security. Your parents may figure prominently in your marriage decisions and you also may seek a mother or father figure as a mate. You enjoy dealing with the public and could do well in business. The person you marry may be very energetic and aggressive, or your business partner may have these traits, but you generally welcome them.

Mercury in 7th house: You may marry an intellectual person, such as a teacher, writer, or someone involved in short trips such as a salesman or truck driver. You are concerned with communicating and tuning in mentally with others. You prefer working in a partnership situation rather than alone. Your skill in dealing with other people indicates careers in sales, law, and public relations.

Venus in 7th house: You are considerate and pleasant with other people, so you will be popular. You will be attracted to a marriage partner who loves art and nature. You work well with others and can be successful in sales, psychology, public relations, and the performing arts.

Mars in 7th house: You will probably marry an aggressive person, someone of great energy, or your business partner will have those traits. You prefer to work together with someone instead of on your own. Your own aggressive nature can be helpful in careers of sales, personnel, or public relations.

Jupiter in 7th house: You are an open, friendly, helpful person who will be lucky in love and career. You have a very strong sense of justice and fair play for others. You will show good judgment in choosing a business or marriage partner. Careers indicated are law, public relations, sales, mediating.

Saturn in 7th house: You have a strong sense of justice and responsibility regarding your public and private dealings with others. You may marry later in life or choose an older or more stable person as a mate or business partner. You could do well in law or business organization or management.

Uranus in 7th house: You want freedom in your marriage or business partnership. If you do marry, it could be sudden and under unusual circumstances. Your marriage or business partner may be eccentric.

Neptune in 7th house: Mystical or religious overtones may dominate your marriage or business partnership. In any case, you and your partner will enjoy a shared sympathy. You have musical or artistic talent and an appreciation of the arts.

Pluto in 7th house: You want to drastically change your mate or partner. There is a tendency for divorce or separation, primarily because of jealousy. Your mate or partner may be too domineering for you. You could be successful as a lawyer, judge, or psychologist.

8th house—This house holds the secrets of life and death and also indicates an ability to use the energies of others.

Sun in 8th house: You will be interested in the mysteries of life and the after-life, especially as you grow older. You will make good use of your inner resources to benefit through self-improvement. With a strong will and faith, you can overcome great obstacles and be a success in life.

Moon in 8th house: You understand power and how to use it for your advantage. You may have strong psychic ability and a desire to communicate with deceased relatives.

Mercury in 8th house: You have a deep interest in psychic and occult matters, including communicating with those who are deceased. You love reading or writing mystery stories.

Venus in 8th house: You will have strong affections for someone deceased. You may come into wealth through marriage or a partnership.

Mars in 8th house: You have strong emotions and desires, but probably will keep them hidden from others. Your energy and persistence will help you get things done. You will have a powerful sex drive.

Jupiter in 8th house: Philosophy and the occult are of great interest to you. Partnerships, insurance, or inheritances may bring you wealth.

Saturn in 8th house: Your fortunes will change, and you will need to find a sense of security beyond change. You will be involved with others' money or property besides your own, involving you in heavy responsibility.

Uranus in 8th house: You are interested in the occult and life beyond this world. You may have a very deep insight into the workings of nature and the universe.

Neptune in 8th house: You may be psychic and even be able to predict coming events. Your partner may be involved in deceptive practices.

Pluto in 8th house: A subtle knowledge of energy gives you deep insight into physics. You have a very strong sexual drive and want to use sex for power.

9th house—This house rules your philosophy of life and also indicates the foreign countries you may travel to.

Sun in 9th house: Philosophy or the priestly life interests you. You may travel to sunny climes.

Moon in 9th house: You are the dreamy type of person and could be a philosopher. You may visit dreamy, misty places.

Mercury in 9th house: You could be a writer of philosophy. You may travel to Europe, especially Switzerland.

Venus in 9th house: Your philosophy of life is peace and harmony. Beautiful, green countries attract you.

Mars in 9th house: Your philosophy of life is to fight for what you want. You may travel to England and Germany.

Jupiter in 9th house: You have talent to become a doctor or minister. You will journey to far-off places such as Australia.

Saturn in 9th house: You will work hard for what you want in life and never give up. Mountainous places attract you.

Uranus in 9th house: You take a different view of traditional views and become interested in the occult sciences. You will travel to other planets, either physically or mentally.

Neptune in 9th house: You are drawn to mystical religions and have an intuitive mind. You will travel to dreamy, watery places.

Pluto in 9th house: Your philosophy is to get what you want in life. You will travel to desert countries.

10th house—This house tells what contribution you will make to the world. It also indicates your attitude toward your career.

Sun in 10th house: Your ambition is toward positions of power and responsibility. You have a strong will to succeed, and desire honor and recognition by others. You could do well in politics or managerial positions, or as an actor.

Moon in 10th house: You have a strong need to establish yourself in a position of prominence and to be recognized and admired. Women will greatly influence your career. A political life is indicated.

Mercury in 10th house: Your contribution to the world will be through communications, perhaps as a writer, journalist, or teacher. Education is of great importance to you, to enhance your career.

Venus in 10th house: Your future is in social and artistic directions. Your mate is likely to be influential and wealthy. You will be fortunate in dealing with the opposite sex, both romantically and in business. Careers in clothing, including fashion design, are indicated.

Mars in 10th house: You have strong needs for status and fame. Your strong competitive drive can help you in politics, corporate management, or the military life.

Jupiter in 10th house: You are ambitious and apply ethical and religious principles to your career. You could be a philosopher, doctor, minister, or pharmacist.

Saturn in 10th house: Hard work and integrity help you to achieve success and status as a leader. However, success and happiness come only if your motives concern serving others rather than just yourself.

Uranus in 10th house: Your career success involves innovations; ideas you bring to methods and techniques. Careers in electronics and mathematics are indicated.

Neptune in 10th house: Intuition plays a major role in your career. Careers indicated include minister, psychologist, psychiatrist. Actors, artists, musicians also often have this placement.

Pluto in 10th house: You have a strong will and drive to be a success. You could be a leader in politics and fields in which you can reform the system.

11th house—This house describes how you function in groups and with other people. It tells who your friends will be and what your fondest wishes are.

Sun in 11th house: You want to have many friends and hope they will be loving. Your fondest wish is to have your personal expression recognized.

Moon in 11th house: You tend to be a dreamer and your wishes will be other-worldly. You have a strong need for friends and to take part in group activities.

Mercury in 11th house: You want others to admire you for being clever and intelligent. You will seek friends who are intellectual.

Venus in 11th house: You want peace and harmony and for others to love you. Your friends will be loving and affectionate.

Mars in 11th house: You desire friendships, especially masculine and aggressive types, and enjoy group activities.

Jupiter in 11th house: You will achieve success through friendships and group activities. Your friends will be enthusiastic and optimistic. You will love giving and going to parties.

Saturn in 11th house: You take on responsibility in regard to friendships and group situations. You are eager to meet and know influential people so they can advance your career. You will be selective regarding friends and only have one or two really close friends.

Uranus in 11th house: You are open-minded, not bound by tradition or the approval of other people. You will have many friends, but they may be unconventional or eccentric.

Neptune in 11th house: You are drawn to idealistic friends and groups, and have a close spiritual tie to them. You want to become one with the universe.

Pluto in 11th house: You want power and to have your desires fulfilled. It will be difficult for you to avoid sexual relationships with friends. You want to reform your friends and group associates.

12th house—Your subconscious mind tells you things about yourself and your life that are otherwise hidden from you.

Sun in 12th house: You tend to retreat from reality and pursue your subconscious personality. Some expression of yourself is not being recognized by others.

Moon in 12th house: Your moods and emotions are greatly influenced by your unconscious mind and by past experiences. You have to see into and understand your own subconscious in order to achieve peace and fulfillment.

Mercury in 12th house: Your own mind is hidden from you. You find it difficult to think about yourself.

Venus in 12th house: You love quiet and solitude. Your own sense of affection may be hidden from you. You may acquire a secret lover.

Mars in 12th house: Your actions and desires are hidden from your conscious mind. Your work may be carried on in a secret or secluded way. Men with this placement may tend to be too feminine.

Jupiter in 12th house You seek inner peace by way of meditation, seclusion, and have some hidden protection, like a guardian angel, watching over you. Whatever you do will turn out all right for you.

Saturn in 12th house: You will work in seclusion or behind-the-scenes, perhaps in government, at a university, or hospital. If you can find out what you were afraid of in your past life, it can help you overcome much of your fear in this life.

Uranus in 12th house: You will search for a greater spiritual identity, perhaps through the occult. Friends trust you with their secrets.

Neptune in 12th house: You are very compassionate for the sick and suffering. You have an intuitive connection to your subconscious mind.

Pluto in 12th house: You have many hidden needs and desires and you repress your negative feelings. You are interested in psychology or the occult, in order to bring out your subconscious mind.

THE MOON'S NODES IN THE HOUSES

North Node glyph: ☊   South Node glyph: ☋

Another important factor in your birth chart is the placement of the Moon's nodes. The nodes are the two points where the Moon's orbit passes through the ecliptic. The ecliptic is the apparent path of the Sun.

The house where you find the Moon's North Node in your chart is considered to be a place of blessing. The South Node, always exactly opposite the North Node in the chart, shows a place of self-undoing.

Both nodes work together, as if they were one aspect. The North Node offers an area of new growth in your life. The South Node shows where you will be tempted to coast or slide along through life, because it is easy for you.

North Node in 1st house, South Node in 7th house: Your point of blessing is your own self. Rely less on influences from others. Happiness comes from your own independence and self-reliance.

North Node in 2nd house, South Node in 8th house: Stay out of the financial and emotional affairs of others. Be self-reliant and confident you can handle your own affairs without leaning on others.

North Node in 3rd house, South Node in 9th house: Don't spend too much time thinking on lofty or philosophical planes. You will do better concentrating on little things that must be done right now.

North Node in 4th house, South Node in 10th house: You want success and recognition through a career in the public eye, but will find more happiness and security through your home, family, and personal affairs.

North Node in 5th house, South Node in 11th house: You will achieve the greatest personal fulfillment by means of your own creativity and self-expression.

North Node in 6th house, South Node in 12th house: Concentrate on everyday affairs and your work and you can put your life together. You could be happiest if you make your work the most important thing in your life.

Up to now we have looked at the North Node in the personal houses of the chart. If you have the North Node in any of the personal houses of your chart, you have to concentrate on your private affairs before you can get involved in social matters.

Houses 7 through 12 describe the North Node in the social houses. If your North Node is in the social half of the chart, you may be putting too much energy into yourself or your personal affairs. You need to broaden your horizons by getting out of yourself more and becoming more involved with other people. The house in which your North Node is located will show you the best way to accomplish this.

North Node in 7th house, South Node in 1st house: You could get along well as a loner, but your real challenge is to stop concentrating on yourself first and start thinking more of others.

North Node in 8th house, South Node in 2nd house: You find it easy to manage your own personal affairs, but you will be happier if you cooperate, work with, and share with others.

North Node in 9th house, South Node in 3rd house: You are comfortable in your familiar corner of the world. However, greater satisfaction can come if you explore new places or ideas.

North Node in 10th house, South Node in 4th house: You lead a very comfortable and quiet life centered around your home, but you need some public activity that can bring you more respect.

North Node in 11th house, South Node in 5th house: The center of your life is your close friends, hobbies, love affairs, and other personal enjoyments. You will be a richer person if you get out more into the world and meet more people and be of service to others.

North Node in 12th house, South Node in 6th house: You are too wrapped up in your own work and the drudgery of every-day life. Your subconscious mind can tune you in to answers to your deepest questions and lead you to a greater happiness.

Analyzing Your Aspects

**What the planets in your chart do to each
other, and what that does to you**

As the planets travel through the Zodiac they form various angles to each other in relation to the Earth. As the planets form these angles to each other (with the Earth as the vertex, geometrically speaking), they create times of prosperity or hardship on Earth.

It is interesting to note that the most dreaded angles of astrology—45°, 90°, and 180°—are the angles that we almost always use in building our homes, offices, factories, civic buildings, furniture, and other possessions.

ANGLES THAT BRING GOOD LUCK

The lucky, good, or harmonious angles in astrology are 30°, 60°, and 120°; and we seldom build houses, cities, cars, boxes or anything else that use very many of these triangular or hexagonal angles, which astrology has shown to be so lucky and full of harmony. Perhaps our lives would be more peaceful and pleasant if we lived in triangular houses.

American Plains Indians, who were very wise in the ways of nature, often lived in triangular-shaped teepees. When they were forced to live on reservations, they complained that the square-shaped houses they were moved to held no power in them.

Only recently has Western civilization become interested in studying the energy effects of certain angles and shapes, such as pyramids, as "collectors" of some kind of cosmic energy which we do not yet fully understand.

CHALLENGES YOU CAN PROFIT FROM

The angles that the planets made to each other when you were born are permanently recorded on your birth chart, and they are permanently recorded in you. The planets with "easy" angles in your chart will always bring ease and good luck to you. The planets that form "hard" angles in your chart will always bring hard luck and challenges to you—problems to be overcome.

When you know which planets are causing problems, which planets you can count on for help, and which areas of your life are involved (which houses), then you can set about improving your life in new and perhaps unexpected ways, because you will finally know what's going on in these areas.

THE SUN-MOON CYCLE

From our place of viewing on Earth, the aspect cycle that affects us most on a day-to-day level, and is easiest to observe, is the Sun-Moon cycle.

PHASES OF THE MOON

The New Moon is considered to be the beginning point of the Sun-Moon cycle. At this time the Sun, Moon, and Earth are all situated along one line.

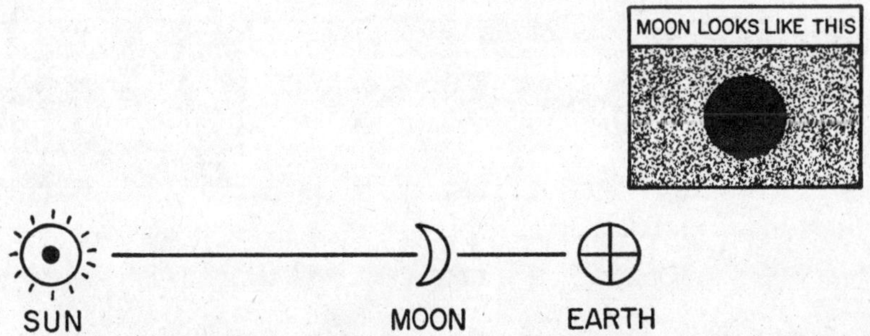

New Moon: Sun and Moon are "conjunct" (☌) : 0° angle

Astrologically, the Sun and Moon are forming a conjunction at this time—a 0° angle: a 0° aspect.

The New Moon is often considered a symbolic mating of the male principle (the Sun) and the female principle (the Moon), at which time the Moon receives energy from the light-giving Sun, which she distributes gradually to the Earth for the rest of the month, until the next symbolic "mating," 29 days later.

The New Moon is a time of new beginnings. In general, it is a good time to start any new project or relationship (unless some other astrological factors are strongly negative at that time).

Any conjunction of two planets is the beginning of a new cycle for that pair of planets and is a good time to begin a venture associated with the character of that pair of planets.

For instance, a Mars-Saturn conjunction would be the ideal time to start a new project requiring energy, efficiency, and perseverence. Mars provides the boundless energy in this "planetary partnership," while Saturn provides discipline, perseverance, and efficiency. A Mars-Saturn conjunction would not be an especially good time to start a project requiring sensitivity, diplomacy, or flexibility, however. That kind of enterprise is best begun under a planetary combination involving Moon, Venus, or Mercury.

About five days after the New Moon, the Moon will have traveled through two signs (30° each), and will be 60° away from the Sun—a sextile aspect. While the visible area of the Moon is growing larger (from the New Moon to the Full Moon), the Moon is said to be "waxing." When the visible area is becoming smaller, in the second half of the cycle (Full Moon to New Moon), it is said to be "waning."

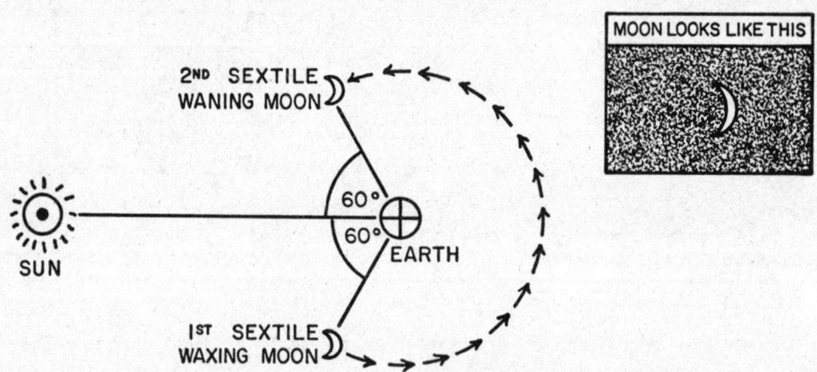

The Crescent Moon: A "Sextile" aspect: 60° angle

The sextile is a fortunate aspect, bringing opportunities and ideas which will bear fruit if you act on them. Sextiles are not considered quite as lucky as trines, since they provide only an opportunity, a possibility—which you must then fulfill through effort. Trines, as you will see shortly, are famous for simply dumping good luck into your lap for no apparent reason.

About a week after the New Moon, the first major stressful aspect of the cycle occurs. This is the Half Moon. The Sun and Moon form a 90° angle to the Earth at this time.

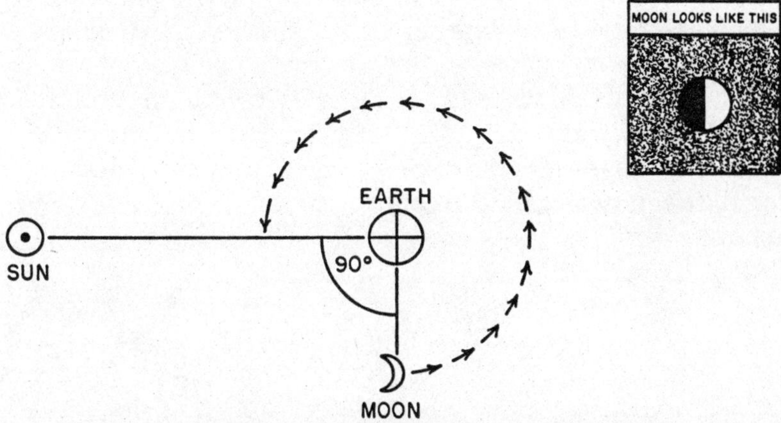

The Half Moon: A "Square" aspect: 90° angle

The square is a difficult aspect which brings a test or a challenge: a problem to be overcome, usually through effort and discipline.

The square is a dynamic aspect that creates definite problems, obstacles, and frustrations. It is the greatest character-builder, because it impels us to grow by struggling to overcome flaws in ourselves and our environments.

Powerful square aspects are almost always found in the charts of famous people, celebrities or historical figures. An exciting life, like a good movie or novel, contains a conflict, and the hero must grow and test himself in meeting the challenge. So it is with natives who have powerful square aspects in their chart.

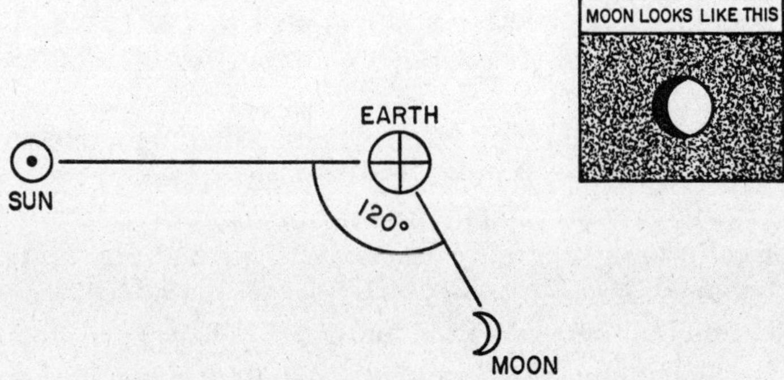

The "Gibbous" Moon: A "Trine" aspect: 120°

The next major aspect is the trine, which first occurs about 10 days after the New Moon.

The trine is the luckiest of all aspects. It brings so much abundance that a person with a lot of trines and few "hard" aspects can have such an easy, unchallenging life that they never see any reason to work very hard at anything, and wind up not really developing their talents. Having a trine is sort of like getting a raise every week, or making the big sale of the year every month.

The Sun-Moon trine, then, is a fortunate time for any activity that has abundance as its goal.

The last major aspect is the opposition. This occurs when the Earth is situated between two other planets.

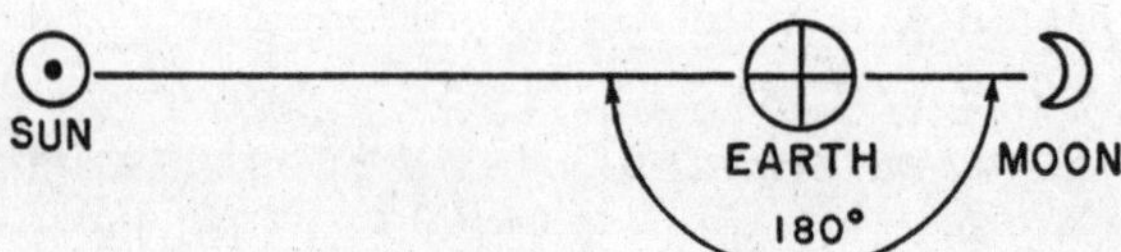

The Full Moon: An "Opposition" Aspect: 180°

The opposition is a difficult aspect that is a little more subtle than the square. The square brings clear, obvious obstacles to be overcome, while the opposition can create psychological conflicts with others or within yourself—conflicts that may be hidden by withdrawal or emotional isolation.

The opposition creates problems in relationships, often caused by images that you project on others. You see others as feeling hostile toward you, and then proceed to act in such a way as to make them feel hostile toward you. Then you believe that your initial suspicions were accurate.

Each month as the Full Moon approaches, policemen, bartenders, and attendants at mental hospitals and general hospital emergency rooms around the world prepare themselves for an evening of crisis and even craziness. Family quarrels, barroom brawls, vandalism, and other disturbances become more common when the rays of the Full Moon fuel the paranoid feelings of unstable personalities.

Scientific experiments have shown that many species of animals, oysters for instance, know exactly when the Full Moon occurs, even when they are isolated in controlled environments and cannot see the Moon or feel its light.

The Sun-Moon cycle influences us in obvious ways (such as variation in tides and moonlight), and in subtle ways through psychological influences of the aspects formed by the Sun and Moon. As the 10 "planets" (the Sun, Moon, and the eight planets) travel around the Zodiac, they form an everchanging pattern of aspects. Each planetary aspect in your chart shows a potential pathway for the flow or clash of planetary energies.

FINDING YOUR ASPECTS

Before you can analyze the aspects in your chart, you must first find them, and then record them in a convenient form.

Here are some helpful hints for easy aspect-finding:

Conjunction: Easy to spot because the planets involved are "touching" in the chart.

Sextile: Planets that are two signs apart, in the same degree or about the same degree, are sextile. Planets that are two signs apart are in compatible elements.

Square: Planets that are three signs apart in about the same degree form a square. Check your chart visually for planets that look like they are 90° apart, then check mathematically. Planets that are three signs apart are in signs of the same type, i.e., cardinal, fixed, or mutable.

Trine: Look for planets that are four signs apart, in about the same degree. Planets that are four signs apart are in signs of the same element—fire, earth, air, or water.

Opposition: These planets will be opposite in the chart.

If a planet is near a cusp, it may form an aspect to a planet on the opposite side of the "wrong" sign. For instance, if your Jupiter is at 29° Aries, it would form a conjunction to Mars at 1° Taurus, even though conjunctions are usually between two planets in the same sign. Your Jupiter would also form an opposition to a planet at 1° Scorpio, even though you would normally expect an opposition only to the opposite sign (which would have been Libra).

These cusp-crossover aspects are called "hidden" aspects, and are said to be a little weaker than normal aspects.

If you have a planet at 29° Aries, first look for aspects to 29°. Then pretend that your planet is at 0° Taurus and look around for aspects to that point.

The Orb of Influence

An aspect does not have to be exact to work. Each planet has an orb of influence (or "orb") around it, of about 6° on each side. Any two planets that are within 6° of an exact aspect can be considered to be in aspect.

The closer an aspect is to being exact, the more powerful the aspect. Since the Sun and Moon are so powerful in the chart, they are allowed an orb of 8° when they aspect a planet, and 10° when they aspect each other.

Your Whole Chart in One Picture

One very convenient way to record your aspects is by making a donut-shaped chart, with a hole in the center for colored lines that represent the aspects. This gives a picture of the whole chart in one unified form, and it is easy to see the overall aspect pattern in one glance.

Here is an example of a chart drawn by this "donut" method:

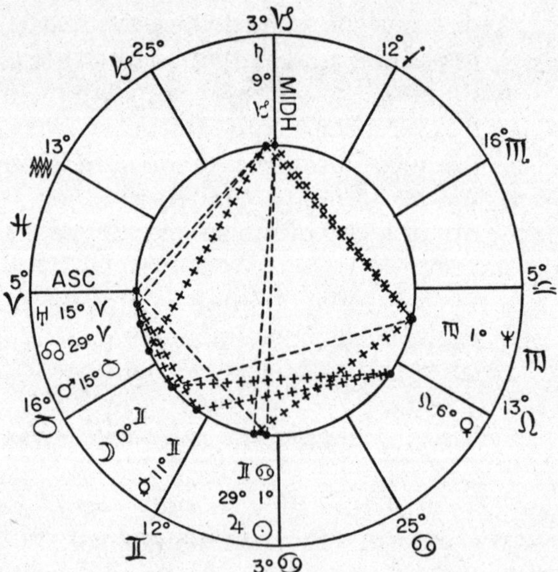

In this diagram, the pluses represent positive aspects, and the minuses represent negative aspects. Conjunctions are symbolized by a tiny arc connecting the conjuncting planets.

Using colored pencils or pens for the aspect lines puts a stronger visual emphasis on the difference between the aspects. A two-color system—red for negative and blue or black for positive—creates an "aspect picture" that is clear and easy to read, but the best system uses five colors—one for each major aspect. You can use whatever colors you like to represent the aspects.

Here are the colors that we have chosen to symbolize the natures of the aspects:

Conjunction: a sky-blue blob connecting the conjuncting planets.
Sextile: an orange-yellow line, or a yellow line with orange dots.
Square: a deep red line.
Trine: a medium-brown line.
Opposition: a thick black line.

You can visually show how exact an aspect is, or how strong you feel it is in the chart, by how heavily you draw the line representing the aspect.

A good way to hunt for aspects is to start with the Sun and look for the Sun-Moon aspects, Sun-Mercury aspects, Sun-Venus aspects, etc., and record them in your chart as you find them.

Aspect delineations are organized in this book, and in most other astrology books, in the following order: Sun, Moon, Mercury, Venus, Mars, Jupiter, Saturn, Uranus, Neptune, Pluto. Happy hunting!

SUN ASPECTS

Planets in aspect with the Sun have a great deal of energy. By being aspected to the Sun, they are given an added creative force and importance in the chart.

Sun-Moon Aspects

Sun-Moon aspects tell you how you get along with the opposite sex and with your mother and father. They also show how your conscious and subconscious minds work together.

Sun-Moon conjunction: Your conscious and subconscious minds work harmoniously together. You generally will get what you wish for. You are self-confident and self-motivated.

Sun-Moon positive: A general harmony exists because your ego and emotions work well together. Your temperament is well-balanced. You will enjoy happy family relationships, especially with young people.

Sun-Moon negative: You need to try to get your conscious and subconscious wishes to work together. You may have a conflict between career and home.

Sun-Mercury Aspects

Mercury is so close to the Sun, the only possible aspect between the planet and the Sun is the conjunction.

Sun-Mercury conjunction: Your mind is forceful and keen, but you may be too self-centered, preoccupied with your own affairs and ideas.

Sun-Venus Aspects

The only Sun-Venus aspect possible is the conjunction, since Venus always stays close to the Sun.

Sun-Venus conjuction: You are attractive, pleasant to be with, and generous, so you are likely to be well-regarded.

Sun-Mars Aspects

Sun-Mars conjunction: You have a great deal of physical strength, but could misuse it when you have a temper. You are both physically and mentally courageous, and will go out on a limb to help others.

Sun-Mars positive: You are very energetic and possess strong leadership qualities, partly because you are so tactful. This is the "hero aspect," because of your physical strength and courage.

Sun-Mars negative: You are courageous and have great physical strength but like to flirt with danger. You may be too impulsive or reckless.

Sun-Jupiter Aspects

Sun-Jupiter conjunction and *positive aspects:* You are optimistic, enjoy life, and have a good sense of humor. These qualities are so natural to you, they influence others toward you.

Sun-Jupiter negative: The above qualities tend to make you feel you must justify or prove your sincerity to others. Your love for travel may make it difficult for you to stay in one place very long. You also may be overindulgent in food and may be rebellious.

Sun-Saturn Aspects

Sun-Saturn conjunction: You are a hard worker. What you want to achieve in life may come in later years, but it will be yours to keep.

Sun-Saturn positive: You have a rather fixed, rigid ego and may be a serious person, conservative and well-disciplined. You will be a steady and patient worker. You will achieve your goals in life, but they will come in later years.

Sun-Saturn negative: Your ego may be the same as above, but may tend to be even more rigid and inflexible. You may take on too many responsibilities and often feel burdened.

Sun-Uranus Aspects

These aspects make a person eccentric and inventive, individualistic and unpredictable. They can be good or bad, or good one day and bad the next.

Sun-Uranus conjunction: People may consider you to be a genius and you are very original. But you may be high-strung, stubborn, and irrational at times.

Sun-Uranus positive: You are a strong leader, very scientific and inventive, but you may lack tact.

Sun-Uranus negative: You want something different and may try too hard to be different, becoming eccentric.

Sun-Neptune Aspects

Sun-Neptune aspects tend to make people dreamers.

Sun-Neptune conjunction: You may lack self-confidence and not be sure of your identity. You find it difficult to make decisions. The important thing is to do something. Decide on a course of action and follow it.

Sun-Neptune positive: You are very imaginative and intuitive and probably have psychic powers. You are gifted in music and may be a dreamer.

Sun-Neptune negative: You tend to be indecisive, irresponsible, and may depend too much on others. You may be impractical and live too much in a dream world escape from reality.

Sun-Pluto Aspects

All Sun-Pluto aspects give the native a desire for power, but also a talent for handling it well.

Sun-Pluto conjunction: You are driven by power and may be boastful and temperamental. Because of your strength of character and will, you can have great effect on changing your environment. You can see into other people's minds and their hidden motives.

Sun-Pluto positive: You have a powerful personality, a strong will, and could be a good leader of groups. You are a very progressive person, bent on reforming others and the system.

Sun-Pluto negative: You can be ruthless in going after what you want. You could even be devious in manipulating people so you can achieve your desires.

MOON ASPECTS

Moon aspects deal with your emotions, personality, habits, and relationship with women.

Moon-Mercury Aspects

Moon-Mercury conjunction: You are strongly influenced by what you think and read and also by what people say to you. You have above-average intelligence and a good memory. Your love for change may make you restless and disrupt your life.

Moon-Mercury positive: You communicate and express your feelings very well. You relate well to women and children. People find you charming. You are intelligent, alert, and have good common sense.

Moon-Mercury negative: You are restless, high-strung, and have difficulty concentrating. You may have trouble making decisions and could be quarrelsome with relatives and neighbors.

Moon-Venus Aspects

Moon-Venus aspects deal with your search for peace, love, harmony, beauty, and the wishes of your heart.

Moon-Venus conjunction: Your inner need is to be surrounded by beauty and nature. You have lots of charisma. You are refined, artistic, and love luxury. You will be happy in marriage.

Moon-Venus positive: People are attracted to you because of your harmonious, pleasing nature. You have a soothing, even healing, effect on others. You will have a happy home life and good relations with women.

Moon-Venus negative: You may be moody and overly sensitive or self-indulgent. You have a strong need for love but may be disappointed in your love life and find it hard to communicate with women.

Moon-Mars Aspects

These aspects deal with the energy of your subconscious wishes.

Moon-Mars conjunction: You have a great deal of energy, but may be restless and irritable. You are courageous but impulsive.

Moon-Mars positive: You will enjoy good health, have a strong interest in sports, and be a "country" kind of person. You have ambition and drive, and can make a lot of money. You need security.

Moon-Mars negative: You are moody and temperamental, often irritable and argumentative. You may try to control other people in subtle ways. You may have financial difficulties.

Moon-Jupiter Aspects

These are good aspects and make people feel lucky and looked after by some unseen protector.

Moon-Jupiter conjunction: You will be healthy and have a great enthusiasm for life. You will enjoy yourself most of the time. Optimism is a strong character trait.

Moon-Jupiter positive: You are optimistic and don't take things seriously. You always bounce right back from adversity. You will be lucky and will inherit from or be helped by others.

Moon-Jupiter negative: You are inclined toward excessives, especially in food and alcohol. You may be emotionally rash and extravagant, likely to be taken in by schemes, unreliable people.

Moon-Saturn Aspects

Moon-Saturn conjunction: You are serious and may not be able to express your subconscious emotions.

Moon-Saturn positive: You are very stable, conservative, and loyal to your friends. You will achieve your subconscious wishes, but not until later in life. You are thrifty and practical, able to handle responsibility.

Moon-Saturn negative: You may be too defensive, afraid to express your emotions, and may even be afraid of other people. You also may be morbid, jealous, and critical.

Moon-Uranus Aspects

These are good aspects because they make people creative in unusual ways. They are called the "Alice in Wonderland" aspects.

Moon-Uranus conjunction: You are very gifted and constantly need outlets for your creative self-expression. You are inventive, independent, eccentric, but have lots of charisma.

Moon-Uranus positive: You are ambitious and imaginative, with psychic or intuitive powers. You are full of energy, a romantic, and will enjoy many friends. Your moods change quickly.

Moon-Uranus negative: Your energies are scattered; you try to do too many things at the same time. You are high-strung, rebellious, unstable and need to structure your life better and relax more.

Moon-Neptune Aspects

Moon-Nepturn conjunction: You tend to be too receptive to other people's thoughts and lose your own identity. You are overly sensitive and retiring, prone to daydreaming and escapism.

Moon-Neptune positive: You are very receptive and probably psychic. You are imaginative and artistic. You love to travel and are popular with people, partly because you are so sympathetic.

Moon-Neptune negative: You daydream a lot and tend to live in an unreal world you have created. You have a strong dependence on others and may be deceived by women. Be careful of alcohol and drugs.

Moon-Pluto Aspects

Moon-Pluto conjunction: You are impulsive and your mood may change often. You are sensual and sensitive. You may not be aware of how devious you can be in pursuing your goals.

Moon-Pluto positive: Your emotions are very strong and you should be careful not to become too emotional. You have visionary abilities. You will be an achiever.

Moon-Pluto negative: When you are frustrated, especially in sex and power matters, you can be quite devious. You may be obstinate and have a bad temper.

MERCURY ASPECTS

All aspects of Mercury deal with your mind, how you think, and how you communicate with others.

Mercury-Venus Aspects

It is possible only to form a conjunction or sextile. Both aspects make a person good at expressing themself by means of the spoken and written word. These people are popular and well-liked.

Mercury-Venus conjunction: You are a calm and charming person in your manner and speech. You love pleasure and the arts, and could be successful as a dress designer or hairdresser or work in crafts.

Mercury-Venus positive: You have a charming way about you, especially in how you speak.

Mercury-Mars Aspects

With these aspects, people tend to talk a lot. That can be both good and bad.

Mercury-Mars conjunction: You are good at public speaking, but could be rude and even crude. You are quick both physically and mentally, but could be too impulsive.

Mercury-Mars positive: You are skilled at public speaking and have the courage to say what you believe. Your physical and mental expression is coordinated and smooth.

Mercury-Mars negative: You are argumentative and like conflicts with other people. You are very critical and can be bad-tempered. Little things upset you easily. You should reason things out before you draw conclusions.

Mercury-Jupiter Aspects

Mercury-Jupiter conjunction: You are optimistic and inspire others. You are gifted in oratory, science, and philosophy, but may tend to be superior to others. You can cheer people up.

Mercury-Jupiter positive: You have a strong ability to integrate facts and abstract figures. You will be very thorough in intellectual pursuits and could be a philosopher, religious leader, or teacher.

Mercury-Jupiter negative: You are optimistic and lucky, but tend to say the wrong thing at the wrong time or to the wrong person. You also may be untruthful and could become involved in fraud.

Mercury-Saturn Aspects

Mercury-Saturn conjunction: You are a serious person with great powers of concentration. You may be too conservative and inhibited or skeptical. You probably don't believe you are as intelligent as you really are.

Mercury-Saturn positive: You have an orderly mind and are a deep thinker. You are methodical and well-organized, able to make decisions based on a lot of serious thinking.

Mercury-Saturn negative: You are rigid and obstinate, somewhat brusque in what you write and say. You are shy and even inhibited. You put on a cool or harsh exterior to cover your shyness, which can keep you from making friends.

Mercury-Uranus Aspects

Mercury-Uranus conjunction: You are very inventive and perceptive. Ideas come to you like a bolt out of the blue. Though you could be a genius, you may be somewhat irrational in your thinking. You could be restless and hasty. Because your mind is hyperactive, you need to take time to relax and get away from thinking too much or too deeply.

Mercury-Uranus positive: You are very inventive, especially in scientific ways, and excel in debate. Your inspiration and genius come to you from outside the known world.

Mercury-Uranus negative: You are nervous and your energies are scattered. You are unconventional and headstrong. You also are skeptical to the point where you won't listen to reason, even when the advice is good for you.

Mercury-Neptune Aspects

Mercury-Neptune conjunction: You are very imaginative, a relaxed and peaceful person who may be too sensitive to other people. You need to think more for yourself and need more time to relax.

Mercury-Neptune positive: You are psychic and poetic, a refined, artistic person who is sympathetic to others and at peace with life. You love music and also could be an imaginative writer, especially writing about the future.

Mercury-Neptune negative: You have a very vivid imagination but are lacking in areas of ability to reason. You are inclined toward deception and may be both gullible and unreliable.

Mercury-Pluto Aspects

Mercury-Pluto conjunction: You are quite intelligent and subtle, but also restless and irritable. You tend to dominate people and want them to change their minds and agree with you. You may be nagging.

Mercury-Pluto positive: You are clever and diplomatic, aware of subtle forces in the universe. You have strong powers of concentration and can psychoanalyze people. You could be a good critic.

Mercury-Pluto negative: You are sarcastic and cynical, even violent. You want to play mind games and change other people's minds to suit your own desires.

VENUS ASPECTS

Venus aspects deal with your affections and matters of the heart.

Venus-Mars Aspects

Venus-Mars conjunction: You are a sexually-oriented person with lots of charisma. You are self-confident, optimistic, and love excitement and sports. You are especially creative and artistic in the arts and crafts.

Venus-Mars positive: You are an affectionate, sensuous person and very popular, though you like to flirt. The opposite sex is easily attracted to you. You are artistic and creative, with good senses of rhythm, timing, and also color.

Venus-Mars negative: You may have difficulty with the opposite sex and in social situations. You are highly sexed and self-indulgent. You may lack tact and be careless with money. You may not realize how physically attractive you really are.

Venus-Jupiter Aspects

Venus-Jupiter conjunction: You are a popular person with a happy-go-lucky outlook that others enjoy. You will have many love affairs because you are so charming. You are very artistic and could be more successful working with a partner than alone.

Venus-Jupiter positive: You have a great enthusiasm for life. You are able to be happy or content even when things go wrong. You will enjoy financial security, perhaps through your artistic abilities. You will have good relationships with others.

Venus-Jupiter negative: You may abuse your natural charm by being conceited, or by self-indulgence. You have a strong need for a partner. You may be lazy, careless, and even sloppy. You may overindulge in buying things or in drinking.

Venus-Saturn Aspects

Venus-Saturn conjunction: This is called "the Romeo and Juliet aspect." It can be tragic and cause loss of a lover or separation from someone you love. It may mean a late marriage or marriage to an older person. It could also mean jealousy or emotional problems.

Venus-Saturn positive: You have good relationships with older people. You tend to be lonely. You could have a stable marriage because you are loyal, faithful, have a good business head, and are responsible.

Venus-Saturn negative: You may sacrifice a lot in order to become successful in something, but you sacrifice because of a sense of duty to a person or a cause. Jealousy, unhappiness, emotional problems, estrangements may occur often in life. You may never marry.

Venus-Uranus Aspects

Venus-Uranus conjunction: You have original and even unusual ideas concerning both art and love. Though flirtatious and often irrational in love, you are charismatic and attractive. You will enjoy financial advantages and be independent.

Venus-Uranus positive: You do things in a charming and even whimsical way. You have a great deal of charisma and are popular. You want freedom and excitement in your romantic life. You will have many financial opportunities and love to speculate.

Venus-Uranus negative: You will have difficulty creating stable love relationships. You may form unconventional partnerships and unusual love relationships. You may suffer losses through speculation.

Venus-Neptune Aspects

Venus-Neptune conjunction: You are very sensitive, romantic, imaginative, and sentimental. You have a tendency toward self-delusion and an unrealistic outlook on life.

Venus-Neptune positive: You have a very delicate sensitivity, are sentimental, and psychic. You have strong artistic abilities and could also be successful working in fields where you can be of help to others.

Venus-Neptune negative: You may be self-indulgent, but also can get carried away about other people's feelings and become dependent on drugs or love. An impractical side to your nature may cause financial losses. Others may deceive you, especially women.

Venus-Pluto Aspects

Venus-Pluto conjunction: You have very powerful desires and may even have a secret love. You are very sensitive, possessive, and easily hurt.

Venus-Pluto positive: You are creative, even ingenious, and have a strong sense of color. You are very perceptive and have the ability to be a success. You give off a lot of strength and have a magnetic personality.

Venus-Pluto negative: You are easily hurt and can be rather coarse or crude, all of which can cause difficulty getting along with others. You may be too self-serving and immoral. You will have romantic reversals. But despite all this, you have a desire to see the ugly as being beautiful.

MARS ASPECTS

Mars aspects deal with your energies and desires.

Mars-Jupiter Aspects

Mars-Jupiter conjunction: You have a great deal of energy and are courageous, adventurous, and daring. You can inspire other people to action and also make them happy. Though you have strong leadership abilities, you could also be reckless and unscrupulous. You may make a lot of money but will spend it fast.

Mars-Jupiter positive: You are a fun-loving, adventurous person with lots of physical energy. You have tremendous energy and could do well in sports. You need financial security or protection and are likely to get help when you need it.

Mars-Jupiter negative: You are reckless and extravagant. You tend to be opinionated and rebellious. You have a gambling instinct and want something for nothing. Avoid smuggling and get-rich-quick schemes.

Mars-Saturn Aspects

Mars-Saturn conjunction: You tend to be suspicious and untrusting, and can be temperamental. But you have the ability to construct things and could be good in architectural and mechancial work. Careful, though, because you're accident-prone.

Mars-Saturn positive: You have incredible endurance and possess strong leadership qualities. You are materialistic and good at details because you are so thorough. You can endure just about anything and you accept difficulty and hardships. You even seem to enjoy rough times.

Mars-Saturn negative: You are impatient, bad-tempered, suspicious, and could be ruthless. You suffer from both physical and emotional strains. You may have a lot of bitterness in you and a tendency toward violence.

Mars-Uranus Aspects

Mars-Uranus conjunction: You are high-strung and nervous, stubborn and irritable. But you are very inventive and energetic. Success in science is indicated. You need freedom of thought and action.

Mars-Uranus positive: You are inventive, especially along scientific lines. You are an original thinker, very practical and fearless. You love anything in fast travel, especially fast cars and motorcycles.

Mars-Uranus negative: You are high-strung, temperamental, and bull-headed, often tactless. You tend to leap before you look.

Mars-Neptune Aspects

Mars-Neptune conjunction: You are very sensitive and self-centered, even conceited. You tend to be too self-indulgent and also feel persecuted. You are sometimes so afraid about deciding what to do that you won't do anything.

Mars-Neptune positive: You are enthusiastic and popular, possessing abundant charisma. You have inspirational insight and also considerable executive ability, both of which could serve you well in the ministry. You have a fine imagination and insight. Be careful of slipping and falling.

Mars-Neptune negative: You may get carried away by your imagination and be fearful or unrealistic. You have a tendency toward an inferiority complex and could be self-destructive, especially regarding addiction to alcohol or drugs. Be careful of your feet and of falling and cutting them. Men with this placement may doubt their masculinity.

Mars-Pluto Aspects

Mars-Pluto conjunction: You are extremely masculine, whether you are male or female. You need an outlet for your abundant physical energy. Sports may be the answer. You are explosive and temperamental, often stubborn, with strong destructive tendencies.

Mars-Pluto positive: You have tremendous courage and can be capable of great achievements. You are ambitious and self-confident. You have great physical and mental energy. You are keenly interested in moving things and could be involved in race car driving.

Mars-Pluto negative: You may have a bad temper and be argumentative, even cruel at times, or brutal. You may meet with physical danger. Be careful of explosives and chemicals.

JUPITER ASPECTS

Jupiter deals with a person's philosophy and source of joy in his or her life.

Jupiter-Saturn Aspects

Jupiter-Saturn conjunction: You are an honest person, but one who is subject to fluctuating periods of optimism and depression. You can make sound investments but also tend to be penny-wise and pound-foolish. You like to work with old, established institutions.

Jupiter-Saturn positive: You are a very practical person, patient, confident, and possess common sense. You will be prosperous, perhaps through inheriting land and money or a good position.

Jupiter-Saturn negative: Problems or tests early in life bring maturity beyond your years. You have a long struggle in life and have to work hard for what you get. You may swing back and forth from being very exuberant to being very depressed. You will have to work to achieve a balance.

Jupiter-Uranus Aspects

Jupiter-Uranus conjunction: You are a religious person, optimistic and philosophic. You are freedom-loving and enjoy travel. Some people may believe in you, because of your prophetic ideas, as if you were the "chosen one."

Jupiter-Uranus positive: You are very inventive and have an unique, pioneering philosophy. You have strong leadership qualities. You want to improve yourself.

Jupiter-Uranus negative: You are emotional and nervous, a headstrong person who is rebellious and opinionated. You can suffer from hasty actions or decisions. You may be wasteful.

Jupiter-Neptune Aspects

Jupiter-Neptune conjunction: You are religious and mystical, a poetic, emotional person with artistic ability. You have the gift of prophecy, as well as musical talent. You get money easily but may spend too freely.

Jupiter-Neptune positive: You are poetic and imaginative, with strong psychic abilities. You want to help less fortunate people, perhaps in a spiritual way.

Jupiter-Neptune negative: You are extremely sensitive, often misunderstood by yourself as well as others. You may suffer emotional problems and financial misfortune, primarily because you can't handle money well. You are very likely to depend on other people or drugs. You should avoid excesses of any kind.

Jupiter-Pluto Aspects

Jupiter-Pluto conjunction: You are very ambitious and have a great deal of enthusiasm and willpower. You can change the world on a very large scale with your own thinking. Inwardly, you are an adventurer, exploring your mind and the minds of others.

Jupiter-Pluto positive: You have very strong leadership and organizational abilities and can greatly influence others. You are psychologically equipped to work with groups and to use them for the common good.

Jupiter-Pluto negative: You are likely to have trouble with large corporations; your nature is in conflict with authority. You are often arrogant and may even be fanatical. Be careful of contracts and of get-rich-quick schemes.

SATURN ASPECTS

Saturn-Uranus Aspects

Saturn-Uranus conjunction: You have trouble concentrating and are very emotional. You may have difficulty in dealing with change. You may be inhibited and eccentric and waste your energy.

Saturn-Uranus positive: You are very ambitious and inventive, possessing an unique, pioneering philosophy and a fine sense of humor. You are a serious and honorable person.

Saturn-Uranus negative: You are very emotional and nervous, usually wasting your energy. You may be vague and find it hard to concentrate. You also could be restless and impulsive, as well as accident-prone, especially involving your feet and bones.

Saturn-Neptune Aspects:

Saturn-Neptune conjunction: You have a tendency to delude yourself and may have an inferiority complex. But you have abilities in musical and mechanical ways and could be a builder, even a spiritual builder.

Saturn-Neptune positive: You are practical, self-reliant, and intuitive. You are good at organizing things and can be successful in business. Your sense of timing and perception is excellent, especially concerning the past.

Saturn-Neptune negative: You are critical and inhibited, with an inferiority complex. You may have difficulty trying to structure your life.

Saturn-Pluto Aspects

Saturn-Pluto conjunction: You may be impatient and suspicious, even self-destructive. Unpleasant subjects, such as murder or torture, may preoccupy your mind.

Saturn-Pluto positive: You have great self-discipline and are tenacious, able to endure just about anything. You love projects involving research. You also are mechanically inclined.

Saturn-Pluto negative: You are an egotist, tend to become depressed, and may be unsympathetic to others. You have trouble forgiving others and not being bitter or vindictive.

URANUS ASPECTS

Uranus-Neptune Aspects

Uranus-Neptune conjunction: You are extremely sensitive and somewhat naive, an easy mark for new ideas. You may be restless and self-deluded.

Uranus-Neptune positive: You have an inventive, intuitive mind, and are idealistic. You love to travel and possess strong executive abilities. You are tuned in to mysticism, magic, science.

Uranus-Neptune negative: You are overly sensitive and may be nervous and confused. You may have unusual psychic experiences and illusions that may fool you.

Uranus-Pluto Aspects

Uranus-Pluto conjunction: You are inventive but excitable, subject to sudden changes and even violence. You have a "science fiction mind" and could be a science fiction writer.

Uranus-Pluto positive: You have great stamina and lots of energy to work to do good. You have strong abilities to re-create.

Uranus-Pluto negative: Inner tensions may cause you to blow your top and have emotional outbursts. You may be fanatical and have destructive tendencies.

NEPTUNE ASPECTS

Nepturne-Pluto Aspects

Neptune-Pluto conjunction: You may have scattered, confused energy and unusual or odd ideas and objectives. Your approach to occult matters is intellectual, thoughtful.

Neptune-Pluto positive: You are mystical, spiritual, and are tuned in to psychic matters, able to use them for good purposes.

Nepturn-Pluto negative: You understand the motives of others, and are attuned toward black magic and an ability to predict the future.

How to Read the Chart

Learning to unlock the storehouse of
knowledge that is "hidden" in the birth chart

Your birth chart shows who you are, but more important than that, it shows who you could be; what your life could be—a road map to your ideal destination.

You could view your chart as a picture of the opportunities and challenges that are presented to you in this lifetime. Experience shows that people are happier and more successful when the conditions and potentials of their own individual charts are fulfilled in their lives.

In looking at your chart, you must determine:

(a) *what each factor means*, and

(b) *how to put the different factors together properly.*

Step (a) would be very easy if it weren't for the fact that no part of the chart stands alone. You can only look at each part first as if it stood alone, and then imagine how the different parts will work when they are put together. This is somewhat like picking separate players from different professional football teams, forming a team of these individuals, and then predicting how they will play together.

POSSIBLE CONTRADICTIONS

Different parts of the birth chart will seem, at first glance, to contradict each other. Well-aspected Mars, for example, may show you to be strong-willed, self-reliant, dynamic, active, and assertive. Yet your Mercury square Neptune indicates shyness, hesitance, indecisiveness, lack of self-confidence, and confusion or anxiety in planning future actions.

You should look for the areas (by house, sign, and planet) where you have problems, and try to shift your emphasis out of those areas and into the areas where you are stronger.

In this case, since Mercury (thinking and speaking) and Neptune (imagination) are a problem area, while Mars (desire and action) is very well-aspected, the best advice would be for you to try not to think (Mercury) about future actions very much. You should wait until you feel a direct desire for action (Mars), and then act on that. You would be wise not to cross your bridges until you come to them.

However, if you have an afflicted Mars but a good Mercury-Neptune aspect, you should follow the opposite course, because your immediate emotional-level desires and actions are rash and often turn out wrong, while your advance thinking-about and visualizing of a situation would be very clear. You should look before you leap.

CONCENTRATE ON YOUR CHART

The ability to look at a chart and understand it well comes with experience. If you do not have the time to develop a general experience in astrology, the best thing is to concentrate on an in-depth study of your own chart and perhaps the charts of a few people that are very close to you. That way, astrology will be of maximum benefit in your life and you will come to understand well the charts that you do study.

12 STEPS TO READING A BIRTH CHART

Here are some very valuable methods to use, and points to remember, when analyzing a birth chart:

1. House and Quadrant Emphasis

First look for overall shape and emphasis of the chart. Planets concentrated in one house or area of the chart mean that that house or area of the chart will be a focal point of concern in the person's life.

The houses that are empty, containing no planets, show areas of life that are not especially crucial to the native—areas that tend to take care of themselves when the native handles properly the houses that *are* emphasized.

The chart can be divided into four quadrants. The quadrant or quadrants that are heavily "populated" by planets will be the areas of most concern to the native.

The 1st quadrant, houses 1-3, is the area of *personal accomplishment*, achieved mainly to satisfy one's own desires to do and to feel productive and capable.

The 2nd quadrant, houses 4-6, is the area of *security*. If you have many planets here, you are highly concerned with maintaining your personal security.

The 3rd quadrant, houses 7-9, signifies *human relations:* people you know, how you relate to their values, and how you share knowledge and thought with others.

The 4th quadrant, houses 10-12, represents *public career.* People with an emphasis in this quadrant are strongly motivated to achieve in a public way, wanting to influence society, as opposed to the 1st quadrant achiever who accomplishes for his own personal satisfaction.

2. House Cusp Rulers

The sign on each house cusp rules that house. The entire area of the native's life that is ruled by a house will be strongly flavored by the nature of the sign on the cusp.

For instance, if you have Cancer on the cusp of your 6th house (work and service), both the kind of work and the way that you do that work would show a Cancerian influence. The kinds of work or service that you are especially likely to become involved in would be housing, food or restaurant business, domestic services, products for children, plant nursery work, etc. Anything involving food, shelter, children, or growing things.

Even if you did not go into those types of fields for a living, your place of work would have a Cancerian quality. You would make it as much like a home as possible. You also would be concerned about the interests of coworkers or employees, treating them almost like family.

In this way you can discover quite a lot about a person's orientation toward different areas of life, just by considering the signs on his various house cusps.

3. Career Indicators in the Chart

When studying a chart for vocational guidance, there are many factors to consider. Sometimes, each of these factors represents a type of work that the native will do at some time in his life. The kind of work that he will really be happy in, and is truly suited for, will be indicated in the chart in at least three different ways (see the "Rule of Three", Step No. 6, in this chapter).

For instance, success in working with machinery is indicated primarily by positive aspects to Mars and Pluto (good aspects to Uranus help by adding inventive genius), and to the signs they rule—Aries (Mars), Scorpio (Pluto), and Aquarius (Uranus) to some extent. Planets in Virgo are also helpful, especially if the machinery is to be very precise.

If any of these planets or signs appear in the 2nd, 6th, or 10th houses, the native has some probability of working with machinery, as a job, at some time in his life. If he has three or more of these planets or signs influencing houses 2, 6, or 10, then he is almost certain to become involved in a line of work that involves machinery, and to be happy in it, at least for a while.

If there are no other significant patterns affecting these houses, then the native probably would stay with machinery, and feel satisfied there. If there is another configuration (such as a Venus-Neptune/Taurus-Libra-Pisces, which indicates art), then he is likely to switch to that other field at some time, or to enter a career that blends both fields, such as in this example, a commercial artist for a machinery firm.

Self-employment is generally indicated by the presence of Uranus (planet of independence and freedom) in the 2nd, 6th, or 10th house; or by Uranus in the 1st house, which puts the Uranian stamp of independent self-reliance on the entire personality.

Good career possibilities are also indicated by especially good aspects to the planets that rule a particular field, no matter which house those planets are located in; or by a concentration of mostly well-aspected planets in any house, because each house relates to the same kind of work as the house's natural ruler. For example, the 3rd house (ruled by Gemini) indicates communications or writing, the 6th house (ruled by Virgo) indicates health-care professions, etc.

The 2nd house indicates specifically how you earn your income, and the 6th shows the type of service that you render to your group or society, and the 10th house is the indicator of your reputation—how you will be thought of and remembered by the world. The sign on your 10th house cusp—your midheaven—relates to the way your work will be thought of and remembered, even if that sign does not specifically rule the kind of work you do.

For instance, if you have Leo on your midheaven, you may not actually become an actor or professional adventurer. But you will be seen as a courageous, outspoken person in your field, or you will be "lionized" as one of the showmen or spokesmen within your field. You will be regarded as a person of authority. If you are expressing the negative side of Leo, however, you will be thought of simply as being domineering or an egotist.

4. Elevated Planets

Planets located within 30° of the midheaven are considered to be "elevated," and indicate honor and recognition.

The character of the planet will have something to do with the type of honor and recognition received.

5. Indicators for Love and Marriage

Here again, we have a few different indicators, each showing one aspect of this major area of life.

First consider the Sun and Moon. These show one's general attitude about men (Sun) and women (Moon). The Moon also indicates the domestic and family life in general, in the charts of men and women.

In a man's chart, Venus shows what kind of women turn him on. A man with Venus in Aries likes a high-spirited tigress. A man with Venus in Cancer wants a woman who likes to cook like a gourmet, and who enjoys children. A man with Venus in Pisces likes women that are sensitive, feminine, artistic, and mysterious. Mars in a man's chart shows what he will do for a woman, and Venus in a woman's chart shows what she will do for a man.

In a woman's chart, Mars shows the kind of man she is looking for, the kind that really "turns her on." If men want to find out how to please the woman of their dreams, or if they are really her type at all, they should see what sign her Mars is in.

If the woman's Mars is in Aries, she wants a Tarzan or macho-man. Mars in Gemini women want intellectual men. Mars in Pisces has a fondness for the sensitive, poetic, or spiritual type of man. You can figure out the others based on the natures of the signs.

The sign on your 5th house shows how you feel about love and romance. For instance, Taurus on the 5th indicates fidelity, while Gemini on the 5th tends to prefer variety. The 8th house shows how you feel about sex in and of itself.

Finally, the sign on your 7th house cusp shows what kind of partner you will actually wind up with in marriage. The best match, of course, is with someone who matches fairly well with you in all of these areas.

6. The "Rule of Three"

Professional astrologers consider that anything that is not shown in at least three different ways in your chart is not significant.

For instance, Mars in the 2nd house tends to indicate working with machinery, but it does not mean much unless it is backed up by at least two other indicators, such as Aries in the 6th house and Uranus in Virgo in the 10th.

As a beginner, you will not see every factor in the chart, so you should consider things that you find shown only once or twice. Of course, something that is shown three different ways is more significant.

7. Finding Your Overall Temperament

The "overall temperament" of a person is a significant factor that is often overlooked. It is actually more revealing than the Sun sign in describing just what it says—the "overall temperament".

To find the overall temperament of a native, count the number of planets you have in Fire signs, in Earth signs, Air signs, and Water signs. Make a note of which element contains the most planets (in case of a tie, count the ascendant, and then the midheaven, if necessary). Then note how many planets you have in cardinal, fixed, and mutable signs, and see which type holds the most planets.

Now put the "winning" element and type together to find your basic temperament. For instance, if you come up with cardinal fire, your temperament is basically Arien (if this isn't clear, refer back to the last part of Chapter 4).

8. Releasing Aspects

Whenever a negative ("bad") aspect occurs, look for a positive aspect that ties into one or both ends of the negative aspect. This positive aspect can be used to "release" or reduce the problems caused by the difficult aspect.

For instance, if your Sun is at 20° Leo, conjunct your ascendant, and your Mars is at 20° Aquarius in your 7th house, you have a powerful opposition that gives a tendency to arguments and even physical fights with other aggressive people (whom you tend to attract).

If you happen to have Jupiter at 20° Aries, in the 9th house, it would form a trine to your Sun and a sextile to your Mars. It would have the potential of "releasing" the opposition, if you utilize it. Since Jupiter rules sports, and the 9th is Jupiter's native house, sports would be a perfect outlet, drawing off the problematic energy of the opposition and channeling it into a positive expression.

9. Ascendant Ruler

The planet that rules the sign on the ascendant is said to be the ruler of the chart. For instance, if you are rising on Pisces, then Neptune is the ruler of your chart, and aspects to Neptune would be especially important, particularly in relation to your appearance and health (the ascendant rules the body and appearance). The house that holds this planet is also a place of special emphasis in the chart, and you will have a special interest in the kinds of things ruled by that house.

10. House Ruler and Energy Flow

This is one idea that many beginners find hard to grasp or remember.

It can reveal some interesting information, however, if you pursue it.

The energy that you accumulate in each house of your chart tends to flow to the planet that rules the cusp of that house, and to the house that holds the ruling planet.

For example, if the sign on the cusp of your 2nd house (resources and money) is Scorpio, then the energy accumulated there goes to Pluto (ruler of Scorpio), and to the house that Pluto is in. If Pluto is in your 9th house, then you would tend to spend your money on travel and education (9th house things). If Pluto were in your 4th, then you would spend most of your money on home and family (4th house things).

11. "Best" and "Worst" Points in the Chart

When you look at a chart, notice the strongest, most positive point in the chart (the point where the most positive aspects converge), and you can encourage the native to develop and utilize that area to the maximum.

Then look for the most difficult point in the chart and make the native aware of what is happening there and why. Then look for releasing aspects or other means of alleviating this major problem. Sometimes, just focusing a great deal of energy on the positive point will take the pressure off of the negative point.

12. Tips on Interpreting a Chart

(a) Look at the whole chart in terms of just one question at a time, rather than trying to see every facet of the native's life at one sitting. That is, look only at love, or career, or family, or friendship, health, self-image, or some other single issue. Professional astrologers do this when a client comes to them with a specific question.

(b) Another way to focus as you read the chart is to go around the houses from 1 to 12, addressing yourself, as you go, to the issues of each house, including how things in other houses influence the affairs of the house in question.

This, briefly, is how to read a chart. You will probably not see all the possibilities in your own or someone else's birth chart on your first reading. Analyzing a chart takes time and knowledge, plus an ability to use that knowledge thoughtfully.

Once you become familiar with casting horoscopes and chart reading, you will start to realize how much information is there to be learned and used, in virtually every facet of your life or the life of the native whose chart you are doing.

Forecasting the Future

*What lies ahead, and how to
make the best use of it*

Astrologers cannot always tell you exactly what events will take place in your life at what time, because a lot of how you choose to live your life is strictly a matter of your own choice. A good astrologer *can* tell you what kinds of energies, opportunities, changes, and crises are almost certain to occur at certain times, and he can also predict with some degree of accuracy how you will feel about and react to these events, based on your character as it is revealed in your birth chart.

An astrologer forecasts the future in much the same way that a meteorologist forecasts the weather—he can tell you what kinds of conditions will prevail, but he can't guarantee how you will react to them.

The weatherman can tell you that there will be a storm, but he can't predict whether you will choose to stay safe at home or go out sailing on that day. An astrologer can tell by looking at your chart that you are a cautious person, or an adventurous person, and he can even predict whether you will be feeling unusually cautious or unusually careless on that particular day. He can make a highly educated guess as to what you will decide to do on that day, but the ultimate decision is always up to you. As it is said, "The planets impel, they do not compel."

THE RIGHT TIMES TO ACT

Despite this freedom of choice, there is a wealth of knowledge about future trends and timing in your life that you can gain by studying the transits and progressions of your chart.

Certain times are more favorable than others for certain things, and certain opportunities will come to you at certain times.

TRANSITS TIME THE EVENTS OF YOUR LIFE

Every day the planets are passing through, or "transitting," the various houses of your chart. Each time one of the slow-moving planets (Jupiter, Saturn, Uranus, Neptune, and Pluto) passes from one of your houses to another, a major change takes place in your life.

Transits of the faster planets (Sun, Moon, Mercury, Venus, and Mars) have an influence also, but it is more short-lived and not as profound a change. The Moon, for instance, transits through your entire chart every 28 days, doing little more than triggering-off the aspects set up by the other planets.

Predicting Future Events

Prediction by transit follows the same general rules that you have already learned. Each planet influences the house that it is in for as long as it remains in that house.

For instance, when Saturn, planet of scarcity, toughness, efficiency, and work, enters your 2nd house (the house of money), your income is likely to become more limited, or you may have to work harder or plan your budget more carefully.

When Jupiter enters your 2nd house, a period of relative prosperity is likely to begin and to continue until Jupiter leaves your 2nd and enters your 3rd house. If you happen to be a writer or a professional communicator of some kind, Jupiter could bring even greater career luck to you in your 3rd house (communication) than it did in your 2nd, since it would strengthen your ability to communicate, and bring luck in that area.

Even Stronger Effects

The transitting planets have an especially strong effect when they pass over the degree occupied by one of the planets in your birth chart.

For instance, if Saturn in your birth chart is at 17° Leo, then the power of Saturn in your birth chart will be activated whenever a planet passes over 17° Leo.

If Saturn is strong in your birth chart (heavily aspected, such as ruler of your ascendant, etc.), then transits of 17° Leo will have a tremendous influence in your life. If Saturn is not particularly strong in your birth chart, then transits to 17° Leo will not be of such great importance.

If Saturn in your birth chart is well-aspected, then transits to 17° Leo will bring opportunities and recognition. If Saturn in your birth chart is negatively aspected, then planets approaching 17° Leo are likely to bring problems.

The Range of Influence

The transitting planets only operate within the limits of the possibilities shown in your birth chart. If your birth chart shows great financial genius, then negative influences transitting your 2nd house will not make you a pauper, but they could make things a little rough for a while.

The transits also form aspects to your planets as they go around your chart. For instance, when Jupiter hits 17° Aquarius it will form an opposition to your Saturn at 17° Leo. When Mars hits 17° Aries it forms a trine to your Saturn at 17° Leo, etc.

The transitting aspects, like the aspects at birth, do not have to be exact to work. Transitting aspects are allowed an orb of only 2 or 3 degrees. The influence of the transitting aspect fades in and out gradually with the strongest influence occuring during the period just before the aspect becomes exact. At this time the aspect is said to be "forming," and its influence is stronger than when it is "separating" (after the exact aspect occurs).

HOW PROGRESSIONS FORECAST THE FUTURE

Another important tool that astrologers use to assess future trends and be able to better understand the present is the progression.

Progressions reveal information about changes in a person's own nature, while transits deal more with changes in one's external environment and circumstances, although there is quite a bit of overlap in this distinction.

The method of progression that is most popularly used, and the easiest one to use, is the "day-for-a-year" method. Why it works is not easy to understand, but it does work, and is easy to learn.

The "Day-for-a-Year" Method

In this method, every day after you were born represents a year of your life. Therefore, in order to learn about what you will be experiencing at age 30, look and see where the planets were, and what aspects they formed, thirty days after your birthday.

For instance, if you were born on January 1, 1958, both the Sun and Mercury changed signs within 30 days (30 years, by progression) after you were born.

The Sun left Capricorn and moved into Aquarius 20 days after your birth, so your 20th year would have been a milestone year for you.

Your basic nature would have become much more open-minded and interested in humanitarian causes and all things new at this time (since

this is the nature of Aquarians). You would have become less conservative, less serious, less rigid and less pessimistic when your progressed
Sun left Capricorn at age 20.

Further Refinements

Planets in progression also enter and leave houses and form aspects
just as the transitting planets do.

When an astrologer plots a chart including the progressions and
transits, it is generally done in the form of a regular chart with two exact
rings added outside of the ring which holds the planets' positions at
birth.

The first outer ring holds the progressed planets, and the outside ring
holds the transitting planets. This creates a very complex picture with a
multitude of variables to consider.

WHAT EACH TRANSIT MEANS IN YOUR LIFE

In this chapter, you have learned the basic principles of progression
and transit, and can add these to your chart and analyze what they mean
through your basic knowledge of house, sign, and aspect.

If you would like to find out, in detail, what each transit signifies in
your life, we highly recommend the book Planets in Transit (listed in
Recommended Reading).

If you would like to explore the technical aspects of future trend
prediction, we recommend the A to Z Horoscope Maker and Delineator,
also listed in Recommended Reading.

AN EASY METHOD OF PREDICTING THE FUTURE

An easier means of planning for the future and analyzing the present is
simply to follow the Moon as it goes through the signs.

Man is said to be composed of about 90 percent water. Does the Moon,
which controls the tides, also control man? Some say that the Moon has
its strong influence over us because, for example, during the Full Moon
we tend to become dehydrated. Drinking large quantities of nonal-
coholic liquids can protect you from "Full Moon Madness."

Every two and a half days or so, the Moon changes signs, and everyone
is subtly influenced by these changes. When the Moon is in Aries, people
are more energetic and enthusiastic than usual. When it is in Taurus,
people tend to slow down and want to enjoy sensual pleasures. Moon in
Gemini is ideal for conversation, writing, and anything that should
happen quickly.

If you want to follow these changes in the Moon, the best thing to do is to get an astrological calendar, which lists the exact minute when the Moon changes signs, as well as many other things of astrological interest. There are pocket-size and wall-size calendars published (see Recommended Reading).

These calendars also tell, to the minute, *when the Moon will be "void of course."* The Moon is considered to be void of course from the time that it makes its last aspect in the sign that it is in until the time that it enters the next sign. These periods occur every few days, and last anywhere from a few seconds to a day or more. During this time it is best to avoid doing anything that is important and practical. These are considered to be very good times to play, but very bad times to work. Work done at this time often goes wrong and has to be re-done later. For instance, Presidential candidates who were nominated during void-of-course Moons have always lost the election.

Of course, if you have to work when the Moon is void of course, try to do the more routine things and avoid starting anything new and important, and you will probably manage to get something done despite this lunar handicap. A strong will can succeed even when the astrological "weather" is rough.

Tricks of the Trade

This chapter is a round-up of various small facts that will be helpful to you in pursuing astrology further.

1. How to Obtain Computerized Horoscopes

Computerized horoscopes offer two advantages to casting the horoscope yourself:

(a) you save time, and

(b) the computer-cast chart is highly accurate, and free from human error. For about $3, you can obtain a chart that is more detailed and accurate than the kind of chart that a professional astrologer would produce in an hour without help of a computer.

When sending for a computer-cast chart, do be sure to check that you send the company the exact time, and know whether you are sending them Standard Time or Daylight Savings Time.

Here are the addresses of services that offer chart-computing services:

ACA, Inc., Box 395, Weston, Mass., 02193

Astro-Computing, Neil Michelsen, Box 16297, San Diego, Calif., 92116.

Astro-Graphics Services, Robert Hand, 217 Rock Harbor Rd., Orleans, Mass., 02653.

Astro-Numeric Services, Greg Howe, Box 512, El Cerrito, Calif., 94530.

Astrological Bureau of Ideas, Box 251, Wethersfield, Conn., 06109.

Para Research, Inc., Box 7B, Lanesville, Mass., 01930.

2. A Guide to the Crazy-Quilt Time History of the U.S.

There are many towns, cities, counties, and states that have used time laws that differ from those of the rest of the country. Illinois, for instance, recorded all births on the birth certificate in Standard Time until July 1, 1959, even in summer, while Daylight Savings Time was in effect.

The best guide through the maze of time changes is the series by Doris Chase Doane: *Time Changes in the U.S., Time Changes in Canada and Mexico,* and *Time Changes in the World.*

In the *Time Changes in the U.S.,* be sure to notice the update supplement on blue paper at the end of the book, which contains vital information which modifies some of the information given in the main body of the book.

3. If You Were Born Outside the U.S.

Consult an atlas to see how many hours you need to add to, or subtract from, your time of birth to find Greenwich Mean Time. Since there have been various changes in time-keeping systems around the world, you may want to consult *Time Changes in Canada and Mexico* or *Time Changes in the World.*

4. How to Achieve Greater Accuracy

You will need to buy some reference books and to add some difficult steps to your chart-casting procedure.

You will need books containing:

(a) Latitude, longitude, and Local Mean Time variations for each town and city (see Longitudes and Latitudes in the U.S. in Recommended Reading).

(b) Tables of houses for the various latitudes.

(c) A daily ephemeris for all years that you wish to work with.

(d) The Time Changes books mentioned in Number 2 above.

(e) A book describing how to cast a chart in the full professional manner (or a person who would show you how to do this). This procedure is much more difficult than the method described in this book, but it can give you results that are accurate to the minute (1/60th of a degree) or even the second (1/60th of 1/60th of a degree). A good guide to this exact method of chart-casting is the *Master Guide to Preparing Your Natal Horoscope,* by King Keyes (Parker Publishing Co.) The entire book is devoted to the technical procedures involved in casting a precise chart.

If you want to add considerable mathematical accuracy without becoming involved in a major mathematical project, simply convert your birth time from Standard Time to Local Mean Time (the correction factors for each town are given in the Longitudes and Latitudes books, U.S. or World); use a table of houses for your exact latitude, and use a daily ephemeris (such as *Raphael's Ephemeris* or the *American Ephemeris*).

Glyphs and Glossary

THE GLYPHS—AND HOW TO REMEMBER THEM

The glyphs are a very important and convenient form of astrological shorthand. Each glyph artistically symbolizes the unique character of the sign, planet, or aspect that it represents.

The Zodiac

Glyph	Sign	Interpretation or Memory Cue
♈	**Aries**	Horns of the ram Angular shape: aggressive
♉	**Taurus**	Bull's head and horns Round shape: patient
♊	**Gemini**	Simple straight lines: logical Roman numeral "2": duality
♋	**Cancer**	Round, protected shape Harbors of safety, looks like "C's"
♌	**Leo**	A lion's mane Dramatic, open shape: outgoing
♍	**Virgo**	Precise shape Closed area at end symbolizes virginity
♎	**Libra**	The scales Equality, balance
♏	**Scorpio**	Arrow is the scorpion's stinger Flowing: a water sign
♐	**Sagittarius**	The archer's arrow Onward, upward, optimism
♑	**Capricorn**	A seagoat: Sharp horn and curvy tail

Glyph	Sign	Interpretation or Memory Cue
♒	**Aquarius**	Waves in the air: Electricity, radio
♓	**Pisces**	Two fish tied together: Duality

The Planets

Glyph	Planet	Memory Cue
☉	**Sun**	The center
☽	**Moon**	The crescent Moon's shape
☿	**Mercury**	Messenger with feet and winged hat
♀	**Venus**	The female symbol: attraction
♂	**Mars**	Arrow: weapon or tool: action
♃	**Jupiter**	An open cup gathering abundance from the heavens
♄	**Saturn**	Opposite of Jupiter: an empty cup (overturned): hardship, scarcity, hard work
♅	**Uranus**	A TV antenna: rules inventions
♆	**Neptune**	Neptune's trident
♇	**Pluto**	Old symbol: a man with arms upraised: Power; New symbol: Pl for Pluto

Review of Aspect Glyphs

Glyph	Angle	Name	Nature of Aspect
☌	0°	**Conjunction**	"Good" or "bad" concentrated energy

Glyph	Angle	Name	Nature of Aspect
✳	60°	**Sextile**	Opportunity to create "good": talent
☐	90°	**Square**	Problems you cause and obstacles to overcome
△	120°	**Trine**	Good luck; abundance; protection
☍	180°	**Opposition**	Problems that come to you, especially in relationships

GLOSSARY

Affliction.   A planet or house cusp that is involved in a negative ("bad") aspect is said to be afflicted. If a planet or a point in the chart is involved in an overall pattern of negative aspects, it is said to be "heavily afflicted." "Bad" aspects are actually challenges, which bring growth, development, and eventually good fortune if they are properly handled.

Ascendant.   The "rising point." The point in the Zodiac that was on the Eastern horizon at the moment that you were born, or at any other moment in question. Planets on the Eastern horizon are said to be "on the ascendant" or "conjunct the ascendant." The sign that was on the Eastern horizon at the moment of your birth is often called your "rising sign." Your ascendant influences your appearance, body build, personality projection, and qualities that you are striving to develop in yourself in this lifetime.

Aspects.   The aspects are the angles that the planets form to each other and to other important points in the chart, such as the ascendant and midheaven. Geometrically, your position on Earth is the vertex of the angle. In this book we deal only with the five "major aspects": conjunction, sextile, square, trine, and opposition. Some astrologers also consider the "minor aspects": quintile, semisquare, sesquiquadrate, etc. These do influence the chart, but are much less powerful than the major aspects.

Asteroids.   Pallas, Juno, Ceres, and other large asteroids have regular orbits and influence life on Earth. But their influence is weak in comparison to that of the planets. Many astrologers include these asteroids in their charts.

Benefic.   In Latin, "benefic" means "to make good." Jupiter and Venus are called "the benefics"—they bring good luck, love, harmony, and abundance. Venus, the "lesser benefic," operates on a personal level and is not always above selfishness. Jupiter, the "greater benefic," operates on a more spiritual level, bringing education, knowledge, and abundance for everyone he influences. The Sun will act as a benefic if it is not heavily afflicted.

Cardinal houses.   The four houses that are on the four cardinal points in the chart (ascendant, descendant, midheaven, and Nadir). These houses—1, 4, 7, and 10—are in the same positions in the chart as the cardinal signs are in the Natural Zodiac. These houses show areas of your life where you begin new things. The cardinal, fixed, and mutable houses are often called the "angular, succeedent, and cadent" houses.

Cardinal signs.   The signs that begin the four seasons—Aries, Cancer, Libra, and Capricorn. Cardinal sign people love to begin new projects, learn new things, and be very active.

Common signs.   Older astrology books sometimes refer to the mutable signs as the "common" signs.

Conjunction.   The aspect formed by two or more planets that are within 6° of each other. If the Sun or Moon is involved in the aspect, an orb of 8° or more is allowable. Naturally, a 1° conjunction is much stronger than an 8° conjunction. The conjunction causes blending and strengthening of the planets involved.

Constellation.   A group of stars that appear to form an animal, a person, or some other image in the sky (like the Big Dipper). The images of the signs of the Zodiac are all constellations, forming a belt around the Earth, and you can see them in the sky if you have a clear night, a constellation map, and a good imagination.

Cusp.   In Latin, "a point." The dividing point between two signs or two houses is called a cusp. The ascendant is the 1st house cusp. The midheaven (in the prevailing Placidean house cusp system) is the 10th house cusp, i.e., the beginning point of the 10th house. The cusps of the signs occur at 30° of each sign. If you have a planet at 27°, 28°, or 29°, or at 0°, 1°, or 2° of any sign, that planet will also have some qualities of the neighboring sign.

Ecliptic.   The apparent path of the Sun. Eclipses always occur along the ecliptic.

Ephemeris.   A book, booklet, or section of a book which lists the "ephemeral" (quickly-changing) positions of the planets, usually at zero hour (12:00 a.m.) Greenwich Mean Time. The zero hour ephemeris is often called a "midnight" ephemeris. Also common is the "noon" ephemeris, calculated for noon G.M.T.

Fixed stars.   Distant stars which, from our place of viewing, appear to stay in fixed, unchanging positions year after year. The fixed stars do influence life on Earth, but their influence is weak in comparison to the astrological effects of the planets.

Grand trine.   When three planets are each 120° from each other, they form an equilateral triangle around the chart which is called a grand trine. This triple trine in a birth chart brings good luck that is so abundant that it can cause one to become lazy and unambitious, coasting along in an easy life without challenge. The grand trine also can be formed with the ascendant or midheaven as one of the points of the triangle.

Horoscope.   A diagram of the positions of the planets, houses, and signs at the moment of birth, or any other moment.

Houses.   The circle of the horoscope chart divides the sky into 12 pie-shaped sectors called houses. The astrological factors affecting each house in your chart show what has happened, is happening, and can happen in each area of your life.

Luminaries.   The Sun and Moon—the givers of light. In astrology, the Sun and Moon are often referred to as "planets" for the sake of convenience, even though the Sun is technically a star and the Moon a satellite.

Malefic.   A Latin word meaning "to make bad." The planets Mars, Saturn, Uranus, and Pluto have been called malefic, but no planet is really "bad." If these planets are well-aspected, they will bring good fortune. Even if they are "afflicted" (negatively aspected), they can be a positive, constructive force in your life, if you use them well.

Nadir.   The point at the "bottom of the chart," opposite the midheaven. The nadir is the cusp of the 4th house (in the Placidean, and most other house-division systems).

Natal.   "Of or pertaining to one's birth." Astrologers often call the birth chart the natal chart.

Native.   "The one who is born." The person whose chart is being discussed. For example, "The native's blunt manner of speech is indicated by the placement of Mercury in Aries in his natal chart."

Nodes.   Usually refers to the nodes of the Moon. The points where the Moon's path crosses the ecliptic.

Orb.   The area of influence around a planet. Most astrologers allow an orb of 6° or so for the planets, and 8° or 10° for the Sun and Moon.

Retrograde.   A planet that, from our point of view on Earth, appears to be traveling backward through the Zodiac is said at that time to be "retrograding" or "in retrograde motion." Any planet that was in retrograde motion at the time of your birth shows an energy that you feel inwardly but have a difficult time expressing to others.

Rising sign.   The sign of the Zodiac that is on the Eastern horizon at the moment of birth. The sign that is on the ascendant.

Signs.   The signs of the Zodiac divide the sky into 12 equal sectors of 30 degrees each. The Sun enters each sign at a slightly different time each year.

Transit.   Transit means "traveling through." As the planets travel through the Zodiac, they form aspects to each other and to the permanent positions of the planets in your birth chart.

Zero Hour.   12:00 a.m., the first moment of the day. Practically speaking, Midnight of July 1st, for example, equals zero hour of July 2nd.

Zodiac.   An imaginary belt, in the heavens, around the Earth. Most of the planets spend all of their time within this belt, which extends for 8 degrees on each side of the ecliptic. The Zodiac is divided into 12 equal parts, each containing 30 degrees of Zodiacal longitude.

Recommended Reading

We strongly encourage you to go farther in your study of yourself and your life through astrology. Now that you have your complete chart, the simplest way to examine some different professional points of view of what the stars say about you is by looking up your various aspects and placements in different books and seeing what each astrologer's experience has told him about each of your aspects.

Always keep in mind that the birth chart is only accurately read as a whole, since the different parts all modify each other, so not every word of every description will be true of you.

Now that you have done the "hard part"—learning the concepts and setting up your chart—going on to further explore your chart is easy and very rewarding.

Here are some books that contain penetrating, useful analysis of your aspects, including valuable personal and career-oriented advice based on your chart.

INTERPRETATION

Hand, Robert. *Planets in Transit.* Gloucester, Mass.: Para Research, 1976. Detailed, accurate, specific analysis of what changes to expect in your life as the planets transit through the houses of your chart and aspect your natal planets. Also valuable in helping you understand what you're going through in the present, and in gaining a different perspective on your past.

Maynard, Jim. *The Pocket Astrologer.* Ashland, Oregon: Quicksilver Productions, published annually. Pocket-sized paperback with complete ephemeris for the current year and many other features.

Moore, Marcia, and Douglas, Mark, *Astrology, the Divine Science.* York Harbor, Maine: Arcane Publications, 1971. Sections show how planets influenced history and how they shape social events now and in the future.

Pelletier, Robert. *Planets in Aspect.* Gloucester, Mass.: Para Research, 1974. Helpful and practical advice including vocational information, based on your planetary aspects.

Rosenblum, Art, and Jackson, Leah. *The Natural Birth Control Book.*
    Philadelphia, Pa.: Aquarian Research Foundation, 1974. Contains
    long section on astrological birth control.
Sakoian, Frances, and Acker, Louis S. *The Astrologer's Handbook.* New
    York: Harper & Row, 1973. Specific descriptions of the placements
    and aspects are very useful.
Wickenburg, Joanne. *In Search of a Fulfilling Career.* Seattle, Wash.:
    Search publishers, 1977. Astrologically helpful guide stressing the
    career that is right for you.

TECHNICAL

Dernay, Eugene. *Longitudes and Latitudes in the U.S.* and *Longitudes
    and Latitudes Throughout the World.* Washington, D.C.: National
    Astrological Library.
Doane, Doris Chase. *Time Changes in the U.S., Time Changes in
    Canada and Mexico,* and *Time Changes in the World.* Hollywood,
    Calif: Professional Astrologers, Inc.
George, Llewellyn. *A to Z Horoscope Maker and Delineator.* St. Paul,
    Minn: Llewellyn Publications, 1973. A thick encyclopedia of astrol-
    ogy in one volume.
Keyes, King. *Master Guide to Preparing Your Natal Horoscope.* West
    Nyack, N.Y.: Parker Publishing Company, Inc., 1974. A complete
    explanation of how to cast a precise birth chart.
Raphael's Ephemeris, published by W. Foursham and Co., Toronto,
    Ontario, Canada.
Rice, Hugh S. *American Astrology Table of Houses.* Los Angeles, Calif.:
    The Church of Light.

*Ephemeris
for the years 1922-1990*

1922

	Sun	Merc	Venus	Mars
Jan. 1	10 Cp	12 Cp	0 Cp	3 Sc
6	15 Cp	21 Cp	7 Cp	6 Sc
11	20 Cp	29 Cp	13 Cp	9 Sc
16	25 Cp	7 Aq	19 Cp	12 Sc
21	0 Aq	15 Aq	26 Cp	15 Sc
26	5 Aq	23 Aq	2 Aq	17 Sc
31	10 Aq	29 Aq	8 Aq	20 Sc

Jan. 1/Jup 17 Lb/Sat 7 Lb/Uran 7 Pc
Nep 15 Lo/Plut 9 Ce/N Node 14 Lb

	Sun	Merc	Venus	Mars
Feb. 1	11 Aq	29 Aq	9 Aq	21 Sc
6	16 Aq	1 Pc	16 Aq	23 Sc
11	21 Aq	29 Aq	22 Aq	26 Sc
16	27 Aq	23 Aq	28 Aq	29 Sc
21	2 Pc	18 Aq	4 Pc	1 Sg
26	7 Pc	16 Aq	11 Pc	4 Sg

Feb. 1/Jup 19 Lb/Sat 7 Lb/Uran 8 Pc
Nep 15 Lo/Plut 8 Ce/N Node 12 Lb

	Sun	Merc	Venus	Mars
Mar. 1	10 Pc	16 Aq	14 Pc	5 Sg
6	15 Pc	18 Aq	21 Pc	7 Sg
11	20 Pc	22 Aq	27 Pc	10 Sg
16	25 Pc	27 Aq	3 Ar	12 Sg
21	0 Ar	3 Pc	9 Ar	14 Sg
26	5 Ar	10 Pc	16 Ar	16 Sg
31	10 Ar	18 Pc	22 Ar	18 Sg

Mar. 1/Jup 18 Lb/Sat 6 Lb/Uran 10 Pc
Nep 14 Lo/Plut 8 Ce/N Node 11 Lb

	Sun	Merc	Venus	Mars
Apr. 1	10 Ar	19 Pc	23 Ar	18 Sg
6	15 Ar	28 Pc	29 Ar	20 Sg
11	20 Ar	6 Ar	5 Tr	21 Sg
16	25 Ar	16 Ar	12 Tr	22 Sg
21	0 Tr	26 Ar	18 Tr	24 Sg
26	5 Tr	6 Tr	24 Tr	24 Sg

Apr. 1/Jup 14 Lb/Sat 4 Lb/Uran 11 Pc
Nep 13 Lo/Plut 8 Ce/N Node 9 Lb

	Sun	Merc	Venus	Mars
May 1	10 Tr	17 Tr	0 Gm	25 Sg
6	15 Tr	27 Tr	6 Gm	25 Sg
11	20 Tr	7 Gm	12 Gm	25 Sg
16	24 Tr	15 Gm	18 Gm	25 Sg
21	29 Tr	21 Gm	24 Gm	24 Sg
26	4 Gm	26 Gm	0 Ce	23 Sg
31	9 Gm	0 Ce	6 Ce	22 Sg

May 1/Jup 11 Lb/Sat 2 Lb/Uran 13 Pc
Nep 13 Lo/Plut 8 Ce/N Node 7 Lb

	Sun	Merc	Venus	Mars
June 1	10 Gm	0 Ce	8 Ce	22 Sg
6	15 Gm	1 Ce	14 Ce	20 Sg
11	19 Gm	0 Ce	20 Ce	19 Sg
16	24 Gm	28 Gm	26 Ce	17 Sg
21	29 Gm	25 Gm	2 Lo	16 Sg
26	4 Ce	23 Gm	8 Lo	14 Sg

June 1/Jup 9 Lb/Sat 1 Lb/Uran 13 Pc
Nep 14 Lo/Plut 9 Ce/N Node 6 Lb

	Sun	Merc	Venus	Mars
July 1	8 Ce	22 Gm	13 Lo	13 Sg
6	13 Ce	24 Gm	19 Lo	12 Sg
11	18 Ce	27 Gm	25 Lo	11 Sg
16	23 Ce	3 Ce	1 Vr	11 Sg
21	27 Ce	10 Ce	7 Vr	11 Sg
26	2 Lo	19 Ce	13 Vr	12 Sg
31	7 Lo	29 Ce	18 Vr	12 Sg

July 1/Jup 10 Lb/Sat 1 Lb/Uran 14 Pc
Nep 14 Lo/Plut 10 Ce/N Node 4 Lb

	Sun	Merc	Venus	Mars
Aug. 1	8 Lo	1 Lo	19 Vr	13 Sg
6	13 Lo	11 Lo	25 Vr	14 Sg
11	18 Lo	22 Lo	1 Lb	15 Sg
16	22 Lo	1 Vr	6 Lb	17 Sg
21	27 Lo	10 Vr	12 Lb	19 Sg
26	2 Vr	19 Vr	17 Lb	21 Sg
31	7 Vr	27 Vr	22 Lb	23 Sg

Aug. 1/Jup 13 Lb/Sat 4 Lb/Uran 13 Pc
Nep 15 Lo/Plut 10 Ce/N Node 2 Lb

1922

	Sun	Merc	Venus	Mars
Sept 1	8 Vr	28 Vr	23 Lb	24 Sg
6	13 Vr	6 Lb	29 Lb	26 Sg
11	17 Vr	12 Lb	4 Sc	29 Sg
16	22 Vr	18 Lb	9 Sc	1 Cp
21	27 Vr	24 Lb	13 Sc	4 Cp
26	2 Lb	28 Lb	18 Sc	7 Cp

Sept 1/Jup 18 Lb/Sat 7 Lb/Uran 12 Pc
Nep 17 Lo/Plut 11 Ce/N Node 1 Lb

	Sun	Merc	Venus	Mars
Oct. 1	7 Lb	0 Sc	22 Sc	10 Cp
6	12 Lb	0 Sc	26 Sc	13 Cp
11	17 Lb	26 Lb	0 Sg	17 Cp
16	22 Lb	21 Lb	3 Sg	20 Cp
21	27 Lb	16 Lb	6 Sg	23 Cp
26	2 Sc	15 Lb	8 Sg	27 Cp
31	7 Sc	18 Lb	9 Sg	0 Aq

Oct. 1/Jup 24 Lb/Sat 10 Lb/Uran 11 Pc
Nep 17 Lo/Plut 11 Ce/N Node 29 Vr

	Sun	Merc	Venus	Mars
Nov. 1	8 Sc	19 Lb	10 Sg	1 Aq
6	13 Sc	26 Lb	10 Sg	4 Aq
11	18 Sc	3 Sc	9 Sg	8 Aq
16	23 Sc	11 Sc	7 Sg	11 Aq
21	28 Sc	19 Sc	5 Sg	15 Aq
26	3 Sg	27 Sc	2 Sg	19 Aq

Nov. 1/Jup 1 Sc/Sat 14 Lb/Uran 10 Pc
Nep 18 Lo/Plut 11 Ce/N Node 28 Vr

	Sun	Merc	Venus	Mars
Dec. 1	8 Sg	5 Sg	29 Sc	22 Aq
6	13 Sg	13 Sg	26 Sc	26 Aq
11	18 Sg	21 Sg	25 Sc	0 Pc
16	23 Sg	28 Sg	25 Sc	3 Pc
21	28 Sg	6 Cp	25 Sc	7 Pc
26	3 Cp	14 Cp	27 Sc	11 Pc
31	9 Cp	22 Cp	29 Sc	14 Pc

Dec. 1/Jup 7 Sc/Sat 17 Lb/Uran 10 Pc
Nep 18 Lo/Plut 11 Ce/N Node 26 Vr

Moon's Positions

	1	4	7	10	13	16	19	22	25	28	31
Jan.	11 Aq	16 Pc	22 Ar	1 Gm	14 Ce	29 Lo	12 Lb	23 Sc	1 Cp	7 Aq	13 Pc
Feb.	25 Pc	1 Tr	9 Gm	22 Ce	7 Vr	22 Lb	2 Sg	10 Cp	16 Aq	22 Pc	
Mar.	4 Ar	10 Tr	18 Gm	30 Ce	15 Vr	30 Lb	11 Sg	19 Cp	25 Aq	1 Ar	7 Tr
Apr.	19 Tr	28 Gm	9 Lo	23 Vr	8 Sc	20 Sg	28 Cp	4 Pc	9 Ar	16 Tr	
May	25 Gm	6 Lo	18 Vr	2 Sc	14 Sg	23 Cp	30 Aq	5 Ar	12 Tr	21 Gm	3 Lo
June	17 Lo	29 Vr	11 Sc	23 Sg	1 Aq	8 Pc	13 Ar	20 Tr	0 Ce	13 Lo	
July	26 Vr	8 Sc	18 Sg	27 Cp	4 Pc	9 Ar	16 Tr	25 Gm	8 Lo	22 Vr	5 Sc
Aug.	18 Sc	28 Sg	6 Aq	12 Pc	18 Ar	24 Tr	3 Ce	16 Lo	1 Lb	15 Sc	25 Sg
Sept	8 Cp	15 Aq	21 Pc	26 Ar	3 Gm	12 Ce	24 Lo	10 Lb	24 Sc	5 Cp	
Oct.	12 Aq	18 Pc	23 Ar	30 Tr	8 Ce	19 Lo	3 Lb	18 Sc	0 Cp	9 Aq	15 Pc
Nov.	27 Pc	2 Tr	9 Gm	18 Ce	28 Lo	12 Lb	26 Sc	8 Cp	17 Aq	23 Pc	
Dec.	28 Ar	5 Gm	15 Ce	25 Lo	7 Lb	20 Sc	3 Cp	12 Aq	19 Pc	24 Ar	1 Gm

1923

	Sun	Merc	Venus	Mars
Jan. 1	10 Cp	24 Cp	29 Sc	15 Pc
6	15 Cp	2 Aq	2 Sg	19 Pc
11	20 Cp	8 Aq	6 Sg	22 Pc
16	25 Cp	13 Aq	10 Sg	26 Pc
21	0 Aq	15 Aq	14 Sg	0 Ar
26	5 Aq	12 Aq	19 Sg	3 Ar
31	10 Aq	6 Aq	23 Sg	7 Ar

Jan. 1/Jup 13 Sc/Sat 19 Lb/Uran 10 Pc
Nep 18 Lo/Plut 10 Ce/N Node 24 Vr

	Sun	Merc	Venus	Mars
Feb. 1	11 Aq	5 Aq	24 Sg	8 Ar
6	16 Aq	0 Aq	29 Sg	11 Ar
11	21 Aq	29 Cp	5 Cp	15 Ar
16	26 Aq	1 Aq	10 Cp	19 Ar
21	1 Pc	5 Aq	15 Cp	22 Ar
26	6 Pc	10 Aq	21 Cp	26 Ar

Feb. 1/Jup 17 Sc/Sat 20 Lb/Uran 12 Pc
Nep 17 Lo/Plut 10 Ce/N Node 23 Vr

	Sun	Merc	Venus	Mars
Mar. 1	9 Pc	13 Aq	24 Cp	28 Ar
6	14 Pc	20 Aq	0 Aq	1 Tr
11	19 Pc	27 Aq	5 Aq	5 Tr
16	24 Pc	4 Pc	11 Aq	8 Tr
21	29 Pc	13 Pc	17 Aq	12 Tr
26	4 Ar	21 Pc	23 Aq	15 Tr
31	9 Ar	0 Ar	29 Aq	19 Tr

Mar. 1/Jup 19 Sc/Sat 19 Lb/Uran 13 Pc
Nep 16 Lo/Plut 9 Ce/N Node 21 Vr

	Sun	Merc	Venus	Mars
Apr. 1	10 Ar	2 Ar	0 Pc	20 Tr
6	15 Ar	12 Ar	6 Pc	23 Tr
11	20 Ar	23 Ar	12 Pc	27 Tr
16	25 Ar	3 Tr	17 Pc	0 Gm
21	0 Tr	13 Tr	23 Pc	3 Gm
26	5 Tr	22 Tr	29 Pc	7 Gm

Apr. 1/Jup 18 Sc/Sat 17 Lb/Uran 15 Pc
Nep 16 Lo/Plut 9 Ce/N Node 20 Vr

	Sun	Merc	Venus	Mars
May 1	10 Tr	0 Gm	5 Ar	10 Gm
6	14 Tr	5 Gm	11 Ar	13 Gm
11	19 Tr	9 Gm	17 Ar	17 Gm
16	24 Tr	11 Gm	23 Ar	20 Gm
21	29 Tr	10 Gm	29 Ar	23 Gm
26	4 Gm	8 Gm	5 Tr	27 Gm
31	9 Gm	6 Gm	11 Tr	0 Ce

May 1/Jup 15 Sc/Sat 15 Lb/Uran 16 Pc
Nep 15 Lo/Plut 9 Ce/N Node 18 Vr

	Sun	Merc	Venus	Mars
June 1	9 Gm	5 Gm	13 Tr	1 Ce
6	14 Gm	3 Gm	19 Tr	4 Ce
11	19 Gm	2 Gm	25 Tr	7 Ce
16	24 Gm	3 Gm	1 Gm	11 Ce
21	29 Gm	7 Gm	7 Gm	14 Ce
26	3 Ce	11 Gm	13 Gm	17 Ce

June 1/Jup 11 Sc/Sat 14 Lb/Uran 17 Pc
Nep 16 Lo/Plut 10 Ce/N Node 16 Vr

	Sun	Merc	Venus	Mars
July 1	8 Ce	18 Gm	19 Gm	20 Ce
6	13 Ce	26 Gm	25 Gm	24 Ce
11	18 Ce	5 Ce	1 Ce	27 Ce
16	22 Ce	15 Ce	7 Ce	0 Lo
21	27 Ce	26 Ce	13 Ce	3 Lo
26	2 Lo	6 Lo	19 Ce	6 Lo
31	7 Lo	16 Lo	25 Ce	10 Lo

July 1/Jup 9 Sc/Sat 14 Lb/Uran 18 Pc
Nep 16 Lo/Plut 11 Ce/N Node 15 Vr

	Sun	Merc	Venus	Mars
Aug. 1	8 Lo	18 Lo	27 Ce	10 Lo
6	13 Lo	27 Lo	3 Lo	13 Lo
11	17 Lo	6 Vr	9 Lo	17 Lo
16	22 Lo	14 Vr	15 Lo	20 Lo
21	27 Lo	21 Vr	21 Lo	23 Lo
26	2 Vr	28 Vr	28 Lo	26 Lo
31	7 Vr	3 Lb	4 Vr	29 Lo

Aug. 1/Jup 10 Sc/Sat 15 Lb/Uran 17 Pc
Nep 18 Lo/Plut 11 Ce/N Node 13 Vr

1923

		Sun	Merc	Venus	Mars
Sept	1	8 Vr	5 Lb	5 Vr	0 Vr
	6	12 Vr	9 Lb	11 Vr	3 Vr
	11	17 Vr	12 Lb	17 Vr	6 Vr
	16	22 Vr	14 Lb	24 Vr	10 Vr
	21	27 Vr	13 Lb	0 Lb	13 Vr
	26	2 Lb	8 Lb	6 Lb	16 Vr

Sept 1/Jup 13 Sc/Sat 18 Lb/Uran 16 Pc
Nep 19 Lo/Plut 12 Ce/N Node 11 Vr

		Sun	Merc	Venus	Mars
Oct.	1	7 Lb	3 Lb	12 Lb	19 Vr
	6	12 Lb	29 Vr	19 Lb	22 Vr
	11	17 Lb	29 Vr	25 Lb	25 Vr
	16	22 Lb	4 Lb	1 Sc	29 Vr
	21	27 Lb	10 Lb	7 Sc	2 Lb
	26	2 Sc	18 Lb	14 Sc	5 Lb
	31	7 Sc	27 Lb	20 Sc	8 Lb

Oct. 1/Jup 18 Sc/Sat 21 Lb/Uran 15 Pc
Nep 20 Lo/Plut 12 Ce/N Node 10 Vr

		Sun	Merc	Venus	Mars
Nov.	1	8 Sc	28 Lb	21 Sc	9 Lb
	6	13 Sc	6 Sc	27 Sc	12 Lb
	11	18 Sc	15 Sc	3 Sg	15 Lb
	16	23 Sc	23 Sc	10 Sg	18 Lb
	21	28 Sc	1 Sg	16 Sg	22 Lb
	26	3 Sg	8 Sg	22 Sg	25 Lb

Nov. 1/Jup 25 Sc/Sat 25 Lb/Uran 14 Pc
Nep 20 Lo/Plut 12 Ce/N Node 8 Vr

		Sun	Merc	Venus	Mars
Dec.	1	8 Sg	16 Sg	28 Sg	28 Lb
	6	13 Sg	24 Sg	5 Cp	1 Sc
	11	18 Sg	2 Cp	11 Cp	4 Sc
	16	23 Sg	9 Cp	17 Cp	8 Sc
	21	28 Sg	16 Cp	23 Cp	11 Sc
	26	3 Cp	23 Cp	0 Aq	14 Sc
	31	8 Cp	27 Cp	6 Aq	17 Sc

Dec. 1/Jup 1 Sg/Sat 28 Lb/Uran 14 Pc
Nep 20 Lo/Plut 12 Ce/N Node 7 Vr

Moon's Positions

	1	4	7	10	13	16	19	22	25	28	31
Jan.	14 Gm	24 Ce	6 Vr	18 Lb	0 Sg	11 Cp	20 Aq	27 Pc	2 Tr	9 Gm	18 Ce
Feb.	2 Lo	16 Vr	29 Lb	11 Sg	21 Cp	29 Aq	5 Ar	10 Tr	17 Gm	26 Ce	
Mar.	10 Lo	24 Vr	9 Sc	21 Sg	1 Aq	8 Pc	13 Ar	19 Tr	25 Gm	4 Lo	17 Vr
Apr.	2 Lb	18 Sc	1 Cp	10 Aq	17 Pc	22 Ar	28 Tr	4 Ce	13 Lo	26 Vr	
May	11 Sc	26 Sg	6 Aq	14 Pc	19 Ar	25 Tr	2 Ce	10 Lo	21 Vr	5 Sc	19 Sg
June	4 Cp	15 Aq	22 Pc	28 Ar	4 Gm	11 Ce	20 Lo	1 Lb	14 Sc	28 Sg	
July	10 Aq	18 Pc	24 Ar	30 Tr	7 Ce	17 Lo	28 Vr	11 Sc	23 Sg	5 Aq	13 Pc
Aug.	26 Pc	2 Tr	8 Gm	15 Ce	26 Lo	9 Lb	22 Sc	4 Cp	14 Aq	22 Pc	28 Ar
Sept	10 Tr	16 Gm	23 Ce	5 Vr	18 Lb	2 Sg	14 Cp	23 Aq	0 Ar	6 Tr	
Oct.	12 Gm	19 Ce	28 Lo	12 Lb	27 Sc	11 Cp	20 Aq	27 Pc	3 Tr	9 Gm	15 Ce
Nov.	27 Ce	7 Vr	20 Lb	6 Sg	20 Cp	30 Aq	6 Ar	12 Tr	18 Gm	24 Ce	
Dec.	3 Vr	14 Lb	29 Sc	14 Cp	25 Aq	3 Ar	9 Tr	14 Gm	21 Ce	30 Lo	10 Lb

1924

```
           Sun    Merc   Venus   Mars              Sun     Merc   Venus   Mars
Jan. 1    9 Cp   28 Cp    7 Aq   18 Sc    Feb. 1  11 Aq   16 Cp   15 Pc    8 Sg
      6   14 Cp   29 Cp   13 Aq   21 Sc         6  16 Aq   20 Cp   21 Pc   11 Sg
     11   20 Cp   25 Cp   19 Aq   24 Sc        11  21 Aq   26 Cp   27 Pc   14 Sg
     16   25 Cp   18 Cp   26 Aq   28 Sc        16  26 Aq    2 Aq    3 Ar   17 Sg
     21    0 Aq   14 Cp    2 Pc    1 Sg        21   1 Pc    9 Aq    9 Ar   21 Sg
     26    5 Aq   13 Cp    8 Pc    4 Sg        26   6 Pc   17 Aq   15 Ar   24 Sg
     31   10 Aq   15 Cp   14 Pc    7 Sg
Jan. 1/Jup  8 Sg/Sat  1 Sc/Uran 14 Pc    Feb. 1/Jup 14 Sg/Sat  2 Sc/Uran 16 Pc
Nep 20 Lo/Plut 11 Ce/N Node  5 Vr        Nep 19 Lo/Plut 11 Ce/N Node  3 Vr


           Sun    Merc   Venus   Mars              Sun     Merc   Venus   Mars
Mar. 1   10 Pc   23 Aq   20 Ar   26 Sg    Apr. 1  11 Ar   21 Ar   25 Tr   16 Cp
      6   15 Pc    1 Pc   26 Ar    0 Cp         6  16 Ar    1 Tr    1 Gm   19 Cp
     11   20 Pc   10 Pc    2 Tr    3 Cp        11  21 Ar    9 Tr    6 Gm   22 Cp
     16   25 Pc   19 Pc    7 Tr    6 Cp        16  26 Ar   15 Tr   11 Gm   25 Cp
     21    0 Ar   29 Pc   13 Tr    9 Cp        21   1 Tr   20 Tr   16 Gm   28 Cp
     26    5 Ar    9 Ar   19 Tr   12 Cp        26   5 Tr   21 Tr   21 Gm    1 Aq
     31   10 Ar   19 Ar   24 Tr   15 Cp
Mar. 1/Jup 18 Sg/Sat  2 Sc/Uran 17 Pc    Apr. 1/Jup 20 Sg/Sat  0 Sc/Uran 19 Pc
Nep 18 Lo/Plut 10 Ce/N Node  2 Vr        Nep 18 Lo/Plut 10 Ce/N Node  0 Vr


           Sun    Merc   Venus   Mars              Sun     Merc   Venus   Mars
May 1    10 Tr   21 Tr   26 Gm    4 Aq    June 1  10 Gm   16 Tr   16 Ce   20 Aq
      6   15 Tr   18 Tr    0 Ce    7 Aq         6  15 Gm   21 Tr   17 Ce   23 Aq
     11   20 Tr   15 Tr    4 Ce    9 Aq        11  20 Gm   27 Tr   18 Ce   25 Aq
     16   25 Tr   13 Tr    8 Ce   12 Aq        16  25 Gm    4 Gm   17 Ce   27 Aq
     21    0 Gm   12 Tr   11 Ce   15 Aq        21  29 Gm   13 Gm   15 Ce   29 Aq
     26    4 Gm   13 Tr   14 Ce   17 Aq        26   4 Ce   23 Gm   13 Ce    0 Pc
     31    9 Gm   16 Tr   16 Ce   20 Aq
May 1/Jup 19 Sg/Sat 28 Lb/Uran 20 Pc     June 1/Jup 16 Sg/Sat 26 Lb/Uran 21 Pc
Nep 18 Lo/Plut 11 Ce/N Node 29 Lo        Nep 18 Lo/Plut 11 Ce/N Node 27 Lo


           Sun    Merc   Venus   Mars              Sun     Merc   Venus   Mars
July 1    9 Ce    3 Ce   10 Ce    2 Pc    Aug. 1   8 Lo    2 Vr    2 Ce    5 Pc
      6   14 Ce   14 Ce    7 Ce    3 Pc         6  13 Lo    9 Vr    4 Ce    4 Pc
     11   18 Ce   25 Ce    4 Ce    4 Pc        11  18 Lo   15 Vr    7 Ce    3 Pc
     16   23 Ce    5 Lo    2 Ce    5 Pc        16  23 Lo   20 Vr   10 Ce    2 Pc
     21   28 Ce   14 Lo    1 Ce    5 Pc        21  28 Lo   24 Vr   14 Ce    1 Pc
     26    3 Lo   23 Lo    1 Ce    5 Pc        26   2 Vr   26 Vr   18 Ce    0 Pc
     31    7 Lo    0 Vr    2 Ce    5 Pc        31   7 Vr   27 Vr   22 Ce   28 Aq
July 1/Jup 12 Sg/Sat 26 Lb/Uran 22 Pc    Aug. 1/Jup 10 Sg/Sat 27 Lb/Uran 21 Pc
Nep 19 Lo/Plut 12 Ce/N Node 25 Lo        Nep 20 Lo/Plut 13 Ce/N Node 24 Lo
```

1924

```
          Sun    Merc   Venus  Mars                    Sun    Merc   Venus  Mars
Sept 1   8 Vr   27 Vr   23 Ce   28 Aq      Oct. 1    8 Lb   20 Vr   23 Lo   26 Aq
     6  13 Vr   24 Vr   27 Ce   27 Aq           6   12 Lb   28 Vr   28 Lo   27 Aq
    11  18 Vr   19 Vr    2 Lo   26 Aq          11   17 Lb    7 Lb    4 Vr   28 Aq
    16  23 Vr   14 Vr    7 Lo   26 Aq          16   22 Lb   15 Lb    9 Vr   29 Aq
    21  28 Vr   13 Vr   12 Lo   25 Aq          21   27 Lb   24 Lb   15 Vr    0 Pc
    26   3 Lb   15 Vr   17 Lo   25 Aq          26    2 Sc    2 Sc   21 Vr    2 Pc
                                              31    7 Sc   10 Sc   27 Vr    4 Pc

Sept 1/Jup 11 Sg/Sat 29 Lb/Uran 20 Pc    Oct. 1/Jup 14 Sg/Sat  2 Sc/Uran 19 Pc
Nep 21 Lo/Plut 13 Ce/N Node 22 Lo        Nep 22 Lo/Plut 14 Ce/N Node 21 Lo


          Sun    Merc   Venus  Mars                    Sun    Merc   Venus  Mars
Nov. 1   8 Sc   12 Sc   28 Vr    5 Pc      Dec. 1    9 Sg   27 Sg    4 Sc   19 Pc
     6  13 Sc   20 Sc    4 Lb    7 Pc           6   14 Sg    4 Cp   10 Sc   22 Pc
    11  18 Sc   28 Sc   10 Lb    9 Pc          11   19 Sg    9 Cp   17 Sc   25 Pc
    16  23 Sc    5 Sg   16 Lb   11 Pc          16   24 Sg   13 Cp   23 Sc   28 Pc
    21  28 Sc   13 Sg   22 Lb   14 Pc          21   29 Sg   12 Cp   29 Sc    1 Ar
    26   3 Sg   20 Sg   28 Lb   17 Pc          26    4 Cp    7 Cp    5 Sg    4 Ar
                                              31    9 Cp    1 Cp   11 Sg    7 Ar

Nov. 1/Jup 20 Sg/Sat  6 Sc/Uran 18 Pc    Dec. 1/Jup 26 Sg/Sat  9 Sc/Uran 18 Pc
Nep 22 Lo/Plut 13 Ce/N Node 19 Lo        Nep 23 Lo/Plut 13 Ce/N Node 17 Lo
```

Moon's Positions

	1	4	7	10	13	16	19	22	25	28	31
Jan.	24 Lb	8 Sg	22 Cp	3 Pc	11 Ar	17 Tr	23 Gm	0 Lo	10 Vr	21 Lb	3 Sg
Feb.	17 Sg	0 Aq	11 Pc	19 Ar	25 Tr	1 Ce	9 Lo	19 Vr	1 Sc	14 Sg	
Mar.	12 Cp	23 Aq	2 Ar	9 Tr	14 Gm	21 Ce	30 Lo	12 Lb	26 Sc	9 Cp	20 Aq
Apr.	3 Pc	10 Ar	17 Tr	23 Gm	29 Ce	8 Vr	20 Lb	6 Sg	19 Cp	30 Aq	
May	7 Ar	14 Tr	19 Gm	25 Ce	3 Vr	14 Lb	29 Sc	14 Cp	26 Aq	4 Ar	11 Tr
June	23 Tr	28 Gm	4 Lo	12 Vr	23 Lb	7 Sg	23 Cp	5 Pc	14 Ar	20 Tr	
July	25 Gm	1 Lo	9 Vr	19 Lb	2 Sg	16 Cp	30 Aq	9 Ar	16 Tr	22 Gm	28 Ce
Aug.	11 Lo	19 Vr	29 Lb	12 Sg	25 Cp	8 Pc	18 Ar	24 Tr	0 Ce	7 Lo	15 Vr
Sept	29 Vr	10 Sc	22 Sg	5 Aq	16 Pc	25 Ar	2 Gm	8 Ce	15 Lo	24 Vr	
Oct.	6 Sc	19 Sg	2 Aq	12 Pc	21 Ar	28 Tr	4 Ce	10 Lo	18 Vr	0 Sc	15 Sg
Nov.	30 Sg	12 Aq	22 Pc	0 Tr	7 Gm	12 Ce	18 Lo	26 Vr	8 Sc	24 Sg	
Dec.	8 Aq	19 Pc	27 Ar	4 Gm	9 Ce	15 Lo	22 Vr	2 Sc	16 Sg	2 Aq	15 Pc

1925

	Sun	Merc	Venus	Mars
Jan. 1	10 Cp	0 Cp	13 Sg	8 Ar
6	15 Cp	27 Sg	19 Sg	11 Ar
11	20 Cp	28 Sg	25 Sg	14 Ar
16	25 Cp	1 Cp	1 Cp	17 Ar
21	0 Aq	7 Cp	8 Cp	20 Ar
26	6 Aq	13 Cp	14 Cp	23 Ar
31	11 Aq	19 Cp	20 Cp	27 Ar

Jan. 1/Jup 3 Cp/Sat 12 Sc/Uran 18 Pc
Nep 22 Lo/Plut 13 Ce/N Node 16 Lo

	Sun	Merc	Venus	Mars
Feb. 1	12 Aq	21 Cp	21 Cp	27 Ar
6	17 Aq	28 Cp	28 Cp	0 Tr
11	22 Aq	6 Aq	4 Aq	4 Tr
16	27 Aq	14 Aq	10 Aq	7 Tr
21	2 Pc	22 Aq	16 Aq	10 Tr
26	7 Pc	1 Pc	23 Aq	13 Tr

Feb. 1/Jup 10 Cp/Sat 14 Sc/Uran 19 Pc
Nep 21 Lo/Plut 12 Ce/N Node 14 Lo

	Sun	Merc	Venus	Mars
Mar. 1	10 Pc	6 Pc	26 Aq	15 Tr
6	15 Pc	15 Pc	2 Pc	18 Tr
11	20 Pc	25 Pc	9 Pc	22 Tr
16	25 Pc	5 Ar	15 Pc	25 Tr
21	0 Ar	14 Ar	21 Pc	28 Tr
26	5 Ar	22 Ar	27 Pc	1 Gm
31	10 Ar	29 Ar	4 Ar	4 Gm

Mar. 1/Jup 16 Cp/Sat 14 Sc/Uran 21 Pc
Nep 21 Lo/Plut 12 Ce/N Node 13 Lo

	Sun	Merc	Venus	Mars
Apr. 1	11 Ar	29 Ar	5 Ar	5 Gm
6	16 Ar	2 Tr	11 Ar	8 Gm
11	21 Ar	2 Tr	17 Ar	12 Gm
16	25 Ar	0 Tr	23 Ar	15 Gm
21	0 Tr	27 Ar	0 Tr	18 Gm
26	5 Tr	24 Ar	6 Tr	21 Gm

Apr. 1/Jup 20 Cp/Sat 13 Sc/Uran 23 Pc
Nep 20 Lo/Plut 11 Ce/N Node 11 Lo

	Sun	Merc	Venus	Mars
May 1	10 Tr	22 Ar	12 Tr	24 Gm
6	15 Tr	23 Ar	18 Tr	28 Gm
11	20 Tr	25 Ar	24 Tr	1 Ce
16	25 Tr	29 Ar	0 Gm	4 Ce
21	29 Tr	4 Tr	7 Gm	7 Ce
26	4 Gm	11 Tr	13 Gm	10 Ce
31	9 Gm	18 Tr	19 Gm	13 Ce

May 1/Jup 22 Cp/Sat 11 Sc/Uran 24 Pc
Nep 20 Lo/Plut 12 Ce/N Node 9 Lo

	Sun	Merc	Venus	Mars
June 1	10 Gm	20 Tr	20 Gm	14 Ce
6	15 Gm	29 Tr	26 Gm	17 Ce
11	20 Gm	9 Gm	2 Ce	20 Ce
16	24 Gm	19 Gm	8 Ce	23 Ce
21	29 Gm	0 Ce	15 Ce	27 Ce
26	4 Ce	11 Ce	21 Ce	0 Lo

June 1/Jup 22 Cp/Sat 9 Sc/Uran 25 Pc
Nep 20 Lo/Plut 12 Ce/N Node 8 Lo

	Sun	Merc	Venus	Mars
July 1	9 Ce	21 Ce	27 Ce	3 Lo
6	13 Ce	0 Lo	3 Lo	6 Lo
11	18 Ce	9 Lo	9 Lo	9 Lo
16	23 Ce	17 Lo	15 Lo	12 Lo
21	28 Ce	24 Lo	21 Lo	16 Lo
26	2 Lo	29 Lo	27 Lo	19 Lo
31	7 Lo	4 Vr	3 Vr	22 Lo

July 1/Jup 19 Cp/Sat 8 Sc/Uran 25 Pc
Nep 21 Lo/Plut 13 Ce/N Node 6 Lo

	Sun	Merc	Venus	Mars
Aug. 1	8 Lo	5 Vr	5 Vr	22 Lo
6	13 Lo	8 Vr	11 Vr	26 Lo
11	18 Lo	9 Vr	17 Vr	29 Lo
16	23 Lo	9 Vr	23 Vr	2 Vr
21	27 Lo	5 Vr	29 Vr	5 Vr
26	2 Vr	1 Vr	5 Lb	8 Vr
31	7 Vr	27 Lo	11 Lb	12 Vr

Aug. 1/Jup 15 Cp/Sat 8 Sc/Uran 25 Pc
Nep 22 Lo/Plut 14 Ce/N Node 4 Lo

1925

	Sun	Merc	Venus	Mars
Sept 1	8 Vr	27 Lo	12 Lb	12 Vr
6	13 Vr	27 Lo	18 Lb	15 Vr
11	18 Vr	0 Vr	24 Lb	19 Vr
16	23 Vr	6 Vr	0 Sc	22 Vr
21	27 Vr	14 Vr	6 Sc	25 Vr
26	2 Lb	23 Vr	12 Sc	28 Vr

Sept 1/Jup 13 Cp/Sat 10 Sc/Uran 24 Pc
Nep 23 Lo/Plut 14 Ce/N Node 3 Lo

	Sun	Merc	Venus	Mars
Oct. 1	7 Lb	2 Lb	18 Sc	1 Lb
6	12 Lb	11 Lb	23 Sc	5 Lb
11	17 Lb	20 Lb	29 Sc	8 Lb
16	22 Lb	28 Lb	5 Sg	11 Lb
21	27 Lb	6 Sc	11 Sg	14 Lb
26	2 Sc	14 Sc	17 Sg	18 Lb
31	7 Sc	22 Sc	22 Sg	21 Lb

Oct. 1/Jup 13 Cp/Sat 12 Sc/Uran 23 Pc
Nep 24 Lo/Plut 15 Ce/N Node 1 Lo

	Sun	Merc	Venus	Mars
Nov. 1	8 Sc	23 Sc	23 Sg	22 Lb
6	13 Sc	0 Sg	29 Sg	25 Lb
11	18 Sc	7 Sg	4 Cp	28 Lb
16	23 Sc	14 Sg	10 Cp	2 Sc
21	28 Sc	20 Sg	15 Cp	5 Sc
26	3 Sg	25 Sg	20 Cp	8 Sc

Nov. 1/Jup 17 Cp/Sat 16 Sc/Uran 22 Pc
Nep 25 Lo/Plut 15 Ce/N Node 30 Ce

	Sun	Merc	Venus	Mars
Dec. 1	8 Sg	27 Sg	25 Cp	12 Sc
6	13 Sg	26 Sg	0 Aq	15 Sc
11	18 Sg	20 Sg	5 Aq	18 Sc
16	24 Sg	14 Sg	9 Aq	22 Sc
21	29 Sg	11 Sg	13 Aq	25 Sc
26	4 Cp	12 Sg	17 Aq	29 Sc
31	9 Cp	16 Sg	20 Aq	2 Sg

Dec. 1/Jup 22 Cp/Sat 20 Sc/Uran 22 Pc
Nep 25 Lo/Plut 14 Ce/N Node 28 Ce

Moon's Positions

	1	4	7	10	13	16	19	22	25	28	31
Jan.	28 Pc	6 Tr	12 Gm	18 Ce	24 Lo	1 Lb	11 Sc	25 Sg	10 Aq	23 Pc	3 Tr
Feb.	15 Tr	21 Gm	27 Ce	3 Vr	11 Lb	22 Sc	4 Cp	18 Aq	1 Ar	11 Tr	
Mar.	23 Tr	29 Gm	5 Lo	12 Vr	21 Lb	2 Sg	15 Cp	27 Aq	9 Ar	18 Tr	25 Gm
Apr.	7 Ce	13 Lo	20 Vr	1 Sc	13 Sg	26 Cp	7 Pc	18 Ar	27 Tr	3 Ce	
May	9 Lo	15 Vr	25 Lb	8 Sg	22 Cp	4 Pc	15 Ar	23 Tr	29 Gm	5 Lo	11 Vr
June	23 Vr	3 Sc	17 Sg	2 Aq	15 Pc	25 Ar	2 Gm	8 Ce	13 Lo	20 Vr	
July	28 Lb	10 Sg	26 Cp	10 Pc	21 Ar	29 Tr	5 Ce	11 Lo	16 Vr	24 Lb	5 Sg
Aug.	19 Sg	4 Aq	19 Pc	0 Tr	8 Gm	14 Ce	19 Lo	26 Vr	4 Sc	14 Sg	28 Cp
Sept	13 Aq	27 Pc	9 Tr	17 Gm	22 Ce	28 Lo	5 Lb	14 Sc	25 Sg	7 Aq	
Oct.	21 Pc	3 Tr	12 Gm	19 Ce	24 Lo	1 Lb	11 Sc	22 Sg	4 Aq	16 Pc	28 Ar
Nov.	12 Tr	20 Gm	26 Ce	2 Vr	9 Lb	19 Sc	2 Cp	15 Aq	27 Pc	7 Tr	
Dec.	16 Gm	22 Ce	28 Lo	4 Lb	13 Sc	26 Sg	11 Aq	24 Pc	4 Tr	12 Gm	19 Cn

1926

```
        Sun    Merc   Venus  Mars                    Sun    Merc   Venus  Mars
Jan. 1  10 Cp  17 Sg  21 Aq   3 Sg      Feb. 1  11 Aq   1 Aq  22 Aq  24 Sg
     6  15 Cp  23 Sg  23 Aq   6 Sg           6  16 Aq   9 Aq  19 Aq  28 Sg
    11  20 Cp   0 Cp  25 Aq  10 Sg          11  22 Aq  18 Aq  16 Aq   1 Cp
    16  25 Cp   7 Cp  26 Aq  13 Sg          16  27 Aq  27 Aq  13 Aq   5 Cp
    21   0 Aq  14 Cp  26 Aq  17 Sg          21   2 Pc   6 Pc  11 Aq   8 Cp
    26   5 Aq  21 Cp  25 Aq  20 Sg          26   7 Pc  15 Pc  10 Aq  12 Cp
    31  10 Aq  29 Cp  23 Aq  24 Sg
Jan. 1/Jup 29 Cp/Sat 23 Sc/Uran 22 Pc    Feb. 1/Jup  6 Aq/Sat 25 Sc/Uran 23 Pc
Nep 24 Lo/Plut 14 Ce/N Node 26 Ce        Nep 24 Lo/Plut 13 Ce/N Node 25 Ce


        Sun    Merc   Venus  Mars                    Sun    Merc   Venus  Mars
Mar. 1  10 Pc  21 Pc  10 Aq  14 Cp      Apr. 1  11 Ar   9 Ar  26 Aq   6 Aq
     6  15 Pc   0 Ar  11 Aq  18 Cp           6  15 Ar   5 Ar   0 Pc  10 Aq
    11  20 Pc   7 Ar  13 Aq  21 Cp          11  20 Ar   3 Ar   4 Pc  14 Aq
    16  25 Pc  13 Ar  15 Aq  25 Cp          16  25 Ar   3 Ar   9 Pc  17 Aq
    21   0 Ar  15 Ar  18 Aq  28 Cp          21   0 Tr   5 Ar  14 Pc  21 Aq
    26   5 Ar  14 Ar  21 Aq   2 Aq          26   5 Tr   8 Ar  19 Pc  24 Aq
    31  10 Ar  10 Ar  25 Aq   6 Aq
Mar. 1/Jup 13 Aq/Sat 26 Sc/Uran 25 Pc    Apr. 1/Jup 19 Aq/Sat 26 Sc/Uran 26 Pc
Nep 23 Lo/Plut 13 Ce/N Node 23 Ce        Nep 22 Lo/Plut 13 Ce/N Node 22 Ce


        Sun    Merc   Venus  Mars                    Sun    Merc   Venus  Mars
May  1  10 Tr  13 Ar  24 Pc  28 Aq      June 1  10 Gm   5 Gm  28 Ar  20 Pc
     6  15 Tr  19 Ar  29 Pc   2 Pc           6  15 Gm  16 Gm   4 Tr  24 Pc
    11  20 Tr  26 Ar   5 Ar   5 Pc          11  19 Gm  27 Gm   9 Tr  27 Pc
    16  24 Tr   4 Tr  10 Ar   9 Pc          16  24 Gm   7 Ce  15 Tr   1 Ar
    21  29 Tr  13 Tr  16 Ar  12 Pc          21  29 Gm  17 Ce  21 Tr   4 Ar
    26   4 Gm  23 Tr  21 Ar  16 Pc          26   4 Ce  25 Ce  27 Tr   7 Ar
    31   9 Gm   3 Gm  27 Ar  20 Pc
May  1/Jup 24 Aq/Sat 24 Sc/Uran 28 Pc    June 1/Jup 27 Aq/Sat 21 Sc/Uran 29 Pc
Nep 22 Lo/Plut 13 Ce/N Node 20 Ce        Nep 22 Lo/Plut 13 Ce/N Node 18 Ce


        Sun    Merc   Venus  Mars                    Sun    Merc   Venus  Mars
July 1   8 Ce   3 Lo   2 Gm  11 Ar      Aug. 1   8 Lo  19 Lo   9 Ce   0 Tr
     6  13 Ce   9 Lo   8 Gm  14 Ar           6  13 Lo  16 Lo  15 Ce   3 Tr
    11  18 Ce  14 Lo  14 Gm  17 Ar          11  18 Lo  12 Lo  21 Ce   5 Tr
    16  23 Ce  18 Lo  20 Gm  20 Ar          16  22 Lo  10 Lo  27 Ce   8 Tr
    21  27 Ce  21 Lo  26 Gm  23 Ar          21  27 Lo  10 Lo   3 Lo  10 Tr
    26   2 Lo  21 Lo   2 Ce  26 Ar          26   2 Vr  14 Lo  10 Lo  12 Tr
    31   7 Lo  20 Lo   8 Ce  29 Ar          31   7 Vr  20 Lo  16 Lo  14 Tr
July 1/Jup 27 Aq/Sat 20 Sc/Uran 29 Pc    Aug. 1/Jup 24 Aq/Sat 19 Sc/Uran 29 Pc
Nep 23 Lo/Plut 14 Ce/N Node 17 Ce        Nep 24 Lo/Plut 15 Ce/N Node 15 Ce
```

1926

	Sun	Merc	Venus	Mars
Sept 1	8 Vr	22 Lo	17 Lo	14 Tr
6	13 Vr	0 Vr	23 Lo	16 Tr
11	18 Vr	10 Vr	29 Lo	17 Tr
16	22 Vr	19 Vr	5 Vr	18 Tr
21	27 Vr	28 Vr	12 Vr	19 Tr
26	2 Lb	7 Lb	18 Vr	19 Tr

Sept 1/Jup 20 Aq/Sat 21 Sc/Uran 28 Pc
Nep 25 Lo/Plut 16 Ce/N Node 13 Ce

	Sun	Merc	Venus	Mars
Oct. 1	7 Lb	16 Lb	24 Vr	19 Tr
6	12 Lb	24 Lb	0 Lb	19 Tr
11	17 Lb	2 Sc	6 Lb	18 Tr
16	22 Lb	9 Sc	13 Lb	17 Tr
21	27 Lb	16 Sc	19 Lb	16 Tr
26	2 Sc	23 Sc	25 Lb	14 Tr
31	7 Sc	29 Sc	1 Sc	13 Tr

Oct. 1/Jup 18 Aq/Sat 23 Sc/Uran 27 Pc
Nep 26 Lo/Plut 16 Ce/N Node 12 Ce

	Sun	Merc	Venus	Mars
Nov. 1	8 Sc	1 Sg	3 Sc	12 Tr
6	13 Sc	6 Sg	9 Sc	11 Tr
11	18 Sc	10 Sg	15 Sc	9 Tr
16	23 Sc	11 Sg	22 Sc	8 Tr
21	28 Sc	9 Sg	28 Sc	6 Tr
26	3 Sg	3 Sg	4 Sg	5 Tr

Nov. 1/Jup 18 Aq/Sat 26 Sc/Uran 26 Pc
Nep 27 Lo/Plut 16 Ce/N Node 10 Ce

	Sun	Merc	Venus	Mars
Dec. 1	8 Sg	27 Sc	10 Sg	5 Tr
6	13 Sg	25 Sc	17 Sg	5 Tr
11	18 Sg	27 Sc	23 Sg	5 Tr
16	23 Sg	2 Sg	29 Sg	5 Tr
21	28 Sg	8 Sg	6 Cp	6 Tr
26	3 Cp	15 Sg	12 Cp	7 Tr
31	9 Cp	22 Sg	18 Cp	8 Tr

Dec. 1/Jup 21 Aq/Sat 30 Sc/Uran 26 Pc
Nep 27 Lo/Plut 16 Ce/N Node 9 Ce

Moon's Positions

	1	4	7	10	13	16	19	22	25	28	31
Jan.	1 Lo	6 Vr	12 Lb	21 Sc	4 Cp	19 Aq	4 Ar	14 Tr	22 Gm	28 Ce	3 Vr
Feb.	15 Vr	21 Lb	30 Sc	12 Cp	28 Aq	12 Ar	23 Tr	1 Ce	6 Lo	12 Vr	
Mar.	24 Vr	1 Sc	10 Sg	21 Cp	6 Pc	20 Ar	2 Gm	9 Ce	15 Lo	21 Vr	28 Lb
Apr.	10 Sc	20 Sg	1 Aq	15 Pc	28 Ar	10 Gm	17 Ce	23 Lo	29 Vr	7 Sc	
May	17 Sg	28 Cp	10 Pc	23 Ar	5 Gm	13 Ce	19 Lo	25 Vr	2 Sc	12 Sg	24 Cp
June	9 Aq	21 Pc	3 Tr	13 Gm	21 Ce	27 Lo	3 Lb	10 Sc	21 Sg	4 Aq	
July	18 Pc	0 Tr	10 Gm	17 Ce	24 Lo	29 Vr	6 Sc	15 Sg	28 Cp	13 Pc	27 Ar
Aug.	10 Tr	20 Gm	26 Ce	2 Vr	8 Lb	14 Sc	23 Sg	7 Aq	22 Pc	6 Tr	16 Gm
Sept	29 Gm	5 Lo	11 Vr	17 Lb	24 Sc	2 Cp	15 Aq	0 Ar	15 Tr	25 Gm	
Oct.	2 Lo	8 Vr	14 Lb	21 Sc	29 Sg	10 Aq	24 Pc	9 Tr	21 Gm	29 Ce	5 Vr
Nov.	16 Vr	23 Lb	0 Sg	9 Cp	20 Aq	3 Ar	17 Tr	28 Gm	7 Lo	13 Vr	
Dec.	18 Lb	26 Sc	6 Cp	17 Aq	30 Pc	12 Tr	23 Gm	2 Lo	8 Vr	14 Lb	21 Sc

                                                                 Ephemeris

1927

```
        Sun    Merc   Venus  Mars
Jan. 1  10 Cp  24 Sg  19 Cp   8 Tr
      6  15 Cp   1 Cp  26 Cp  10 Tr
     11  20 Cp   9 Cp   2 Aq  11 Tr
     16  25 Cp  17 Cp   8 Aq  13 Tr
     21   0 Aq  25 Cp  14 Aq  15 Tr
     26   5 Aq   3 Aq  21 Aq  17 Tr
     31  10 Aq  12 Aq  27 Aq  19 Tr
```
Jan. 1/Jup 26 Aq/Sat 3 Sg/Uran 26 Pc
Nep 27 Lo/Plut 15 Ce/N Node 7 Ce

```
        Sun    Merc   Venus  Mars
Feb. 1  11 Aq  14 Aq  28 Aq  20 Tr
      6  16 Aq  22 Aq   4 Pc  22 Tr
     11  21 Aq   1 Pc  11 Pc  24 Tr
     16  26 Aq  10 Pc  17 Pc  27 Tr
     21   1 Pc  18 Pc  23 Pc  29 Tr
     26   6 Pc  24 Pc  29 Pc   2 Gm
```
Feb. 1/Jup 3 Pc/Sat 6 Sg/Uran 27 Pc
Nep 26 Lo/Plut 14 Ce/N Node 5 Ce

```
        Sun    Merc   Venus  Mars
Mar. 1   9 Pc  27 Pc   3 Ar   4 Gm
      6  14 Pc  27 Pc   9 Ar   6 Gm
     11  19 Pc  24 Pc  15 Ar   9 Gm
     16  24 Pc  20 Pc  22 Ar  12 Gm
     21  29 Pc  16 Pc  28 Ar  15 Gm
     26   4 Ar  14 Pc   4 Tr  17 Gm
     31   9 Ar  15 Pc  10 Tr  20 Gm
```
Mar. 1/Jup 10 Pc/Sat 7 Sg/Uran 28 Pc
Nep 25 Lo/Plut 14 Ce/N Node 4 Ce

```
        Sun    Merc   Venus  Mars
Apr. 1  10 Ar  15 Pc  11 Tr  21 Gm
      6  15 Ar  18 Pc  17 Tr  24 Gm
     11  20 Ar  22 Pc  23 Tr  26 Gm
     16  25 Ar  28 Pc  29 Tr  29 Gm
     21   0 Tr   5 Ar   5 Gm   2 Ce
     26   5 Tr  12 Ar  11 Gm   5 Ce
```
Apr. 1/Jup 17 Pc/Sat 8 Sg/Uran
Nep 25 Lo/Plut 14 Ce/N Node 2 Ce

```
        Sun    Merc   Venus  Mars
May  1  10 Tr  20 Ar  17 Gm   8 Ce
      6  14 Tr  29 Ar  23 Gm  11 Ce
     11  19 Tr   9 Tr  28 Gm  14 Ce
     16  24 Tr  19 Tr   4 Ce  17 Ce
     21  29 Tr   0 Gm  10 Ce  20 Ce
     26   4 Gm  11 Gm  16 Ce  23 Ce
     31   9 Gm  21 Gm  21 Ce  26 Ce
```
May 1/Jup 24 Pc/Sat 6 Sg/Uran 2 Ar
Nep 24 Lo/Plut 14 Ce/N Node 1 Ce

```
        Sun    Merc   Venus  Mars
June 1  10 Gm  23 Gm  22 Ce  27 Ce
      6  14 Gm   3 Ce  28 Ce   0 Lo
     11  19 Gm  11 Ce   3 Lo   3 Lo
     16  24 Gm  18 Ce   8 Lo   6 Lo
     21  29 Gm  24 Ce  14 Lo   9 Lo
     26   3 Ce  28 Ce  19 Lo  12 Lo
```
June 1/Jup 29 Pc/Sat 4 Sg/Uran 3 Ar
Nep 24 Lo/Plut 15 Ce/N Node 29 Gm

```
        Sun    Merc   Venus  Mars
July 1   8 Ce   1 Lo  24 Lo  15 Lo
      6  13 Ce   2 Lo  28 Lo  18 Lo
     11  18 Ce   1 Lo   3 Vr  21 Lo
     16  22 Ce  29 Ce   7 Vr  24 Lo
     21  27 Ce  26 Ce  11 Vr  27 Lo
     26   2 Lo  23 Ce  15 Vr   0 Vr
     31   7 Lo  22 Ce  18 Vr   4 Vr
```
July 1/Jup 3 Ar/Sat 2 Sg/Uran 3 Ar
Nep 25 Lo/Plut 15 Ce/N Node 27 Gm

```
        Sun    Merc   Venus  Mars
Aug. 1   8 Lo  22 Ce  19 Vr   4 Vr
      6  13 Lo  24 Ce  21 Vr   7 Vr
     11  17 Lo  29 Ce  23 Vr  10 Vr
     16  22 Lo   6 Lo  25 Vr  14 Vr
     21  27 Lo  14 Lo  25 Vr  17 Vr
     26   2 Vr  24 Lo  24 Vr  20 Vr
     31   7 Vr   4 Vr  23 Vr  23 Vr
```
Aug. 1/Jup 3 Ar/Sat 1 Sg/Uran 3 Ar
Nep 26 Lo/Plut 16 Ce/N Node 26 Gm

1927

	Sun	Merc	Venus	Mars
Sept 1	8 Vr	6 Vr	22 Vr	24 Vr
6	12 Vr	16 Vr	20 Vr	27 Vr
11	17 Vr	25 Vr	17 Vr	0 Lb
16	22 Vr	3 Lb	14 Vr	4 Lb
21	27 Vr	11 Lb	11 Vr	7 Lb
26	2 Lb	19 Lb	10 Vr	10 Lb

Sept 1/Jup 1 Ar/Sat 2 Sg/Uran 2 Ar
Nep 27 Lo/Plut 17 Ce/N Node 24 Gm

	Sun	Merc	Venus	Mars
Oct. 1	7 Lb	27 Lb	9 Vr	13 Lb
6	12 Lb	4 Sc	9 Vr	17 Lb
11	17 Lb	10 Sc	10 Vr	20 Lb
16	22 Lb	16 Sc	12 Vr	23 Lb
21	27 Lb	21 Sc	15 Vr	27 Lb
26	2 Sc	24 Sc	18 Vr	0 Sc
31	7 Sc	26 Sc	22 Vr	3 Sc

Oct. 1/Jup 27 Pc/Sat 3 Sg/Uran 1 Ar
Nep 28 Lo/Plut 17 Ce/N Node 23 Gm

	Sun	Merc	Venus	Mars
Nov. 1	8 Sc	25 Sc	23 Vr	4 Sc
6	13 Sc	22 Sc	27 Vr	7 Sc
11	18 Sc	16 Sc	1 Lb	11 Sc
16	23 Sc	11 Sc	6 Lb	14 Sc
21	28 Sc	10 Sc	11 Lb	18 Sc
26	3 Sg	13 Sc	16 Lb	21 Sc

Nov. 1/Jup 24 Pc/Sat 6 Sg/Uran
Nep 29 Lo/Plut 17 Ce/N Node 21 Gm

	Sun	Merc	Venus	Mars
Dec. 1	8 Sg	18 Sc	21 Lb	25 Sc
6	13 Sg	25 Sc	27 Lb	28 Sc
11	18 Sg	2 Sg	2 Sc	2 Sg
16	23 Sg	10 Sg	8 Sc	5 Sg
21	28 Sg	17 Sg	14 Sc	9 Sg
26	3 Cp	25 Sg	19 Sc	13 Sg
31	8 Cp	3 Cp	25 Sc	16 Sg

Dec. 1/Jup 24 Pc/Sat 10 Sg/Uran 30 Pc
Nep 29 Lo/Plut 17 Ce/N Node 19 Gm

Moon's Positions

	1	4	7	10	13	16	19	22	25	28	31
Jan.	4 Sg	15 Cp	28 Aq	11 Ar	22 Tr	2 Ce	10 Lo	16 Vr	22 Lb	29 Sc	8 Cp
Feb.	23 Cp	7 Pc	21 Ar	3 Gm	12 Ce	19 Lo	25 Vr	0 Sc	7 Sg	16 Cp	
Mar.	0 Aq	15 Pc	1 Tr	13 Gm	21 Ce	28 Lo	4 Lb	9 Sc	16 Sg	25 Cp	8 Pc
Apr.	23 Pc	9 Tr	22 Gm	1 Lo	7 Vr	12 Lb	18 Sc	25 Sg	5 Aq	17 Pc	
May	2 Tr	16 Gm	26 Ce	3 Vr	9 Lb	15 Sc	22 Sg	2 Aq	13 Pc	26 Ar	10 Gm
June	24 Gm	4 Lo	12 Vr	17 Lb	24 Sc	2 Cp	12 Aq	24 Pc	7 Tr	19 Gm	
July	30 Ce	7 Vr	13 Lb	19 Sc	27 Sg	8 Aq	20 Pc	3 Tr	15 Gm	25 Ce	3 Vr
Aug.	16 Vr	21 Lb	27 Sc	5 Cp	17 Aq	1 Ar	14 Tr	25 Gm	4 Lo	12 Vr	18 Lb
Sept	30 Lb	5 Sg	13 Cp	25 Aq	10 Ar	24 Tr	6 Ce	14 Lo	21 Vr	27 Lb	
Oct.	2 Sg	9 Cp	19 Aq	3 Ar	19 Tr	2 Ce	11 Lo	18 Vr	24 Lb	29 Sc	5 Cp
Nov.	18 Cp	28 Aq	11 Ar	27 Tr	10 Ce	20 Lo	27 Vr	2 Sc	8 Sg	15 Cp	
Dec.	24 Aq	6 Ar	20 Tr	4 Ce	15 Lo	23 Vr	29 Lb	5 Sg	12 Cp	21 Aq	2 Ar

1928

```
        Sun    Merc   Venus  Mars                      Sun    Merc   Venus  Mars
Jan. 1  11 Cp   8 Cp  29 Sc  18 Sg        Feb. 1  13 Aq  29 Aq   6 Cp  11 Cp
     6  16 Cp  16 Cp   5 Sg  22 Sg             6  18 Aq   6 Pc  12 Cp  15 Cp
    11  22 Cp  24 Cp  11 Sg  26 Sg            11  23 Aq  10 Pc  18 Cp  19 Cp
    16  27 Cp   2 Aq  17 Sg  29 Sg            16  28 Aq  10 Pc  24 Cp  22 Cp
    21   2 Aq  11 Aq  23 Sg   3 Cp            21   3 Pc   7 Pc   0 Aq  26 Cp
    26   7 Aq  20 Aq  29 Sg   7 Cp            26   8 Pc   1 Pc   7 Aq   0 Aq
    31  12 Aq  28 Aq   5 Cp  10 Cp
```
Jan. 1/Jup 27 Pc/Sat 14 Sg/Uran 30 Pc   Feb. 1/Jup 2 Ar/Sat 17 Sg/Uran 1 Ar
Nep 29 Lo/Plut 16 Ce/N Node 18 Gm   Nep 28 Lo/Plut 16 Ce/N Node 16 Gm

```
        Sun    Merc   Venus  Mars                      Sun    Merc   Venus  Mars
Mar. 1  10 Pc  29 Aq   9 Aq   1 Aq        Apr. 1  11 Ar  15 Pc  17 Pc  25 Aq
     6  15 Pc  26 Aq  15 Aq   5 Aq             6  16 Ar  22 Pc  23 Pc  29 Aq
    11  20 Pc  26 Aq  21 Aq   9 Aq            11  21 Ar   0 Ar  29 Pc   3 Pc
    16  25 Pc  29 Aq  27 Aq  13 Aq            16  26 Ar   8 Ar   5 Ar   6 Pc
    21   0 Ar   2 Pc   4 Pc  17 Aq            21   1 Tr  17 Ar  12 Ar  10 Pc
    26   5 Ar   8 Pc  10 Pc  20 Aq            26   6 Tr  27 Ar  18 Ar  14 Pc
    31  10 Ar  14 Pc  16 Pc  24 Aq
```
Mar. 1/Jup 8 Ar/Sat 18 Sg/Uran 2 Ar   Apr. 1/Jup 15 Ar/Sat 19 Sg/Uran 4 Ar
Nep 27 Lo/Plut 15 Ce/N Node 14 Gm   Nep 27 Lo/Plut 15 Ce/N Node 13 Gm

```
        Sun    Merc   Venus  Mars                      Sun    Merc   Venus  Mars
May 1   10 Tr   7 Tr  24 Ar  18 Pc        June 1  10 Gm   4 Ce   2 Gm  11 Ar
     6  15 Tr  18 Tr   0 Tr  22 Pc             6  15 Gm   8 Ce   8 Gm  15 Ar
    11  20 Tr  29 Tr   6 Tr  26 Pc            11  20 Gm  11 Ce  14 Gm  19 Ar
    16  25 Tr   9 Gm  12 Tr  29 Pc            16  25 Gm  12 Ce  20 Gm  22 Ar
    21   0 Gm  18 Gm  18 Tr   3 Ar            21  29 Gm  12 Ce  26 Gm  26 Ar
    26   4 Gm  26 Gm  25 Tr   7 Ar            26   4 Ce  10 Ce   3 Ce   0 Tr
    31   9 Gm   2 Ce   1 Gm  11 Ar
```
May 1/Jup 22 Ar/Sat 18 Sg/Uran 5 Ar   June 1/Jup 29 Ar/Sat 16 Sg/Uran 7 Ar
Nep 26 Lo/Plut 15 Ce/N Node 11 Gm   Nep 27 Lo/Plut 16 Ce/N Node 10 Gm

```
        Sun    Merc   Venus  Mars                      Sun    Merc   Venus  Mars
July 1   9 Ce   7 Ce   9 Ce   3 Tr        Aug. 1   8 Lo  23 Ce  17 Lo  25 Tr
     6  14 Ce   4 Ce  15 Ce   7 Tr             6  13 Lo   2 Lo  23 Lo  28 Tr
    11  18 Ce   3 Ce  21 Ce  10 Tr            11  18 Lo  12 Lo  29 Lo   1 Gm
    16  23 Ce   4 Ce  27 Ce  14 Tr            16  23 Lo  23 Lo   5 Vr   4 Gm
    21  28 Ce   8 Ce   3 Lo  17 Tr            21  28 Lo   3 Vr  12 Vr   7 Gm
    26   3 Lo  14 Ce   9 Lo  21 Tr            26   3 Vr  12 Vr  18 Vr  10 Gm
    31   8 Lo  21 Ce  16 Lo  24 Tr            31   7 Vr  21 Vr  24 Vr  13 Gm
```
July 1/Jup 5 Tr/Sat 14 Sg/Uran 7 Ar   Aug. 1/Jup 9 Tr/Sat 13 Sg/Uran 7 Ar
Nep 27 Lo/Plut 16 Ce/N Node 8 Gm   Nep 28 Lo/Plut 17 Ce/N Node 6 Gm

1928

```
            Sun     Merc    Venus    Mars                      Sun     Merc    Venus    Mars
Sept  1    8 Vr   22 Vr   25 Vr   14 Gm         Oct.  1    8 Lb    3 Sc    2 Sc   29 Gm
      6   13 Vr    1 Lb    1 Lb   17 Gm               6   12 Lb    7 Sc    8 Sc    1 Ce
     11   18 Vr    8 Lb    7 Lb   19 Gm              11   17 Lb    9 Sc   14 Sc    3 Ce
     16   23 Vr   15 Lb   14 Lb   22 Gm              16   22 Lb    9 Sc   21 Sc    5 Ce
     21   28 Vr   22 Lb   20 Lb   25 Gm              21   27 Lb    5 Sc   27 Sc    6 Ce
     26    3 Lb   28 Lb   26 Lb   27 Gm              26    2 Sc   29 Lb    3 Sg    7 Ce
                                                     31    7 Sc   24 Lb    9 Sg    8 Ce
```

Sept 1/Jup 10 Tr/Sat 13 Sg/Uran 6 Ar   Oct. 1/Jup 9 Tr/Sat 14 Sg/Uran 5 Ar
Nep 29 Lo/Plut 18 Ce/N Node 5 Gm   Nep 0 Vr/Plut 18 Ce/N Node 3 Gm

```
            Sun     Merc    Venus    Mars                      Sun     Merc    Venus    Mars
Nov.  1    8 Sc   24 Lb   10 Sg    8 Ce         Dec.  1    9 Sg   29 Sc   17 Cp    7 Ce
      6   13 Sc   25 Lb   16 Sg    9 Ce               6   14 Sg    7 Sg   23 Cp    5 Ce
     11   18 Sc    0 Sc   22 Sg    9 Ce              11   19 Sg   15 Sg   29 Cp    4 Ce
     16   23 Sc    6 Sc   28 Sg    9 Ce              16   24 Sg   22 Sg    5 Aq    2 Ce
     21   28 Sc   13 Sc    5 Cp    9 Ce              21   29 Sg    0 Cp   11 Aq    0 Ce
     26    4 Sg   21 Sc   11 Cp    8 Ce              26    4 Cp    8 Cp   17 Aq   28 Gm
                                                     31    9 Cp   16 Cp   22 Aq   26 Gm
```

Nov. 1/Jup 5 Tr/Sat 17 Sg/Uran 4 Ar   Dec. 1/Jup 1 Tr/Sat 20 Sg/Uran 4 Ar
Nep 1 Vr/Plut 18 Ce/N Node 1 Gm   Nep 1 Vr/Plut 18 Ce/N Node 30 Tr

Moon's Positions

```
           1        4        7       10       13       16       19       22       25       28       31
Jan.   15 Tr   28 Gm   10 Lo   19 Vr   25 Lb    0 Sg    8 Cp   17 Aq   29 Pc   11 Tr   23 Gm
Feb.    7 Ce   18 Lo   26 Vr    3 Sc    8 Sg   15 Cp   26 Aq    9 Ar   22 Tr    4 Ce
Mar.    4 Ce   14 Lo   22 Vr   29 Lb    4 Sg   11 Cp   20 Aq    3 Ar   18 Tr    1 Ce   11 Lo
Apr.   24 Lo    1 Lb    7 Sc   13 Sg   19 Cp   28 Aq   11 Ar   27 Tr   10 Ce   21 Lo
May    28 Vr    4 Sc   10 Sg   16 Cp   24 Aq    5 Ar   20 Tr    5 Ce   17 Lo   25 Vr    1 Sc
June   13 Sc   18 Sg   25 Cp    3 Pc   15 Ar   28 Tr   13 Ce   25 Lo    4 Lb   10 Sc
July   15 Sg   22 Cp    0 Pc   11 Ar   23 Tr    7 Ce   20 Lo   29 Vr    6 Sc   12 Sg   18 Cp
Aug.    1 Aq   10 Pc   22 Ar    4 Gm   17 Ce   28 Lo    7 Lb   14 Sc   20 Sg   26 Cp    6 Pc
Sept   20 Pc    2 Tr   15 Gm   27 Ce    7 Vr   16 Lb   22 Sc   27 Sg    4 Aq   14 Pc
Oct.   28 Ar   11 Gm   24 Ce    4 Vr   12 Lb   18 Sc   24 Sg   30 Cp    8 Pc   21 Ar    6 Gm
Nov.   21 Gm    4 Lo   14 Vr   21 Lb   27 Sc    2 Cp    8 Aq   17 Pc   29 Ar   14 Gm
Dec.   29 Ce   10 Vr   18 Lb   24 Sc   29 Sg    5 Aq   13 Pc   23 Ar    7 Gm   22 Ce    6 Vr
```

1929

```
        Sun     Merc    Venus   Mars                    Sun     Merc    Venus   Mars
Jan. 1  10 Cp   18 Cp   24 Aq   26 Gm        Feb. 1   12 Aq   24 Aq   28 Pc   21 Gm
     6  15 Cp   26 Cp   29 Aq   24 Gm             6   17 Aq   19 Aq    4 Ar   22 Gm
    11  20 Cp    4 Aq    5 Pc   23 Gm            11   22 Aq   13 Aq    9 Ar   22 Gm
    16  25 Cp   12 Aq   11 Pc   22 Gm            16   27 Aq   10 Aq   13 Ar   23 Gm
    21   0 Aq   19 Aq   16 Pc   21 Gm            21    2 Pc    9 Aq   18 Ar   24 Gm
    26   6 Aq   23 Aq   22 Pc   21 Gm            26    7 Pc   11 Aq   22 Ar   26 Gm
    31  11 Aq   24 Aq   27 Pc   21 Gm
```

Jan. 1/Jup 0 Tr/Sat 24 Sg/Uran 4 Ar   Feb. 1/Jup 3 Tr/Sat 27 Sg/Uran 5 Ar
Nep 1 Vr/Plut 17 Ce/N Node 28 Tr   Nep 1 Vr/Plut 17 Ce/N Node 27 Tr

```
        Sun     Merc    Venus   Mars                    Sun     Merc    Venus   Mars
Mar. 1  10 Pc   13 Aq   25 Ar   27 Gm        Apr. 1   11 Ar   25 Pc    8 Tr    9 Ce
     6  15 Pc   18 Aq   28 Ar   28 Gm             6   16 Ar    4 Ar    7 Tr   11 Ce
    11  20 Pc   23 Aq    2 Tr    0 Ce            11   21 Ar   14 Ar    5 Tr   13 Ce
    16  25 Pc    0 Pc    4 Tr    2 Ce            16   26 Ar   24 Ar    3 Tr   16 Ce
    21   0 Ar    7 Pc    6 Tr    4 Ce            21    0 Tr    4 Tr   29 Ar   18 Ce
    26   5 Ar   15 Pc    8 Tr    6 Ce            26    5 Tr   15 Tr   26 Ar   21 Ce
    31  10 Ar   23 Pc    8 Tr    8 Ce
```

Mar. 1/Jup 7 Tr/Sat 29 Sg/Uran 6 Ar   Apr. 1/Jup 13 Tr/Sat 0 Cp/Uran 8 Ar
Nep 30 Lo/Plut 16 Ce/N Node 25 Tr   Nep 29 Lo/Plut 16 Ce/N Node 24 Tr

```
        Sun     Merc    Venus   Mars                    Sun     Merc    Venus   Mars
May  1  10 Tr   25 Tr   24 Ar   24 Ce        June 1   10 Gm   22 Gm   28 Ar   11 Lo
     6  15 Tr    4 Gm   22 Ar   26 Ce             6   15 Gm   20 Gm    2 Tr   13 Lo
    11  20 Tr   11 Gm   22 Ar   29 Ce            11   20 Gm   17 Gm    5 Tr   16 Lo
    16  25 Tr   16 Gm   22 Ar    2 Lo            16   24 Gm   15 Gm    9 Tr   19 Lo
    21  29 Tr   20 Gm   23 Ar    4 Lo            21   29 Gm   14 Gm   14 Tr   22 Lo
    26   4 Gm   22 Gm   25 Ar    7 Lo            26    4 Ce   15 Gm   18 Tr   25 Lo
    31   9 Gm   22 Gm   28 Ar   10 Lo
```

May 1/Jup 20 Tr/Sat 0 Cp/Uran 9 Ar   June 1/Jup 27 Tr/Sat 29 Sg/Uran 11 Ar
Nep 29 Lo/Plut 16 Ce/N Node 22 Tr   Nep 29 Lo/Plut 17 Ce/N Node 20 Tr

```
        Sun     Merc    Venus   Mars                    Sun     Merc    Venus   Mars
July 1   9 Ce   18 Gm   23 Tr   28 Lo        Aug. 1    8 Lo    9 Lo   25 Gm   17 Vr
     6  13 Ce   22 Gm   28 Tr    1 Vr             6   13 Lo   19 Lo    1 Ce   20 Vr
    11  18 Ce   29 Gm    3 Gm    4 Vr            11   18 Lo   29 Lo    6 Ce   23 Vr
    16  23 Ce    7 Ce    8 Gm    7 Vr            16   23 Lo    8 Vr   12 Ce   26 Vr
    21  28 Ce   16 Ce   13 Gm   10 Vr            21   27 Lo   16 Vr   18 Ce   29 Vr
    26   3 Lo   27 Ce   19 Gm   13 Vr            26    2 Vr   24 Vr   24 Ce    3 Lb
    31   7 Lo    7 Lo   24 Gm   16 Vr            31    7 Vr    1 Lb   29 Ce    6 Lb
```

July 1/Jup 4 Gm/Sat 26 Sg/Uran 11 Ar   Aug. 1/Jup 10 Gm/Sat 25 Sg/Uran 11 Ar
Nep 29 Lo/Plut 18 Ce/N Node 19 Tr   Nep 0 Vr/Plut 18 Ce/N Node 17 Tr

1929

	Sun	Merc	Venus	Mars
Sept 1	8 Vr	2 Lb	1 Lo	6 Lb
6	13 Vr	9 Lb	7 Lo	10 Lb
11	18 Vr	14 Lb	12 Lo	13 Lb
16	23 Vr	19 Lb	18 Lo	16 Lb
21	28 Vr	22 Lb	24 Lo	20 Lb
26	2 Lb	23 Lb	0 Vr	23 Lb

Sept 1/Jup 15 Gm/Sat 24 Sg/Uran 11 Ar
Nep 1 Vr/Plut 19 Ce/N Node 15 Tr

	Sun	Merc	Venus	Mars
Oct. 1	7 Lb	22 Lb	6 Vr	26 Lb
6	12 Lb	17 Lb	13 Vr	0 Sc
11	17 Lb	11 Lb	19 Vr	3 Sc
16	22 Lb	8 Lb	25 Vr	6 Sc
21	27 Lb	9 Lb	1 Lb	10 Sc
26	2 Sc	14 Lb	7 Lb	13 Sc
31	7 Sc	21 Lb	13 Lb	17 Sc

Oct. 1/Jup 16 Gm/Sat 25 Sg/Uran 9 Ar
Nep 2 Vr/Plut 20 Ce/N Node 14 Tr

	Sun	Merc	Venus	Mars
Nov. 1	8 Sc	22 Lb	15 Lb	18 Sc
6	13 Sc	0 Sc	21 Lb	21 Sc
11	18 Sc	8 Sc	27 Lb	25 Sc
16	23 Sc	16 Sc	3 Sc	28 Sc
21	28 Sc	24 Sc	10 Sc	2 Sg
26	3 Sg	2 Sg	16 Sc	5 Sg

Nov. 1/Jup 15 Gm/Sat 27 Sg/Uran 8 Ar
Nep 3 Vr/Plut 20 Ce/N Node 12 Tr

	Sun	Merc	Venus	Mars
Dec. 1	8 Sg	10 Sg	22 Sc	9 Sg
6	13 Sg	18 Sg	28 Sc	13 Sg
11	18 Sg	26 Sg	5 Sg	16 Sg
16	24 Sg	4 Cp	11 Sg	20 Sg
21	29 Sg	12 Cp	17 Sg	24 Sg
26	4 Cp	19 Cp	24 Sg	27 Sg
31	9 Cp	27 Cp	0 Cp	1 Cp

Dec. 1/Jup 12 Gm/Sat 0 Cp/Uran 8 Ar
Nep 4 Vr/Plut 19 Ce/N Node 11 Tr

Moon's Positions

	1	4	7	10	13	16	19	22	25	28	31
Jan.	19 Vr	27 Lb	3 Sg	8 Cp	15 Aq	23 Pc	3 Tr	16 Gm	0 Lo	14 Vr	23 Lb
Feb.	5 Sc	11 Sg	16 Cp	24 Aq	3 Ar	14 Tr	26 Gm	9 Lo	21 Vr	1 Sc	
Mar.	13 Sc	19 Sg	25 Cp	2 Pc	13 Ar	25 Tr	7 Ce	19 Lo	30 Vr	8 Sc	15 Sg
Apr.	27 Sg	2 Aq	10 Pc	22 Ar	5 Gm	18 Ce	29 Lo	9 Lb	17 Sc	23 Sg	
May	28 Cp	5 Pc	16 Ar	29 Tr	14 Ce	26 Lo	6 Lb	13 Sc	19 Sg	25 Cp	1 Pc
June	14 Pc	24 Ar	8 Gm	23 Ce	6 Vr	16 Lb	23 Sc	28 Sg	4 Aq	10 Pc	
July	19 Ar	1 Gm	16 Ce	1 Vr	12 Lb	20 Sc	25 Sg	1 Aq	7 Pc	15 Ar	26 Tr
Aug.	10 Gm	25 Ce	9 Vr	21 Lb	28 Sc	4 Cp	10 Aq	17 Pc	26 Ar	6 Gm	19 Ce
Sept	4 Lo	18 Vr	29 Lb	6 Sg	12 Cp	18 Aq	26 Pc	6 Tr	17 Gm	30 Ce	
Oct.	12 Vr	24 Lb	2 Sg	8 Cp	14 Aq	21 Pc	1 Tr	14 Gm	26 Ce	9 Vr	19 Lb
Nov.	2 Sc	10 Sg	16 Cp	22 Aq	29 Pc	10 Tr	23 Gm	7 Lo	19 Vr	29 Lb	
Dec.	6 Sg	12 Cp	18 Aq	24 Pc	4 Tr	17 Gm	2 Lo	16 Vr	26 Lb	3 Sg	9 Cp

                                    Ephemeris

1930

	Sun	Merc	Venus	Mars
Jan. 1	10 Cp	28 Cp	1 Cp	2 Cp
6	15 Cp	4 Aq	7 Cp	6 Cp
11	20 Cp	8 Aq	14 Cp	9 Cp
16	25 Cp	7 Aq	20 Cp	13 Cp
21	0 Aq	3 Aq	26 Cp	17 Cp
26	5 Aq	26 Cp	3 Aq	21 Cp
31	10 Aq	23 Cp	9 Aq	25 Cp

Jan. 1/Jup 8 Gm/Sat 4 Cp/Uran 8 Ar
Nep 3 Vr/Plut 19 Ce/N Node 9 Tr

	Sun	Merc	Venus	Mars
Feb. 1	11 Aq	22 Cp	10 Aq	26 Cp
6	16 Aq	23 Cp	16 Aq	29 Cp
11	22 Aq	26 Cp	23 Aq	3 Aq
16	27 Aq	0 Aq	29 Aq	7 Aq
21	2 Pc	6 Aq	5 Pc	11 Aq
26	7 Pc	12 Aq	11 Pc	15 Aq

Feb. 1/Jup 6 Gm/Sat 7 Cp/Uran 8 Ar
Nep 3 Vr/Plut 18 Ce/N Node 7 Tr

	Sun	Merc	Venus	Mars
Mar. 1	10 Pc	17 Aq	15 Pc	17 Aq
6	15 Pc	24 Aq	21 Pc	21 Aq
11	20 Pc	2 Pc	28 Pc	25 Aq
16	25 Pc	10 Pc	4 Ar	29 Aq
21	0 Ar	19 Pc	10 Ar	3 Pc
26	5 Ar	28 Pc	16 Ar	7 Pc
31	10 Ar	8 Ar	22 Ar	11 Pc

Mar. 1/Jup 8 Gm/Sat 10 Cp/Uran 10 Ar
Nep 2 Vr/Plut 18 Ce/N Node 6 Tr

	Sun	Merc	Venus	Mars
Apr. 1	11 Ar	10 Ar	24 Ar	12 Pc
6	15 Ar	20 Ar	0 Tr	15 Pc
11	20 Ar	1 Tr	6 Tr	19 Pc
16	25 Ar	10 Tr	12 Tr	23 Pc
21	0 Tr	19 Tr	18 Tr	27 Pc
26	5 Tr	25 Tr	24 Tr	1 Ar

Apr. 1/Jup 12 Gm/Sat 12 Cp/Uran 11 Ar
Nep 1 Vr/Plut 17 Ce/N Node 4 Tr

	Sun	Merc	Venus	Mars
May 1	10 Tr	0 Gm	1 Gm	5 Ar
6	15 Tr	2 Gm	7 Gm	9 Ar
11	20 Tr	2 Gm	13 Gm	13 Ar
16	24 Tr	1 Gm	19 Gm	16 Ar
21	29 Tr	28 Tr	25 Gm	20 Ar
26	4 Gm	25 Tr	1 Ce	24 Ar
31	9 Gm	24 Tr	7 Ce	28 Ar

May 1/Jup 17 Gm/Sat 12 Cp/Uran 13 Ar
Nep 1 Vr/Plut 18 Ce/N Node 3 Tr

	Sun	Merc	Venus	Mars
June 1	10 Gm	24 Tr	8 Ce	28 Ar
6	15 Gm	24 Tr	14 Ce	2 Tr
11	19 Gm	27 Tr	20 Ce	6 Tr
16	24 Gm	1 Gm	26 Ce	10 Tr
21	29 Gm	7 Gm	2 Lo	13 Tr
26	4 Ce	14 Gm	8 Lo	17 Tr

June 1/Jup 24 Gm/Sat 11 Cp/Uran 14 Ar
Nep 1 Vr/Plut 18 Ce/N Node 1 Tr

	Sun	Merc	Venus	Mars
July 1	8 Ce	22 Gm	14 Lo	20 Tr
6	13 Ce	2 Ce	20 Lo	24 Tr
11	18 Ce	13 Ce	26 Lo	28 Tr
16	23 Ce	23 Ce	2 Vr	1 Gm
21	28 Ce	4 Lo	7 Vr	5 Gm
26	2 Lo	14 Lo	13 Vr	8 Gm
31	7 Lo	23 Lo	19 Vr	11 Gm

July 1/Jup 1 Ce/Sat 9 Cp/Uran 15 Ar
Nep 1 Vr/Plut 19 Ce/N Node 29 Ar

	Sun	Merc	Venus	Mars
Aug. 1	8 Lo	25 Lo	20 Vr	12 Gm
6	13 Lo	3 Vr	25 Vr	15 Gm
11	18 Lo	11 Vr	1 Lb	19 Gm
16	22 Lo	18 Vr	7 Lb	22 Gm
21	27 Lo	24 Vr	12 Lb	25 Gm
26	2 Vr	29 Vr	17 Lb	28 Gm
31	7 Vr	3 Lb	23 Lb	2 Ce

Aug. 1/Jup 8 Ce/Sat 6 Cp/Uran 15 Ar
Nep 2 Vr/Plut 20 Ce/N Node 28 Ar

1930

```
          Sun      Merc     Venus    Mars                    Sun      Merc     Venus    Mars
Sept 1    8 Vr     4 Lb    24 Lb     2 Ce       Oct. 1      7 Lb    22 Vr    22 Sc    20 Ce
     6   13 Vr     6 Lb    29 Lb     5 Ce            6     12 Lb    24 Vr    26 Sc    23 Ce
    11   18 Vr     7 Lb     4 Sc     8 Ce           11     17 Lb     0 Lb    29 Sc    25 Ce
    16   22 Vr     4 Lb     9 Sc    11 Ce           16     22 Lb     7 Lb     2 Sg    28 Ce
    21   27 Vr    29 Vr    13 Sc    14 Ce           21     27 Lb    15 Lb     5 Sg     0 Lo
    26    2 Lb    24 Vr    18 Sc    17 Ce           26      2 Sc    24 Lb     6 Sg     3 Lo
                                                    31      7 Sc     2 Sc     7 Sg     5 Lo
```

```
Sept 1/Jup 14 Ce/Sat  5 Cp/Uran 15 Ar        Oct. 1/Jup 18 Ce/Sat  6 Cp/Uran 14 Ar
Nep  4 Vr/Plut 20 Ce/N Node 26 Ar            Nep  5 Vr/Plut 21 Ce/N Node 24 Ar
```

```
          Sun      Merc     Venus    Mars                    Sun      Merc     Venus    Mars
Nov. 1    8 Sc     4 Sc     7 Sg     5 Lo       Dec. 1      8 Sg    21 Sg    25 Sc    15 Lo
     6   13 Sc    12 Sc     7 Sg     7 Lo            6     13 Sg    29 Sg    23 Sc    16 Lo
    11   18 Sc    20 Sc     6 Sg     9 Lo           11     18 Sg     6 Cp    22 Sc    16 Lo
    16   23 Sc    28 Sc     4 Sg    11 Lo           16     23 Sg    13 Cp    22 Sc    17 Lo
    21   28 Sc     6 Sg     1 Sg    12 Lo           21     28 Sg    19 Cp    23 Sc    17 Lo
    26    3 Sg    14 Sg    28 Sc    14 Lo           26      4 Cp    22 Cp    25 Sc    16 Lo
                                                    31      9 Cp    21 Cp    28 Sc    16 Lo
```

```
Nov. 1/Jup 20 Ce/Sat  7 Cp/Uran 12 Ar        Dec. 1/Jup 20 Ce/Sat 10 Cp/Uran 12 Ar
Nep  5 Vr/Plut 21 Ce/N Node 23 Ar            Nep  6 Vr/Plut 21 Ce/N Node 21 Ar
```

Moon's Positions

```
            1        4        7       10       13       16       19       22       25       28       31
Jan.   21 Cp    26 Aq     3 Ar    12 Tr    25 Gm    10 Lo    25 Vr     5 Sc    12 Sg    18 Cp    24 Aq
Feb.    6 Pc    12 Ar    21 Tr     3 Ce    18 Lo     3 Lb    14 Sc    21 Sg    27 Cp     2 Pc
Mar.   15 Pc    22 Ar     1 Gm    13 Ce    27 Lo    11 Lb    22 Sc    29 Sg     5 Aq    11 Pc    18 Ar
Apr.    1 Tr    11 Gm    23 Ce     7 Vr    19 Lb    30 Sc     7 Cp    13 Aq    19 Pc    27 Ar
May     8 Cm    20 Ce     3 Vr    15 Lb    25 Sc     3 Cp     9 Aq    15 Pc    22 Ar     3 Cm    16 Ce
June    1 Lo    14 Vr    25 Lb     4 Sg    11 Cp    17 Aq    23 Pc     0 Tr    11 Gm    26 Ce
July   10 Vr    22 Lb     1 Sg     8 Cp    14 Aq    19 Pc    26 Ar     5 Gm    19 Ce     5 Vr    18 Lb
Aug.    2 Sc    10 Sg    17 Cp    23 Aq    28 Pc     5 Tr    14 Gm    28 Ce    13 Vr    27 Lb     7 Sg
Sept   19 Sg    26 Cp     1 Pc     7 Ar    14 Tr    24 Gm     7 Lo    21 Vr     5 Sc    15 Sg
Oct.   22 Cp    28 Aq     4 Ar    11 Tr    21 Gm     2 Lo    16 Vr    29 Lb    10 Sg    18 Cp    24 Aq
Nov.    6 Pc    12 Ar    21 Tr     1 Ce    13 Lo    26 Vr     8 Sc    18 Sg    26 Cp     2 Pc
Dec.    8 Ar    16 Tr    27 Gm    10 Lo    22 Vr     4 Sc    14 Sg    22 Cp    28 Aq     4 Ar    11 Tr
```

                                                    Ephemeris

1931

```
        Sun    Merc   Venus  Mars                    Sun    Merc   Venus  Mars
Jan. 1  10 Cp  21 Cp  28 Sc  16 Lo         Feb. 1   11 Aq  16 Cp  24 Sg   5 Lo
     6  15 Cp  15 Cp   1 Sg  15 Lo              6   16 Aq  23 Cp  29 Sg   3 Lo
    11  20 Cp   9 Cp   5 Sg  13 Lo             11   21 Aq  29 Cp   5 Cp   2 Lo
    16  25 Cp   6 Cp   9 Sg  11 Lo             16   26 Aq   6 Aq  10 Cp   0 Lo
    21   0 Aq   7 Cp  14 Sg  10 Lo             21    1 Pc  14 Aq  16 Cp  29 Ce
    26   5 Aq  10 Cp  18 Sg   8 Lo             26    6 Pc  22 Aq  21 Cp  28 Ce
    31  10 Aq  15 Cp  23 Sg   6 Lo
Jan. 1/Jup 16 Ce/Sat 14 Cp/Uran 11 Ar     Feb. 1/Jup 12 Ce/Sat 17 Cp/Uran 12 Ar
Nep  6 Vr/Plut 20 Ce/N Node 20 Ar         Nep  5 Vr/Plut 19 Ce/N Node 18 Ar


        Sun    Merc   Venus  Mars                    Sun    Merc   Venus  Mars
Mar. 1   9 Pc  27 Aq  24 Cp  28 Ce         Apr. 1   10 Ar  26 Ar   0 Pc   0 Lo
     6  14 Pc   6 Pc   0 Aq  27 Ce              6   15 Ar   4 Tr   6 Pc   2 Lo
    11  19 Pc  15 Pc   6 Aq  27 Ce             11   20 Ar   9 Tr  12 Pc   3 Lo
    16  24 Pc  24 Pc  12 Aq  28 Ce             16   25 Ar  13 Tr  18 Pc   5 Lo
    21  29 Pc   4 Ar  17 Aq  28 Ce             21    0 Tr  13 Tr  24 Pc   7 Lo
    26   4 Ar  14 Ar  23 Aq  29 Ce             26    5 Tr  12 Tr   0 Ar   8 Lo
    31   9 Ar  24 Ar  29 Aq   0 Lo
Mar. 1/Jup 11 Ce/Sat 20 Cp/Uran 13 Ar     Apr. 1/Jup 11 Ce/Sat 22 Cp/Uran 15 Ar
Nep  4 Vr/Plut 19 Ce/N Node 16 Ar         Nep  3 Vr/Plut 19 Ce/N Node 15 Ar


        Sun    Merc   Venus  Mars                    Sun    Merc   Venus  Mars
May  1  10 Tr   9 Tr   6 Ar  11 Lo         June 1   10 Gm  15 Tr  13 Tr  25 Lo
     6  15 Tr   6 Tr  12 Ar  13 Lo              6   14 Gm  22 Tr  19 Tr  28 Lo
    11  19 Tr   4 Tr  18 Ar  15 Lo             11   19 Gm  29 Tr  25 Tr   0 Vr
    16  24 Tr   4 Tr  24 Ar  17 Lo             16   24 Gm   8 Gm   1 Gm   3 Vr
    21  29 Tr   6 Tr   0 Tr  20 Lo             21   29 Gm  18 Gm   7 Gm   6 Vr
    26   4 Gm   9 Tr   6 Tr  22 Lo             26    3 Ce  29 Gm  13 Gm   8 Vr
    31   9 Gm  14 Tr  12 Tr  24 Lo
May  1/Jup 15 Ce/Sat 23 Cp/Uran 17 Ar     June 1/Jup 20 Ce/Sat 23 Cp/Uran 18 Ar
Nep  3 Vr/Plut 19 Ce/N Node 13 Ar         Nep  3 Vr/Plut 19 Ce/N Node 12 Ar


        Sun    Merc   Venus  Mars                    Sun    Merc   Venus  Mars
July 1   8 Ce  10 Ce  19 Gm  11 Vr         Aug. 1    8 Lo   4 Vr  27 Ce   0 Lb
     6  13 Ce  20 Ce  26 Gm  14 Vr              6   13 Lo  10 Vr   4 Lo   3 Lb
    11  18 Ce   0 Lo   2 Ce  17 Vr             11   17 Lo  15 Vr  10 Lo   6 Lb
    16  23 Ce  10 Lo   8 Ce  20 Vr             16   22 Lo  18 Vr  16 Lo   9 Lb
    21  27 Ce  18 Lo  14 Ce  23 Vr             21   27 Lo  20 Vr  22 Lo  12 Lb
    26   2 Lo  26 Lo  20 Ce  26 Vr             26    2 Vr  19 Vr  28 Lo  15 Lb
    31   7 Lo   3 Vr  26 Ce  29 Vr             31    7 Vr  16 Vr   4 Vr  19 Lb
July 1/Jup 26 Ce/Sat 21 Cp/Uran 19 Ar     Aug. 1/Jup  3 Lo/Sat 19 Cp/Uran 19 Ar
Nep  4 Vr/Plut 20 Ce/N Node 10 Ar         Nep  4 Vr/Plut 21 Ce/N Node  8 Ar
```

1931

```
           Sun      Merc     Venus    Mars                    Sun      Merc     Venus    Mars
Sept 1    8 Vr    15 Vr     6 Vr   19 Lb       Oct. 1    7 Lb    23 Vr    13 Lb    9 Sc
     6   12 Vr    11 Vr    12 Vr   22 Lb            6   12 Lb     2 Lb    19 Lb   13 Sc
    11   17 Vr     7 Vr    18 Vr   26 Lb           11   17 Lb    11 Lb    25 Lb   16 Sc
    16   22 Vr     6 Vr    24 Vr   29 Lb           16   22 Lb    20 Lb     2 Sc   20 Sc
    21   27 Vr     9 Vr     1 Lb    2 Sc           21   27 Lb    28 Lb     8 Sc   23 Sc
    26    2 Lb    15 Vr     7 Lb    6 Sc           26    2 Sc     6 Sc    14 Sc   27 Sc
                                                   31    7 Sc    14 Sc    20 Sc    0 Sg
```

Sept 1/Jup 10 Lo/Sat 17 Cp/Uran 19 Ar
Nep 6 Vr/Plut 22 Ce/N Node 7 Ar

Oct. 1/Jup 16 Lo/Sat 17 Cp/Uran 18 Ar
Nep 7 Vr/Plut 22 Ce/N Node 5 Ar

```
           Sun      Merc     Venus    Mars                    Sun      Merc     Venus    Mars
Nov. 1    8 Sc    16 Sc    22 Sc    1 Sg       Dec. 1    8 Sg    29 Sg    29 Sg   23 Sg
     6   13 Sc    24 Sc    28 Sc    5 Sg            6   13 Sg     4 Cp     5 Cp   27 Sg
    11   18 Sc     1 Sg     4 Sg    8 Sg           11   18 Sg     6 Cp    12 Cp    1 Cp
    16   23 Sc     9 Sg    10 Sg   12 Sg           16   23 Sg     5 Cp    18 Cp    4 Cp
    21   28 Sc    16 Sg    17 Sg   16 Sg           21   28 Sg    29 Sg    24 Cp    8 Cp
    26    3 Sg    23 Sg    23 Sg   19 Sg           26    3 Cp    23 Sg     0 Aq   12 Cp
                                                   31    8 Cp    20 Sg     6 Aq   16 Cp
```

Nov. 1/Jup 20 Lo/Sat 18 Cp/Uran 17 Ar
Nep 8 Vr/Plut 22 Ce/N Node 4 Ar

Dec. 1/Jup 23 Lo/Sat 20 Cp/Uran 16 Ar
Nep 8 Vr/Plut 22 Ce/N Node 2 Ar

Moon's Positions

	1	4	7	10	13	16	19	22	25	28	31
Jan.	24 Tr	5 Ce	19 Lo	3 Lb	14 Sc	23 Sg	0 Aq	6 Pc	12 Ar	19 Tr	29 Gm
Feb.	13 Ce	28 Lo	13 Lb	24 Sc	3 Cp	9 Aq	15 Pc	21 Ar	27 Tr	7 Ce	
Mar.	21 Ce	6 Vr	21 Lb	4 Sg	12 Cp	18 Aq	24 Pc	30 Ar	7 Gm	16 Ce	29 Lo
Apr.	14 Vr	29 Lb	12 Sg	21 Cp	27 Aq	3 Ar	9 Tr	17 Gm	27 Ce	9 Vr	
May	23 Lb	6 Sg	17 Cp	24 Aq	29 Pc	5 Tr	13 Gm	23 Ce	5 Vr	18 Lb	1 Sg
June	15 Sg	24 Cp	1 Pc	7 Ar	13 Tr	22 Gm	4 Lo	16 Vr	29 Lb	10 Sg	
July	20 Cp	27 Aq	3 Ar	9 Tr	17 Gm	29 Ce	13 Vr	25 Lb	7 Sg	16 Cp	24 Aq
Aug.	6 Pc	11 Ar	17 Tr	25 Gm	8 Lo	22 Vr	6 Sc	17 Sg	26 Cp	2 Pc	8 Ar
Sept	20 Ar	26 Tr	4 Ce	16 Lo	1 Lb	15 Sc	27 Sg	5 Aq	11 Pc	17 Ar	
Oct.	22 Tr	30 Gm	10 Lo	24 Vr	9 Sc	22 Sg	2 Aq	8 Pc	14 Ar	19 Tr	27 Gm
Nov.	9 Ce	19 Lo	2 Lb	17 Sc	1 Cp	10 Aq	17 Pc	22 Ar	28 Tr	6 Ce	
Dec.	16 Lo	28 Vr	11 Sc	25 Sg	5 Aq	13 Pc	18 Ar	24 Tr	3 Ce	13 Lo	25 Vr

1932

	Sun	Merc	Venus	Mars
Jan. 1	9 Cp	20 Sg	8 Aq	17 Cp
6	14 Cp	22 Sg	14 Aq	21 Cp
11	20 Cp	26 Sg	20 Aq	25 Cp
16	25 Cp	2 Cp	26 Aq	28 Cp
21	0 Aq	8 Cp	2 Pc	2 Aq
26	5 Aq	15 Cp	9 Pc	6 Aq
31	10 Aq	22 Cp	15 Pc	10 Aq

Jan. 1/Jup 22 Lo/Sat 24 Cp/Uran 15 Ar
Nep 8 Vr/Plut 21 Ce/N Node 0 Ar

	Sun	Merc	Venus	Mars
Feb. 1	11 Aq	24 Cp	16 Pc	11 Aq
6	16 Aq	1 Aq	22 Pc	15 Aq
11	21 Aq	9 Aq	28 Pc	19 Aq
16	26 Aq	18 Aq	4 Ar	23 Aq
21	1 Pc	26 Aq	10 Ar	27 Aq
26	6 Pc	5 Pc	16 Ar	1 Pc

Feb. 1/Jup 19 Lo/Sat 27 Cp/Uran 16 Ar
Nep 7 Vr/Plut 21 Ce/N Node 29 Pc

	Sun	Merc	Venus	Mars
Mar. 1	10 Pc	13 Pc	21 Ar	4 Pc
6	15 Pc	23 Pc	26 Ar	8 Pc
11	20 Pc	2 Ar	2 Tr	12 Pc
16	25 Pc	11 Ar	8 Tr	16 Pc
21	0 Ar	18 Ar	14 Tr	20 Pc
26	5 Ar	23 Ar	19 Tr	24 Pc
31	10 Ar	25 Ar	25 Tr	27 Pc

Mar. 1/Jup 15 Lo/Sat 1 Aq/Uran 17 Ar
Nep 7 Vr/Plut 20 Ce/N Node 27 Pc

	Sun	Merc	Venus	Mars
Apr. 1	11 Ar	25 Ar	26 Tr	28 Pc
6	16 Ar	23 Ar	1 Gm	2 Ar
11	21 Ar	20 Ar	6 Gm	6 Ar
16	26 Ar	16 Ar	11 Gm	10 Ar
21	1 Tr	14 Ar	16 Gm	14 Ar
26	6 Tr	14 Ar	21 Gm	18 Ar

Apr. 1/Jup 13 Lo/Sat 3 Aq/Uran 19 Ar
Nep 6 Vr/Plut 20 Ce/N Node 25. Pc

	Sun	Merc	Venus	Mars
May 1	10 Tr	16 Ar	25 Gm	21 Ar
6	15 Tr	19 Ar	0 Ce	25 Ar
11	20 Tr	24 Ar	4 Ce	29 Ar
16	25 Tr	0 Tr	7 Ce	3 Tr
21	0 Gm	7 Tr	10 Ce	6 Tr
26	5 Gm	15 Tr	13 Ce	10 Tr
31	9 Gm	24 Tr	14 Ce	14 Tr

May 1/Jup 13 Lo/Sat 5 Aq/Uran 21 Ar
Nep 5 Vr/Plut 20 Ce/N Node 24 Pc

	Sun	Merc	Venus	Mars
June 1	10 Gm	26 Tr	15 Ce	15 Tr
6	15 Gm	6 Gm	15 Ce	18 Tr
11	20 Gm	17 Gm	15 Ce	22 Tr
16	25 Gm	28 Gm	14 Ce	25 Tr
21	29 Gm	9 Ce	12 Ce	29 Tr
26	4 Ce	19 Ce	9 Ce	3 Gm

June 1/Jup 17 Lo/Sat 5 Aq/Uran 22 Ar
Nep 5 Vr/Plut 21 Ce/N Node 22 Pc

	Sun	Merc	Venus	Mars
July 1	9 Ce	28 Ce	6 Ce	6 Gm
6	14 Ce	6 Lo	3 Ce	10 Gm
11	18 Ce	13 Lo	1 Ce	13 Gm
16	23 Ce	20 Lo	29 Gm	17 Gm
21	28 Ce	25 Lo	29 Gm	20 Gm
26	3 Lo	29 Lo	29 Gm	23 Gm
31	8 Lo	1 Vr	1 Ce	27 Gm

July 1/Jup 22 Lo/Sat 3 Aq/Uran 23 Ar
Nep 6 Vr/Plut 21 Ce/N Node 21 Pc

	Sun	Merc	Venus	Mars
Aug. 1	9 Lo	2 Vr	1 Ce	27 Gm
6	13 Lo	2 Vr	3 Ce	1 Ce
11	18 Lo	0 Vr	6 Ce	4 Ce
16	23 Lo	26 Lo	10 Ce	7 Ce
21	28 Lo	22 Lo	13 Ce	11 Ce
26	3 Vr	19 Lo	17 Ce	14 Ce
31	7 Vr	20 Lo	22 Ce	17 Ce

Aug. 1/Jup 28 Lo/Sat 1 Aq/Uran 23 Ar
Nep 7 Vr/Plut 22 Ce/N Node 19 Pc

1932

```
          Sun    Merc   Venus   Mars              Sun    Merc   Venus   Mars
Sept 1    8 Vr   21 Lo  23 Ce  18 Ce     Oct. 1   8 Lb   9 Lb  23 Lo   6 Lo
     6   13 Vr   25 Lo  27 Ce  21 Ce          6  13 Lb  17 Lb  29 Lo   9 Lo
    11   18 Vr    3 Vr   2 Lo  24 Ce         11  17 Lb  26 Lb   4 Vr  12 Lo
    16   23 Vr   11 Vr   7 Lo  27 Ce         16  22 Lb   4 Sc  10 Vr  15 Lo
    21   28 Vr   21 Vr  12 Lo   0 Lo         21  27 Lb  11 Sc  16 Vr  18 Lo
    26    3 Lb    0 Lb  18 Lo   3 Lo         26   2 Sc  19 Sc  22 Vr  20 Lo
                                             31   7 Sc  26 Sc  27 Vr  23 Lo
```

Sept 1/Jup   4 Vr/Sat 29 Cp/Uran 23 Ar   Oct. 1/Jup 11 Vr/Sat 28 Cp/Uran 22 Ar
Nep   8 Vr/Plut 23 Ce/N Node 17 Pc   Nep   9 Vr/Plut 23 Ce/N Node 16 Pc

```
          Sun    Merc   Venus   Mars              Sun    Merc   Venus   Mars
Nov. 1    8 Sc   27 Sc  29 Vr  23 Lo     Dec. 1   9 Sg  17 Sg   5 Sc   8 Vr
     6   13 Sc    4 Sg   5 Lb  26 Lo          6  14 Sg  11 Sg  11 Sc  10 Vr
    11   18 Sc   10 Sg  11 Lb  29 Lo         11  19 Sg   5 Sg  17 Sc  12 Vr
    16   23 Sc   16 Sg  17 Lb   1 Vr         16  24 Sg   5 Sg  23 Sc  14 Vr
    21   28 Sc   20 Sg  23 Lb   3 Vr         21  29 Sg   7 Sg   0 Sg  15 Vr
    26    4 Sg   20 Sg  29 Lb   6 Vr         26   4 Cp  12 Sg   6 Sg  17 Vr
                                             31   9 Cp  18 Sg  12 Sg  18 Vr
```

Nov. 1/Jup 17 Vr/Sat 29 Cp/Uran 21 Ar   Dec. 1/Jup 21 Vr/Sat 1 Aq/Uran 20 Ar
Nep 10 Vr/Plut 23 Ce/N Node 14 Pc   Nep 10 Vr/Plut 23 Ce/N Node 13 Pc

Moon's Positions

```
         1       4       7      10      13      16      19      22      25      28      31
Jan.   9 Lb   21 Sc    3 Cp   13 Aq   20 Pc   26 Ar    2 Gm   11 Ce   22 Lo    5 Lb   18 Sc
Feb.   2 Sg   13 Cp   21 Aq   28 Pc    4 Tr   10 Gm   19 Ce    1 Vr   15 Lb   28 Sc
Mar.  26 Sg    5 Aq   13 Pc   19 Ar   24 Tr    1 Ce   10 Lo   24 Vr    9 Sc   22 Sg    2 Aq
Apr.  15 Aq   22 Pc   27 Ar    3 Gm    9 Ce   19 Lo    2 Lb   17 Sc    2 Cp   12 Aq
May   19 Pc   24 Ar   30 Tr    6 Ce   15 Lo   26 Vr   11 Sc   26 Sg    8 Aq   15 Pc   21 Ar
June   3 Tr    9 Gm   16 Ce   25 Lo    6 Lb   20 Sc    4 Cp   16 Aq   24 Pc   29 Ar
July   5 Gm   13 Ce   22 Lo    3 Lb   15 Sc   28 Sg   10 Aq   19 Pc   26 Ar    1 Gm    8 Ce
Aug.  21 Ce    2 Vr   14 Lb   26 Sc    8 Cp   19 Aq   27 Pc    4 Tr    9 Gm   16 Ce   27 Lo
Sept  11 Vr   24 Lb    7 Sg   19 Cp   28 Aq    6 Ar   12 Tr   17 Gm   24 Ce    5 Vr
Oct.  18 Lb    3 Sg   16 Cp   25 Aq    2 Ar    8 Tr   14 Gm   20 Ce   29 Lo   11 Lb   27 Sc
Nov.  12 Sg   25 Cp    5 Pc   11 Ar   17 Tr   23 Gm   29 Ce    8 Vr   20 Lb    5 Sg
Dec.  20 Cp    1 Pc    8 Ar   14 Tr   20 Gm   26 Ce    4 Vr   15 Lb   28 Sc   13 Cp   26 Aq
```

1933

```
        Sun    Merc   Venus   Mars                     Sun    Merc   Venus   Mars
Jan. 1  10 Cp  20 Sg  13 Sg   18 Vr       Feb. 1  12 Aq   7 Aq   22 Cp   19 Vr
     6  15 Cp  27 Sg  20 Sg   19 Vr            6  17 Aq  15 Aq   28 Cp   19 Vr
    11  20 Cp   4 Cp  26 Sg   20 Vr           11  22 Aq  24 Aq    4 Aq   17 Vr
    16  25 Cp  11 Cp   2 Cp   20 Vr           16  27 Aq   3 Pc   11 Aq   16 Vr
    21   1 Aq  19 Cp   8 Cp   20 Vr           21   2 Pc  13 Pc   17 Aq   14 Vr
    26   6 Aq  27 Cp  14 Cp   20 Vr           26   7 Pc  22 Pc   23 Aq   12 Vr
    31  11 Aq   5 Aq  21 Cp   20 Vr
Jan. 1/Jup 23 Vr/Sat  4 Aq/Uran 19 Ar    Feb. 1/Jup 22 Vr/Sat  8 Aq/Uran 20 Ar
Nep 10 Vr/Plut 23 Ce/N Node 11 Pc        Nep 10 Vr/Plut 22 Ce/N Node  9 Pc


        Sun    Merc   Venus   Mars                     Sun    Merc   Venus   Mars
Mar. 1  10 Pc  26 Pc  27 Aq   11 Vr       Apr. 1  11 Ar  26 Pc    5 Ar    2 Vr
     6  15 Pc   3 Ar   3 Pc    9 Vr            6  16 Ar  25 Pc   12 Ar    1 Vr
    11  20 Pc   7 Ar   9 Pc    7 Vr           11  21 Ar  26 Pc   18 Ar    1 Vr
    16  25 Pc   7 Ar  16 Pc    6 Vr           16  26 Ar  29 Pc   24 Ar    1 Vr
    21   0 Ar   4 Ar  22 Pc    4 Vr           21   0 Tr   3 Ar    0 Tr    1 Vr
    26   5 Ar   0 Ar  28 Pc    3 Vr           26   5 Tr   9 Ar    6 Tr    2 Vr
    31  10 Ar  26 Pc   4 Ar    2 Vr
Mar. 1/Jup 19 Vr/Sat 11 Aq/Uran 21 Ar    Apr. 1/Jup 16 Vr/Sat 14 Aq/Uran 23 Ar
Nep  9 Vr/Plut 21 Ce/N Node  8 Pc        Nep  8 Vr/Plut 21 Ce/N Node  6 Pc


        Sun    Merc   Venus   Mars                      Sun    Merc   Venus   Mars
May  1  10 Tr  15 Ar  13 Tr    3 Vr       June 1  10 Gm  14 Gm   21 Gm   13 Vr
     6  15 Tr  23 Ar  19 Tr    4 Vr            6  15 Gm  25 Gm   27 Gm   15 Vr
    11  20 Tr   1 Tr  25 Tr    5 Vr           11  20 Gm   5 Ce    3 Ce   17 Vr
    16  25 Tr  10 Tr   1 Gm    7 Vr           16  24 Gm  14 Ce    9 Ce   19 Vr
    21  29 Tr  20 Tr   7 Gm    9 Vr           21  29 Gm  22 Ce   15 Ce   22 Vr
    26   4 Gm   1 Gm  13 Gm   10 Vr           26   4 Ce  29 Ce   21 Ce   24 Vr
    31   9 Gm  12 Gm  20 Gm   12 Vr
May  1/Jup 13 Vr/Sat 16 Aq/Uran 24 Ar    June 1/Jup 14 Vr/Sat 16 Aq/Uran 26 Ar
Nep  7 Vr/Plut 21 Ce/N Node  5 Pc        Nep  7 Vr/Plut 22 Ce/N Node  3 Pc


         Sun    Merc   Venus   Mars                     Sun    Merc   Venus   Mars
July 1   9 Ce   5 Lo  27 Ce   27 Vr       Aug. 1   8 Lo   6 Lo    5 Vr   14 Lb
     6  13 Ce   9 Lo   4 Lo    0 Lb            6  13 Lo   3 Lo   11 Vr   17 Lb
    11  18 Ce  12 Lo  10 Lo    2 Lb           11  18 Lo   2 Lo   17 Vr   20 Lb
    16  23 Ce  13 Lo  16 Lo    5 Lb           16  23 Lo   4 Lo   23 Vr   23 Lb
    21  28 Ce  13 Lo  22 Lo    8 Lb           21  27 Lo   9 Lo   29 Vr   27 Lb
    26   3 Lo  10 Lo  28 Lo   11 Lb           26   2 Vr  17 Lo    5 Lb    0 Sc
    31   7 Lo   6 Lo   4 Vr   14 Lb           31   7 Vr  26 Lo   11 Lb    3 Sc
July 1/Jup 17 Vr/Sat 15 Aq/Uran 27 Ar    Aug. 1/Jup 22 Vr/Sat 13 Aq/Uran 27 Ar
Nep  8 Vr/Plut 23 Ce/N Node  1 Pc        Nep  9 Vr/Plut 23 Ce/N Node 30 Aq
```

1933

```
        Sun    Merc    Venus   Mars                    Sun    Merc    Venus   Mars
Sept 1  8 Vr   28 Lo   13 Lb    4 Sc        Oct. 1   7 Lb   21 Lb   18 Sc   24 Sc
     6  13 Vr   7 Vr   19 Lb    7 Sc             6   12 Lb  29 Lb   24 Sc   28 Sc
    11  18 Vr  17 Vr   25 Lb   10 Sc            11   17 Lb   6 Sc    0 Sg    1 Sg
    16  23 Vr  26 Vr    0 Sc   14 Sc            16   22 Lb  13 Sc    6 Sg    5 Sg
    21  28 Vr   5 Lb    6 Sc   17 Sc            21   27 Lb  20 Sc   11 Sg    8 Sg
    26   2 Lb  13 Lb   12 Sc   21 Sc            26    2 Sc  26 Sc   17 Sg   12 Sg
                                               31    7 Sc   1 Sg   23 Sg   16 Sg

Sept 1/Jup 28 Vr/Sat 11 Aq/Uran 27 Ar      Oct. 1/Jup  4 Lb/Sat 10 Aq/Uran 26 Ar
Nep 10 Vr/Plut 24 Ce/N Node 28 Aq          Nep 11 Vr/Plut 25 Ce/N Node 26 Aq


        Sun    Merc    Venus   Mars                    Sun    Merc    Venus   Mars
Nov. 1  8 Sc    2 Sg   24 Sg   16 Sg        Dec. 1   8 Sg   19 Sc   25 Cp    9 Cp
     6  13 Sc   4 Sg   29 Sg   20 Sg             6   13 Sg  23 Sc    0 Aq   13 Cp
    11  18 Sc   4 Sg    5 Cp   24 Sg            11   19 Sg  29 Sc    5 Aq   17 Cp
    16  23 Sc   0 Sg   10 Cp   28 Sg            16   24 Sg   5 Sg    9 Aq   21 Cp
    21  28 Sc  24 Sc   15 Cp    1 Cp            21   29 Sg  12 Sg   13 Aq   24 Cp
    26   3 Sg  19 Sc   20 Cp    5 Cp            26    4 Cp  20 Sg   16 Aq   28 Cp
                                               31    9 Cp  27 Sg   19 Aq    2 Aq

Nov. 1/Jup 11 Lb/Sat 10 Aq/Uran 25 Ar      Dec. 1/Jup 17 Lb/Sat 12 Aq/Uran 24 Ar
Nep 12 Vr/Plut 25 Ce/N Node 25 Aq          Nep 12 Vr/Plut 24 Ce/N Node 23 Aq
```

Moon's Positions

	1	4	7	10	13	16	19	22	25	28	31
Jan.	9 Pc	17 Ar	22 Tr	28 Gm	6 Lo	14 Vr	25 Lb	8 Sg	22 Cp	4 Pc	12 Ar
Feb.	25 Ar	0 Gm	6 Ce	14 Lo	24 Vr	6 Sc	19 Sg	1 Aq	12 Pc	20 Ar	
Mar.	2 Tr	8 Gm	14 Ce	22 Lo	3 Lb	17 Sc	30 Sg	11 Aq	20 Pc	28 Ar	4 Gm
Apr.	16 Gm	22 Ce	0 Vr	12 Lb	26 Sc	10 Cp	21 Aq	30 Pc	7 Tr	13 Gm	
May	18 Ce	25 Lo	6 Lb	20 Sc	5 Cp	18 Aq	27 Pc	4 Tr	10 Gm	15 Ce	22 Lo
June	4 Vr	14 Lb	28 Sc	14 Cp	27 Aq	6 Ar	13 Tr	19 Gm	24 Ce	1 Vr	
July	10 Lb	22 Sc	7 Cp	22 Aq	2 Ar	10 Tr	15 Gm	21 Ce	28 Lo	7 Lb	18 Sc
Aug.	2 Sg	16 Cp	30 Aq	11 Ar	18 Tr	24 Gm	30 Ce	7 Vr	17 Lb	29 Sc	11 Cp
Sept	26 Cp	8 Pc	19 Ar	26 Tr	2 Ce	8 Lo	16 Vr	27 Lb	10 Sg	22 Cp	
Oct.	4 Pc	14 Ar	22 Tr	28 Gm	4 Lo	11 Vr	22 Lb	6 Sg	19 Cp	0 Pc	10 Ar
Nov.	23 Ar	30 Tr	6 Ce	11 Lo	19 Vr	0 Sc	15 Sg	29 Cp	11 Pc	20 Ar	
Dec.	27 Tr	3 Ce	8 Lo	14 Vr	24 Lb	8 Sg	23 Cp	7 Pc	17 Ar	24 Tr	29 Gm

1934

	Sun	Merc	Venus	Mars
Jan. 1	10 Cp	29 Sg	20 Aq	3 Aq
6	15 Cp	7 Cp	22 Aq	7 Aq
11	20 Cp	14 Cp	23 Aq	11 Aq
16	25 Cp	23 Cp	24 Aq	15 Aq
21	0 Aq	1 Aq	23 Aq	19 Aq
26	5 Aq	9 Aq	21 Aq	23 Aq
31	10 Aq	18 Aq	19 Aq	27 Aq

Jan. 1/Jup 21 Lb/Sat 14 Aq/Uran 23 Ar
Nep 12 Vr/Plut 24 Ce/N Node 22 Aq

	Sun	Merc	Venus	Mars
Feb. 1	11 Aq	20 Aq	18 Aq	28 Aq
6	17 Aq	29 Aq	15 Aq	1 Pc
11	22 Aq	7 Pc	12 Aq	5 Pc
16	27 Aq	14 Pc	10 Aq	9 Pc
21	2 Pc	19 Pc	8 Aq	13 Pc
26	7 Pc	20 Pc	8 Aq	17 Pc

Feb. 1/Jup 23 Lb/Sat 18 Aq/Uran 24 Ar
Nep 12 Vr/Plut 23 Ce/N Node 20 Aq

	Sun	Merc	Venus	Mars
Mar. 1	10 Pc	19 Pc	8 Aq	20 Pc
6	15 Pc	15 Pc	9 Aq	23 Pc
11	20 Pc	10 Pc	11 Aq	27 Pc
16	25 Pc	7 Pc	14 Aq	1 Ar
21	0 Ar	6 Pc	17 Aq	5 Ar
26	5 Ar	8 Pc	20 Aq	9 Ar
31	10 Ar	12 Pc	24 Aq	13 Ar

Mar. 1/Jup 22 Lb/Sat 21 Aq/Uran 25 Ar
Nep 11 Vr/Plut 23 Ce/N Node 18 Aq

	Sun	Merc	Venus	Mars
Apr. 1	11 Ar	13 Pc	25 Aq	14 Ar
6	16 Ar	18 Pc	0 Pc	17 Ar
11	20 Ar	24 Pc	4 Pc	21 Ar
16	25 Ar	1 Ar	9 Pc	25 Ar
21	0 Tr	9 Ar	14 Pc	29 Ar
26	5 Tr	17 Ar	19 Pc	3 Tr

Apr. 1/Jup 19 Lb/Sat 25 Aq/Uran 26 Ar
Nep 10 Vr/Plut 23 Ce/N Node 17 Aq

	Sun	Merc	Venus	Mars
May 1	10 Tr	27 Ar	24 Pc	6 Tr
6	15 Tr	6 Tr	0 Ar	10 Tr
11	20 Tr	17 Tr	5 Ar	14 Tr
16	24 Tr	28 Tr	10 Ar	17 Tr
21	29 Tr	9 Gm	16 Ar	21 Tr
26	4 Gm	19 Gm	22 Ar	25 Tr
31	9 Gm	28 Gm	27 Ar	28 Tr

May 1/Jup 16 Lb/Sat 27 Aq/Uran 28 Ar
Nep 10 Vr/Plut 23 Ce/N Node 15 Aq

	Sun	Merc	Venus	Mars
June 1	10 Gm	29 Gm	28 Ar	29 Tr
6	15 Gm	7 Ce	4 Tr	2 Gm
11	19 Gm	13 Ce	10 Tr	6 Gm
16	24 Gm	19 Ce	16 Tr	9 Gm
21	29 Gm	22 Ce	21 Tr	13 Gm
26	4 Ce	24 Ce	27 Tr	16 Gm

June 1/Jup 13 Lb/Sat 28 Aq/Uran 30 Ar
Nep 10 Vr/Plut 23 Ce/N Node 14 Aq

	Sun	Merc	Venus	Mars
July 1	8 Ce	24 Ce	3 Gm	20 Gm
6	13 Ce	22 Ce	9 Gm	23 Gm
11	18 Ce	19 Ce	15 Gm	27 Gm
16	23 Ce	16 Ce	21 Gm	0 Ce
21	28 Ce	14 Ce	27 Gm	3 Ce
26	2 Lo	15 Ce	3 Ce	7 Ce
31	7 Lo	18 Ce	9 Ce	10 Ce

July 1/Jup 14 Lb/Sat 28 Aq/Uran 1 Tr
Nep 10 Vr/Plut 24 Ce/N Node 12 Aq

	Sun	Merc	Venus	Mars
Aug. 1	8 Lo	19 Ce	10 Ce	11 Ce
6	13 Lo	25 Ce	16 Ce	14 Ce
11	18 Lo	2 Lo	22 Ce	17 Ce
16	22 Lo	12 Lo	28 Ce	21 Ce
21	27 Lo	22 Lo	4 Lo	24 Ce
26	2 Vr	2 Vr	10 Lo	27 Ce
31	7 Vr	11 Vr	16 Lo	0 Lo

Aug. 1/Jup 17 Lb/Sat 26 Aq/Uran 1 Tr
Nep 11 Vr/Plut 25 Ce/N Node 10 Aq

1934

```
          Sun      Merc     Venus    Mars                    Sun      Merc     Venus    Mars
Sept  1   8 Vr    13 Vr    18 Lo     1 Lo        Oct.  1    7 Lb     1 Sc    25 Vr    20 Lo
      6  13 Vr    22 Vr    24 Lo     4 Lo              6   12 Lb     7 Sc     1 Lb    23 Lo
     11  18 Vr     1 Lb     0 Vr     7 Lo             11   17 Lb    12 Sc     7 Lb    26 Lo
     16  22 Vr     9 Lb     6 Vr    10 Lo             16   22 Lb    16 Sc    13 Lb    29 Lo
     21  27 Vr    17 Lb    12 Vr    13 Lo             21   27 Lb    19 Sc    20 Lb     2 Vr
     26   2 Lb    24 Lb    18 Vr    17 Lo             26    2 Sc    18 Sc    26 Lb     5 Vr
                                                     31    7 Sc    14 Sc     2 Sc     7 Vr
```

Sept 1/Jup 22 Lb/Sat 24 Aq/Uran 1 Tr   Oct. 1/Jup 28 Lb/Sat 22 Aq/Uran 0 Tr
Nep 12 Vr/Plut 25 Ce/N Node 9 Aq   Nep 13 Vr/Plut 26 Ce/N Node 7 Aq

```
          Sun      Merc     Venus    Mars                    Sun      Merc     Venus    Mars
Nov.  1   8 Sc    13 Sc     3 Sc     8 Vr        Dec.  1    8 Sg    22 Sc    11 Sg    25 Vr
      6  13 Sc     7 Sc    10 Sc    11 Vr              6   13 Sg     0 Sg    17 Sg    27 Vr
     11  18 Sc     3 Sc    16 Sc    14 Vr             11   18 Sg     7 Sg    24 Sg     0 Lb
     16  23 Sc     4 Sc    22 Sc    17 Vr             16   23 Sg    15 Sg     0 Cp     2 Lb
     21  28 Sc     9 Sc    28 Sc    19 Vr             21   28 Sg    23 Sg     6 Cp     5 Lb
     26   3 Sg    15 Sc     5 Sg    22 Vr             26    4 Cp     1 Cp    12 Cp     7 Lb
                                                     31    9 Cp     9 Cp    19 Cp     9 Lb
```

Nov. 1/Jup 5 Sc/Sat 22 Aq/Uran 29 Ar   Dec. 1/Jup 11 Sc/Sat 23 Aq/Uran 28 Ar
Nep 14 Vr/Plut 26 Ce/N Node 5 Aq   Nep 14 Vr/Plut 26 Ce/N Node 4 Aq

Moon's Positions

```
           1       4       7      10      13      16      19      22      25      28      31
Jan.   11 Ce   17 Lo   24 Vr    3 Sc   16 Sg    1 Aq   15 Pc   26 Ar    3 Gm    8 Ce   14 Lo
Feb.   26 Lo    3 Lb   13 Sc   25 Sg    9 Aq   23 Pc    4 Tr   11 Gm   17 Ce   22 Lo
Mar.    5 Vr   13 Lb   23 Sc    5 Cp   18 Aq    1 Ar   12 Tr   19 Gm   25 Ce    1 Vr    9 Lb
Apr.   22 Lb    4 Sg   16 Cp   28 Aq   10 Ar   20 Tr   27 Gm    2 Lo    9 Vr   17 Lb
May    29 Sc   13 Cp   25 Aq    6 Ar   15 Tr   23 Gm   29 Ce    4 Vr   12 Lb   24 Sc    8 Cp
June   23 Cp    6 Pc   16 Ar   25 Tr    1 Ce    7 Lo   13 Vr   20 Lb    2 Sg   17 Cp
July    1 Pc   13 Ar   22 Tr   28 Gm    4 Lo    9 Vr   16 Lb   26 Sc   10 Cp   25 Aq    9 Ar
Aug.   23 Ar    1 Gm    7 Ce   13 Lo   19 Vr   26 Lb    6 Sg   19 Cp    4 Pc   17 Ar   27 Tr
Sept   10 Gm   16 Ce   21 Lo   28 Vr    6 Sc   16 Sg   28 Cp   12 Pc   25 Ar    6 Gm
Oct.   12 Ce   18 Lo   24 Vr    2 Sc   13 Sg   24 Cp    7 Pc   20 Ar    1 Gm    8 Ce   14 Lo
Nov.   26 Lo    2 Lb   11 Sc   23 Sg    5 Aq   18 Pc   29 Ar    9 Gm   16 Ce   22 Lo
Dec.   28 Vr    6 Sc   18 Sg    1 Aq   14 Pc   26 Ar    5 Gm   12 Ce   18 Lo   23 Vr    1 Sc
```

1935

Jan.	Sun	Merc	Venus	Mars
1	10 Cp	10 Cp	20 Cp	10 Lb
6	15 Cp	18 Cp	26 Cp	12 Lb
11	20 Cp	27 Cp	3 Aq	14 Lb
16	25 Cp	5 Aq	9 Aq	16 Lb
21	0 Aq	13 Aq	15 Aq	17 Lb
26	5 Aq	21 Aq	21 Aq	19 Lb
31	10 Aq	28 Aq	28 Aq	21 Lb

Jan. 1/Jup 17 Sc/Sat 25 Aq/Uran 28 Ar
Nep 15 Vr/Plut 25 Ce/N Node 2 Aq

Feb.	Sun	Merc	Venus	Mars
1	11 Aq	29 Aq	29 Aq	21 Lb
6	16 Aq	3 Pc	5 Pc	22 Lb
11	21 Aq	3 Pc	11 Pc	23 Lb
16	26 Aq	29 Aq	18 Pc	24 Lb
21	1 Pc	24 Aq	24 Pc	24 Lb
26	6 Pc	20 Aq	0 Ar	25 Lb

Feb. 1/Jup 21 Sc/Sat 28 Aq/Uran 28 Ar
Nep 14 Vr/Plut 25 Ce/N Node 1 Aq

Mar.	Sun	Merc	Venus	Mars
1	9 Pc	19 Aq	4 Ar	25 Lb
6	14 Pc	20 Aq	10 Ar	24 Lb
11	19 Pc	22 Aq	16 Ar	24 Lb
16	24 Pc	27 Aq	22 Ar	23 Lb
21	29 Pc	2 Pc	28 Ar	22 Lb
26	4 Ar	9 Pc	4 Tr	20 Lb
31	9 Ar	16 Pc	10 Tr	18 Lb

Mar. 1/Jup 23 Sc/Sat 2 Pc/Uran 29 Ar
Nep 13 Vr/Plut 24 Ce/N Node 29 Cp

Apr.	Sun	Merc	Venus	Mars
1	10 Ar	17 Pc	12 Tr	18 Lb
6	15 Ar	25 Pc	18 Tr	16 Lb
11	20 Ar	4 Ar	24 Tr	14 Lb
16	25 Ar	13 Ar	0 Gm	12 Lb
21	0 Tr	23 Ar	6 Gm	11 Lb
26	5 Tr	3 Tr	11 Gm	9 Lb

Apr. 1/Jup 23 Sc/Sat 5 Pc/Uran 0 Tr
Nep 12 Vr/Plut 24 Ce/N Node 27 Cp

May	Sun	Merc	Venus	Mars
1	10 Tr	14 Tr	17 Gm	8 Lb
6	15 Tr	24 Tr	23 Gm	7 Lb
11	19 Tr	4 Gm	29 Gm	6 Lb
16	24 Tr	13 Gm	5 Ce	6 Lb
21	29 Tr	21 Gm	10 Ce	6 Lb
26	4 Gm	27 Gm	16 Ce	6 Lb
31	9 Gm	1 Ce	22 Ce	7 Lb

May 1/Jup 20 Sc/Sat 8 Pc/Uran 2 Tr
Nep 12 Vr/Plut 24 Ce/N Node 26 Cp

June	Sun	Merc	Venus	Mars
1	10 Gm	2 Ce	23 Ce	7 Lb
6	14 Gm	4 Ce	28 Ce	8 Lb
11	19 Gm	4 Ce	3 Lo	9 Lb
16	24 Gm	2 Ce	9 Lo	11 Lb
21	29 Gm	0 Ce	14 Lo	12 Lb
26	3 Ce	27 Gm	19 Lo	14 Lb

June 1/Jup 16 Sc/Sat 10 Pc/Uran 4 Tr
Nep 12 Vr/Plut 24 Ce/N Node 24 Cp

July	Sun	Merc	Venus	Mars
1	8 Ce	25 Gm	24 Lo	16 Lb
6	13 Ce	26 Gm	28 Lo	18 Lb
11	18 Ce	28 Gm	3 Vr	21 Lb
16	23 Ce	2 Ce	7 Vr	23 Lb
21	27 Ce	8 Ce	11 Vr	25 Lb
26	2 Lo	16 Ce	14 Vr	28 Lb
31	7 Lo	26 Ce	17 Vr	1 Sc

July 1/Jup 14 Sc/Sat 10 Pc/Uran 5 Tr
Nep 12 Vr/Plut 25 Ce/N Node 23 Cp

Aug.	Sun	Merc	Venus	Mars
1	8 Lo	28 Ce	18 Vr	1 Sc
6	13 Lo	8 Lo	20 Vr	4 Sc
11	17 Lo	18 Lo	22 Vr	7 Sc
16	22 Lo	28 Lo	23 Vr	10 Sc
21	27 Lo	8 Vr	23 Vr	13 Sc
26	2 Vr	16 Vr	22 Vr	16 Sc
31	7 Vr	25 Vr	20 Vr	19 Sc

Aug. 1/Jup 14 Sc/Sat 9 Pc/Uran 5 Tr
Nep 13 Vr/Plut 26 Ce/N Node 21 Cp

1935

```
              Sun    Merc    Venus    Mars                  Sun    Merc    Venus    Mars
Sept  1    8 Vr   26 Vr   19 Vr   20 Sc     Oct.  1    7 Lb    1 Sc    7 Vr   10 Sg
       6   12 Vr    4 Lb   16 Vr   23 Sc            6   12 Lb    3 Sc    7 Vr   13 Sg
      11   17 Vr   11 Lb   13 Vr   26 Sc           11   17 Lb    1 Sc    9 Vr   17 Sg
      16   22 Vr   17 Lb   10 Vr    0 Sg           16   22 Lb   27 Lb   11 Vr   21 Sg
      21   27 Vr   23 Lb    8 Vr    3 Sg           21   27 Lb   21 Lb   14 Vr   24 Sg
      26    2 Lb   28 Lb    7 Vr    6 Sg           26    2 Sc   17 Lb   18 Vr   28 Sg
                                                   31    7 Sc   19 Lb   22 Vr    2 Cp
```

Sept 1/Jup 17 Sc/Sat 7 Pc/Uran 5 Tr   Oct. 1/Jup 22 Sc/Sat 5 Pc/Uran 5 Tr
Nep 14 Vr/Plut 27 Ce/N Node 19 Cp   Nep 15 Vr/Plut 27 Ce/N Node 18 Cp

```
              Sun    Merc    Venus    Mars                  Sun    Merc    Venus    Mars
Nov.  1    8 Sc   19 Lb   22 Vr    2 Cp     Dec.  1    8 Sg    3 Sg   22 Lb   25 Cp
       6   13 Sc   24 Lb   27 Vr    6 Cp            6   13 Sg   11 Sg   27 Lb   29 Cp
      11   18 Sc    1 Sc    1 Lb   10 Cp           11   18 Sg   18 Sg    3 Sc    3 Aq
      16   23 Sc    9 Sc    6 Lb   14 Cp           16   23 Sg   26 Sg    8 Sc    7 Aq
      21   28 Sc   17 Sc   11 Lb   18 Cp           21   28 Sg    4 Cp   14 Sc   11 Aq
      26    3 Sg   25 Sc   16 Lb   21 Cp           26    3 Cp   12 Cp   20 Sc   15 Aq
                                                   31    8 Cp   20 Cp   26 Sc   19 Aq
```

Nov. 1/Jup 28 Sc/Sat 4 Pc/Uran 3 Tr   Dec. 1/Jup 5 Sg/Sat 4 Pc/Uran 2 Tr
Nep 16 Vr/Plut 27 Ce/N Node 16 Cp   Nep 17 Vr/Plut 27 Ce/N Node 15 Cp

Moon's Positions

	1	4	7	10	13	16	19	22	25	28	31
Jan.	14 Sc	26 Sg	11 Aq	25 Pc	6 Tr	14 Gm	21 Ce	26 Lo	2 Lb	9 Sc	19 Sg
Feb.	4 Cp	19 Aq	4 Ar	16 Tr	24 Gm	30 Ce	5 Vr	11 Lb	18 Sc	28 Sg	
Mar.	12 Cp	27 Aq	12 Ar	24 Tr	3 Ce	8 Lo	14 Vr	20 Lb	28 Sc	8 Cp	21 Aq
Apr.	5 Pc	20 Ar	2 Gm	11 Ce	17 Lo	22 Vr	29 Lb	8 Sg	19 Cp	1 Pc	
May	14 Ar	27 Tr	6 Ce	13 Lo	19 Vr	25 Lb	4 Sg	15 Cp	27 Aq	10 Ar	22 Tr
June	5 Gm	14 Ce	21 Lo	27 Vr	3 Sc	13 Sg	25 Cp	8 Pc	21 Ar	2 Gm	
July	10 Ce	17 Lo	23 Vr	29 Lb	8 Sg	20 Cp	4 Pc	18 Ar	29 Tr	7 Ce	14 Lo
Aug.	25 Lo	1 Lb	7 Sc	16 Sg	28 Cp	13 Pc	28 Ar	9 Gm	16 Ce	22 Lo	28 Vr
Sept	10 Lb	16 Sc	24 Sg	6 Aq	21 Pc	7 Tr	18 Gm	26 Ce	1 Vr	7 Lb	
Oct.	13 Sc	21 Sg	1 Aq	15 Pc	0 Tr	13 Gm	22 Ce	28 Lo	4 Lb	10 Sc	18 Sg
Nov.	1 Cp	11 Aq	24 Pc	8 Tr	21 Gm	0 Lo	6 Vr	12 Lb	19 Sc	28 Sg	
Dec.	8 Aq	20 Pc	3 Tr	15 Gm	25 Ce	2 Vr	8 Lb	14 Sc	23 Sg	4 Aq	17 Pc

1936

```
          Sun    Merc   Venus  Mars                    Sun    Merc   Venus  Mars
Jan. 1   9 Cp   22 Cp   27 Sc  19 Aq      Feb. 1   11 Aq   11 Aq    4 Cp  14 Pc
     6  14 Cp    0 Aq    3 Sg  23 Aq           6   16 Aq    5 Aq   10 Cp  18 Pc
    11  20 Cp    7 Aq    9 Sg  27 Aq          11   21 Aq    2 Aq   16 Cp  21 Pc
    16  25 Cp   14 Aq   15 Sg   1 Pc          16   26 Aq    2 Aq   22 Cp  25 Pc
    21   0 Aq   17 Aq   21 Sg   5 Pc          21    1 Pc    5 Aq   29 Cp  29 Pc
    26   5 Aq   17 Aq   27 Sg   9 Pc          26    6 Pc    9 Aq    5 Aq   3 Ar
    31  10 Aq   12 Aq    3 Cp  13 Pc
Jan. 1/Jup 12 Sg/Sat  6 Pc/Uran  2 Tr    Feb. 1/Jup 18 Sg/Sat  9 Pc/Uran  2 Tr
Nep 17 Vr/Plut 27 Ce/N Node 13 Cp        Nep 16 Vr/Plut 26 Ce/N Node 11 Cp


          Sun    Merc   Venus  Mars                    Sun    Merc   Venus  Mars
Mar. 1  10 Pc   14 Aq   10 Aq   6 Ar      Apr. 1   11 Ar    1 Ar   18 Pc  29 Ar
     6  15 Pc   20 Aq   16 Aq  10 Ar           6   16 Ar   11 Ar   24 Pc   3 Tr
    11  20 Pc   27 Aq   22 Aq  14 Ar          11   21 Ar   21 Ar    0 Ar   7 Tr
    16  25 Pc    4 Pc   28 Aq  17 Ar          16   26 Ar    2 Tr    6 Ar  10 Tr
    21   0 Ar   12 Pc    4 Pc  21 Ar          21    1 Tr   12 Tr   12 Ar  14 Tr
    26   5 Ar   21 Pc   10 Pc  25 Ar          26    6 Tr   22 Tr   18 Ar  18 Tr
    31  10 Ar    0 Ar   16 Pc  29 Ar
Mar. 1/Jup 22 Sg/Sat 13 Pc/Uran  3 Tr    Apr. 1/Jup 24 Sg/Sat 16 Pc/Uran  4 Tr
Nep 16 Vr/Plut 25 Ce/N Node 10 Cp        Nep 15 Vr/Plut 25 Ce/N Node  8 Cp


          Sun    Merc   Venus  Mars                    Sun    Merc   Venus  Mars
May  1  10 Tr    0 Gm   25 Ar  21 Tr      June 1   10 Gm   10 Gm    3 Gm  13 Gm
     6  15 Tr    6 Gm    1 Tr  25 Tr           6   15 Gm    7 Gm    9 Gm  16 Gm
    11  20 Tr   11 Gm    7 Tr  28 Tr          11   20 Gm    6 Gm   15 Gm  20 Gm
    16  25 Tr   13 Gm   13 Tr   2 Gm          16   25 Gm    6 Gm   21 Gm  23 Gm
    21   0 Gm   14 Gm   19 Tr   5 Gm          21   29 Gm    8 Gm   27 Gm  27 Gm
    26   5 Gm   13 Gm   25 Tr   9 Gm          26    4 Ce   12 Gm    3 Ce   0 Ce
    31   9 Gm   10 Gm    1 Gm  12 Gm
May  1/Jup 24 Sg/Sat 19 Pc/Uran  6 Tr    June 1/Jup 21 Sg/Sat 22 Pc/Uran  7 Tr
Nep 14 Vr/Plut 25 Ce/N Node  7 Cp        Nep 14 Vr/Plut 26 Ce/N Node  5 Cp


          Sun    Merc   Venus  Mars                    Sun    Merc   Venus  Mars
July 1   9 Ce   18 Gm    9 Ce   3 Ce      Aug. 1    9 Lo   17 Lo   18 Lo  24 Ce
     6  14 Ce   25 Gm   16 Ce   7 Ce           6   13 Lo   26 Lo   24 Lo  27 Ce
    11  19 Ce    4 Ce   22 Ce  10 Ce          11   18 Lo    5 Vr    0 Vr   0 Lo
    16  23 Ce   14 Ce   28 Ce  13 Ce          16   23 Lo   13 Vr    6 Vr   4 Lo
    21  28 Ce   24 Ce    4 Lo  17 Ce          21   28 Lo   21 Vr   12 Vr   7 Lo
    26   3 Lo    5 Lo   10 Lo  20 Ce          26    3 Vr   28 Vr   18 Vr  10 Lo
    31   8 Lo   15 Lo   16 Lo  23 Ce          31    7 Vr    4 Lb   25 Vr  13 Lo
July 1/Jup 17 Sg/Sat 23 Pc/Uran  9 Tr    Aug. 1/Jup 15 Sg/Sat 22 Pc/Uran 10 Tr
Nep 14 Vr/Plut 26 Ce/N Node  3 Cp        Nep 15 Vr/Plut 27 Ce/N Node  2 Cp
```

1936

```
          Sun      Merc     Venus    Mars                    Sun      Merc     Venus    Mars
Sept 1    8 Vr     5 Lb    26 Vr    14 Lo        Oct. 1     8 Lb     8 Lb     3 Sc     3 Vr
     6   13 Vr    10 Lb     2 Lb    17 Lo             6    13 Lb     3 Lb     9 Sc     6 Vr
    11   18 Vr    14 Lb     8 Lb    20 Lo            11    17 Lb     1 Lb    15 Sc     9 Vr
    16   23 Vr    16 Lb    14 Lb    23 Lo            16    22 Lb     4 Lb    21 Sc    12 Vr
    21   28 Vr    16 Lb    20 Lb    26 Lo            21    27 Lb    10 Lb    27 Sc    15 Vr
    26    3 Lb    13 Lb    27 Lb     0 Vr            26     2 Sc    18 Lb     3 Sg    18 Vr
                                                    31     7 Sc    26 Lb    10 Sg    21 Vr
```

Sept 1/Jup 15 Sg/Sat 20 Pc/Uran 9 Tr   Oct. 1/Jup 18 Sg/Sat 18 Pc/Uran 9 Tr
Nep 16 Vr/Plut 28 Ce/N Node 30 Sg   Nep 17 Vr/Plut 29 Ce/N Node 28 Sg

```
          Sun      Merc     Venus    Mars                    Sun      Merc     Venus    Mars
Nov. 1    8 Sc    28 Lb    11 Sg    22 Vr        Dec. 1     9 Sg    16 Sg    17 Cp    10 Lb
     6   13 Sc     6 Sc    17 Sg    25 Vr             6    14 Sg    23 Sg    23 Cp    13 Lb
    11   18 Sc    14 Sc    23 Sg    28 Vr            11    19 Sg     1 Cp    29 Cp    16 Lb
    16   23 Sc    22 Sc    29 Sg     1 Lb            16    24 Sg     9 Cp     5 Aq    18 Lb
    21   29 Sc     0 Sg     5 Cp     4 Lb            21    29 Sg    16 Cp    11 Aq    21 Lb
    26    4 Sg     8 Sg    11 Cp     7 Lb            26     4 Cp    23 Cp    17 Aq    24 Lb
                                                    31     9 Cp    29 Cp    23 Aq    27 Lb
```

Nov. 1/Jup 23 Sg/Sat 16 Pc/Uran 8 Tr   Dec. 1/Jup 30 Sg/Sat 16 Pc/Uran 6 Tr
Nep 18 Vr/Plut 29 Ce/N Node 27 Sg   Nep 19 Vr/Plut 29 Ce/N Node 25 Sg

Moon's Positions

```
          1        4        7       10       13       16       19       22       25       28       31
Jan.    1 Ar    13 Tr    24 Gm     3 Lo    10 Vr    16 Lb    22 Sc     1 Cp    13 Aq    27 Pc    10 Tr
Feb.   24 Tr     4 Ce    12 Lo    18 Vr    24 Lb     0 Sg     9 Cp    21 Aq     7 Ar    20 Tr
Mar.   18 Gm    26 Ce     3 Vr     9 Lb    14 Sc    21 Sg     1 Aq    14 Pc     0 Tr    14 Gm    23 Ce
Apr.    6 Lo    12 Vr    18 Lb    23 Sc     0 Cp    10 Aq    23 Pc     8 Tr    22 Gm     2 Lo
May     9 Vr    14 Lb    20 Sc    27 Sg     6 Aq    18 Pc     2 Tr    16 Gm    27 Ce     5 Vr    11 Lb
June   23 Lb    29 Sc     7 Cp    17 Aq    28 Pc    12 Tr    25 Gm     5 Lo    13 Vr    19 Lb
July   25 Sc     3 Cp    13 Aq    25 Pc     8 Tr    20 Gm     1 Lo     9 Vr    15 Lb    21 Sc    28 Sg
Aug.   11 Cp    22 Aq     6 Ar    19 Tr     0 Ce    10 Lo    17 Vr    23 Lb    29 Sc     6 Cp    17 Aq
Sept    1 Pc    16 Ar    29 Tr    10 Ce    19 Lo    26 Vr     2 Sc     7 Sg    14 Cp    25 Aq
Oct.    9 Ar    25 Tr     7 Ce    16 Lo    23 Vr    29 Lb     4 Sg    10 Cp    19 Aq     2 Ar    18 Tr
Nov.    3 Gm    16 Ce    25 Lo     2 Lb     7 Sc    13 Sg    20 Cp    29 Aq    11 Ar    26 Tr
Dec.   10 Ce    21 Lo    29 Vr     4 Sc    10 Sg    17 Cp    26 Aq     7 Ar    20 Tr     4 Ce    16 Lo
```

1937

	Sun	Merc	Venus	Mars
Jan. 1	10 Cp	29 Cp	24 Aq	27 Lb
6	15 Cp	2 Aq	0 Pc	0 Sc
11	20 Cp	29 Cp	6 Pc	3 Sc
16	25 Cp	23 Cp	11 Pc	5 Sc
21	1 Aq	17 Cp	17 Pc	8 Sc
26	6 Aq	15 Cp	22 Pc	11 Sc
31	11 Aq	17 Cp	27 Pc	13 Sc

Jan. 1/Jup 7 Cp/Sat 17 Pc/Uran 6 Tr
Nep 19 Vr/Plut 28 Ce/N Node 24 Sg

	Sun	Merc	Venus	Mars
Feb. 1	12 Aq	17 Cp	29 Pc	14 Sc
6	17 Aq	21 Cp	4 Ar	16 Sc
11	22 Aq	26 Cp	9 Ar	18 Sc
16	27 Aq	3 Aq	13 Ar	20 Sc
21	2 Pc	9 Aq	18 Ar	23 Sc
26	7 Pc	16 Aq	22 Ar	25 Sc

Feb. 1/Jup 14 Cp/Sat 20 Pc/Uran 6 Tr
Nep 18 Vr/Plut 27 Ce/N Node 22 Sg

	Sun	Merc	Venus	Mars
Mar. 1	10 Pc	21 Aq	24 Ar	26 Sc
6	15 Pc	29 Aq	28 Ar	28 Sc
11	20 Pc	7 Pc	1 Tr	29 Sc
16	25 Pc	16 Pc	3 Tr	1 Sg
21	0 Ar	26 Pc	5 Tr	2 Sg
26	5 Ar	6 Ar	6 Tr	3 Sg
31	10 Ar	16 Ar	6 Tr	4 Sg

Mar. 1/Jup 19 Cp/Sat 23 Pc/Uran 7 Tr
Nep 18 Vr/Plut 27 Ce/N Node 20 Sg

	Sun	Merc	Venus	Mars
Apr. 1	11 Ar	18 Ar	5 Tr	4 Sg
6	16 Ar	28 Ar	4 Tr	5 Sg
11	21 Ar	7 Tr	2 Tr	5 Sg
16	26 Ar	15 Tr	29 Ar	6 Sg
21	0 Tr	20 Tr	26 Ar	5 Sg
26	5 Tr	24 Tr	23 Ar	5 Sg

Apr. 1/Jup 24 Cp/Sat 27 Pc/Uran 8 Tr
Nep 17 Vr/Plut 27 Ce/N Node 19 Sg

	Sun	Merc	Venus	Mars
May 1	10 Tr	24 Tr	21 Ar	4 Sg
6	15 Tr	23 Tr	20 Ar	3 Sg
11	20 Tr	21 Tr	19 Ar	1 Sg
16	25 Tr	18 Tr	20 Ar	0 Sg
21	0 Gm	16 Tr	22 Ar	28 Sc
26	4 Gm	15 Tr	24 Ar	26 Sc
31	9 Gm	17 Tr	27 Ar	24 Sc

May 1/Jup 27 Cp/Sat 1 Ar/Uran 10 Tr
Nep 16 Vr/Plut 27 Ce/N Node 17 Sg

	Sun	Merc	Venus	Mars
June 1	10 Gm	18 Tr	28 Ar	24 Sc
6	15 Gm	21 Tr	1 Tr	23 Sc
11	20 Gm	26 Tr	5 Tr	21 Sc
16	24 Gm	3 Gm	9 Tr	20 Sc
21	29 Gm	11 Gm	14 Tr	20 Sc
26	4 Ce	20 Gm	18 Tr	20 Sc

June 1/Jup 27 Cp/Sat 3 Ar/Uran 11 Tr
Nep 16 Vr/Plut 27 Ce/N Node 16 Sg

	Sun	Merc	Venus	Mars
July 1	9 Ce	0 Ce	23 Tr	20 Sc
6	14 Ce	11 Ce	28 Tr	20 Sc
11	18 Ce	21 Ce	3 Gm	21 Sc
16	23 Ce	2 Lo	8 Gm	22 Sc
21	28 Ce	11 Lo	14 Gm	23 Sc
26	3 Lo	20 Lo	19 Gm	25 Sc
31	7 Lo	29 Lo	25 Gm	26 Sc

July 1/Jup 24 Cp/Sat 5 Ar/Uran 13 Tr
Nep 16 Vr/Plut 28 Ce/N Node 14 Sg

	Sun	Merc	Venus	Mars
Aug. 1	8 Lo	0 Vr	26 Gm	27 Sc
6	13 Lo	8 Vr	1 Ce	29 Sc
11	18 Lo	14 Vr	7 Ce	1 Sg
16	23 Lo	20 Vr	13 Ce	3 Sg
21	28 Lo	25 Vr	18 Ce	6 Sg
26	2 Vr	28 Vr	24 Ce	8 Sg
31	7 Vr	0 Lb	0 Lo	11 Sg

Aug. 1/Jup 20 Cp/Sat 5 Ar/Uran 14 Tr
Nep 17 Vr/Plut 29 Ce/N Node 12 Sg

1937

	Sun	Merc	Venus	Mars
Sept 1	8 Vr	0 Lb	1 Lo	12 Sg
6	13 Vr	28 Vr	7 Lo	15 Sg
11	18 Vr	25 Vr	13 Lo	18 Sg
16	23 Vr	20 Vr	19 Lo	21 Sg
21	28 Vr	16 Vr	25 Lo	24 Sg
26	2 Lb	16 Vr	1 Vr	27 Sg

Sept 1/Jup 18 Cp/Sat 3 Ar/Uran 14 Tr
Nep 18 Vr/Plut 29 Ce/N Node 11 Sg

	Sun	Merc	Venus	Mars
Oct. 1	7 Lb	20 Vr	7 Vr	0 Cp
6	12 Lb	26 Vr	13 Vr	4 Cp
11	17 Lb	4 Lb	19 Vr	7 Cp
16	22 Lb	13 Lb	25 Vr	11 Cp
21	27 Lb	21 Lb	2 Lb	14 Cp
26	2 Sc	0 Sc	8 Lb	18 Cp
31	7 Sc	8 Sc	14 Lb	21 Cp

Oct. 1/Jup 18 Cp/Sat 1 Ar/Uran 13 Tr
Nep 19 Vr/Plut 30 Ce/N Node 9 Sg

	Sun	Merc	Venus	Mars
Nov. 1	8 Sc	10 Sc	15 Lb	22 Cp
6	13 Sc	18 Sc	21 Lb	26 Cp
11	18 Sc	26 Sc	28 Lb	29 Cp
16	23 Sc	3 Sg	4 Sc	3 Aq
21	28 Sc	11 Sg	10 Sc	7 Aq
26	3 Sg	18 Sg	17 Sc	11 Aq

Nov. 1/Jup 21 Cp/Sat 29 Pc/Uran 12 Tr
Nep 20 Vr/Plut 0 Lo/N Node 7 Sg

	Sun	Merc	Venus	Mars
Dec. 1	8 Sg	26 Sg	23 Sc	14 Aq
6	13 Sg	3 Cp	29 Sc	18 Aq
11	19 Sg	9 Cp	5 Sg	22 Aq
16	24 Sg	14 Cp	12 Sg	26 Aq
21	29 Sg	16 Cp	18 Sg	29 Aq
26	4 Cp	13 Cp	24 Sg	3 Pc
31	9 Cp	7 Cp	0 Cp	7 Pc

Dec. 1/Jup 26 Cp/Sat 28 Pc/Uran 11 Tr
Nep 21 Vr/Plut 30 Ce/N Node 6 Sg

Moon's Positions

	1	4	7	10	13	16	19	22	25	28	31
Jan.	29 Lo	7 Lb	12 Sc	18 Sg	26 Cp	6 Pc	18 Ar	0 Gm	13 Ce	24 Lo	2 Lb
Feb.	14 Lb	20 Sc	26 Sg	4 Aq	16 Pc	28 Ar	11 Gm	22 Ce	2 Vr	10 Lb	
Mar.	22 Lb	28 Sc	4 Cp	12 Aq	25 Pc	9 Tr	22 Gm	2 Lo	11 Vr	19 Lb	24 Sc
Apr.	6 Sg	12 Cp	20 Aq	3 Ar	18 Tr	2 Ce	13 Lo	21 Vr	27 Lb	3 Sg	
May	9 Cp	16 Aq	27 Pc	11 Tr	26 Gm	9 Lo	18 Vr	24 Lb	30 Sc	6 Cp	12 Aq
June	25 Aq	6 Ar	19 Tr	5 Ce	18 Lo	27 Vr	3 Sc	9 Sg	15 Cp	22 Aq	
July	2 Ar	14 Tr	28 Gm	12 Lo	22 Vr	30 Lb	5 Sg	11 Cp	19 Aq	29 Pc	10 Tr
Aug.	24 Tr	7 Ce	20 Lo	1 Lb	8 Sc	13 Sg	20 Cp	28 Aq	9 Ar	21 Tr	3 Ce
Sept	18 Ce	29 Lo	9 Lb	16 Sc	21 Sg	27 Cp	7 Pc	19 Ar	2 Gm	14 Ce	
Oct.	25 Lo	5 Lb	12 Sc	17 Sg	23 Cp	1 Pc	13 Ar	27 Tr	11 Ce	22 Lo	1 Lb
Nov.	14 Lb	20 Sc	26 Sg	1 Aq	9 Pc	21 Ar	6 Gm	20 Ce	2 Vr	11 Lb	
Dec.	17 Sc	23 Sg	28 Cp	5 Pc	15 Ar	28 Tr	14 Ce	28 Lo	8 Lb	14 Sc	20 Sg

1938

```
            Sun    Merc   Venus  Mars                    Sun    Merc   Venus  Mars
Jan. 1    10 Cp   5 Cp   2 Cp   8 Pc       Feb. 1    11 Aq  19 Cp  11 Aq   1 Ar
      6    15 Cp   0 Cp   8 Cp  12 Pc             6    17 Aq  26 Cp  17 Aq   5 Ar
     11    20 Cp  29 Sg  14 Cp  15 Pc            11    22 Aq   4 Aq  23 Aq   9 Ar
     16    25 Cp   2 Cp  21 Cp  19 Pc            16    27 Aq  11 Aq   0 Pc  12 Ar
     21     0 Aq   6 Cp  27 Cp  23 Pc            21     2 Pc  20 Aq   6 Pc  16 Ar
     26     5 Aq  12 Cp   3 Aq  27 Pc            26     7 Pc  28 Aq  12 Pc  20 Ar
     31    10 Aq  18 Cp   9 Aq   0 Ar
Jan. 1/Jup  3 Aq/Sat 29 Pc/Uran 10 Tr      Feb. 1/Jup 10 Aq/Sat  1 Ar/Uran 10 Tr
Nep 21 Vr/Plut 29 Ce/N Node  4 Sg          Nep 21 Vr/Plut 29 Ce/N Node  3 Sg
```

```
            Sun    Merc   Venus  Mars                    Sun    Merc   Venus  Mars
Mar. 1    10 Pc   3 Pc  16 Pc  22 Ar       Apr. 1    11 Ar  29 Ar  24 Ar  14 Tr
      6    15 Pc  13 Pc  22 Pc  25 Ar             6    16 Ar   4 Tr   1 Tr  18 Tr
     11    20 Pc  22 Pc  28 Pc  29 Ar            11    20 Ar   6 Tr   7 Tr  21 Tr
     16    25 Pc   2 Ar   5 Ar   3 Tr            16    25 Ar   5 Tr  13 Tr  25 Tr
     21     0 Ar  12 Ar  11 Ar   6 Tr            21     0 Tr   2 Tr  19 Tr  28 Tr
     26     5 Ar  21 Ar  17 Ar  10 Tr            26     5 Tr  28 Ar  25 Tr   2 Gm
     31    10 Ar  28 Ar  23 Ar  13 Tr
Mar. 1/Jup 16 Aq/Sat  4 Ar/Uran 10 Tr      Apr. 1/Jup 23 Aq/Sat  8 Ar/Uran 12 Tr
Nep 20 Vr/Plut 28 Ce/N Node  1 Sg          Nep 19 Vr/Plut 28 Ce/N Node 29 Sc
```

```
            Sun    Merc   Venus  Mars                    Sun    Merc   Venus  Mars
May  1    10 Tr  26 Ar   1 Gm   5 Gm       June 1    10 Gm  18 Tr   9 Ce  26 Gm
      6    15 Tr  25 Ar   7 Gm   8 Gm             6    15 Gm  26 Tr  15 Ce  29 Gm
     11    20 Tr  26 Ar  13 Gm  12 Gm            11    19 Gm   6 Gm  21 Ce   3 Ce
     16    24 Tr  29 Ar  20 Gm  15 Gm            16    24 Gm  16 Gm  27 Ce   6 Ce
     21    29 Tr   4 Tr  26 Gm  19 Gm            21    29 Gm  27 Gm   3 Lo   9 Ce
     26     4 Gm  10 Tr   2 Ce  22 Gm            26     4 Ce   8 Ce   9 Lo  13 Ce
     31     9 Gm  17 Tr   8 Ce  25 Gm
May  1/Jup 28 Aq/Sat 12 Ar/Uran 13 Tr      June 1/Jup  2 Pc/Sat 15 Ar/Uran 15 Tr
Nep 19 Vr/Plut 28 Ce/N Node 28 Sc          Nep 18 Vr/Plut 28 Ce/N Node 26 Sc
```

```
            Sun    Merc   Venus  Mars                    Sun    Merc   Venus  Mars
July 1     9 Ce  18 Ce  15 Lo  16 Ce       Aug. 1     8 Lo   5 Vr  20 Vr   6 Lo
      6    13 Ce  28 Ce  20 Lo  19 Ce             6    13 Lo   9 Vr  26 Vr   9 Lo
     11    18 Ce   7 Lo  26 Lo  22 Ce            11    18 Lo  12 Vr   1 Lb  12 Lo
     16    23 Ce  15 Lo   2 Vr  26 Ce            16    22 Lo  12 Vr   7 Lb  15 Lo
     21    28 Ce  22 Lo   8 Vr  29 Ce            21    27 Lo  10 Vr  12 Lb  19 Lo
     26     2 Lo  29 Lo  14 Vr   2 Lo            26     2 Vr   7 Vr  18 Lb  22 Lo
     31     7 Lo   4 Vr  19 Vr   5 Lo            31     7 Vr   2 Vr  23 Lb  25 Lo
July 1/Jup  2 Pc/Sat 17 Ar/Uran 17 Tr      Aug. 1/Jup 30 Aq/Sat 18 Ar/Uran 18 Tr
Nep 19 Vr/Plut 29 Ce/N Node 25 Sc          Nep 19 Vr/Plut 30 Ce/N Node 23 Sc
```

1938

	Sun	Merc	Venus	Mars
Sept 1	8 Vr	1 Vr	24 Lb	26 Lo
6	13 Vr	29 Lo	29 Lb	29 Lo
11	18 Vr	0 Vr	4 Sc	2 Vr
16	22 Vr	5 Vr	9 Sc	5 Vr
21	27 Vr	12 Vr	13 Sc	8 Vr
26	2 Lb	21 Vr	17 Sc	12 Vr

Sept 1/Jup 26 Aq/Sat 17 Ar/Uran 18 Tr
Nep 20 Vr/Plut 1 Lo/N Node 21 Sc

	Sun	Merc	Venus	Mars
Oct. 1	7 Lb	0 Lb	22 Sc	15 Vr
6	12 Lb	9 Lb	25 Sc	18 Vr
11	17 Lb	17 Lb	28 Sc	21 Vr
16	22 Lb	26 Lb	1 Sg	24 Vr
21	27 Lb	4 Sc	3 Sg	27 Vr
26	2 Sc	12 Sc	5 Sg	0 Lb
31	7 Sc	20 Sc	5 Sg	4 Lb

Oct. 1/Jup 23 Aq/Sat 15 Ar/Uran 17 Tr
Nep 21 Vr/Plut 1 Lo/N Node 20 Sc

	Sun	Merc	Venus	Mars
Nov. 1	8 Sc	21 Sc	5 Sg	4 Lb
6	13 Sc	29 Sc	4 Sg	7 Lb
11	18 Sc	6 Sg	2 Sg	11 Lb
16	23 Sc	13 Sg	0 Sg	14 Lb
21	28 Sc	19 Sg	27 Sc	17 Lb
26	3 Sg	25 Sg	24 Sc	20 Lb

Nov. 1/Jup 23 Aq/Sat 13 Ar/Uran 16 Tr
Nep 23 Vr/Plut 2 Lo/N Node 18 Sc

	Sun	Merc	Venus	Mars
Dec. 1	8 Sg	29 Sg	22 Sc	23 Lb
6	13 Sg	0 Cp	20 Sc	26 Lb
11	18 Sg	26 Sg	20 Sc	29 Lb
16	23 Sg	20 Sg	20 Sc	3 Sc
21	28 Sg	14 Sg	22 Sc	6 Sc
26	4 Cp	14 Sg	24 Sc	9 Sc
31	9 Cp	16 Sg	27 Sc	12 Sc

Dec. 1/Jup 25 Aq/Sat 11 Ar/Uran 15 Tr
Nep 23 Vr/Plut 1 Lo/N Node 17 Sc

Moon's Positions

	1	4	7	10	13	16	19	22	25	28	31
Jan.	1 Cp	7 Aq	15 Pc	24 Ar	7 Gm	22 Ce	6 Vr	16 Lb	23 Sc	28 Sg	4 Aq
Feb.	16 Aq	25 Pc	5 Tr	16 Gm	0 Lo	14 Vr	24 Lb	1 Sg	6 Cp	13 Aq	
Mar.	25 Aq	4 Ar	15 Tr	27 Gm	10 Lo	22 Vr	2 Sc	8 Sg	14 Cp	21 Aq	30 Pc
Apr.	13 Ar	26 Tr	8 Ce	20 Lo	1 Lb	10 Sc	16 Sg	22 Cp	28 Aq	8 Ar	
May	20 Tr	4 Ce	17 Lo	28 Vr	6 Sc	13 Sg	18 Cp	24 Aq	2 Ar	14 Tr	29 Gm
June	14 Ce	27 Lo	8 Lb	15 Sc	21 Sg	27 Cp	3 Pc	11 Ar	22 Tr	7 Ce	
July	22 Lo	4 Lb	12 Sc	18 Sg	24 Cp	0 Pc	7 Ar	17 Tr	1 Ce	16 Lo	30 Vr
Aug.	13 Lb	21 Sc	27 Sg	3 Aq	9 Pc	17 Ar	27 Tr	10 Ce	25 Lo	8 Lb	17 Sc
Sept	30 Sc	6 Cp	11 Aq	18 Pc	27 Ar	8 Gm	20 Ce	4 Vr	16 Lb	25 Sc	
Oct.	2 Cp	7 Aq	14 Pc	23 Ar	5 Gm	17 Ce	29 Lo	11 Lb	21 Sc	28 Sg	3 Aq
Nov.	15 Aq	22 Pc	2 Tr	14 Gm	28 Ce	10 Vr	21 Lb	29 Sc	6 Cp	11 Aq	
Dec.	17 Pc	26 Ar	8 Gm	23 Ce	7 Vr	17 Lb	26 Sc	2 Cp	8 Aq	14 Pc	21 Ar

1939

```
          Sun    Merc    Venus   Mars                Sun     Merc    Venus   Mars
Jan. 1   10 Cp   17 Sg   27 Sc   12 Sc    Feb. 1    11 Aq   29 Cp   24 Sg    2 Sg
     6   15 Cp   22 Sg    1 Sg   16 Sc         6    16 Aq    7 Aq    0 Cp    5 Sg
    11   20 Cp   28 Sg    5 Sg   19 Sc        11    21 Aq   15 Aq    5 Cp    8 Sg
    16   25 Cp    5 Cp    9 Sg   22 Sc        16    26 Aq   24 Aq   10 Cp   11 Sg
    21    0 Aq   12 Cp   14 Sg   25 Sc        21     1 Pc    3 Pc   16 Cp   14 Sg
    26    5 Aq   20 Cp   18 Sg   28 Sc        26     6 Pc   12 Pc   21 Cp   17 Sg
    31   10 Aq   27 Cp   23 Sg    1 Sg
```
Jan. 1/Jup 0 Pc/Sat 12 Ar/Uran 14 Tr   Feb. 1/Jup 7 Pc/Sat 13 Ar/Uran 14 Tr
Nep 23 Vr/Plut 1 Lo/N Node 15 Sc   Nep 23 Vr/Plut 0 Lo/N Node 13 Sc

```
          Sun    Merc    Venus   Mars                Sun     Merc    Venus   Mars
Mar. 1   10 Pc   18 Pc   25 Cp   18 Sg    Apr. 1    10 Ar   14 Ar    1 Pc    6 Cp
     6   15 Pc   28 Pc    1 Aq   21 Sg         6    15 Ar   11 Ar    7 Pc    9 Cp
    11   20 Pc    6 Ar    6 Aq   24 Sg        11    20 Ar    7 Ar   13 Pc   11 Cp
    16   25 Pc   13 Ar   12 Aq   27 Sg        16    25 Ar    6 Ar   19 Pc   14 Cp
    21   29 Pc   17 Ar   18 Aq    0 Cp        21     0 Tr    6 Ar   25 Pc   16 Cp
    26    4 Ar   17 Ar   24 Aq    3 Cp        26     5 Tr    9 Ar    0 Ar   19 Cp
    31    9 Ar   15 Ar    0 Pc    5 Cp
```
Mar. 1/Jup 14 Pc/Sat 16 Ar/Uran 14 Tr   Apr. 1/Jup 21 Pc/Sat 20 Ar/Uran 16 Tr
Nep 22 Vr/Plut 30 Ce/N Node 12 Sc   Nep 21 Vr/Plut 29 Ce/N Node 10 Sc

```
          Sun    Merc    Venus   Mars                Sun     Merc    Venus   Mars
May  1   10 Tr   13 Ar    6 Ar   21 Cp    June 1    10 Gm    2 Gm   14 Tr    2 Aq
     6   15 Tr   18 Ar   12 Ar   23 Cp         6    14 Gm   13 Gm   20 Tr    3 Aq
    11   19 Tr   25 Ar   18 Ar   25 Cp        11    19 Gm   24 Gm   26 Tr    4 Aq
    16   24 Tr    2 Tr   24 Ar   27 Cp        16    24 Gm    4 Ce    2 Gm    4 Aq
    21   29 Tr   11 Tr    0 Tr   29 Cp        21    29 Gm   14 Ce    8 Gm    5 Aq
    26    4 Gm   20 Tr    7 Tr    0 Aq        26     4 Ce   23 Ce   14 Gm    5 Aq
    31    9 Gm    0 Gm   13 Tr    2 Aq
```
May 1/Jup 28 Pc/Sat 23 Ar/Uran 17 Tr   June 1/Jup 4 Ar/Sat 27 Ar/Uran 19 Tr
Nep 21 Vr/Plut 29 Ce/N Node 9 Sc   Nep 21 Vr/Plut 30 Ce/N Node 7 Sc

```
          Sun    Merc    Venus   Mars                Sun     Merc    Venus   Mars
July 1    8 Ce    1 Lo   20 Gm    4 Aq    Aug. 1     8 Lo   23 Lo   28 Ce   27 Cp
     6   13 Ce    8 Lo   26 Gm    4 Aq         6    13 Lo   21 Lo    4 Lo   26 Cp
    11   18 Ce   14 Lo    2 Ce    3 Aq        11    17 Lo   17 Lo   10 Lo   25 Cp
    16   23 Ce   19 Lo    8 Ce    2 Aq        16    22 Lo   13 Lo   17 Lo   24 Cp
    21   27 Ce   22 Lo   15 Ce    0 Aq        21    27 Lo   12 Lo   23 Lo   24 Cp
    26    2 Lo   24 Lo   21 Ce   29 Cp        26     2 Vr   14 Lo   29 Lo   24 Cp
    31    7 Lo   24 Lo   27 Ce   28 Cp        31     7 Vr   19 Lo    5 Vr   24 Cp
```
July 1/Jup 7 Ar/Sat 30 Ar/Uran 21 Tr   Aug. 1/Jup 9 Ar/Sat 1 Tr/Uran 22 Tr
Nep 21 Vr/Plut 0 Lo/N Node 5 Sc   Nep 21 Vr/Plut 1 Lo/N Node 4 Sc

1939

```
        Sun    Merc    Venus    Mars                    Sun     Merc    Venus    Mars
Sept 1   8 Vr  20 Lo    6 Vr   24 Cp        Oct. 1    7 Lb   13 Lb    14 Lb    3 Aq
     6  13 Vr  28 Lo   13 Vr   25 Cp             6   12 Lb   22 Lb    20 Lb    5 Aq
    11  17 Vr   7 Vr   19 Vr   26 Cp            11   17 Lb    0 Sc    26 Lb    7 Aq
    16  22 Vr  16 Vr   25 Vr   27 Cp            16   22 Lb    7 Sc     2 Sc   10 Aq
    21  27 Vr  26 Vr    1 Lb   29 Cp            21   27 Lb   15 Sc     9 Sc   12 Aq
    26   2 Lb   5 Lb    7 Lb    1 Aq            26    2 Sc   22 Sc    15 Sc   15 Aq
                                               31    7 Sc   28 Sc    21 Sc   18 Aq
```

Sept 1/Jup 7 Ar/Sat 1 Tr/Uran 22 Tr   Oct. 1/Jup 3 Ar/Sat 29 Ar/Uran 22 Tr
Nep 22 Vr/Plut 2 Lo/N Node 2 Sc   Nep 24 Vr/Plut 3 Lo/N Node 0 Sc

```
        Sun    Merc    Venus    Mars                    Sun     Merc    Venus    Mars
Nov. 1   8 Sc   0 Sg   22 Sc   19 Aq        Dec. 1    8 Sg    3 Sg     0 Cp    7 Pc
     6  13 Sc   6 Sg   29 Sc   22 Aq             6   13 Sg   28 Sc     6 Cp   11 Pc
    11  18 Sc  10 Sg    5 Sg   25 Aq            11   18 Sg   28 Sc    12 Cp   14 Pc
    16  23 Sc  14 Sg   11 Sg   28 Aq            16   23 Sg    2 Sg    18 Cp   17 Pc
    21  28 Sc  13 Sg   17 Sg    1 Pc            21   28 Sg    7 Sg    25 Cp   21 Pc
    26   3 Sg   9 Sg   24 Sg    4 Pc            26    3 Cp   14 Sg     1 Aq   24 Pc
                                               31    8 Cp   21 Sg     7 Aq   27 Pc
```

Nov. 1/Jup 30 Pc/Sat 27 Ar/Uran 20 Tr   Dec. 1/Jup 29 Pc/Sat 25 Ar/Uran 19 Tr
Nep 25 Vr/Plut 3 Lo/N Node 29 Lb   Nep 25 Vr/Plut 3 Lo/N Node 27 Lb

Moon's Positions

	1	4	7	10	13	16	19	22	25	28	31
Jan.	4 Tr	16 Gm	2 Lo	16 Vr	27 Lb	5 Sg	11 Cp	17 Aq	23 Pc	30 Ar	10 Gm
Feb.	24 Gm	10 Lo	25 Vr	6 Sc	14 Sg	20 Cp	26 Aq	2 Ar	9 Tr	19 Gm	
Mar.	3 Ce	18 Lo	3 Lb	15 Sc	23 Sg	29 Cp	4 Pc	11 Ar	19 Tr	30 Gm	13 Lo
Apr.	27 Lo	11 Lb	22 Sc	1 Cp	7 Aq	13 Pc	20 Ar	29 Tr	11 Ce	23 Lo	
May	6 Lb	17 Sc	26 Sg	3 Aq	8 Pc	15 Ar	25 Tr	7 Ce	20 Lo	2 Lb	13 Sc
June	26 Sc	4 Cp	11 Aq	16 Pc	23 Ar	3 Gm	16 Ce	1 Vr	13 Lb	23 Sc	
July	1 Cp	7 Aq	13 Pc	19 Ar	28 Tr	10 Ce	26 Lo	9 Lb	20 Sc	28 Sg	4 Aq
Aug.	16 Aq	21 Pc	28 Ar	6 Gm	19 Ce	4 Vr	19 Lb	29 Sc	7 Cp	13 Aq	18 Pc
Sept	0 Ar	7 Tr	15 Gm	27 Ce	13 Vr	27 Lb	8 Sg	16 Cp	22 Aq	27 Pc	
Oct.	4 Tr	12 Gm	23 Ce	6 Vr	21 Lb	3 Sg	12 Cp	18 Aq	24 Pc	0 Tr	9 Gm
Nov.	22 Gm	3 Lo	16 Vr	29 Lb	11 Sg	20 Cp	26 Aq	2 Ar	9 Tr	18 Gm	
Dec.	0 Lo	13 Vr	25 Lb	6 Sg	15 Cp	22 Aq	27 Pc	4 Tr	13 Gm	26 Ce	9 Vr

1940

	Sun	Merc	Venus	Mars
Jan. 1	9 Cp	22 Sg	8 Aq	28 Pc
6	15 Cp	0 Cp	14 Aq	1 Ar
11	20 Cp	7 Cp	21 Aq	5 Ar
16	25 Cp	15 Cp	27 Aq	8 Ar
21	0 Aq	23 Cp	3 Pc	12 Ar
26	5 Aq	1 Aq	9 Pc	15 Ar
31	10 Aq	9 Aq	15 Pc	18 Ar

Jan. 1/Jup 1 Ar/Sat 24 Ar/Uran 18 Tr
Nep 26 Vr/Plut 2 Lo/N Node 26 Lb

	Sun	Merc	Venus	Mars
Feb. 1	11 Aq	11 Aq	16 Pc	19 Ar
6	16 Aq	20 Aq	22 Pc	22 Ar
11	21 Aq	29 Aq	29 Pc	26 Ar
16	26 Aq	8 Pc	5 Ar	29 Ar
21	1 Pc	17 Pc	10 Ar	3 Tr
26	6 Pc	24 Pc	16 Ar	6 Tr

Feb. 1/Jup 6 Ar/Sat 26 Ar/Uran 18 Tr
Nep 25 Vr/Plut 2 Lo/N Node 24 Lb

	Sun	Merc	Venus	Mars
Mar. 1	10 Pc	28 Pc	21 Ar	9 Tr
6	15 Pc	0 Ar	27 Ar	12 Tr
11	20 Pc	29 Pc	3 Tr	15 Tr
16	25 Pc	24 Pc	8 Tr	19 Tr
21	0 Ar	20 Pc	14 Tr	22 Tr
26	5 Ar	17 Pc	20 Tr	25 Tr
31	10 Ar	17 Pc	25 Tr	29 Tr

Mar. 1/Jup 12 Ar/Sat 28 Ar/Uran 19 Tr
Nep 25 Vr/Plut 1 Lo/N Node 22 Lb

	Sun	Merc	Venus	Mars
Apr. 1	11 Ar	17 Pc	26 Tr	29 Tr
6	16 Ar	19 Pc	1 Gm	3 Gm
11	21 Ar	23 Pc	6 Gm	6 Gm
16	26 Ar	29 Pc	11 Gm	9 Gm
21	1 Tr	5 Ar	16 Gm	13 Gm
26	6 Tr	12 Ar	21 Gm	16 Gm

Apr. 1/Jup 19 Ar/Sat 1 Tr/Uran 20 Tr
Nep 24 Vr/Plut 1 Lo/N Node 21 Lb

	Sun	Merc	Venus	Mars
May 1	10 Tr	20 Ar	25 Gm	19 Gm
6	15 Tr	28 Ar	29 Gm	22 Gm
11	20 Tr	8 Tr	3 Ce	26 Gm
16	25 Tr	18 Tr	6 Ce	29 Gm
21	0 Gm	29 Tr	9 Ce	2 Ce
26	5 Gm	10 Gm	11 Ce	5 Ce
31	9 Gm	20 Gm	13 Ce	9 Ce

May 1/Jup 26 Ar/Sat 5 Tr/Uran 21 Tr
Nep 23 Vr/Plut 1 Lo/N Node 19 Lb

	Sun	Merc	Venus	Mars
June 1	10 Gm	22 Gm	13 Ce	9 Ce
6	15 Gm	2 Ce	13 Ce	12 Ce
11	20 Gm	11 Ce	13 Ce	16 Ce
16	25 Gm	18 Ce	11 Ce	19 Ce
21	29 Gm	24 Ce	9 Ce	22 Ce
26	4 Ce	29 Ce	6 Ce	25 Ce

June 1/Jup 3 Tr/Sat 9 Tr/Uran 23 Tr
Nep 23 Vr/Plut 1 Lo/N Node 18 Lb

	Sun	Merc	Venus	Mars
July 1	9 Ce	3 Lo	3 Ce	28 Ce
6	14 Ce	5 Lo	0 Ce	2 Lo
11	19 Ce	5 Lo	28 Gm	5 Lo
16	23 Ce	3 Lo	27 Gm	8 Lo
21	28 Ce	0 Lo	27 Gm	11 Lo
26	3 Lo	27 Ce	28 Gm	14 Lo
31	8 Lo	25 Ce	0 Ce	18 Lo

July 1/Jup 9 Tr/Sat 12 Tr/Uran 25 Tr
Nep 23 Vr/Plut 2 Lo/N Node 16 Lb

	Sun	Merc	Venus	Mars
Aug. 1	9 Lo	25 Ce	0 Ce	18 Lo
6	13 Lo	26 Ce	2 Ce	21 Lo
11	18 Lo	29 Ce	6 Ce	25 Lo
16	23 Lo	5 Lo	9 Ce	28 Lo
21	28 Lo	14 Lo	13 Ce	1 Vr
26	3 Vr	23 Lo	17 Ce	4 Vr
31	7 Vr	3 Vr	22 Ce	7 Vr

Aug. 1/Jup 14 Tr/Sat 14 Tr/Uran 26 Tr
Nep 24 Vr/Plut 3 Lo/N Node 14 Lb

1940

	Sun	Merc	Venus	Mars
Sept 1	8 Vr	5 Vr	23 Ce	8 Vr
6	13 Vr	15 Vr	27 Ce	11 Vr
11	18 Vr	24 Vr	2 Lo	14 Vr
16	23 Vr	3 Lb	7 Lo	17 Vr
21	28 Vr	11 Lb	13 Lo	21 Vr
26	3 Lb	19 Lb	18 Lo	24 Vr

Sept 1/Jup 16 Tr/Sat 15 Tr/Uran 26 Tr
Nep 25 Vr/Plut 3 Lo/N Node 13 Lb

	Sun	Merc	Venus	Mars
Oct. 1	8 Lb	26 Lb	23 Lo	27 Vr
6	13 Lb	4 Sc	29 Lo	0 Lb
11	18 Lb	10 Sc	5 Vr	3 Lb
16	22 Lb	16 Sc	10 Vr	7 Lb
21	27 Lb	22 Sc	16 Vr	10 Lb
26	2 Sc	26 Sc	22 Vr	13 Lb
31	7 Sc	28 Sc	28 Vr	16 Lb

Oct. 1/Jup 15 Tr/Sat 14 Tr/Uran 26 Tr
Nep 26 Vr/Plut 4 Lo/N Node 11 Lb

	Sun	Merc	Venus	Mars
Nov. 1	8 Sc	28 Sc	29 Vr	17 Lb
6	13 Sc	26 Sc	5 Lb	20 Lb
11	18 Sc	21 Sc	11 Lb	24 Lb
16	23 Sc	15 Sc	17 Lb	27 Lb
21	29 Sc	12 Sc	23 Lb	0 Sc
26	4 Sg	14 Sc	29 Lb	3 Sc

Nov. 1/Jup 11 Tr/Sat 12 Tr/Uran 25 Tr
Nep 27 Vr/Plut 4 Lo/N Node 9 Lb

	Sun	Merc	Venus	Mars
Dec. 1	9 Sg	19 Sc	6 Sc	7 Sc
6	14 Sg	25 Sc	12 Sc	10 Sc
11	19 Sg	2 Sg	18 Sc	13 Sc
16	24 Sg	10 Sg	24 Sc	17 Sc
21	29 Sg	17 Sg	0 Sg	20 Sc
26	4 Cp	25 Sg	6 Sg	23 Sc
31	9 Cp	3 Cp	13 Sg	27 Sc

Dec. 1/Jup 7 Tr/Sat 9 Tr/Uran 24 Tr
Nep 27 Vr/Plut 4 Lo/N Node 8 Lb

Moon's Positions

	1	4	7	10	13	16	19	22	25	28	31
Jan.	24 Vr	5 Sc	15 Sg	23 Cp	30 Aq	5 Ar	12 Tr	21 Gm	4 Lo	19 Vr	2 Sc
Feb.	16 Sc	25 Sg	2 Aq	8 Pc	14 Ar	20 Tr	29 Gm	12 Lo	28 Vr	12 Sc	
Mar.	9 Sg	17 Cp	24 Aq	29 Pc	5 Tr	12 Gm	22 Ce	5 Vr	21 Lb	4 Sg	14 Cp
Apr.	26 Cp	2 Pc	8 Ar	14 Tr	21 Gm	1 Lo	14 Vr	29 Lb	12 Sg	22 Cp	
May	29 Aq	5 Ar	11 Tr	18 Gm	28 Ce	10 Vr	23 Lb	7 Sg	17 Cp	25 Aq	1 Ar
June	13 Ar	19 Tr	28 Gm	9 Lo	21 Vr	3 Sc	15 Sg	26 Cp	3 Pc	9 Ar	
July	15 Tr	23 Gm	5 Lo	17 Vr	30 Lb	11 Sg	21 Cp	29 Aq	5 Ar	11 Tr	18 Gm
Aug.	1 Ce	14 Lo	28 Vr	11 Sc	22 Sg	0 Aq	7 Pc	13 Ar	19 Tr	26 Gm	7 Lo
Sept	22 Lo	7 Lb	21 Sc	2 Cp	10 Aq	16 Pc	22 Ar	27 Tr	5 Ce	16 Lo	
Oct.	0 Lb	15 Sc	28 Sg	7 Aq	13 Pc	19 Ar	24 Tr	1 Ce	11 Lo	23 Vr	9 Sc
Nov.	24 Sc	7 Cp	16 Aq	22 Pc	27 Ar	4 Gm	11 Ce	21 Lo	3 Lb	17 Sc	
Dec.	1 Cp	11 Aq	18 Pc	24 Ar	30 Tr	8 Ce	18 Lo	29 Vr	12 Sc	25 Sg	6 Aq

1941

	Sun	Merc	Venus	Mars
Jan. 1	10 Cp	4 Cp	14 Sg	27 Sc
6	15 Cp	12 Cp	20 Sg	1 Sg
11	20 Cp	20 Cp	26 Sg	4 Sg
16	25 Cp	28 Cp	3 Cp	8 Sg
21	1 Aq	7 Aq	9 Cp	11 Sg
26	6 Aq	16 Aq	15 Cp	14 Sg
31	11 Aq	24 Aq	21 Cp	18 Sg

Jan. 1/Jup 6 Tr/Sat 8 Tr/Uran 23 Tr
Nep 28 Vr/Plut 4 Lo/N Node 6 Lb

	Sun	Merc	Venus	Mars
Feb. 1	12 Aq	26 Aq	23 Cp	18 Sg
6	17 Aq	4 Pc	29 Cp	22 Sg
11	22 Aq	10 Pc	5 Aq	25 Sg
16	27 Aq	13 Pc	11 Aq	29 Sg
21	2 Pc	12 Pc	18 Aq	2 Cp
26	7 Pc	8 Pc	24 Aq	6 Cp

Feb. 1/Jup 7 Tr/Sat 8 Tr/Uran 22 Tr
Nep 27 Vr/Plut 3 Lo/N Node 5 Lb

	Sun	Merc	Venus	Mars
Mar. 1	10 Pc	5 Pc	28 Aq	8 Cp
6	15 Pc	1 Pc	4 Pc	11 Cp
11	20 Pc	29 Aq	10 Pc	14 Cp
16	25 Pc	0 Pc	16 Pc	18 Cp
21	0 Ar	3 Pc	23 Pc	21 Cp
26	5 Ar	7 Pc	29 Pc	25 Cp
31	10 Ar	13 Pc	5 Ar	28 Cp

Mar. 1/Jup 11 Tr/Sat 10 Tr/Uran 23 Tr
Nep 27 Vr/Plut 2 Lo/N Node 3 Lb

	Sun	Merc	Venus	Mars
Apr. 1	11 Ar	14 Pc	6 Ar	29 Cp
6	16 Ar	21 Pc	12 Ar	2 Aq
11	21 Ar	28 Pc	19 Ar	6 Aq
16	26 Ar	6 Ar	25 Ar	9 Aq
21	1 Tr	15 Ar	1 Tr	13 Aq
26	5 Tr	24 Ar	7 Tr	16 Aq

Apr. 1/Jup 17 Tr/Sat 13 Tr/Uran 24 Tr
Nep 26 Vr/Plut 2 Lo/N Node 1 Lb

	Sun	Merc	Venus	Mars
May 1	10 Tr	4 Tr	13 Tr	20 Aq
6	15 Tr	15 Tr	19 Tr	23 Aq
11	20 Tr	26 Tr	26 Tr	26 Aq
16	25 Tr	6 Gm	2 Gm	0 Pc
21	0 Gm	16 Gm	8 Gm	3 Pc
26	4 Gm	24 Gm	14 Gm	7 Pc
31	9 Gm	2 Ce	20 Gm	10 Pc

May 1/Jup 24 Tr/Sat 17 Tr/Uran 25 Tr
Nep 25 Vr/Plut 2 Lo/N Node 30 Vr

	Sun	Merc	Venus	Mars
June 1	10 Gm	3 Ce	21 Gm	11 Pc
6	15 Gm	9 Ce	28 Gm	14 Pc
11	20 Gm	13 Ce	4 Ce	17 Pc
16	24 Gm	15 Ce	10 Ce	20 Pc
21	29 Gm	16 Ce	16 Ce	23 Pc
26	4 Ce	14 Ce	22 Ce	26 Pc

June 1/Jup 1 Gm/Sat 21 Tr/Uran 27 Tr
Nep 25 Vr/Plut 3 Lo/N Node 28 Vr

	Sun	Merc	Venus	Mars
July 1	9 Ce	12 Ce	28 Ce	29 Pc
6	14 Ce	9 Ce	4 Lo	2 Ar
11	18 Ce	7 Ce	10 Lo	5 Ar
16	23 Ce	6 Ce	16 Lo	8 Ar
21	28 Ce	8 Ce	23 Lo	10 Ar
26	3 Lo	13 Ce	29 Lo	13 Ar
31	7 Lo	19 Ce	5 Vr	15 Ar

July 1/Jup 8 Gm/Sat 24 Tr/Uran 29 Tr
Nep 25 Vr/Plut 3 Lo/N Node 27 Vr

	Sun	Merc	Venus	Mars
Aug. 1	8 Lo	21 Ce	6 Vr	15 Ar
6	13 Lo	0 Lo	12 Vr	17 Ar
11	18 Lo	9 Lo	18 Vr	19 Ar
16	23 Lo	20 Lo	24 Vr	21 Ar
21	28 Lo	0 Vr	0 Lb	22 Ar
26	2 Vr	9 Vr	6 Lb	23 Ar
31	7 Vr	18 Vr	12 Lb	23 Ar

Aug. 1/Jup 14 Gm/Sat 27 Tr/Uran 30 Tr
Nep 26 Vr/Plut 4 Lo/N Node 25 Vr

1941

```
           Sun    Merc   Venus   Mars                    Sun    Merc   Venus   Mars
Sept  1   8 Vr   20 Vr   13 Lb   24 Ar      Oct.  1   7 Lb    3 Sc   19 Sc   20 Ar
      6  13 Vr   28 Vr   19 Lb   24 Ar            6  12 Lb    8 Sc   24 Sc   18 Ar
     11  18 Vr    6 Lb   25 Lb   24 Ar           11  17 Lb   11 Sc    0 Sg   17 Ar
     16  23 Vr   14 Lb    1 Sc   23 Ar           16  22 Lb   12 Sc    6 Sg   15 Ar
     21  28 Vr   21 Lb    7 Sc   22 Ar           21  27 Lb   10 Sc   12 Sg   14 Ar
     26   3 Lb   27 Lb   13 Sc   21 Ar           26   2 Sc    5 Sc   17 Sg   13 Ar
                                                 31   7 Sc   29 Lb   23 Sg   12 Ar
```

Sept 1/Jup 19 Gm/Sat 28 Tr/Uran 0 Gm   Oct. 1/Jup 21 Gm/Sat 28 Tr/Uran 0 Gm
Nep 27 Vr/Plut 5 Lo/N Node 23 Vr   Nep 28 Vr/Plut 5 Lo/N Node 22 Vr

```
           Sun    Merc   Venus   Mars                    Sun    Merc   Venus   Mars
Nov.  1   8 Sc   28 Lb   24 Sg   12 Ar      Dec.  1   8 Sg   27 Sc   25 Cp   14 Ar
      6  13 Sc   26 Lb    0 Cp   11 Ar            6  13 Sg    5 Sg    0 Aq   15 Ar
     11  18 Sc   29 Lb    5 Cp   11 Ar           11  19 Sg   12 Sg    4 Aq   17 Ar
     16  23 Sc    5 Sc   10 Cp   11 Ar           16  24 Sg   20 Sg    9 Aq   18 Ar
     21  28 Sc   12 Sc   15 Cp   12 Ar           21  29 Sg   28 Sg   12 Aq   20 Ar
     26   3 Sg   19 Sc   21 Cp   13 Ar           26   4 Cp    6 Cp   15 Aq   22 Ar
                                                 31   9 Cp   14 Cp   18 Aq   24 Ar
```

Nov. 1/Jup 21 Gm/Sat 26 Tr/Uran 29 Tr   Dec. 1/Jup 17 Gm/Sat 24 Tr/Uran 28 Tr
Nep 29 Vr/Plut 6 Lo/N Node 20 Vr   Nep 30 Vr/Plut 6 Lo/N Node 18 Vr

Moon's Positions

```
         1       4       7      10      13      16      19      22      25      28      31
Jan.  19 Aq  26 Pc   2 Tr   8 Gm  17 Ce  28 Lo  10 Lb  22 Sc   4 Cp  14 Aq  22 Pc
Feb.   4 Ar  10 Tr  16 Gm  25 Ce   7 Vr  20 Lb   3 Sg  14 Cp  23 Aq   0 Ar
Mar.  12 Ar  18 Tr  24 Gm   3 Lo  15 Vr  30 Lb  14 Sg  24 Cp   2 Pc   9 Ar  14 Tr
Apr.  26 Tr   2 Ce  11 Lo  23 Vr   9 Sc  23 Sg   4 Aq  12 Pc  18 Ar  23 Tr
May   29 Gm   7 Lo  17 Vr   2 Sc  17 Sg  30 Cp   9 Pc  15 Ar  20 Tr  26 Gm   4 Lo
June  16 Lo  27 Vr  10 Sc  25 Sg   8 Aq  17 Pc  23 Ar  29 Tr   5 Ce  14 Lo
July  24 Vr   6 Sc  19 Sg   3 Aq  13 Pc  19 Ar  25 Tr   1 Ce  10 Lo  20 Vr   2 Sc
Aug.  16 Sc  29 Sg  11 Aq  20 Pc  27 Ar   3 Gm  10 Ce  19 Lo   0 Lb  13 Sc  26 Sg
Sept  10 Cp  20 Aq  29 Pc   5 Tr  11 Gm  17 Ce  27 Lo  10 Lb  24 Sc   7 Cp
Oct.  17 Aq  25 Pc   2 Tr   7 Gm  13 Ce  21 Lo   3 Lb  18 Sc   3 Cp  14 Aq  22 Pc
Nov.   4 Ar  10 Tr  16 Gm  22 Ce  30 Lo  11 Lb  26 Sc  12 Cp  23 Aq   1 Ar
Dec.   7 Tr  13 Gm  19 Ce  26 Lo   6 Lb  19 Sc   5 Cp  18 Aq  28 Pc   4 Tr  10 Gm
```

1942

	Sun	Merc	Venus	Mars
Jan. 1	10 Cp	16 Cp	18 Aq	25 Ar
6	15 Cp	24 Cp	20 Aq	27 Ar
11	20 Cp	2 Aq	21 Aq	0 Tr
16	25 Cp	10 Aq	21 Aq	2 Tr
21	0 Aq	18 Aq	20 Aq	5 Tr
26	5 Aq	24 Aq	18 Aq	7 Tr
31	10 Aq	27 Aq	15 Aq	10 Tr

Jan. 1/Jup 13 Gm/Sat 22 Tr/Uran 27 Tr
Nep 30 Vr/Plut 5 Lo/N Node 17 Vr

	Sun	Merc	Venus	Mars
Feb. 1	12 Aq	27 Aq	14 Aq	10 Tr
6	17 Aq	25 Aq	11 Aq	13 Tr
11	22 Aq	19 Aq	9 Aq	16 Tr
16	27 Aq	14 Aq	7 Aq	19 Tr
21	2 Pc	12 Aq	6 Aq	22 Tr
26	7 Pc	12 Aq	6 Aq	25 Tr

Feb. 1/Jup 11 Gm/Sat 22 Tr/Uran 26 Tr
Nep 30 Vr/Plut 4 Lo/N Node 15 Vr

	Sun	Merc	Venus	Mars
Mar. 1	10 Pc	14 Aq	6 Aq	26 Tr
6	15 Pc	18 Aq	8 Aq	29 Tr
11	20 Pc	23 Aq	10 Aq	2 Gm
16	25 Pc	29 Aq	13 Aq	5 Gm
21	0 Ar	5 Pc	16 Aq	8 Gm
26	5 Ar	13 Pc	20 Aq	11 Gm
31	10 Ar	21 Pc	24 Aq	14 Gm

Mar. 1/Jup 12 Gm/Sat 23 Tr/Uran 27 Tr
Nep 29 Vr/Plut 4 Lo/N Node 14 Vr

	Sun	Merc	Venus	Mars
Apr. 1	11 Ar	23 Pc	25 Aq	15 Gm
6	16 Ar	1 Ar	0 Pc	18 Gm
11	20 Ar	11 Ar	4 Pc	21 Gm
16	25 Ar	21 Ar	9 Pc	24 Gm
21	0 Tr	1 Tr	14 Pc	27 Gm
26	5 Tr	12 Tr	19 Pc	0 Ce

Apr. 1/Jup 16 Gm/Sat 26 Tr/Uran 28 Tr
Nep 28 Vr/Plut 4 Lo/N Node 12 Vr

	Sun	Merc	Venus	Mars
May 1	10 Tr	22 Tr	25 Pc	3 Ce
6	15 Tr	1 Gm	0 Ar	6 Ce
11	20 Tr	10 Gm	5 Ar	9 Ce
16	25 Tr	16 Gm	11 Ar	12 Ce
21	29 Tr	21 Gm	16 Ar	15 Ce
26	4 Gm	24 Gm	22 Ar	18 Ce
31	9 Gm	26 Gm	28 Ar	21 Ce

May 1/Jup 21 Gm/Sat 29 Tr/Uran 29 Tr
Nep 27 Vr/Plut 4 Lo/N Node 10 Vr

	Sun	Merc	Venus	Mars
June 1	10 Gm	26 Gm	29 Ar	22 Ce
6	15 Gm	25 Gm	5 Tr	25 Ce
11	19 Gm	22 Gm	10 Tr	28 Ce
16	24 Gm	20 Gm	16 Tr	1 Lo
21	29 Gm	18 Gm	22 Tr	4 Lo
26	4 Ce	17 Gm	28 Tr	7 Lo

June 1/Jup 28 Gm/Sat 3 Gm/Uran 1 Gm
Nep 27 Vr/Plut 4 Lo/N Node 9 Vr

	Sun	Merc	Venus	Mars
July 1	9 Ce	19 Gm	4 Gm	10 Lo
6	13 Ce	22 Gm	10 Gm	14 Lo
11	18 Ce	28 Gm	15 Gm	17 Lo
16	23 Ce	5 Ce	21 Gm	20 Lo
21	28 Ce	13 Ce	27 Gm	23 Lo
26	2 Lo	23 Ce	3 Ce	26 Lo
31	7 Lo	4 Lo	9 Ce	29 Lo

July 1/Jup 5 Ce/Sat 7 Gm/Uran 3 Gm
Nep 27 Vr/Plut 5 Lo/N Node 7 Vr

	Sun	Merc	Venus	Mars
Aug. 1	8 Lo	6 Lo	10 Ce	0 Vr
6	13 Lo	16 Lo	17 Ce	3 Vr
11	18 Lo	26 Lo	23 Ce	6 Vr
16	23 Lo	5 Vr	29 Ce	9 Vr
21	27 Lo	14 Vr	5 Lo	12 Vr
26	2 Vr	22 Vr	11 Lo	16 Vr
31	7 Vr	0 Lb	17 Lo	19 Vr

Aug. 1/Jup 12 Ce/Sat 10 Gm/Uran 4 Gm
Nep 28 Vr/Plut 5 Lo/N Node 6 Vr

1942

```
            Sun    Merc   Venus   Mars              Sun    Merc   Venus   Mars
Sept 1    8 Vr    1 Lb   18 Lo   19 Vr    Oct. 1   7 Lb   26 Lb   25 Vr    9 Lb
     6   13 Vr    8 Lb   24 Lo   23 Vr         6  12 Lb   23 Lb    2 Lb   12 Lb
    11   18 Vr   14 Lb    0 Vr   26 Vr        11  17 Lb   17 Lb    8 Lb   15 Lb
    16   23 Vr   19 Lb    7 Vr   29 Vr        16  22 Lb   12 Lb   14 Lb   19 Lb
    21   27 Vr   23 Lb   13 Vr    2 Lb        21  27 Lb   11 Lb   20 Lb   22 Lb
    26    2 Lb   26 Lb   19 Vr    6 Lb        26   2 Sc   14 Lb   27 Lb   25 Lb
                                              31   7 Sc   19 Lb    3 Sc   29 Lb
```

Sept 1/Jup 18 Ce/Sat 12 Gm/Uran 5 Gm   Oct. 1/Jup 22 Ce/Sat 12 Gm/Uran 4 Gm
Nep 29 Vr/Plut 6 Lo/N Node 4 Vr   Nep 30 Vr/Plut 7 Lo/N Node 2 Vr

```
            Sun    Merc   Venus   Mars              Sun    Merc   Venus   Mars
Nov. 1    8 Sc   21 Lb    4 Sc   29 Lb    Dec. 1   8 Sg    8 Sg   12 Sg   20 Sc
     6   13 Sc   28 Lb   10 Sc    3 Sc         6  13 Sg   16 Sg   18 Sg   23 Sc
    11   18 Sc    6 Sc   17 Sc    6 Sc        11  18 Sg   24 Sg   24 Sg   27 Sc
    16   23 Sc   14 Sc   23 Sc   10 Sc        16  23 Sg    2 Cp    1 Cp    0 Sg
    21   28 Sc   22 Sc   29 Sc   13 Sc        21  28 Sg   10 Cp    7 Cp    4 Sg
    26    3 Sg    0 Sg    5 Sg   16 Sc        26   4 Cp   17 Cp   13 Cp    7 Sg
                                              31   9 Cp   25 Cp   19 Cp   11 Sg
```

Nov. 1/Jup 25 Ce/Sat 11 Gm/Uran 4 Gm   Dec. 1/Jup 25 Ce/Sat 9 Gm/Uran 2 Gm
Nep 1 Lb/Plut 7 Lo/N Node 1 Vr   Nep 2 Lb/Plut 7 Lo/N Node 29 Lo

Moon's Positions

	1	4	7	10	13	16	19	22	25	28	31
Jan.	22 Gm	28 Ce	6 Vr	16 Lb	28 Sc	13 Cp	26 Aq	6 Ar	12 Tr	18 Gm	24 Ce
Feb.	7 Lo	16 Vr	27 Lb	9 Sg	22 Cp	4 Pc	13 Ar	20 Tr	26 Gm	3 Lo	
Mar.	15 Lo	25 Vr	7 Sc	20 Sg	2 Aq	13 Pc	21 Ar	28 Tr	4 Ce	10 Lo	20 Vr
Apr.	4 Lb	17 Sc	1 Cp	13 Aq	22 Pc	30 Ar	6 Gm	12 Ce	18 Lo	28 Vr	
May	11 Sc	26 Sg	9 Aq	19 Pc	27 Ar	3 Gm	8 Ce	14 Lo	23 Vr	5 Sc	20 Sg
June	5 Cp	19 Aq	29 Pc	6 Tr	12 Gm	17 Ce	24 Lo	2 Lb	13 Sc	28 Sg	
July	13 Aq	25 Pc	3 Tr	9 Gm	14 Ce	21 Lo	28 Vr	9 Sc	22 Sg	7 Aq	20 Pc
Aug.	3 Ar	11 Tr	17 Gm	23 Ce	30 Lo	8 Lb	19 Sc	2 Cp	16 Aq	28 Pc	7 Tr
Sept	20 Tr	26 Gm	1 Lo	9 Vr	18 Lb	0 Sg	13 Cp	25 Aq	6 Ar	15 Tr	
Oct.	22 Gm	27 Ce	4 Vr	14 Lb	26 Sc	9 Cp	21 Aq	2 Ar	11 Tr	18 Gm	23 Ce
Nov.	5 Lo	12 Vr	22 Lb	6 Sg	20 Cp	2 Pc	12 Ar	19 Tr	26 Gm	1 Lo	
Dec.	7 Vr	16 Lb	29 Sc	14 Cp	28 Aq	9 Ar	16 Tr	23 Gm	28 Ce	4 Vr	11 Lb

1943

	Sun	Merc	Venus	Mars
Jan. 1	10 Cp	27 Cp	21 Cp	12 Sg
6	15 Cp	4 Aq	27 Cp	15 Sg
11	20 Cp	9 Aq	3 Aq	19 Sg
16	25 Cp	11 Aq	10 Aq	22 Sg
21	0 Aq	8 Aq	16 Aq	26 Sg
26	5 Aq	2 Aq	22 Aq	29 Sg
31	10 Aq	27 Cp	28 Aq	3 Cp

Jan. 1/Jup 22 Ce/Sat 7 Gm/Uran 1 Gm
Nep 2 Lb/Plut 7 Lo/N Node 28 Lo

	Sun	Merc	Venus	Mars
Feb. 1	11 Aq	26 Cp	0 Pc	4 Cp
6	16 Aq	25 Cp	6 Pc	7 Cp
11	21 Aq	27 Cp	12 Pc	11 Cp
16	26 Aq	0 Aq	18 Pc	15 Cp
21	1 Pc	5 Aq	24 Pc	18 Cp
26	7 Pc	11 Aq	1 Ar	22 Cp

Feb. 1/Jup 18 Ce/Sat 6 Gm/Uran 1 Gm
Nep 2 Lb/Plut 6 Lo/N Node 26 Lo

	Sun	Merc	Venus	Mars
Mar. 1	10 Pc	15 Aq	4 Ar	24 Cp
6	15 Pc	22 Aq	11 Ar	28 Cp
11	20 Pc	0 Pc	17 Ar	2 Aq
16	25 Pc	8 Pc	23 Ar	6 Aq
21	0 Ar	16 Pc	29 Ar	9 Aq
26	4 Ar	25 Pc	5 Tr	13 Aq
31	9 Ar	5 Ar	11 Tr	17 Aq

Mar. 1/Jup 15 Ce/Sat 6 Gm/Uran 1 Gm
Nep 1 Lb/Plut 5 Lo/N Node 24 Lo

	Sun	Merc	Venus	Mars
Apr. 1	10 Ar	7 Ar	12 Tr	18 Aq
6	15 Ar	17 Ar	18 Tr	21 Aq
11	20 Ar	28 Ar	24 Tr	25 Aq
16	25 Ar	8 Tr	0 Gm	29 Aq
21	0 Tr	17 Tr	6 Gm	3 Pc
26	5 Tr	25 Tr	12 Gm	6 Pc

Apr. 1/Jup 16 Ce/Sat 8 Gm/Uran 2 Gm
Nep 0 Lb/Plut 5 Lo/N Node 23 Lo

	Sun	Merc	Venus	Mars
May 1	10 Tr	0 Gm	18 Gm	10 Pc
6	15 Tr	4 Gm	24 Gm	14 Pc
11	19 Tr	6 Gm	29 Gm	18 Pc
16	24 Tr	5 Gm	5 Ce	22 Pc
21	29 Tr	3 Gm	11 Ce	25 Pc
26	4 Gm	0 Gm	16 Ce	29 Pc
31	9 Gm	28 Tr	22 Ce	3 Ar

May 1/Jup 19 Ce/Sat 11 Gm/Uran 3 Gm
Nep 30 Vr/Plut 5 Lo/N Node 21 Lo

	Sun	Merc	Venus	Mars
June 1	10 Gm	28 Tr	23 Ce	3 Ar
6	14 Gm	27 Tr	28 Ce	7 Ar
11	19 Gm	28 Tr	4 Lo	11 Ar
16	24 Gm	1 Gm	9 Lo	14 Ar
21	29 Gm	6 Gm	14 Lo	18 Ar
26	4 Ce	12 Gm	19 Lo	22 Ar

June 1/Jup 24 Ce/Sat 15 Gm/Uran 5 Gm
Nep 29 Vr/Plut 5 Lo/N Node 20 Lo

	Sun	Merc	Venus	Mars
July 1	8 Ce	20 Gm	24 Lo	25 Ar
6	13 Ce	29 Gm	28 Lo	29 Ar
11	18 Ce	9 Ce	3 Vr	2 Tr
16	23 Ce	20 Ce	7 Vr	6 Tr
21	27 Ce	1 Lo	10 Vr	9 Tr
26	2 Lo	11 Lo	14 Vr	12 Tr
31	7 Lo	20 Lo	16 Vr	15 Tr

July 1/Jup 0 Lo/Sat 19 Gm/Uran 7 Gm
Nep 29 Vr/Plut 6 Lo/N Node 18 Lo

	Sun	Merc	Venus	Mars
Aug. 1	8 Lo	22 Lo	17 Vr	16 Tr
6	13 Lo	1 Vr	19 Vr	19 Tr
11	17 Lo	9 Vr	20 Vr	22 Tr
16	22 Lo	16 Vr	21 Vr	25 Tr
21	27 Lo	23 Vr	20 Vr	28 Tr
26	2 Vr	29 Vr	18 Vr	1 Gm
31	7 Vr	4 Lb	16 Vr	4 Gm

Aug. 1/Jup 7 Lo/Sat 23 Gm/Uran 8 Gm
Nep 30 Vr/Plut 7 Lo/N Node 16 Lo

1943

```
             Sun      Merc    Venus    Mars                    Sun      Merc    Venus    Mars
Sept 1     8 Vr     5 Lb    16 Vr     4 Gm      Oct. 1      7 Lb    25 Vr     5 Vr    17 Gm
     6    13 Vr     8 Lb    13 Vr     7 Gm           6     12 Lb    25 Vr     6 Vr    19 Gm
    11    17 Vr     9 Lb    10 Vr     9 Gm          11     17 Lb    29 Vr     8 Vr    20 Gm
    16    22 Vr     8 Lb     7 Vr    12 Gm          16     22 Lb     5 Lb    10 Vr    21 Gm
    21    27 Vr     5 Lb     5 Vr    14 Gm          21     27 Lb    13 Lb    13 Vr    22 Gm
    26     2 Lb    29 Vr     4 Vr    16 Gm          26      2 Sc    22 Lb    17 Vr    22 Gm
                                                    31      7 Sc     0 Sc    21 Vr    22 Gm
```

Sept 1/Jup 14 Lo/Sat 25 Gm/Uran 9 Gm   Oct. 1/Jup 19 Lo/Sat 27 Gm/Uran 9 Gm
Nep 1 Lb/Plut 8 Lo/N Node 15 Lo   Nep 2 Lb/Plut 8 Lo/N Node 13 Lo

```
             Sun      Merc    Venus    Mars                    Sun      Merc    Venus    Mars
Nov. 1     8 Sc     2 Sc    22 Vr    22 Gm      Dec. 1      8 Sg    19 Sg    22 Lb    15 Gm
     6    13 Sc    10 Sc    26 Vr    22 Gm           6     13 Sg    27 Sg    27 Lb    13 Gm
    11    18 Sc    18 Sc     1 Lb    21 Gm          11     18 Sg     4 Cp     3 Sc    11 Gm
    16    23 Sc    26 Sc     6 Lb    20 Gm          16     23 Sg    12 Cp     9 Sc     9 Gm
    21    28 Sc     4 Sg    11 Lb    18 Gm          21     28 Sg    18 Cp    15 Sc     8 Gm
    26     3 Sg    12 Sg    16 Lb    16 Gm          26      3 Cp    23 Cp    20 Sc     6 Gm
                                                    31      8 Cp    25 Cp    26 Sc     6 Gm
```

Nov. 1/Jup 24 Lo/Sat 26 Gm/Uran 8 Gm   Dec. 1/Jup 27 Lo/Sat 24 Gm/Uran 7 Gm
Nep 3 Lb/Plut 9 Lo/N Node 11 Lo   Nep 4 Lb/Plut 9 Lo/N Node 10 Lo

Moon's Positions

	1	4	7	10	13	16	19	22	25	28	31
Jan.	25 Lb	7 Sg	23 Cp	7 Pc	18 Ar	26 Tr	2 Ce	7 Lo	13 Vr	21 Lb	1 Sg
Feb.	16 Sg	1 Aq	15 Pc	27 Ar	4 Gm	10 Ce	16 Lo	22 Vr	1 Sc	12 Sg	
Mar.	26 Sg	9 Aq	23 Pc	4 Tr	13 Gm	18 Ce	24 Lo	1 Lb	11 Sc	22 Sg	5 Aq
Apr.	19 Aq	2 Ar	12 Tr	20 Gm	26 Ce	2 Vr	10 Lb	21 Sc	3 Cp	16 Aq	
May	27 Pc	8 Tr	16 Gm	22 Ce	28 Lo	5 Lb	15 Sc	29 Sg	12 Aq	24 Pc	4 Tr
June	17 Tr	25 Gm	0 Lo	6 Vr	13 Lb	24 Sc	8 Cp	22 Aq	5 Ar	14 Tr	
July	21 Gm	27 Ce	3 Vr	9 Lb	18 Sc	1 Cp	17 Aq	1 Ar	11 Tr	18 Gm	24 Ce
Aug.	6 Lo	11 Vr	18 Lb	27 Sc	10 Cp	25 Aq	9 Ar	20 Tr	27 Gm	3 Lo	9 Vr
Sept	21 Vr	28 Lb	7 Sg	19 Cp	3 Pc	17 Ar	29 Tr	6 Ce	12 Lo	17 Vr	
Oct.	25 Lb	4 Sg	15 Cp	28 Aq	11 Ar	23 Tr	2 Ce	8 Lo	13 Vr	21 Lb	0 Sg
Nov.	14 Sg	26 Cp	8 Pc	20 Ar	1 Gm	10 Ce	16 Lo	21 Vr	29 Lb	10 Sg	
Dec.	22 Cp	5 Pc	17 Ar	27 Tr	5 Ce	12 Lo	17 Vr	24 Lb	4 Sg	17 Cp	1 Pc

1944

```
             Sun    Merc   Venus   Mars                    Sun    Merc   Venus   Mars
Jan. 1    9 Cp   25 Cp   27 Sc    5 Gm      Feb. 1   11 Aq   16 Cp    5 Cp    8 Gm
      6   15 Cp   21 Cp    3 Sg    5 Gm            6   16 Aq   22 Cp   11 Cp    9 Gm
     11   20 Cp   15 Cp    9 Sg    5 Gm           11   21 Aq   28 Cp   17 Cp   10 Gm
     16   25 Cp   10 Cp   15 Sg    5 Gm           16   26 Aq    5 Aq   23 Cp   12 Gm
     21    0 Aq    9 Cp   21 Sg    6 Gm           21    1 Pc   12 Aq   29 Cp   14 Gm
     26    5 Aq   11 Cp   27 Sg    6 Gm           26    6 Pc   20 Aq    5 Aq   16 Gm
     31   10 Aq   15 Cp    3 Cp    7 Gm
Jan. 1/Jup 27 Lo/Sat 22 Gm/Uran  6 Gm      Feb. 1/Jup 23 Lo/Sat 20 Gm/Uran  5 Gm
Nep  4 Lb/Plut  8 Lo/N Node  8 Lo          Nep  4 Lb/Plut  8 Lo/N Node  7 Lo
```

```
             Sun    Merc   Venus   Mars                    Sun    Merc   Venus   Mars
Mar. 1   10 Pc   26 Aq   10 Aq   17 Gm      Apr. 1   11 Ar   25 Ar   18 Pc    2 Ce
      6   15 Pc    5 Pc   16 Aq   19 Gm            6   16 Ar    4 Tr   24 Pc    4 Ce
     11   20 Pc   14 Pc   22 Aq   22 Gm           11   21 Ar   10 Tr    1 Ar    7 Ce
     16   25 Pc   23 Pc   29 Aq   24 Gm           16   26 Ar   15 Tr    7 Ar   10 Ce
     21    0 Ar    3 Ar    5 Pc   26 Gm           21    1 Tr   16 Tr   13 Ar   12 Ce
     26    5 Ar   13 Ar   11 Pc   29 Gm           26    6 Tr   16 Tr   19 Ar   15 Ce
     31   10 Ar   23 Ar   17 Pc    1 Ce
Mar. 1/Jup 20 Lo/Sat 20 Gm/Uran  5 Gm      Apr. 1/Jup 17 Lo/Sat 21 Gm/Uran  6 Gm
Nep  3 Lb/Plut  7 Lo/N Node  5 Lo          Nep  3 Lb/Plut  6 Lo/N Node  3 Lo
```

```
             Sun    Merc   Venus   Mars                    Sun    Merc   Venus   Mars
May  1   11 Tr   13 Tr   25 Ar   18 Ce      June 1   10 Gm   16 Tr    3 Gm    5 Lo
      6   15 Tr   10 Tr    1 Tr   21 Ce            6   15 Gm   22 Tr    9 Gm    8 Lo
     11   20 Tr    8 Tr    7 Tr   23 Ce           11   20 Gm   29 Tr   16 Gm   11 Lo
     16   25 Tr    7 Tr   14 Tr   26 Ce           16   25 Gm    8 Gm   22 Gm   14 Lo
     21    0 Gm    8 Tr   20 Tr   29 Ce           21   29 Gm   17 Gm   28 Gm   17 Lo
     26    5 Gm   11 Tr   26 Tr    2 Lo           26    4 Ce   28 Gm    4 Ce   20 Lo
     31    9 Gm   15 Tr    2 Gm    5 Lo
May  1/Jup 18 Lo/Sat 24 Gm/Uran  7 Gm      June 1/Jup 20 Lo/Sat 28 Gm/Uran  9 Gm
Nep  2 Lb/Plut  6 Lo/N Node  2 Lo          Nep  1 Lb/Plut  7 Lo/N Node  0 Lo
```

```
             Sun    Merc   Venus   Mars                    Sun    Merc   Venus   Mars
July 1    9 Ce    8 Ce   10 Ce   23 Lo      Aug. 1    9 Lo    4 Vr   18 Lo   12 Vr
      6   14 Ce   19 Ce   16 Ce   26 Lo            6   13 Lo   10 Vr   24 Lo   15 Vr
     11   19 Ce   29 Ce   22 Ce   29 Lo           11   18 Lo   16 Vr    1 Vr   19 Vr
     16   23 Ce    9 Lo   29 Ce    2 Vr           16   23 Lo   20 Vr    7 Vr   22 Vr
     21   28 Ce   18 Lo    5 Lo    5 Vr           21   28 Lo   22 Vr   13 Vr   25 Vr
     26    3 Lo   26 Lo   11 Lo    9 Vr           26    3 Vr   22 Vr   19 Vr   28 Vr
     31    8 Lo    3 Vr   17 Lo   12 Vr           31    7 Vr   20 Vr   25 Vr    1 Lb
July 1/Jup 25 Lo/Sat  1 Ce/Uran 11 Gm      Aug. 1/Jup  1 Vr/Sat  5 Ce/Uran 12 Gm
Nep  2 Lb/Plut  7 Lo/N Node 29 Ce          Nep  2 Lb/Plut  8 Lo/N Node 27 Ce
```

1944

	Sun	Merc	Venus	Mars
Sept 1	8 Vr	20 Vr	26 Vr	2 Lb
6	13 Vr	15 Vr	3 Lb	5 Lb
11	18 Vr	11 Vr	9 Lb	8 Lb
16	23 Vr	9 Vr	15 Lb	12 Lb
21	28 Vr	10 Vr	21 Lb	15 Lb
26	3 Lb	16 Vr	27 Lb	18 Lb

Sept 1/Jup 8 Vr/Sat 8 Ce/Uran 13 Gm
Nep 3 Lb/Plut 9 Lo/N Node 25 Ce

	Sun	Merc	Venus	Mars
Oct. 1	8 Lb	23 Vr	3 Sc	22 Lb
6	13 Lb	2 Lb	10 Sc	25 Lb
11	18 Lb	10 Lb	16 Sc	28 Lb
16	23 Lb	19 Lb	22 Sc	2 Sc
21	27 Lb	28 Lb	28 Sc	5 Sc
26	2 Sc	6 Sc	4 Sg	9 Sc
31	7 Sc	14 Sc	10 Sg	12 Sc

Oct. 1/Jup 14 Vr/Sat 10 Ce/Uran 13 Gm
Nep 4 Lb/Plut 10 Lo/N Node 24 Ce

	Sun	Merc	Venus	Mars
Nov. 1	8 Sc	15 Sc	11 Sg	13 Sc
6	13 Sc	23 Sc	17 Sg	16 Sc
11	18 Sc	1 Sg	24 Sg	20 Sc
16	24 Sc	8 Sg	0 Cp	23 Sc
21	29 Sc	16 Sg	6 Cp	27 Sc
26	4 Sg	23 Sg	12 Cp	0 Sg

Nov. 1/Jup 20 Vr/Sat 11 Ce/Uran 12 Gm
Nep 5 Lb/Plut 10 Lo/N Node 22 Ce

	Sun	Merc	Venus	Mars
Dec. 1	9 Sg	29 Sg	18 Cp	4 Sg
6	14 Sg	5 Cp	24 Cp	7 Sg
11	19 Sg	8 Cp	0 Aq	11 Sg
16	24 Sg	8 Cp	6 Aq	15 Sg
21	29 Sg	4 Cp	12 Aq	18 Sg
26	4 Cp	27 Sg	18 Aq	22 Sg
31	9 Cp	23 Sg	23 Aq	26 Sg

Dec. 1/Jup 25 Vr/Sat 9 Ce/Uran 11 Gm
Nep 6 Lb/Plut 10 Lo/N Node 20 Ce

Moon's Positions

	1	4	7	10	13	16	19	22	25	28	31
Jan.	15 Pc	27 Ar	7 Gm	14 Ce	20 Lo	25 Vr	2 Sc	11 Sg	25 Cp	10 Pc	24 Ar
Feb.	7 Tr	16 Gm	23 Ce	28 Lo	4 Lb	11 Sc	20 Sg	3 Aq	18 Pc	3 Tr	
Mar.	30 Tr	8 Ce	14 Lo	19 Vr	25 Lb	3 Sg	13 Cp	26 Aq	11 Ar	25 Tr	4 Ce
Apr.	16 Ce	22 Lo	28 Vr	5 Sc	13 Sg	23 Cp	6 Pc	20 Ar	3 Gm	12 Ce	
May	19 Lo	24 Vr	1 Sc	10 Sg	20 Cp	2 Pc	15 Ar	27 Tr	7 Ce	15 Lo	20 Vr
June	2 Lb	9 Sc	19 Sg	0 Aq	13 Pc	25 Ar	7 Gm	16 Ce	23 Lo	28 Vr	
July	5 Sc	14 Sg	26 Cp	9 Pc	22 Ar	3 Gm	12 Ce	19 Lo	25 Vr	0 Sc	8 Sg
Aug.	22 Sg	4 Aq	19 Pc	3 Tr	13 Gm	21 Ce	28 Lo	3 Lb	9 Sc	17 Sg	28 Cp
Sept	12 Aq	28 Pc	12 Tr	23 Gm	1 Lo	6 Vr	12 Lb	18 Sc	26 Sg	6 Aq	
Oct.	21 Pc	6 Tr	19 Gm	27 Ce	3 Vr	9 Lb	15 Sc	23 Sg	2 Aq	15 Pc	30 Ar
Nov.	14 Tr	27 Gm	6 Lo	12 Vr	18 Lb	24 Sc	3 Cp	13 Aq	25 Pc	8 Tr	
Dec.	21 Gm	1 Lo	8 Vr	14 Lb	20 Sc	29 Sg	9 Aq	21 Pc	4 Tr	16 Gm	26 Ce

1945

```
        Sun    Merc   Venus  Mars              Sun    Merc   Venus  Mars
Jan. 1  10 Cp  23 Sg  24 Aq  26 Sg     Feb. 1  12 Aq  23 Cp  29 Pc  20 Cp
     6  15 Cp  23 Sg   0 Pc   0 Cp          6  17 Aq   1 Aq   4 Ar  24 Cp
    11  20 Cp  27 Sg   6 Pc   4 Cp         11  22 Aq   9 Aq   9 Ar  27 Cp
    16  26 Cp   2 Cp  12 Pc   8 Cp         16  27 Aq  17 Aq  13 Ar   1 Aq
    21   1 Aq   8 Cp  17 Pc  11 Cp         21   2 Pc  26 Aq  17 Ar   5 Aq
    26   6 Aq  15 Cp  22 Pc  15 Cp         26   7 Pc   5 Pc  21 Ar   9 Aq
    31  11 Aq  22 Cp  28 Pc  19 Cp
```
Jan. 1/Jup 27 Vr/Sat 7 Ce/Uran 10 Gm   Feb. 1/Jup 27 Vr/Sat 5 Ce/Uran 9 Gm
Nep 6 Lb/Plut 10 Lo/N Node 19 Ce   Nep 6 Lb/Plut 9 Lo/N Node 17 Ce

```
        Sun    Merc   Venus  Mars              Sun    Merc   Venus  Mars
Mar. 1  10 Pc  10 Pc  24 Ar  11 Aq     Apr. 1  11 Ar  28 Ar   3 Tr   5 Pc
     6  15 Pc  20 Pc  27 Ar  15 Aq          6  16 Ar  28 Ar   1 Tr   9 Pc
    11  20 Pc  29 Pc   0 Tr  19 Aq         11  21 Ar  25 Ar  28 Ar  13 Pc
    16  25 Pc   9 Ar   2 Tr  23 Aq         16  26 Ar  22 Ar  25 Ar  17 Pc
    21   0 Ar  17 Ar   3 Tr  27 Aq         21   1 Tr  18 Ar  22 Ar  21 Pc
    26   5 Ar  24 Ar   4 Tr   1 Pc         26   5 Tr  17 Ar  20 Ar  25 Pc
    31  10 Ar  27 Ar   3 Tr   5 Pc
```
Mar. 1/Jup 24 Vr/Sat 4 Ce/Uran 9 Gm   Apr. 1/Jup 20 Vr/Sat 4 Ce/Uran 10 Gm
Nep 6 Lb/Plut 8 Lo/N Node 16 Ce   Nep 5 Lb/Plut 8 Lo/N Node 14 Ce

```
        Sun    Merc   Venus  Mars              Sun    Merc   Venus  Mars
May  1  10 Tr  17 Ar  18 Ar  29 Pc     June 1  10 Gm  24 Tr  27 Ar  22 Ar
     6  15 Tr  20 Ar  17 Ar   2 Ar          6  15 Gm   3 Gm   1 Tr  26 Ar
    11  20 Tr  24 Ar  18 Ar   6 Ar         11  20 Gm  14 Gm   5 Tr   0 Tr
    16  25 Tr  29 Ar  19 Ar  10 Ar         16  24 Gm  25 Gm   9 Tr   3 Tr
    21   0 Gm   6 Tr  21 Ar  14 Ar         21  29 Gm   5 Ce  14 Tr   7 Tr
    26   4 Gm  13 Tr  23 Ar  18 Ar         26   4 Ce  16 Ce  18 Tr  11 Tr
    31   9 Gm  22 Tr  26 Ar  21 Ar
```
May 1/Jup 18 Vr/Sat 7 Ce/Uran 11 Gm   June 1/Jup 18 Vr/Sat 10 Ce/Uran 13 Gm
Nep 4 Lb/Plut 8 Lo/N Node 12 Ce   Nep 4 Lb/Plut 8 Lo/N Node 11 Ce

```
        Sun    Merc   Venus  Mars              Sun    Merc   Venus  Mars
July 1   9 Ce  25 Ce  23 Tr  14 Tr     Aug. 1   8 Lo   3 Vr  26 Gm   6 Gm
     6  14 Ce   4 Lo  28 Tr  18 Tr          6  13 Lo   5 Vr   2 Ce   9 Gm
    11  18 Ce  12 Lo   3 Gm  21 Tr         11  18 Lo   4 Vr   7 Ce  13 Gm
    16  23 Ce  19 Lo   9 Gm  25 Tr         16  23 Lo   1 Vr  13 Ce  16 Gm
    21  28 Ce  25 Lo  14 Gm  28 Tr         21  28 Lo  27 Lo  19 Ce  19 Gm
    26   3 Lo   0 Vr  20 Gm   2 Gm         26   2 Vr  23 Lo  25 Ce  22 Gm
    31   7 Lo   3 Vr  25 Gm   5 Gm         31   7 Vr  22 Lo   1 Lo  25 Gm
```
July 1/Jup 21 Vr/Sat 14 Ce/Uran 15 Gm   Aug. 1/Jup 25 Vr/Sat 18 Ce/Uran 16 Gm
Nep 4 Lb/Plut 9 Lo/N Node 9 Ce   Nep 4 Lb/Plut 10 Lo/N Node 8 Ce

1945

	Sun	Merc	Venus	Mars
Sept 1	8 Vr	22 Lo	2 Lo	26 Gm
6	13 Vr	25 Lo	8 Lo	29 Gm
11	18 Vr	1 Vr	14 Lo	2 Ce
16	23 Vr	9 Vr	20 Lo	5 Ce
21	28 Vr	18 Vr	26 Lo	8 Ce
26	3 Lb	27 Vr	2 Vr	10 Ce

Sept 1/Jup 1 Lb/Sat 21 Ce/Uran 17 Gm
Nep 5 Lb/Plut 11 Lo/N Node 6 Ce

	Sun	Merc	Venus	Mars
Oct. 1	7 Lb	6 Lb	8 Vr	13 Ce
6	12 Lb	15 Lb	14 Vr	15 Ce
11	17 Lb	23 Lb	20 Vr	18 Ce
16	22 Lb	2 Sc	26 Vr	20 Ce
21	27 Lb	9 Sc	2 Lb	22 Ce
26	2 Sc	17 Sc	8 Lb	24 Ce
31	7 Sc	24 Sc	15 Lb	26 Ce

Oct. 1/Jup 8 Lb/Sat 24 Ce/Uran 17 Gm
Nep 6 Lb/Plut 11 Lo/N Node 4 Ce

	Sun	Merc	Venus	Mars
Nov. 1	8 Sc	26 Sc	16 Lb	27 Ce
6	13 Sc	3 Sg	22 Lb	28 Ce
11	18 Sc	9 Sg	28 Lb	0 Lo
16	23 Sc	15 Sg	5 Sc	1 Lo
21	28 Sc	20 Sg	11 Sc	2 Lo
26	3 Sg	23 Sg	17 Sc	3 Lo

Nov. 1/Jup 14 Lb/Sat 25 Ce/Uran 17 Gm
Nep 7 Lb/Plut 12 Lo/N Node 3 Ce

	Sun	Merc	Venus	Mars
Dec. 1	8 Sg	22 Sg	23 Sc	3 Lo
6	14 Sg	17 Sg	0 Sg	3 Lo
11	19 Sg	10 Sg	6 Sg	3 Lo
16	24 Sg	7 Sg	12 Sg	2 Lo
21	29 Sg	8 Sg	19 Sg	1 Lo
26	4 Cp	12 Sg	25 Sg	0 Lo
31	9 Cp	17 Sg	1 Cp	29 Ce

Dec. 1/Jup 20 Lb/Sat 24 Ce/Uran 16 Gm
Nep 8 Lb/Plut 12 Lo/N Node 1 Ce

Moon's Positions

	1	4	7	10	13	16	19	22	25	28	31
Jan.	9 Lo	16 Vr	21 Lb	28 Sc	7 Cp	19 Aq	2 Ar	15 Tr	26 Gm	4 Lo	12 Vr
Feb.	24 Vr	29 Lb	6 Sg	15 Cp	28 Aq	12 Ar	25 Tr	6 Ce	14 Lo	20 Vr	
Mar.	2 Lb	8 Sc	14 Sg	23 Cp	6 Pc	21 Ar	5 Gm	15 Ce	23 Lo	29 Vr	5 Sc
Apr.	16 Sc	23 Sg	1 Aq	14 Pc	30 Ar	14 Gm	25 Ce	2 Vr	8 Lb	13 Sc	
May	20 Sg	28 Cp	9 Pc	23 Ar	8 Gm	20 Ce	28 Lo	5 Lb	10 Sc	17 Sg	25 Cp
June	8 Aq	19 Pc	2 Tr	16 Gm	28 Ce	7 Vr	13 Lb	19 Sc	26 Sg	5 Aq	
July	16 Pc	28 Ar	11 Gm	23 Ce	2 Vr	9 Lb	15 Sc	21 Sg	0 Aq	12 Pc	25 Ar
Aug.	9 Tr	21 Gm	2 Lo	10 Vr	17 Lb	23 Sc	29 Sg	9 Aq	22 Pc	6 Tr	18 Gm
Sept	2 Ce	11 Lo	19 Vr	25 Lb	1 Sg	7 Cp	17 Aq	1 Ar	16 Tr	29 Gm	
Oct.	8 Lo	16 Vr	22 Lb	27 Sc	3 Cp	11 Aq	24 Pc	9 Tr	24 Gm	5 Lo	13 Vr
Nov.	25 Vr	1 Sc	6 Sg	12 Cp	20 Aq	2 Ar	17 Tr	2 Ce	14 Lo	22 Vr	
Dec.	28 Lb	3 Sg	9 Cp	17 Aq	28 Pc	11 Tr	25 Gm	8 Lo	18 Vr	24 Lb	30 Sc

                                   Ephemeris

1946

		Sun	Merc	Venus	Mars
Jan.	1	10 Cp	19 Sg	2 Cp	28 Ce
	6	15 Cp	25 Sg	9 Cp	26 Ce
	11	20 Cp	2 Cp	15 Cp	24 Ce
	16	25 Cp	9 Cp	21 Cp	22 Ce
	21	0 Aq	17 Cp	28 Cp	21 Ce
	26	5 Aq	25 Cp	4 Aq	19 Ce
	31	11 Aq	3 Aq	10 Aq	17 Ce

Jan. 1/Jup 25 Lb/Sat 22 Ce/Uran 14 Gm
Nep 9 Lb/Plut 11 Lo/N Node 29 Gm

		Sun	Merc	Venus	Mars
Feb.	1	12 Aq	4 Aq	11 Aq	17 Ce
	6	17 Aq	13 Aq	18 Aq	16 Ce
	11	22 Aq	22 Aq	24 Aq	15 Ce
	16	27 Aq	1 Pc	0 Pc	14 Ce
	21	2 Pc	10 Pc	6 Pc	14 Ce
	26	7 Pc	19 Pc	13 Pc	14 Ce

Feb. 1/Jup 27 Lb/Sat 20 Ce/Uran 14 Gm
Nep 8 Lb/Plut 11 Lo/N Node 28 Gm

		Sun	Merc	Venus	Mars
Mar.	1	10 Pc	25 Pc	16 Pc	14 Ce
	6	15 Pc	2 Ar	23 Pc	15 Ce
	11	20 Pc	8 Ar	29 Pc	16 Ce
	16	25 Pc	10 Ar	5 Ar	17 Ce
	21	0 Ar	9 Ar	11 Ar	18 Ce
	26	5 Ar	5 Ar	18 Ar	19 Ce
	31	10 Ar	1 Ar	24 Ar	21 Ce

Mar. 1/Jup 27 Lb/Sat 18 Ce/Uran 13 Gm
Nep 8 Lb/Plut 10 Lo/N Node 26 Gm

		Sun	Merc	Venus	Mars
Apr.	1	11 Ar	1 Ar	25 Ar	21 Ce
	6	16 Ar	28 Pc	1 Tr	23 Ce
	11	21 Ar	28 Pc	7 Tr	25 Ce
	16	25 Ar	0 Ar	14 Tr	27 Ce
	21	0 Tr	3 Ar	20 Tr	29 Ce
	26	5 Tr	8 Ar	26 Tr	1 Lo

Apr. 1/Jup 24 Lb/Sat 18 Ce/Uran 14 Gm
Nep 7 Lb/Plut 10 Lo/N Node 25 Gm

		Sun	Merc	Venus	Mars
May	1	10 Tr	14 Ar	2 Gm	4 Lo
	6	15 Tr	21 Ar	8 Gm	6 Lo
	11	20 Tr	29 Ar	14 Gm	9 Lo
	16	25 Tr	8 Tr	20 Gm	11 Lo
	21	29 Tr	17 Tr	26 Gm	14 Lo
	26	4 Gm	28 Tr	2 Ce	16 Lo
	31	9 Gm	8 Gm	8 Ce	19 Lo

May 1/Jup 20 Lb/Sat 19 Ce/Uran 15 Gm
Nep 6 Lb/Plut 9 Lo/N Node 23 Gm

		Sun	Merc	Venus	Mars
June	1	10 Gm	11 Gm	9 Ce	19 Lo
	6	15 Gm	21 Gm	15 Ce	22 Lo
	11	19 Gm	2 Ce	21 Ce	25 Lo
	16	24 Gm	11 Ce	27 Ce	28 Lo
	21	29 Gm	20 Ce	3 Lo	0 Vr
	26	4 Ce	28 Ce	9 Lo	3 Vr

June 1/Jup 18 Lb/Sat 22 Ce/Uran 17 Gm
Nep 6 Lb/Plut 10 Lo/N Node 21 Gm

		Sun	Merc	Venus	Mars
July	1	9 Ce	4 Lo	15 Lo	6 Vr
	6	13 Ce	9 Lo	21 Lo	9 Vr
	11	18 Ce	13 Lo	27 Lo	12 Vr
	16	23 Ce	16 Lo	3 Vr	15 Vr
	21	28 Ce	16 Lo	8 Vr	18 Vr
	26	2 Lo	15 Lo	14 Vr	21 Vr
	31	7 Lo	12 Lo	20 Vr	24 Vr

July 1/Jup 18 Lb/Sat 26 Ce/Uran 19 Gm
Nep 6 Lb/Plut 10 Lo/N Node 20 Gm

		Sun	Merc	Venus	Mars
Aug.	1	8 Lo	11 Lo	21 Vr	25 Vr
	6	13 Lo	7 Lo	26 Vr	28 Vr
	11	18 Lo	5 Lo	2 Lb	1 Lb
	16	23 Lo	5 Lo	7 Lb	4 Lb
	21	27 Lo	9 Lo	13 Lb	7 Lb
	26	2 Vr	15 Lo	18 Lb	10 Lb
	31	7 Vr	23 Lo	23 Lb	14 Lb

Aug. 1/Jup 21 Lb/Sat 30 Ce/Uran 20 Gm
Nep 6 Lb/Plut 11 Lo/N Node 18 Gm

1946

```
            Sun      Merc     Venus    Mars              Sun      Merc     Venus    Mars
Sept 1    8 Vr    25 Lo    24 Lb    14 Lb    Oct. 1    7 Lb    19 Lb    21 Sc     4 Sc
     6   13 Vr     4 Vr    29 Lb    18 Lb         6   12 Lb    27 Lb    24 Sc     8 Sc
    11   18 Vr    14 Vr     4 Sc    21 Lb        11   17 Lb     5 Sc    27 Sc    11 Sc
    16   23 Vr    23 Vr     9 Sc    24 Lb        16   22 Lb    12 Sc     0 Sg    15 Sc
    21   27 Vr     2 Lb    13 Sc    28 Lb        21   27 Lb    19 Sc     2 Sg    18 Sc
    26    2 Lb    11 Lb    17 Sc     1 Sc        26    2 Sc    25 Sc     2 Sg    22 Sc
                                                31    7 Sc     1 Sg     2 Sg    25 Sc
```

Sept 1/Jup 25 Lb/Sat 4 Lo/Uran 21 Gm   Oct. 1/Jup 1 Sc/Sat 7 Lo/Uran 22 Gm
Nep 7 Lb/Plut 12 Lo/N Node 17 Gm   Nep 8 Lb/Plut 13 Lo/N Node 15 Gm

```
            Sun      Merc     Venus    Mars              Sun      Merc     Venus    Mars
Nov. 1    8 Sc     2 Sg     2 Sg    26 Sc    Dec. 1    8 Sg    21 Sc    18 Sc    18 Sg
     6   13 Sc     6 Sg     1 Sg    29 Sc         6   13 Sg    23 Sc    17 Sc    21 Sg
    11   18 Sc     7 Sg    29 Sc     3 Sg        11   18 Sg    28 Sc    17 Sc    25 Sg
    16   23 Sc     5 Sg    26 Sc     7 Sg        16   23 Sg     4 Sg    18 Sc    29 Sg
    21   28 Sc     0 Sg    23 Sc    10 Sg        21   29 Sg    11 Sg    20 Sc     3 Cp
    26    3 Sg    24 Sc    20 Sc    14 Sg        26    4 Cp    18 Sg    23 Sc     6 Cp
                                                31    9 Cp    25 Sg    26 Sc    10 Cp
```

Nov. 1/Jup 8 Sc/Sat 9 Lo/Uran 21 Gm   Dec. 1/Jup 14 Sc/Sat 9 Lo/Uran 20 Gm
Nep 9 Lb/Plut 13 Lo/N Node 13 Gm   Nep 10 Lb/Plut 13 Lo/N Node 12 Gm

Moon's Positions

	1	4	7	10	13	16	19	22	25	28	31
Jan.	12 Sg	19 Cp	27 Aq	8 Ar	21 Tr	4 Ce	16 Lo	26 Vr	2 Sc	8 Sg	14 Cp
Feb.	27 Cp	7 Pc	19 Ar	1 Gm	13 Ce	24 Lo	3 Lb	10 Sc	15 Sg	22 Cp	
Mar.	5 Aq	16 Pc	29 Ar	12 Gm	24 Ce	4 Vr	12 Lb	18 Sc	23 Sg	0 Aq	10 Pc
Apr.	24 Pc	9 Tr	23 Gm	4 Lo	13 Vr	20 Lb	26 Sc	2 Cp	8 Aq	18 Pc	
May	2 Tr	17 Gm	1 Lo	10 Vr	17 Lb	23 Sc	29 Sg	5 Aq	13 Pc	26 Ar	11 Gm
June	26 Gm	10 Lo	20 Vr	26 Lb	2 Sg	8 Cp	14 Aq	23 Pc	5 Tr	19 Gm	
July	4 Lo	15 Vr	23 Lb	29 Sc	4 Cp	11 Aq	20 Pc	1 Tr	14 Gm	28 Ce	10 Vr
Aug.	23 Vr	1 Sc	7 Sg	13 Cp	20 Aq	0 Ar	12 Tr	24 Gm	7 Lo	18 Vr	27 Lb
Sept	9 Sc	15 Sg	21 Cp	29 Aq	10 Ar	22 Tr	5 Ce	17 Lo	27 Vr	5 Sc	
Oct.	11 Sg	17 Cp	24 Aq	5 Ar	18 Tr	2 Ce	13 Lo	23 Vr	1 Sc	7 Sg	13 Cp
Nov.	25 Cp	2 Pc	13 Ar	27 Tr	11 Ce	24 Lo	3 Lb	10 Sc	16 Sg	21 Cp	
Dec.	28 Aq	7 Ar	20 Tr	5 Ce	19 Lo	30 Vr	7 Sc	13 Sg	18 Cp	24 Aq	2 Ar

1947

```
            Sun    Merc   Venus   Mars                   Sun    Merc   Venus  Mars
Jan. 1    10 Cp  27 Sg   27 Sc  11 Cp        Feb. 1    11 Aq  17 Aq   25 Sg  5 Aq
     6    15 Cp   5 Cp    0 Sg  15 Cp             6    16 Aq  26 Aq    0 Cp  9 Aq
    11    20 Cp  12 Cp    4 Sg  19 Cp            11    21 Aq   5 Pc    5 Cp  13 Aq
    16    25 Cp  20 Cp    9 Sg  23 Cp            16    26 Aq  13 Pc   11 Cp  17 Aq
    21     0 Aq  29 Cp   13 Sg  27 Cp            21     2 Pc  20 Pc   16 Cp  21 Aq
    26     5 Aq   7 Aq   18 Sg   0 Aq            26     7 Pc  23 Pc   22 Cp  25 Aq
    31    10 Aq  16 Aq   23 Sg   4 Aq
Jan. 1/Jup 20 Sc/Sat  7 Lo/Uran 19 Gm       Feb. 1/Jup 25 Sc/Sat  5 Lo/Uran 18 Gm
Nep 11 Lb/Plut 13 Lo/N Node 10 Gm           Nep 11 Lb/Plut 12 Lo/N Node  9 Gm


            Sun    Merc   Venus   Mars                   Sun    Merc   Venus  Mars
Mar. 1    10 Pc  23 Pc   25 Cp  27 Aq        Apr. 1    10 Ar  13 Pc    1 Pc  21 Pc
     6    15 Pc  20 Pc    1 Aq   1 Pc             6    15 Ar  18 Pc    7 Pc  25 Pc
    11    20 Pc  15 Pc    7 Aq   5 Pc            11    20 Ar  23 Pc   13 Pc  29 Pc
    16    25 Pc  11 Pc   12 Aq   9 Pc            16    25 Ar   0 Ar   19 Pc   3 Ar
    21     0 Ar   9 Pc   18 Aq  13 Pc            21     0 Tr   7 Ar   25 Pc   7 Ar
    26     5 Ar  10 Pc   24 Aq  17 Pc            26     5 Tr  15 Ar    1 Ar  11 Ar
    31     9 Ar  12 Pc    0 Pc  21 Pc
Mar. 1/Jup 27 Sc/Sat  3 Lo/Uran 18 Gm       Apr. 1/Jup 27 Sc/Sat  2 Lo/Uran 18 Gm
Nep 10 Lb/Plut 12 Lo/N Node  7 Gm           Nep  9 Lb/Plut 11 Lo/N Node  5 Gm


            Sun    Merc   Venus   Mars                   Sun    Merc   Venus  Mars
May  1    10 Tr  24 Ar    7 Ar  15 Ar        June 1    10 Gm  27 Gm   14 Tr   8 Tr
     6    15 Tr   3 Tr   13 Ar  19 Ar             6    14 Gm   6 Ce   20 Tr  12 Tr
    11    19 Tr  14 Tr   19 Ar  22 Ar            11    19 Gm  13 Ce   26 Tr  15 Tr
    16    24 Tr  24 Tr   25 Ar  26 Ar            16    24 Gm  19 Ce    3 Gm  19 Tr
    21    29 Tr   5 Gm    1 Tr   0 Tr            21    29 Gm  23 Ce    9 Gm  23 Tr
    26     4 Gm  16 Gm    7 Tr   4 Tr            26     4 Ce  26 Ce   15 Gm  26 Tr
    31     9 Gm  25 Gm   13 Tr   7 Tr
May  1/Jup 24 Sc/Sat  3 Lo/Uran 19 Gm       June 1/Jup 21 Sc/Sat  5 Lo/Uran 21 Gm
Nep  9 Lb/Plut 11 Lo/N Node  4 Gm           Nep  8 Lb/Plut 11 Lo/N Node  2 Gm


            Sun    Merc   Venus   Mars                   Sun    Merc   Venus  Mars
July 1     8 Ce  27 Ce   21 Gm   0 Gm        Aug. 1     8 Lo  19 Ce   29 Ce  21 Gm
     6    13 Ce  26 Ce   27 Gm   3 Gm             6    13 Lo  24 Ce    5 Lo  25 Gm
    11    18 Ce  24 Ce    3 Ce   7 Gm            11    18 Lo   0 Lo   11 Lo  28 Gm
    16    23 Ce  21 Ce    9 Ce  10 Gm            16    22 Lo   9 Lo   17 Lo   1 Ce
    21    27 Ce  18 Ce   15 Ce  14 Gm            21    27 Lo  19 Lo   23 Lo   5 Ce
    26     2 Lo  17 Ce   21 Ce  17 Gm            26     2 Vr  29 Lo    0 Vr   8 Ce
    31     7 Lo  19 Ce   27 Ce  21 Gm            31     7 Vr   9 Vr    6 Vr  11 Ce
July 1/Jup 18 Sc/Sat  8 Lo/Uran 23 Gm       Aug. 1/Jup 18 Sc/Sat 12 Lo/Uran 25 Gm
Nep  8 Lb/Plut 12 Lo/N Node  1 Gm           Nep  8 Lb/Plut 13 Lo/N Node 29 Tr
```

1947

```
          Sun    Merc   Venus   Mars                    Sun    Merc   Venus   Mars
Sept  1   8 Vr  11 Vr   7 Vr   12 Ce    Oct.  1   7 Lb  29 Lb  14 Lb    0 Lo
      6  13 Vr  20 Vr  13 Vr   15 Ce          6  12 Lb   6 Sc  21 Lb    3 Lo
     11  17 Vr  29 Vr  19 Vr   18 Ce         11  17 Lb  12 Sc  27 Lb    6 Lo
     16  22 Vr   7 Lb  26 Vr   21 Ce         16  22 Lb  17 Sc   3 Sc    8 Lo
     21  27 Vr  15 Lb   2 Lb   24 Ce         21  27 Lb  20 Sc   9 Sc   11 Lo
     26   2 Lb  22 Lb   8 Lb   27 Ce         26   2 Sc  21 Sc  16 Sc   14 Lo
                                             31   7 Sc  19 Sc  22 Sc   16 Lo
```
Sept 1/Jup 21 Sc/Sat 16 Lo/Uran 26 Gm   Oct. 1/Jup 26 Sc/Sat 19 Lo/Uran 26 Gm
Nep 9 Lb/Plut 14 Lo/N Node 27 Tr   Nep 10 Lb/Plut 14 Lo/N Node 26 Tr

```
          Sun    Merc   Venus   Mars                    Sun    Merc   Venus   Mars
Nov.  1   8 Sc  19 Sc  23 Sc   17 Lo    Dec.  1   8 Sg  20 Sc   0 Cp    0 Vr
      6  13 Sc  13 Sc  29 Sc   19 Lo          6  13 Sg  28 Sc   7 Cp    2 Vr
     11  18 Sc   7 Sc   5 Sg   22 Lo         11  18 Sg   5 Sg  13 Cp    3 Vr
     16  23 Sc   6 Sc  12 Sg   24 Lo         16  23 Sg  13 Sg  19 Cp    4 Vr
     21  28 Sc   8 Sc  18 Sg   26 Lo         21  28 Sg  21 Sg  25 Cp    6 Vr
     26   3 Sg  14 Sc  24 Sg   28 Lo         26   3 Cp  28 Sg   2 Aq    7 Vr
                                             31   8 Cp   6 Cp   8 Aq    7 Vr
```
Nov. 1/Jup 2 Sg/Sat 22 Lo/Uran 26 Gm Dec. 1/Jup 8 Sg/Sat 23 Lo/Uran 25 Gm
Nep 12 Lb/Plut 15 Lo/N Node 24 Tr   Nep 12 Lb/Plut 15 Lo/N Node 22 Tr

Moon's Positions

```
         1       4       7      10      13      16      19      22      25      28      31
Jan.  16 Ar  28 Tr  13 Ce  28 Lo   9 Lb  16 Sc  22 Sg  27 Cp   4 Pc  12 Ar  23 Tr
Feb.   7 Gm  21 Ce   6 Vr  17 Lb  24 Sc  30 Sg   6 Aq  13 Pc  23 Ar   4 Gm
Mar.  18 Gm   1 Lo  14 Vr  25 Lb   2 Sg   8 Cp  14 Aq  22 Pc   3 Tr  14 Gm  27 Ce
Apr.  11 Lo  23 Vr   3 Sc  10 Sg  16 Cp  22 Aq   0 Ar  12 Tr  25 Gm   8 Lo
May   19 Vr  29 Lb   6 Sg  12 Cp  18 Aq  25 Pc   6 Tr  20 Gm   4 Lo  16 Vr  25 Lb
June   8 Sc  15 Sg  20 Cp  26 Aq   3 Ar  14 Tr  28 Gm  14 Lo  26 Vr   5 Sc
July  12 Sg  17 Cp  23 Aq  30 Pc   9 Tr  22 Gm   7 Lo  22 Vr   2 Sc   9 Sg  14 Cp
Aug.  26 Cp   2 Pc   9 Ar  18 Tr   1 Ce  16 Lo  30 Vr  10 Sc  17 Sg  23 Cp  29 Aq
Sept  11 Pc  19 Ar  29 Tr  11 Ce  25 Lo   8 Lb  18 Sc  26 Sg   1 Aq   7 Pc
Oct.  16 Ar  26 Tr   7 Ce  20 Lo   3 Lb  13 Sc  21 Sg  27 Cp   3 Pc  11 Ar  22 Tr
Nov.   5 Gm  18 Ce   1 Vr  12 Lb  22 Sc  29 Sg   5 Aq  11 Pc  19 Ar   0 Gm
Dec.  14 Ce  27 Lo   9 Lb  18 Sc  25 Sg   1 Aq   7 Pc  14 Ar  24 Tr   7 Ce  23 Lo
```

1948

```
          Sun     Merc     Venus    Mars                    Sun      Merc     Venus    Mars
Jan. 1    9 Cp    8 Cp     9 Aq     7 Vr          Feb. 1   11 Aq    29 Aq    17 Pc     4 Vr
      6   15 Cp   16 Cp    15 Aq    8 Vr                6   16 Aq    4 Pc     23 Pc     2 Vr
     11   20 Cp   24 Cp    21 Aq    8 Vr               11   21 Aq    7 Pc     29 Pc     1 Vr
     16   25 Cp    3 Aq    27 Aq    7 Vr               16   26 Aq    4 Pc      5 Ar    29 Lo
     21    0 Aq   11 Aq     4 Pc    7 Vr               21    1 Pc    29 Aq    11 Ar    27 Lo
     26    5 Aq   20 Aq    10 Pc    6 Vr               26    6 Pc    24 Aq    17 Ar    25 Lo
     31   10 Aq   27 Aq    16 Pc    4 Vr
```

Jan. 1/Jup 15 Sg/Sat 22 Lo/Uran 24 Gm

Nep 13 Lb/Plut 14 Lo/N Node 21 Tr

Feb. 1/Jup 21 Sg/Sat 20 Lo/Uran 22 Gm

Nep 13 Lb/Plut 14 Lo/N Node 19 Tr

```
          Sun     Merc     Venus    Mars                    Sun      Merc     Venus    Mars
Mar. 1   10 Pc   22 Aq    22 Ar    23 Lo          Apr. 1   11 Ar    17 Pc    26 Tr    18 Lo
      6   15 Pc   22 Aq    27 Ar    22 Lo                6   16 Ar    25 Pc     2 Gm    18 Lo
     11   20 Pc   24 Aq     3 Tr    20 Lo               11   21 Ar     3 Ar     7 Gm    19 Lo
     16   25 Pc   28 Aq     9 Tr    19 Lo               16   26 Ar    12 Ar    12 Gm    20 Lo
     21    0 Ar    3 Pc    14 Tr    19 Lo               21    1 Tr    22 Ar    16 Gm    21 Lo
     26    5 Ar    9 Pc    20 Tr    18 Lo               26    6 Tr     2 Tr    21 Gm    22 Lo
     31   10 Ar   16 Pc    25 Tr    18 Lo
```

Mar. 1/Jup 26 Sg/Sat 18 Lo/Uran 22 Gm

Nep 12 Lb/Plut 13 Lo/N Node 18 Tr

Apr. 1/Jup 29 Sg/Sat 16 Lo/Uran 23 Gm

Nep 12 Lb/Plut 13 Lo/N Node 16 Tr

```
          Sun     Merc     Venus    Mars                     Sun      Merc     Venus    Mars
May  1   11 Tr   13 Tr    25 Gm    24 Lo          June 1   10 Gm     3 Ce    11 Ce     6 Vr
      6   15 Tr   23 Tr    29 Gm    25 Lo                6   15 Gm     6 Ce    11 Ce     8 Vr
     11   20 Tr    4 Gm     3 Ce    27 Lo               11   20 Gm     7 Ce    10 Ce    10 Vr
     16   25 Tr   13 Gm     6 Ce    29 Lo               16   25 Gm     7 Ce     8 Ce    13 Vr
     21    0 Gm   21 Gm     8 Ce     1 Vr               21    0 Ce     4 Ce     5 Ce    16 Vr
     26    5 Gm   27 Gm    10 Ce     3 Vr               26    4 Ce     1 Ce     2 Ce    18 Vr
     31    9 Gm    2 Ce    11 Ce     5 Vr
```

May 1/Jup 29 Sg/Sat 16 Lo/Uran 24 Gm

Nep 11 Lb/Plut 13 Lo/N Node 14 Tr

June 1/Jup 26 Sg/Sat 17 Lo/Uran 25 Gm

Nep 10 Lb/Plut 13 Lo/N Node 13 Tr

```
           Sun     Merc     Venus    Mars                    Sun      Merc     Venus    Mars
July 1    9 Ce   29 Gm    29 Gm    21 Vr          Aug. 1    9 Lo    27 Ce    29 Gm     9 Lb
      6   14 Ce   28 Gm    27 Gm    24 Vr                6   13 Lo     7 Lo     2 Ce    12 Lb
     11   19 Ce    0 Ce    25 Gm    26 Vr               11   18 Lo    17 Lo     5 Ce    15 Lb
     16   23 Ce    3 Ce    25 Gm    29 Vr               16   23 Lo    27 Lo     9 Ce    18 Lb
     21   28 Ce    8 Ce    25 Gm     2 Lb               21   28 Lo     7 Vr    13 Ce    21 Lb
     26    3 Lo   16 Ce    26 Gm     5 Lb               26    3 Vr    16 Vr    17 Ce    24 Lb
     31    8 Lo   25 Ce    28 Gm     8 Lb               31    7 Vr    24 Vr    22 Ce    28 Lb
```

July 1/Jup 22 Sg/Sat 20 Lo/Uran 27 Gm

Nep 10 Lb/Plut 13 Lo/N Node 11 Tr

Aug. 1/Jup 19 Sg/Sat 24 Lo/Uran 29 Gm

Nep 11 Lb/Plut 14 Lo/N Node 10 Tr

1948

```
          Sun    Merc   Venus   Mars              Sun    Merc   Venus   Mars
Sept 1   8 Vr   26 Vr   23 Ce   28 Lb     Oct. 1   8 Lb    3 Sc   24 Lo   19 Sc
     6  13 Vr    4 Lb   27 Ce    2 Sc          6  13 Lb    5 Sc   29 Lo   22 Sc
    11  18 Vr   11 Lb    2 Lo    5 Sc         11  18 Lb    5 Sc    5 Vr   26 Sc
    16  23 Vr   18 Lb    8 Lo    8 Sc         16  23 Lb    1 Sc   11 Vr   29 Sc
    21  28 Vr   24 Lb   13 Lo   12 Sc         21  28 Lb   25 Lb   17 Vr    3 Sg
    26   3 Lb   29 Lb   18 Lo   15 Sc         26   2 Sc   21 Lb   23 Vr    6 Sg
                                              31   7 Sc   20 Lb   28 Vr   10 Sg
```

```
Sept 1/Jup 20 Sg/Sat 28 Lo/Uran   0 Ce     Oct. 1/Jup 22 Sg/Sat  1 Vr/Uran   1 Ce
Nep 11 Lb/Plut 15 Lo/N Node  8 Tr          Nep 13 Lb/Plut 16 Lo/N Node  6 Tr
```

```
          Sun    Merc   Venus   Mars              Sun    Merc   Venus   Mars
Nov. 1   8 Sc   21 Lb    0 Lb   11 Sg     Dec. 1   9 Sg    2 Sg    6 Sc    3 Cp
     6  13 Sc   25 Lb    6 Lb   14 Sg          6  14 Sg   10 Sg   12 Sc    7 Cp
    11  19 Sc    1 Sc   12 Lb   18 Sg         11  19 Sg   18 Sg   18 Sc   11 Cp
    16  24 Sc    9 Sc   18 Lb   22 Sg         16  24 Sg   26 Sg   25 Sc   15 Cp
    21  29 Sc   16 Sc   24 Lb   26 Sg         21  29 Sg    4 Cp    1 Sg   18 Cp
    26   4 Sg   24 Sc    0 Sc   29 Sg         26   4 Cp   12 Cp    7 Sg   22 Cp
                                              31   9 Cp   20 Cp   13 Sg   26 Cp
```

```
Nov. 1/Jup 27 Sg/Sat  4 Vr/Uran   0 Ce     Dec. 1/Jup  3 Cp/Sat  6 Vr/Uran 29 Gm
Nep 14 Lb/Plut 16 Lo/N Node  5 Tr          Nep 15 Lb/Plut 17 Lo/N Node  3 Tr
```

Moon's Positions

```
          1       4       7      10      13      16      19      22      25      28      31
Jan.    7 Vr   19 Lb   28 Sc    4 Cp   10 Aq   16 Pc   22 Ar    2 Gm   15 Ce    1 Vr   15 Lb
Feb.   29 Lb    7 Sg   13 Cp   19 Aq   25 Pc    1 Tr   11 Gm   24 Ce    9 Vr   23 Lb
Mar.   20 Sc   28 Sg    4 Aq   10 Pc   16 Ar   24 Tr    4 Ce   18 Lo    2 Lb   15 Sc   24 Sg
Apr.    6 Cp   12 Aq   18 Pc   25 Ar    4 Gm   15 Ce   28 Lo   11 Lb   23 Sc    2 Cp
May     8 Aq   14 Pc   21 Ar    0 Gm   12 Ce   25 Lo    7 Lb   18 Sc   27 Sg    4 Aq   10 Pc
June   22 Pc   29 Ar    9 Gm   22 Ce    6 Vr   18 Lb   28 Sc    6 Cp   12 Aq   18 Pc
July   24 Ar    4 Gm   16 Ce    1 Vr   14 Lb   25 Sc    2 Cp    9 Aq   15 Pc   21 Ar   28 Tr
Aug.   12 Gm   25 Ce   10 Vr   24 Lb    4 Sg   12 Cp   18 Aq   24 Pc   29 Ar    7 Gm   19 Ce
Sept    3 Lo   19 Vr    3 Sc   14 Sg   21 Cp   27 Aq    2 Ar    9 Tr   17 Gm   28 Ce
Oct.   12 Vr   27 Lb    9 Sg   17 Cp   24 Aq   29 Pc    6 Tr   14 Gm   24 Ce    7 Vr   21 Lb
Nov.    5 Sc   17 Sg   26 Cp    2 Pc    7 Ar   14 Tr   24 Gm    5 Lo   17 Vr   30 Lb
Dec.   11 Sg   21 Cp   28 Aq    3 Ar   10 Tr   19 Gm    1 Lo   14 Vr   26 Lb    7 Sg   16 Cp
```

1949

Jan.	Sun	Merc	Venus	Mars
1	10 Cp	21 Cp	15 Sg	27 Cp
6	15 Cp	29 Cp	21 Sg	1 Aq
11	20 Cp	7 Aq	27 Sg	5 Aq
16	26 Cp	14 Aq	3 Cp	9 Aq
21	1 Aq	19 Aq	10 Cp	13 Aq
26	6 Aq	20 Aq	16 Cp	17 Aq
31	11 Aq	17 Aq	22 Cp	21 Aq

Jan. 1/Jup 10 Cp/Sat 6 Vr/Uran 28 Gm
Nep 15 Lb/Plut 16 Lo/N Node 1 Tr

Feb.	Sun	Merc	Venus	Mars
1	12 Aq	16 Aq	23 Cp	21 Aq
6	17 Aq	10 Aq	0 Aq	25 Aq
11	22 Aq	6 Aq	6 Aq	29 Aq
16	27 Aq	5 Aq	12 Aq	3 Pc
21	2 Pc	6 Aq	18 Aq	7 Pc
26	7 Pc	10 Aq	25 Aq	11 Pc

Feb. 1/Jup 17 Cp/Sat 4 Vr/Uran 27 Gm
Nep 15 Lb/Plut 15 Lo/N Node 30 Ar

Mar.	Sun	Merc	Venus	Mars
1	10 Pc	13 Aq	28 Aq	14 Pc
6	15 Pc	19 Aq	4 Pc	18 Pc
11	20 Pc	25 Aq	11 Pc	21 Pc
16	25 Pc	2 Pc	17 Pc	25 Pc
21	0 Ar	10 Pc	23 Pc	29 Pc
26	5 Ar	18 Pc	29 Pc	3 Ar
31	10 Ar	27 Pc	6 Ar	7 Ar

Mar. 1/Jup 23 Cp/Sat 2 Vr/Uran 27 Gm
Nep 15 Lb/Plut 15 Lo/N Node 28 Ar

Apr.	Sun	Merc	Venus	Mars
1	11 Ar	29 Pc	7 Ar	8 Ar
6	16 Ar	8 Ar	13 Ar	12 Ar
11	21 Ar	18 Ar	19 Ar	16 Ar
16	26 Ar	29 Ar	25 Ar	19 Ar
21	1 Tr	9 Tr	2 Tr	23 Ar
26	5 Tr	19 Tr	8 Tr	27 Ar

Apr. 1/Jup 29 Cp/Sat 0 Vr/Uran 27 Gm
Nep 14 Lb/Plut 14 Lo/N Node 27 Ar

May	Sun	Merc	Venus	Mars
1	10 Tr	28 Tr	14 Tr	1 Tr
6	15 Tr	6 Gm	20 Tr	4 Tr
11	20 Tr	11 Gm	26 Tr	8 Tr
16	25 Tr	15 Gm	2 Gm	12 Tr
21	0 Gm	17 Gm	9 Gm	16 Tr
26	4 Gm	17 Gm	15 Gm	19 Tr
31	9 Gm	15 Gm	21 Gm	23 Tr

May 1/Jup 2 Aq/Sat 29 Lo/Uran 28 Gm
Nep 13 Lb/Plut 14 Lo/N Node 25 Ar

June	Sun	Merc	Venus	Mars
1	10 Gm	15 Gm	22 Gm	24 Tr
6	15 Gm	12 Gm	28 Gm	27 Tr
11	20 Gm	10 Gm	4 Ce	1 Gm
16	25 Gm	9 Gm	10 Ce	4 Gm
21	29 Gm	10 Gm	17 Ce	8 Gm
26	4 Ce	12 Gm	23 Ce	11 Gm

June 1/Jup 2 Aq/Sat 0 Vr/Uran 29 Gm
Nep 13 Lb/Plut 14 Lo/N Node 23 Ar

July	Sun	Merc	Venus	Mars
1	9 Ce	17 Gm	29 Ce	15 Gm
6	14 Ce	24 Gm	5 Lo	18 Gm
11	18 Ce	1 Ce	11 Lo	22 Gm
16	23 Ce	11 Ce	17 Lo	25 Gm
21	28 Ce	21 Ce	23 Lo	28 Gm
26	3 Lo	2 Lo	29 Lo	2 Ce
31	7 Lo	12 Lo	5 Vr	5 Ce

July 1/Jup 30 Cp/Sat 2 Vr/Uran 1 Ce
Nep 12 Lb/Plut 15 Lo/N Node 22 Ar

Aug.	Sun	Merc	Venus	Mars
1	8 Lo	14 Lo	6 Vr	6 Ce
6	13 Lo	24 Lo	13 Vr	9 Ce
11	18 Lo	3 Vr	19 Vr	12 Ce
16	23 Lo	11 Vr	25 Vr	16 Ce
21	28 Lo	19 Vr	1 Lb	19 Ce
26	2 Vr	26 Vr	7 Lb	22 Ce
31	7 Vr	3 Lb	13 Lb	25 Ce

Aug. 1/Jup 26 Cp/Sat 6 Vr/Uran 3 Ce
Nep 13 Lb/Plut 16 Lo/N Node 20 Ar

1949

```
        Sun     Merc    Venus   Mars                    Sun     Merc    Venus   Mars
Sept  1  8 Vr   4 Lb   14 Lb   26 Ce        Oct.  1  7 Lb   13 Lb   19 Sc   15 Lo
      6 13 Vr  10 Lb   20 Lb   29 Ce              6 12 Lb    8 Lb   25 Sc   18 Lo
     11 18 Vr  15 Lb   26 Lb    2 Lo             11 17 Lb    4 Lb    1 Sg   21 Lo
     16 23 Vr  18 Lb    2 Sc    6 Lo             16 22 Lb    5 Lb    6 Sg   24 Lo
     21 28 Vr  19 Lb    7 Sc    9 Lo             21 27 Lb    9 Lb   12 Sg   27 Lo
     26  3 Lb  18 Lb   13 Sc   12 Lo             26  2 Sc   16 Lb   18 Sg   29 Lo
                                                 31  7 Sc   24 Lb   23 Sg    2 Vr
```

Sept 1/Jup 23 Cp/Sat 9 Vr/Uran 4 Ce   Oct. 1/Jup 23 Cp/Sat 13 Vr/Uran 5 Ce
Nep 14 Lb/Plut 17 Lo/N Node 19 Ar   Nep 15 Lb/Plut 18 Lo/N Node 17 Ar

```
        Sun     Merc    Venus   Mars                    Sun     Merc    Venus   Mars
Nov.  1  8 Sc  25 Lb   24 Sg    3 Vr        Dec.  1  8 Sg   14 Sg   25 Cp   19 Vr
      6 13 Sc   4 Sc    0 Cp    6 Vr              6 14 Sg   21 Sg    0 Aq   21 Vr
     11 18 Sc  12 Sc    5 Cp    8 Vr             11 19 Sg   29 Sg    4 Aq   23 Vr
     16 23 Sc  20 Sc   10 Cp   11 Vr             16 24 Sg    7 Cp    8 Aq   26 Vr
     21 28 Sc  28 Sc   16 Cp   14 Vr             21 29 Sg   15 Cp   11 Aq   28 Vr
     26  3 Sg   6 Sg   20 Cp   16 Vr             26  4 Cp   22 Cp   14 Aq    0 Lb
                                                 31  9 Cp   28 Cp   17 Aq    2 Lb
```

Nov. 1/Jup 25 Cp/Sat 16 Vr/Uran 5 Ce   Dec. 1/Jup 0 Aq/Sat 19 Vr/Uran 4 Ce
Nep 16 Lb/Plut 18 Lo/N Node 15 Ar   Nep 17 Lb/Plut 18 Lo/N Node 14 Ar

Moon's Positions

	1	4	7	10	13	16	19	22	25	28	31
Jan.	29 Cp	5 Pc	11 Ar	17 Tr	27 Gm	10 Lo	25 Vr	7 Sc	17 Sg	25 Cp	2 Pc
Feb.	14 Pc	19 Ar	25 Tr	5 Ce	19 Lo	4 Lb	17 Sc	27 Sg	4 Aq	10 Pc	
Mar.	22 Pc	28 Ar	4 Gm	13 Ce	27 Lo	12 Lb	26 Sc	6 Cp	14 Aq	19 Pc	25 Ar
Apr.	7 Tr	13 Gm	23 Ce	5 Vr	20 Lb	5 Sg	15 Cp	22 Aq	28 Pc	4 Tr	
May	10 Gm	19 Ce	0 Vr	14 Lb	28 Sc	10 Cp	19 Aq	25 Pc	0 Tr	7 Gm	16 Ce
June	30 Ce	11 Vr	24 Lb	7 Sg	18 Cp	27 Aq	3 Ar	8 Tr	16 Gm	26 Ce	
July	8 Vr	20 Lb	2 Sg	13 Cp	22 Aq	29 Pc	4 Tr	11 Gm	21 Ce	4 Vr	17 Lb
Aug.	1 Sc	13 Sg	23 Cp	1 Pc	7 Ar	12 Tr	19 Gm	29 Ce	13 Vr	27 Lb	10 Sg
Sept	23 Sg	2 Aq	9 Pc	15 Ar	21 Tr	27 Gm	7 Lo	21 Vr	7 Sc	20 Sg	
Oct.	29 Cp	6 Pc	12 Ar	18 Tr	24 Gm	2 Lo	15 Vr	30 Lb	15 Sg	26 Cp	3 Pc
Nov.	15 Pc	21 Ar	27 Tr	3 Ce	12 Lo	24 Vr	8 Sc	23 Sg	4 Aq	12 Pc	
Dec.	18 Ar	23 Tr	0 Ce	9 Lo	20 Vr	2 Sc	16 Sg	29 Cp	8 Pc	14 Ar	19 Tr

1950

	Sun	Merc	Venus	Mars
Jan. 1	10 Cp	29 Cp	17 Aq	2 Lb
6	15 Cp	3 Aq	18 Aq	4 Lb
11	20 Cp	4 Aq	19 Aq	6 Lb
16	25 Cp	29 Cp	18 Aq	7 Lb
21	0 Aq	23 Cp	17 Aq	8 Lb
26	5 Aq	19 Cp	14 Aq	9 Lb
31	11 Aq	18 Cp	11 Aq	10 Lb

Jan. 1/Jup 7 Aq/Sat 19 Vr/Uran 3 Ce
Nep 17 Lb/Plut 18 Lo/N Node 12 Ar

	Sun	Merc	Venus	Mars
Feb. 1	12 Aq	19 Cp	10 Aq	10 Lb
6	17 Aq	21 Cp	7 Aq	11 Lb
11	22 Aq	26 Cp	5 Aq	11 Lb
16	27 Aq	1 Aq	4 Aq	11 Lb
21	2 Pc	8 Aq	3 Aq	11 Lb
26	7 Pc	15 Aq	4 Aq	10 Lb

Feb. 1/Jup 14 Aq/Sat 18 Vr/Uran 2 Ce
Nep 17 Lb/Plut 17 Lo/N Node 10 Ar

	Sun	Merc	Venus	Mars
Mar. 1	10 Pc	19 Aq	4 Aq	9 Lb
6	15 Pc	27 Aq	6 Aq	8 Lb
11	20 Pc	5 Pc	9 Aq	7 Lb
16	25 Pc	14 Pc	12 Aq	5 Lb
21	0 Ar	23 Pc	16 Aq	3 Lb
26	5 Ar	3 Ar	20 Aq	1 Lb
31	10 Ar	13 Ar	24 Aq	29 Vr

Mar. 1/Jup 20 Aq/Sat 17 Vr/Uran 1 Ce
Nep 17 Lb/Plut 16 Lo/N Node 9 Ar

	Sun	Merc	Venus	Mars
Apr. 1	11 Ar	15 Ar	25 Aq	29 Vr
6	16 Ar	25 Ar	29 Aq	27 Vr
11	21 Ar	5 Tr	4 Pc	25 Vr
16	25 Ar	13 Tr	9 Pc	24 Vr
21	0 Tr	20 Tr	14 Pc	23 Vr
26	5 Tr	25 Tr	19 Pc	22 Vr

Apr. 1/Jup 27 Aq/Sat 14 Vr/Uran 1 Ce
Nep 16 Lb/Plut 16 Lo/N Node 7 Ar

	Sun	Merc	Venus	Mars
May 1	10 Tr	27 Tr	25 Pc	22 Vr
6	15 Tr	27 Tr	0 Ar	22 Vr
11	20 Tr	25 Tr	6 Ar	22 Vr
16	25 Tr	23 Tr	11 Ar	23 Vr
21	29 Tr	20 Tr	17 Ar	24 Vr
26	4 Gm	19 Tr	22 Ar	25 Vr
31	9 Gm	19 Tr	28 Ar	26 Vr

May 1/Jup 3 Pc/Sat 13 Vr/Uran 2 Ce
Nep 15 Lb/Plut 16 Lo/N Node 6 Ar

	Sun	Merc	Venus	Mars
June 1	10 Gm	19 Tr	29 Ar	26 Vr
6	15 Gm	22 Tr	5 Tr	28 Vr
11	20 Gm	26 Tr	11 Tr	0 Lb
16	24 Gm	2 Gm	17 Tr	2 Lb
21	29 Gm	9 Gm	22 Tr	4 Lb
26	4 Ce	17 Gm	28 Tr	6 Lb

June 1/Jup 6 Pc/Sat 13 Vr/Uran 4 Ce
Nep 15 Lb/Plut 16 Lo/N Node 4 Ar

	Sun	Merc	Venus	Mars
July 1	9 Ce	27 Gm	4 Gm	8 Lb
6	13 Ce	7 Ce	10 Gm	10 Lb
11	18 Ce	18 Ce	16 Gm	13 Lb
16	23 Ce	29 Ce	22 Gm	15 Lb
21	28 Ce	9 Lo	28 Gm	18 Lb
26	2 Lo	18 Lo	4 Ce	21 Lb
31	7 Lo	27 Lo	10 Ce	24 Lb

July 1/Jup 7 Pc/Sat 14 Vr/Uran 5 Ce
Nep 15 Lb/Plut 17 Lo/N Node 3 Ar

	Sun	Merc	Venus	Mars
Aug. 1	8 Lo	28 Lo	11 Ce	24 Lb
6	13 Lo	6 Vr	17 Ce	27 Lb
11	18 Lo	13 Vr	23 Ce	0 Sc
16	23 Lo	19 Vr	29 Ce	3 Sc
21	27 Lo	25 Vr	5 Lo	6 Sc
26	2 Vr	29 Vr	11 Lo	9 Sc
31	7 Vr	2 Lb	18 Lo	13 Sc

Aug. 1/Jup 6 Pc/Sat 17 Vr/Uran 7 Ce
Nep 15 Lb/Plut 18 Lo/N Node 1 Ar

1950

	Sun	Merc	Venus	Mars
Sept 1	8 Vr	2 Lb	19 Lo	13 Sc
6	13 Vr	2 Lb	25 Lo	17 Sc
11	18 Vr	0 Lb	1 Vr	20 Sc
16	23 Vr	25 Vr	7 Vr	23 Sc
21	27 Vr	20 Vr	14 Vr	27 Sc
26	2 Lb	18 Vr	20 Vr	0 Sg

Sept 1/Jup 2 Pc/Sat 21 Vr/Uran 9 Ce
Nep 16 Lb/Plut 18 Lo/N Node 29 Pc

	Sun	Merc	Venus	Mars
Oct. 1	7 Lb	20 Vr	26 Vr	4 Sg
6	12 Lb	25 Vr	2 Lb	7 Sg
11	17 Lb	2 Lb	8 Lb	11 Sg
16	22 Lb	11 Lb	15 Lb	14 Sg
21	27 Lb	19 Lb	21 Lb	18 Sg
26	2 Sc	28 Lb	27 Lb	22 Sg
31	7 Sc	6 Sc	3 Sc	25 Sg

Oct. 1/Jup 29 Aq/Sat 25 Vr/Uran 9 Ce
Nep 17 Lb/Plut 19 Lo/N Node 28 Pc

	Sun	Merc	Venus	Mars
Nov. 1	8 Sc	8 Sc	5 Sc	26 Sg
6	13 Sc	16 Sc	11 Sc	0 Cp
11	18 Sc	24 Sc	17 Sc	4 Cp
16	23 Sc	1 Sg	24 Sc	7 Cp
21	28 Sc	9 Sg	0 Sg	11 Cp
26	3 Sg	17 Sg	6 Sg	15 Cp

Nov. 1/Jup 28 Aq/Sat 28 Vr/Uran 9 Ce
Nep 18 Lb/Plut 20 Lo/N Node 26 Pc

	Sun	Merc	Venus	Mars
Dec. 1	8 Sg	24 Sg	12 Sg	19 Cp
6	13 Sg	1 Cp	19 Sg	23 Cp
11	18 Sg	8 Cp	25 Sg	27 Cp
16	23 Sg	14 Cp	1 Cp	0 Aq
21	29 Sg	18 Cp	8 Cp	4 Aq
26	4 Cp	18 Cp	14 Cp	8 Aq
31	9 Cp	13 Cp	20 Cp	12 Aq

Dec. 1/Jup 30 Aq/Sat 1 Lb/Uran 9 Ce
Nep 19 Lb/Plut 20 Lo/N Node 24 Pc

Moon's Positions

	1	4	7	10	13	16	19	22	25	28	31
Jan.	1 Gm	9 Ce	19 Lo	1 Lb	13 Sc	25 Sg	7 Aq	15 Pc	22 Ar	27 Tr	4 Ce
Feb.	17 Ce	28 Lo	11 Lb	24 Sc	5 Cp	15 Aq	23 Pc	29 Ar	5 Gm	12 Ce	
Mar.	25 Ce	7 Vr	21 Lb	4 Sg	16 Cp	25 Aq	2 Ar	8 Tr	13 Gm	20 Ce	1 Vr
Apr.	15 Vr	30 Lb	14 Sg	26 Cp	4 Pc	11 Ar	16 Tr	22 Gm	29 Ce	9 Vr	
May	23 Lb	8 Sg	22 Cp	1 Pc	8 Ar	13 Tr	19 Gm	26 Ce	5 Vr	16 Lb	1 Sg
June	17 Sg	0 Aq	10 Pc	17 Ar	22 Tr	28 Gm	5 Lo	15 Vr	26 Lb	10 Sg	
July	24 Cp	6 Pc	13 Ar	19 Tr	25 Gm	2 Lo	12 Vr	23 Lb	5 Sg	19 Cp	0 Pc
Aug.	14 Pc	21 Ar	27 Tr	3 Ce	11 Lo	22 Vr	4 Sc	16 Sg	28 Cp	9 Pc	17 Ar
Sept	29 Ar	5 Gm	11 Ce	19 Lo	1 Lb	14 Sc	27 Sg	8 Aq	18 Pc	25 Ar	
Oct.	1 Gm	7 Ce	14 Lo	25 Vr	9 Sc	23 Sg	5 Aq	14 Pc	21 Ar	27 Tr	3 Ce
Nov.	15 Ce	22 Lo	3 Lb	17 Sc	3 Cp	15 Aq	24 Pc	0 Tr	6 Gm	12 Ce	
Dec.	18 Lo	27 Vr	10 Sc	26 Sg	10 Aq	21 Pc	27 Ar	3 Gm	9 Ce	16 Lo	24 Vr

                                                                 Ephemeris

1951

	Sun	Merc	Venus	Mars
Jan. 1	10 Cp	12 Cp	21 Cp	13 Aq
6	15 Cp	5 Cp	28 Cp	17 Aq
11	20 Cp	2 Cp	4 Aq	21 Aq
16	25 Cp	3 Cp	10 Aq	25 Aq
21	0 Aq	6 Cp	16 Aq	29 Aq
26	5 Aq	11 Cp	23 Aq	3 Pc
31	10 Aq	17 Cp	29 Aq	7 Pc

Jan. 1/Jup 5 Pc/Sat 2 Lb/Uran 7 Ce
Nep 19 Lb/Plut 19 Lo/N Node 23 Pc

	Sun	Merc	Venus	Mars
Feb. 1	11 Aq	18 Cp	0 Pc	7 Pc
6	16 Aq	25 Cp	6 Pc	11 Pc
11	21 Aq	2 Aq	13 Pc	15 Pc
16	27 Aq	9 Aq	19 Pc	19 Pc
21	2 Pc	17 Aq	25 Pc	23 Pc
26	7 Pc	26 Aq	1 Ar	27 Pc

Feb. 1/Jup 11 Pc/Sat 2 Lb/Uran 6 Ce
Nep 19 Lb/Plut 19 Lo/N Node 21 Pc

	Sun	Merc	Venus	Mars
Mar. 1	10 Pc	1 Pc	5 Ar	29 Pc
6	15 Pc	10 Pc	11 Ar	3 Ar
11	20 Pc	19 Pc	17 Ar	7 Ar
16	25 Pc	29 Pc	23 Ar	11 Ar
21	0 Ar	9 Ar	29 Ar	15 Ar
26	5 Ar	19 Ar	6 Tr	18 Ar
31	9 Ar	27 Ar	12 Tr	22 Ar

Mar. 1/Jup 18 Pc/Sat 0 Lb/Uran 5 Ce
Nep 19 Lb/Plut 18 Lo/N Node 20 Pc

	Sun	Merc	Venus	Mars
Apr. 1	10 Ar	28 Ar	13 Tr	23 Ar
6	15 Ar	4 Tr	19 Tr	27 Ar
11	20 Ar	8 Tr	25 Tr	0 Tr
16	25 Ar	8 Tr	1 Gm	4 Tr
21	0 Tr	7 Tr	7 Gm	8 Tr
26	5 Tr	4 Tr	13 Gm	12 Tr

Apr. 1/Jup 25 Pc/Sat 28 Vr/Uran 6 Ce
Nep 18 Lb/Plut 18 Lo/N Node 18 Pc

	Sun	Merc	Venus	Mars
May 1	10 Tr	0 Tr	18 Gm	15 Tr
6	15 Tr	29 Ar	24 Gm	19 Tr
11	20 Tr	29 Ar	0 Ce	22 Tr
16	24 Tr	0 Tr	6 Ce	26 Tr
21	29 Tr	4 Tr	11 Ce	0 Gm
26	4 Gm	9 Tr	17 Ce	3 Gm
31	9 Gm	15 Tr	22 Ce	7 Gm

May 1/Jup 2 Ar/Sat 26 Vr/Uran 6 Ce
Nep 18 Lb/Plut 17 Lo/N Node 16 Pc

	Sun	Merc	Venus	Mars
June 1	10 Gm	17 Tr	23 Ce	7 Gm
6	15 Gm	24 Tr	29 Ce	11 Gm
11	19 Gm	3 Gm	4 Lo	14 Gm
16	24 Gm	13 Gm	9 Lo	18 Gm
21	29 Gm	23 Gm	14 Lo	21 Gm
26	4 Ce	4 Ce	19 Lo	25 Gm

June 1/Jup 8 Ar/Sat 26 Vr/Uran 8 Ce
Nep 17 Lb/Plut 18 Lo/N Node 15 Pc

	Sun	Merc	Venus	Mars
July 1	8 Ce	15 Ce	24 Lo	28 Gm
6	13 Ce	25 Ce	28 Lo	1 Ce
11	18 Ce	4 Lo	2 Vr	5 Ce
16	23 Ce	13 Lo	6 Vr	8 Ce
21	27 Ce	21 Lo	10 Vr	11 Ce
26	2 Lo	28 Lo	13 Vr	15 Ce
31	7 Lo	4 Vr	15 Vr	18 Ce

July 1/Jup 12 Ar/Sat 26 Vr/Uran 10 Ce
Nep 17 Lb/Plut 18 Lo/N Node 13 Pc

	Sun	Merc	Venus	Mars
Aug. 1	8 Lo	5 Vr	16 Vr	19 Ce
6	13 Lo	10 Vr	17 Vr	22 Ce
11	18 Lo	13 Vr	18 Vr	25 Ce
16	22 Lo	15 Vr	18 Vr	28 Ce
21	27 Lo	15 Vr	17 Vr	2 Lo
26	2 Vr	12 Vr	15 Vr	5 Lo
31	7 Vr	7 Vr	13 Vr	8 Lo

Aug. 1/Jup 14 Ar/Sat 29 Vr/Uran 11 Ce
Nep 17 Lb/Plut 19 Lo/N Node 12 Pc

1951

	Sun	Merc	Venus	Mars
Sept 1	8 Vr	7 Vr	12 Vr	9 Lo
6	13 Vr	3 Vr	9 Vr	12 Lo
11	17 Vr	2 Vr	6 Vr	15 Lo
16	22 Vr	4 Vr	4 Vr	18 Lo
21	27 Vr	10 Vr	2 Vr	21 Lo
26	2 Lb	18 Vr	2 Vr	24 Lo

Sept 1/Jup 13 Ar/Sat 2 Lb/Uran 13 Ce
Nep 18 Lb/Plut 20 Lo/N Node 10 Pc

	Sun	Merc	Venus	Mars
Oct. 1	7 Lb	27 Vr	3 Vr	28 Lo
6	12 Lb	6 Lb	4 Vr	1 Vr
11	17 Lb	15 Lb	7 Vr	4 Vr
16	22 Lb	24 Lb	9 Vr	7 Vr
21	27 Lb	2 Sc	13 Vr	10 Vr
26	2 Sc	10 Sc	17 Vr	13 Vr
31	7 Sc	18 Sc	21 Vr	16 Vr

Oct. 1/Jup 9 Ar/Sat 6 Lb/Uran 14 Ce
Nep 19 Lb/Plut 21 Lo/N Node 8 Pc

	Sun	Merc	Venus	Mars
Nov. 1	8 Sc	19 Sc	22 Vr	16 Vr
6	13 Sc	27 Sc	26 Vr	19 Vr
11	18 Sc	4 Sg	1 Lb	22 Vr
16	23 Sc	11 Sg	6 Lb	25 Vr
21	28 Sc	18 Sg	11 Lb	28 Vr
26	3 Sg	24 Sg	17 Lb	1 Lb

Nov. 1/Jup 6 Ar/Sat 9 Lb/Uran 14 Ce
Nep 20 Lb/Plut 21 Lo/N Node 7 Pc

	Sun	Merc	Venus	Mars
Dec. 1	8 Sg	29 Sg	22 Lb	4 Lb
6	13 Sg	2 Cp	28 Lb	7 Lb
11	18 Sg	1 Cp	3 Sc	9 Lb
16	23 Sg	26 Sg	9 Sc	12 Lb
21	28 Sg	19 Sg	15 Sc	15 Lb
26	3 Cp	16 Sg	21 Sc	18 Lb
31	8 Cp	17 Sg	27 Sc	20 Lb

Dec. 1/Jup 4 Ar/Sat 12 Lb/Uran 13 Ce
Nep 21 Lb/Plut 22 Lo/N Node 5 Pc

Moon's Positions

	1	4	7	10	13	16	19	22	25	28	31
Jan.	7 Lb	19 Sc	4 Cp	18 Aq	29 Pc	6 Tr	12 Gm	18 Ce	25 Lo	4 Lb	15 Sc
Feb.	29 Sc	13 Cp	26 Aq	7 Ar	14 Tr	20 Gm	26 Ce	4 Vr	14 Lb	26 Sc	
Mar.	10 Sg	23 Cp	5 Pc	14 Ar	22 Tr	27 Gm	4 Lo	12 Vr	24 Lb	7 Sg	20 Cp
Apr.	3 Aq	14 Pc	23 Ar	30 Tr	5 Ce	12 Lo	20 Vr	2 Sc	17 Sg	0 Aq	
May	11 Pc	19 Ar	26 Tr	2 Ce	8 Lo	15 Vr	26 Lb	11 Sg	26 Cp	8 Pc	16 Ar
June	29 Ar	5 Gm	11 Ce	16 Lo	24 Vr	5 Sc	19 Sg	5 Aq	17 Pc	26 Ar	
July	2 Gm	8 Ce	13 Lo	20 Vr	30 Lb	13 Sg	28 Cp	12 Pc	22 Ar	29 Tr	5 Ce
Aug.	16 Ce	23 Lo	0 Lb	10 Sc	22 Sg	7 Aq	20 Pc	0 Tr	7 Gm	13 Ce	19 Lo
Sept	2 Vr	10 Lb	21 Sc	3 Cp	16 Aq	28 Pc	8 Tr	15 Gm	21 Ce	27 Lo	
Oct.	6 Lb	17 Sc	30 Sg	12 Aq	24 Pc	3 Tr	11 Gm	17 Ce	23 Lo	1 Lb	12 Sc
Nov.	27 Sc	10 Cp	23 Aq	3 Ar	12 Tr	19 Gm	25 Ce	1 Vr	9 Lb	21 Sc	
Dec.	5 Cp	19 Aq	0 Ar	9 Tr	16 Gm	22 Ce	27 Lo	4 Lb	14 Sc	28 Sg	14 Aq

1952

```
        Sun    Merc   Venus   Mars
Jan. 1  10 Cp  18 Sg  28 Sc   21 Lb
     6  15 Cp  22 Sg   4 Sg   23 Lb
    11  20 Cp  27 Sg  10 Sg   26 Lb
    16  25 Cp   4 Cp  16 Sg   28 Lb
    21   0 Aq  10 Cp  22 Sg    0 Sc
    26   5 Aq  18 Cp  28 Sg    3 Sc
    31  10 Aq  25 Cp   4 Cp    5 Sc
Jan. 1/Jup  6 Ar/Sat 14 Lb/Uran 12 Ce
Nep 22 Lb/Plut 21 Lo/N Node  3 Pc
```

```
        Sun    Merc   Venus   Mars
Feb. 1  11 Aq  27 Cp   5 Cp    5 Sc
     6  16 Aq   5 Aq  11 Cp    7 Sc
    11  21 Aq  13 Aq  18 Cp    9 Sc
    16  26 Aq  21 Aq  24 Cp   11 Sc
    21   1 Pc   0 Pc   0 Aq   13 Sc
    26   6 Pc  10 Pc   6 Aq   14 Sc
Feb. 1/Jup 10 Ar/Sat 15 Lb/Uran 11 Ce
Nep 22 Lb/Plut 21 Lo/N Node  2 Pc
```

```
        Sun    Merc   Venus   Mars
Mar. 1  10 Pc  17 Pc  11 Aq   15 Sc
     6  15 Pc  27 Pc  17 Aq   16 Sc
    11  20 Pc   6 Ar  23 Aq   17 Sc
    16  25 Pc  13 Ar  29 Aq   18 Sc
    21   0 Ar  18 Ar   5 Pc   18 Sc
    26   5 Ar  20 Ar  12 Pc   18 Sc
    31  10 Ar  19 Ar  18 Pc   18 Sc
Mar. 1/Jup 16 Ar/Sat 14 Lb/Uran 10 Ce
Nep 21 Lb/Plut 20 Lo/N Node  0 Pc
```

```
        Sun    Merc   Venus   Mars
Apr. 1  11 Ar  19 Ar  19 Pc   18 Sc
     6  16 Ar  15 Ar  25 Pc   18 Sc
    11  21 Ar  11 Ar   1 Ar   17 Sc
    16  26 Ar   9 Ar   7 Ar   16 Sc
    21   1 Tr   9 Ar  14 Ar   14 Sc
    26   6 Tr  11 Ar  20 Ar   12 Sc
Apr. 1/Jup 23 Ar/Sat 12 Lb/Uran 10 Ce
Nep 21 Lb/Plut 19 Lo/N Node 29 Aq
```

```
        Sun    Merc   Venus   Mars
May  1  11 Tr  14 Ar  26 Ar   11 Sc
     6  15 Tr  19 Ar   2 Tr    9 Sc
    11  20 Tr  25 Ar   8 Tr    7 Sc
    16  25 Tr   2 Tr  14 Tr    5 Sc
    21   0 Gm  10 Tr  20 Tr    4 Sc
    26   5 Gm  19 Tr  27 Tr    3 Sc
    31   9 Gm  29 Tr   3 Gm    2 Sc
May  1/Jup  1 Tr/Sat  9 Lb/Uran 11 Ce
Nep 20 Lb/Plut 19 Lo/N Node 27 Aq
```

```
        Sun    Merc   Venus   Mars
June 1  10 Gm   1 Gm   4 Gm    2 Sc
     6  15 Gm  11 Gm  10 Gm    1 Sc
    11  20 Gm  22 Gm  16 Gm    1 Sc
    16  25 Gm   3 Ce  22 Gm    1 Sc
    21   0 Ce  13 Ce  28 Gm    2 Sc
    26   4 Ce  23 Ce   5 Ce    3 Sc
June 1/Jup  8 Tr/Sat  8 Lb/Uran 12 Ce
Nep 19 Lb/Plut 19 Lo/N Node 25 Aq
```

```
        Sun    Merc   Venus   Mars
July 1   9 Ce   1 Lo  11 Ce    4 Sc
     6  14 Ce   8 Lo  17 Ce    5 Sc
    11  19 Ce  15 Lo  23 Ce    7 Sc
    16  23 Ce  20 Lo  29 Ce    9 Sc
    21  28 Ce  24 Lo   5 Lo   11 Sc
    26   3 Lo  27 Lo  12 Lo   13 Sc
    31   8 Lo  27 Lo  18 Lo   15 Sc
July 1/Jup 14 Tr/Sat  9 Lb/Uran 14 Ce
Nep 19 Lb/Plut 20 Lo/N Node 24 Aq
```

```
        Sun    Merc   Venus   Mars
Aug. 1   9 Lo  27 Lo  19 Lo   15 Sc
     6  13 Lo  25 Lo  25 Lo   18 Sc
    11  18 Lo  21 Lo   1 Vr   20 Sc
    16  23 Lo  17 Lo   7 Vr   23 Sc
    21  28 Lo  15 Lo  14 Vr   26 Sc
    26   3 Vr  16 Lo  20 Vr   29 Sc
    31   8 Vr  19 Lo  26 Vr    2 Sg
Aug. 1/Jup 18 Tr/Sat 10 Lb/Uran 16 Ce
Nep 19 Lb/Plut 21 Lo/N Node 22 Aq
```

1952

```
           Sun    Merc   Venus   Mars                Sun    Merc   Venus   Mars
Sept 1    8 Vr   20 Lo   27 Vr    3 Sg     Oct. 1   8 Lb   13 Lb    4 Sc   22 Sg
     6   13 Vr   28 Lo    3 Lb    6 Sg          6  13 Lb   21 Lb   10 Sc   26 Sg
    11   18 Vr    6 Vr    9 Lb    9 Sg         11  18 Lb   29 Lb   16 Sc   29 Sg
    16   23 Vr   16 Vr   16 Lb   12 Sg         16  23 Lb    7 Sc   22 Sc    3 Cp
    21   28 Vr   25 Vr   22 Lb   15 Sg         21  28 Lb   14 Sc   29 Sc    6 Cp
    26    3 Lb    4 Lb   28 Lb   19 Sg         26   3 Sc   22 Sc    5 Sg   10 Cp
                                               31   8 Sc   28 Sc   11 Sg   14 Cp
```

Sept 1/Jup 21 Tr/Sat 13 Lb/Uran 17 Ce
Nep 20 Lb/Plut 22 Lo/N Node 21 Aq

Oct. 1/Jup 20 Tr/Sat 17 Lb/Uran 18 Ce
Nep 21 Lb/Plut 23 Lo/N Node 19 Aq

```
           Sun    Merc   Venus   Mars                Sun    Merc   Venus   Mars
Nov. 1    9 Sc    0 Sg   12 Sg   14 Cp     Dec. 1   9 Sg    7 Sg   18 Cp    7 Aq
     6   14 Sc    6 Sg   18 Sg   18 Cp          6  14 Sg    2 Sg   24 Cp   11 Aq
    11   19 Sc   11 Sg   24 Sg   22 Cp         11  19 Sg    0 Sg    0 Aq   15 Aq
    16   24 Sc   15 Sg    0 Cp   26 Cp         16  24 Sg    3 Sg    6 Aq   19 Aq
    21   29 Sc   16 Sg    6 Cp   29 Cp         21  29 Sg    8 Sg   12 Aq   22 Aq
    26    4 Sg   14 Sg   12 Cp    3 Aq         26   4 Cp   14 Sg   18 Aq   26 Aq
                                               31   9 Cp   21 Sg   24 Aq    0 Pc
```

Nov. 1/Jup 17 Tr/Sat 20 Lb/Uran 19 Ce
Nep 22 Lb/Plut 23 Lo/N Node 17 Aq

Dec. 1/Jup 13 Tr/Sat 24 Lb/Uran 18 Ce
Nep 23 Lb/Plut 23 Lo/N Node 16 Aq

Moon's Positions

```
             1       4       7      10      13      16      19      22      25      28      31
Jan.   29 Aq   10 Ar   18 Tr   25 Gm    0 Lo    6 Vr   13 Lb   23 Sc    7 Cp   22 Aq    5 Ar
Feb.   19 Ar   27 Tr    4 Ce    9 Lo   15 Vr   23 Lb    2 Sg   15 Cp   30 Aq   13 Ar
Mar.   10 Tr   18 Gm   24 Ce   30 Lo    7 Lb   16 Sc   27 Sg   10 Aq   23 Pc    5 Tr   14 Gm
Apr.   26 Gm    2 Lo    8 Vr   16 Lb   26 Sc    8 Cp   20 Aq    2 Ar   13 Tr   22 Gm
May    28 Ce    4 Vr   11 Lb   21 Sc    4 Cp   17 Aq   29 Pc    9 Tr   18 Gm   24 Ce   30 Lo
June   11 Vr   19 Lb   30 Sc   14 Cp   28 Aq    9 Ar   19 Tr   26 Gm    2 Lo    8 Vr
July   14 Lb   24 Sc    7 Cp   23 Aq    6 Ar   16 Tr   23 Gm   29 Ce    5 Vr   11 Lb   19 Sc
Aug.    3 Sg   16 Cp    1 Pc   15 Ar   25 Tr    3 Ce    8 Lo   14 Vr   20 Lb   28 Sc   10 Cp
Sept   24 Cp    9 Pc   24 Ar    4 Gm   11 Ce   17 Lo   23 Vr   30 Lb    9 Sg   20 Cp
Oct.    3 Pc   17 Ar   29 Tr    8 Ce   13 Lo   19 Vr   26 Lb    5 Sg   16 Cp   29 Aq   12 Ar
Nov.   26 Ar    7 Gm   15 Ce   21 Lo   27 Vr    5 Sc   15 Sg   27 Cp    9 Pc   21 Ar
Dec.    2 Gm   11 Ce   17 Lo   23 Vr   30 Lb   10 Sg   23 Cp    6 Pc   18 Ar   28 Tr    7 Ce
```

1953

```
          Sun    Merc    Venus   Mars                    Sun    Merc    Venus   Mars
Jan.  1  10 Cp  22 Sg   25 Aq    1 Pc        Feb.  1   12 Aq  10 Aq   29 Pc   25 Pc
      6  15 Cp  29 Sg    1 Pc    5 Pc              6   17 Aq  19 Aq    4 Ar   28 Pc
     11  20 Cp   7 Cp    6 Pc    9 Pc             11   22 Aq  28 Aq    8 Ar    2 Ar
     16  26 Cp  14 Cp   12 Pc   12 Pc             16   27 Aq   7 Pc   13 Ar    6 Ar
     21   1 Aq  22 Cp   17 Pc   16 Pc             21    2 Pc  16 Pc   17 Ar   10 Ar
     26   6 Aq   0 Aq   23 Pc   20 Pc             26    7 Pc  24 Pc   21 Ar   14 Ar
     31  11 Aq   9 Aq   28 Pc   24 Pc
Jan. 1/Jup 11 Tr/Sat 26 Lb/Uran 17 Ce       Feb. 1/Jup 12 Tr/Sat 27 Lb/Uran 15 Ce
Nep 24 Lb/Plut 23 Lo/N Node 14 Aq           Nep 24 Lb/Plut 22 Lo/N Node 12 Aq


          Sun    Merc    Venus   Mars                    Sun    Merc    Venus   Mars
Mar.  1  10 Pc  28 Pc   23 Ar   16 Ar        Apr.  1   11 Ar  20 Pc    0 Tr    9 Tr
      6  15 Pc   2 Ar   26 Ar   19 Ar              6   16 Ar  21 Pc   27 Ar   12 Tr
     11  20 Pc   3 Ar   29 Ar   23 Ar             11   21 Ar  24 Pc   25 Ar   16 Tr
     16  25 Pc   0 Ar    0 Tr   27 Ar             16   26 Ar  28 Pc   21 Ar   19 Tr
     21   0 Ar  25 Pc    1 Tr    1 Tr             21    1 Tr   4 Ar   19 Ar   23 Tr
     26   5 Ar  22 Pc    1 Tr    4 Tr             26    5 Tr  10 Ar   16 Ar   26 Tr
     31  10 Ar  20 Pc    0 Tr    8 Tr
Mar. 1/Jup 16 Tr/Sat 27 Lb/Uran 15 Ce       Apr. 1/Jup 21 Tr/Sat 25 Lb/Uran 14 Ce
Nep 24 Lb/Plut 22 Lo/N Node 11 Aq           Nep 23 Lb/Plut 21 Lo/N Node  9 Aq


          Sun    Merc    Venus   Mars                    Sun    Merc    Venus   Mars
May   1  10 Tr  18 Ar   15 Ar    0 Gm        June  1   10 Gm  19 Gm   27 Ar   21 Gm
      6  15 Tr  26 Ar   15 Ar    3 Gm              6   15 Gm  29 Gm    0 Tr   25 Gm
     11  20 Tr   5 Tr   16 Ar    7 Gm             11   20 Gm   9 Ce    5 Tr   28 Gm
     16  25 Tr  15 Tr   17 Ar   10 Gm             16   25 Gm  17 Ce    9 Tr    1 Ce
     21   0 Gm  25 Tr   20 Ar   14 Gm             21   29 Gm  24 Ce   14 Tr    5 Ce
     26   4 Gm   6 Gm   23 Ar   17 Gm             26    4 Ce   0 Lo   18 Tr    8 Ce
     31   9 Gm  17 Gm   26 Ar   20 Gm
May  1/Jup 28 Tr/Sat 23 Lb/Uran 15 Ce       June 1/Jup  5 Gm/Sat 21 Lb/Uran 16 Ce
Nep 22 Lb/Plut 21 Lo/N Node  8 Aq           Nep 21 Lb/Plut 21 Lo/N Node  6 Aq


          Sun    Merc    Venus   Mars                    Sun    Merc    Venus   Mars
July  1   9 Ce   4 Lo   23 Tr   11 Ce        Aug.  1    8 Lo  28 Ce   27 Gm    1 Lo
      6  14 Ce   7 Lo   29 Tr   14 Ce              6   13 Lo  28 Ce    2 Ce    5 Lo
     11  18 Ce   8 Lo    4 Gm   18 Ce             11   18 Lo   0 Lo    8 Ce    8 Lo
     16  23 Ce   8 Lo    9 Gm   21 Ce             16   23 Lo   4 Lo   14 Ce   11 Lo
     21  28 Ce   5 Lo   14 Gm   24 Ce             21   28 Lo  12 Lo   19 Ce   14 Lo
     26   3 Lo   2 Lo   20 Gm   28 Ce             26    2 Vr  20 Lo   25 Ce   17 Lo
     31   7 Lo  29 Ce   25 Gm    1 Lo             31    7 Vr   0 Vr    1 Lo   21 Lo
July 1/Jup 12 Gm/Sat 21 Lb/Uran 18 Ce       Aug. 1/Jup 18 Gm/Sat 22 Lb/Uran 20 Ce
Nep 21 Lb/Plut 22 Lo/N Node  4 Aq           Nep 21 Lb/Plut 22 Lo/N Node  3 Aq
```

1953

	Sun	Merc	Venus	Mars
Sept 1	8 Vr	2 Vr	2 Lo	21 Lo
6	13 Vr	12 Vr	8 Lo	24 Lo
11	18 Vr	21 Vr	14 Lo	28 Lo
16	23 Vr	0 Lb	20 Lo	1 Vr
21	28 Vr	9 Lb	26 Lo	4 Vr
26	3 Lb	17 Lb	2 Vr	7 Vr

Sept 1/Jup 23 Gm/Sat 24 Lb/Uran 22 Ce
Nep 22 Lb/Plut 23 Lo/N Node 1 Aq

	Sun	Merc	Venus	Mars
Oct. 1	8 Lb	25 Lb	8 Vr	10 Vr
6	12 Lb	2 Sc	14 Vr	13 Vr
11	17 Lb	9 Sc	21 Vr	17 Vr
16	22 Lb	15 Sc	27 Vr	20 Vr
21	27 Lb	21 Sc	3 Lb	23 Vr
26	2 Sc	26 Sc	9 Lb	26 Vr
31	7 Sc	0 Sg	15 Lb	29 Vr

Oct. 1/Jup 26 Gm/Sat 27 Lb/Uran 23 Ce
Nep 23 Lb/Plut 24 Lo/N Node 30 Cp

	Sun	Merc	Venus	Mars
Nov. 1	8 Sc	0 Sg	17 Lb	0 Lb
6	13 Sc	0 Sg	23 Lb	3 Lb
11	18 Sc	27 Sc	29 Lb	6 Lb
16	23 Sc	20 Sc	5 Sc	9 Lb
21	28 Sc	15 Sc	12 Sc	12 Lb
26	3 Sg	15 Sc	18 Sc	15 Lb

Nov. 1/Jup 26 Gm/Sat 1 Sc/Uran 23 Ce
Nep 24 Lb/Plut 25 Lo/N Node 28 Cp

	Sun	Merc	Venus	Mars
Dec. 1	9 Sg	18 Sc	24 Sc	18 Lb
6	14 Sg	24 Sc	0 Sg	21 Lb
11	19 Sg	1 Sg	7 Sg	24 Lb
16	24 Sg	8 Sg	13 Sg	27 Lb
21	29 Sg	15 Sg	19 Sg	0 Sc
26	4 Cp	23 Sg	26 Sg	3 Sc
31	9 Cp	0 Cp	2 Cp	6 Sc

Dec. 1/Jup 23 Gm/Sat 5 Sc/Uran 23 Ce
Nep 25 Lb/Plut 25 Lo/N Node 26 Cp

Moon's Positions

	1	4	7	10	13	16	19	22	25	28	31
Jan.	19 Ce	25 Lo	1 Lb	8 Sc	18 Sg	1 Aq	16 Pc	29 Ar	8 Gm	16 Ce	22 Lo
Feb.	4 Vr	9 Lb	16 Sc	26 Sg	9 Aq	25 Pc	8 Tr	18 Gm	25 Ce	1 Vr	
Mar.	12 Vr	18 Lb	25 Sc	4 Cp	17 Aq	3 Ar	17 Tr	27 Gm	4 Lo	9 Vr	15 Lb
Apr.	27 Lb	5 Sg	14 Cp	26 Aq	11 Ar	25 Tr	5 Ce	12 Lo	18 Vr	24 Lb	
May	2 Sg	11 Cp	22 Aq	6 Ar	19 Tr	0 Ce	8 Lo	14 Vr	20 Lb	28 Sc	8 Cp
June	21 Cp	3 Pc	16 Ar	28 Tr	9 Ce	16 Lo	22 Vr	28 Lb	6 Sg	17 Cp	9 Ar
July	30 Aq	13 Ar	24 Tr	4 Ce	12 Lo	18 Vr	24 Lb	1 Sg	12 Cp	25 Aq	9 Ar
Aug.	24 Ar	5 Gm	14 Ce	21 Lo	26 Vr	2 Sc	9 Sg	20 Cp	4 Pc	19 Ar	2 Gm
Sept	15 Gm	23 Ce	30 Lo	5 Lb	11 Sc	18 Sg	28 Cp	12 Pc	28 Ar	11 Gm	
Oct.	20 Ce	27 Lo	2 Lb	8 Sc	15 Sg	23 Cp	5 Pc	21 Ar	5 Gm	16 Ce	23 Lo
Nov.	5 Vr	11 Lb	17 Sc	25 Sg	4 Aq	15 Pc	29 Ar	13 Gm	24 Ce	2 Vr	9 Sc
Dec.	7 Lb	13 Sc	21 Sg	1 Aq	12 Pc	24 Ar	7 Gm	19 Ce	27 Lo	3 Lb	9 Sc

                                                  Ephemeris

1954

	Sun	Merc	Venus	Mars
Jan. 1	10 Cp	2 Cp	3 Cp	7 Sc
6	15 Cp	10 Cp	9 Cp	10 Sc
11	20 Cp	18 Cp	16 Cp	13 Sc
16	25 Cp	26 Cp	22 Cp	16 Sc
21	0 Aq	5 Aq	28 Cp	19 Sc
26	6 Aq	13 Aq	5 Aq	22 Sc
31	11 Aq	22 Aq	11 Aq	24 Sc

Jan. 1/Jup 19 Gm/Sat 7 Sc/Uran 22 Ce
Nep 26 Lb/Plut 25 Lo/N Node 25 Cp

	Sun	Merc	Venus	Mars
Feb. 1	12 Aq	24 Aq	12 Aq	25 Sc
6	17 Aq	2 Pc	18 Aq	28 Sc
11	22 Aq	9 Pc	25 Aq	1 Sg
16	27 Aq	15 Pc	1 Pc	3 Sg
21	2 Pc	16 Pc	7 Pc	6 Sg
26	7 Pc	14 Pc	13 Pc	9 Sg

Feb. 1/Jup 17 Gm/Sat 9 Sc/Uran 20 Ce
Nep 26 Lb/Plut 24 Lo/N Node 23 Cp

	Sun	Merc	Venus	Mars
Mar. 1	10 Pc	11 Pc	17 Pc	10 Sg
6	15 Pc	6 Pc	23 Pc	13 Sg
11	20 Pc	2 Pc	0 Ar	16 Sg
16	25 Pc	2 Pc	6 Ar	18 Sg
21	0 Ar	4 Pc	12 Ar	20 Sg
26	5 Ar	7 Pc	18 Ar	23 Sg
31	10 Ar	12 Pc	24 Ar	25 Sg

Mar. 1/Jup 17 Gm/Sat 9 Sc/Uran 19 Ce
Nep 26 Lb/Plut 23 Lo/N Node 22 Cp

	Sun	Merc	Venus	Mars
Apr. 1	11 Ar	13 Pc	26 Ar	25 Sg
6	16 Ar	19 Pc	2 Tr	27 Sg
11	21 Ar	26 Pc	8 Tr	29 Sg
16	25 Ar	4 Ar	14 Tr	1 Cp
21	0 Tr	12 Ar	20 Tr	3 Cp
26	5 Tr	21 Ar	26 Tr	4 Cp

Apr. 1/Jup 20 Gm/Sat 8 Sc/Uran 19 Ce
Nep 25 Lb/Plut 23 Lo/N Node 20 Cp

	Sun	Merc	Venus	Mars
May 1	10 Tr	1 Tr	3 Gm	6 Cp
6	15 Tr	11 Tr	9 Gm	7 Cp
11	20 Tr	22 Tr	15 Gm	8 Cp
16	25 Tr	3 Gm	21 Gm	8 Cp
21	29 Tr	13 Gm	27 Gm	8 Cp
26	4 Gm	22 Gm	3 Ce	8 Cp
31	9 Gm	0 Ce	9 Ce	8 Cp

May 1/Jup 25 Gm/Sat 6 Sc/Uran 20 Ce
Nep 24 Lb/Plut 23 Lo/N Node 18 Cp

	Sun	Merc	Venus	Mars
June 1	10 Gm	2 Ce	10 Ce	8 Cp
6	15 Gm	8 Ce	16 Ce	7 Cp
11	20 Gm	13 Ce	22 Ce	6 Cp
16	24 Gm	17 Ce	28 Ce	5 Cp
21	29 Gm	19 Ce	4 Lo	4 Cp
26	4 Ce	19 Ce	10 Lo	2 Cp

June 1/Jup 2 Ce/Sat 4 Sc/Uran 21 Ce
Nep 24 Lb/Plut 23 Lo/N Node 17 Cp

	Sun	Merc	Venus	Mars
July 1	9 Ce	17 Ce	16 Lo	1 Cp
6	13 Ce	14 Ce	21 Lo	29 Sg
11	18 Ce	11 Ce	27 Lo	28 Sg
16	23 Ce	9 Ce	3 Vr	27 Sg
21	28 Ce	10 Ce	9 Vr	26 Sg
26	2 Lo	13 Ce	14 Vr	26 Sg
31	7 Lo	18 Ce	20 Vr	26 Sg

July 1/Jup 8 Ce/Sat 3 Sc/Uran 22 Ce
Nep 23 Lb/Plut 23 Lo/N Node 15 Cp

	Sun	Merc	Venus	Mars
Aug. 1	8 Lo	19 Ce	21 Vr	26 Sg
6	13 Lo	27 Ce	27 Vr	26 Sg
11	18 Lo	6 Lo	2 Lb	27 Sg
16	23 Lo	16 Lo	8 Lb	28 Sg
21	27 Lo	27 Lo	13 Lb	29 Sg
26	2 Vr	6 Vr	18 Lb	0 Cp
31	7 Vr	16 Vr	23 Lb	2 Cp

Aug. 1/Jup 15 Ce/Sat 3 Sc/Uran 24 Ce
Nep 23 Lb/Plut 24 Lo/N Node 14 Cp

1954

```
           Sun    Merc   Venus   Mars                    Sun    Merc   Venus   Mars
Sept 1   8 Vr   17 Vr   24 Lb    3 Cp      Oct. 1   7 Lb    2 Sc   20 Sc   17 Cp
      6  13 Vr   26 Vr   29 Lb    5 Cp            6  12 Lb    8 Sc   24 Sc   20 Cp
     11  18 Vr    4 Lb    4 Sc    7 Cp           11  17 Lb   12 Sc   26 Sc   23 Cp
     16  23 Vr   12 Lb    8 Sc    9 Cp           16  22 Lb   14 Sc   28 Sc   26 Cp
     21  27 Vr   19 Lb   13 Sc   12 Cp           21  27 Lb   14 Sc    0 Sg    0 Aq
     26   2 Lb   26 Lb   17 Sc   15 Cp           26   2 Sc   11 Sc    0 Sg    3 Aq
                                                 31   7 Sc    4 Sc   29 Sc    6 Aq
```

Sept 1/Jup 22 Ce/Sat 5 Sc/Uran 26 Ce   Oct. 1/Jup 27 Ce/Sat 8 Sc/Uran 27 Ce
Nep 24 Lb/Plut 25 Lo/N Node 12 Cp   Nep 25 Lb/Plut 26 Lo/N Node 10 Cp

```
           Sun    Merc   Venus   Mars                    Sun    Merc   Venus   Mars
Nov. 1   8 Sc    3 Sc   29 Sc    7 Aq      Dec. 1   8 Sg   25 Sc   15 Sc   28 Aq
      6  13 Sc   29 Lb   28 Sc   10 Aq            6  13 Sg    3 Sg   15 Sc    1 Pc
     11  18 Sc    0 Sc   25 Sc   14 Aq           11  18 Sg   10 Sg   15 Sc    5 Pc
     16  23 Sc    4 Sc   22 Sc   17 Aq           16  23 Sg   18 Sg   17 Sc    8 Pc
     21  28 Sc   10 Sc   19 Sc   21 Aq           21  29 Sg   26 Sg   19 Sc   12 Pc
     26   3 Sg   17 Sc   17 Sc   24 Aq           26   4 Cp    4 Cp   22 Sc   15 Pc
                                                 31   9 Cp   12 Cp   25 Sc   19 Pc
```

Nov. 1/Jup 30 Ce/Sat 12 Sc/Uran 28 Ce   Dec. 1/Jup 30 Ce/Sat 15 Sc/Uran 27 Ce
Nep 26 Lb/Plut 27 Lo/N Node 9 Cp   Nep 27 Lb/Plut 27 Lo/N Node 7 Cp

Moon's Positions

	1	4	7	10	13	16	19	22	25	28	31
Jan.	21 Sc	30 Sg	10 Aq	23 Pc	5 Tr	17 Gm	27 Ce	5 Vr	11 Lb	17 Sc	24 Sg
Feb.	7 Cp	19 Aq	3 Ar	16 Tr	27 Gm	6 Lo	13 Vr	19 Lb	25 Sc	2 Cp	
Mar.	15 Cp	27 Aq	12 Ar	26 Tr	7 Ce	15 Lo	22 Vr	28 Lb	4 Sg	11 Cp	21 Aq
Apr.	5 Pc	21 Ar	6 Gm	17 Ce	25 Lo	1 Lb	7 Sc	13 Sg	20 Cp	30 Aq	
May	14 Ar	29 Tr	12 Ce	22 Lo	28 Vr	4 Sc	10 Sg	17 Cp	26 Aq	8 Ar	23 Tr
June	8 Gm	21 Ce	30 Lo	6 Lb	12 Sc	19 Sg	26 Cp	6 Pc	18 Ar	2 Gm	
July	15 Ce	25 Lo	3 Lb	8 Sc	15 Sg	23 Cp	3 Pc	15 Ar	28 Tr	10 Ce	20 Lo
Aug.	3 Vr	11 Lb	16 Sc	23 Sg	1 Aq	13 Pc	26 Ar	9 Gm	20 Ce	29 Lo	7 Lb
Sept	19 Lb	24 Sc	0 Cp	9 Aq	22 Pc	6 Tr	20 Gm	30 Ce	8 Vr	15 Lb	
Oct.	21 Sc	26 Sg	4 Aq	15 Pc	0 Tr	15 Gm	27 Ce	5 Vr	12 Lb	18 Sc	23 Sg
Nov.	5 Cp	13 Aq	24 Pc	8 Tr	24 Gm	6 Lo	15 Vr	21 Lb	27 Sc	2 Cp	
Dec.	9 Aq	19 Pc	2 Tr	17 Gm	1 Lo	11 Vr	18 Lb	23 Sc	29 Sg	6 Aq	15 Pc

1955

	Sun	Merc	Venus	Mars
Jan. 1	10 Cp	14 Cp	26 Sc	20 Pc
6	15 Cp	22 Cp	0 Sg	23 Pc
11	20 Cp	0 Aq	4 Sg	27 Pc
16	25 Cp	8 Aq	9 Sg	1 Ar
21	0 Aq	16 Aq	13 Sg	4 Ar
26	5 Aq	23 Aq	18 Sg	8 Ar
31	10 Aq	28 Aq	24 Sg	11 Ar

Jan. 1/Jup 27 Ce/Sat 18 Sc/Uran 26 Ce
Nep 28 Lb/Plut 27 Lo/N Node 5 Cp

	Sun	Merc	Venus	Mars
Feb. 1	11 Aq	29 Aq	25 Sg	12 Ar
6	16 Aq	29 Aq	0 Cp	16 Ar
11	21 Aq	25 Aq	5 Cp	19 Ar
16	27 Aq	20 Aq	11 Cp	23 Ar
21	2 Pc	16 Aq	16 Cp	26 Ar
26	7 Pc	14 Aq	22 Cp	0 Tr

Feb. 1/Jup 23 Ce/Sat 20 Sc/Uran 25 Ce
Nep 28 Lb/Plut 26 Lo/N Node 4 Cp

	Sun	Merc	Venus	Mars
Mar. 1	10 Pc	15 Aq	26 Cp	2 Tr
6	15 Pc	18 Aq	1 Aq	5 Tr
11	20 Pc	22 Aq	7 Aq	9 Tr
16	25 Pc	28 Aq	13 Aq	12 Tr
21	0 Ar	4 Pc	19 Aq	16 Tr
26	5 Ar	11 Pc	25 Aq	19 Tr
31	10 Ar	19 Pc	1 Pc	23 Tr

Mar. 1/Jup 20 Ce/Sat 21 Sc/Uran 24 Ce
Nep 28 Lb/Plut 25 Lo/N Node 2 Cp

	Sun	Merc	Venus	Mars
Apr. 1	10 Ar	20 Pc	2 Pc	23 Tr
6	15 Ar	29 Pc	8 Pc	27 Tr
11	20 Ar	8 Ar	14 Pc	0 Gm
16	25 Ar	17 Ar	20 Pc	3 Gm
21	0 Tr	28 Ar	26 Pc	7 Gm
26	5 Tr	8 Tr	2 Ar	10 Gm

Apr. 1/Jup 20 Ce/Sat 20 Sc/Uran 24 Ce
Nep 27 Lb/Plut 25 Lo/N Node 1 Cp

	Sun	Merc	Venus	Mars
May 1	10 Tr	19 Tr	8 Ar	13 Gm
6	15 Tr	29 Tr	14 Ar	17 Gm
11	20 Tr	8 Gm	20 Ar	20 Gm
16	24 Tr	15 Gm	26 Ar	23 Gm
21	29 Tr	21 Gm	2 Tr	27 Gm
26	4 Gm	26 Gm	8 Tr	0 Ce
31	9 Gm	28 Gm	14 Tr	3 Ce

May 1/Jup 23 Ce/Sat 18 Sc/Uran 24 Ce
Nep 27 Lb/Plut 24 Lo/N Node 29 Sg

	Sun	Merc	Venus	Mars
June 1	10 Gm	29 Gm	15 Tr	4 Ce
6	15 Gm	29 Gm	21 Tr	7 Ce
11	19 Gm	27 Gm	27 Tr	10 Ce
16	24 Gm	24 Gm	3 Gm	14 Ce
21	29 Gm	22 Gm	9 Gm	17 Ce
26	4 Ce	20 Gm	15 Gm	20 Ce

June 1/Jup 28 Ce/Sat 16 Sc/Uran 25 Ce
Nep 26 Lb/Plut 24 Lo/N Node 27 Sg

	Sun	Merc	Venus	Mars
July 1	8 Ce	21 Gm	21 Gm	23 Ce
6	13 Ce	23 Gm	28 Gm	27 Ce
11	18 Ce	27 Gm	4 Ce	0 Lo
16	23 Ce	3 Ce	10 Ce	3 Lo
21	27 Ce	11 Ce	16 Ce	6 Lo
26	2 Lo	20 Ce	22 Ce	9 Lo
31	7 Lo	1 Lo	28 Ce	13 Lo

July 1/Jup 4 Lo/Sat 15 Sc/Uran 27 Ce
Nep 25 Lb/Plut 25 Lo/N Node 26 Sg

	Sun	Merc	Venus	Mars
Aug. 1	8 Lo	3 Lo	29 Ce	13 Lo
6	13 Lo	13 Lo	6 Lo	16 Lo
11	18 Lo	23 Lo	12 Lo	20 Lo
16	22 Lo	3 Vr	18 Lo	23 Lo
21	27 Lo	12 Vr	24 Lo	26 Lo
26	2 Vr	20 Vr	0 Vr	29 Lo
31	7 Vr	28 Vr	6 Vr	2 Vr

Aug. 1/Jup 10 Lo/Sat 15 Sc/Uran 29 Ce
Nep 26 Lb/Plut 26 Lo/N Node 24 Sg

1955

```
           Sun    Merc   Venus   Mars                    Sun    Merc   Venus   Mars
Sept 1    8 Vr   29 Vr    8 Vr   3 Vr        Oct. 1     7 Lb   29 Lb   15 Lb   22 Vr
     6   13 Vr    6 Lb   14 Vr   6 Vr             6    12 Lb   27 Lb   21 Lb   25 Vr
    11   17 Vr   13 Lb   20 Vr   9 Vr            11    17 Lb   23 Lb   27 Lb   28 Vr
    16   22 Vr   19 Lb   26 Vr  12 Vr            16    22 Lb   17 Lb    4 Sc    2 Lb
    21   27 Vr   24 Lb    3 Lb  16 Vr            21    27 Lb   13 Lb   10 Sc    5 Lb
    26    2 Lb   27 Lb    9 Lb  19 Vr            26     2 Sc   14 Lb   16 Sc    8 Lb
                                                31     7 Sc   18 Lb   22 Sc   11 Lb
```

Sept 1/Jup 17 Lo/Sat 16 Sc/Uran 0 Lo   Oct. 1/Jup 23 Lo/Sat 19 Sc/Uran 2 Lo
Nep 26 Lb/Plut 27 Lo/N Node 23 Sg   Nep 27 Lb/Plut 28 Lo/N Node 21 Sg

```
           Sun    Merc   Venus   Mars                    Sun    Merc   Venus   Mars
Nov. 1    8 Sc   20 Lb   24 Sc  12 Lb        Dec. 1     8 Sg    6 Sg    1 Cp    1 Sc
     6   13 Sc   27 Lb    0 Sg  15 Lb             6    13 Sg   14 Sg    7 Cp    5 Sc
    11   18 Sc    4 Sc    6 Sg  18 Lb            11    18 Sg   22 Sg   14 Cp    8 Sc
    16   23 Sc   12 Sc   12 Sg  22 Lb            16    23 Sg    0 Cp   20 Cp   11 Sc
    21   28 Sc   20 Sc   19 Sg  25 Lb            21    28 Sg    8 Cp   26 Cp   14 Sc
    26    3 Sg   28 Sc   25 Sg  28 Lb            26     3 Cp   15 Cp    2 Aq   18 Sc
                                                31     9 Cp   23 Cp    8 Aq   21 Sc
```

Nov. 1/Jup 28 Lo/Sat 22 Sc/Uran 2 Lo   Dec. 1/Jup 1 Vr/Sat 25 Sc/Uran 2 Lo
Nep 28 Lb/Plut 28 Lo/N Node 19 Sg   Nep 29 Lb/Plut 29 Lo/N Node 18 Sg

Moon's Positions

```
          1       4       7      10      13      16      19      22      25      28      31
Jan.  29 Pc   11 Tr   25 Gm    8 Lo   19 Vr   26 Lb    1 Sg    8 Cp   16 Aq   26 Pc    8 Tr
Feb.  22 Tr    4 Ce   17 Lo   27 Vr    4 Sc    9 Sg   16 Cp   24 Aq    6 Ar   19 Tr
Mar.   3 Gm   15 Ce   25 Lo    5 Lb   12 Sc   17 Sg   23 Cp    2 Pc   15 Ar   29 Tr   12 Ce
Apr.  25 Ce    5 Vr   13 Lb   20 Sc   25 Sg    1 Aq   10 Pc   23 Ar    8 Gm   22 Ce
May    2 Vr   10 Lb   16 Sc   22 Sg   28 Cp    5 Pc   17 Ar    2 Gm   17 Ce   29 Lo    7 Lb
June  19 Lb   25 Sc    1 Cp    7 Aq   15 Pc   26 Ar   10 Gm   25 Ce    8 Vr   16 Lb
July  22 Sc   28 Sg    4 Aq   12 Pc   22 Ar    4 Gm   19 Ce    2 Vr   12 Lb   19 Sc   24 Sg
Aug.   6 Cp   13 Aq   22 Pc    2 Tr   14 Gm   28 Ce   10 Vr   20 Lb   27 Sc    2 Cp    9 Aq
Sept  22 Aq    1 Ar   13 Tr   25 Gm    8 Lo   19 Vr   28 Lb    5 Sg   10 Cp   17 Aq
Oct.  27 Pc    9 Tr   22 Gm    4 Lo   15 Vr   24 Lb    1 Sg    6 Cp   12 Aq   21 Pc    3 Tr
Nov.  18 Tr    2 Ce   15 Lo   25 Vr    3 Sc    9 Sg   15 Cp   21 Aq   29 Pc   11 Tr
Dec.  26 Gm   11 Lo   22 Vr    0 Sc    6 Sg   12 Cp   17 Aq   25 Pc    5 Tr   19 Gm    5 Lo
```

1956

	Sun	Merc	Venus	Mars
Jan. 1	10 Cp	25 Cp	10 Aq	21 Sc
6	15 Cp	2 Aq	16 Aq	25 Sc
11	20 Cp	9 Aq	22 Aq	28 Sc
16	25 Cp	13 Aq	28 Aq	1 Sg
21	0 Aq	13 Aq	4 Pc	5 Sg
26	5 Aq	9 Aq	10 Pc	8 Sg
31	10 Aq	2 Aq	16 Pc	11 Sg

Jan. 1/Jup 1 Vr/Sat 29 Sc/Uran 1 Lo
Nep 0 Sc/Plut 28 Lo/N Node 16 Sg

	Sun	Merc	Venus	Mars
Feb. 1	11 Aq	1 Aq	18 Pc	12 Sg
6	16 Aq	28 Cp	24 Pc	15 Sg
11	21 Aq	28 Cp	0 Ar	18 Sg
16	26 Aq	0 Aq	6 Ar	22 Sg
21	1 Pc	5 Aq	12 Ar	25 Sg
26	6 Pc	10 Aq	17 Ar	28 Sg

Feb. 1/Jup 28 Lo/Sat 1 Sg/Uran 30 Ce
Nep 0 Sc/Plut 28 Lo/N Node 14 Sg

	Sun	Merc	Venus	Mars
Mar. 1	10 Pc	15 Aq	22 Ar	1 Cp
6	15 Pc	22 Aq	28 Ar	4 Cp
11	20 Pc	29 Aq	4 Tr	7 Cp
16	25 Pc	7 Pc	9 Tr	11 Cp
21	0 Ar	16 Pc	15 Tr	14 Cp
26	5 Ar	25 Pc	20 Tr	17 Cp
31	10 Ar	4 Ar	26 Tr	20 Cp

Mar. 1/Jup 25 Lo/Sat 3 Sg/Uran 29 Ce
Nep 0 Sc/Plut 27 Lo/N Node 13 Sg

	Sun	Merc	Venus	Mars
Apr. 1	11 Ar	6 Ar	27 Tr	21 Cp
6	16 Ar	16 Ar	2 Gm	24 Cp
11	21 Ar	26 Ar	7 Gm	27 Cp
16	26 Ar	7 Tr	12 Gm	1 Aq
21	1 Tr	16 Tr	16 Gm	4 Aq
26	6 Tr	25 Tr	21 Gm	7 Aq

Apr. 1/Jup 22 Lo/Sat 2 Sg/Uran 28 Ce
Nep 30 Lb/Plut 26 Lo/N Node 11 Sg

	Sun	Merc	Venus	Mars
May 1	11 Tr	1 Gm	25 Gm	10 Aq
6	15 Tr	6 Gm	29 Gm	13 Aq
11	20 Tr	8 Gm	2 Ce	16 Aq
16	25 Tr	9 Gm	5 Ce	19 Aq
21	0 Gm	7 Gm	7 Ce	22 Aq
26	5 Gm	5 Gm	8 Ce	25 Aq
31	10 Gm	2 Gm	9 Ce	28 Aq

May 1/Jup 22 Lo/Sat 1 Sg/Uran 29 Ce
Nep 29 Lb/Plut 26 Lo/N Node 10 Sg

	Sun	Merc	Venus	Mars
June 1	10 Gm	2 Gm	9 Ce	29 Aq
6	15 Gm	0 Gm	8 Ce	1 Pc
11	20 Gm	1 Gm	7 Ce	4 Pc
16	25 Gm	3 Gm	5 Ce	7 Pc
21	0 Ce	7 Gm	2 Ce	9 Pc
26	4 Ce	13 Gm	28 Gm	12 Pc

June 1/Jup 24 Lo/Sat 29 Sc/Uran 30 Ce
Nep 28 Lb/Plut 26 Lo/N Node 8 Sg

	Sun	Merc	Venus	Mars
July 1	9 Ce	20 Gm	26 Gm	14 Pc
6	14 Ce	29 Gm	24 Gm	16 Pc
11	19 Ce	8 Ce	23 Gm	18 Pc
16	23 Ce	19 Ce	23 Gm	19 Pc
21	28 Ce	0 Lo	23 Gm	21 Pc
26	3 Lo	10 Lo	25 Gm	22 Pc
31	8 Lo	20 Lo	27 Gm	23 Pc

July 1/Jup 29 Lo/Sat 27 Sc/Uran 1 Lo
Nep 28 Lb/Plut 27 Lo/N Node 6 Sg

	Sun	Merc	Venus	Mars
Aug. 1	9 Lo	21 Lo	28 Gm	23 Pc
6	13 Lo	0 Vr	1 Ce	24 Pc
11	18 Lo	9 Vr	5 Ce	24 Pc
16	23 Lo	16 Vr	8 Ce	23 Pc
21	28 Lo	23 Vr	13 Ce	23 Pc
26	3 Vr	29 Vr	17 Ce	22 Pc
31	8 Vr	5 Lb	22 Ce	21 Pc

Aug. 1/Jup 5 Vr/Sat 26 Sc/Uran 3 Lo
Nep 28 Lb/Plut 28 Lo/N Node 5 Sg

1956

```
        Sun    Merc    Venus   Mars              Sun    Merc    Venus   Mars
Sept 1  9 Vr   6 Lb   23 Ce   21 Pc     Oct. 1  8 Lb   29 Vr   24 Lo   14 Pc
     6  13 Vr  10 Lb  28 Ce   20 Pc          6  13 Lb  27 Vr    0 Vr   13 Pc
    11  18 Vr  12 Lb   3 Lo   18 Pc         11  18 Lb   0 Lb    6 Vr   13 Pc
    16  23 Vr  12 Lb   8 Lo   17 Pc         16  23 Lb   5 Lb   11 Vr   13 Pc
    21  28 Vr   9 Lb  13 Lo   16 Pc         21  28 Lb  13 Lb   17 Vr   14 Pc
    26   3 Lb   4 Lb  19 Lo   15 Pc         26   3 Sc  21 Lb   23 Vr   15 Pc
                                            31   8 Sc  29 Lb   29 Vr   16 Pc
```

```
Sept 1/Jup 11 Vr/Sat 27 Sc/Uran  5 Lo     Oct. 1/Jup 18 Vr/Sat 29 Sc/Uran  6 Lo
Nep 28 Lb/Plut 29 Lo/N Node  3 Sg         Nep 29 Lb/Plut 30 Lo/N Node  2 Sg
```

```
        Sun    Merc    Venus   Mars              Sun    Merc    Venus   Mars
Nov. 1  9 Sc   1 Sc    0 Lb   16 Pc     Dec. 1  9 Sg   19 Sg    7 Sc   27 Pc
     6  14 Sc   9 Sc   6 Lb   17 Pc          6  14 Sg  26 Sg   13 Sc    0 Ar
    11  19 Sc  17 Sc  12 Lb   19 Pc         11  19 Sg   4 Cp   19 Sc    2 Ar
    16  24 Sc  25 Sc  18 Lb   21 Pc         16  24 Sg  11 Cp   25 Sc    5 Ar
    21  29 Sc   3 Sg  24 Lb   23 Pc         21  29 Sg  18 Cp    2 Sg    8 Ar
    26   4 Sg  11 Sg   1 Sc   25 Pc         26   4 Cp  24 Cp    8 Sg   10 Ar
                                            31   9 Cp  27 Cp   14 Sg   13 Ar
```

```
Nov. 1/Jup 24 Vr/Sat  2 Sg/Uran  7 Lo     Dec. 1/Jup 29 Vr/Sat  6 Sg/Uran  7 Lo
Nep  0 Sc/Plut  0 Vr/N Node 30 Sc         Nep  2 Sc/Plut  0 Vr/N Node 28 Sc
```

Moon's Positions

```
        1      4      7     10     13     16     19     22     25     28     31
Jan.  19 Lo   1 Lb   9 Sc  15 Sg  20 Cp  27 Aq   4 Ar  14 Tr  27 Gm  12 Lo  26 Vr
Feb.  10 Lb  18 Sc  24 Sg  29 Cp   6 Pc  14 Ar  24 Tr   7 Ce  21 Lo   4 Lb
Mar.   1 Sc   8 Sg  13 Cp  20 Aq  28 Pc   8 Tr  19 Gm   1 Lo  14 Vr  25 Lb   4 Sg
Apr.  16 Sg  21 Cp  28 Aq   6 Ar  17 Tr  30 Gm  12 Lo  24 Vr   4 Sc  12 Sg
May   17 Cp  23 Aq   1 Ar  12 Tr  26 Gm   9 Lo  21 Vr   0 Sc   8 Sg  14 Cp  19 Aq
June   1 Pc   9 Ar  20 Tr   5 Ce  19 Lo   1 Lb  10 Sc  17 Sg  22 Cp  28 Aq
July   5 Ar  14 Tr  28 Gm  13 Lo  27 Vr   7 Sc  14 Sg  19 Cp  25 Aq   2 Ar  10 Tr
Aug.  24 Tr   6 Ce  22 Lo   6 Lb  16 Sc  23 Sg  28 Cp   4 Pc  11 Ar  20 Tr   1 Ce
Sept  16 Ce   0 Vr  14 Lb  24 Sc   1 Cp   7 Aq  13 Pc  21 Ar   0 Gm  12 Ce
Oct.  25 Lo   8 Lb  19 Sc  27 Sg   3 Aq   9 Pc  17 Ar  27 Tr   9 Ce  21 Lo   3 Lb
Nov.  17 Lb  27 Sc   5 Cp  11 Aq  17 Pc  25 Ar   6 Gm  19 Ce   2 Vr  14 Lb
Dec.  23 Sc   1 Cp   7 Aq  12 Pc  20 Ar  30 Tr  14 Ce  28 Lo  10 Lb  20 Sc  27 Sg
```

1957

	Sun	Merc	Venus	Mars
Jan. 1	10 Cp	27 Cp	15 Sg	14 Ar
6	15 Cp	25 Cp	21 Sg	17 Ar
11	21 Cp	20 Cp	28 Sg	19 Ar
16	26 Cp	14 Cp	4 Cp	22 Ar
21	1 Aq	11 Cp	10 Cp	25 Ar
26	6 Aq	12 Cp	16 Cp	28 Ar
31	11 Aq	16 Cp	23 Cp	1 Tr

Jan. 1/Jup 1 Lb/Sat 9 Sg/Uran 6 Lo
Nep 2 Sc/Plut 0 Vr/N Node 27 Sc

	Sun	Merc	Venus	Mars
Feb. 1	12 Aq	17 Cp	24 Cp	2 Tr
6	17 Aq	22 Cp	0 Aq	5 Tr
11	22 Aq	28 Cp	6 Aq	8 Tr
16	27 Aq	5 Aq	13 Aq	11 Tr
21	2 Pc	12 Aq	19 Aq	14 Tr
26	7 Pc	19 Aq	25 Aq	18 Tr

Feb. 1/Jup 1 Lb/Sat 12 Sg/Uran 5 Lo
Nep 3 Sc/Plut 30 Lo/N Node 25 Sc

	Sun	Merc	Venus	Mars
Mar. 1	10 Pc	24 Aq	29 Aq	19 Tr
6	15 Pc	3 Pc	5 Pc	23 Tr
11	20 Pc	11 Pc	11 Pc	26 Tr
16	25 Pc	21 Pc	18 Pc	29 Tr
21	0 Ar	0 Ar	24 Pc	2 Gm
26	5 Ar	10 Ar	0 Ar	5 Gm
31	10 Ar	21 Ar	6 Ar	8 Gm

Mar. 1/Jup 29 Vr/Sat 14 Sg/Uran 4 Lo
Nep 2 Sc/Plut 29 Lo/N Node 24 Sc

	Sun	Merc	Venus	Mars
Apr. 1	11 Ar	23 Ar	8 Ar	9 Gm
6	16 Ar	2 Tr	14 Ar	12 Gm
11	21 Ar	10 Tr	20 Ar	15 Gm
16	26 Ar	15 Tr	26 Ar	18 Gm
21	1 Tr	19 Tr	2 Tr	21 Gm
26	6 Tr	19 Tr	8 Tr	25 Gm

Apr. 1/Jup 25 Vr/Sat 14 Sg/Uran 3 Lo
Nep 2 Sc/Plut 28 Lo/N Node 22 Sc

	Sun	Merc	Venus	Mars
May 1	10 Tr	18 Tr	15 Tr	28 Gm
6	15 Tr	15 Tr	21 Tr	1 Ce
11	20 Tr	12 Tr	27 Tr	4 Ce
16	25 Tr	10 Tr	3 Gm	7 Ce
21	0 Gm	10 Tr	9 Gm	10 Ce
26	4 Gm	12 Tr	15 Gm	13 Ce
31	9 Gm	15 Tr	22 Gm	17 Ce

May 1/Jup 22 Vr/Sat 13 Sg/Uran 3 Lo
Nep 1 Sc/Plut 28 Lo/N Node 20 Sc

	Sun	Merc	Venus	Mars
June 1	10 Gm	16 Tr	23 Gm	17 Ce
6	15 Gm	21 Tr	29 Gm	20 Ce
11	20 Gm	28 Tr	5 Ce	23 Ce
16	25 Gm	5 Gm	11 Ce	27 Ce
21	29 Gm	14 Gm	17 Ce	0 Lo
26	4 Ce	24 Gm	23 Ce	3 Lo

June 1/Jup 22 Vr/Sat 11 Sg/Uran 4 Lo
Nep 0 Sc/Plut 28 Lo/N Node 19 Sc

	Sun	Merc	Venus	Mars
July 1	9 Ce	5 Ce	29 Ce	6 Lo
6	14 Ce	16 Ce	6 Lo	9 Lo
11	18 Ce	26 Ce	12 Lo	12 Lo
16	23 Ce	6 Lo	18 Lo	15 Lo
21	28 Ce	15 Lo	24 Lo	19 Lo
26	3 Lo	24 Lo	0 Vr	22 Lo
31	8 Lo	1 Vr	6 Vr	25 Lo

July 1/Jup 24 Vr/Sat 9 Sg/Uran 6 Lo
Nep 30 Lb/Plut 29 Lo/N Node 17 Sc

	Sun	Merc	Venus	Mars
Aug. 1	8 Lo	3 Vr	7 Vr	25 Lo
6	13 Lo	9 Vr	13 Vr	29 Lo
11	18 Lo	15 Vr	19 Vr	2 Vr
16	23 Lo	20 Vr	25 Vr	5 Vr
21	28 Lo	24 Vr	1 Lb	8 Vr
26	2 Vr	25 Vr	7 Lb	11 Vr
31	7 Vr	25 Vr	13 Lb	14 Vr

Aug. 1/Jup 29 Vr/Sat 8 Sg/Uran 7 Lo
Nep 30 Lb/Plut 29 Lo/N Node 15 Sc

1957

	Sun	Merc	Venus	Mars
Sept 1	8 Vr	24 Vr	14 Lb	15 Vr
6	13 Vr	21 Vr	20 Lb	18 Vr
11	18 Vr	16 Vr	26 Lb	22 Vr
16	23 Vr	12 Vr	2 Sc	25 Vr
21	28 Vr	11 Vr	8 Sc	28 Vr
26	3 Lb	15 Vr	14 Sc	1 Lb

Sept 1/Jup 5 Lb/Sat 8 Sg/Uran 9 Lo
Nep 1 Sc/Plut 0 Vr/N Node 14 Sc

	Sun	Merc	Venus	Mars
Oct. 1	8 Lb	21 Vr	20 Sc	4 Lb
6	12 Lb	29 Vr	25 Sc	8 Lb
11	17 Lb	8 Lb	1 Sg	11 Lb
16	22 Lb	17 Lb	7 Sg	14 Lb
21	27 Lb	25 Lb	12 Sg	17 Lb
26	2 Sc	4 Sc	18 Sg	21 Lb
31	7 Sc	12 Sc	24 Sg	24 Lb

Oct. 1/Jup 11 Lb/Sat 10 Sg/Uran 11 Lo
Nep 1 Sc/Plut 1 Vr/N Node 12 Sc

	Sun	Merc	Venus	Mars
Nov. 1	8 Sc	13 Sc	25 Sg	25 Lb
6	13 Sc	21 Sc	0 Cp	28 Lb
11	18 Sc	29 Sc	5 Cp	1 Sc
16	23 Sc	6 Sg	11 Cp	5 Sc
21	28 Sc	14 Sg	16 Cp	8 Sc
26	3 Sg	21 Sg	20 Cp	12 Sc

Nov. 1/Jup 18 Lb/Sat 12 Sg/Uran 12 Lo
Nep 3 Sc/Plut 2 Vr/N Node 11 Sc

	Sun	Merc	Venus	Mars
Dec. 1	9 Sg	28 Sg	25 Cp	15 Sc
6	14 Sg	4 Cp	29 Cp	18 Sc
11	19 Sg	9 Cp	4 Aq	22 Sc
16	24 Sg	12 Cp	7 Aq	25 Sc
21	29 Sg	10 Cp	10 Aq	29 Sc
26	4 Cp	4 Cp	13 Aq	2 Sg
31	9 Cp	28 Sg	15 Aq	6 Sg

Dec. 1/Jup 24 Lb/Sat 16 Sg/Uran 12 Lo
Nep 4 Sc/Plut 2 Vr/N Node 9 Sc

Moon's Positions

	1	4	7	10	13	16	19	22	25	28	31
Jan.	9 Cp	15 Aq	21 Pc	28 Ar	8 Gm	22 Ce	7 Vr	20 Lb	30 Sc	6 Cp	12 Aq
Feb.	24 Aq	30 Pc	6 Tr	16 Gm	30 Ce	16 Vr	29 Lb	9 Sg	15 Cp	21 Aq	
Mar.	3 Pc	9 Ar	16 Tr	26 Gm	9 Lo	24 Vr	7 Sc	17 Sg	24 Cp	30 Aq	6 Ar
Apr.	18 Ar	26 Tr	6 Ce	18 Lo	2 Lb	15 Sc	25 Sg	2 Aq	8 Pc	14 Ar	
May	22 Tr	3 Ce	15 Lo	28 Vr	10 Sc	20 Sg	28 Cp	4 Pc	10 Ar	18 Tr	29 Gm
June	13 Ce	26 Lo	8 Lb	19 Sc	29 Sg	6 Aq	12 Pc	18 Ar	26 Tr	8 Ce	
July	22 Lo	5 Lb	16 Sc	25 Sg	2 Aq	8 Pc	14 Ar	21 Tr	2 Ce	16 Lo	1 Lb
Aug.	15 Lb	26 Sc	4 Cp	11 Aq	17 Pc	22 Ar	30 Tr	10 Ce	25 Lo	10 Lb	23 Sc
Sept	6 Sg	14 Cp	20 Aq	26 Pc	2 Tr	9 Gm	19 Ce	3 Vr	18 Lb	1 Sg	
Oct.	11 Cp	17 Aq	23 Pc	29 Ar	6 Gm	15 Ce	27 Lo	12 Lb	26 Sc	6 Cp	13 Aq
Nov.	25 Aq	1 Ar	7 Tr	16 Gm	26 Ce	8 Vr	21 Lb	4 Sg	14 Cp	21 Aq	
Dec.	27 Pc	3 Tr	11 Gm	22 Ce	4 Vr	17 Lb	29 Sc	9 Cp	17 Aq	23 Pc	29 Ar

1958

	Sun	Merc	Venus	Mars
Jan. 1	10 Cp	27 Sg	15 Aq	6 Sg
6	15 Cp	25 Sg	16 Aq	10 Sg
11	20 Cp	27 Sg	16 Aq	13 Sg
16	25 Cp	2 Cp	15 Aq	17 Sg
21	0 Aq	7 Cp	13 Aq	20 Sg
26	6 Aq	13 Cp	10 Aq	24 Sg
31	11 Aq	20 Cp	7 Aq	27 Sg

Jan. 1/Jup 29 Lb/Sat 19 Sg/Uran 11 Lo
Nep 4 Sc/Plut 2 Vr/N Node 7 Sc

	Sun	Merc	Venus	Mars
Feb. 1	12 Aq	22 Cp	6 Aq	28 Sg
6	17 Aq	29 Cp	4 Aq	2 Cp
11	22 Aq	7 Aq	2 Aq	5 Cp
16	27 Aq	15 Aq	1 Aq	9 Cp
21	2 Pc	23 Aq	1 Aq	12 Cp
26	7 Pc	2 Pc	2 Aq	16 Cp

Feb. 1/Jup 1 Sc/Sat 23 Sg/Uran 10 Lo
Nep 5 Sc/Plut 2 Vr/N Node 6 Sc

	Sun	Merc	Venus	Mars
Mar. 1	10 Pc	7 Pc	3 Aq	18 Cp
6	15 Pc	17 Pc	5 Aq	22 Cp
11	20 Pc	27 Pc	8 Aq	25 Cp
16	25 Pc	6 Ar	11 Aq	29 Cp
21	0 Ar	15 Ar	15 Aq	3 Aq
26	5 Ar	23 Ar	19 Aq	6 Aq
31	10 Ar	28 Ar	24 Aq	10 Aq

Mar. 1/Jup 1 Sc/Sat 25 Sg/Uran 8 Lo
Nep 5 Sc/Plut 1 Vr/N Node 4 Sc

	Sun	Merc	Venus	Mars
Apr. 1	11 Ar	29 Ar	25 Aq	11 Aq
6	16 Ar	1 Tr	29 Aq	14 Aq
11	21 Ar	0 Tr	4 Pc	18 Aq
16	26 Ar	27 Ar	9 Pc	22 Aq
21	0 Tr	23 Ar	14 Pc	26 Aq
26	5 Tr	21 Ar	20 Pc	29 Aq

Apr. 1/Jup 29 Lb/Sat 26 Sg/Uran 8 Lo
Nep 4 Sc/Plut 0 Vr/N Node 3 Sc

	Sun	Merc	Venus	Mars
May 1	10 Tr	20 Ar	25 Pc	3 Pc
6	15 Tr	21 Ar	1 Ar	7 Pc
11	20 Tr	24 Ar	6 Ar	10 Pc
16	25 Tr	29 Ar	12 Ar	14 Pc
21	29 Tr	5 Tr	17 Ar	18 Pc
26	4 Gm	12 Tr	23 Ar	21 Pc
31	9 Gm	19 Tr	29 Ar	25 Pc

May 1/Jup 25 Lb/Sat 25 Sg/Uran 8 Lo
Nep 3 Sc/Plut 30 Lo/N Node 1 Sc

	Sun	Merc	Venus	Mars
June 1	10 Gm	21 Tr	0 Tr	26 Pc
6	15 Gm	0 Gm	6 Tr	29 Pc
11	20 Gm	10 Gm	11 Tr	3 Ar
16	24 Gm	21 Gm	17 Tr	6 Ar
21	29 Gm	2 Ce	23 Tr	10 Ar
26	4 Ce	13 Ce	29 Tr	13 Ar

June 1/Jup 22 Lb/Sat 23 Sg/Uran 8 Lo
Nep 2 Sc/Plut 30 Lo/N Node 29 Lb

	Sun	Merc	Venus	Mars
July 1	9 Ce	23 Ce	5 Gm	17 Ar
6	13 Ce	2 Lo	11 Gm	20 Ar
11	18 Ce	10 Lo	17 Gm	23 Ar
16	23 Ce	18 Lo	23 Gm	27 Ar
21	28 Ce	24 Lo	29 Gm	0 Tr
26	3 Lo	0 Vr	5 Ce	3 Tr
31	7 Lo	4 Vr	11 Ce	6 Tr

July 1/Jup 22 Lb/Sat 21 Sg/Uran 10 Lo
Nep 2 Sc/Plut 0 Vr/N Node 28 Lb

	Sun	Merc	Venus	Mars
Aug. 1	8 Lo	5 Vr	12 Ce	7 Tr
6	13 Lo	7 Vr	18 Ce	10 Tr
11	18 Lo	8 Vr	24 Ce	12 Tr
16	23 Lo	6 Vr	0 Lo	15 Tr
21	27 Lo	2 Vr	6 Lo	18 Tr
26	2 Vr	28 Lo	12 Lo	20 Tr
31	7 Vr	25 Lo	18 Lo	22 Tr

Aug. 1/Jup 24 Lb/Sat 20 Sg/Uran 12 Lo
Nep 2 Sc/Plut 1 Vr/N Node 26 Lb

1958

```
          Sun    Merc   Venus  Mars                    Sun    Merc   Venus  Mars
Sept 1   8 Vr   25 Lo   20 Lo  23 Tr    Oct. 1   7 Lb    4 Lb   27 Vr   2 Gm
      6  13 Vr   26 Lo   26 Lo  25 Tr         6  12 Lb   13 Lb    3 Lb   2 Gm
     11  18 Vr    0 Vr    2 Vr  27 Tr        11  17 Lb   21 Lb    9 Lb   3 Gm
     16  23 Vr    7 Vr    8 Vr  29 Tr        16  22 Lb   29 Lb   15 Lb   2 Gm
     21  28 Vr   15 Vr   14 Vr   0 Gm        21  27 Lb    7 Sc   22 Lb   2 Gm
     26   2 Lb   25 Vr   20 Vr   1 Gm        26   2 Sc   15 Sc   28 Lb   1 Gm
                                             31   7 Sc   23 Sc    4 Sc  29 Tr
```

Sept 1/Jup 29 Lb/Sat 19 Sg/Uran 14 Lo   Oct. 1/Jup 5 Sc/Sat 20 Sg/Uran 15 Lo
Nep 3 Sc/Plut 2 Vr/N Node 25 Lb   Nep 4 Sc/Plut 3 Vr/N Node 23 Lb

```
          Sun    Merc   Venus  Mars                    Sun    Merc   Venus  Mars
Nov. 1   8 Sc   24 Sc    5 Sc  29 Tr    Dec. 1   8 Sg   26 Sg   13 Sg  19 Tr
      6  13 Sc    1 Sg   12 Sc  28 Tr         6  13 Sg   23 Sg   19 Sg  18 Tr
     11  18 Sc    8 Sg   18 Sc  26 Tr        11  18 Sg   16 Sg   26 Sg  17 Tr
     16  23 Sc   15 Sg   24 Sc  24 Tr        16  24 Sg   11 Sg    2 Cp  17 Tr
     21  28 Sc   20 Sg    1 Sg  22 Tr        21  29 Sg    9 Sg    8 Cp  17 Tr
     26   3 Sg   24 Sg    7 Sg  21 Tr        26   4 Cp   12 Sg   15 Cp  17 Tr
                                             31   9 Cp   17 Sg   21 Cp  17 Tr
```

Nov. 1/Jup 11 Sc/Sat 23 Sg/Uran 16 Lo   Dec. 1/Jup 18 Sc/Sat 26 Sg/Uran 16 Lo
Nep 5 Sc/Plut 4 Vr/N Node 21 Lb   Nep 6 Sc/Plut 4 Vr/N Node 20 Lb

Moon's Positions

	1	4	7	10	13	16	19	22	25	28	31
Jan.	11 Tr	20 Gm	2 Lo	15 Vr	28 Lb	8 Sg	18 Cp	25 Aq	1 Ar	7 Tr	14 Gm
Feb.	27 Gm	10 Lo	25 Vr	8 Sc	19 Sg	27 Cp	4 Pc	9 Ar	15 Tr	22 Gm	
Mar.	5 Ce	18 Lo	3 Lb	18 Sc	29 Sg	6 Aq	13 Pc	18 Ar	24 Tr	1 Ce	12 Lo
Apr.	26 Lo	12 Lb	26 Sc	8 Cp	16 Aq	21 Pc	27 Ar	3 Gm	11 Ce	21 Lo	
May	5 Lb	20 Sc	3 Cp	12 Aq	18 Pc	24 Ar	30 Tr	8 Ce	18 Lo	0 Lb	14 Sc
June	28 Sc	11 Cp	20 Aq	26 Pc	2 Tr	9 Gm	18 Ce	29 Lo	11 Lb	23 Sc	
July	5 Cp	15 Aq	22 Pc	28 Ar	4 Gm	13 Ce	25 Lo	8 Lb	20 Sc	1 Cp	11 Aq
Aug.	24 Aq	0 Ar	6 Tr	12 Gm	22 Ce	4 Vr	18 Lb	1 Sg	11 Cp	20 Aq	27 Pc
Sept	9 Ar	14 Tr	20 Gm	30 Ce	13 Vr	28 Lb	11 Sg	21 Cp	29 Aq	5 Ar	
Oct.	11 Tr	17 Gm	25 Ce	6 Vr	21 Lb	6 Sg	18 Cp	26 Aq	2 Ar	8 Tr	14 Gm
Nov.	26 Gm	4 Lo	15 Vr	29 Lb	14 Sg	27 Cp	5 Pc	11 Ar	17 Tr	23 Gm	
Dec.	1 Lo	11 Vr	23 Lb	7 Sg	21 Cp	1 Pc	8 Ar	13 Tr	19 Gm	28 Ce	8 Vr

1959

		Sun	Merc	Venus	Mars			Sun	Merc	Venus	Mars
Jan.	1	10 Cp	18 Sg	22 Cp	17 Tr	Feb.	1	11 Aq	2 Aq	1 Pc	26 Tr
	6	15 Cp	24 Sg	28 Cp	18 Tr		6	16 Aq	10 Aq	7 Pc	28 Tr
	11	20 Cp	0 Cp	5 Aq	19 Tr		11	22 Aq	19 Aq	13 Pc	0 Gm
	16	25 Cp	8 Cp	11 Aq	21 Tr		16	27 Aq	28 Aq	20 Pc	2 Gm
	21	0 Aq	15 Cp	17 Aq	22 Tr		21	2 Pc	7 Pc	26 Pc	5 Gm
	26	5 Aq	23 Cp	23 Aq	24 Tr		26	7 Pc	17 Pc	2 Ar	7 Gm
	31	10 Aq	1 Aq	0 Pc	26 Tr						

Jan. 1/Jup 24 Sc/Sat 29 Sg/Uran 16 Lo
Nep 7 Sc/Plut 4 Vr/N Node 18 Lb

Feb. 1/Jup 29 Sc/Sat 3 Cp/Uran 14 Lo
Nep 7 Sc/Plut 3 Vr/N Node 16 Lb

		Sun	Merc	Venus	Mars			Sun	Merc	Venus	Mars
Mar.	1	10 Pc	22 Pc	6 Ar	9 Gm	Apr.	1	11 Ar	6 Ar	13 Tr	25 Gm
	6	15 Pc	1 Ar	12 Ar	11 Gm		6	15 Ar	2 Ar	19 Tr	28 Gm
	11	20 Pc	8 Ar	18 Ar	14 Gm		11	20 Ar	1 Ar	25 Tr	0 Ce
	16	25 Pc	12 Ar	24 Ar	16 Gm		16	25 Ar	1 Ar	1 Gm	3 Ce
	21	0 Ar	13 Ar	0 Tr	19 Gm		21	0 Tr	4 Ar	7 Gm	6 Ce
	26	5 Ar	11 Ar	6 Tr	22 Gm		26	5 Tr	8 Ar	13 Gm	9 Ce
	31	10 Ar	7 Ar	12 Tr	24 Gm						

Mar. 1/Jup 1 Sg/Sat 5 Cp/Uran 13 Lo
Nep 7 Sc/Plut 3 Vr/N Node 15 Lb

Apr. 1/Jup 2 Sg/Sat 7 Cp/Uran 12 Lo
Nep 6 Sc/Plut 2 Vr/N Node 13 Lb

		Sun	Merc	Venus	Mars			Sun	Merc	Venus	Mars
May	1	10 Tr	13 Ar	19 Gm	12 Ce	June	1	10 Gm	7 Gm	24 Ce	0 Lo
	6	15 Tr	20 Ar	25 Gm	15 Ce		6	15 Gm	18 Gm	29 Ce	3 Lo
	11	20 Tr	27 Ar	0 Ce	18 Ce		11	19 Gm	29 Gm	4 Lo	6 Lo
	16	24 Tr	5 Tr	6 Ce	20 Ce		16	24 Gm	9 Ce	9 Lo	9 Lo
	21	29 Tr	14 Tr	12 Ce	23 Ce		21	29 Gm	18 Ce	14 Lo	12 Lo
	26	4 Gm	24 Tr	17 Ce	26 Ce		26	4 Ce	26 Ce	19 Lo	15 Lo
	31	9 Gm	5 Gm	23 Ce	29 Ce						

May 1/Jup 29 Sc/Sat 7 Cp/Uran 12 Lo
Nep 5 Sc/Plut 2 Vr/N Node 12 Lb

June 1/Jup 25 Sc/Sat 6 Cp/Uran 13 Lo
Nep 5 Sc/Plut 2 Vr/N Node 10 Lb

		Sun	Merc	Venus	Mars			Sun	Merc	Venus	Mars
July	1	8 Ce	3 Lo	24 Lo	18 Lo	Aug.	1	8 Lo	16 Lo	14 Vr	7 Vr
	6	13 Ce	9 Lo	28 Lo	21 Lo		6	13 Lo	12 Lo	16 Vr	10 Vr
	11	18 Ce	14 Lo	2 Vr	24 Lo		11	18 Lo	9 Lo	16 Vr	13 Vr
	16	23 Ce	18 Lo	6 Vr	27 Lo		16	22 Lo	8 Lo	16 Vr	17 Vr
	21	28 Ce	19 Lo	9 Vr	0 Vr		21	27 Lo	9 Lo	14 Vr	20 Vr
	26	2 Lo	19 Lo	12 Vr	3 Vr		26	2 Vr	14 Lo	12 Vr	23 Vr
	31	7 Lo	17 Lo	14 Vr	7 Vr		31	7 Vr	21 Lo	9 Vr	26 Vr

July 1/Jup 23 Sc/Sat 3 Cp/Uran 14 Lo
Nep 4 Sc/Plut 2 Vr/N Node 8 Lb

Aug. 1/Jup 22 Sc/Sat 1 Cp/Uran 16 Lo
Nep 4 Sc/Plut 3 Vr/N Node 7 Lb

1959

```
          Sun    Merc   Venus  Mars                  Sun    Merc   Venus  Mars
Sept 1   8 Vr  23 Lo   8 Vr  27 Vr      Oct. 1   7 Lb  17 Lb   1 Vr  16 Lb
     6  13 Vr   2 Vr   5 Vr   0 Lb           6  12 Lb  25 Lb   3 Vr  20 Lb
    11  18 Vr  11 Vr   3 Vr   3 Lb          11  17 Lb   3 Sc   6 Vr  23 Lb
    16  22 Vr  21 Vr   1 Vr   7 Lb          16  22 Lb  10 Sc   9 Vr  26 Lb
    21  27 Vr   0 Lb   0 Vr  10 Lb          21  27 Lb  17 Sc  12 Vr   0 Sc
    26   2 Lb   9 Lb   0 Vr  13 Lb          26   2 Sc  24 Sc  16 Vr   3 Sc
                                            31   7 Sc   0 Sg  21 Vr   7 Sc

Sept 1/Jup 25 Sc/Sat  0 Cp/Uran 18 Lo   Oct. 1/Jup 29 Sc/Sat  1 Cp/Uran 20 Lo
Nep  5 Sc/Plut  4 Vr/N Node  5 Lb       Nep  6 Sc/Plut  5 Vr/N Node  4 Lb
```

```
          Sun    Merc   Venus  Mars                  Sun    Merc   Venus  Mars
Nov. 1   8 Sc   1 Sg  22 Vr   7 Sc       Dec. 1   8 Sg  24 Sc  22 Lb  28 Sc
     6  13 Sc   6 Sg  26 Vr  11 Sc            6  13 Sg  24 Sc  28 Lb   2 Sg
    11  18 Sc   9 Sg   1 Lb  14 Sc           11  18 Sg  27 Sc   4 Sc   5 Sg
    16  23 Sc  10 Sg   6 Lb  18 Sc           16  23 Sg   3 Sg  10 Sc   9 Sg
    21  28 Sc   6 Sg  12 Lb  21 Sc           21  28 Sg   9 Sg  15 Sc  12 Sg
    26   3 Sg  29 Sc  17 Lb  25 Sc           26   3 Cp  16 Sg  21 Sc  16 Sg
                                             31   9 Cp  23 Sg  27 Sc  20 Sg

Nov. 1/Jup  5 Sg/Sat  3 Cp/Uran 21 Lo   Dec. 1/Jup 12 Sg/Sat  6 Cp/Uran 21 Lo
Nep  7 Sc/Plut  6 Vr/N Node  2 Lb       Nep  8 Sc/Plut  6 Vr/N Node  0 Lb
```

Moon's Positions

```
         1       4       7      10      13      16      19      22      25      28      31
Jan.  21 Vr   3 Sc  16 Sg  29 Cp   9 Pc  15 Ar  21 Tr  27 Gm   7 Lo  18 Vr  30 Lb
Feb.  14 Sc  26 Sg   7 Aq  17 Pc  23 Ar  29 Tr   5 Ce  15 Lo  27 Vr  11 Sc
Mar.  25 Sc   7 Cp  17 Aq  25 Pc   1 Tr   7 Gm  13 Ce  23 Lo   6 Lb  20 Sc   4 Cp
Apr.  17 Cp  27 Aq   4 Ar  10 Tr  15 Gm  22 Ce   1 Vr  14 Lb  29 Sc  13 Cp
May   24 Aq   1 Ar   7 Tr  12 Gm  18 Ce  26 Lo   8 Lb  22 Sc   8 Cp  20 Aq  28 Pc
June  10 Ar  15 Tr  21 Gm  28 Ce   6 Vr  17 Lb   1 Sg  16 Cp  28 Aq   6 Ar
July  12 Tr  18 Gm  25 Ce   3 Vr  13 Lb  26 Sc  10 Cp  23 Aq   2 Ar   9 Tr  14 Gm
Aug.  26 Gm   4 Lo  13 Vr  24 Lb   7 Sg  19 Cp   1 Pc  10 Ar  16 Tr  22 Gm  29 Ce
Sept  12 Lo  23 Vr   5 Sc  18 Sg  30 Cp  10 Pc  18 Ar  24 Tr   0 Ce   7 Lo
Oct.  17 Vr   0 Sc  14 Sg  26 Cp   6 Pc  14 Ar  21 Tr  26 Gm   3 Lo  11 Vr  24 Lb
Nov.   9 Sc  24 Sg   7 Aq  16 Pc  23 Ar  29 Tr   5 Ce  11 Lo  19 Vr   2 Sc
Dec.  17 Sg   2 Aq  13 Pc  20 Ar  26 Tr   2 Ce   8 Lo  16 Vr  26 Lb  10 Sg  25 Cp
```

1960

	Sun	Merc	Venus	Mars
Jan. 1	10 Cp	25 Sg	28 Sc	20 Sg
6	15 Cp	3 Cp	4 Sg	24 Sg
11	20 Cp	10 Cp	10 Sg	28 Sg
16	25 Cp	18 Cp	16 Sg	1 Cp
21	0 Aq	26 Cp	22 Sg	5 Cp
26	5 Aq	5 Aq	29 Sg	9 Cp
31	10 Aq	13 Aq	5 Cp	12 Cp

Jan. 1/Jup 19 Sg/Sat 9 Cp/Uran 21 Lo
Nep 9 Sc/Plut 6 Vr/N Node 29 Vr

	Sun	Merc	Venus	Mars
Feb. 1	11 Aq	15 Aq	6 Cp	13 Cp
6	16 Aq	24 Aq	12 Cp	17 Cp
11	21 Aq	3 Pc	18 Cp	21 Cp
16	26 Aq	11 Pc	24 Cp	25 Cp
21	1 Pc	19 Pc	0 Aq	28 Cp
26	6 Pc	24 Pc	7 Aq	2 Aq

Feb. 1/Jup 25 Sg/Sat 13 Cp/Uran 19 Lo
Nep 9 Sc/Plut 5 Vr/N Node 27 Vr

	Sun	Merc	Venus	Mars
Mar. 1	10 Pc	26 Pc	11 Aq	5 Aq
6	15 Pc	24 Pc	18 Aq	9 Aq
11	20 Pc	20 Pc	24 Aq	13 Aq
16	25 Pc	16 Pc	0 Pc	17 Aq
21	0 Ar	13 Pc	6 Pc	21 Aq
26	5 Ar	12 Pc	12 Pc	24 Aq
31	10 Ar	14 Pc	18 Pc	28 Aq

Mar. 1/Jup 30 Sg/Sat 16 Cp/Uran 18 Lo
Nep 9 Sc/Plut 5 Vr/N Node 26 Vr

	Sun	Merc	Venus	Mars
Apr. 1	11 Ar	15 Pc	20 Pc	29 Aq
6	16 Ar	19 Pc	26 Pc	3 Pc
11	21 Ar	24 Pc	2 Ar	7 Pc
16	26 Ar	0 Ar	8 Ar	11 Pc
21	1 Tr	7 Ar	14 Ar	14 Pc
26	6 Tr	15 Ar	20 Ar	18 Pc

Apr. 1/Jup 3 Cp/Sat 18 Cp/Uran 17 Lo
Nep 8 Sc/Plut 4 Vr/N Node 24 Vr

	Sun	Merc	Venus	Mars
May 1	11 Tr	23 Ar	27 Ar	22 Pc
6	15 Tr	2 Tr	3 Tr	26 Pc
11	20 Tr	13 Tr	9 Tr	0 Ar
16	25 Tr	23 Tr	15 Tr	4 Ar
21	0 Gm	4 Gm	21 Tr	7 Ar
26	5 Gm	15 Gm	27 Tr	11 Ar
31	10 Gm	25 Gm	3 Gm	15 Ar

May 1/Jup 3 Cp/Sat 18 Cp/Uran 17 Lo
Nep 8 Sc/Plut 4 Vr/N Node 22 Vr

	Sun	Merc	Venus	Mars
June 1	11 Gm	27 Gm	5 Gm	16 Ar
6	15 Gm	5 Ce	11 Gm	19 Ar
11	20 Gm	13 Ce	17 Gm	23 Ar
16	25 Gm	19 Ce	23 Gm	27 Ar
21	0 Ce	24 Ce	29 Gm	0 Tr
26	4 Ce	28 Ce	5 Ce	4 Tr

June 1/Jup 1 Cp/Sat 18 Cp/Uran 18 Lo
Nep 7 Sc/Plut 4 Vr/N Node 21 Vr

	Sun	Merc	Venus	Mars
July 1	9 Ce	0 Lo	11 Ce	8 Tr
6	14 Ce	0 Lo	18 Ce	11 Tr
11	19 Ce	28 Ce	24 Ce	15 Tr
16	23 Ce	25 Ce	0 Lo	18 Tr
21	28 Ce	22 Ce	6 Lo	22 Tr
26	3 Lo	20 Ce	12 Lo	25 Tr
31	8 Lo	20 Ce	18 Lo	29 Tr

July 1/Jup 27 Sg/Sat 16 Cp/Uran 19 Lo
Nep 6 Sc/Plut 4 Vr/N Node 19 Vr

	Sun	Merc	Venus	Mars
Aug. 1	9 Lo	21 Ce	20 Lo	29 Tr
6	14 Lo	24 Ce	26 Lo	3 Gm
11	18 Lo	0 Lo	2 Vr	6 Gm
16	23 Lo	8 Lo	8 Vr	9 Gm
21	28 Lo	18 Lo	14 Vr	12 Gm
26	3 Vr	28 Lo	20 Vr	15 Gm
31	8 Vr	8 Vr	27 Vr	18 Gm

Aug. 1/Jup 24 Sg/Sat 13 Cp/Uran 21 Lo
Nep 6 Sc/Plut 5 Vr/N Node 17 Vr

1960

```
            Sun     Merc    Venus   Mars                        Sun     Merc    Venus   Mars
Sept  1    9 Vr   10 Vr   28 Vr   19 Gm        Oct.  1    8 Lb   29 Lb    5 Sc    5 Ce
      6   13 Vr   19 Vr    4 Lb   22 Gm              6   13 Lb    6 Sc   11 Sc    7 Ce
     11   18 Vr   28 Vr   10 Lb   25 Gm             11   18 Lb   12 Sc   17 Sc    9 Ce
     16   23 Vr    6 Lb   16 Lb   27 Gm             16   23 Lb   17 Sc   23 Sc   11 Ce
     21   28 Vr   14 Lb   22 Lb    0 Ce             21   28 Lb   22 Sc   29 Sc   13 Ce
     26    3 Lb   22 Lb   29 Lb    2 Ce             26    3 Sc   24 Sc    5 Sg   15 Ce
                                                    31    8 Sc   23 Sc   11 Sg   16 Ce

Sept  1/Jup 24 Sg/Sat 12 Cp/Uran 23 Lo        Oct.  1/Jup 26 Sg/Sat 12 Cp/Uran 24 Lo
Nep  7 Sc/Plut  6 Vr/N Node 16 Vr             Nep  8 Sc/Plut  7 Vr/N Node 14 Vr
```

```
            Sun     Merc    Venus   Mars                        Sun     Merc    Venus   Mars
Nov.  1    9 Sc   23 Sc   13 Sg   16 Ce        Dec.  1    9 Sg   20 Sc   19 Cp   18 Ce
      6   14 Sc   18 Sc   19 Sg   17 Ce              6   14 Sg   27 Sc   25 Cp   17 Ce
     11   19 Sc   11 Sc   25 Sg   18 Ce             11   19 Sg    5 Sg    1 Aq   16 Ce
     16   24 Sc    8 Sc    1 Cp   19 Ce             16   24 Sg   12 Sg    7 Aq   14 Ce
     21   29 Sc    9 Sc    7 Cp   19 Ce             21   29 Sg   20 Sg   13 Aq   12 Ce
     26    4 Sg   14 Sc   13 Cp   18 Ce             26    4 Cp   28 Sg   18 Aq   11 Ce
                                                    31    9 Cp    6 Cp   24 Aq    9 Ce

Nov.  1/Jup  1 Cp/Sat 14 Cp/Uran 25 Lo        Dec.  1/Jup  7 Cp/Sat 16 Cp/Uran 26 Lo
Nep  9 Sc/Plut  8 Vr/N Node 13 Vr             Nep 10 Sc/Plut  8 Vr/N Node 11 Vr
```

Moon's Positions

```
          1        4        7       10       13       16       19       22       25       28       31
Jan.  10 Aq   22 Pc   29 Ar    5 Gm   11 Ce   17 Lo   26 Vr    6 Sc   19 Sg    3 Aq   16 Pc
Feb.  30 Pc    8 Tr   13 Gm   19 Ce   27 Lo    6 Lb   16 Sc   29 Sg   12 Aq   24 Pc
Mar.  20 Ar   27 Tr    3 Ce   10 Lo   18 Vr   29 Lb   11 Sg   24 Cp    6 Pc   15 Ar   23 Tr
Apr.   5 Gm   11 Ce   17 Lo   26 Vr    8 Sc   22 Sg    5 Aq   16 Pc   24 Ar    1 Gm
May    7 Ce   13 Lo   21 Vr    2 Sc   17 Sg    1 Aq   13 Pc   21 Ar   28 Tr    4 Ce   10 Lo
June  22 Lo   29 Vr   11 Sc   26 Sg   11 Aq   22 Pc    1 Tr    7 Gm   13 Ce   18 Lo
July  25 Vr    5 Sc   19 Sg    5 Aq   18 Pc   27 Ar    4 Gm   10 Ce   16 Lo   22 Vr    1 Sc
Aug.  15 Sc   28 Sg   13 Aq   26 Pc    6 Tr   13 Gm   18 Ce   25 Lo    2 Lb   12 Sc   23 Sg
Sept   8 Cp   22 Aq    4 Ar   14 Tr   21 Gm   27 Ce    3 Vr   11 Lb   22 Sc    4 Cp
Oct.  17 Aq   29 Pc    9 Tr   17 Gm   23 Ce   29 Lo    7 Lb   18 Sc    1 Cp   14 Aq   25 Pc
Nov.   8 Ar   17 Tr   25 Gm    1 Lo    6 Vr   15 Lb   27 Sc   11 Cp   24 Aq    5 Ar
Dec.  14 Tr   21 Gm   27 Ce    2 Vr    9 Lb   20 Sc    5 Cp   20 Aq    2 Ar   11 Tr   18 Gm
```

                                                           Ephemeris

1961

	Sun	Merc	Venus	Mars
Jan. 1	10 Cp	7 Cp	25 Aq	8 Ce
6	15 Cp	15 Cp	1 Pc	6 Ce
11	21 Cp	24 Cp	7 Pc	4 Ce
16	26 Cp	2 Aq	12 Pc	3 Ce
21	1 Aq	11 Aq	17 Pc	2 Ce
26	6 Aq	19 Aq	23 Pc	1 Ce
31	11 Aq	27 Aq	28 Pc	0 Ce

Jan. 1/Jup 14 Cp/Sat 20 Cp/Uran 25 Lo
Nep 11 Sc/Plut 8 Vr/N Node 9 Vr

	Sun	Merc	Venus	Mars
Feb. 1	12 Aq	29 Aq	29 Pc	0 Ce
6	17 Aq	5 Pc	4 Ar	0 Ce
11	22 Aq	9 Pc	8 Ar	0 Ce
16	27 Aq	8 Pc	13 Ar	1 Ce
21	2 Pc	4 Pc	17 Ar	1 Ce
26	7 Pc	29 Aq	20 Ar	2 Ce

Feb. 1/Jup 21 Cp/Sat 23 Cp/Uran 24 Lo
Nep 11 Sc/Plut 7 Vr/N Node 8 Vr

	Sun	Merc	Venus	Mars
Mar. 1	10 Pc	26 Aq	22 Ar	3 Ce
6	15 Pc	24 Aq	25 Ar	4 Ce
11	20 Pc	25 Aq	27 Ar	6 Ce
16	25 Pc	28 Aq	29 Ar	7 Ce
21	0 Ar	2 Pc	29 Ar	9 Ce
26	5 Ar	8 Pc	29 Ar	11 Ce
31	10 Ar	14 Pc	27 Ar	13 Ce

Mar. 1/Jup 27 Cp/Sat 26 Cp/Uran 23 Lo
Nep 11 Sc/Plut 7 Vr/N Node 6 Vr

	Sun	Merc	Venus	Mars
Apr. 1	11 Ar	16 Pc	27 Ar	13 Ce
6	16 Ar	23 Pc	24 Ar	16 Ce
11	21 Ar	1 Ar	21 Ar	18 Ce
16	26 Ar	10 Ar	18 Ar	20 Ce
21	1 Tr	19 Ar	15 Ar	22 Ce
26	6 Tr	29 Ar	14 Ar	25 Ce

Apr. 1/Jup 3 Aq/Sat 29 Cp/Uran 22 Lo
Nep 11 Sc/Plut 6 Vr/N Node 5 Vr

	Sun	Merc	Venus	Mars
May 1	10 Tr	9 Tr	13 Ar	27 Ce
6	15 Tr	20 Tr	13 Ar	0 Lo
11	20 Tr	1 Gm	14 Ar	3 Lo
16	25 Tr	11 Gm	16 Ar	5 Lo
21	0 Gm	19 Gm	19 Ar	8 Lo
26	5 Gm	27 Gm	22 Ar	11 Lo
31	9 Gm	3 Ce	25 Ar	13 Lo

May 1/Jup 6 Aq/Sat 30 Cp/Uran 22 Lo
Nep 10 Sc/Plut 6 Vr/N Node 3 Vr

	Sun	Merc	Venus	Mars
June 1	10 Gm	4 Ce	26 Ar	14 Lo
6	15 Gm	8 Ce	0 Tr	17 Lo
11	20 Gm	10 Ce	4 Tr	20 Lo
16	25 Gm	10 Ce	9 Tr	22 Lo
21	29 Gm	9 Ce	14 Tr	25 Lo
26	4 Ce	6 Ce	19 Tr	28 Lo

June 1/Jup 7 Aq/Sat 29 Cp/Uran 22 Lo
Nep 9 Sc/Plut 6 Vr/N Node 1 Vr

	Sun	Merc	Venus	Mars
July 1	9 Ce	4 Ce	24 Tr	1 Vr
6	14 Ce	2 Ce	29 Tr	4 Vr
11	18 Ce	2 Ce	4 Gm	7 Vr
16	23 Ce	4 Ce	9 Gm	10 Vr
21	28 Ce	8 Ce	15 Gm	13 Vr
26	3 Lo	14 Ce	20 Gm	16 Vr
31	8 Lo	22 Ce	26 Gm	19 Vr

July 1/Jup 5 Aq/Sat 28 Cp/Uran 23 Lo
Nep 9 Sc/Plut 6 Vr/N Node 30 Lo

	Sun	Merc	Venus	Mars
Aug. 1	9 Lo	24 Ce	27 Gm	20 Vr
6	13 Lo	4 Lo	3 Ce	23 Vr
11	18 Lo	14 Lo	8 Ce	26 Vr
16	23 Lo	24 Lo	14 Ce	29 Vr
21	28 Lo	4 Vr	20 Ce	3 Lb
26	3 Vr	13 Vr	26 Ce	6 Lb
31	7 Vr	22 Vr	2 Lo	9 Lb

Aug. 1/Jup 1 Aq/Sat 26 Cp/Uran 25 Lo
Nep 9 Sc/Plut 7 Vr/N Node 28 Lo

1961

```
          Sun    Merc   Venus   Mars                    Sun    Merc   Venus   Mars
Sept 1   8 Vr   24 Vr   3 Lo   10 Lb        Oct. 1    8 Lb    3 Sc    9 Vr   29 Lb
     6  13 Vr    2 Lb   9 Lo   13 Lb             6   13 Lb    7 Sc   15 Vr    3 Sc
    11  18 Vr    9 Lb  15 Lo   16 Lb            11   17 Lb    8 Sc   21 Vr    6 Sc
    16  23 Vr   16 Lb  21 Lo   19 Lb            16   22 Lb    6 Sc   27 Vr   10 Sc
    21  28 Vr   23 Lb  27 Lo   23 Lb            21   27 Lb    1 Sc    4 Lb   13 Sc
    26   3 Lb   28 Lb   3 Vr   26 Lb            26    2 Sc   25 Lb   10 Lb   17 Sc
                                               31    7 Sc   22 Lb   16 Lb   20 Sc
```

Sept 1/Jup 28 Cp/Sat 24 Cp/Uran 27 Lo   Oct. 1/Jup 27 Cp/Sat 23 Cp/Uran 29 Lo
Nep 9 Sc/Plut 8 Vr/N Node 26 Lo   Nep 10 Sc/Plut 9 Vr/N Node 25 Lo

```
          Sun    Merc   Venus   Mars                    Sun    Merc   Venus   Mars
Nov. 1   8 Sc   22 Lb  17 Lb   21 Sc        Dec. 1    9 Sg    0 Sg   25 Sc   12 Sg
     6  13 Sc   25 Lb  23 Lb   24 Sc             6   14 Sg    8 Sg    1 Sg   16 Sg
    11  18 Sc    0 Sc   0 Sc   28 Sc            11   19 Sg   16 Sg    7 Sg   20 Sg
    16  23 Sc    7 Sc   6 Sc    2 Sg            16   24 Sg   24 Sg   14 Sg   23 Sg
    21  28 Sc   14 Sc  12 Sc    5 Sg            21   29 Sg    2 Cp   20 Sg   27 Sg
    26   4 Sg   22 Sc  19 Sc    9 Sg            26    4 Cp   10 Cp   26 Sg    1 Cp
                                               31    9 Cp   18 Cp    3 Cp    5 Cp
```

Nov. 1/Jup 30 Cp/Sat 24 Cp/Uran 30 Lo   Dec. 1/Jup 4 Aq/Sat 26 Cp/Uran 1 Vr
Nep 11 Sc/Plut 10 Vr/N Node 23 Lo   Nep 12 Sc/Plut 10 Vr/N Node 22 Lo

Moon's Positions

```
          1       4       7      10      13      16      19      22      25      28      31
Jan.   30 Gm    5 Lo   11 Vr   18 Lb   28 Sc   13 Cp   28 Aq   11 Ar   20 Tr   27 Gm    2 Lo
Feb.   14 Lo   20 Vr   27 Lb    7 Sg   21 Cp    6 Pc   20 Ar   29 Tr    6 Ce   11 Lo
Mar.   23 Lo   29 Vr    7 Sc   18 Sg    0 Aq   14 Pc   27 Ar    7 Gm   14 Ce   19 Lo   26 Vr
Apr.    8 Lb   17 Sc   28 Sg   11 Aq   24 Pc    6 Tr   15 Gm   22 Ce   27 Lo    4 Lb
May    13 Sc   25 Sg    7 Aq   20 Pc    1 Tr   10 Gm   18 Ce   23 Lo   29 Vr    8 Sc   20 Sg
June    5 Cp   18 Aq    0 Ar   11 Tr   19 Gm   26 Ce    1 Vr    7 Lb   16 Sc   29 Sg
July   13 Aq   27 Pc    8 Tr   16 Gm   23 Ce   28 Lo    4 Lb   11 Sc   22 Sg    7 Aq   22 Pc
Aug.    7 Ar   18 Tr   25 Gm    2 Lo    7 Vr   13 Lb   20 Sc    1 Cp   15 Aq    1 Ar   13 Tr
Sept   27 Tr    5 Ce   10 Lo   16 Vr   22 Lb    0 Sg   11 Cp   24 Aq    9 Ar   22 Tr
Oct.    1 Ce    7 Lo   12 Vr   19 Lb   27 Sc    7 Cp   19 Aq    3 Ar   16 Tr   26 Gm    3 Lo
Nov.   15 Lo   21 Vr   28 Lb    7 Sg   18 Cp   30 Aq   12 Ar   24 Tr    4 Ce   11 Lo
Dec.   17 Vr   23 Lb    2 Sg   14 Cp   27 Aq    9 Ar   20 Tr   30 Gm    7 Lo   13 Vr   18 Lb
```

1962

	Sun	Merc	Venus	Mars
Jan. 1	10 Cp	19 Cp	4 Cp	5 Cp
6	15 Cp	27 Cp	10 Cp	9 Cp
11	20 Cp	5 Aq	16 Cp	13 Cp
16	25 Cp	13 Aq	23 Cp	17 Cp
21	0 Aq	19 Aq	29 Cp	21 Cp
26	6 Aq	23 Aq	5 Aq	25 Cp
31	11 Aq	22 Aq	12 Aq	28 Cp

Jan. 1/Jup 10 Aq/Sat 30 Cp/Uran 0 Vr
Nep 13 Sc/Plut 10 Vr/N Node 20 Lo

	Sun	Merc	Venus	Mars
Feb. 1	12 Aq	21 Aq	13 Aq	29 Cp
6	17 Aq	16 Aq	19 Aq	3 Aq
11	22 Aq	10 Aq	25 Aq	7 Aq
16	27 Aq	7 Aq	2 Pc	11 Aq
21	2 Pc	8 Aq	8 Pc	15 Aq
26	7 Pc	10 Aq	14 Pc	19 Aq

Feb. 1/Jup 18 Aq/Sat 3 Aq/Uran 29 Lo
Nep 13 Sc/Plut 10 Vr/N Node 18 Lo

	Sun	Merc	Venus	Mars
Mar. 1	10 Pc	13 Aq	18 Pc	21 Aq
6	15 Pc	18 Aq	24 Pc	25 Aq
11	20 Pc	24 Aq	0 Ar	29 Aq
16	25 Pc	1 Pc	7 Ar	3 Pc
21	0 Ar	8 Pc	13 Ar	7 Pc
26	5 Ar	16 Pc	19 Ar	11 Pc
31	10 Ar	24 Pc	25 Ar	15 Pc

Mar. 1/Jup 24 Aq/Sat 7 Aq/Uran 28 Lo
Nep 13 Sc/Plut 9 Vr/N Node 17 Lo

	Sun	Merc	Venus	Mars
Apr. 1	11 Ar	26 Pc	26 Ar	15 Pc
6	16 Ar	5 Ar	3 Tr	19 Pc
11	21 Ar	15 Ar	9 Tr	23 Pc
16	26 Ar	25 Ar	15 Tr	27 Pc
21	0 Tr	6 Tr	21 Tr	1 Ar
26	5 Tr	16 Tr	27 Tr	5 Ar

Apr. 1/Jup 1 Pc/Sat 9 Aq/Uran 27 Lo
Nep 13 Sc/Plut 8 Vr/N Node 15 Lo

	Sun	Merc	Venus	Mars
May 1	10 Tr	26 Tr	3 Gm	9 Ar
6	15 Tr	4 Gm	9 Gm	13 Ar
11	20 Tr	11 Gm	15 Gm	16 Ar
16	25 Tr	16 Gm	21 Gm	20 Ar
21	29 Tr	19 Gm	27 Gm	24 Ar
26	4 Gm	20 Gm	3 Ce	28 Ar
31	9 Gm	20 Gm	9 Ce	2 Tr

May 1/Jup 7 Pc/Sat 11 Aq/Uran 26 Lo
Nep 12 Sc/Plut 8 Vr/N Node 14 Lo

	Sun	Merc	Venus	Mars
June 1	10 Gm	19 Gm	11 Ce	2 Tr
6	15 Gm	17 Gm	17 Ce	6 Tr
11	20 Gm	14 Gm	23 Ce	10 Tr
16	24 Gm	12 Gm	29 Ce	13 Tr
21	29 Gm	12 Gm	4 Lo	17 Tr
26	4 Ce	14 Gm	10 Lo	21 Tr

June 1/Jup 11 Pc/Sat 11 Aq/Uran 27 Lo
Nep 11 Sc/Plut 8 Vr/N Node 12 Lo

	Sun	Merc	Venus	Mars
July 1	9 Ce	17 Gm	16 Lo	24 Tr
6	13 Ce	22 Gm	22 Lo	28 Tr
11	18 Ce	0 Ce	28 Lo	1 Gm
16	23 Ce	8 Ce	4 Vr	5 Gm
21	28 Ce	18 Ce	9 Vr	8 Gm
26	3 Lo	28 Ce	15 Vr	12 Gm
31	7 Lo	9 Lo	20 Vr	15 Gm

July 1/Jup 13 Pc/Sat 10 Aq/Uran 28 Lo
Nep 11 Sc/Plut 8 Vr/N Node 10 Lo

	Sun	Merc	Venus	Mars
Aug. 1	8 Lo	11 Lo	22 Vr	16 Gm
6	13 Lo	21 Lo	27 Vr	19 Gm
11	18 Lo	0 Vr	2 Lb	23 Gm
16	23 Lo	9 Vr	8 Lb	26 Gm
21	27 Lo	17 Vr	13 Lb	29 Gm
26	2 Vr	25 Vr	18 Lb	2 Ce
31	7 Vr	2 Lb	23 Lb	5 Ce

Aug. 1/Jup 11 Pc/Sat 8 Aq/Uran 29 Lo
Nep 11 Sc/Plut 9 Vr/N Node 9 Lo

1962

```
           Sun    Merc    Venus   Mars                    Sun     Merc    Venus   Mars
Sept 1    8 Vr    3 Lb    24 Lb    6 Ce      Oct. 1     7 Lb    19 Lb    20 Sc   24 Ce
     6   13 Vr    9 Lb    29 Lb    9 Ce           6    12 Lb    14 Lb    23 Sc   27 Ce
    11   18 Vr   15 Lb     4 Sc   12 Ce          11    17 Lb     8 Lb    25 Sc   29 Ce
    16   23 Vr   19 Lb     8 Sc   15 Ce          16    22 Lb     7 Lb    27 Sc    2 Lo
    21   28 Vr   21 Lb    12 Sc   18 Ce          21    27 Lb     9 Lb    28 Sc    5 Lo
    26    2 Lb   22 Lb    16 Sc   21 Ce          26     2 Sc    15 Lb    27 Sc    7 Lo
                                                 31     7 Sc    22 Lb    26 Sc    9 Lo
```

Sept 1/Jup 8 Pc/Sat 6 Aq/Uran 1 Vr
Nep 11 Sc/Plut 10 Vr/N Node 7 Lo

Oct. 1/Jup 4 Pc/Sat 5 Aq/Uran 3 Vr
Nep 12 Sc/Plut 11 Vr/N Node 6 Lo

```
           Sun    Merc    Venus   Mars                    Sun     Merc    Venus   Mars
Nov. 1    8 Sc   23 Lb    26 Sc   10 Lo      Dec. 1     8 Sg    11 Sg    12 Sc   21 Lo
     6   13 Sc    1 Sc    24 Sc   12 Lo           6    13 Sg    19 Sg    12 Sc   22 Lo
    11   18 Sc   10 Sc    21 Sc   14 Lo          11    18 Sg    27 Sg    13 Sc   23 Lo
    16   23 Sc   18 Sc    18 Sc   16 Lo          16    24 Sg     5 Cp    15 Sc   24 Lo
    21   28 Sc   26 Sc    15 Sc   18 Lo          21    29 Sg    13 Cp    18 Sc   25 Lo
    26    3 Sg    4 Sg    13 Sc   20 Lo          26     4 Cp    20 Cp    21 Sc   25 Lo
                                                 31     9 Cp    27 Cp    24 Sc   25 Lo
```

Nov. 1/Jup 3 Pc/Sat 5 Aq/Uran 5 Vr
Nep 13 Sc/Plut 12 Vr/N Node 4 Lo

Dec. 1/Jup 5 Pc/Sat 7 Aq/Uran 5 Vr
Nep 14 Sc/Plut 12 Vr/N Node 2 Lo

Moon's Positions

```
           1        4        7       10       13       16       19       22       25       28       31
Jan.    1 Sc    10 Sg    23 Cp     7 Pc    20 Ar     0 Gm     9 Ce    15 Lo    21 Vr    27 Lb     4 Sg
Feb.   18 Sg     1 Aq    16 Pc    30 Ar    10 Gm    18 Ce    24 Lo    29 Vr     5 Sc    13 Sg
Mar.   26 Sg     9 Aq    24 Pc     9 Tr    20 Gm    27 Ce     3 Vr     8 Lb    15 Sc    22 Sg     3 Aq
Apr.   17 Aq     2 Ar    17 Tr    28 Gm     6 Lo    11 Vr    17 Lb    24 Sc     3 Cp    13 Aq
May    26 Pc    11 Tr    23 Gm     2 Lo     8 Vr    13 Lb    20 Sc    29 Sg    10 Aq    22 Pc     5 Tr
June   20 Tr     1 Ce    10 Lo    16 Vr    22 Lb    29 Sc     9 Cp    21 Aq     3 Ar    15 Tr
July   26 Gm     5 Lo    12 Vr    17 Lb    24 Sc     4 Cp    16 Aq    30 Pc    12 Tr    23 Gm     1 Lo
Aug.   14 Lo    20 Vr    26 Lb     2 Sg    12 Cp    25 Aq    10 Ar    23 Tr     3 Ce    11 Lo    17 Vr
Sept   29 Vr     4 Sc    11 Sg    20 Cp     3 Pc    19 Ar     3 Gm    13 Ce    20 Lo    26 Vr
Oct.    1 Sc     7 Sg    15 Cp    27 Aq    12 Ar    27 Tr     9 Ce    17 Lo    23 Vr    28 Lb     4 Sg
Nov.   17 Sg    25 Cp     6 Pc    20 Ar     5 Gm    17 Ce    25 Lo     1 Lb     7 Sc    14 Sg
Dec.   22 Cp     2 Pc    15 Ar    29 Tr    11 Ce    21 Lo    27 Vr     3 Sc    10 Sg    18 Cp    29 Aq
```

1963

	Sun	Merc	Venus	Mars
Jan. 1	10 Cp	29 Cp	25 Sc	25 Lo
6	15 Cp	4 Aq	29 Sc	24 Lo
11	20 Cp	7 Aq	4 Sg	23 Lo
16	25 Cp	5 Aq	9 Sg	22 Lo
21	0 Aq	29 Cp	13 Sg	20 Lo
26	5 Aq	23 Cp	18 Sg	19 Lo
31	10 Aq	21 Cp	24 Sg	17 Lo

Jan. 1/Jup 9 Pc/Sat 10 Aq/Uran 5 Vr
Nep 15 Sc/Plut 12 Vr/N Node 1 Lo

	Sun	Merc	Venus	Mars
Feb. 1	11 Aq	21 Cp	25 Sg	16 Lo
6	16 Aq	22 Cp	0 Cp	14 Lo
11	22 Aq	26 Cp	6 Cp	12 Lo
16	27 Aq	1 Aq	11 Cp	11 Lo
21	2 Pc	7 Aq	17 Cp	9 Lo
26	7 Pc	13 Aq	23 Cp	8 Lo

Feb. 1/Jup 15 Pc/Sat 14 Aq/Uran 4 Vr
Nep 16 Sc/Plut 12 Vr/N Node 29 Ce

	Sun	Merc	Venus	Mars
Mar. 1	10 Pc	17 Aq	26 Cp	7 Lo
6	15 Pc	25 Aq	2 Aq	6 Lo
11	20 Pc	3 Pc	8 Aq	6 Lo
16	25 Pc	11 Pc	13 Aq	5 Lo
21	0 Ar	20 Pc	19 Aq	5 Lo
26	5 Ar	0 Ar	25 Aq	6 Lo
31	10 Ar	10 Ar	1 Pc	7 Lo

Mar. 1/Jup 22 Pc/Sat 17 Aq/Uran 3 Vr
Nep 16 Sc/Plut 11 Vr/N Node 28 Ce

	Sun	Merc	Venus	Mars
Apr. 1	11 Ar	12 Ar	2 Pc	7 Lo
6	15 Ar	22 Ar	8 Pc	8 Lo
11	20 Ar	2 Tr	14 Pc	9 Lo
16	25 Ar	12 Tr	20 Pc	10 Lo
21	0 Tr	19 Tr	26 Pc	12 Lo
26	5 Tr	25 Tr	2 Ar	13 Lo

Apr. 1/Jup 29 Pc/Sat 20 Aq/Uran 2 Vr
Nep 15 Sc/Plut 10 Vr/N Node 26 Ce

	Sun	Merc	Venus	Mars
May 1	10 Tr	29 Tr	8 Ar	15 Lo
6	15 Tr	1 Gm	14 Ar	17 Lo
11	20 Tr	0 Gm	20 Ar	19 Lo
16	24 Tr	28 Tr	26 Ar	21 Lo
21	29 Tr	25 Tr	2 Tr	24 Lo
26	4 Gm	23 Tr	8 Tr	26 Lo
31	9 Gm	22 Tr	14 Tr	28 Lo

May 1/Jup 6 Ar/Sat 22 Aq/Uran 1 Vr
Nep 14 Sc/Plut 10 Vr/N Node 24 Ce

	Sun	Merc	Venus	Mars
June 1	10 Gm	22 Tr	16 Tr	29 Lo
6	15 Gm	23 Tr	22 Tr	1 Vr
11	19 Gm	26 Tr	28 Tr	4 Vr
16	24 Gm	1 Gm	4 Gm	7 Vr
21	29 Gm	7 Gm	10 Gm	9 Vr
26	4 Ce	15 Gm	16 Gm	12 Vr

June 1/Jup 12 Ar/Sat 23 Aq/Uran 1 Vr
Nep 14 Sc/Plut 10 Vr/N Node 23 Ce

	Sun	Merc	Venus	Mars
July 1	8 Ce	24 Gm	22 Gm	15 Vr
6	13 Ce	4 Ce	28 Gm	18 Vr
11	18 Ce	15 Ce	4 Ce	20 Vr
16	23 Ce	25 Ce	10 Ce	23 Vr
21	28 Ce	6 Lo	17 Ce	26 Vr
26	2 Lo	15 Lo	23 Ce	29 Vr
31	7 Lo	24 Lo	29 Ce	2 Lb

July 1/Jup 17 Ar/Sat 23 Aq/Uran 2 Vr
Nep 13 Sc/Plut 10 Vr/N Node 21 Ce

	Sun	Merc	Venus	Mars
Aug. 1	8 Lo	26 Lo	0 Lo	3 Lb
6	13 Lo	4 Vr	6 Lo	6 Lb
11	18 Lo	12 Vr	12 Lo	9 Lb
16	22 Lo	18 Vr	19 Lo	12 Lb
21	27 Lo	24 Vr	25 Lo	15 Lb
26	2 Vr	29 Vr	1 Vr	19 Lb
31	7 Vr	3 Lb	7 Vr	22 Lb

Aug. 1/Jup 19 Ar/Sat 21 Aq/Uran 4 Vr
Nep 13 Sc/Plut 11 Vr/N Node 19 Ce

1963

```
           Sun     Merc     Venus    Mars                    Sun     Merc     Venus    Mars
Sept 1     8 Vr     4 Lb     8 Vr    23 Lb       Oct. 1      7 Lb    21 Vr    16 Lb    13 Sc
     6     13 Vr    5 Lb    15 Vr    26 Lb            6      12 Lb    24 Vr    22 Lb    16 Sc
    11     18 Vr    4 Lb    21 Vr    29 Lb           11      17 Lb     0 Lb    28 Lb    20 Sc
    16     22 Vr    1 Lb    27 Vr     2 Sc           16      22 Lb     8 Lb     4 Sc    23 Sc
    21     27 Vr   26 Vr     3 Lb     6 Sc           21      27 Lb    17 Lb    11 Sc    27 Sc
    26      2 Lb   21 Vr     9 Lb     9 Sc           26       2 Sc    25 Lb    17 Sc     0 Sg
                                                    31       7 Sc     4 Sc    23 Sc     4 Sg
```

Sept 1/Jup 19 Ar/Sat 18 Aq/Uran 6 Vr
Nep 13 Sc/Plut 12 Vr/N Node 18 Ce

Oct. 1/Jup 15 Ar/Sat 17 Aq/Uran 8 Vr
Nep 14 Sc/Plut 13 Vr/N Node 16 Ce

```
           Sun     Merc     Venus    Mars                    Sun     Merc     Venus    Mars
Nov. 1     8 Sc     5 Sc    24 Sc     5 Sg       Dec. 1      8 Sg    22 Sg     2 Cp    27 Sg
     6     13 Sc    13 Sc     1 Sg     8 Sg           6      13 Sg     0 Cp     8 Cp     0 Cp
    11     18 Sc    21 Sc     7 Sg    12 Sg          11      18 Sg     7 Cp    14 Cp     4 Cp
    16     23 Sc    29 Sc    13 Sg    16 Sg          16      23 Sg    13 Cp    20 Cp     8 Cp
    21     28 Sc     7 Sg    19 Sg    19 Sg          21      28 Sg    18 Cp    27 Cp    12 Cp
    26      3 Sg    15 Sg    25 Sg    23 Sg          26       3 Cp    21 Cp     3 Aq    16 Cp
                                                    31       9 Cp    19 Cp     9 Aq    20 Cp
```

Nov. 1/Jup 11 Ar/Sat 17 Aq/Uran 9 Vr
Nep 15 Sc/Plut 14 Vr/N Node 15 Ce

Dec. 1/Jup 10 Ar/Sat 18 Aq/Uran 10 Vr
Nep 16 Sc/Plut 14 Vr/N Node 13 Ce

Moon's Positions

	1	4	7	10	13	16	19	22	25	28	31
Jan.	13 Pc	26 Ar	8 Gm	19 Ce	28 Lo	5 Lb	11 Sc	17 Sg	27 Cp	9 Pc	22 Ar
Feb.	7 Tr	18 Gm	28 Ce	6 Vr	13 Lb	19 Sc	25 Sg	5 Aq	18 Pc	3 Tr	
Mar.	17 Tr	29 Gm	8 Lo	15 Vr	21 Lb	27 Sc	3 Cp	13 Aq	26 Pc	12 Tr	25 Gm
Apr.	9 Ce	17 Lo	24 Vr	30 Lb	6 Sg	12 Cp	21 Aq	5 Ar	20 Tr	4 Ce	
May	14 Lo	21 Vr	27 Lb	3 Sg	9 Cp	17 Aq	29 Pc	14 Tr	28 Gm	10 Lo	18 Vr
June	30 Vr	6 Sc	12 Sg	19 Cp	28 Aq	9 Ar	23 Tr	7 Ce	18 Lo	26 Vr	
July	2 Sc	8 Sg	15 Cp	24 Aq	6 Ar	18 Tr	1 Ce	13 Lo	22 Vr	28 Lb	4 Sg
Aug.	16 Sg	24 Cp	4 Pc	17 Ar	29 Tr	11 Ce	21 Lo	30 Vr	6 Sc	12 Sg	19 Cp
Sept	2 Aq	13 Pc	27 Ar	10 Gm	21 Ce	1 Vr	8 Lb	14 Sc	20 Sg	27 Cp	
Oct.	7 Pc	21 Ar	6 Gm	18 Ce	28 Lo	5 Lb	11 Sc	16 Sg	23 Cp	1 Pc	14 Ar
Nov.	30 Ar	15 Gm	28 Ce	7 Vr	14 Lb	20 Sc	25 Sg	2 Aq	10 Pc	23 Ar	
Dec.	8 Gm	23 Ce	4 Vr	11 Lb	17 Sc	22 Sg	29 Cp	7 Pc	18 Ar	1 Gm	16 Ce

1964

	Sun	Merc	Venus	Mars
Jan. 1	10 Cp	18 Cp	10 Aq	20 Cp
6	15 Cp	11 Cp	16 Aq	24 Cp
11	20 Cp	6 Cp	23 Aq	28 Cp
16	25 Cp	5 Cp	29 Aq	2 Aq
21	0 Aq	6 Cp	5 Pc	6 Aq
26	5 Aq	10 Cp	11 Pc	10 Aq
31	10 Aq	16 Cp	17 Pc	14 Aq

Jan. 1/Jup 11 Ar/Sat 20 Aq/Uran 10 Vr
Nep 17 Sc/Plut 14 Vr/N Node 11 Ce

	Sun	Merc	Venus	Mars
Feb. 1	11 Aq	17 Cp	18 Pc	15 Aq
6	16 Aq	23 Cp	24 Pc	19 Aq
11	21 Aq	0 Aq	0 Ar	23 Aq
16	26 Aq	7 Aq	6 Ar	27 Aq
21	1 Pc	15 Aq	12 Ar	1 Pc
26	6 Pc	23 Aq	18 Ar	5 Pc

Feb. 1/Jup 15 Ar/Sat 24 Aq/Uran 9 Vr
Nep 18 Sc/Plut 14 Vr/N Node 10 Ce

	Sun	Merc	Venus	Mars
Mar. 1	10 Pc	0 Pc	23 Ar	8 Pc
6	15 Pc	9 Pc	28 Ar	12 Pc
11	20 Pc	18 Pc	4 Tr	16 Pc
16	25 Pc	28 Pc	10 Tr	19 Pc
21	0 Ar	8 Ar	15 Tr	23 Pc
26	5 Ar	18 Ar	20 Tr	27 Pc
31	10 Ar	27 Ar	26 Tr	1 Ar

Mar. 1/Jup 20 Ar/Sat 27 Aq/Uran 8 Vr
Nep 18 Sc/Plut 13 Vr/N Node 8 Ce

	Sun	Merc	Venus	Mars
Apr. 1	11 Ar	28 Ar	27 Tr	2 Ar
6	16 Ar	5 Tr	2 Gm	6 Ar
11	21 Ar	10 Tr	7 Gm	10 Ar
16	26 Ar	11 Tr	12 Gm	14 Ar
21	1 Tr	11 Tr	16 Gm	17 Ar
26	6 Tr	8 Tr	20 Gm	21 Ar

Apr. 1/Jup 27 Ar/Sat 1 Pc/Uran 7 Vr
Nep 17 Sc/Plut 12 Vr/N Node 7 Ce

	Sun	Merc	Venus	Mars
May 1	11 Tr	5 Tr	24 Gm	25 Ar
6	16 Tr	2 Tr	28 Gm	29 Ar
11	20 Tr	2 Tr	1 Ce	3 Tr
16	25 Tr	3 Tr	4 Ce	6 Tr
21	0 Gm	5 Tr	6 Ce	10 Tr
26	5 Gm	10 Tr	7 Ce	14 Tr
31	10 Gm	16 Tr	7 Ce	17 Tr

May 1/Jup 4 Tr/Sat 3 Pc/Uran 6 Vr
Nep 17 Sc/Plut 12 Vr/N Node 5 Ce

	Sun	Merc	Venus	Mars
June 1	11 Gm	17 Tr	7 Ce	18 Tr
6	15 Gm	24 Tr	6 Ce	22 Tr
11	20 Gm	2 Gm	4 Ce	25 Tr
16	25 Gm	12 Gm	1 Ce	29 Tr
21	0 Ce	22 Gm	28 Gm	3 Gm
26	4 Ce	3 Ce	25 Gm	6 Gm

June 1/Jup 12 Tr/Sat 5 Pc/Uran 6 Vr
Nep 16 Sc/Plut 12 Vr/N Node 3 Ce

	Sun	Merc	Venus	Mars
July 1	9 Ce	14 Ce	23 Gm	10 Gm
6	14 Ce	24 Ce	21 Gm	13 Gm
11	19 Ce	4 Lo	20 Gm	17 Gm
16	23 Ce	13 Lo	21 Gm	20 Gm
21	28 Ce	21 Lo	22 Gm	23 Gm
26	3 Lo	28 Lo	24 Gm	27 Gm
31	8 Lo	4 Vr	27 Gm	0 Ce

July 1/Jup 18 Tr/Sat 5 Pc/Uran 7 Vr
Nep 15 Sc/Plut 12 Vr/N Node 2 Ce

	Sun	Merc	Venus	Mars
Aug. 1	9 Lo	6 Vr	27 Gm	1 Ce
6	14 Lo	11 Vr	0 Ce	4 Ce
11	18 Lo	15 Vr	4 Ce	7 Ce
16	23 Lo	17 Vr	8 Ce	11 Ce
21	28 Lo	18 Vr	12 Ce	14 Ce
26	3 Vr	16 Vr	17 Ce	17 Ce
31	8 Vr	12 Vr	22 Ce	20 Ce

Aug. 1/Jup 23 Tr/Sat 3 Pc/Uran 8 Vr
Nep 15 Sc/Plut 13 Vr/N Node 0 Ce

1964

```
        Sun     Merc    Venus   Mars                    Sun     Merc    Venus   Mars
Sept 1   9 Vr   11 Vr   23 Ce   21 Ce        Oct. 1    8 Lb   26 Vr   25 Lo   10 Lo
     6  13 Vr    7 Vr   28 Ce   24 Ce             6   13 Lb    5 Lb    0 Vr   13 Lo
    11  18 Vr    4 Vr    3 Lo   27 Ce            11   18 Lb   14 Lb    6 Vr   15 Lo
    16  23 Vr    6 Vr    8 Lo    0 Lo            16   23 Lb   23 Lb   12 Vr   18 Lo
    21  28 Vr   11 Vr   14 Lo    4 Lo            21   28 Lb    1 Sc   18 Vr   21 Lo
    26   3 Lb   18 Vr   19 Lo    7 Lo            26    3 Sc    9 Sc   24 Vr   24 Lo
                                                 31    8 Sc   17 Sc    0 Lb   27 Lo
```

```
Sept 1/Jup 26 Tr/Sat  1 Pc/Uran 10 Vr        Oct. 1/Jup 26 Tr/Sat 29 Aq/Uran 12 Vr
Nep 15 Sc/Plut 14 Vr/N Node 28 Gm            Nep 16 Sc/Plut 15 Vr/N Node 27 Gm
```

```
        Sun     Merc    Venus   Mars                    Sun     Merc    Venus   Mars
Nov. 1   9 Sc   19 Sc    1 Lb   27 Lo        Dec. 1    9 Sg    0 Cp    7 Sc   12 Vr
     6  14 Sc   26 Sc    7 Lb    0 Vr             6   14 Sg    4 Cp   14 Sc   14 Vr
    11  19 Sc    4 Sg   13 Lb    3 Vr            11   19 Sg    5 Cp   20 Sc   17 Vr
    16  24 Sc   11 Sg   19 Lb    5 Vr            16   24 Sg    1 Cp   26 Sc   18 Vr
    21  29 Sc   18 Sg   25 Lb    8 Vr            21   29 Sg   24 Sg    2 Sg   20 Vr
    26   4 Sg   25 Sg    1 Sc   10 Vr            26    4 Cp   19 Sg    8 Sg   22 Vr
                                                 31    9 Cp   19 Sg   15 Sg   24 Vr
```

```
Nov. 1/Jup 23 Tr/Sat 28 Aq/Uran 14 Vr        Dec. 1/Jup 19 Tr/Sat 29 Aq/Uran 15 Vr
Nep 17 Sc/Plut 16 Vr/N Node 25 Gm            Nep 18 Sc/Plut 16 Vr/N Node 24 Gm
```

Moon's Positions

	1	4	7	10	13	16	19	22	25	28	31
Jan.	1 Lo	12 Vr	19 Lb	25 Sc	1 Cp	8 Aq	17 Pc	28 Ar	11 Gm	24 Ce	6 Vr
Feb.	19 Vr	27 Lb	3 Sg	9 Cp	17 Aq	27 Pc	9 Tr	21 Gm	3 Lo	14 Vr	
Mar.	10 Lb	17 Sc	23 Sg	29 Cp	8 Pc	21 Ar	4 Gm	16 Ce	27 Lo	6 Lb	13 Sc
Apr.	25 Sc	1 Cp	7 Aq	16 Pc	30 Ar	14 Gm	27 Ce	7 Vr	15 Lb	22 Sc	
May	27 Sg	3 Aq	11 Pc	23 Ar	8 Gm	23 Ce	4 Vr	12 Lb	19 Sc	24 Sg	30 Cp
June	12 Aq	20 Pc	2 Tr	17 Gm	1 Lo	13 Vr	21 Lb	28 Sc	3 Cp	9 Aq	
July	16 Pc	27 Ar	10 Gm	25 Ce	8 Vr	18 Lb	24 Sc	30 Sg	6 Aq	13 Pc	23 Ar
Aug.	7 Tr	20 Gm	4 Lo	16 Vr	26 Lb	3 Sg	8 Cp	15 Aq	23 Pc	4 Tr	16 Gm
Sept	30 Gm	13 Lo	25 Vr	4 Sc	11 Sg	16 Cp	23 Aq	2 Ar	14 Tr	27 Gm	
Oct.	9 Lo	20 Vr	30 Lb	7 Sg	12 Cp	18 Aq	27 Pc	9 Tr	23 Gm	6 Lo	17 Vr
Nov.	30 Vr	8 Sc	15 Sg	20 Cp	26 Aq	5 Ar	18 Tr	2 Ce	16 Lo	27 Vr	
Dec.	5 Sc	11 Sg	17 Cp	22 Aq	30 Pc	11 Tr	26 Gm	11 Lo	23 Vr	2 Sc	8 Sg

1965

```
        Sun    Merc   Venus  Mars              Sun    Merc   Venus  Mars
Jan. 1  10 Cp  19 Sg  16 Sg  24 Vr    Feb. 1  12 Aq  26 Cp  25 Cp  28 Vr
     6  15 Cp  22 Sg  22 Sg  25 Vr         6  17 Aq   4 Aq   1 Aq  28 Vr
    11  21 Cp  28 Sg  28 Sg  26 Vr        11  22 Aq  12 Aq   7 Aq  27 Vr
    16  26 Cp   4 Cp   5 Cp  27 Vr        16  27 Aq  21 Aq  13 Aq  26 Vr
    21   1 Aq  10 Cp  11 Cp  28 Vr        21   2 Pc   0 Pc  20 Aq  25 Vr
    26   6 Aq  17 Cp  17 Cp  28 Vr        26   7 Pc   9 Pc  26 Aq  23 Vr
    31  11 Aq  25 Cp  23 Cp  28 Vr
Jan. 1/Jup 16 Tr/Sat  1 Pc/Uran 15 Vr    Feb. 1/Jup 17 Tr/Sat  5 Pc/Uran 14 Vr
Nep 19 Sc/Plut 16 Vr/N Node 22 Gm        Nep 20 Sc/Plut 16 Vr/N Node 20 Gm


        Sun    Merc   Venus  Mars              Sun    Merc   Venus  Mars
Mar. 1  10 Pc  14 Pc   0 Pc  22 Vr    Apr. 1  11 Ar  23 Ar   8 Ar  11 Vr
     6  15 Pc  24 Pc   6 Pc  20 Vr         6  16 Ar  20 Ar  14 Ar  10 Vr
    11  20 Pc   4 Ar  12 Pc  18 Vr        11  21 Ar  17 Ar  21 Ar   9 Vr
    16  25 Pc  12 Ar  18 Pc  16 Vr        16  26 Ar  13 Ar  27 Ar   9 Vr
    21   0 Ar  19 Ar  25 Pc  14 Vr        21   1 Tr  12 Ar   3 Tr   9 Vr
    26   5 Ar  22 Ar   1 Ar  13 Vr        26   6 Tr  12 Ar   9 Tr   9 Vr
    31  10 Ar  23 Ar   7 Ar  11 Vr
Mar. 1/Jup 20 Tr/Sat  8 Pc/Uran 13 Vr    Apr. 1/Jup 25 Tr/Sat 12 Pc/Uran 12 Vr
Nep 20 Sc/Plut 15 Vr/N Node 19 Gm        Nep 20 Sc/Plut 14 Vr/N Node 17 Gm


        Sun    Merc   Venus  Mars              Sun    Merc   Venus  Mars
May  1  10 Tr  15 Ar  15 Tr   9 Vr    June 1  10 Gm  28 Tr  23 Gm  18 Vr
     6  15 Tr  19 Ar  21 Tr  10 Vr         6  15 Gm   8 Gm   0 Ce  20 Vr
    11  20 Tr  24 Ar  28 Tr  11 Vr        11  20 Gm  19 Gm   6 Ce  22 Vr
    16  25 Tr   1 Tr   4 Gm  12 Vr        16  25 Gm   0 Ce  12 Ce  24 Vr
    21   0 Gm   8 Tr  10 Gm  14 Vr        21  29 Gm  10 Ce  18 Ce  26 Vr
    26   5 Gm  16 Tr  16 Gm  15 Vr        26   4 Ce  20 Ce  24 Ce  29 Vr
    31   9 Gm  26 Tr  22 Gm  17 Vr
May  1/Jup  2 Gm/Sat 15 Pc/Uran 11 Vr    June 1/Jup  9 Gm/Sat 17 Pc/Uran 11 Vr
Nep 19 Sc/Plut 14 Vr/N Node 16 Gm        Nep 18 Sc/Plut 14 Vr/N Node 14 Gm


        Sun    Merc   Venus  Mars              Sun    Merc   Venus  Mars
July 1   9 Ce  29 Ce   0 Lo   1 Lb    Aug. 1   9 Lo   0 Vr   8 Vr  18 Lb
     6  14 Ce   7 Lo   6 Lo   4 Lb         6  13 Lo  29 Lo  14 Vr  21 Lb
    11  18 Ce  14 Lo  12 Lo   6 Lb        11  18 Lo  27 Lo  20 Vr  24 Lb
    16  23 Ce  20 Lo  18 Lo   9 Lb        16  23 Lo  23 Lo  26 Vr  27 Lb
    21  28 Ce  25 Lo  24 Lo  12 Lb        21  28 Lo  19 Lo   2 Lb   0 Sc
    26   3 Lo  28 Lo   0 Vr  15 Lb        26   3 Vr  18 Lo   8 Lb   4 Sc
    31   8 Lo   0 Vr   7 Vr  17 Lb        31   7 Vr  20 Lo  14 Lb   7 Sc
July 1/Jup 16 Gm/Sat 17 Pc/Uran 12 Vr    Aug. 1/Jup 22 Gm/Sat 16 Pc/Uran 13 Vr
Nep 17 Sc/Plut 14 Vr/N Node 12 Gm        Nep 17 Sc/Plut 15 Vr/N Node 11 Gm
```

1965

	Sun	Merc	Venus	Mars
Sept 1	8 Vr	20 Lo	15 Lb	7 Sc
6	13 Vr	26 Lo	21 Lb	11 Sc
11	18 Vr	4 Vr	27 Lb	14 Sc
16	23 Vr	13 Vr	3 Sc	17 Sc
21	28 Vr	22 Vr	8 Sc	21 Sc
26	3 Lb	1 Lb	14 Sc	24 Sc

Sept 1/Jup 28 Gm/Sat 14 Pc/Uran 15 Vr
Nep 18 Sc/Plut 16 Vr/N Node 9 Gm

	Sun	Merc	Venus	Mars
Oct. 1	8 Lb	10 Lb	20 Sc	28 Sc
6	13 Lb	19 Lb	26 Sc	1 Sg
11	17 Lb	27 Lb	1 Sg	5 Sg
16	22 Lb	5 Sc	7 Sg	8 Sg
21	27 Lb	13 Sc	13 Sg	12 Sg
26	2 Sc	20 Sc	18 Sg	16 Sg
31	7 Sc	27 Sc	24 Sg	19 Sg

Oct. 1/Jup 1 Ce/Sat 12 Pc/Uran 17 Vr
Nep 18 Sc/Plut 17 Vr/N Node 8 Gm

	Sun	Merc	Venus	Mars
Nov. 1	8 Sc	28 Sc	25 Sg	20 Sg
6	13 Sc	5 Sg	0 Cp	24 Sg
11	18 Sc	11 Sg	5 Cp	28 Sg
16	23 Sc	16 Sg	11 Cp	1 Cp
21	28 Sc	19 Sg	16 Cp	5 Cp
26	4 Sg	18 Sg	20 Cp	9 Cp

Nov. 1/Jup 1 Ce/Sat 11 Pc/Uran 18 Vr
Nep 19 Sc/Plut 18 Vr/N Node 6 Gm

	Sun	Merc	Venus	Mars
Dec. 1	9 Sg	14 Sg	25 Cp	13 Cp
6	14 Sg	7 Sg	29 Cp	17 Cp
11	19 Sg	3 Sg	3 Aq	20 Cp
16	24 Sg	4 Sg	6 Aq	24 Cp
21	29 Sg	7 Sg	9 Aq	28 Cp
26	4 Cp	13 Sg	12 Aq	2 Aq
31	9 Cp	19 Sg	13 Aq	6 Aq

Dec. 1/Jup 29 Gm/Sat 11 Pc/Uran 19 Vr
Nep 20 Sc/Plut 18 Vr/N Node 4 Gm

Moon's Positions

	1	4	7	10	13	16	19	22	25	28	31
Jan.	20 Sg	26 Cp	1 Pc	9 Ar	19 Tr	3 Ce	19 Lo	2 Lb	11 Sc	17 Sg	22 Cp
Feb.	4 Aq	11 Pc	19 Ar	29 Tr	12 Ce	27 Lo	10 Lb	19 Sc	25 Sg	1 Aq	
Mar.	13 Aq	20 Pc	29 Ar	10 Gm	22 Ce	5 Vr	18 Lb	27 Sc	3 Cp	9 Aq	16 Pc
Apr.	29 Pc	9 Tr	20 Gm	3 Lo	15 Vr	26 Lb	5 Sg	11 Cp	17 Aq	24 Pc	
May	4 Tr	16 Gm	30 Ce	12 Vr	22 Lb	1 Sg	7 Cp	13 Aq	19 Pc	28 Ar	11 Gm
June	26 Gm	10 Lo	22 Vr	2 Sc	10 Sg	16 Cp	21 Aq	28 Pc	7 Tr	19 Gm	
July	4 Lo	19 Vr	29 Lb	7 Sg	13 Cp	18 Aq	24 Pc	2 Tr	13 Gm	28 Ce	13 Vr
Aug.	28 Vr	9 Sc	16 Sg	22 Cp	27 Aq	4 Ar	12 Tr	22 Gm	6 Lo	22 Vr	4 Sc
Sept	17 Sc	25 Sg	0 Aq	6 Pc	13 Ar	22 Tr	2 Ce	16 Lo	30 Vr	12 Sc	
Oct.	21 Sg	27 Cp	2 Pc	10 Ar	18 Tr	29 Gm	11 Lo	24 Vr	7 Sc	16 Sg	23 Cp
Nov.	5 Aq	10 Pc	18 Ar	28 Tr	10 Ce	22 Lo	5 Lb	15 Sc	24 Sg	0 Aq	
Dec.	6 Pc	13 Ar	22 Tr	5 Ce	19 Lo	1 Lb	12 Sc	20 Sg	27 Cp	2 Pc	8 Ar

                                          Ephemeris

1966

```
           Sun     Merc    Venus   Mars                    Sun     Merc    Venus   Mars
Jan. 1   10 Cp   20 Sg   13 Aq    7 Aq      Feb. 1   12 Aq    8 Aq    3 Aq    1 Pc
      6   15 Cp   27 Sg   14 Aq   11 Aq            6   17 Aq   17 Aq    0 Aq    5 Pc
     11   20 Cp    5 Cp   13 Aq   15 Aq           11   22 Aq   26 Aq   29 Cp    9 Pc
     16   25 Cp   12 Cp   12 Aq   19 Aq           16   27 Aq    5 Pc   28 Cp   13 Pc
     21    1 Aq   20 Cp    9 Aq   23 Aq           21    2 Pc   14 Pc   29 Cp   17 Pc
     26    6 Aq   28 Cp    6 Aq   27 Aq           26    7 Pc   23 Pc    0 Aq   21 Pc
     31   11 Aq    6 Aq    3 Aq    1 Pc
Jan. 1/Jup 24 Gm/Sat 12 Pc/Uran 20 Vr      Feb. 1/Jup 22 Gm/Sat 15 Pc/Uran 19 Vr
Nep 21 Sc/Plut 18 Vr/N Node 3 Gm           Nep 22 Sc/Plut 18 Vr/N Node 1 Gm


           Sun     Merc    Venus   Mars                    Sun     Merc    Venus   Mars
Mar. 1   10 Pc   27 Pc    1 Aq   23 Pc      Apr. 1   11 Ar   23 Pc   25 Aq   17 Ar
      6   15 Pc    3 Ar    4 Aq   27 Pc            6   16 Ar   23 Pc   29 Aq   21 Ar
     11   20 Pc    6 Ar    7 Aq    1 Ar           11   21 Ar   25 Pc    4 Pc   25 Ar
     16   25 Pc    5 Ar   11 Aq    5 Ar           16   26 Ar   28 Pc    9 Pc   29 Ar
     21    0 Ar    1 Ar   15 Aq    9 Ar           21    0 Tr    3 Ar   15 Pc    2 Tr
     26    5 Ar   27 Pc   19 Aq   13 Ar           26    5 Tr    9 Ar   20 Pc    6 Tr
     31   10 Ar   24 Pc   24 Aq   17 Ar
Mar. 1/Jup 22 Gm/Sat 19 Pc/Uran 18 Vr      Apr. 1/Jup 24 Gm/Sat 22 Pc/Uran 17 Vr
Nep 22 Sc/Plut 17 Vr/N Node 30 Tr          Nep 22 Sc/Plut 17 Vr/N Node 28 Tr


           Sun     Merc    Venus   Mars                    Sun     Merc    Venus   Mars
May  1   10 Tr   16 Ar   25 Pc   10 Tr      June 1   10 Gm   16 Gm    0 Tr    2 Gm
      6   15 Tr   24 Ar    1 Ar   13 Tr            6   15 Gm   26 Gm    6 Tr    6 Gm
     11   20 Tr    2 Tr    6 Ar   17 Tr           11   20 Gm    6 Ce   12 Tr    9 Gm
     16   25 Tr   12 Tr   12 Ar   21 Tr           16   24 Gm   15 Ce   18 Tr   13 Gm
     21    0 Gm   22 Tr   18 Ar   24 Tr           21   29 Gm   23 Ce   24 Tr   16 Gm
     26    4 Gm    3 Gm   23 Ar   28 Tr           26    4 Ce   29 Ce   29 Tr   20 Gm
     31    9 Gm   14 Gm   29 Ar    1 Gm
May 1/Jup 29 Gm/Sat 26 Pc/Uran 16 Vr       June 1/Jup  5 Ce/Sat 28 Pc/Uran 16 Vr
Nep 21 Sc/Plut 16 Vr/N Node 26 Tr          Nep 20 Sc/Plut 16 Vr/N Node 25 Tr


           Sun     Merc    Venus   Mars                    Sun     Merc    Venus   Mars
July 1    9 Ce    4 Lo    5 Gm   23 Gm      Aug. 1    8 Lo    3 Lo   12 Ce   14 Ce
      6   13 Ce    8 Lo   11 Gm   27 Gm            6   13 Lo    1 Lo   18 Ce   17 Ce
     11   18 Ce   11 Lo   17 Gm    0 Ce           11   18 Lo    1 Lo   24 Ce   21 Ce
     16   23 Ce   11 Lo   23 Gm    3 Ce           16   23 Lo    4 Lo    1 Lo   24 Ce
     21   28 Ce   10 Lo   29 Gm    7 Ce           21   28 Lo   10 Lo    7 Lo   27 Ce
     26    3 Lo    7 Lo    5 Ce   10 Ce           26    2 Vr   18 Lo   13 Lo    0 Lo
     31    7 Lo    3 Lo   11 Ce   13 Ce           31    7 Vr   27 Lo   19 Lo    3 Lo
July 1/Jup 12 Ce/Sat 30 Pc/Uran 16 Vr      Aug. 1/Jup 19 Ce/Sat 29 Pc/Uran 17 Vr
Nep 20 Sc/Plut 16 Vr/N Node 23 Tr          Nep 19 Sc/Plut 17 Vr/N Node 21 Tr
```

1966

```
           Sun     Merc    Venus    Mars              Sun     Merc    Venus    Mars
Sept 1    8 Vr   29 Lo   20 Lo    4 Lo     Oct. 1    7 Lb   23 Lb   27 Vr   23 Lo
     6   13 Vr    9 Vr   26 Lo    7 Lo          6   12 Lb    0 Sc    4 Lb   26 Lo
    11   18 Vr   18 Vr    3 Vr   10 Lo         11   17 Lb    7 Sc   10 Lb   29 Lo
    16   23 Vr   28 Vr    9 Vr   14 Lo         16   22 Lb   14 Sc   16 Lb    2 Vr
    21   28 Vr    6 Lb   15 Vr   17 Lo         21   27 Lb   20 Sc   22 Lb    5 Vr
    26    2 Lb   15 Lb   21 Vr   20 Lo         26    2 Sc   26 Sc   29 Lb    8 Vr
                                               31    7 Sc    1 Sg    5 Sc   11 Vr
```

Sept 1/Jup 25 Ce/Sat 28 Pc/Uran 19 Vr
Nep 20 Sc/Plut 18 Vr/N Node 20 Tr

Oct. 1/Jup 1 Lo/Sat 25 Pc/Uran 21 Vr
Nep 20 Sc/Plut 19 Vr/N Node 18 Tr

```
           Sun     Merc    Venus    Mars              Sun     Merc    Venus    Mars
Nov. 1    8 Sc    1 Sg    6 Sc   11 Vr     Dec. 1    8 Sg   19 Sc   14 Sg   28 Vr
     6   13 Sc    3 Sg   12 Sc   14 Vr          6   13 Sg   23 Sc   20 Sg    1 Lb
    11   18 Sc    2 Sg   19 Sc   17 Vr         11   19 Sg   29 Sc   26 Sg    4 Lb
    16   23 Sc   27 Sc   25 Sc   20 Vr         16   24 Sg    6 Sg    3 Cp    6 Lb
    21   28 Sc   20 Sc    1 Sg   23 Vr         21   29 Sg   13 Sg    9 Cp    9 Lb
    26    3 Sg   17 Sc    7 Sg   26 Vr         26    4 Cp   21 Sg   15 Cp   11 Lb
                                               31    9 Cp   28 Sg   21 Cp   14 Lb
```

Nov. 1/Jup 4 Lo/Sat 23 Pc/Uran 23 Vr
Nep 21 Sc/Plut 20 Vr/N Node 17 Tr

Dec. 1/Jup 4 Lo/Sat 23 Pc/Uran 24 Vr
Nep 23 Sc/Plut 21 Vr/N Node 15 Tr

Moon's Positions

```
          1       4       7      10      13      16      19      22      25      28      31
Jan.   21 Ar   30 Tr   13 Ce   28 Lo   12 Lb   22 Sc   29 Sg    5 Aq   11 Pc   17 Ar   25 Tr
Feb.    8 Gm   21 Ce    7 Vr   21 Lb    1 Sg    8 Cp   14 Aq   20 Pc   26 Ar    4 Gm
Mar.   17 Gm   29 Ce   15 Vr   30 Lb   10 Sg   17 Cp   23 Aq   29 Pc    5 Tr   14 Gm   25 Ce
Apr.    9 Lo   23 Vr    7 Sc   18 Sg   26 Cp    1 Pc    7 Ar   15 Tr   24 Gm    5 Lo
May    18 Vr    2 Sc   13 Sg   21 Cp   28 Aq    3 Ar   11 Tr   20 Gm    2 Lo   15 Vr   27 Lb
June   11 Sc   21 Sg   29 Cp    5 Pc   11 Ar   19 Tr   29 Gm   12 Lo   26 Vr    7 Sc
July   17 Sg   25 Cp    2 Pc    7 Ar   14 Tr   24 Gm    7 Lo   22 Vr    4 Sc   14 Sg   22 Cp
Aug.    4 Aq   10 Pc   16 Ar   22 Tr    2 Ce   16 Lo    1 Lb   14 Sc   24 Sg    1 Aq    7 Pc
Sept   19 Pc   25 Ar    1 Gm   11 Ce   24 Lo   10 Lb   24 Sc    3 Cp   10 Aq   16 Pc
Oct.   22 Ar   28 Tr    6 Ce   18 Lo    3 Lb   18 Sc   29 Sg    7 Aq   13 Pc   18 Ar   25 Tr
Nov.    8 Gm   17 Ce   28 Lo   12 Lb   25 Sc    7 Cp   15 Aq   21 Pc   27 Ar    4 Gm
Dec.   14 Ce   25 Lo    7 Lb   20 Sc    1 Cp   10 Aq   17 Pc   22 Ar   29 Tr    9 Ce   21 Lo
```

1967

	Sun	Merc	Venus	Mars
Jan. 1	10 Cp	0 Cp	23 Cp	14 Lb
6	15 Cp	8 Cp	29 Cp	16 Lb
11	20 Cp	16 Cp	5 Aq	19 Lb
16	25 Cp	24 Cp	12 Aq	21 Lb
21	0 Aq	2 Aq	18 Aq	23 Lb
26	5 Aq	11 Aq	24 Aq	25 Lb
31	10 Aq	20 Aq	0 Pc	26 Lb

Jan. 1/Jup 2 Lo/Sat 24 Pc/Uran 24 Vr
Nep 24 Sc/Plut 21 Vr/N Node 13 Tr

	Sun	Merc	Venus	Mars
Feb. 1	11 Aq	21 Aq	2 Pc	27 Lb
6	17 Aq	0 Pc	8 Pc	28 Lb
11	22 Aq	8 Pc	14 Pc	0 Sc
16	27 Aq	15 Pc	20 Pc	1 Sc
21	2 Pc	18 Pc	26 Pc	2 Sc
26	7 Pc	18 Pc	3 Ar	3 Sc

Feb. 1/Jup 28 Ce/Sat 27 Pc/Uran 24 Vr
Nep 24 Sc/Plut 20 Vr/N Node 12 Tr

	Sun	Merc	Venus	Mars
Mar. 1	10 Pc	16 Pc	6 Ar	3 Sc
6	15 Pc	11 Pc	12 Ar	3 Sc
11	20 Pc	7 Pc	19 Ar	3 Sc
16	25 Pc	5 Pc	25 Ar	3 Sc
21	0 Ar	5 Pc	1 Tr	2 Sc
26	5 Ar	8 Pc	7 Tr	1 Sc
31	10 Ar	12 Pc	13 Tr	0 Sc

Mar. 1/Jup 25 Ce/Sat 30 Pc/Uran 23 Vr
Nep 24 Sc/Plut 20 Vr/N Node 10 Tr

	Sun	Merc	Venus	Mars
Apr. 1	11 Ar	13 Pc	14 Tr	0 Sc
6	16 Ar	18 Pc	20 Tr	28 Lb
11	20 Ar	25 Pc	26 Tr	26 Lb
16	25 Ar	2 Ar	2 Gm	25 Lb
21	0 Tr	10 Ar	8 Gm	23 Lb
26	5 Tr	19 Ar	14 Gm	21 Lb

Apr. 1/Jup 25 Ce/Sat 3 Ar/Uran 22 Vr
Nep 24 Sc/Plut 19 Vr/N Node 9 Tr

	Sun	Merc	Venus	Mars
May 1	10 Tr	28 Ar	19 Gm	19 Lb
6	15 Tr	8 Tr	25 Gm	18 Lb
11	20 Tr	19 Tr	1 Ce	17 Lb
16	24 Tr	0 Gm	6 Ce	16 Lb
21	29 Tr	10 Gm	12 Ce	15 Lb
26	4 Gm	20 Gm	18 Ce	15 Lb
31	9 Gm	29 Gm	23 Ce	15 Lb

May 1/Jup 27 Ce/Sat 7 Ar/Uran 21 Vr
Nep 23 Sc/Plut 18 Vr/N Node 7 Tr

	Sun	Merc	Venus	Mars
June 1	10 Gm	0 Ce	24 Ce	15 Lb
6	15 Gm	8 Ce	29 Ce	16 Lb
11	19 Gm	14 Ce	4 Lo	16 Lb
16	24 Gm	18 Ce	9 Lo	18 Lb
21	29 Gm	21 Ce	14 Lo	19 Lb
26	4 Ce	22 Ce	19 Lo	20 Lb

June 1/Jup 1 Lo/Sat 10 Ar/Uran 20 Vr
Nep 23 Sc/Plut 18 Vr/N Node 5 Tr

	Sun	Merc	Venus	Mars
July 1	8 Ce	21 Ce	23 Lo	22 Lb
6	13 Ce	19 Ce	28 Lo	24 Lb
11	18 Ce	16 Ce	2 Vr	26 Lb
16	23 Ce	13 Ce	5 Vr	28 Lb
21	28 Ce	12 Ce	8 Vr	1 Sc
26	2 Lo	14 Ce	11 Vr	3 Sc
31	7 Lo	18 Ce	13 Vr	6 Sc

July 1/Jup 7 Lo/Sat 12 Ar/Uran 21 Vr
Nep 22 Sc/Plut 18 Vr/N Node 4 Tr

	Sun	Merc	Venus	Mars
Aug. 1	8 Lo	19 Ce	13 Vr	6 Sc
6	13 Lo	25 Ce	14 Vr	9 Sc
11	18 Lo	4 Lo	14 Vr	12 Sc
16	22 Lo	13 Lo	13 Vr	14 Sc
21	27 Lo	23 Lo	11 Vr	17 Sc
26	2 Vr	3 Vr	8 Vr	20 Sc
31	7 Vr	13 Vr	5 Vr	24 Sc

Aug. 1/Jup 14 Lo/Sat 12 Ar/Uran 22 Vr
Nep 22 Sc/Plut 19 Vr/N Node 2 Tr

1967

	Sun	Merc	Venus	Mars
Sept 1	8 Vr	15 Vr	5 Vr	24 Sc
6	13 Vr	24 Vr	2 Vr	27 Sc
11	18 Vr	2 Lb	29 Lo	1 Sg
16	22 Vr	10 Lb	28 Lo	4 Sg
21	27 Vr	18 Lb	28 Lo	7 Sg
26	2 Lb	25 Lb	28 Lo	11 Sg

Sept 1/Jup 21 Lo/Sat 11 Ar/Uran 24 Vr
Nep 22 Sc/Plut 20 Vr/N Node 0 Tr

	Sun	Merc	Venus	Mars
Oct. 1	7 Lb	1 Sc	0 Vr	14 Sg
6	12 Lb	7 Sc	2 Vr	18 Sg
11	17 Lb	12 Sc	5 Vr	21 Sg
16	22 Lb	16 Sc	8 Vr	25 Sg
21	27 Lb	17 Sc	12 Vr	28 Sg
26	2 Sc	16 Sc	16 Vr	2 Cp
31	7 Sc	11 Sc	21 Vr	6 Cp

Oct. 1/Jup 27 Lo/Sat 9 Ar/Uran 26 Vr
Nep 22 Sc/Plut 21 Vr/N Node 29 Ar

	Sun	Merc	Venus	Mars
Nov. 1	8 Sc	9 Sc	22 Vr	7 Cp
6	13 Sc	4 Sc	26 Vr	10 Cp
11	18 Sc	1 Sc	1 Lb	14 Cp
16	23 Sc	4 Sc	6 Lb	18 Cp
21	28 Sc	9 Sc	12 Lb	22 Cp
26	3 Sg	16 Sc	17 Lb	26 Cp

Nov. 1/Jup 2 Vr/Sat 7 Ar/Uran 27 Vr
Nep 23 Sc/Plut 22 Vr/N Node 27 Ar

	Sun	Merc	Venus	Mars
Dec. 1	8 Sg	23 Sc	23 Lb	29 Cp
6	13 Sg	1 Sg	28 Lb	3 Aq
11	18 Sg	8 Sg	4 Sc	7 Aq
16	23 Sg	16 Sg	10 Sc	11 Aq
21	28 Sg	24 Sg	16 Sc	15 Aq
26	4 Cp	2 Cp	22 Sc	19 Aq
31	9 Cp	10 Cp	28 Sc	23 Aq

Dec. 1/Jup 5 Vr/Sat 6 Ar/Uran 29 Vr
Nep 25 Sc/Plut 23 Vr/N Node 26 Ar

Moon's Positions

	1	4	7	10	13	16	19	22	25	28	31
Jan.	6 Vr	18 Lb	30 Sc	10 Cp	18 Aq	25 Pc	0 Tr	7 Gm	17 Ce	1 Vr	15 Lb
Feb.	29 Lb	10 Sg	19 Cp	27 Aq	3 Ar	8 Tr	15 Gm	25 Ce	9 Vr	24 Lb	
Mar.	9 Sc	20 Sg	29 Cp	6 Pc	11 Ar	17 Tr	24 Gm	3 Lo	17 Vr	3 Sc	16 Sg
Apr.	30 Sg	8 Aq	15 Pc	20 Ar	26 Tr	3 Ce	13 Lo	26 Vr	11 Sc	25 Sg	
May	5 Aq	12 Pc	17 Ar	23 Tr	30 Gm	9 Lo	21 Vr	5 Sc	19 Sg	0 Aq	8 Pc
June	20 Pc	26 Ar	2 Gm	10 Ce	20 Lo	1 Lb	14 Sc	27 Sg	8 Aq	16 Pc	
July	22 Ar	28 Tr	6 Ce	16 Lo	28 Vr	10 Sc	23 Sg	3 Aq	12 Pc	18 Ar	23 Tr
Aug.	6 Gm	14 Ce	25 Lo	9 Lb	21 Sc	3 Cp	12 Aq	20 Pc	26 Ar	1 Gm	9 Ce
Sept	22 Ce	4 Vr	19 Lb	2 Sg	13 Cp	22 Aq	29 Pc	4 Tr	10 Gm	17 Ce	
Oct.	28 Lo	12 Lb	27 Sc	10 Cp	19 Aq	26 Pc	1 Tr	7 Gm	13 Ce	22 Lo	5 Lb
Nov.	20 Lb	6 Sg	19 Cp	28 Aq	4 Ar	10 Tr	16 Gm	23 Ce	2 Vr	14 Lb	
Dec.	29 Sc	13 Cp	24 Aq	1 Ar	7 Tr	12 Gm	20 Ce	29 Lo	10 Lb	23 Sc	7 Cp

1968

```
        Sun    Merc   Venus   Mars                    Sun    Merc   Venus   Mars
Jan. 1  10 Cp  11 Cp  29 Sc  23 Aq        Feb. 1  11 Aq   0 Pc   6 Cp  18 Pc
     6  15 Cp  20 Cp   5 Sg  27 Aq             6  16 Aq   2 Pc  13 Cp  21 Pc
    11  20 Cp  28 Cp  11 Sg   1 Pc            11  21 Aq   1 Pc  19 Cp  25 Pc
    16  25 Cp   6 Aq  17 Sg   5 Pc            16  26 Aq  26 Aq  25 Cp  29 Pc
    21   0 Aq  14 Aq  23 Sg   9 Pc            21   1 Pc  20 Aq   1 Aq   3 Ar
    26   5 Aq  22 Aq  29 Sg  13 Pc            26   6 Pc  17 Aq   7 Aq   7 Ar
    31  10 Aq  29 Aq   5 Cp  17 Pc
Jan. 1/Jup  6 Vr/Sat  6 Ar/Uran 29 Vr     Feb. 1/Jup  3 Vr/Sat  8 Ar/Uran 29 Vr
Nep 26 Sc/Plut 23 Vr/N Node 24 Ar         Nep 26 Sc/Plut 23 Vr/N Node 22 Ar
```

```
        Sun    Merc   Venus   Mars                    Sun    Merc   Venus   Mars
Mar. 1  10 Pc  17 Aq  12 Aq  10 Ar        Apr. 1  11 Ar  20 Pc  20 Pc   3 Tr
     6  15 Pc  19 Aq  18 Aq  14 Ar             6  16 Ar  28 Pc  26 Pc   7 Tr
    11  20 Pc  23 Aq  24 Aq  17 Ar            11  21 Ar   7 Ar   3 Ar  10 Tr
    16  25 Pc  28 Aq   1 Pc  21 Ar            16  26 Ar  16 Ar   9 Ar  14 Tr
    21   0 Ar   4 Pc   7 Pc  25 Ar            21   1 Tr  27 Ar  15 Ar  17 Tr
    26   5 Ar  11 Pc  13 Pc  29 Ar            26   6 Tr   7 Tr  21 Ar  21 Tr
    31  10 Ar  18 Pc  19 Pc   2 Tr
Mar. 1/Jup 30 Lo/Sat 11 Ar/Uran 28 Vr     Apr. 1/Jup 27 Lo/Sat 15 Ar/Uran 27 Vr
Nep 27 Sc/Plut 22 Vr/N Node 21 Ar         Nep 26 Sc/Plut 21 Vr/N Node 19 Ar
```

```
        Sun    Merc   Venus   Mars                    Sun    Merc   Venus   Mars
May  1  11 Tr  18 Tr  27 Ar  25 Tr        June 1  11 Gm   1 Ce   5 Gm  16 Gm
     6  16 Tr  28 Tr   3 Tr  28 Tr             6  15 Gm   2 Ce  11 Gm  20 Gm
    11  20 Tr   8 Gm   9 Tr   2 Gm            11  20 Gm   1 Ce  18 Gm  23 Gm
    16  25 Tr  16 Gm  16 Tr   5 Gm            16  25 Gm  29 Gm  24 Gm  26 Gm
    21   0 Gm  22 Gm  22 Tr   9 Gm            21   0 Ce  26 Gm   0 Ce   0 Ce
    26   5 Gm  27 Gm  28 Tr  12 Gm            26   4 Ce  24 Gm   6 Ce   3 Ce
    31  10 Gm   1 Ce   4 Gm  16 Gm
May  1/Jup 26 Lo/Sat 19 Ar/Uran 26 Vr     June 1/Jup 28 Lo/Sat 22 Ar/Uran 25 Vr
Nep 26 Sc/Plut 20 Vr/N Node 18 Ar         Nep 25 Sc/Plut 20 Vr/N Node 16 Ar
```

```
        Sun    Merc   Venus   Mars                    Sun    Merc   Venus   Mars
July 1   9 Ce  23 Gm  12 Ce   7 Ce        Aug. 1   9 Lo   2 Lo  20 Lo  27 Ce
     6  14 Ce  25 Gm  18 Ce  10 Ce             6  14 Lo  12 Lo  26 Lo   0 Lo
    11  19 Ce  28 Gm  24 Ce  13 Ce            11  18 Lo  22 Lo   3 Vr   3 Lo
    16  24 Ce   3 Ce   1 Lo  16 Ce            16  23 Lo   2 Vr   9 Vr   7 Lo
    21  28 Ce  11 Ce   7 Lo  20 Ce            21  28 Lo  11 Vr  15 Vr  10 Lo
    26   3 Lo  20 Ce  13 Lo  23 Ce            26   3 Vr  19 Vr  21 Vr  13 Lo
    31   8 Lo  29 Ce  19 Lo  26 Ce            31   8 Vr  27 Vr  27 Vr  16 Lo
July 1/Jup  2 Vr/Sat 24 Ar/Uran 25 Vr     Aug. 1/Jup  8 Vr/Sat 26 Ar/Uran 27 Vr
Nep 24 Sc/Plut 20 Vr/N Node 14 Ar         Nep 24 Sc/Plut 21 Vr/N Node 13 Ar
```

1968

	Sun	Merc	Venus	Mars
Sept 1	9 Vr	29 Vr	28 Vr	17 Lo
6	13 Vr	6 Lb	5 Lb	20 Lo
11	18 Vr	13 Lb	11 Lb	23 Lo
16	23 Vr	19 Lb	17 Lb	26 Lo
21	28 Vr	24 Lb	23 Lb	0 Vr
26	3 Lb	28 Lb	29 Lb	3 Vr

Sept 1/Jup 15 Vr/Sat 25 Ar/Uran 28 Vr
Nep 24 Sc/Plut 22 Vr/N Node 11 Ar

	Sun	Merc	Venus	Mars
Oct. 1	8 Lb	1 Sc	5 Sc	6 Vr
6	13 Lb	1 Sc	11 Sc	9 Vr
11	18 Lb	28 Lb	18 Sc	12 Vr
16	23 Lb	22 Lb	24 Sc	15 Vr
21	28 Lb	17 Lb	0 Sg	18 Vr
26	3 Sc	16 Lb	6 Sg	21 Vr
31	8 Sc	19 Lb	12 Sg	24 Vr

Oct. 1/Jup 21 Vr/Sat 23 Ar/Uran 0 Lb
Nep 25 Sc/Plut 23 Vr/N Node 9 Ar

	Sun	Merc	Venus	Mars
Nov. 1	9 Sc	20 Lb	13 Sg	25 Vr
6	14 Sc	26 Lb	19 Sg	28 Vr
11	19 Sc	4 Sc	25 Sg	1 Lb
16	24 Sc	12 Sc	1 Cp	4 Lb
21	29 Sc	20 Sc	7 Cp	7 Lb
26	4 Sg	28 Sc	13 Cp	10 Lb

Nov. 1/Jup 27 Vr/Sat 21 Ar/Uran 2 Lb
Nep 26 Sc/Plut 24 Vr/N Node 8 Ar

	Sun	Merc	Venus	Mars
Dec. 1	9 Sg	5 Sg	19 Cp	13 Lb
6	14 Sg	13 Sg	25 Cp	16 Lb
11	19 Sg	21 Sg	1 Aq	19 Lb
16	24 Sg	29 Sg	7 Aq	22 Lb
21	29 Sg	7 Cp	13 Aq	25 Lb
26	4 Cp	15 Cp	19 Aq	28 Lb
31	9 Cp	23 Cp	25 Aq	1 Sc

Dec. 1/Jup 2 Lb/Sat 19 Ar/Uran 3 Lb
Nep 27 Sc/Plut 25 Vr/N Node 6 Ar

Moon's Positions

	1	4	7	10	13	16	19	22	25	28	31
Jan.	21 Cp	2 Pc	9 Ar	15 Tr	21 Gm	29 Ce	9 Vr	20 Lb	3 Sg	15 Cp	27 Aq
Feb.	10 Pc	17 Ar	23 Tr	29 Gm	7 Lo	19 Vr	1 Sc	14 Sg	25 Cp	5 Pc	
Mar.	0 Ar	7 Tr	12 Gm	19 Ce	29 Lo	12 Lb	26 Sc	8 Cp	19 Aq	27 Pc	3 Tr
Apr.	15 Tr	20 Gm	27 Ce	7 Vr	20 Lb	5 Sg	19 Cp	29 Aq	6 Ar	12 Tr	
May	17 Gm	23 Ce	2 Vr	14 Lb	29 Sc	14 Cp	25 Aq	3 Ar	9 Tr	14 Gm	20 Ce
June	3 Lo	11 Vr	22 Lb	7 Sg	22 Cp	4 Pc	12 Ar	18 Tr	23 Gm	30 Ce	
July	8 Vr	18 Lb	1 Sg	16 Cp	29 Aq	8 Ar	14 Tr	20 Gm	26 Ce	5 Vr	15 Lb
Aug.	29 Lb	11 Sg	25 Cp	7 Pc	16 Ar	22 Tr	28 Gm	5 Lo	14 Vr	26 Lb	8 Sg
Sept	22 Sg	4 Aq	15 Pc	24 Ar	0 Gm	6 Ce	13 Lo	23 Vr	6 Sc	19 Sg	
Oct.	1 Aq	11 Pc	20 Ar	26 Tr	2 Ce	8 Lo	17 Vr	30 Lb	15 Sg	28 Cp	8 Pc
Nov.	21 Pc	28 Ar	5 Gm	10 Ce	16 Lo	25 Vr	8 Sc	23 Sg	8 Aq	18 Pc	
Dec.	25 Ar	1 Gm	7 Ce	13 Lo	21 Vr	1 Sc	16 Sg	2 Aq	14 Pc	22 Ar	28 Tr

 Ephemeris

1969

	Sun	Merc	Venus	Mars
Jan. 1	10 Cp	25 Cp	26 Aq	1 Sc
6	16 Cp	2 Aq	1 Pc	4 Sc
11	21 Cp	9 Aq	7 Pc	7 Sc
16	26 Cp	14 Aq	12 Pc	10 Sc
21	1 Aq	16 Aq	18 Pc	12 Sc
26	6 Aq	13 Aq	23 Pc	15 Sc
31	11 Aq	7 Aq	28 Pc	18 Sc

Jan. 1/Jup 5 Lb/Sat 19 Ar/Uran 4 Lb
Nep 28 Sc/Plut 25 Vr/N Node 5 Ar

	Sun	Merc	Venus	Mars
Feb. 1	12 Aq	6 Aq	29 Pc	18 Sc
6	17 Aq	2 Aq	4 Ar	21 Sc
11	22 Aq	0 Aq	8 Ar	23 Sc
16	27 Aq	2 Aq	12 Ar	26 Sc
21	2 Pc	6 Aq	16 Ar	28 Sc
26	7 Pc	11 Aq	20 Ar	0 Sg

Feb. 1/Jup 6 Lb/Sat 20 Ar/Uran 4 Lb
Nep 28 Sc/Plut 25 Vr/N Node 3 Ar

	Sun	Merc	Venus	Mars
Mar. 1	10 Pc	14 Aq	21 Ar	2 Sg
6	15 Pc	21 Aq	24 Ar	4 Sg
11	20 Pc	28 Aq	26 Ar	6 Sg
16	25 Pc	5 Pc	27 Ar	8 Sg
21	0 Ar	13 Pc	27 Ar	10 Sg
26	5 Ar	22 Pc	26 Ar	11 Sg
31	10 Ar	1 Ar	24 Ar	13 Sg

Mar. 1/Jup 4 Lb/Sat 23 Ar/Uran 3 Lb
Nep 29 Sc/Plut 24 Vr/N Node 1 Ar

	Sun	Merc	Venus	Mars
Apr. 1	11 Ar	3 Ar	23 Ar	13 Sg
6	16 Ar	13 Ar	20 Ar	14 Sg
11	21 Ar	23 Ar	17 Ar	15 Sg
16	26 Ar	4 Tr	14 Ar	16 Sg
21	1 Tr	14 Tr	12 Ar	17 Sg
26	6 Tr	23 Tr	11 Ar	17 Sg

Apr. 1/Jup 30 Vr/Sat 26 Ar/Uran 2 Lb
Nep 28 Sc/Plut 23 Vr/N Node 30 Pc

	Sun	Merc	Venus	Mars
May 1	10 Tr	1 Gm	11 Ar	17 Sg
6	15 Tr	6 Gm	11 Ar	16 Sg
11	20 Tr	10 Gm	13 Ar	16 Sg
16	25 Tr	12 Gm	15 Ar	15 Sg
21	0 Gm	12 Gm	18 Ar	13 Sg
26	5 Gm	10 Gm	21 Ar	12 Sg
31	9 Gm	7 Gm	25 Ar	10 Sg

May 1/Jup 27 Vr/Sat 0 Tr/Uran 0 Lb
Nep 28 Sc/Plut 23 Vr/N Node 28 Pc

	Sun	Merc	Venus	Mars
June 1	10 Gm	6 Gm	26 Ar	10 Sg
6	15 Gm	4 Gm	0 Tr	8 Sg
11	20 Gm	3 Gm	4 Tr	7 Sg
16	25 Gm	5 Gm	9 Tr	5 Sg
21	29 Gm	7 Gm	14 Tr	4 Sg
26	4 Ce	12 Gm	19 Tr	3 Sg

June 1/Jup 26 Vr/Sat 4 Tr/Uran 30 Vr
Nep 27 Sc/Plut 22 Vr/N Node 27 Pc

	Sun	Merc	Venus	Mars
July 1	9 Ce	18 Gm	24 Tr	2 Sg
6	14 Ce	26 Gm	29 Tr	2 Sg
11	19 Ce	5 Ce	4 Gm	2 Sg
16	23 Ce	16 Ce	10 Gm	2 Sg
21	28 Ce	26 Ce	15 Gm	3 Sg
26	3 Lo	7 Lo	21 Gm	4 Sg
31	8 Lo	17 Lo	26 Gm	5 Sg

July 1/Jup 28 Vr/Sat 7 Tr/Uran 0 Lb
Nep 26 Sc/Plut 23 Vr/N Node 25 Pc

	Sun	Merc	Venus	Mars
Aug. 1	9 Lo	19 Lo	27 Gm	5 Sg
6	13 Lo	28 Lo	3 Ce	7 Sg
11	18 Lo	7 Vr	9 Ce	9 Sg
16	23 Lo	14 Vr	15 Ce	11 Sg
21	28 Lo	22 Vr	20 Ce	13 Sg
26	3 Vr	28 Vr	26 Ce	15 Sg
31	7 Vr	4 Lb	2 Lo	18 Sg

Aug. 1/Jup 2 Lb/Sat 9 Tr/Uran 1 Lb
Nep 26 Sc/Plut 23 Vr/N Node 23 Pc

1969

```
          Sun    Merc   Venus   Mars                    Sun    Merc   Venus   Mars
Sept 1    8 Vr   5 Lb    3 Lo   18 Sg      Oct. 1    8 Lb   4 Lb   10 Vr    6 Cp
     6   13 Vr  10 Lb    9 Lo   21 Sg           6   13 Lb   0 Lb   16 Vr    9 Cp
    11   18 Vr  13 Lb   15 Lo   24 Sg          11   18 Lb   0 Lb   22 Vr   13 Cp
    16   23 Vr  15 Lb   21 Lo   27 Sg          16   22 Lb   4 Lb   28 Vr   16 Cp
    21   28 Vr  14 Lb   27 Lo    0 Cp          21   27 Lb  11 Lb    4 Lb   20 Cp
    26    3 Lb  10 Lb    3 Vr    3 Cp          26    2 Sc  19 Lb   10 Lb   23 Cp
                                               31    7 Sc  27 Lb   17 Lb   27 Cp
```

Sept 1/Jup 8 Lb/Sat 9 Tr/Uran 3 Lb   Oct. 1/Jup 14 Lb/Sat 8 Tr/Uran 5 Lb
Nep 26 Sc/Plut 24 Vr/N Node 22 Pc   Nep 27 Sc/Plut 25 Vr/N Node 20 Pc

```
          Sun    Merc   Venus   Mars                    Sun    Merc   Venus   Mars
Nov. 1    8 Sc  29 Lb   18 Lb   27 Cp      Dec. 1    9 Sg   17 Sg   25 Sc   19 Aq
     6   13 Sc   7 Sc   24 Lb    1 Aq           6   14 Sg   25 Sg    2 Sg   23 Aq
    11   18 Sc  15 Sc    0 Sc    4 Aq          11   19 Sg    2 Cp    8 Sg   27 Aq
    16   23 Sc  23 Sc    7 Sc    8 Aq          16   24 Sg   10 Cp   14 Sg    0 Pc
    21   29 Sc   1 Sg   13 Sc   12 Aq          21   29 Sg   17 Cp   21 Sg    4 Pc
    26    4 Sg   9 Sg   19 Sc   15 Aq          26    4 Cp   24 Cp   27 Sg    8 Pc
                                               31    9 Cp   28 Cp    3 Cp   11 Pc
```

Nov. 1/Jup 21 Lb/Sat 5 Tr/Uran 6 Lb   Dec. 1/Jup 27 Lb/Sat 3 Tr/Uran 8 Lb
Nep 28 Sc/Plut 26 Vr/N Node 19 Pc   Nep 29 Sc/Plut 27 Vr/N Node 17 Pc

Moon's Positions

	1	4	7	10	13	16	19	22	25	28	31
Jan.	10 Gm	16 Ce	22 Lo	0 Lb	11 Sc	25 Sg	10 Aq	22 Pc	1 Tr	7 Gm	13 Ce
Feb.	25 Ce	2 Vr	10 Lb	21 Sc	4 Cp	18 Aq	0 Ar	9 Tr	15 Gm	21 Ce	
Mar.	3 Lo	11 Vr	20 Lb	2 Sg	14 Cp	27 Aq	8 Ar	17 Tr	23 Gm	29 Ce	6 Vr
Apr.	19 Vr	30 Lb	13 Sg	25 Cp	7 Pc	17 Ar	25 Tr	1 Ce	7 Lo	14 Vr	
May	24 Lb	8 Sg	22 Cp	4 Pc	13 Ar	21 Tr	27 Gm	3 Lo	9 Vr	18 Lb	2 Sg
June	17 Sg	2 Aq	14 Pc	23 Ar	0 Gm	6 Ce	12 Lo	18 Vr	27 Lb	10 Sg	
July	26 Cp	10 Pc	20 Ar	27 Tr	3 Ce	9 Lo	15 Vr	23 Lb	4 Sg	19 Cp	4 Pc
Aug.	18 Pc	29 Ar	6 Gm	12 Ce	18 Lo	24 Vr	3 Sc	14 Sg	28 Cp	12 Pc	24 Ar
Sept	7 Tr	15 Gm	20 Ce	26 Lo	4 Lb	13 Sc	25 Sg	8 Aq	21 Pc	2 Tr	
Oct.	10 Gm	16 Ce	22 Lo	30 Vr	9 Sc	21 Sg	4 Aq	16 Pc	27 Ar	6 Gm	12 Ce
Nov.	24 Ce	0 Vr	8 Lb	18 Sc	2 Cp	15 Aq	26 Pc	6 Tr	14 Gm	20 Ce	
Dec.	26 Lo	2 Lb	12 Sc	26 Sg	11 Aq	23 Pc	3 Tr	11 Gm	17 Ce	22 Lo	28 Vr

1970

	Sun	Merc	Venus	Mars
Jan. 1	10 Cp	29 Cp	4 Cp	12 Pc
6	15 Cp	0 Aq	11 Cp	16 Pc
11	20 Cp	26 Cp	17 Cp	20 Pc
16	25 Cp	19 Cp	23 Cp	23 Pc
21	1 Aq	15 Cp	0 Aq	27 Pc
26	6 Aq	14 Cp	6 Aq	1 Ar
31	11 Aq	16 Cp	12 Aq	5 Ar

Jan. 1/Jup 2 Sc/Sat 2 Tr/Uran 9 Lb
Nep 30 Sc/Plut 27 Vr/N Node 15 Pc

	Sun	Merc	Venus	Mars
Feb. 1	12 Aq	17 Cp	13 Aq	5 Ar
6	17 Aq	21 Cp	20 Aq	9 Ar
11	22 Aq	27 Cp	26 Aq	13 Ar
16	27 Aq	3 Aq	2 Pc	16 Ar
21	2 Pc	10 Aq	9 Pc	20 Ar
26	7 Pc	18 Aq	15 Pc	23 Ar

Feb. 1/Jup 5 Sc/Sat 3 Tr/Uran 9 Lb
Nep 1 Sg/Plut 27 Vr/N Node 14 Pc

	Sun	Merc	Venus	Mars
Mar. 1	10 Pc	22 Aq	19 Pc	26 Ar
6	15 Pc	0 Pc	25 Pc	29 Ar
11	20 Pc	9 Pc	1 Ar	3 Tr
16	25 Pc	18 Pc	7 Ar	6 Tr
21	0 Ar	27 Pc	13 Ar	10 Tr
26	5 Ar	7 Ar	20 Ar	13 Tr
31	10 Ar	18 Ar	26 Ar	17 Tr

Mar. 1/Jup 6 Sc/Sat 5 Tr/Uran 8 Lb
Nep 1 Sg/Plut 26 Vr/N Node 12 Pc

	Sun	Merc	Venus	Mars
Apr. 1	11 Ar	20 Ar	27 Ar	18 Tr
6	16 Ar	29 Ar	3 Tr	21 Tr
11	21 Ar	8 Tr	9 Tr	25 Tr
16	26 Ar	15 Tr	15 Tr	28 Tr
21	0 Tr	20 Tr	22 Tr	2 Gm
26	5 Tr	22 Tr	28 Tr	5 Gm

Apr. 1/Jup 4 Sc/Sat 8 Tr/Uran 7 Lb
Nep 1 Sg/Plut 26 Vr/N Node 11 Pc

	Sun	Merc	Venus	Mars
May 1	10 Tr	22 Tr	4 Gm	8 Gm
6	15 Tr	20 Tr	10 Gm	12 Gm
11	20 Tr	17 Tr	16 Gm	15 Gm
16	25 Tr	15 Tr	22 Gm	18 Gm
21	0 Gm	13 Tr	28 Gm	22 Gm
26	4 Gm	14 Tr	4 Ce	25 Gm
31	9 Gm	16 Tr	10 Ce	28 Gm

May 1/Jup 30 Lb/Sat 12 Tr/Uran 5 Lb
Nep 0 Sg/Plut 25 Vr/N Node 9 Pc

	Sun	Merc	Venus	Mars
June 1	10 Gm	17 Tr	11 Ce	29 Gm
6	15 Gm	21 Tr	17 Ce	2 Ce
11	20 Gm	27 Tr	23 Ce	6 Ce
16	24 Gm	4 Gm	29 Ce	9 Ce
21	29 Gm	12 Gm	5 Lo	12 Ce
26	4 Ce	21 Gm	11 Lo	16 Ce

June 1/Jup 27 Lb/Sat 16 Tr/Uran 5 Lb
Nep 29 Sc/Plut 25 Vr/N Node 7 Pc

	Sun	Merc	Venus	Mars
July 1	9 Ce	2 Ce	17 Lo	19 Ce
6	14 Ce	12 Ce	23 Lo	22 Ce
11	18 Ce	23 Ce	28 Lo	25 Ce
16	23 Ce	3 Lo	4 Vr	29 Ce
21	28 Ce	13 Lo	10 Vr	2 Lo
26	3 Lo	22 Lo	15 Vr	5 Lo
31	7 Lo	0 Vr	21 Vr	8 Lo

July 1/Jup 26 Lb/Sat 19 Tr/Uran 5 Lb
Nep 29 Sc/Plut 25 Vr/N Node 6 Pc

	Sun	Merc	Venus	Mars
Aug. 1	8 Lo	1 Vr	22 Vr	9 Lo
6	13 Lo	8 Vr	27 Vr	12 Lo
11	18 Lo	15 Vr	3 Lb	15 Lo
16	23 Lo	20 Vr	8 Lb	18 Lo
21	28 Lo	24 Vr	13 Lb	22 Lo
26	2 Vr	27 Vr	18 Lb	25 Lo
31	7 Vr	28 Vr	23 Lb	28 Lo

Aug. 1/Jup 28 Lb/Sat 22 Tr/Uran 6 Lb
Nep 28 Sc/Plut 26 Vr/N Node 4 Pc

1970

	Sun	Merc	Venus	Mars
Sept 1	8 Vr	28 Vr	24 Lb	29 Lo
6	13 Vr	26 Vr	29 Lb	2 Vr
11	18 Vr	21 Vr	4 Sc	5 Vr
16	23 Vr	17 Vr	8 Sc	8 Vr
21	28 Vr	14 Vr	12 Sc	11 Vr
26	2 Lb	15 Vr	15 Sc	14 Vr

Sept 1/Jup 2 Sc/Sat 23 Tr/Uran 7 Lb
Nep 28 Sc/Plut 27 Vr/N Node 2 Pc

	Sun	Merc	Venus	Mars
Oct. 1	7 Lb	20 Vr	19 Sc	18 Vr
6	12 Lb	27 Vr	21 Sc	21 Vr
11	17 Lb	6 Lb	23 Sc	24 Vr
16	22 Lb	14 Lb	25 Sc	27 Vr
21	27 Lb	23 Lb	25 Sc	0 Lb
26	2 Sc	1 Sc	25 Sc	4 Lb
31	7 Sc	9 Sc	23 Sc	7 Lb

Oct. 1/Jup 8 Sc/Sat 22 Tr/Uran 9 Lb
Nep 29 Sc/Plut 28 Vr/N Node 1 Pc

	Sun	Merc	Venus	Mars
Nov. 1	8 Sc	11 Sc	23 Sc	7 Lb
6	13 Sc	19 Sc	20 Sc	11 Lb
11	18 Sc	27 Sc	17 Sc	14 Lb
16	23 Sc	5 Sg	14 Sc	17 Lb
21	28 Sc	12 Sg	12 Sc	20 Lb
26	3 Sg	19 Sg	10 Sc	23 Lb

Nov. 1/Jup 15 Sc/Sat 20 Tr/Uran 11 Lb
Nep 30 Sc/Plut 29 Vr/N Node 29 Aq

	Sun	Merc	Venus	Mars
Dec. 1	8 Sg	27 Sg	10 Sc	26 Lb
6	13 Sg	3 Cp	10 Sc	0 Sc
11	19 Sg	9 Cp	12 Sc	3 Sc
16	24 Sg	13 Cp	14 Sc	6 Sc
21	29 Sg	14 Cp	17 Sc	9 Sc
26	4 Cp	10 Cp	20 Sc	12 Sc
31	9 Cp	3 Cp	24 Sc	15 Sc

Dec. 1/Jup 21 Sc/Sat 18 Tr/Uran 13 Lb
Nep 1 Sg/Plut 29 Vr/N Node 28 Aq

Moon's Positions

	1	4	7	10	13	16	19	22	25	28	31
Jan.	11 Lb	20 Sc	4 Cp	20 Aq	3 Ar	13 Tr	20 Gm	26 Ce	1 Vr	7 Lb	15 Sc
Feb.	29 Sc	12 Cp	28 Aq	12 Ar	22 Tr	29 Gm	4 Lo	10 Vr	17 Lb	25 Sc	
Mar.	9 Sg	21 Cp	6 Pc	20 Ar	0 Gm	7 Ce	13 Lo	19 Vr	26 Lb	6 Sg	17 Cp
Apr.	1 Aq	15 Pc	28 Ar	8 Gm	15 Ce	21 Lo	27 Vr	5 Sc	16 Sg	28 Cp	
May	10 Pc	22 Ar	3 Gm	11 Ce	17 Lo	23 Vr	1 Sc	12 Sg	24 Cp	7 Pc	19 Ar
June	2 Tr	12 Gm	19 Ce	25 Lo	1 Lb	9 Sc	20 Sg	4 Aq	18 Pc	29 Ar	
July	8 Gm	16 Ce	22 Lo	27 Vr	4 Sc	14 Sg	28 Cp	13 Pc	26 Ar	5 Gm	13 Ce
Aug.	25 Ce	0 Vr	6 Lb	13 Sc	23 Sg	7 Aq	22 Pc	5 Tr	15 Gm	22 Ce	27 Lo
Sept	9 Vr	15 Lb	22 Sc	2 Cp	15 Aq	0 Ar	14 Tr	24 Gm	1 Lo	6 Vr	
Oct.	12 Lb	19 Sc	28 Sg	10 Aq	24 Pc	8 Tr	19 Gm	27 Ce	2 Vr	8 Lb	16 Sc
Nov.	29 Sc	9 Cp	20 Aq	3 Ar	16 Tr	27 Gm	5 Lo	10 Vr	16 Lb	24 Sc	
Dec.	5 Cp	17 Aq	29 Pc	11 Tr	22 Gm	0 Lo	6 Vr	12 Lb	19 Sc	30 Sg	13 Aq

1971

	Sun	Merc	Venus	Mars
Jan. 1	10 Cp	2 Cp	25 Sc	16 Sc
6	15 Cp	28 Sg	29 Sc	19 Sc
11	20 Cp	28 Sg	4 Sg	22 Sc
16	25 Cp	1 Cp	8 Sg	26 Sc
21	0 Aq	6 Cp	13 Sg	29 Sc
26	5 Aq	12 Cp	19 Sg	2 Sg
31	10 Aq	19 Cp	24 Sg	5 Sg

Jan. 1/Jup 28 Sc/Sat 16 Tr/Uran 13 Lb
Nep 2 Sg/Plut 30 Vr/N Node 26 Aq

	Sun	Merc	Venus	Mars
Feb. 1	11 Aq	20 Cp	25 Sg	6 Sg
6	17 Aq	27 Cp	0 Cp	9 Sg
11	22 Aq	5 Aq	6 Cp	12 Sg
16	27 Aq	13 Aq	12 Cp	15 Sg
21	2 Pc	21 Aq	17 Cp	18 Sg
26	7 Pc	29 Aq	23 Cp	21 Sg

Feb. 1/Jup 3 Sg/Sat 16 Tr/Uran 13 Lb
Nep 3 Sg/Plut 29 Vr/N Node 24 Aq

	Sun	Merc	Venus	Mars
Mar. 1	10 Pc	5 Pc	26 Cp	23 Sg
6	15 Pc	14 Pc	2 Aq	26 Sg
11	20 Pc	24 Pc	8 Aq	29 Sg
16	25 Pc	4 Ar	14 Aq	2 Cp
21	0 Ar	13 Ar	20 Aq	5 Cp
26	5 Ar	22 Ar	26 Aq	8 Cp
31	10 Ar	28 Ar	2 Pc	11 Cp

Mar. 1/Jup 6 Sg/Sat 17 Tr/Uran 13 Lb
Nep 3 Sg/Plut 29 Vr/N Node 23 Aq

	Sun	Merc	Venus	Mars
Apr. 1	11 Ar	29 Ar	3 Pc	12 Cp
6	16 Ar	3 Tr	9 Pc	15 Cp
11	20 Ar	4 Tr	15 Pc	17 Cp
16	25 Ar	2 Tr	21 Pc	20 Cp
21	0 Tr	29 Ar	27 Pc	23 Cp
26	5 Tr	25 Ar	3 Ar	26 Cp

Apr. 1/Jup 6 Sg/Sat 20 Tr/Uran 12 Lb
Nep 3 Sg/Plut 28 Vr/N Node 21 Aq

	Sun	Merc	Venus	Mars
May 1	10 Tr	23 Ar	9 Ar	28 Cp
6	15 Tr	23 Ar	15 Ar	1 Aq
11	20 Tr	25 Ar	21 Ar	4 Aq
16	24 Tr	29 Ar	27 Ar	6 Aq
21	29 Tr	4 Tr	3 Tr	8 Aq
26	4 Gm	10 Tr	9 Tr	11 Aq
31	9 Gm	18 Tr	15 Tr	13 Aq

May 1/Jup 4 Sg/Sat 24 Tr/Uran 10 Lb
Nep 2 Sg/Plut 27 Vr/N Node 20 Aq

	Sun	Merc	Venus	Mars
June 1	10 Gm	19 Tr	16 Tr	13 Aq
6	15 Gm	28 Tr	22 Tr	15 Aq
11	19 Gm	7 Gm	28 Tr	17 Aq
16	24 Gm	18 Gm	5 Gm	18 Aq
21	29 Gm	29 Gm	11 Gm	19 Aq
26	4 Ce	9 Ce	17 Gm	21 Aq

June 1/Jup 1 Sg/Sat 28 Tr/Uran 10 Lb
Nep 1 Sg/Plut 27 Vr/N Node 18 Aq

	Sun	Merc	Venus	Mars
July 1	9 Ce	20 Ce	23 Gm	21 Aq
6	13 Ce	29 Ce	29 Gm	22 Aq
11	18 Ce	8 Lo	5 Ce	22 Aq
16	23 Ce	16 Lo	11 Ce	22 Aq
21	28 Ce	23 Lo	17 Ce	21 Aq
26	2 Lo	29 Lo	23 Ce	21 Aq
31	7 Lo	4 Vr	0 Lo	20 Aq

July 1/Jup 27 Sc/Sat 1 Gm/Uran 10 Lb
Nep 1 Sg/Plut 27 Vr/N Node 16 Aq

	Sun	Merc	Venus	Mars
Aug. 1	8 Lo	5 Vr	1 Lo	19 Aq
6	13 Lo	9 Vr	7 Lo	18 Aq
11	18 Lo	10 Vr	13 Lo	17 Aq
16	22 Lo	10 Vr	19 Lo	15 Aq
21	27 Lo	8 Vr	25 Lo	14 Aq
26	2 Vr	3 Vr	2 Vr	13 Aq
31	7 Vr	29 Lo	8 Vr	12 Aq

Aug. 1/Jup 27 Sc/Sat 4 Gm/Uran 10 Lb
Nep 0 Sg/Plut 28 Vr/N Node 15 Aq

1971

```
         Sun     Merc    Venus   Mars              Sun     Merc    Venus   Mars
Sept 1   8 Vr   29 Lo    9 Vr   12 Aq     Oct. 1   7 Lb    1 Lb   16 Lb   15 Aq
     6  13 Vr   27 Lo   15 Vr   12 Aq          6  12 Lb   10 Lb   23 Lb   16 Aq
    11  18 Vr    0 Vr   21 Vr   12 Aq         11  17 Lb   19 Lb   29 Lb   18 Aq
    16  22 Vr    5 Vr   28 Vr   12 Aq         16  22 Lb   27 Lb    5 Sc   20 Aq
    21  27 Vr   13 Vr    4 Lb   13 Aq         21  27 Lb    5 Sc   11 Sc   22 Aq
    26   2 Lb   22 Vr   10 Lb   14 Aq         26   2 Sc   13 Sc   18 Sc   24 Aq
                                              31   7 Sc   21 Sc   24 Sc   27 Aq

Sept 1/Jup 29 Sc/Sat  6 Gm/Uran 12 Lb    Oct. 1/Jup  3 Sg/Sat  6 Gm/Uran 14 Lb
Nep  0 Sg/Plut 29 Vr/N Node 13 Aq        Nep  1 Sg/Plut 30 Vr/N Node 12 Aq
```

```
         Sun     Merc    Venus   Mars              Sun     Merc    Venus   Mars
Nov. 1   8 Sc   22 Sc   25 Sc   27 Aq     Dec. 1   8 Sg   28 Sg    2 Cp   14 Pc
     6  13 Sc    0 Sg    1 Sg    0 Pc          6  13 Sg   28 Sg    9 Cp   17 Pc
    11  18 Sc    7 Sg    7 Sg    2 Pc         11  18 Sg   23 Sg   15 Cp   20 Pc
    16  23 Sc   13 Sg   14 Sg    5 Pc         16  23 Sg   16 Sg   21 Cp   23 Pc
    21  28 Sc   20 Sg   20 Sg    8 Pc         21  28 Sg   12 Sg   27 Cp   26 Pc
    26   3 Sg   25 Sg   26 Sg   11 Pc         26   4 Cp   13 Sg    3 Aq    0 Ar
                                              31   9 Cp   16 Sg   10 Aq    3 Ar

Nov. 1/Jup  9 Sg/Sat  5 Gm/Uran 15 Lb    Dec. 1/Jup 15 Sg/Sat  3 Gm/Uran 17 Lb
Nep  2 Sg/Plut  1 Lb/N Node 10 Aq        Nep  3 Sg/Plut  2 Lb/N Node  8 Aq
```

Moon's Positions

```
          1        4        7       10       13       16       19       22       25       28       31
Jan.   28 Aq   10 Ar   22 Tr    1 Ce    8 Lo   14 Vr   20 Lb   27 Sc    8 Cp   22 Aq    6 Ar
Feb.   21 Ar    2 Gm   10 Ce   17 Lo   23 Vr   28 Lb    5 Sg   16 Cp   30 Aq   15 Ar
Mar.    0 Tr   12 Gm   20 Ce   26 Lo    1 Lb    7 Sc   15 Sg   24 Cp    8 Pc   24 Ar    7 Gm
Apr.   21 Gm   29 Ce    5 Vr   10 Lb   17 Sc   24 Sg    4 Aq   17 Pc    2 Tr   15 Gm
May    25 Ce    1 Vr    7 Lb   13 Sc   21 Sg    1 Aq   13 Pc   26 Ar    9 Gm   20 Ce   28 Lo
June   10 Vr   15 Lb   22 Sc    1 Cp   11 Aq   23 Pc    6 Tr   18 Gm   28 Ce    5 Vr
July   11 Lb   17 Sc   26 Sg    7 Aq   20 Pc    3 Tr   14 Gm   24 Ce    1 Vr    7 Lb   13 Sc
Aug.   25 Sc    4 Cp   16 Aq    0 Ar   14 Tr   25 Gm    3 Lo   10 Vr   16 Lb   21 Sc   29 Sg
Sept   12 Cp   25 Aq   10 Ar   24 Tr    5 Ce   13 Lo   19 Vr   24 Lb    0 Sg    8 Cp
Oct.   18 Aq    3 Ar   18 Tr    1 Ce   10 Lo   16 Vr   21 Lb   27 Sc    4 Cp   13 Aq   26 Pc
Nov.   11 Ar   27 Tr   10 Ce   18 Lo   25 Vr    0 Sc    6 Sg   14 Cp   23 Aq    5 Ar
Dec.   20 Tr    4 Ce   14 Lo   21 Vr   27 Lb    3 Sg   11 Cp   20 Aq    2 Ar   15 Tr   28 Gm
```

                                                    Ephemeris

1972

	Sun	Merc	Venus	Mars
Jan. 1	10 Cp	17 Sg	11 Aq	3 Ar
6	15 Cp	23 Sg	17 Aq	7 Ar
11	20 Cp	29 Sg	23 Aq	10 Ar
16	25 Cp	6 Cp	29 Aq	13 Ar
21	0 Aq	13 Cp	5 Pc	16 Ar
26	5 Aq	21 Cp	11 Pc	20 Ar
31	10 Aq	28 Cp	17 Pc	23 Ar

Jan. 1/Jup 22 Sg/Sat 0 Gm/Uran 18 Lb
Nep 4 Sg/Plut 2 Lb/N Node 7 Aq

	Sun	Merc	Venus	Mars
Feb. 1	11 Aq	0 Aq	19 Pc	24 Ar
6	16 Aq	8 Aq	25 Pc	27 Ar
11	21 Aq	17 Aq	1 Ar	0 Tr
16	26 Aq	25 Aq	7 Ar	4 Tr
21	1 Pc	5 Pc	13 Ar	7 Tr
26	6 Pc	14 Pc	18 Ar	10 Tr

Feb. 1/Jup 29 Sg/Sat 30 Tr/Uran 18 Lb
Nep 5 Sg/Plut 2 Lb/N Node 5 Aq

	Sun	Merc	Venus	Mars
Mar. 1	11 Pc	21 Pc	23 Ar	13 Tr
6	16 Pc	1 Ar	29 Ar	16 Tr
11	21 Pc	8 Ar	4 Tr	19 Tr
16	26 Pc	14 Ar	10 Tr	23 Tr
21	0 Ar	16 Ar	15 Tr	26 Tr
26	5 Ar	15 Ar	21 Tr	29 Tr
31	10 Ar	11 Ar	26 Tr	2 Gm

Mar. 1/Jup 4 Cp/Sat 0 Gm/Uran 18 Lb
Nep 5 Sg/Plut 1 Lb/N Node 3 Aq

	Sun	Merc	Venus	Mars
Apr. 1	11 Ar	10 Ar	27 Tr	3 Gm
6	16 Ar	7 Ar	2 Gm	6 Gm
11	21 Ar	4 Ar	7 Gm	10 Gm
16	26 Ar	4 Ar	12 Gm	13 Gm
21	1 Tr	6 Ar	16 Gm	16 Gm
26	6 Tr	9 Ar	20 Gm	19 Gm

Apr. 1/Jup 7 Cp/Sat 3 Gm/Uran 16 Lb
Nep 5 Sg/Plut 0 Lb/N Node 2 Aq

	Sun	Merc	Venus	Mars
May 1	11 Tr	14 Ar	24 Gm	23 Gm
6	16 Tr	20 Ar	27 Gm	26 Gm
11	20 Tr	27 Ar	0 Ce	29 Gm
16	25 Tr	5 Tr	2 Ce	2 Ce
21	0 Gm	14 Tr	4 Ce	5 Ce
26	5 Gm	23 Tr	5 Ce	9 Ce
31	10 Gm	4 Gm	4 Ce	12 Ce

May 1/Jup 8 Cp/Sat 6 Gm/Uran 15 Lb
Nep 4 Sg/Plut 30 Vr/N Node 0 Aq

	Sun	Merc	Venus	Mars
June 1	11 Gm	6 Gm	4 Ce	12 Ce
6	15 Gm	17 Gm	3 Ce	16 Ce
11	20 Gm	28 Gm	0 Ce	19 Ce
16	25 Gm	8 Ce	28 Gm	22 Ce
21	0 Ce	17 Ce	24 Gm	25 Ce
26	4 Ce	26 Ce	22 Gm	28 Ce

June 1/Jup 6 Cp/Sat 10 Gm/Uran 14 Lb
Nep 4 Sg/Plut 29 Vr/N Node 29 Cp

	Sun	Merc	Venus	Mars
July 1	9 Ce	3 Lo	20 Gm	1 Lo
6	14 Ce	10 Lo	18 Gm	5 Lo
11	19 Ce	15 Lo	18 Gm	8 Lo
16	24 Ce	19 Lo	19 Gm	11 Lo
21	28 Ce	22 Lo	21 Gm	14 Lo
26	3 Lo	22 Lo	23 Gm	17 Lo
31	8 Lo	21 Lo	26 Gm	20 Lo

July 1/Jup 3 Cp/Sat 14 Gm/Uran 14 Lb
Nep 3 Sg/Plut 29 Vr/N Node 27 Cp

	Sun	Merc	Venus	Mars
Aug. 1	9 Lo	20 Lo	26 Gm	21 Lo
6	14 Lo	17 Lo	0 Ce	24 Lo
11	18 Lo	13 Lo	4 Ce	27 Lo
16	23 Lo	11 Lo	8 Ce	1 Vr
21	28 Lo	11 Lo	12 Ce	4 Vr
26	3 Vr	15 Lo	17 Ce	7 Vr
31	8 Vr	21 Lo	22 Ce	10 Vr

Aug. 1/Jup 29 Sg/Sat 17 Gm/Uran 15 Lb
Nep 3 Sg/Plut 0 Lb/N Node 25 Cp

1972

	Sun	Merc	Venus	Mars
Sept 1	9 Vr	22 Lo	23 Ce	11 Vr
6	13 Vr	1 Vr	28 Ce	14 Vr
11	18 Vr	10 Vr	3 Lo	17 Vr
16	23 Vr	20 Vr	8 Lo	20 Vr
21	28 Vr	29 Vr	14 Lo	24 Vr
26	3 Lb	8 Lb	19 Lo	27 Vr

Sept 1/Jup 29 Sg/Sat 20 Gm/Uran 16 Lb
Nep 3 Sg/Plut 1 Lb/N Node 24 Cp

	Sun	Merc	Venus	Mars
Oct. 1	8 Lb	16 Lb	25 Lo	0 Lb
6	13 Lb	25 Lb	1 Vr	3 Lb
11	18 Lb	2 Sc	7 Vr	6 Lb
16	23 Lb	10 Sc	12 Vr	10 Lb
21	28 Lb	17 Sc	18 Vr	13 Lb
26	3 Sc	24 Sc	24 Vr	16 Lb
31	8 Sc	0 Sg	0 Lb	20 Lb

Oct. 1/Jup 1 Cp/Sat 21 Gm/Uran 18 Lb
Nep 3 Sg/Plut 2 Lb/N Node 22 Cp

	Sun	Merc	Venus	Mars
Nov. 1	9 Sc	1 Sg	1 Lb	20 Lb
6	14 Sc	7 Sg	7 Lb	23 Lb
11	19 Sc	11 Sg	13 Lb	27 Lb
16	24 Sc	12 Sg	20 Lb	0 Sc
21	29 Sc	10 Sg	26 Lb	3 Sc
26	4 Sg	4 Sg	2 Sc	7 Sc

Nov. 1/Jup 5 Cp/Sat 20 Gm/Uran 20 Lb
Nep 4 Sg/Plut 3 Lb/N Node 20 Cp

	Sun	Merc	Venus	Mars
Dec. 1	9 Sg	28 Sc	8 Sc	10 Sc
6	14 Sg	26 Sc	14 Sc	13 Sc
11	19 Sg	28 Sc	20 Sc	17 Sc
16	24 Sg	3 Sg	27 Sc	20 Sc
21	29 Sg	9 Sg	3 Sg	23 Sc
26	4 Cp	16 Sg	9 Sg	27 Sc
31	9 Cp	23 Sg	15 Sg	0 Sg

Dec. 1/Jup 11 Cp/Sat 18 Gm/Uran 22 Lb
Nep 5 Sg/Plut 4 Lb/N Node 19 Cp

Moon's Positions

	1	4	7	10	13	16	19	22	25	28	31
Jan.	12 Ce	22 Lo	29 Vr	4 Sc	11 Sg	19 Cp	0 Pc	13 Ar	25 Tr	7 Ce	17 Lo
Feb.	30 Lo	6 Lb	12 Sc	19 Sg	27 Cp	9 Pc	23 Ar	6 Gm	17 Ce	25 Lo	
Mar.	20 Vr	27 Lb	2 Sg	9 Cp	19 Aq	3 Ar	18 Tr	0 Ce	10 Lo	17 Vr	23 Lb
Apr.	5 Sc	11 Sg	17 Cp	27 Aq	11 Ar	27 Tr	10 Ce	19 Lo	26 Vr	2 Sc	
May	8 Sg	14 Cp	22 Aq	5 Ar	20 Tr	5 Ce	16 Lo	23 Vr	29 Lb	5 Sg	11 Cp
June	24 Cp	2 Pc	14 Ar	28 Tr	13 Ce	24 Lo	2 Lb	8 Sc	13 Sg	20 Cp	
July	29 Aq	10 Ar	23 Tr	7 Ce	19 Lo	28 Vr	4 Sc	10 Sg	17 Cp	26 Aq	7 Ar
Aug.	21 Ar	4 Gm	16 Ce	27 Lo	5 Lb	12 Sc	18 Sg	25 Cp	5 Pc	18 Ar	1 Gm
Sept	15 Gm	26 Ce	6 Vr	14 Lb	20 Sc	25 Sg	3 Aq	13 Pc	27 Ar	11 Gm	
Oct.	23 Ce	2 Vr	10 Lb	16 Sc	22 Sg	28 Cp	7 Pc	21 Ar	6 Gm	20 Ce	29 Lo
Nov.	12 Vr	19 Lb	25 Sc	0 Cp	7 Aq	16 Pc	29 Ar	15 Gm	29 Ce	9 Vr	
Dec.	16 Lb	22 Sc	27 Sg	4 Aq	12 Pc	23 Ar	7 Gm	22 Ce	4 Vr	13 Lb	19 Sc

          Ephemeris

1973

	Sun	Merc	Venus	Mars
Jan. 1	10 Cp	25 Sg	17 Sg	1 Sg
6	16 Cp	2 Cp	23 Sg	4 Sg
11	21 Cp	10 Cp	29 Sg	8 Sg
16	26 Cp	18 Cp	5 Cp	11 Sg
21	1 Aq	26 Cp	12 Cp	15 Sg
26	6 Aq	4 Aq	18 Cp	18 Sg
31	11 Aq	13 Aq	24 Cp	22 Sg

Jan. 1/Jup 18 Cp/Sat 15 Gm/Uran 23 Lb
Nep 6 Sg/Plut 4 Lb/N Node 17 Cp

	Sun	Merc	Venus	Mars
Feb. 1	12 Aq	14 Aq	25 Cp	22 Sg
6	17 Aq	23 Aq	2 Aq	26 Sg
11	22 Aq	2 Pc	8 Aq	29 Sg
16	27 Aq	11 Pc	14 Aq	3 Cp
21	2 Pc	19 Pc	20 Aq	6 Cp
26	7 Pc	25 Pc	27 Aq	10 Cp

Feb. 1/Jup 25 Cp/Sat 14 Gm/Uran 23 Lb
Nep 7 Sg/Plut 4 Lb/N Node 16 Cp

	Sun	Merc	Venus	Mars
Mar. 1	10 Pc	28 Pc	0 Pc	12 Cp
6	15 Pc	28 Pc	7 Pc	15 Cp
11	20 Pc	26 Pc	13 Pc	19 Cp
16	25 Pc	21 Pc	19 Pc	22 Cp
21	0 Ar	17 Pc	25 Pc	26 Cp
26	5 Ar	15 Pc	1 Ar	29 Cp
31	10 Ar	16 Pc	8 Ar	3 Aq

Mar. 1/Jup 1 Aq/Sat 14 Gm/Uran 23 Lb
Nep 7 Sg/Plut 4 Lb/N Node 14 Cp

	Sun	Merc	Venus	Mars
Apr. 1	11 Ar	16 Pc	9 Ar	4 Aq
6	16 Ar	19 Pc	15 Ar	7 Aq
11	21 Ar	23 Pc	21 Ar	11 Aq
16	26 Ar	29 Pc	27 Ar	14 Aq
21	1 Tr	5 Ar	4 Tr	18 Aq
26	6 Tr	13 Ar	10 Tr	21 Aq

Apr. 1/Jup 7 Aq/Sat 16 Gm/Uran 21 Lb
Nep 7 Sg/Plut 3 Lb/N Node 12 Cp

	Sun	Merc	Venus	Mars
May 1	10 Tr	21 Ar	16 Tr	25 Aq
6	15 Tr	0 Tr	22 Tr	28 Aq
11	20 Tr	9 Tr	28 Tr	2 Pc
16	25 Tr	20 Tr	4 Gm	6 Pc
21	0 Gm	1 Gm	11 Gm	9 Pc
26	5 Gm	12 Gm	17 Gm	12 Pc
31	9 Gm	22 Gm	23 Gm	16 Pc

May 1/Jup 11 Aq/Sat 18 Gm/Uran 20 Lb
Nep 7 Sg/Plut 2 Lb/N Node 11 Cp

	Sun	Merc	Venus	Mars
June 1	10 Gm	24 Gm	24 Gm	17 Pc
6	15 Gm	3 Ce	0 Ce	20 Pc
11	20 Gm	12 Ce	6 Ce	23 Pc
16	25 Gm	19 Ce	12 Ce	27 Pc
21	29 Gm	25 Ce	19 Ce	0 Ar
26	4 Ce	29 Ce	25 Ce	3 Ar

June 1/Jup 12 Aq/Sat 22 Gm/Uran 19 Lb
Nep 6 Sg/Plut 2 Lb/N Node 9 Cp

	Sun	Merc	Venus	Mars
July 1	9 Ce	2 Lo	1 Lo	7 Ar
6	14 Ce	3 Lo	7 Lo	10 Ar
11	19 Ce	3 Lo	13 Lo	13 Ar
16	23 Ce	0 Lo	19 Lo	16 Ar
21	28 Ce	27 Ce	25 Lo	19 Ar
26	3 Lo	24 Ce	1 Vr	21 Ar
31	8 Lo	23 Ce	7 Vr	24 Ar

July 1/Jup 11 Aq/Sat 26 Gm/Uran 19 Lb
Nep 5 Sg/Plut 2 Lb/N Node 8 Cp

	Sun	Merc	Venus	Mars
Aug. 1	9 Lo	23 Ce	8 Vr	24 Ar
6	13 Lo	25 Ce	14 Vr	27 Ar
11	18 Lo	29 Ce	20 Vr	29 Ar
16	23 Lo	6 Lo	26 Vr	1 Tr
21	28 Lo	15 Lo	2 Lb	3 Tr
26	3 Vr	25 Lo	8 Lb	5 Tr
31	7 Vr	5 Vr	14 Lb	7 Tr

Aug. 1/Jup 7 Aq/Sat 30 Gm/Uran 19 Lb
Nep 5 Sg/Plut 2 Lb/N Node 6 Cp

1973

	Sun	Merc	Venus	Mars
Sept 1	8 Vr	7 Vr	15 Lb	7 Tr
6	13 Vr	16 Vr	21 Lb	8 Tr
11	18 Vr	25 Vr	27 Lb	9 Tr
16	23 Vr	4 Lb	3 Sc	9 Tr
21	28 Vr	12 Lb	9 Sc	9 Tr
26	3 Lb	20 Lb	15 Sc	9 Tr

Sept 1/Jup 4 Aq/Sat 3 Ce/Uran 21 Lb
Nep 5 Sg/Plut 3 Lb/N Node 4 Cp

	Sun	Merc	Venus	Mars
Oct. 1	8 Lb	27 Lb	20 Sc	8 Tr
6	13 Lb	4 Sc	26 Sc	7 Tr
11	18 Lb	11 Sc	2 Sg	6 Tr
16	22 Lb	17 Sc	8 Sg	5 Tr
21	27 Lb	22 Sc	13 Sg	3 Tr
26	2 Sc	25 Sc	19 Sg	1 Tr
31	7 Sc	27 Sc	24 Sg	0 Tr

Oct. 1/Jup 2 Aq/Sat 5 Ce/Uran 22 Lb
Nep 5 Sg/Plut 4 Lb/N Node 3 Cp

	Sun	Merc	Venus	Mars
Nov. 1	8 Sc	26 Sc	25 Sg	29 Ar
6	13 Sc	23 Sc	0 Cp	28 Ar
11	18 Sc	17 Sc	6 Cp	27 Ar
16	23 Sc	12 Sc	11 Cp	26 Ar
21	29 Sc	11 Sc	15 Cp	25 Ar
26	4 Sg	14 Sc	20 Cp	25 Ar

Nov. 1/Jup 4 Aq/Sat 5 Ce/Uran 24 Lb
Nep 6 Sg/Plut 6 Lb/N Node 1 Cp

	Sun	Merc	Venus	Mars
Dec. 1	9 Sg	19 Sc	24 Cp	25 Ar
6	14 Sg	26 Sc	29 Cp	26 Ar
11	19 Sg	3 Sg	2 Aq	27 Ar
16	24 Sg	11 Sg	5 Aq	28 Ar
21	29 Sg	18 Sg	8 Aq	29 Ar
26	4 Cp	26 Sg	10 Aq	1 Tr
31	9 Cp	4 Cp	11 Aq	2 Tr

Dec. 1/Jup 8 Aq/Sat 3 Ce/Uran 26 Lb
Nep 7 Sg/Plut 6 Lb/N Node 30 Sg

Moon's Positions

	1	4	7	10	13	16	19	22	25	28	31
Jan.	1 Sg	6 Cp	13 Aq	22 Pc	3 Tr	16 Gm	0 Lo	12 Vr	21 Lb	27 Sc	3 Cp
Feb.	15 Cp	22 Aq	2 Ar	13 Tr	26 Gm	9 Lo	20 Vr	29 Lb	5 Sg	10 Cp	
Mar.	23 Cp	1 Pc	12 Ar	24 Tr	7 Ce	18 Lo	28 Vr	7 Sc	13 Sg	18 Cp	26 Aq
Apr.	9 Pc	21 Ar	5 Gm	18 Ce	28 Lo	8 Lb	15 Sc	21 Sg	26 Cp	4 Pc	
May	15 Ar	29 Tr	14 Ce	25 Lo	4 Lb	12 Sc	17 Sg	23 Cp	29 Aq	9 Ar	23 Tr
June	8 Gm	23 Ce	5 Vr	14 Lb	21 Sc	26 Sg	2 Aq	9 Pc	18 Ar	1 Gm	
July	16 Ce	0 Vr	11 Lb	18 Sc	23 Sg	29 Cp	6 Pc	14 Ar	26 Tr	10 Ce	24 Lo
Aug.	9 Vr	19 Lb	26 Sc	2 Cp	8 Aq	15 Pc	25 Ar	6 Gm	19 Ce	3 Vr	14 Lb
Sept	27 Lb	4 Sg	10 Cp	16 Aq	24 Pc	5 Tr	17 Gm	29 Ce	12 Vr	22 Lb	
Oct.	0 Sg	6 Cp	12 Aq	20 Pc	1 Tr	14 Gm	26 Ce	8 Vr	18 Lb	26 Sc	2 Cp
Nov.	14 Cp	20 Aq	28 Pc	9 Tr	23 Gm	7 Lo	18 Vr	27 Lb	4 Sg	10 Cp	
Dec.	16 Aq	23 Pc	3 Tr	17 Gm	2 Lo	15 Vr	24 Lb	1 Sg	7 Cp	12 Aq	19 Pc

   Ephemeris

1974

	Sun	Merc	Venus	Mars
Jan. 1	10 Cp	5 Cp	11 Aq	3 Tr
6	15 Cp	13 Cp	11 Aq	4 Tr
11	20 Cp	21 Cp	10 Aq	6 Tr
16	25 Cp	0 Aq	8 Aq	9 Tr
21	1 Aq	8 Aq	5 Aq	11 Tr
26	6 Aq	17 Aq	2 Aq	13 Tr
31	11 Aq	25 Aq	29 Cp	16 Tr

Jan. 1/Jup 14 Aq/Sat 1 Ce/Uran 27 Lb
Nep 8 Sg/Plut 7 Lb/N Node 28 Sg

	Sun	Merc	Venus	Mars
Feb. 1	12 Aq	27 Aq	29 Cp	16 Tr
6	17 Aq	4 Pc	27 Cp	19 Tr
11	22 Aq	10 Pc	26 Cp	21 Tr
16	27 Aq	12 Pc	26 Cp	24 Tr
21	2 Pc	10 Pc	27 Cp	26 Tr
26	7 Pc	5 Pc	29 Cp	29 Tr

Feb. 1/Jup 22 Aq/Sat 28 Gm/Uran 28 Lb
Nep 9 Sg/Plut 7 Lb/N Node 26 Sg

	Sun	Merc	Venus	Mars
Mar. 1	10 Pc	2 Pc	0 Aq	1 Gm
6	15 Pc	28 Aq	3 Aq	4 Gm
11	20 Pc	27 Aq	6 Aq	6 Gm
16	25 Pc	29 Aq	10 Aq	9 Gm
21	0 Ar	2 Pc	14 Aq	12 Gm
26	5 Ar	7 Pc	19 Aq	15 Gm
31	10 Ar	13 Pc	24 Aq	18 Gm

Mar. 1/Jup 28 Aq/Sat 28 Gm/Uran 27 Lb
Nep 10 Sg/Plut 6 Lb/N Node 25 Sg

	Sun	Merc	Venus	Mars
Apr. 1	11 Ar	15 Pc	25 Aq	19 Gm
6	16 Ar	21 Pc	29 Aq	22 Gm
11	21 Ar	29 Pc	4 Pc	24 Gm
16	26 Ar	7 Ar	10 Pc	27 Gm
21	1 Tr	16 Ar	15 Pc	0 Ce
26	5 Tr	26 Ar	20 Pc	3 Ce

Apr. 1/Jup 5 Pc/Sat 29 Gm/Uran 26 Lb
Nep 9 Sg/Plut 5 Lb/N Node 23 Sg

	Sun	Merc	Venus	Mars
May 1	10 Tr	6 Tr	26 Pc	6 Ce
6	15 Tr	17 Tr	1 Ar	9 Ce
11	20 Tr	27 Tr	7 Ar	12 Ce
16	25 Tr	8 Gm	12 Ar	15 Ce
21	0 Gm	17 Gm	18 Ar	18 Ce
26	4 Gm	25 Gm	24 Ar	21 Ce
31	9 Gm	2 Ce	0 Tr	24 Ce

May 1/Jup 11 Pc/Sat 1 Ce/Uran 25 Lb
Nep 9 Sg/Plut 5 Lb/N Node 22 Sg

	Sun	Merc	Venus	Mars
June 1	10 Gm	3 Ce	1 Tr	25 Ce
6	15 Gm	8 Ce	7 Tr	28 Ce
11	20 Gm	12 Ce	12 Tr	1 Lo
16	24 Gm	13 Ce	18 Tr	4 Lo
21	29 Gm	13 Ce	24 Tr	7 Lo
26	4 Ce	11 Ce	0 Gm	10 Lo

June 1/Jup 16 Pc/Sat 5 Ce/Uran 24 Lb
Nep 8 Sg/Plut 4 Lb/N Node 20 Sg

	Sun	Merc	Venus	Mars
July 1	9 Ce	9 Ce	6 Gm	13 Lo
6	14 Ce	6 Ce	12 Gm	17 Lo
11	18 Ce	4 Ce	18 Gm	20 Lo
16	23 Ce	5 Ce	24 Gm	23 Lo
21	28 Ce	8 Ce	0 Ce	26 Lo
26	3 Lo	13 Ce	6 Ce	29 Lo
31	7 Lo	20 Ce	12 Ce	2 Vr

July 1/Jup 18 Pc/Sat 8 Ce/Uran 24 Lb
Nep 7 Sg/Plut 4 Lb/N Node 18 Sg

	Sun	Merc	Venus	Mars
Aug. 1	8 Lo	22 Ce	13 Ce	3 Vr
6	13 Lo	1 Lo	19 Ce	6 Vr
11	18 Lo	11 Lo	25 Ce	9 Vr
16	23 Lo	21 Lo	1 Lo	12 Vr
21	28 Lo	1 Vr	7 Lo	15 Vr
26	2 Vr	11 Vr	13 Lo	19 Vr
31	7 Vr	20 Vr	20 Lo	22 Vr

Aug. 1/Jup 17 Pc/Sat 12 Ce/Uran 24 Lb
Nep 7 Sg/Plut 5 Lb/N Node 17 Sg

1974

	Sun	Merc	Venus	Mars
Sept 1	8 Vr	21 Vr	21 Lo	22 Vr
6	13 Vr	0 Lb	27 Lo	26 Vr
11	18 Vr	7 Lb	3 Vr	29 Vr
16	23 Vr	15 Lb	9 Vr	2 Lb
21	28 Vr	22 Lb	16 Vr	5 Lb
26	3 Lb	28 Lb	22 Vr	9 Lb

Sept 1/Jup 14 Pc/Sat 16 Ce/Uran 25 Lb
Nep 7 Sg/Plut 6 Lb/N Node 15 Sg

	Sun	Merc	Venus	Mars
Oct. 1	7 Lb	3 Sc	28 Vr	12 Lb
6	12 Lb	7 Sc	4 Lb	15 Lb
11	17 Lb	10 Sc	10 Lb	18 Lb
16	22 Lb	10 Sc	17 Lb	22 Lb
21	27 Lb	7 Sc	23 Lb	25 Lb
26	2 Sc	1 Sc	29 Lb	28 Lb
31	7 Sc	26 Lb	6 Sc	2 Sc

Oct. 1/Jup 10 Pc/Sat 18 Ce/Uran 27 Lb
Nep 7 Sg/Plut 7 Lb/N Node 13 Sg

	Sun	Merc	Venus	Mars
Nov. 1	8 Sc	25 Lb	7 Sc	3 Sc
6	13 Sc	25 Lb	13 Sc	6 Sc
11	18 Sc	29 Lb	19 Sc	9 Sc
16	23 Sc	5 Sc	26 Sc	13 Sc
21	28 Sc	13 Sc	2 Sg	16 Sc
26	3 Sg	20 Sc	8 Sg	20 Sc

Nov. 1/Jup 8 Pc/Sat 19 Ce/Uran 29 Lb
Nep 8 Sg/Plut 8 Lb/N Node 12 Sg

	Sun	Merc	Venus	Mars
Dec. 1	8 Sg	28 Sc	14 Sg	23 Sc
6	13 Sg	6 Sg	21 Sg	27 Sc
11	19 Sg	14 Sg	27 Sg	0 Sg
16	24 Sg	22 Sg	3 Cp	4 Sg
21	29 Sg	29 Sg	10 Cp	7 Sg
26	4 Cp	7 Cp	16 Cp	11 Sg
31	9 Cp	15 Cp	22 Cp	14 Sg

Dec. 1/Jup 9 Pc/Sat 18 Ce/Uran 1 Sc
Nep 9 Sg/Plut 9 Lb/N Node 10 Sg

Moon's Positions

	1	4	7	10	13	16	19	22	25	28	31
Jan.	1 Ar	11 Tr	25 Gm	10 Lo	24 Vr	4 Sc	10 Sg	16 Cp	21 Aq	28 Pc	7 Tr
Feb.	20 Tr	3 Ce	18 Lo	2 Lb	12 Sc	19 Sg	24 Cp	0 Pc	8 Ar	17 Tr	
Mar.	0 Gm	13 Ce	27 Lo	10 Lb	20 Sc	27 Sg	3 Aq	9 Pc	17 Ar	27 Tr	9 Ce
Apr.	23 Ce	6 Vr	18 Lb	28 Sc	5 Cp	11 Aq	17 Pc	26 Ar	7 Gm	20 Ce	
May	2 Vr	14 Lb	24 Sc	1 Cp	7 Aq	13 Pc	21 Ar	2 Gm	16 Ce	29 Lo	11 Lb
June	24 Lb	2 Sg	9 Cp	15 Aq	21 Pc	29 Ar	11 Gm	25 Ce	10 Vr	21 Lb	
July	29 Sc	6 Cp	11 Aq	17 Pc	24 Ar	5 Gm	19 Ce	4 Vr	17 Lb	26 Sc	3 Cp
Aug.	15 Cp	20 Aq	26 Pc	4 Tr	14 Gm	27 Ce	13 Vr	26 Lb	5 Sg	12 Cp	17 Aq
Sept	29 Aq	6 Ar	13 Tr	23 Gm	6 Lo	21 Vr	5 Sc	14 Sg	20 Cp	26 Aq	
Oct.	2 Ar	10 Tr	20 Gm	2 Lo	15 Vr	29 Lb	9 Sg	16 Cp	22 Aq	28 Pc	7 Tr
Nov.	20 Tr	1 Ce	13 Lo	25 Vr	7 Sc	17 Sg	24 Cp	30 Aq	6 Ar	15 Tr	
Dec.	26 Gm	9 Lo	22 Vr	3 Sc	13 Sg	20 Cp	26 Aq	2 Ar	9 Tr	20 Gm	4 Lo

1975

	Sun	Merc	Venus	Mars
Jan. 1	10 Cp	17 Cp	23 Cp	15 Sg
6	15 Cp	25 Cp	0 Aq	19 Sg
11	20 Cp	3 Aq	6 Aq	22 Sg
16	25 Cp	11 Aq	12 Aq	26 Sg
21	0 Aq	18 Aq	18 Aq	29 Sg
26	5 Aq	24 Aq	25 Aq	3 Cp
31	10 Aq	25 Aq	1 Pc	7 Cp

Jan. 1/Jup 13 Pc/Sat 16 Ce/Uran 2 Sc
Nep 10 Sg/Plut 9 Lb/N Node 9 Sg

	Sun	Merc	Venus	Mars
Feb. 1	12 Aq	25 Aq	2 Pc	8 Cp
6	17 Aq	22 Aq	8 Pc	11 Cp
11	22 Aq	16 Aq	15 Pc	15 Cp
16	27 Aq	11 Aq	21 Pc	19 Cp
21	2 Pc	10 Aq	27 Pc	22 Cp
26	7 Pc	11 Aq	3 Ar	26 Cp

Feb. 1/Jup 19 Pc/Sat 13 Ce/Uran 2 Sc
Nep 11 Sg/Plut 9 Lb/N Node 7 Sg

	Sun	Merc	Venus	Mars
Mar. 1	10 Pc	13 Aq	7 Ar	28 Cp
6	15 Pc	18 Aq	13 Ar	2 Aq
11	20 Pc	23 Aq	19 Ar	6 Aq
16	25 Pc	29 Aq	25 Ar	10 Aq
21	0 Ar	6 Pc	1 Tr	13 Aq
26	5 Ar	14 Pc	7 Tr	17 Aq
31	10 Ar	22 Pc	13 Tr	21 Aq

Mar. 1/Jup 26 Pc/Sat 12 Ce/Uran 2 Sc
Nep 12 Sg/Plut 9 Lb/N Node 5 Sg

	Sun	Merc	Venus	Mars
Apr. 1	11 Ar	24 Pc	15 Tr	22 Aq
6	16 Ar	3 Ar	21 Tr	26 Aq
11	20 Ar	12 Ar	27 Tr	29 Aq
16	25 Ar	22 Ar	2 Gm	3 Pc
21	0 Tr	3 Tr	8 Gm	7 Pc
26	5 Tr	13 Tr	14 Gm	11 Pc

Apr. 1/Jup 3 Ar/Sat 12 Ce/Uran 1 Sc
Nep 12 Sg/Plut 8 Lb/N Node 4 Sg

	Sun	Merc	Venus	Mars
May 1	10 Tr	23 Tr	20 Gm	15 Pc
6	15 Tr	3 Gm	26 Gm	18 Pc
11	20 Tr	10 Gm	1 Ce	22 Pc
16	25 Tr	16 Gm	7 Ce	26 Pc
21	29 Tr	21 Gm	12 Ce	0 Ar
26	4 Gm	23 Gm	18 Ce	4 Ar
31	9 Gm	24 Gm	23 Ce	7 Ar

May 1/Jup 10 Ar/Sat 14 Ce/Uran 0 Sc
Nep 11 Sg/Plut 7 Lb/N Node 2 Sg

	Sun	Merc	Venus	Mars
June 1	10 Gm	23 Gm	24 Ce	8 Ar
6	15 Gm	22 Gm	0 Lo	12 Ar
11	19 Gm	19 Gm	5 Lo	15 Ar
16	24 Gm	17 Gm	10 Lo	19 Ar
21	29 Gm	15 Gm	14 Lo	23 Ar
26	4 Ce	15 Gm	19 Lo	26 Ar

June 1/Jup 17 Ar/Sat 17 Ce/Uran 29 Lb
Nep 10 Sg/Plut 7 Lb/N Node 1 Sg

	Sun	Merc	Venus	Mars
July 1	9 Ce	18 Gm	23 Lo	0 Tr
6	13 Ce	22 Gm	27 Lo	3 Tr
11	18 Ce	28 Gm	1 Vr	7 Tr
16	23 Ce	6 Ce	4 Vr	10 Tr
21	28 Ce	15 Ce	7 Vr	14 Tr
26	2 Lo	25 Ce	9 Vr	17 Tr
31	7 Lo	6 Lo	11 Vr	21 Tr

July 1/Jup 22 Ar/Sat 21 Ce/Uran 28 Lb
Nep 10 Sg/Plut 7 Lb/N Node 29 Sc

	Sun	Merc	Venus	Mars
Aug. 1	8 Lo	8 Lo	11 Vr	21 Tr
6	13 Lo	18 Lo	12 Vr	24 Tr
11	18 Lo	28 Lo	11 Vr	28 Tr
16	23 Lo	7 Vr	10 Vr	1 Gm
21	27 Lo	15 Vr	8 Vr	4 Gm
26	2 Vr	23 Vr	5 Vr	7 Gm
31	7 Vr	0 Lb	2 Vr	10 Gm

Aug. 1/Jup 24 Ar/Sat 25 Ce/Uran 29 Lb
Nep 9 Sg/Plut 7 Lb/N Node 27 Sc

1975

	Sun	Merc	Venus	Mars
Sept 1	8 Vr	2 Lb	1 Vr	10 Gm
6	13 Vr	8 Lb	28 Lo	13 Gm
11	18 Vr	14 Lb	26 Lo	15 Gm
16	23 Vr	19 Lb	26 Lo	18 Gm
21	27 Vr	23 Lb	26 Lo	20 Gm
26	2 Lb	24 Lb	27 Lo	23 Gm

Sept 1/Jup 24 Ar/Sat 28 Ce/Uran 30 Lb
Nep 9 Sg/Plut 8 Lb/N Node 26 Sc

	Sun	Merc	Venus	Mars
Oct. 1	7 Lb	23 Lb	28 Lo	25 Gm
6	12 Lb	20 Lb	1 Vr	27 Gm
11	17 Lb	14 Lb	4 Vr	28 Gm
16	22 Lb	10 Lb	8 Vr	0 Ce
21	27 Lb	10 Lb	12 Vr	1 Ce
26	2 Sc	14 Lb	16 Vr	2 Ce
31	7 Sc	20 Lb	21 Vr	2 Ce

Oct. 1/Jup 21 Ar/Sat 1 Lo/Uran 1 Sc
Nep 9 Sg/Plut 9 Lb/N Node 24 Sc

	Sun	Merc	Venus	Mars
Nov. 1	8 Sc	22 Lb	22 Vr	2 Ce
6	13 Sc	29 Lb	26 Vr	3 Ce
11	18 Sc	7 Sc	1 Lb	3 Ce
16	23 Sc	16 Sc	7 Lb	2 Ce
21	28 Sc	24 Sc	12 Lb	1 Ce
26	3 Sg	1 Sg	18 Lb	0 Ce

Nov. 1/Jup 17 Ar/Sat 3 Lo/Uran 3 Sc
Nep 10 Sg/Plut 10 Lb/N Node 22 Sc

	Sun	Merc	Venus	Mars
Dec. 1	8 Sg	9 Sg	23 Lb	28 Gm
6	13 Sg	17 Sg	29 Lb	27 Gm
11	18 Sg	25 Sg	5 Sc	25 Gm
16	23 Sg	3 Cp	10 Sc	23 Gm
21	28 Sg	11 Cp	16 Sc	21 Gm
26	4 Cp	19 Cp	22 Sc	19 Gm
31	9 Cp	26 Cp	28 Sc	18 Gm

Dec. 1/Jup 15 Ar/Sat 3 Lo/Uran 5 Sc
Nep 11 Sg/Plut 11 Lb/N Node 21 Sc

Moon's Positions

	1	4	7	10	13	16	19	22	25	28	31
Jan.	19 Lo	3 Lb	13 Sc	22 Sg	28 Cp	4 Pc	10 Ar	17 Tr	28 Gm	13 Lo	28 Vr
Feb.	13 Lb	23 Sc	1 Cp	7 Aq	13 Pc	19 Ar	26 Tr	6 Ce	21 Lo	6 Lb	
Mar.	21 Lb	3 Sg	10 Cp	16 Aq	22 Pc	28 Ar	5 Gm	16 Ce	29 Lo	15 Lb	28 Sc
Apr.	11 Sg	19 Cp	25 Aq	1 Ar	7 Tr	15 Gm	26 Ce	9 Vr	23 Lb	6 Sg	
May	15 Cp	21 Aq	27 Pc	4 Tr	12 Gm	23 Ce	5 Vr	18 Lb	0 Sg	10 Cp	17 Aq
June	29 Aq	5 Ar	12 Tr	21 Gm	3 Lo	16 Vr	28 Lb	9 Sg	18 Cp	25 Aq	
July	1 Ar	7 Tr	16 Gm	28 Ce	12 Vr	25 Lb	6 Sg	14 Cp	21 Aq	27 Pc	3 Tr
Aug.	15 Tr	24 Gm	7 Lo	22 Vr	6 Sc	16 Sg	24 Cp	0 Pc	6 Ar	12 Tr	19 Gm
Sept	2 Ce	15 Lo	1 Lb	15 Sc	26 Sg	3 Aq	9 Pc	15 Ar	21 Tr	28 Gm	
Oct.	9 Lo	24 Vr	9 Sc	21 Sg	30 Cp	6 Pc	12 Ar	18 Tr	25 Gm	5 Lo	18 Vr
Nov.	3 Lb	17 Sc	30 Sg	8 Aq	15 Pc	20 Ar	27 Tr	5 Ce	15 Lo	28 Vr	
Dec.	11 Sc	24 Sg	4 Aq	11 Pc	16 Ar	23 Tr	1 Ce	12 Lo	24 Vr	7 Sc	18 Sg

1976

	Sun	Merc	Venus	Mars
Jan. 1	10 Cp	27 Cp	29 Sc	17 Gm
6	15 Cp	4 Aq	5 Sg	16 Gm
11	20 Cp	8 Aq	11 Sg	15 Gm
16	25 Cp	9 Aq	18 Sg	15 Gm
21	0 Aq	5 Aq	24 Sg	15 Gm
26	5 Aq	29 Cp	0 Cp	15 Gm
31	10 Aq	24 Cp	6 Cp	15 Gm

Jan. 1/Jup 16 Ar/Sat 1 Lo/Uran 6 Sc
Nep 13 Sg/Plut 12 Lb/N Node 19 Sc

	Sun	Merc	Venus	Mars
Feb. 1	11 Aq	24 Cp	7 Cp	15 Gm
6	16 Aq	24 Cp	13 Cp	16 Gm
11	21 Aq	26 Cp	19 Cp	17 Gm
16	26 Aq	0 Aq	25 Cp	19 Gm
21	1 Pc	6 Aq	2 Aq	20 Gm
26	7 Pc	12 Aq	8 Aq	22 Gm

Feb. 1/Jup 19 Ar/Sat 29 Ce/Uran 7 Sc
Nep 13 Sg/Plut 12 Lb/N Node 18 Sc

	Sun	Merc	Venus	Mars
Mar. 1	11 Pc	17 Aq	13 Aq	23 Gm
6	16 Pc	25 Aq	19 Aq	25 Gm
11	21 Pc	2 Pc	25 Aq	27 Gm
16	26 Pc	11 Pc	1 Pc	29 Gm
21	1 Ar	19 Pc	7 Pc	1 Ce
26	5 Ar	29 Pc	14 Pc	3 Ce
31	10 Ar	9 Ar	20 Pc	6 Ce

Mar. 1/Jup 24 Ar/Sat 27 Ce/Uran 7 Sc
Nep 14 Sg/Plut 11 Lb/N Node 16 Sc

	Sun	Merc	Venus	Mars
Apr. 1	11 Ar	11 Ar	21 Pc	6 Ce
6	16 Ar	21 Ar	27 Pc	9 Ce
11	21 Ar	1 Tr	3 Ar	11 Ce
16	26 Ar	11 Tr	9 Ar	14 Ce
21	1 Tr	19 Tr	16 Ar	16 Ce
26	6 Tr	26 Tr	22 Ar	19 Ce

Apr. 1/Jup 1 Tr/Sat 26 Ce/Uran 6 Sc
Nep 14 Sg/Plut 10 Lb/N Node 14 Sc

	Sun	Merc	Venus	Mars
May 1	11 Tr	1 Gm	28 Ar	22 Ce
6	16 Tr	3 Gm	4 Tr	24 Ce
11	20 Tr	4 Gm	10 Tr	27 Ce
16	25 Tr	2 Gm	16 Tr	0 Lo
21	0 Gm	29 Tr	22 Tr	3 Lo
26	5 Gm	27 Tr	29 Tr	5 Lo
31	10 Gm	25 Tr	5 Gm	8 Lo

May 1/Jup 8 Tr/Sat 27 Ce/Uran 5 Sc
Nep 13 Sg/Plut 10 Lb/N Node 13 Sc

	Sun	Merc	Venus	Mars
June 1	11 Gm	25 Tr	6 Gm	9 Lo
6	15 Gm	26 Tr	12 Gm	12 Lo
11	20 Gm	28 Tr	18 Gm	15 Lo
16	25 Gm	2 Gm	24 Gm	18 Lo
21	0 Ce	8 Gm	1 Ce	20 Lo
26	5 Ce	15 Gm	7 Ce	23 Lo

June 1/Jup 16 Tr/Sat 30 Ce/Uran 4 Sc
Nep 13 Sg/Plut 9 Lb/N Node 11 Sc

	Sun	Merc	Venus	Mars
July 1	9 Ce	23 Gm	13 Ce	26 Lo
6	14 Ce	3 Ce	19 Ce	29 Lo
11	19 Ce	13 Ce	25 Ce	2 Vr
16	24 Ce	24 Ce	1 Lo	5 Vr
21	28 Ce	5 Lo	7 Lo	9 Vr
26	3 Lo	14 Lo	14 Lo	12 Vr
31	8 Lo	24 Lo	20 Lo	15 Vr

July 1/Jup 22 Tr/Sat 3 Lo/Uran 3 Sc
Nep 12 Sg/Plut 9 Lb/N Node 10 Sc

	Sun	Merc	Venus	Mars
Aug. 1	9 Lo	25 Lo	21 Lo	15 Vr
6	14 Lo	4 Vr	27 Lo	18 Vr
11	18 Lo	11 Vr	3 Vr	22 Vr
16	23 Lo	18 Vr	9 Vr	25 Vr
21	28 Lo	25 Vr	16 Vr	28 Vr
26	3 Vr	0 Lb	22 Vr	1 Lb
31	8 Vr	4 Lb	28 Vr	4 Lb

Aug. 1/Jup 27 Tr/Sat 7 Lo/Uran 3 Sc
Nep 11 Sg/Plut 9 Lb/N Node 8 Sc

1976

	Sun	Merc	Venus	Mars
Sept 1	9 Vr	5 Lb	29 Vr	5 Lb
6	14 Vr	7 Lb	5 Lb	8 Lb
11	18 Vr	8 Lb	11 Lb	11 Lb
16	23 Vr	5 Lb	18 Lb	15 Lb
21	28 Vr	0 Lb	24 Lb	18 Lb
26	3 Lb	25 Vr	0 Sc	21 Lb

Sept 1/Jup 1 Gm/Sat 11 Lo/Uran 4 Sc
Nep 11 Sg/Plut 10 Lb/N Node 6 Sc

	Sun	Merc	Venus	Mars
Oct. 1	8 Lb	23 Vr	6 Sc	25 Lb
6	13 Lb	25 Vr	12 Sc	28 Lb
11	18 Lb	1 Lb	18 Sc	1 Sc
16	23 Lb	8 Lb	24 Sc	5 Sc
21	28 Lb	16 Lb	0 Sg	8 Sc
26	3 Sc	25 Lb	6 Sg	12 Sc
31	8 Sc	3 Sc	13 Sg	15 Sc

Oct. 1/Jup 1 Gm/Sat 14 Lo/Uran 6 Sc
Nep 12 Sg/Plut 11 Lb/N Node 5 Sc

	Sun	Merc	Venus	Mars
Nov. 1	9 Sc	5 Sc	14 Sg	16 Sc
6	14 Sc	13 Sc	20 Sg	19 Sc
11	19 Sc	21 Sc	26 Sg	23 Sc
16	24 Sc	29 Sc	2 Cp	26 Sc
21	29 Sc	7 Sg	8 Cp	0 Sg
26	4 Sg	14 Sg	14 Cp	4 Sg

Nov. 1/Jup 28 Tr/Sat 16 Lo/Uran 8 Sc
Nep 12 Sg/Plut 13 Lb/N Node 3 Sc

	Sun	Merc	Venus	Mars
Dec. 1	9 Sg	22 Sg	20 Cp	7 Sg
6	14 Sg	29 Sg	26 Cp	11 Sg
11	19 Sg	7 Cp	2 Aq	14 Sg
16	24 Sg	14 Cp	8 Aq	18 Sg
21	29 Sg	19 Cp	13 Aq	22 Sg
26	4 Cp	23 Cp	19 Aq	26 Sg
31	9 Cp	23 Cp	25 Aq	29 Sg

Dec. 1/Jup 24 Tr/Sat 17 Lo/Uran 9 Sc
Nep 14 Sg/Plut 14 Lb/N Node 2 Sc

Moon's Positions

	1	4	7	10	13	16	19	22	25	28	31
Jan.	2 Cp	11 Aq	18 Pc	24 Ar	0 Gm	10 Ce	22 Lo	5 Lb	17 Sc	28 Sg	7 Aq
Feb.	20 Aq	26 Pc	2 Tr	8 Gm	17 Ce	1 Vr	15 Lb	28 Sc	8 Cp	16 Aq	
Mar.	11 Pc	17 Ar	22 Tr	29 Gm	9 Lo	24 Vr	9 Sc	22 Sg	1 Aq	8 Pc	13 Ar
Apr.	25 Ar	1 Gm	8 Ce	18 Lo	2 Lb	17 Sc	1 Cp	10 Aq	17 Pc	22 Ar	
May	28 Tr	5 Ce	14 Lo	26 Vr	11 Sc	25 Sg	6 Aq	13 Pc	19 Ar	25 Tr	2 Ce
June	14 Ce	24 Lo	6 Lb	20 Sc	3 Cp	14 Aq	22 Pc	27 Ar	3 Gm	11 Ce	
July	21 Lo	3 Lb	15 Sc	28 Sg	9 Aq	17 Pc	24 Ar	29 Tr	7 Ce	17 Lo	29 Vr
Aug.	13 Lb	26 Sc	7 Cp	18 Aq	26 Pc	1 Tr	7 Gm	15 Ce	26 Lo	9 Lb	23 Sc
Sept	7 Sg	18 Cp	27 Aq	4 Ar	10 Tr	15 Gm	23 Ce	4 Vr	18 Lb	3 Sg	
Oct.	15 Cp	24 Aq	1 Ar	6 Tr	12 Gm	18 Ce	28 Lo	12 Lb	27 Sc	11 Cp	21 Aq
Nov.	3 Pc	10 Ar	15 Tr	21 Gm	28 Ce	7 Vr	20 Lb	5 Sg	19 Cp	30 Aq	
Dec.	6 Ar	12 Tr	18 Gm	25 Ce	3 Vr	14 Lb	28 Sc	13 Cp	25 Aq	3 Ar	8 Tr

1977

	Sun	Merc	Venus	Mars
Jan. 1	10 Cp	22 Cp	26 Aq	0 Cp
6	16 Cp	16 Cp	2 Pc	4 Cp
11	21 Cp	10 Cp	7 Pc	7 Cp
16	26 Cp	7 Cp	13 Pc	11 Cp
21	1 Aq	8 Cp	18 Pc	15 Cp
26	6 Aq	11 Cp	23 Pc	19 Cp
31	11 Aq	16 Cp	28 Pc	23 Cp

Jan. 1/Jup 22 Tr/Sat 16 Lo/Uran 11 Sc
Nep 15 Sg/Plut 14 Lb/N Node 30 Lb

	Sun	Merc	Venus	Mars
Feb. 1	12 Aq	17 Cp	29 Pc	23 Cp
6	17 Aq	23 Cp	3 Ar	27 Cp
11	22 Aq	0 Aq	8 Ar	1 Aq
16	27 Aq	7 Aq	12 Ar	5 Aq
21	2 Pc	15 Aq	16 Ar	9 Aq
26	7 Pc	23 Aq	19 Ar	13 Aq

Feb. 1/Jup 22 Tr/Sat 14 Lo/Uran 12 Sc
Nep 16 Sg/Plut 14 Lb/N Node 28 Lb

	Sun	Merc	Venus	Mars
Mar. 1	10 Pc	28 Aq	20 Ar	15 Aq
6	15 Pc	6 Pc	23 Ar	19 Aq
11	20 Pc	16 Pc	24 Ar	23 Aq
16	25 Pc	25 Pc	25 Ar	27 Aq
21	0 Ar	5 Ar	24 Ar	1 Pc
26	5 Ar	15 Ar	23 Ar	5 Pc
31	10 Ar	25 Ar	20 Ar	9 Pc

Mar. 1/Jup 24 Tr/Sat 11 Lo/Uran 12 Sc
Nep 16 Sg/Plut 14 Lb/N Node 27 Lb

	Sun	Merc	Venus	Mars
Apr. 1	11 Ar	26 Ar	20 Ar	9 Pc
6	16 Ar	4 Tr	17 Ar	13 Pc
11	21 Ar	10 Tr	13 Ar	17 Pc
16	26 Ar	14 Tr	11 Ar	21 Pc
21	1 Tr	14 Tr	9 Ar	25 Pc
26	6 Tr	13 Tr	8 Ar	29 Pc

Apr. 1/Jup 29 Tr/Sat 10 Lo/Uran 11 Sc
Nep 16 Sg/Plut 13 Lb/N Node 25 Lb

	Sun	Merc	Venus	Mars
May 1	11 Tr	10 Tr	9 Ar	3 Ar
6	15 Tr	7 Tr	10 Ar	6 Ar
11	20 Tr	5 Tr	12 Ar	10 Ar
16	25 Tr	5 Tr	14 Ar	14 Ar
21	0 Gm	7 Tr	17 Ar	18 Ar
26	5 Gm	10 Tr	21 Ar	22 Ar
31	9 Gm	15 Tr	25 Ar	25 Ar

May 1/Jup 6 Gm/Sat 10 Lo/Uran 10 Sc
Nep 16 Sg/Plut 12 Lb/N Node 24 Lb

	Sun	Merc	Venus	Mars
June 1	10 Gm	16 Tr	26 Ar	26 Ar
6	15 Gm	23 Tr	0 Tr	0 Tr
11	20 Gm	0 Gm	4 Tr	4 Tr
16	25 Gm	9 Gm	9 Tr	7 Tr
21	0 Ce	19 Gm	14 Tr	11 Tr
26	4 Ce	29 Gm	19 Tr	15 Tr

June 1/Jup 13 Gm/Sat 12 Lo/Uran 9 Sc
Nep 15 Sg/Plut 12 Lb/N Node 22 Lb

	Sun	Merc	Venus	Mars
July 1	9 Ce	10 Ce	24 Tr	18 Tr
6	14 Ce	21 Ce	29 Tr	22 Tr
11	19 Ce	1 Lo	5 Gm	25 Tr
16	23 Ce	10 Lo	10 Gm	29 Tr
21	28 Ce	19 Lo	16 Gm	2 Gm
26	3 Lo	27 Lo	21 Gm	6 Gm
31	8 Lo	3 Vr	27 Gm	9 Gm

July 1/Jup 20 Gm/Sat 15 Lo/Uran 8 Sc
Nep 14 Sg/Plut 11 Lb/N Node 20 Lb

	Sun	Merc	Venus	Mars
Aug. 1	9 Lo	5 Vr	28 Gm	10 Gm
6	13 Lo	11 Vr	4 Ce	13 Gm
11	18 Lo	15 Vr	9 Ce	17 Gm
16	23 Lo	19 Vr	15 Ce	20 Gm
21	28 Lo	21 Vr	21 Ce	23 Gm
26	3 Vr	20 Vr	27 Ce	26 Gm
31	7 Vr	17 Vr	3 Lo	29 Gm

Aug. 1/Jup 26 Gm/Sat 19 Lo/Uran 8 Sc
Nep 14 Sg/Plut 12 Lb/N Node 19 Lb

1977

```
          Sun    Merc   Venus   Mars
Sept 1   8 Vr  17 Vr   4 Lo    0 Ce
     6  13 Vr  12 Vr  10 Lo    3 Ce
    11  18 Vr   8 Vr  16 Lo    6 Ce
    16  23 Vr   7 Vr  22 Lo    9 Ce
    21  28 Vr  10 Vr  28 Lo   12 Ce
    26   3 Lb  16 Vr   4 Vr   15 Ce
```

Sept 1/Jup 2 Ce/Sat 23 Lo/Uran 9 Sc
Nep 13 Sg/Plut 13 Lb/N Node 17 Lb

```
          Sun    Merc   Venus   Mars
Oct. 1   8 Lb  24 Vr  10 Vr   17 Ce
     6  13 Lb   3 Lb  16 Vr   20 Ce
    11  18 Lb  12 Lb  23 Vr   23 Ce
    16  23 Lb  20 Lb  29 Vr   25 Ce
    21  27 Lb  29 Lb   5 Lb   27 Ce
    26   2 Sc   7 Sc  11 Lb    0 Lo
    31   7 Sc  15 Sc  17 Lb    2 Lo
```

Oct. 1/Jup 5 Ce/Sat 26 Lo/Uran 10 Sc
Nep 14 Sg/Plut 14 Lb/N Node 15 Lb

```
          Sun    Merc   Venus   Mars
Nov. 1   8 Sc  17 Sc  19 Lb    2 Lo
     6  13 Sc  24 Sc  25 Lb    4 Lo
    11  18 Sc   2 Sg   1 Sc    6 Lo
    16  24 Sc   9 Sg   7 Sc    7 Lo
    21  29 Sc  17 Sg  14 Sc    9 Lo
    26   4 Sg  23 Sg  20 Sc   10 Lo
```

Nov. 1/Jup 6 Ce/Sat 29 Lo/Uran 12 Sc
Nep 15 Sg/Plut 15 Lb/N Node 14 Lb

```
          Sun    Merc   Venus   Mars
Dec. 1   9 Sg   0 Cp  26 Sc   11 Lo
     6  14 Sg   5 Cp   2 Sg   11 Lo
    11  19 Sg   7 Cp   9 Sg   12 Lo
    16  24 Sg   6 Cp  15 Sg   12 Lo
    21  29 Sg   0 Cp  21 Sg   11 Lo
    26   4 Cp  24 Sg  28 Sg   10 Lo
    31   9 Cp  21 Sg   4 Cp    9 Lo
```

Dec. 1/Jup 4 Ce/Sat 0 Vr/Uran 14 Sc
Nep 16 Sg/Plut 16 Lb/N Node 12 Lb

Moon's Positions

	1	4	7	10	13	16	19	22	25	28	31
Jan.	20 Tr	26 Gm	4 Lo	14 Vr	25 Lb	8 Sg	21 Cp	2 Pc	11 Ar	16 Tr	22 Gm
Feb.	4 Ce	13 Lo	24 Vr	6 Sc	18 Sg	0 Aq	11 Pc	18 Ar	24 Tr	30 Gm	
Mar.	12 Ce	21 Lo	3 Lb	16 Sc	29 Sg	10 Aq	19 Pc	26 Ar	2 Gm	8 Ce	16 Lo
Apr.	29 Lo	12 Lb	26 Sc	10 Cp	20 Aq	29 Pc	5 Tr	11 Gm	16 Ce	24 Lo	
May	5 Lb	20 Sc	5 Cp	17 Aq	26 Pc	2 Tr	7 Gm	13 Ce	20 Lo	30 Vr	13 Sc
June	28 Sc	14 Cp	26 Aq	5 Ar	11 Tr	16 Gm	22 Ce	30 Lo	9 Lb	22 Sc	
July	7 Cp	21 Aq	1 Ar	8 Tr	13 Gm	19 Ce	27 Lo	6 Lb	17 Sc	1 Cp	15 Aq
Aug.	29 Aq	9 Ar	16 Tr	21 Gm	28 Ce	6 Vr	16 Lb	28 Sc	11 Cp	24 Aq	4 Ar
Sept	17 Ar	24 Tr	29 Gm	6 Lo	15 Vr	27 Lb	9 Sg	22 Cp	3 Pc	13 Ar	
Oct.	20 Tr	25 Gm	2 Lo	10 Vr	21 Lb	5 Sg	19 Cp	30 Aq	9 Ar	16 Tr	22 Gm
Nov.	4 Ce	10 Lo	18 Vr	30 Lb	14 Sg	29 Cp	10 Pc	18 Ar	25 Tr	0 Ce	
Dec.	6 Lo	13 Vr	23 Lb	7 Sg	23 Cp	6 Pc	15 Ar	22 Tr	27 Gm	3 Lo	10 Vr

1978

	Sun	Merc	Venus	Mars
Jan. 1	10 Cp	21 Sg	5 Cp	9 Lo
6	15 Cp	23 Sg	11 Cp	8 Lo
11	20 Cp	27 Sg	18 Cp	6 Lo
16	26 Cp	3 Cp	24 Cp	4 Lo
21	1 Aq	9 Cp	0 Aq	2 Lo
26	6 Aq	16 Cp	7 Aq	0 Lo
31	11 Aq	23 Cp	13 Aq	28 Ce

Jan. 1/Jup 30 Gm/Sat 0 Vr/Uran 15 Sc
Nep 17 Sg/Plut 17 Lb/N Node 11 Lb

	Sun	Merc	Venus	Mars
Feb. 1	12 Aq	24 Cp	14 Aq	28 Ce
6	17 Aq	2 Aq	20 Aq	26 Ce
11	22 Aq	10 Aq	27 Aq	25 Ce
16	27 Aq	18 Aq	3 Pc	24 Ce
21	2 Pc	27 Aq	9 Pc	23 Ce
26	7 Pc	6 Pc	15 Pc	22 Ce

Feb. 1/Jup 27 Gm/Sat 28 Lo/Uran 16 Sc
Nep 18 Sg/Plut 17 Lb/N Node 9 Lb

	Sun	Merc	Venus	Mars
Mar. 1	10 Pc	12 Pc	19 Pc	22 Ce
6	15 Pc	21 Pc	25 Pc	22 Ce
11	20 Pc	1 Ar	2 Ar	23 Ce
16	25 Pc	10 Ar	8 Ar	23 Ce
21	0 Ar	18 Ar	14 Ar	24 Ce
26	5 Ar	23 Ar	20 Ar	25 Ce
31	10 Ar	26 Ar	26 Ar	27 Ce

Mar. 1/Jup 26 Gm/Sat 26 Lo/Uran 16 Sc
Nep 18 Sg/Plut 16 Lb/N Node 7 Lb

	Sun	Merc	Venus	Mars
Apr. 1	11 Ar	26 Ar	28 Ar	27 Ce
6	16 Ar	25 Ar	4 Tr	28 Ce
11	21 Ar	22 Ar	10 Tr	0 Lo
16	26 Ar	18 Ar	16 Tr	2 Lo
21	1 Tr	16 Ar	22 Tr	4 Lo
26	5 Tr	15 Ar	28 Tr	6 Lo

Apr. 1/Jup 29 Gm/Sat 24 Lo/Uran 16 Sc
Nep 18 Sg/Plut 15 Lb/N Node 6 Lb

	Sun	Merc	Venus	Mars
May 1	10 Tr	16 Ar	4 Gm	8 Lo
6	15 Tr	19 Ar	11 Gm	10 Lo
11	20 Tr	24 Ar	17 Gm	13 Lo
16	25 Tr	0 Tr	23 Gm	15 Lo
21	0 Gm	6 Tr	29 Gm	17 Lo
26	4 Gm	14 Tr	5 Ce	20 Lo
31	9 Gm	23 Tr	11 Ce	22 Lo

May 1/Jup 3 Ce/Sat 24 Lo/Uran 15 Sc
Nep 18 Sg/Plut 15 Lb/N Node 4 Lb

	Sun	Merc	Venus	Mars
June 1	10 Gm	25 Tr	12 Ce	23 Lo
6	15 Gm	5 Gm	18 Ce	26 Lo
11	20 Gm	15 Gm	24 Ce	28 Lo
16	25 Gm	26 Gm	0 Lo	1 Vr
21	29 Gm	7 Ce	6 Lo	4 Vr
26	4 Ce	17 Ce	11 Lo	7 Vr

June 1/Jup 9 Ce/Sat 25 Lo/Uran 13 Sc
Nep 17 Sg/Plut 14 Lb/N Node 3 Lb

	Sun	Merc	Venus	Mars
July 1	9 Ce	27 Ce	17 Lo	9 Vr
6	14 Ce	5 Lo	23 Lo	12 Vr
11	18 Ce	13 Lo	29 Lo	15 Vr
16	23 Ce	19 Lo	4 Vr	18 Vr
21	28 Ce	25 Lo	10 Vr	21 Vr
26	3 Lo	29 Lo	16 Vr	24 Vr
31	7 Lo	2 Vr	21 Vr	27 Vr

July 1/Jup 16 Ce/Sat 27 Lo/Uran 12 Sc
Nep 16 Sg/Plut 14 Lb/N Node 1 Lb

	Sun	Merc	Venus	Mars
Aug. 1	8 Lo	2 Vr	22 Vr	28 Vr
6	13 Lo	3 Vr	28 Vr	1 Lb
11	18 Lo	1 Vr	3 Lb	4 Lb
16	23 Lo	28 Lo	8 Lb	7 Lb
21	28 Lo	24 Lo	13 Lb	10 Lb
26	2 Vr	21 Lo	18 Lb	14 Lb
31	7 Vr	21 Lo	23 Lb	17 Lb

Aug. 1/Jup 23 Ce/Sat 1 Vr/Uran 12 Sc
Nep 16 Sg/Plut 14 Lb/N Node 29 Vr

1978

```
          Sun     Merc    Venus    Mars              Sun     Merc    Venus    Mars
Sept 1   8 Vr   21 Lo   24 Lb   18 Lb      Oct. 1   7 Lb    8 Lb   18 Sc    8 Sc
     6  13 Vr   25 Lo   29 Lb   21 Lb           6  12 Lb   16 Lb   20 Sc   11 Sc
    11  18 Vr    2 Vr    3 Sc   24 Lb          11  17 Lb   25 Lb   22 Sc   14 Sc
    16  23 Vr   10 Vr    7 Sc   27 Lb          16  22 Lb    3 Sc   23 Sc   18 Sc
    21  28 Vr   19 Vr   11 Sc    1 Sc          21  27 Lb   11 Sc   23 Sc   21 Sc
    26   3 Lb   29 Vr   15 Sc    4 Sc          26   2 Sc   18 Sc   22 Sc   25 Sc
                                               31   7 Sc   25 Sc   20 Sc   29 Sc
```

Sept 1/Jup 29 Ce/Sat 5 Vr/Uran 13 Sc   Oct. 1/Jup 4 Lo/Sat 8 Vr/Uran 14 Sc
Nep 16 Sg/Plut 15 Lb/N Node 28 Vr   Nep 16 Sg/Plut 16 Lb/N Node 26 Vr

```
          Sun     Merc    Venus    Mars              Sun     Merc    Venus    Mars
Nov. 1   8 Sc   27 Sc   19 Sc   29 Sc       Dec. 1   8 Sg   19 Sg    7 Sc   21 Sg
     6  13 Sc    4 Sg   16 Sc    3 Sg            6  14 Sg   13 Sg    8 Sc   25 Sg
    11  18 Sc   10 Sg   13 Sc    6 Sg           11  19 Sg    7 Sg   10 Sc   29 Sg
    16  23 Sc   16 Sg   11 Sc   10 Sg           16  24 Sg    5 Sg   13 Sc    2 Cp
    21  28 Sc   20 Sg    9 Sc   14 Sg           21  29 Sg    7 Sg   16 Sc    6 Cp
    26   3 Sg   22 Sg    7 Sc   17 Sg           26   4 Cp   12 Sg   20 Sc   10 Cp
                                                31   9 Cp   18 Sg   24 Sc   14 Cp
```

Nov. 1/Jup 8 Lo/Sat 11 Vr/Uran 16 Sc   Dec. 1/Jup 9 Lo/Sat 13 Vr/Uran 18 Sc
Nep 17 Sg/Plut 17 Lb/N Node 24 Vr   Nep 18 Sg/Plut 18 Lb/N Node 23 Vr

Moon's Positions

	1	4	7	10	13	16	19	22	25	28	31
Jan.	22 Vr	2 Sc	16 Sg	1 Aq	15 Pc	24 Ar	0 Gm	6 Ce	12 Lo	19 Vr	28 Lb
Feb.	12 Sc	25 Sg	9 Aq	23 Pc	2 Tr	9 Gm	14 Ce	21 Lo	29 Vr	9 Sc	
Mar.	22 Sc	5 Cp	18 Aq	0 Ar	10 Tr	17 Gm	22 Ce	29 Lo	8 Lb	19 Sc	2 Cp
Apr.	16 Cp	28 Aq	9 Ar	18 Tr	25 Gm	0 Lo	7 Vr	16 Lb	29 Sc	12 Cp	
May	25 Aq	5 Ar	14 Tr	21 Gm	26 Ce	2 Vr	11 Lb	23 Sc	8 Cp	21 Aq	2 Ar
June	15 Ar	23 Tr	29 Gm	5 Lo	11 Vr	19 Lb	1 Sg	17 Cp	1 Pc	12 Ar	
July	20 Tr	26 Gm	2 Lo	8 Vr	15 Lb	25 Sc	10 Cp	25 Aq	8 Ar	17 Tr	23 Gm
Aug.	5 Ce	11 Lo	17 Vr	24 Lb	5 Sg	19 Cp	4 Pc	17 Ar	26 Tr	2 Ce	8 Lo
Sept	20 Lo	26 Vr	5 Sc	15 Sg	28 Cp	12 Pc	25 Ar	4 Gm	10 Ce	16 Lo	
Oct.	23 Vr	1 Sc	12 Sg	24 Cp	7 Pc	19 Ar	29 Tr	6 Ce	12 Lo	18 Vr	27 Lb
Nov.	10 Sc	22 Sg	5 Aq	17 Pc	28 Ar	7 Gm	14 Ce	20 Lo	26 Vr	5 Sc	
Dec.	17 Sg	1 Aq	14 Pc	25 Ar	3 Gm	10 Ce	16 Lo	22 Vr	29 Lb	11 Sg	26 Cp

1979

Jan.	Sun	Merc	Venus	Mars
1	10 Cp	19 Sg	24 Sc	15 Cp
6	15 Cp	26 Sg	29 Sc	19 Cp
11	20 Cp	3 Cp	4 Sg	22 Cp
16	25 Cp	10 Cp	8 Sg	26 Cp
21	0 Aq	18 Cp	14 Sg	0 Aq
26	5 Aq	26 Cp	19 Sg	4 Aq
31	11 Aq	4 Aq	24 Sg	8 Aq

Jan. 1/Jup 7 Lo/Sat 14 Vr/Uran 20 Sc
Nep 19 Sg/Plut 19 Lb/N Node 21 Vr

Feb.	Sun	Merc	Venus	Mars
1	12 Aq	6 Aq	25 Sg	9 Aq
6	17 Aq	14 Aq	1 Cp	13 Aq
11	22 Aq	23 Aq	6 Cp	17 Aq
16	27 Aq	2 Pc	12 Cp	21 Aq
21	2 Pc	11 Pc	18 Cp	25 Aq
26	7 Pc	20 Pc	23 Cp	29 Aq

Feb. 1/Jup 3 Lo/Sat 13 Vr/Uran 21 Sc
Nep 20 Sg/Plut 19 Lb/N Node 20 Vr

Mar.	Sun	Merc	Venus	Mars
1	10 Pc	26 Pc	27 Cp	1 Pc
6	15 Pc	3 Ar	3 Aq	5 Pc
11	20 Pc	7 Ar	9 Aq	9 Pc
16	25 Pc	8 Ar	14 Aq	13 Pc
21	0 Ar	6 Ar	20 Aq	17 Pc
26	5 Ar	2 Ar	26 Aq	21 Pc
31	10 Ar	28 Pc	2 Pc	25 Pc

Mar. 1/Jup 30 Ce/Sat 11 Vr/Uran 21 Sc
Nep 20 Sg/Plut 19 Lb/N Node 18 Vr

Apr.	Sun	Merc	Venus	Mars
1	11 Ar	28 Pc	3 Pc	25 Pc
6	16 Ar	26 Pc	9 Pc	29 Pc
11	21 Ar	26 Pc	15 Pc	3 Ar
16	25 Ar	29 Pc	21 Pc	7 Ar
21	0 Tr	3 Ar	27 Pc	11 Ar
26	5 Tr	8 Ar	3 Ar	15 Ar

Apr. 1/Jup 29 Ce/Sat 8 Vr/Uran 20 Sc
Nep 20 Sg/Plut 18 Lb/N Node 16 Vr

May	Sun	Merc	Venus	Mars
1	10 Tr	15 Ar	9 Ar	18 Ar
6	15 Tr	22 Ar	15 Ar	22 Ar
11	20 Tr	0 Tr	22 Ar	26 Ar
16	25 Tr	9 Tr	28 Ar	0 Tr
21	29 Tr	19 Tr	4 Tr	4 Tr
26	4 Gm	29 Tr	10 Tr	7 Tr
31	9 Gm	10 Gm	16 Tr	11 Tr

May 1/Jup 1 Lo/Sat 7 Vr/Uran 19 Sc
Nep 20 Sg/Plut 17 Lb/N Node 15 Vr

June	Sun	Merc	Venus	Mars
1	10 Gm	12 Gm	17 Tr	12 Tr
6	15 Gm	23 Gm	23 Tr	15 Tr
11	20 Gm	3 Ce	29 Tr	19 Tr
16	24 Gm	13 Ce	5 Gm	23 Tr
21	29 Gm	21 Ce	11 Gm	26 Tr
26	4 Ce	28 Ce	17 Gm	0 Gm

June 1/Jup 5 Lo/Sat 8 Vr/Uran 18 Sc
Nep 19 Sg/Plut 17 Lb/N Node 13 Vr

July	Sun	Merc	Venus	Mars
1	9 Ce	4 Lo	23 Gm	4 Gm
6	13 Ce	9 Lo	0 Ce	7 Gm
11	18 Ce	13 Lo	6 Ce	11 Gm
16	23 Ce	14 Lo	12 Ce	14 Gm
21	28 Ce	14 Lo	18 Ce	17 Gm
26	2 Lo	12 Lo	24 Ce	21 Gm
31	7 Lo	8 Lo	0 Lo	24 Gm

July 1/Jup 11 Lo/Sat 9 Vr/Uran 17 Sc
Nep 19 Sg/Plut 16 Lb/N Node 12 Vr

Aug.	Sun	Merc	Venus	Mars
1	8 Lo	8 Lo	1 Lo	25 Gm
6	13 Lo	4 Lo	8 Lo	28 Gm
11	18 Lo	3 Lo	14 Lo	2 Ce
16	23 Lo	5 Lo	20 Lo	5 Ce
21	27 Lo	9 Lo	26 Lo	8 Ce
26	2 Vr	16 Lo	2 Vr	11 Ce
31	7 Vr	25 Lo	9 Vr	15 Ce

Aug. 1/Jup 17 Lo/Sat 12 Vr/Uran 17 Sc
Nep 18 Sg/Plut 17 Lb/N Node 10 Vr

1979

```
           Sun     Merc    Venus   Mars                    Sun     Merc    Venus   Mars
Sept 1   8 Vr   26 Lo   10 Vr   15 Ce      Oct. 1   7 Lb   21 Lb   17 Lb    4 Lo
     6  13 Vr    6 Vr   16 Vr   18 Ce           6  12 Lb   28 Lb   23 Lb    7 Lo
    11  18 Vr   16 Vr   22 Vr   22 Ce          11  17 Lb    6 Sc    0 Sc    9 Lo
    16  23 Vr   25 Vr   28 Vr   25 Ce          16  22 Lb   13 Sc    6 Sc   12 Lo
    21  27 Vr    4 Lb    5 Lb   28 Ce          21  27 Lb   19 Sc   12 Sc   15 Lo
    26   2 Lb   12 Lb   11 Lb    1 Lo          26   2 Sc   25 Sc   18 Sc   18 Lo
                                               31   7 Sc    1 Sg   24 Sc   20 Lo
```

Sept 1/Jup 24 Lo/Sat 16 Vr/Uran 17 Sc   Oct. 1/Jup 0 Vr/Sat 20 Vr/Uran 19 Sc
Nep 18 Sg/Plut 18 Lb/N Node 8 Vr   Nep 18 Sg/Plut 19 Lb/N Node 7 Vr

```
           Sun     Merc    Venus   Mars                    Sun     Merc    Venus   Mars
Nov. 1   8 Sc    2 Sg   26 Sc   21 Lo      Dec. 1   8 Sg   20 Sc    3 Cp    5 Vr
     6  13 Sc    5 Sg    2 Sg   23 Lo           6  13 Sg   23 Sc    9 Cp    7 Vr
    11  18 Sc    6 Sg    8 Sg   26 Lo          11  18 Sg   28 Sc   15 Cp    8 Vr
    16  23 Sc    2 Sg   14 Sg   28 Lo          16  23 Sg    5 Sg   22 Cp   10 Vr
    21  28 Sc   26 Sc   21 Sg    0 Vr          21  29 Sg   12 Sg   28 Cp   12 Vr
    26   3 Sg   21 Sc   27 Sg    3 Vr          26   4 Cp   19 Sg    4 Aq   13 Vr
                                               31   9 Cp   26 Sg   10 Aq   14 Vr
```

Nov. 1/Jup 6 Vr/Sat 23 Vr/Uran 20 Sc   Dec. 1/Jup 9 Vr/Sat 26 Vr/Uran 22 Sc
Nep 19 Sg/Plut 20 Lb/N Node 5 Vr   Nep 20 Sg/Plut 21 Lb/N Node 4 Vr

Moon's Positions

```
           1       4       7      10      13      16      19      22      25      28      31
Jan.   11 Aq   24 Pc    5 Tr   13 Gm   19 Ce   25 Lo    0 Lb    8 Sc   19 Sg    4 Aq   19 Pc
Feb.    3 Ar   14 Tr   22 Gm   28 Ce    3 Vr    9 Lb   17 Sc   28 Sg   12 Aq   27 Pc
Mar.   12 Ar   23 Tr    1 Ce    7 Lo   12 Vr   19 Lb   27 Sc    8 Cp   21 Aq    5 Ar   18 Tr
Apr.    1 Gm    9 Ce   15 Lo   20 Vr   28 Lb    7 Sg   18 Cp    1 Pc   14 Ar   26 Tr
May     5 Ce   11 Lo   17 Vr   23 Lb    3 Sg   15 Cp   27 Aq   10 Ar   21 Tr    0 Ce    7 Lo
June   19 Lo   24 Vr    2 Sc   12 Sg   25 Cp    8 Pc   20 Ar    0 Gm    9 Ce   15 Lo
July   21 Vr   27 Lb    6 Sg   19 Cp    4 Pc   17 Ar   27 Tr    5 Ce   12 Lo   17 Vr   23 Lb
Aug.    5 Sc   15 Sg   28 Cp   13 Pc   27 Ar    7 Gm   15 Ce   21 Lo   26 Vr    2 Sc   10 Sg
Sept   23 Sg    6 Aq   21 Pc    6 Tr   17 Gm   24 Ce   29 Lo    5 Lb   11 Sc   20 Sg
Oct.    1 Aq   15 Pc   30 Ar   12 Gm   20 Ce   26 Lo    2 Lb    8 Sc   17 Sg   27 Cp    9 Pc
Nov.   24 Pc    8 Tr   20 Gm   28 Ce    4 Vr   10 Lb   17 Sc   27 Sg    8 Aq   20 Pc
Dec.    2 Tr   14 Gm   24 Ce    0 Vr    6 Lb   12 Sc   22 Sg    4 Aq   17 Pc   29 Ar   10 Gm
```

1980

```
            Sun    Merc   Venus   Mars                      Sun    Merc   Venus   Mars
Jan. 1   10 Cp   28 Sg   11 Aq   14 Vr       Feb. 1   11 Aq   19 Aq   19 Pc   14 Vr
      6   15 Cp    6 Cp   18 Aq   15 Vr             6   16 Aq   28 Aq   25 Pc   13 Vr
     11   20 Cp   14 Cp   24 Aq   15 Vr            11   21 Aq    6 Pc    1 Ar   11 Vr
     16   25 Cp   22 Cp    0 Pc   15 Vr            16   26 Aq   14 Pc    7 Ar    9 Vr
     21    0 Aq    0 Aq    6 Pc   15 Vr            21    2 Pc   19 Pc   13 Ar    7 Vr
     26    5 Aq    8 Aq   12 Pc   15 Vr            26    7 Pc   22 Pc   19 Ar    5 Vr
     31   10 Aq   17 Aq   18 Pc   14 Vr
```

Jan. 1/Jup 10 Vr/Sat 27 Vr/Uran 24 Sc
Nep 21 Sg/Plut 22 Lb/N Node 2 Vr

Feb. 1/Jup 8 Vr/Sat 26 Vr/Uran 25 Sc
Nep 22 Sg/Plut 22 Lb/N Node 0 Vr

```
            Sun    Merc   Venus   Mars                      Sun    Merc   Venus   Mars
Mar. 1   11 Pc   20 Pc   23 Ar    4 Vr       Apr. 1   11 Ar   14 Pc   27 Tr   26 Lo
      6   16 Pc   16 Pc   29 Ar    2 Vr             6   16 Ar   19 Pc    2 Gm   26 Lo
     11   21 Pc   11 Pc    5 Tr    0 Vr            11   21 Ar   25 Pc    7 Gm   26 Lo
     16   26 Pc    8 Pc   10 Tr   29 Lo            16   26 Ar    2 Ar   12 Gm   26 Lo
     21    1 Ar    8 Pc   16 Tr   28 Lo            21    1 Tr   10 Ar   16 Gm   27 Lo
     26    5 Ar    9 Pc   21 Tr   27 Lo            26    6 Tr   18 Ar   20 Gm   28 Lo
     31   10 Ar   13 Pc   26 Tr   26 Lo
```

Mar. 1/Jup 5 Vr/Sat 25 Vr/Uran 26 Sc
Nep 23 Sg/Plut 21 Lb/N Node 29 Lo

Apr. 1/Jup 1 Vr/Sat 22 Vr/Uran 25 Sc
Nep 23 Sg/Plut 21 Lb/N Node 27 Lo

```
            Sun    Merc   Venus   Mars                      Sun    Merc   Venus   Mars
May 1    11 Tr   27 Ar   23 Gm   29 Lo       June 1   11 Gm    0 Ce    2 Ce   10 Vr
      6   16 Tr    7 Tr   27 Gm    1 Vr             6   15 Gm    8 Ce    0 Ce   12 Vr
     11   20 Tr   18 Tr   29 Gm    2 Vr            11   20 Gm   14 Ce   27 Gm   15 Vr
     16   25 Tr   28 Tr    1 Ce    4 Vr            16   25 Gm   19 Ce   24 Gm   17 Vr
     21    0 Gm    9 Gm    2 Ce    6 Vr            21    0 Ce   23 Ce   21 Gm   20 Vr
     26    5 Gm   19 Gm    3 Ce    8 Vr            26    5 Ce   25 Ce   18 Gm   22 Vr
     31   10 Gm   28 Gm    2 Ce   10 Vr
```

May 1/Jup 0 Vr/Sat 21 Vr/Uran 24 Sc
Nep 22 Sg/Plut 20 Lb/N Node 25 Lo

June 1/Jup 2 Vr/Sat 20 Vr/Uran 23 Sc
Nep 22 Sg/Plut 19 Lb/N Node 24 Lo

```
            Sun    Merc   Venus   Mars                      Sun    Merc   Venus   Mars
July 1    9 Ce   25 Ce   17 Gm   25 Vr       Aug. 1    9 Lo   19 Ce   26 Gm   12 Lb
      6   14 Ce   23 Ce   16 Gm   27 Vr             6   14 Lo   25 Ce    0 Ce   15 Lb
     11   19 Ce   20 Ce   16 Gm    0 Lb            11   18 Lo    3 Lo    4 Ce   18 Lb
     16   24 Ce   17 Ce   18 Gm    3 Lb            16   23 Lo   12 Lo    8 Ce   22 Lb
     21   28 Ce   15 Ce   20 Gm    6 Lb            21   28 Lo   22 Lo   12 Ce   25 Lb
     26    3 Lo   16 Ce   22 Gm    9 Lb            26    3 Vr    2 Vr   17 Ce   28 Lb
     31    8 Lo   19 Ce   25 Gm   12 Lb            31    8 Vr   12 Vr   22 Ce    1 Sc
```

July 1/Jup 6 Vr/Sat 21 Vr/Uran 22 Sc
Nep 21 Sg/Plut 19 Lb/N Node 22 Lo

Aug. 1/Jup 12 Vr/Sat 24 Vr/Uran 22 Sc
Nep 20 Sg/Plut 19 Lb/N Node 21 Lo

1980

```
            Sun    Merc    Venus   Mars                    Sun    Merc   Venus   Mars
Sept 1    9 Vr   14 Vr   23 Ce    2 Sc       Oct. 1    8 Lb    1 Sc   25 Lo   22 Sc
     6   14 Vr   23 Vr   28 Ce    5 Sc            6   13 Lb    7 Sc    1 Vr   26 Sc
    11   18 Vr    2 Lb    3 Lo    8 Sc           11   18 Lb   13 Sc    7 Vr   29 Sc
    16   23 Vr   10 Lb    9 Lo   12 Sc           16   23 Lb   17 Sc   13 Vr    3 Sg
    21   28 Vr   17 Lb   14 Lo   15 Sc           21   28 Lb   20 Sc   19 Vr    6 Sg
    26    3 Lb   25 Lb   20 Lo   19 Sc           26    3 Sc   19 Sc   25 Vr   10 Sg
                                                 31    8 Sc   15 Sc    1 Lb   14 Sg
```

Sept 1/Jup 18 Vr/Sat 27 Vr/Uran 22 Sc   Oct. 1/Jup 25 Vr/Sat 1 Lb/Uran 23 Sc
Nep 20 Sg/Plut 20 Lb/N Node 19 Lo   Nep 20 Sg/Plut 21 Lb/N Node 17 Lo

```
            Sun    Merc    Venus   Mars                    Sun    Merc   Venus   Mars
Nov. 1    9 Sc   14 Sc    2 Lb   14 Sg       Dec. 1    9 Sg   23 Sc    9 Sc    7 Cp
     6   14 Sc    8 Sc    8 Lb   18 Sg            6   14 Sg    0 Sg   15 Sc   11 Cp
    11   19 Sc    4 Sc   14 Lb   22 Sg           11   19 Sg    8 Sg   21 Sc   15 Cp
    16   24 Sc    5 Sc   20 Lb   25 Sg           16   24 Sg   16 Sg   27 Sc   18 Cp
    21   29 Sc    9 Sc   26 Lb   29 Sg           21   29 Sg   23 Sg    3 Sg   22 Cp
    26    4 Sg   16 Sc    2 Sc    3 Cp           26    4 Cp    1 Cp   10 Sg   26 Cp
                                                 31    9 Cp    9 Cp   16 Sg    0 Aq
```

Nov. 1/Jup 1 Lb/Sat 5 Lb/Uran 25 Sc   Dec. 1/Jup 6 Lb/Sat 8 Lb/Uran 27 Sc
Nep 21 Sg/Plut 22 Lb/N Node 16 Lo   Nep 22 Sg/Plut 23 Lb/N Node 14 Lo

Moon's Positions

	1	4	7	10	13	16	19	22	25	28	31
Jan.	23 Gm	2 Lo	8 Vr	14 Lb	20 Sc	0 Cp	13 Aq	27 Pc	10 Tr	20 Gm	28 Ce
Feb.	10 Lo	16 Vr	22 Lb	28 Sc	8 Cp	21 Aq	6 Ar	20 Tr	30 Gm	7 Lo	
Mar.	1 Vr	7 Lb	12 Sc	20 Sg	0 Aq	14 Pc	30 Ar	13 Gm	22 Ce	28 Lo	4 Lb
Apr.	15 Lb	22 Sc	29 Sg	9 Aq	23 Pc	8 Tr	21 Gm	1 Lo	7 Vr	12 Lb	
May	18 Sc	26 Sg	6 Aq	17 Pc	2 Tr	15 Gm	26 Ce	3 Vr	9 Lb	15 Sc	23 Sg
June	6 Cp	16 Aq	28 Pc	11 Tr	24 Gm	4 Lo	11 Vr	17 Lb	23 Sc	2 Cp	
July	13 Aq	25 Pc	7 Tr	19 Gm	29 Ce	7 Vr	13 Lb	19 Sc	27 Sg	8 Aq	21 Pc
Aug.	5 Ar	18 Tr	29 Gm	8 Lo	15 Vr	21 Lb	27 Sc	5 Cp	16 Aq	0 Ar	15 Tr
Sept	29 Tr	9 Ce	17 Lo	24 Vr	29 Lb	5 Sg	13 Cp	24 Aq	9 Ar	24 Tr	
Oct.	6 Ce	15 Lo	21 Vr	26 Lb	2 Sg	9 Cp	19 Aq	2 Ar	18 Tr	2 Ce	11 Lo
Nov.	24 Lo	30 Vr	5 Sc	11 Sg	19 Cp	28 Aq	11 Ar	26 Tr	10 Ce	20 Lo	
Dec.	26 Vr	2 Sc	8 Sg	16 Cp	25 Aq	6 Ar	20 Tr	4 Ce	15 Lo	22 Vr	28 Lb

1981

	Sun	Merc	Venus	Mars
Jan. 1	10 Cp	11 Cp	17 Sg	1 Aq
6	16 Cp	19 Cp	23 Sg	5 Aq
11	21 Cp	27 Cp	0 Cp	9 Aq
16	26 Cp	6 Aq	6 Cp	13 Aq
21	1 Aq	14 Aq	12 Cp	17 Aq
26	6 Aq	22 Aq	18 Cp	21 Aq
31	11 Aq	29 Aq	25 Cp	25 Aq

Jan. 1/Jup 10 Lb/Sat 10 Lb/Uran 28 Sc
Nep 23 Sg/Plut 24 Lb/N Node 13 Lo

	Sun	Merc	Venus	Mars
Feb. 1	12 Aq	0 Pc	26 Cp	25 Aq
6	17 Aq	4 Pc	2 Aq	29 Aq
11	22 Aq	4 Pc	8 Aq	3 Pc
16	27 Aq	0 Pc	15 Aq	7 Pc
21	2 Pc	25 Aq	21 Aq	11 Pc
26	7 Pc	21 Aq	27 Aq	15 Pc

Feb. 1/Jup 10 Lb/Sat 10 Lb/Uran 30 Sc
Nep 24 Sg/Plut 24 Lb/N Node 11 Lo

	Sun	Merc	Venus	Mars
Mar. 1	10 Pc	20 Aq	1 Pc	17 Pc
6	15 Pc	21 Aq	7 Pc	21 Pc
11	20 Pc	23 Aq	13 Pc	25 Pc
16	25 Pc	28 Aq	20 Pc	29 Pc
21	0 Ar	3 Pc	26 Pc	3 Ar
26	5 Ar	10 Pc	2 Ar	7 Ar
31	10 Ar	17 Pc	8 Ar	11 Ar

Mar. 1/Jup 9 Lb/Sat 8 Lb/Uran 0 Sg
Nep 25 Sg/Plut 24 Lb/N Node 9 Lo

	Sun	Merc	Venus	Mars
Apr. 1	11 Ar	18 Pc	10 Ar	12 Ar
6	16 Ar	26 Pc	16 Ar	15 Ar
11	21 Ar	5 Ar	22 Ar	19 Ar
16	26 Ar	14 Ar	28 Ar	23 Ar
21	1 Tr	23 Ar	4 Tr	27 Ar
26	6 Tr	4 Tr	11 Tr	1 Tr

Apr. 1/Jup 5 Lb/Sat 6 Lb/Uran 30 Sc
Nep 25 Sg/Plut 23 Lb/N Node 8 Lo

	Sun	Merc	Venus	Mars
May 1	11 Tr	14 Tr	17 Tr	4 Tr
6	15 Tr	25 Tr	23 Tr	8 Tr
11	20 Tr	5 Gm	29 Tr	12 Tr
16	25 Tr	14 Gm	5 Gm	15 Tr
21	0 Gm	21 Gm	11 Gm	19 Tr
26	5 Gm	27 Gm	17 Gm	23 Tr
31	9 Gm	2 Ce	24 Gm	26 Tr

May 1/Jup 2 Lb/Sat 4 Lb/Uran 29 Sc
Nep 25 Sg/Plut 22 Lb/N Node 6 Lo

	Sun	Merc	Venus	Mars
June 1	10 Gm	2 Ce	25 Gm	27 Tr
6	15 Gm	5 Ce	1 Ce	1 Gm
11	20 Gm	5 Ce	7 Ce	4 Gm
16	25 Gm	4 Ce	13 Ce	8 Gm
21	0 Ce	1 Ce	19 Ce	11 Gm
26	4 Ce	28 Gm	25 Ce	15 Gm

June 1/Jup 0 Lb/Sat 3 Lb/Uran 28 Sc
Nep 24 Sg/Plut 22 Lb/N Node 5 Lo

	Sun	Merc	Venus	Mars
July 1	9 Ce	27 Gm	1 Lo	18 Gm
6	14 Ce	27 Gm	8 Lo	22 Gm
11	19 Ce	29 Gm	14 Lo	25 Gm
16	23 Ce	3 Ce	20 Lo	28 Gm
21	28 Ce	9 Ce	26 Lo	2 Ce
26	3 Lo	17 Ce	2 Vr	5 Ce
31	8 Lo	26 Ce	8 Vr	8 Ce

July 1/Jup 2 Lb/Sat 4 Lb/Uran 27 Sc
Nep 23 Sg/Plut 22 Lb/N Node 3 Lo

	Sun	Merc	Venus	Mars
Aug. 1	9 Lo	28 Ce	9 Vr	9 Ce
6	13 Lo	9 Lo	15 Vr	12 Ce
11	18 Lo	19 Lo	21 Vr	16 Ce
16	23 Lo	29 Lo	27 Vr	19 Ce
21	28 Lo	8 Vr	3 Lb	22 Ce
26	3 Vr	17 Vr	9 Lb	25 Ce
31	8 Vr	25 Vr	15 Lb	29 Ce

Aug. 1/Jup 6 Lb/Sat 6 Lb/Uran 26 Sc
Nep 22 Sg/Plut 22 Lb/N Node 1 Lo

1981

```
          Sun    Merc   Venus  Mars                    Sun    Merc   Venus  Mars
Sept 1    8 Vr   27 Vr  16 Lb  29 Ce       Oct. 1     8 Lb   2 Sc   21 Sc  18 Lo
     6   13 Vr    5 Lb  22 Lb   2 Lo            6     13 Lb   4 Sc   27 Sc  21 Lo
    11   18 Vr   12 Lb  28 Lb   6 Lo           11     18 Lb   3 Sc    2 Sg  24 Lo
    16   23 Vr   18 Lb   4 Sc   9 Lo           16     23 Lb  28 Lb    8 Sg  27 Lo
    21   28 Vr   24 Lb   9 Sc  12 Lo           21     28 Lb  22 Lb   13 Sg   0 Vr
    26    3 Lb   29 Lb  15 Sc  15 Lo           26      2 Sc  18 Lb   19 Sg   3 Vr
                                               31      7 Sc  19 Lb   24 Sg   6 Vr
```

Sept 1/Jup 12 Lb/Sat 9 Lb/Uran 26 Sc   Oct. 1/Jup 18 Lb/Sat 12 Lb/Uran 27 Sc
Nep 22 Sg/Plut 23 Lb/N Node 30 Ce   Nep 22 Sg/Plut 24 Lb/N Node 28 Ce

```
          Sun    Merc   Venus  Mars                    Sun    Merc   Venus  Mars
Nov. 1    8 Sc   20 Lb  25 Sg   6 Vr       Dec. 1     9 Sg   3 Sg   24 Cp  23 Vr
     6   13 Sc   25 Lb   0 Cp   9 Vr            6     14 Sg  11 Sg   28 Cp  25 Vr
    11   19 Sc    2 Sc   6 Cp  12 Vr           11     19 Sg  19 Sg    1 Aq  28 Vr
    16   24 Sc   10 Sc  11 Cp  15 Vr           16     24 Sg  27 Sg    4 Aq   0 Lb
    21   29 Sc   18 Sc  15 Cp  17 Vr           21     29 Sg   5 Cp    7 Aq   2 Lb
    26    4 Sg   25 Sc  20 Cp  20 Vr           26      4 Cp  13 Cp    8 Aq   5 Lb
                                               31      9 Cp  21 Cp    9 Aq   7 Lb
```

Nov. 1/Jup 25 Lb/Sat 16 Lb/Uran 29 Sc   Dec. 1/Jup 1 Sc/Sat 19 Lb/Uran 1 Sg
Nep 23 Sg/Plut 25 Lb/N Node 26 Ce   Nep 24 Sg/Plut 26 Lb/N Node 25 Ce

Moon's Positions

```
          1       4       7      10      13      16      19      22      25      28      31
Jan.   10 Sc   17 Sg   25 Cp    5 Pc   17 Ar   30 Tr   12 Ce   22 Lo    0 Lb    6 Sc   12 Sg
Feb.   24 Sg    3 Aq   15 Pc   28 Ar   11 Gm   22 Ce    1 Vr    8 Lb   14 Sc   20 Sg
Mar.    2 Cp   11 Aq   24 Pc    8 Tr   21 Gm    2 Lo   10 Vr   16 Lb   22 Sc   28 Sg    6 Aq
Apr.   19 Aq    2 Ar   18 Tr    1 Ce   12 Lo   19 Vr   25 Lb    1 Sg    7 Cp   14 Aq
May    26 Pc   11 Tr   26 Gm    8 Lo   16 Vr   22 Lb   28 Sc    4 Cp   11 Aq   21 Pc    4 Tr
June   19 Tr    5 Ce   17 Lo   25 Vr    1 Sc    7 Sg   13 Cp   21 Aq    1 Ar   14 Tr
July   28 Gm   11 Lo   21 Vr   27 Lb    3 Sg   10 Cp   18 Aq   28 Pc   10 Tr   23 Gm    6 Lo
Aug.   19 Lo   29 Vr    6 Sc   11 Sg   18 Cp   27 Aq    8 Ar   21 Tr    3 Ce   15 Lo   24 Vr
Sept    7 Lb   13 Sc   19 Sg   26 Cp    5 Pc   18 Ar    2 Gm   14 Ce   24 Lo    3 Lb
Oct.   10 Sc   15 Sg   21 Cp   30 Aq   12 Ar   27 Tr   11 Ce   21 Lo   30 Vr    6 Sc   12 Sg
Nov.   24 Sg   30 Cp    8 Pc   20 Ar    6 Gm   20 Ce    1 Vr    9 Lb   15 Sc   21 Sg
Dec.   26 Cp    4 Pc   14 Ar   28 Tr   14 Ce   27 Lo    6 Lb   12 Sc   18 Sg   23 Cp    1 Pc
```

1982

	Sun	Merc	Venus	Mars
Jan. 1	10 Cp	23 Cp	9 Aq	7 Lb
6	15 Cp	0 Aq	8 Aq	9 Lb
11	20 Cp	8 Aq	7 Aq	11 Lb
16	26 Cp	14 Aq	4 Aq	13 Lb
21	1 Aq	18 Aq	1 Aq	14 Lb
26	6 Aq	18 Aq	28 Cp	16 Lb
31	11 Aq	13 Aq	26 Cp	17 Lb

Jan. 1/Jup 6 Sc/Sat 21 Lb/Uran 3 Sg
Nep 25 Sg/Plut 27 Lb/N Node 23 Ce

	Sun	Merc	Venus	Mars
Feb. 1	12 Aq	12 Aq	25 Cp	17 Lb
6	17 Aq	6 Aq	24 Cp	18 Lb
11	22 Aq	3 Aq	23 Cp	19 Lb
16	27 Aq	3 Aq	24 Cp	19 Lb
21	2 Pc	6 Aq	25 Cp	19 Lb
26	7 Pc	10 Aq	28 Cp	19 Lb

Feb. 1/Jup 9 Sc/Sat 22 Lb/Uran 4 Sg
Nep 26 Sg/Plut 27 Lb/N Node 22 Ce

	Sun	Merc	Venus	Mars
Mar. 1	10 Pc	13 Aq	29 Cp	19 Lb
6	15 Pc	19 Aq	2 Aq	18 Lb
11	20 Pc	26 Aq	6 Aq	17 Lb
16	25 Pc	3 Pc	10 Aq	16 Lb
21	0 Ar	11 Pc	14 Aq	14 Lb
26	5 Ar	19 Pc	19 Aq	12 Lb
31	10 Ar	28 Pc	24 Aq	11 Lb

Mar. 1/Jup 10 Sc/Sat 22 Lb/Uran 5 Sg
Nep 27 Sg/Plut 27 Lb/N Node 20 Ce

	Sun	Merc	Venus	Mars
Apr. 1	11 Ar	0 Ar	25 Aq	10 Lb
6	16 Ar	10 Ar	29 Aq	8 Lb
11	21 Ar	20 Ar	5 Pc	6 Lb
16	26 Ar	0 Tr	10 Pc	5 Lb
21	1 Tr	11 Tr	15 Pc	3 Lb
26	5 Tr	21 Tr	21 Pc	2 Lb

Apr. 1/Jup 8 Sc/Sat 20 Lb/Uran 4 Sg
Nep 27 Sg/Plut 26 Lb/N Node 18 Ce

	Sun	Merc	Venus	Mars
May 1	10 Tr	29 Tr	26 Pc	1 Lb
6	15 Tr	6 Gm	2 Ar	1 Lb
11	20 Tr	11 Gm	7 Ar	0 Lb
16	25 Tr	14 Gm	13 Ar	0 Lb
21	0 Gm	15 Gm	19 Ar	1 Lb
26	4 Gm	14 Gm	24 Ar	2 Lb
31	9 Gm	12 Gm	0 Tr	3 Lb

May 1/Jup 5 Sc/Sat 17 Lb/Uran 4 Sg
Nep 27 Sg/Plut 25 Lb/N Node 17 Ce

	Sun	Merc	Venus	Mars
June 1	10 Gm	11 Gm	1 Tr	3 Lb
6	15 Gm	9 Gm	7 Tr	4 Lb
11	20 Gm	7 Gm	13 Tr	5 Lb
16	25 Gm	7 Gm	19 Tr	7 Lb
21	29 Gm	9 Gm	25 Tr	9 Lb
26	4 Ce	12 Gm	1 Gm	11 Lb

June 1/Jup 1 Sc/Sat 16 Lb/Uran 2 Sg
Nep 26 Sg/Plut 24 Lb/N Node 15 Ce

	Sun	Merc	Venus	Mars
July 1	9 Ce	17 Gm	7 Gm	13 Lb
6	14 Ce	24 Gm	12 Gm	15 Lb
11	18 Ce	3 Ce	18 Gm	18 Lb
16	23 Ce	12 Ce	24 Gm	20 Lb
21	28 Ce	23 Ce	0 Ce	23 Lb
26	3 Lo	3 Lo	6 Ce	25 Lb
31	7 Lo	14 Lo	12 Ce	28 Lb

July 1/Jup 0 Sc/Sat 16 Lb/Uran 1 Sg
Nep 25 Sg/Plut 24 Lb/N Node 14 Ce

	Sun	Merc	Venus	Mars
Aug. 1	8 Lo	16 Lo	14 Ce	29 Lb
6	13 Lo	25 Lo	20 Ce	1 Sc
11	18 Lo	4 Vr	26 Ce	4 Sc
16	23 Lo	13 Vr	2 Lo	7 Sc
21	28 Lo	20 Vr	8 Lo	10 Sc
26	2 Vr	27 Vr	14 Lo	14 Sc
31	7 Vr	4 Lb	20 Lo	17 Sc

Aug. 1/Jup 2 Sc/Sat 17 Lb/Uran 1 Sg
Nep 25 Sg/Plut 24 Lb/N Node 12 Ce

1982

```
          Sun    Merc    Venus   Mars              Sun    Merc    Venus   Mars
Sept 1    8 Vr    5 Lb   22 Lo   17 Sc     Oct. 1  7 Lb   10 Lb   29 Vr    8 Sg
      6   13 Vr   10 Lb   28 Lo   21 Sc          6  12 Lb    5 Lb    5 Lb   11 Sg
     11   18 Vr   14 Lb    4 Vr   24 Sc         11  17 Lb    2 Lb   11 Lb   15 Sg
     16   23 Vr   17 Lb   10 Vr   27 Sc         16  22 Lb    4 Lb   17 Lb   18 Sg
     21   28 Vr   17 Lb   16 Vr    1 Sg         21  27 Lb   10 Lb   24 Lb   22 Sg
     26    3 Lb   15 Lb   22 Vr    4 Sg         26   2 Sc   17 Lb    0 Sc   26 Sg
                                                31   7 Sc   25 Lb    6 Sc   29 Sg
```

Sept 1/Jup 6 Sc/Sat 20 Lb/Uran 1 Sg   Oct. 1/Jup 12 Sc/Sat 23 Lb/Uran 2 Sg
Nep 24 Sg/Plut 25 Lb/N Node 10 Ce   Nep 24 Sg/Plut 26 Lb/N Node 9 Ce

```
          Sun    Merc    Venus   Mars              Sun    Merc    Venus   Mars
Nov. 1    8 Sc   27 Lb    7 Sc    0 Cp     Dec. 1  8 Sg   15 Sg   15 Sg   23 Cp
      6   13 Sc    5 Sc   14 Sc    4 Cp          6  14 Sg   23 Sg   21 Sg   27 Cp
     11   18 Sc   13 Sc   20 Sc    8 Cp         11  19 Sg    0 Cp   28 Sg    1 Aq
     16   23 Sc   21 Sc   26 Sc   11 Cp         16  24 Sg    8 Cp    4 Cp    4 Aq
     21   28 Sc   29 Sc    3 Sg   15 Cp         21  29 Sg   16 Cp   10 Cp    8 Aq
     26    3 Sg    7 Sg    9 Sg   19 Cp         26   4 Cp   23 Cp   17 Cp   12 Aq
                                                31   9 Cp   29 Cp   23 Cp   16 Aq
```

Nov. 1/Jup 18 Sc/Sat 27 Lb/Uran 3 Sg   Dec. 1/Jup 25 Sc/Sat 0 Sc/Uran 5 Sg
Nep 25 Sg/Plut 27 Lb/N Node 7 Ce   Nep 26 Sg/Plut 28 Lb/N Node 6 Ce

Moon's Positions

```
         1        4        7       10       13       16       19       22       25       28       31
Jan.  13 Pc    24 Ar    7 Gm    22 Ce     5 Vr   14 Lb    21 Sc    26 Sg    2 Aq    10 Pc   20 Ar
Feb.   4 Tr    17 Gm    0 Lo    13 Vr    22 Lb   29 Sc     4 Cp    11 Aq   20 Pc     1 Tr
Mar.  15 Tr    27 Gm    9 Lo    21 Vr    30 Lb    6 Sg    12 Cp    19 Aq   28 Pc    11 Tr   24 Gm
Apr.   8 Ce    20 Lo   30 Vr     8 Sc    14 Sg   20 Cp    27 Aq     7 Ar   20 Tr     4 Ce
May   17 Lo    26 Vr    4 Sc    11 Sg    16 Cp   22 Aq     1 Ar    14 Tr   29 Gm    13 Lo   23 Vr
June   6 Lb    14 Sc   20 Sg    25 Cp     1 Pc   10 Ar    22 Tr     7 Ce   22 Lo     3 Lb
July  11 Sc    17 Sg   22 Cp    28 Aq     6 Ar   17 Tr     1 Ce    16 Lo   28 Vr     7 Sc   13 Sg
Aug.  25 Sg     1 Aq    8 Pc    16 Ar    27 Tr   10 Ce    24 Lo     7 Lb   16 Sc    22 Sg   27 Cp
Sept   9 Aq    17 Pc   26 Ar     8 Gm    20 Ce    3 Vr    15 Lb    24 Sc   30 Sg     5 Aq
Oct.  13 Pc    22 Ar    4 Gm    17 Ce    29 Lo   10 Lb    19 Sc    26 Sg    1 Aq     8 Pc   17 Ar
Nov.   1 Tr    14 Gm   28 Ce     9 Vr    19 Lb   28 Sc     4 Cp     9 Aq   16 Pc    25 Ar
Dec.   8 Gm    23 Ce    6 Vr    16 Lb    24 Sc    0 Cp     6 Aq    12 Pc   20 Ar     1 Gm   16 Ce
```

1983

	Sun	Merc	Venus	Mars
Jan. 1	10 Cp	0 Aq	24 Cp	17 Aq
6	15 Cp	2 Aq	0 Aq	21 Aq
11	20 Cp	1 Aq	7 Aq	25 Aq
16	25 Cp	26 Cp	13 Aq	29 Aq
21	0 Aq	20 Cp	19 Aq	3 Pc
26	5 Aq	17 Cp	25 Aq	7 Pc
31	11 Aq	17 Cp	2 Pc	11 Pc

Jan. 1/Jup 1 Sg/Sat 3 Sc/Uran 7 Sg
Nep 27 Sg/Plut 29 Lb/N Node 4 Ce

	Sun	Merc	Venus	Mars
Feb. 1	12 Aq	18 Cp	3 Pc	11 Pc
6	17 Aq	21 Cp	9 Pc	15 Pc
11	22 Aq	26 Cp	15 Pc	19 Pc
16	27 Aq	2 Aq	21 Pc	23 Pc
21	2 Pc	9 Aq	28 Pc	27 Pc
26	7 Pc	16 Aq	4 Ar	1 Ar

Feb. 1/Jup 7 Sg/Sat 4 Sc/Uran 8 Sg
Nep 28 Sg/Plut 30 Lb/N Node 2 Ce

	Sun	Merc	Venus	Mars
Mar. 1	10 Pc	20 Aq	8 Ar	3 Ar
6	15 Pc	28 Aq	14 Ar	7 Ar
11	20 Pc	6 Pc	20 Ar	11 Ar
16	25 Pc	15 Pc	26 Ar	15 Ar
21	0 Ar	25 Pc	2 Tr	18 Ar
26	5 Ar	4 Ar	8 Tr	22 Ar
31	10 Ar	14 Ar	14 Tr	26 Ar

Mar. 1/Jup 10 Sg/Sat 4 Sc/Uran 9 Sg
Nep 29 Sg/Plut 29 Lb/N Node 1 Ce

	Sun	Merc	Venus	Mars
Apr. 1	11 Ar	17 Ar	15 Tr	27 Ar
6	16 Ar	27 Ar	21 Tr	0 Tr
11	21 Ar	6 Tr	27 Tr	4 Tr
16	25 Ar	14 Tr	3 Gm	8 Tr
21	0 Tr	20 Tr	9 Gm	11 Tr
26	5 Tr	24 Tr	15 Gm	15 Tr

Apr. 1/Jup 11 Sg/Sat 3 Sc/Uran 9 Sg
Nep 29 Sg/Plut 29 Lb/N Node 29 Gm

	Sun	Merc	Venus	Mars
May 1	10 Tr	26 Tr	20 Gm	19 Tr
6	15 Tr	25 Tr	26 Gm	22 Tr
11	20 Tr	22 Tr	2 Ce	26 Tr
16	25 Tr	19 Tr	7 Ce	29 Tr
21	29 Tr	17 Tr	13 Ce	3 Gm
26	4 Gm	16 Tr	18 Ce	6 Gm
31	9 Gm	18 Tr	24 Ce	10 Gm

May 1/Jup 9 Sg/Sat 0 Sc/Uran 8 Sg
Nep 29 Sg/Plut 28 Lb/N Node 28 Gm

	Sun	Merc	Venus	Mars
June 1	10 Gm	18 Tr	25 Ce	11 Gm
6	15 Gm	21 Tr	0 Lo	14 Gm
11	20 Gm	26 Tr	5 Lo	18 Gm
16	24 Gm	2 Gm	10 Lo	21 Gm
21	29 Gm	10 Gm	14 Lo	24 Gm
26	4 Ce	18 Gm	19 Lo	28 Gm

June 1/Jup 6 Sg/Sat 28 Lb/Uran 7 Sg
Nep 28 Sg/Plut 27 Lb/N Node 26 Gm

	Sun	Merc	Venus	Mars
July 1	9 Ce	28 Gm	23 Lo	1 Ce
6	13 Ce	9 Ce	27 Lo	5 Ce
11	18 Ce	20 Ce	1 Vr	8 Ce
16	23 Ce	0 Lo	4 Vr	11 Ce
21	28 Ce	10 Lo	6 Vr	15 Ce
26	2 Lo	19 Lo	8 Vr	18 Ce
31	7 Lo	28 Lo	9 Vr	21 Ce

July 1/Jup 2 Sg/Sat 28 Lb/Uran 6 Sg
Nep 28 Sg/Plut 27 Lb/N Node 24 Gm

	Sun	Merc	Venus	Mars
Aug. 1	8 Lo	29 Lo	9 Vr	22 Ce
6	13 Lo	7 Vr	9 Vr	25 Ce
11	18 Lo	14 Vr	8 Vr	28 Ce
16	23 Lo	20 Vr	7 Vr	1 Lo
21	27 Lo	25 Vr	4 Vr	5 Lo
26	2 Vr	28 Vr	1 Vr	8 Lo
31	7 Vr	1 Lb	28 Lo	11 Lo

Aug. 1/Jup 1 Sg/Sat 28 Lb/Uran 5 Sg
Nep 27 Sg/Plut 27 Lb/N Node 23 Gm

1983

	Sun	Merc	Venus	Mars
Sept 1	8 Vr	1 Lb	27 Lo	12 Lo
6	13 Vr	0 Lb	25 Lo	15 Lo
11	18 Vr	27 Vr	24 Lo	18 Lo
16	23 Vr	22 Vr	23 Lo	21 Lo
21	27 Vr	18 Vr	24 Lo	24 Lo
26	2 Lb	17 Vr	25 Lo	28 Lo

Sept 1/Jup 3 Sg/Sat 1 Sc/Uran 5 Sg
Nep 26 Sg/Plut 28 Lb/N Node 21 Gm

	Sun	Merc	Venus	Mars
Oct. 1	7 Lb	19 Vr	27 Lo	1 Vr
6	12 Lb	25 Vr	0 Vr	4 Vr
11	17 Lb	3 Lb	3 Vr	7 Vr
16	22 Lb	12 Lb	7 Vr	10 Vr
21	27 Lb	20 Lb	11 Vr	13 Vr
26	2 Sc	29 Lb	16 Vr	16 Vr
31	7 Sc	7 Sc	21 Vr	19 Vr

Oct. 1/Jup 7 Sg/Sat 4 Sc/Uran 6 Sg
Nep 27 Sg/Plut 29 Lb/N Node 19 Gm

	Sun	Merc	Venus	Mars
Nov. 1	8 Sc	9 Sc	22 Vr	20 Vr
6	13 Sc	17 Sc	26 Vr	23 Vr
11	18 Sc	25 Sc	2 Lb	26 Vr
16	23 Sc	3 Sg	7 Lb	29 Vr
21	28 Sc	10 Sg	12 Lb	2 Lb
26	3 Sg	18 Sg	18 Lb	4 Lb

Nov. 1/Jup 12 Sg/Sat 7 Sc/Uran 8 Sg
Nep 27 Sg/Plut 30 Lb/N Node 18 Gm

	Sun	Merc	Venus	Mars
Dec. 1	8 Sg	25 Sg	24 Lb	7 Lb
6	13 Sg	2 Cp	29 Lb	10 Lb
11	18 Sg	9 Cp	5 Sc	13 Lb
16	23 Sg	14 Cp	11 Sc	16 Lb
21	29 Sg	17 Cp	17 Sc	19 Lb
26	4 Cp	15 Cp	23 Sc	21 Lb
31	9 Cp	9 Cp	29 Sc	24 Lb

Dec. 1/Jup 19 Sg/Sat 11 Sc/Uran 9 Sg
Nep 28 Sg/Plut 1 Sc/N Node 16 Gm

Moon's Positions

	1	4	7	10	13	16	19	22	25	28	31
Jan.	2 Lo	16 Vr	26 Lb	3 Sg	9 Cp	15 Aq	21 Pc	29 Ar	10 Gm	24 Ce	10 Vr
Feb.	24 Vr	5 Sc	12 Sg	18 Cp	23 Aq	0 Ar	8 Tr	19 Gm	3 Lo	18 Vr	
Mar.	2 Lb	13 Sc	21 Sg	26 Cp	2 Pc	10 Ar	19 Tr	29 Gm	12 Lo	26 Vr	8 Sc
Apr.	21 Sc	29 Sg	4 Aq	10 Pc	18 Ar	29 Tr	10 Ce	23 Lo	5 Lb	16 Sc	
May	24 Sg	0 Aq	6 Pc	14 Ar	24 Tr	7 Ce	20 Lo	2 Lb	12 Sc	20 Sg	27 Cp
June	8 Aq	14 Pc	22 Ar	3 Gm	16 Ce	0 Vr	12 Lb	22 Sc	29 Sg	5 Aq	
July	10 Pc	17 Ar	27 Tr	10 Ce	25 Lo	9 Lb	19 Sc	26 Sg	2 Aq	7 Pc	14 Ar
Aug.	26 Ar	5 Gm	18 Ce	4 Vr	18 Lb	28 Sc	5 Cp	11 Aq	16 Pc	23 Ar	1 Gm
Sept	15 Gm	27 Ce	12 Vr	27 Lb	7 Sg	14 Cp	19 Aq	25 Pc	3 Tr	11 Gm	
Oct.	22 Ce	6 Vr	20 Lb	2 Sg	10 Cp	16 Aq	22 Pc	29 Ar	8 Gm	19 Ce	1 Vr
Nov.	16 Vr	29 Lb	10 Sg	18 Cp	24 Aq	30 Pc	7 Tr	18 Gm	30 Ce	12 Vr	
Dec.	24 Lb	5 Sg	13 Cp	20 Aq	25 Pc	2 Tr	12 Gm	25 Ce	9 Vr	21 Lb	1 Sg

1984

```
          Sun    Merc   Venus  Mars                    Sun    Merc   Venus  Mars
Jan. 1  10 Cp   8 Cp   0 Sg  25 Lb        Feb. 1  11 Aq  19 Cp   8 Cp  10 Sc
      6  15 Cp   2 Cp   6 Sg  27 Lb              6  16 Aq  26 Cp  14 Cp  12 Sc
     11  20 Cp   0 Cp  12 Sg   0 Sc             11  21 Aq   3 Aq  20 Cp  15 Sc
     16  25 Cp   2 Cp  18 Sg   2 Sc             16  27 Aq  11 Aq  26 Cp  17 Sc
     21   0 Aq   6 Cp  24 Sg   5 Sc             21   2 Pc  19 Aq   2 Aq  19 Sc
     26   5 Aq  11 Cp   0 Cp   7 Sc             26   7 Pc  27 Aq   8 Aq  21 Sc
     31  10 Aq  17 Cp   6 Cp  10 Sc
Jan. 1/Jup 26 Sg/Sat 14 Sc/Uran 11 Sg    Feb. 1/Jup  3 Cp/Sat 16 Sc/Uran 13 Sg
Nep 29 Sg/Plut  2 Sc/N Node 15 Gm        Nep  0 Cp/Plut  2 Sc/N Node 13 Gm


          Sun    Merc   Venus  Mars                    Sun    Merc   Venus  Mars
Mar. 1  11 Pc   4 Pc  13 Aq  22 Sc        Apr. 1  11 Ar   0 Tr  22 Pc  28 Sc
      6  16 Pc  13 Pc  19 Aq  23 Sc              6  16 Ar   5 Tr  28 Pc  28 Sc
     11  21 Pc  23 Pc  26 Aq  25 Sc             11  21 Ar   7 Tr   4 Ar  28 Sc
     16  26 Pc   3 Ar   2 Pc  26 Sc             16  26 Ar   6 Tr  10 Ar  28 Sc
     21   1 Ar  12 Ar   8 Pc  27 Sc             21   1 Tr   3 Tr  16 Ar  27 Sc
     26   6 Ar  21 Ar  14 Pc  28 Sc             26   6 Tr   0 Tr  22 Ar  26 Sc
     31  10 Ar  29 Ar  20 Pc  28 Sc
Mar. 1/Jup  8 Cp/Sat 16 Sc/Uran 13 Sg    Apr. 1/Jup 12 Cp/Sat 15 Sc/Uran 13 Sg
Nep  1 Cp/Plut  2 Sc/N Node 11 Gm        Nep  1 Cp/Plut  1 Sc/N Node 10 Gm


          Sun    Merc   Venus  Mars                     Sun    Merc   Venus  Mars
May  1  11 Tr  27 Ar  29 Ar  24 Sc        June 1  11 Gm  19 Tr   7 Gm  14 Sc
      6  16 Tr  26 Ar   5 Tr  23 Sc              6  15 Gm  27 Tr  13 Gm  13 Sc
     11  20 Tr  27 Ar  11 Tr  21 Sc             11  20 Gm   6 Gm  19 Gm  12 Sc
     16  25 Tr   0 Tr  17 Tr  19 Sc             16  25 Gm  16 Gm  25 Gm  12 Sc
     21   0 Gm   5 Tr  23 Tr  17 Sc             21   0 Ce  27 Gm   1 Ce  12 Sc
     26   5 Gm  11 Tr  29 Tr  16 Sc             26   5 Ce   8 Ce   7 Ce  12 Sc
     31  10 Gm  17 Tr   5 Gm  14 Sc
May  1/Jup 13 Cp/Sat 13 Sc/Uran 13 Sg    June 1/Jup 11 Cp/Sat 11 Sc/Uran 12 Sg
Nep  1 Cp/Plut  0 Sc/N Node  8 Gm        Nep  1 Cp/Plut 30 Lb/N Node  6 Gm


          Sun    Merc   Venus  Mars                    Sun    Merc   Venus  Mars
July 1   9 Ce  19 Ce  13 Ce  13 Sc        Aug. 1   9 Lo   6 Vr  22 Lo  22 Sc
      6  14 Ce  29 Ce  20 Ce  13 Sc              6  14 Lo  10 Vr  28 Lo  24 Sc
     11  19 Ce   8 Lo  26 Ce  15 Sc             11  19 Lo  13 Vr   4 Vr  27 Sc
     16  24 Ce  16 Lo   2 Lo  16 Sc             16  23 Lo  13 Vr  10 Vr  29 Sc
     21  28 Ce  23 Lo   8 Lo  18 Sc             21  28 Lo  12 Vr  16 Vr   2 Sg
     26   3 Lo   0 Vr  14 Lo  19 Sc             26   3 Vr   8 Vr  22 Vr   4 Sg
     31   8 Lo   5 Vr  20 Lo  21 Sc             31   8 Vr   3 Vr  29 Vr   7 Sg
July 1/Jup  8 Cp/Sat 10 Sc/Uran 10 Sg    Aug. 1/Jup  4 Cp/Sat 10 Sc/Uran 10 Sg
Nep 30 Sg/Plut 29 Lb/N Node  5 Gm        Nep 29 Sg/Plut 29 Lb/N Node  3 Gm
```

1984

	Sun	Merc	Venus	Mars
Sept 1	9 Vr	3 Vr	0 Lb	8 Sg
6	14 Vr	0 Vr	6 Lb	11 Sg
11	18 Vr	1 Vr	12 Lb	14 Sg
16	23 Vr	6 Vr	18 Lb	17 Sg
21	28 Vr	13 Vr	24 Lb	20 Sg
26	3 Lb	21 Vr	0 Sc	24 Sg

Sept 1/Jup 3 Cp/Sat 12 Sc/Uran 10 Sg
Nep 29 Sg/Plut 0 Sc/N Node 2 Gm

	Sun	Merc	Venus	Mars
Oct. 1	8 Lb	0 Lb	7 Sc	27 Sg
6	13 Lb	9 Lb	13 Sc	1 Cp
11	18 Lb	18 Lb	19 Sc	4 Cp
16	23 Lb	27 Lb	25 Sc	8 Cp
21	28 Lb	5 Sc	1 Sg	11 Cp
26	3 Sc	13 Sc	7 Sg	15 Cp
31	8 Sc	20 Sc	13 Sg	18 Cp

Oct. 1/Jup 5 Cp/Sat 14 Sc/Uran 10 Sg
Nep 29 Sg/Plut 1 Sc/N Node 0 Gm

	Sun	Merc	Venus	Mars
Nov. 1	9 Sc	22 Sc	14 Sg	19 Cp
6	14 Sc	29 Sc	20 Sg	23 Cp
11	19 Sc	7 Sg	26 Sg	26 Cp
16	24 Sc	13 Sg	2 Cp	0 Aq
21	29 Sc	20 Sg	8 Cp	4 Aq
26	4 Sg	26 Sg	14 Cp	8 Aq

Nov. 1/Jup 9 Cp/Sat 18 Sc/Uran 12 Sg
Nep 29 Sg/Plut 2 Sc/N Node 28 Tr

	Sun	Merc	Venus	Mars
Dec. 1	9 Sg	0 Cp	20 Cp	11 Aq
6	14 Sg	1 Cp	26 Cp	15 Aq
11	19 Sg	27 Sg	2 Aq	19 Aq
16	24 Sg	21 Sg	8 Aq	23 Aq
21	29 Sg	16 Sg	14 Aq	27 Aq
26	4 Cp	15 Sg	20 Aq	1 Pc
31	10 Cp	17 Sg	25 Aq	4 Pc

Dec. 1/Jup 15 Cp/Sat 21 Sc/Uran 14 Sg
Nep 0 Cp/Plut 3 Sc/N Node 27 Tr

Moon's Positions

	1	4	7	10	13	16	19	22	25	28	31
Jan.	14 Sg	22 Cp	28 Aq	3 Ar	10 Tr	20 Gm	4 Lo	19 Vr	2 Sc	11 Sg	18 Cp
Feb.	0 Aq	6 Pc	12 Ar	18 Tr	28 Gm	12 Lo	28 Vr	11 Sc	21 Sg	27 Cp	
Mar.	21 Aq	27 Pc	3 Tr	10 Gm	21 Ce	5 Vr	21 Lb	4 Sg	12 Cp	18 Aq	24 Pc
Apr.	6 Ar	12 Tr	20 Gm	1 Lo	14 Vr	29 Lb	12 Sg	21 Cp	27 Aq	2 Ar	
May	9 Tr	17 Gm	27 Ce	10 Vr	23 Lb	6 Sg	16 Cp	23 Aq	29 Pc	5 Tr	13 Gm
June	27 Gm	8 Lo	20 Vr	3 Sc	15 Sg	24 Cp	1 Pc	7 Ar	13 Tr	22 Gm	
July	4 Lo	17 Vr	30 Lb	11 Sg	20 Cp	27 Aq	3 Ar	9 Tr	17 Gm	28 Ce	13 Vr
Aug.	28 Vr	10 Sc	21 Sg	29 Cp	5 Pc	11 Ar	17 Tr	25 Gm	7 Lo	22 Vr	6 Sc
Sept	21 Sc	1 Cp	8 Aq	14 Pc	20 Ar	26 Tr	3 Ce	15 Lo	0 Lb	15 Sc	
Oct.	27 Sg	5 Aq	11 Pc	17 Ar	23 Tr	30 Gm	10 Lo	23 Vr	9 Sc	22 Sg	1 Aq
Nov.	14 Aq	20 Pc	26 Ar	2 Gm	10 Ce	20 Lo	3 Lb	17 Sc	30 Sg	10 Aq	
Dec.	16 Pc	22 Ar	28 Tr	7 Ce	17 Lo	29 Vr	12 Sc	24 Sg	4 Aq	12 Pc	18 Ar

1985

```
        Sun    Merc   Venus   Mars                      Sun    Merc   Venus   Mars
Jan. 1  11 Cp  18 Sg  26 Aq   5 Pc          Feb. 1   12 Aq   0 Aq  29 Pc  29 Pc
     6  16 Cp  23 Sg   2 Pc   9 Pc               6   17 Aq   8 Aq   3 Ar   2 Ar
    11  21 Cp  29 Sg   7 Pc  13 Pc              11   22 Aq  16 Aq   8 Ar   6 Ar
    16  26 Cp   6 Cp  13 Pc  17 Pc              16   27 Aq  25 Aq  11 Ar  10 Ar
    21   1 Aq  13 Cp  18 Pc  20 Pc              21    2 Pc   4 Pc  15 Ar  14 Ar
    26   6 Aq  20 Cp  23 Pc  24 Pc              26    7 Pc  13 Pc  18 Ar  17 Ar
    31  11 Aq  28 Cp  28 Pc  28 Pc
```
Jan. 1/Jup 21 Cp/Sat 25 Sc/Uran 15 Sg   Feb. 1/Jup 29 Cp/Sat 27 Sc/Uran 17 Sg
Nep 2 Cp/Plut 4 Sc/N Node 25 Tr   Nep 3 Cp/Plut 5 Sc/N Node 24 Tr

```
        Sun    Merc   Venus   Mars                      Sun    Merc   Venus   Mars
Mar. 1  10 Pc  19 Pc  19 Ar  20 Ar          Apr. 1   11 Ar  16 Ar  16 Ar  12 Tr
     6  15 Pc  28 Pc  21 Ar  23 Ar               6   16 Ar  12 Ar  13 Ar  16 Tr
    11  20 Pc   7 Ar  22 Ar  27 Ar              11   21 Ar   8 Ar  10 Ar  19 Tr
    16  25 Pc  14 Ar  22 Ar   1 Tr              16   26 Ar   7 Ar   8 Ar  23 Tr
    21   0 Ar  18 Ar  21 Ar   4 Tr              21    1 Tr   7 Ar   6 Ar  26 Tr
    26   5 Ar  19 Ar  19 Ar   8 Tr              26    6 Tr  10 Ar   6 Ar   0 Gm
    31  10 Ar  16 Ar  17 Ar  11 Tr
```
Mar. 1/Jup 5 Aq/Sat 28 Sc/Uran 18 Sg   Apr. 1/Jup 11 Aq/Sat 28 Sc/Uran 18 Sg
Nep 3 Cp/Plut 5 Sc/N Node 22 Tr   Nep 4 Cp/Plut 4 Sc/N Node 20 Tr

```
        Sun    Merc   Venus   Mars                      Sun    Merc   Venus   Mars
May  1  11 Tr  14 Ar   7 Ar   3 Gm          June 1   10 Gm   2 Gm  25 Ar  24 Gm
     6  15 Tr  19 Ar   8 Ar   7 Gm               6   15 Gm  13 Gm   0 Tr  28 Gm
    11  20 Tr  26 Ar  10 Ar  10 Gm              11   20 Gm  24 Gm   4 Tr   1 Ce
    16  25 Tr   3 Tr  13 Ar  14 Gm              16   25 Gm   5 Ce   9 Tr   4 Ce
    21   0 Gm  11 Tr  17 Ar  17 Gm              21    0 Ce  15 Ce  14 Tr   8 Ce
    26   5 Gm  20 Tr  20 Ar  20 Gm              26    4 Ce  24 Ce  19 Tr  11 Ce
    31  10 Gm   0 Gm  24 Ar  24 Gm
```
May 1/Jup 15 Aq/Sat 26 Sc/Uran 17 Sg   June 1/Jup 17 Aq/Sat 24 Sc/Uran 16 Sg
Nep 3 Cp/Plut 3 Sc/N Node 19 Tr   Nep 3 Cp/Plut 2 Sc/N Node 17 Tr

```
        Sun    Merc   Venus   Mars                      Sun    Merc   Venus   Mars
July 1   9 Ce   2 Lo  24 Tr  14 Ce          Aug. 1    9 Lo  25 Lo  28 Gm   4 Lo
     6  14 Ce   9 Lo   0 Gm  18 Ce               6   13 Lo  22 Lo   4 Ce   8 Lo
    11  19 Ce  15 Lo   5 Gm  21 Ce              11   18 Lo  18 Lo  10 Ce  11 Lo
    16  23 Ce  20 Lo  11 Gm  24 Ce              16   23 Lo  15 Lo  16 Ce  14 Lo
    21  28 Ce  23 Lo  16 Gm  27 Ce              21   28 Lo  13 Lo  22 Ce  17 Lo
    26   3 Lo  25 Lo  22 Gm   1 Lo              26    3 Vr  15 Lo  27 Ce  20 Lo
    31   8 Lo  25 Lo  27 Gm   4 Lo              31    8 Vr  20 Lo   3 Lo  24 Lo
```
July 1/Jup 16 Aq/Sat 22 Sc/Uran 15 Sg   Aug. 1/Jup 12 Aq/Sat 21 Sc/Uran 14 Sg
Nep 2 Cp/Plut 2 Sc/N Node 16 Tr   Nep 1 Cp/Plut 2 Sc/N Node 14 Tr

1985

```
          Sun    Merc   Venus  Mars                    Sun    Merc   Venus  Mars
Sept 1   9 Vr   21 Lo   5 Lo   24 Lo        Oct. 1    8 Lb   14 Lb  11 Vr   13 Vr
     6  13 Vr   29 Lo  11 Lo   27 Lo             6   13 Lb   22 Lb  17 Vr   16 Vr
    11  18 Vr    8 Vr  17 Lo    1 Vr            11   18 Lb    0 Sc  23 Vr   20 Vr
    16  23 Vr   17 Vr  23 Lo    4 Vr            16   23 Lb    8 Sc  29 Vr   23 Vr
    21  28 Vr   26 Vr  29 Lo    7 Vr            21   28 Lb   15 Sc   6 Lb   26 Vr
    26   3 Lb    5 Lb   5 Vr   10 Vr            26    3 Sc   22 Sc  12 Lb   29 Vr
                                               31    8 Sc   29 Sc  18 Lb    2 Lb
```

Sept 1/Jup 9 Aq/Sat 23 Sc/Uran 14 Sg   Oct. 1/Jup 7 Aq/Sat 25 Sc/Uran 15 Sg
Nep 1 Cp/Plut 3 Sc/N Node 12 Tr   Nep 1 Cp/Plut 4 Sc/N Node 11 Tr

```
          Sun    Merc   Venus  Mars                    Sun    Merc   Venus  Mars
Nov. 1   9 Sc    0 Sg  19 Lb    3 Lb        Dec. 1    9 Sg    4 Sg  27 Sc   21 Lb
     6  14 Sc    6 Sg  25 Lb    6 Lb             6   14 Sg   29 Sc   3 Sg   25 Lb
    11  19 Sc   11 Sg   2 Sc    9 Lb            11   19 Sg   29 Sc   9 Sg   28 Lb
    16  24 Sc   14 Sg   8 Sc   12 Lb            16   24 Sg    3 Sg  16 Sg    1 Sc
    21  29 Sc   15 Sg  14 Sc   15 Lb            21   29 Sg    8 Sg  22 Sg    4 Sc
    26   4 Sg   10 Sg  21 Sc   18 Lb            26    4 Cp   15 Sg  28 Sg    7 Sc
                                               31    9 Cp   21 Sg   5 Cp   10 Sc
```

Nov. 1/Jup 8 Aq/Sat 28 Sc/Uran 16 Sg   Dec. 1/Jup 12 Aq/Sat 2 Sg/Uran 18 Sg
Nep 2 Cp/Plut 5 Sc/N Node 9 Tr   Nep 2 Cp/Plut 6 Sc/N Node 7 Tr

Moon's Positions

```
         1        4        7       10       13       16       19       22       25       28       31
Jan.  30 Ar    6 Gm   15 Ce   27 Lo   10 Lb   22 Sc    3 Cp   13 Aq   20 Pc   26 Ar    2 Gm
Feb.  14 Gm   24 Ce    7 Vr   21 Lb    3 Sg   13 Cp   21 Aq   28 Pc    4 Tr    9 Gm
Mar.  22 Gm    1 Lo   15 Vr    0 Sc   13 Sg   23 Cp    1 Pc    7 Ar   12 Tr   18 Gm   26 Ce
Apr.  10 Lo   23 Vr    9 Sc   23 Sg    3 Aq   10 Pc   16 Ar   21 Tr   27 Gm    5 Lo
May   17 Vr    2 Sc   17 Sg   29 Cp    7 Pc   13 Ar   18 Tr   24 Cm    2 Lo   13 Vr   26 Lb
June  10 Sc   25 Sg    7 Aq   15 Pc   21 Ar   27 Tr    3 Ce   12 Lo   23 Vr    6 Sc
July  19 Sg    1 Aq   11 Pc   17 Ar   23 Tr   30 Gm    9 Lo   20 Vr    2 Sc   15 Sg   26 Cp
Aug.  10 Aq   19 Pc   25 Ar    1 Gm    8 Ce   18 Lo    0 Lb   13 Sc   25 Sg    6 Aq   15 Pc
Sept  27 Pc    3 Tr    9 Gm   16 Ce   26 Lo    9 Lb   24 Sc    6 Cp   16 Aq   24 Pc
Oct.  30 Ar    5 Gm   11 Ce   20 Lo    3 Lb   18 Sc    2 Cp   13 Aq   20 Pc   27 Ar    2 Gm
Nov.  14 Gm   20 Ce   29 Lo   11 Lb   26 Sc   11 Cp   22 Aq   30 Pc    5 Tr   11 Gm
Dec.  17 Ce   25 Lo    5 Lb   19 Sc    4 Cp   17 Aq   26 Pc    2 Tr    8 Gm   14 Ce   22 Lo
```

                                                      Ephemeris

1986

	Sun	Merc	Venus	Mars
Jan. 1	10 Cp	23 Sg	6 Cp	11 Sc
6	15 Cp	0 Cp	12 Cp	14 Sc
11	20 Cp	8 Cp	18 Cp	17 Sc
16	26 Cp	16 Cp	25 Cp	20 Sc
21	1 Aq	23 Cp	1 Aq	23 Sc
26	6 Aq	2 Aq	7 Aq	26 Sc
31	11 Aq	10 Aq	14 Aq	29 Sc

Jan. 1/Jup 18 Aq/Sat 5 Sg/Uran 20 Sg
Nep 4 Cp/Plut 7 Sc/N Node 6 Tr

	Sun	Merc	Venus	Mars
Feb. 1	12 Aq	12 Aq	15 Aq	29 Sc
6	17 Aq	21 Aq	21 Aq	2 Sg
11	22 Aq	0 Pc	27 Aq	5 Sg
16	27 Aq	9 Pc	4 Pc	8 Sg
21	2 Pc	17 Pc	10 Pc	11 Sg
26	7 Pc	25 Pc	16 Pc	14 Sg

Feb. 1/Jup 25 Aq/Sat 8 Sg/Uran 21 Sg
Nep 5 Cp/Plut 7 Sc/N Node 4 Tr

	Sun	Merc	Venus	Mars
Mar. 1	10 Pc	28 Pc	20 Pc	15 Sg
6	15 Pc	1 Ar	26 Pc	18 Sg
11	20 Pc	0 Ar	2 Ar	21 Sg
16	25 Pc	27 Pc	9 Ar	24 Sg
21	0 Ar	22 Pc	15 Ar	26 Sg
26	5 Ar	19 Pc	21 Ar	29 Sg
31	10 Ar	18 Pc	27 Ar	1 Cp

Mar. 1/Jup 2 Pc/Sat 9 Sg/Uran 22 Sg
Nep 5 Cp/Plut 7 Sc/N Node 3 Tr

	Sun	Merc	Venus	Mars
Apr. 1	11 Ar	18 Pc	28 Ar	2 Cp
6	16 Ar	20 Pc	5 Tr	4 Cp
11	21 Ar	23 Pc	11 Tr	7 Cp
16	26 Ar	28 Pc	17 Tr	9 Cp
21	1 Tr	4 Ar	23 Tr	11 Cp
26	5 Tr	11 Ar	29 Tr	13 Cp

Apr. 1/Jup 9 Pc/Sat 10 Sg/Uran 22 Sg
Nep 6 Cp/Plut 7 Sc/N Node 1 Tr

	Sun	Merc	Venus	Mars
May 1	10 Tr	19 Ar	5 Gm	15 Cp
6	15 Tr	27 Ar	11 Gm	17 Cp
11	20 Tr	7 Tr	17 Gm	18 Cp
16	25 Tr	17 Tr	23 Gm	20 Cp
21	0 Gm	27 Tr	29 Gm	21 Cp
26	4 Gm	8 Gm	5 Ce	22 Cp
31	9 Gm	19 Gm	11 Ce	23 Cp

May 1/Jup 15 Pc/Sat 8 Sg/Uran 22 Sg
Nep 6 Cp/Plut 6 Sc/N Node 29 Ar

	Sun	Merc	Venus	Mars
June 1	10 Gm	21 Gm	12 Ce	23 Cp
6	15 Gm	1 Ce	18 Ce	23 Cp
11	20 Gm	10 Ce	24 Ce	23 Cp
16	25 Gm	17 Ce	0 Lo	23 Cp
21	29 Gm	24 Ce	6 Lo	22 Cp
26	4 Ce	29 Ce	12 Lo	21 Cp

June 1/Jup 20 Pc/Sat 6 Sg/Uran 21 Sg
Nep 5 Cp/Plut 5 Sc/N Node 28 Ar

	Sun	Merc	Venus	Mars
July 1	9 Ce	3 Lo	18 Lo	20 Cp
6	14 Ce	6 Lo	24 Lo	19 Cp
11	18 Ce	6 Lo	29 Lo	17 Cp
16	23 Ce	5 Lo	5 Vr	16 Cp
21	28 Ce	2 Lo	11 Vr	15 Cp
26	3 Lo	29 Ce	16 Vr	13 Cp
31	8 Lo	26 Ce	22 Vr	12 Cp

July 1/Jup 23 Pc/Sat 4 Sg/Uran 20 Sg
Nep 4 Cp/Plut 5 Sc/N Node 26 Ar

	Sun	Merc	Venus	Mars
Aug. 1	8 Lo	26 Ce	23 Vr	12 Cp
6	13 Lo	26 Ce	28 Vr	12 Cp
11	18 Lo	29 Ce	3 Lb	11 Cp
16	23 Lo	5 Lo	9 Lb	12 Cp
21	28 Lo	13 Lo	14 Lb	12 Cp
26	2 Vr	22 Lo	19 Lb	13 Cp
31	7 Vr	2 Vr	23 Lb	14 Cp

Aug. 1/Jup 22 Pc/Sat 3 Sg/Uran 19 Sg
Nep 4 Cp/Plut 5 Sc/N Node 25 Ar

1986

```
          Sun    Merc   Venus   Mars                    Sun    Merc   Venus   Mars
Sept 1    8 Vr   4 Vr   24 Lb   14 Cp        Oct. 1    8 Lb   26 Lb   17 Sc   26 Cp
     6   13 Vr  13 Vr   29 Lb   15 Cp              6   12 Lb    3 Sc   19 Sc   28 Cp
    11   18 Vr  23 Vr    3 Sc   17 Cp             11   17 Lb   10 Sc   20 Sc    1 Aq
    16   23 Vr   2 Lb    7 Sc   19 Cp             16   22 Lb   16 Sc   20 Sc    4 Aq
    21   28 Vr  10 Lb   11 Sc   21 Cp             21   27 Lb   22 Sc   20 Sc    7 Aq
    26    3 Lb  18 Lb   14 Sc   23 Cp             26    2 Sc   26 Sc   18 Sc   10 Aq
                                                 31    7 Sc   29 Sc   16 Sc   13 Aq
```

Sept 1/Jup 19 Pc/Sat 4 Sg/Uran 18 Sg   Oct. 1/Jup 15 Pc/Sat 5 Sg/Uran 19 Sg
Nep 3 Cp/Plut 5 Sc/N Node 23 Ar   Nep 3 Cp/Plut 6 Sc/N Node 21 Ar

```
          Sun    Merc   Venus   Mars                    Sun    Merc   Venus   Mars
Nov. 1    8 Sc   29 Sc   15 Sc   14 Aq        Dec. 1    8 Sg   18 Sc    5 Sc    3 Pc
     6   13 Sc  28 Sc   12 Sc   17 Aq              6   14 Sg   24 Sc    7 Sc    7 Pc
    11   18 Sc  23 Sc    9 Sc   20 Aq             11   19 Sg    1 Sg    9 Sc   10 Pc
    16   23 Sc  17 Sc    7 Sc   23 Aq             16   24 Sg    9 Sg   12 Sc   14 Pc
    21   28 Sc  13 Sc    5 Sc   27 Aq             21   29 Sg   16 Sg   15 Sc   17 Pc
    26    3 Sg  14 Sc    5 Sc    0 Pc             26    4 Cp   24 Sg   19 Sc   21 Pc
                                                 31    9 Cp    2 Cp   23 Sc   24 Pc
```

Nov. 1/Jup 13 Pc/Sat 8 Sg/Uran 20 Sg   Dec. 1/Jup 14 Pc/Sat 12 Sg/Uran 22 Sg
Nep 4 Cp/Plut 7 Sc/N Node 20 Ar   Nep 5 Cp/Plut 9 Sc/N Node 18 Ar

Moon's Positions

	1	4	7	10	13	16	19	22	25	28	31
Jan.	5 Vr	16 Lb	28 Sc	12 Cp	25 Aq	4 Ar	10 Tr	16 Gm	23 Ce	2 Vr	12 Lb
Feb.	26 Lb	9 Sg	21 Cp	3 Pc	12 Ar	18 Tr	24 Gm	1 Lo	11 Vr	23 Lb	
Mar.	7 Sc	19 Sg	1 Aq	12 Pc	20 Ar	26 Tr	1 Ce	9 Lo	19 Vr	2 Sc	16 Sg
Apr.	0 Cp	12 Aq	21 Pc	28 Ar	4 Gm	10 Ce	17 Lo	27 Vr	11 Sc	26 Sg	
May	9 Aq	18 Pc	25 Ar	1 Gm	6 Ce	13 Lo	22 Vr	4 Sc	20 Sg	4 Aq	15 Pc
June	28 Pc	4 Tr	10 Gm	15 Ce	22 Lo	1 Lb	13 Sc	28 Sg	13 Aq	24 Pc	
July	1 Tr	7 Gm	12 Ce	19 Lo	27 Vr	8 Sc	22 Sg	7 Aq	19 Pc	27 Ar	3 Gm
Aug.	15 Gm	21 Ce	29 Lo	8 Lb	19 Sc	2 Cp	15 Aq	27 Pc	5 Tr	11 Gm	17 Ce
Sept	29 Ce	8 Vr	18 Lb	30 Sc	12 Cp	25 Aq	5 Ar	13 Tr	19 Gm	25 Ce	
Oct.	3 Vr	13 Lb	26 Sc	9 Cp	21 Aq	1 Ar	9 Tr	15 Gm	21 Ce	28 Lo	7 Lb
Nov.	21 Lb	5 Sg	20 Cp	1 Pc	10 Ar	18 Tr	24 Gm	29 Ce	6 Vr	15 Lb	
Dec.	29 Sc	14 Cp	28 Aq	8 Ar	15 Tr	21 Gm	26 Ce	2 Vr	10 Lb	22 Sc	7 Cp

                                                                                                 Ephemeris

1987

	Sun	Merc	Venus	Mars
Jan. 1	10 Cp	3 Cp	24 Sc	25 Pc
6	15 Cp	11 Cp	29 Sc	28 Pc
11	20 Cp	19 Cp	3 Sg	2 Ar
16	25 Cp	27 Cp	8 Sg	5 Ar
21	0 Aq	6 Aq	14 Sg	9 Ar
26	5 Aq	14 Aq	19 Sg	12 Ar
31	11 Aq	23 Aq	24 Sg	16 Ar

Jan. 1/Jup 18 Pc/Sat 15 Sg/Uran 24 Sg
Nep 6 Cp/Plut 9 Sc/N Node 16 Ar

	Sun	Merc	Venus	Mars
Feb. 1	12 Aq	25 Aq	25 Sg	16 Ar
6	17 Aq	3 Pc	1 Cp	20 Ar
11	22 Aq	10 Pc	7 Cp	23 Ar
16	27 Aq	14 Pc	12 Cp	27 Ar
21	2 Pc	14 Pc	18 Cp	0 Tr
26	7 Pc	10 Pc	24 Cp	4 Tr

Feb. 1/Jup 23 Pc/Sat 18 Sg/Uran 25 Sg
Nep 7 Cp/Plut 10 Sc/N Node 15 Ar

	Sun	Merc	Venus	Mars
Mar. 1	10 Pc	7 Pc	27 Cp	6 Tr
6	15 Pc	3 Pc	3 Aq	9 Tr
11	20 Pc	0 Pc	9 Aq	13 Tr
16	25 Pc	0 Pc	15 Aq	16 Tr
21	0 Ar	3 Pc	21 Aq	19 Tr
26	5 Ar	7 Pc	27 Aq	23 Tr
31	10 Ar	12 Pc	3 Pc	26 Tr

Mar. 1/Jup 30 Pc/Sat 20 Sg/Uran 26 Sg
Nep 8 Cp/Plut 10 Sc/N Node 13 Ar

	Sun	Merc	Venus	Mars
Apr. 1	11 Ar	14 Pc	4 Pc	27 Tr
6	16 Ar	20 Pc	10 Pc	0 Gm
11	21 Ar	27 Pc	16 Pc	4 Gm
16	25 Ar	5 Ar	22 Pc	7 Gm
21	0 Tr	14 Ar	28 Pc	10 Gm
26	5 Tr	23 Ar	4 Ar	14 Gm

Apr. 1/Jup 7 Ar/Sat 21 Sg/Uran 27 Sg
Nep 8 Cp/Plut 9 Sc/N Node 12 Ar

	Sun	Merc	Venus	Mars
May 1	10 Tr	3 Tr	10 Ar	17 Gm
6	15 Tr	13 Tr	16 Ar	20 Gm
11	20 Tr	24 Tr	22 Ar	23 Gm
16	25 Tr	5 Gm	28 Ar	27 Gm
21	29 Tr	15 Gm	4 Tr	0 Ce
26	4 Gm	24 Gm	10 Tr	3 Ce
31	9 Gm	1 Ce	16 Tr	6 Ce

May 1/Jup 14 Ar/Sat 20 Sg/Uran 26 Sg
Nep 8 Cp/Plut 9 Sc/N Node 10 Ar

	Sun	Merc	Venus	Mars
June 1	10 Gm	3 Ce	18 Tr	7 Ce
6	15 Gm	8 Ce	24 Tr	10 Ce
11	20 Gm	13 Ce	0 Gm	14 Ce
16	24 Gm	16 Ce	6 Gm	17 Ce
21	29 Gm	17 Ce	12 Gm	20 Ce
26	4 Ce	16 Ce	18 Gm	23 Ce

June 1/Jup 21 Ar/Sat 18 Sg/Uran 25 Sg
Nep 7 Cp/Plut 8 Sc/N Node 8 Ar

	Sun	Merc	Venus	Mars
July 1	9 Ce	14 Ce	24 Gm	26 Ce
6	13 Ce	11 Ce	0 Ce	0 Lo
11	18 Ce	8 Ce	6 Ce	3 Lo
16	23 Ce	7 Ce	12 Ce	6 Lo
21	28 Ce	9 Ce	19 Ce	9 Lo
26	3 Lo	13 Ce	25 Ce	12 Lo
31	7 Lo	19 Ce	1 Lo	15 Lo

July 1/Jup 26 Ar/Sat 16 Sg/Uran 24 Sg
Nep 7 Cp/Plut 7 Sc/N Node 7 Ar

	Sun	Merc	Venus	Mars
Aug. 1	8 Lo	20 Ce	2 Lo	16 Lo
6	13 Lo	28 Ce	8 Lo	19 Lo
11	18 Lo	8 Lo	14 Lo	22 Lo
16	23 Lo	18 Lo	21 Lo	26 Lo
21	27 Lo	28 Lo	27 Lo	29 Lo
26	2 Vr	8 Vr	3 Vr	2 Vr
31	7 Vr	17 Vr	9 Vr	5 Vr

Aug. 1/Jup 29 Ar/Sat 15 Sg/Uran 23 Sg
Nep 6 Cp/Plut 7 Sc/N Node 5 Ar

1987

```
            Sun    Merc    Venus    Mars                      Sun    Merc    Venus    Mars
Sept  1    8 Vr   19 Vr   10 Vr    6 Vr        Oct.  1    7 Lb    3 Sc   18 Lb   25 Vr
      6   13 Vr   27 Vr   17 Vr    9 Vr              6   12 Lb    8 Sc   24 Lb   28 Vr
     11   18 Vr    5 Lb   23 Vr   12 Vr             11   17 Lb   11 Sc    0 Sc    1 Lb
     16   23 Vr   13 Lb   29 Vr   15 Vr             16   22 Lb   13 Sc    6 Sc    5 Lb
     21   27 Vr   20 Lb    5 Lb   19 Vr             21   27 Lb   12 Sc   13 Sc    8 Lb
     26    2 Lb   27 Lb   12 Lb   22 Vr             26    2 Sc    7 Sc   19 Sc   11 Lb
                                                   31    7 Sc    1 Sc   25 Sc   14 Lb

Sept  1/Jup 29 Ar/Sat 15 Sg/Uran 23 Sg        Oct.  1/Jup 27 Ar/Sat 16 Sg/Uran 23 Sg
Nep  5 Cp/Plut  8 Sc/N Node  4 Ar             Nep  5 Cp/Plut  9 Sc/N Node  2 Ar


            Sun    Merc    Venus    Mars                      Sun    Merc    Venus    Mars
Nov.  1    8 Sc    0 Sc   26 Sc   15 Lb        Dec.  1    8 Sg   26 Sc    4 Cp    4 Sc
      6   13 Sc   27 Lb    3 Sg   18 Lb              6   13 Sg    4 Sg   10 Cp    8 Sc
     11   18 Sc   29 Lb    9 Sg   21 Lb             11   18 Sg   12 Sg   16 Cp   11 Sc
     16   23 Sc    4 Sc   15 Sg   25 Lb             16   23 Sg   19 Sg   22 Cp   14 Sc
     21   28 Sc   11 Sc   21 Sg   28 Lb             21   29 Sg   27 Sg   28 Cp   18 Sc
     26    3 Sg   18 Sc   27 Sg    1 Sc             26    4 Cp    5 Cp    5 Aq   21 Sc
                                                   31    9 Cp   13 Cp   11 Aq   24 Sc

Nov.  1/Jup 23 Ar/Sat 19 Sg/Uran 24 Sg        Dec.  1/Jup 20 Ar/Sat 22 Sg/Uran 26 Sg
Nep  6 Cp/Plut 10 Sc/N Node  0 Ar             Nep  7 Cp/Plut 11 Sc/N Node 29 Pc
```

Moon's Positions

	1	4	7	10	13	16	19	22	25	28	31
Jan.	22 Cp	7 Pc	17 Ar	24 Tr	29 Gm	5 Lo	12 Vr	20 Lb	1 Sg	15 Cp	0 Pc
Feb.	15 Pc	25 Ar	2 Gm	8 Ce	14 Lo	21 Vr	30 Lb	11 Sg	24 Cp	8 Pc	
Mar.	23 Pc	3 Tr	10 Gm	16 Ce	22 Lo	0 Lb	10 Sc	22 Sg	5 Aq	17 Pc	28 Ar
Apr.	11 Tr	18 Gm	24 Ce	0 Vr	9 Lb	20 Sc	3 Cp	15 Aq	27 Pc	6 Tr	
May	14 Gm	20 Ce	26 Lo	4 Lb	15 Sc	28 Sg	12 Aq	24 Pc	3 Tr	10 Gm	16 Ce
June	28 Ce	4 Vr	12 Lb	23 Sc	8 Cp	22 Aq	4 Ar	13 Tr	19 Gm	25 Ce	
July	1 Vr	7 Lb	17 Sc	1 Cp	17 Aq	30 Pc	10 Tr	16 Gm	22 Ce	28 Lo	4 Lb
Aug.	17 Lb	26 Sc	9 Cp	25 Aq	9 Ar	19 Tr	25 Gm	1 Lo	7 Vr	14 Lb	22 Sc
Sept	6 Sg	19 Cp	3 Pc	17 Ar	27 Tr	4 Ce	9 Lo	16 Vr	23 Lb	3 Sg	
Oct.	15 Cp	28 Aq	11 Ar	22 Tr	30 Gm	6 Lo	12 Vr	19 Lb	29 Sc	11 Cp	24 Aq
Nov.	8 Pc	20 Ar	30 Tr	8 Ce	13 Lo	19 Vr	27 Lb	9 Sg	22 Cp	5 Pc	
Dec.	16 Ar	26 Tr	3 Ce	10 Lo	15 Vr	22 Lb	3 Sg	17 Cp	1 Pc	13 Ar	22 Tr

1988

```
        Sun    Merc   Venus  Mars
Jan. 1  10 Cp  15 Cp  12 Aq  25 Sc
     6  15 Cp  23 Cp  18 Aq  28 Sc
    11  20 Cp   1 Aq  24 Aq   2 Sg
    16  25 Cp   9 Aq   0 Pc   5 Sg
    21   0 Aq  17 Aq   7 Pc   8 Sg
    26   5 Aq  24 Aq  13 Pc  12 Sg
    31  10 Aq  28 Aq  19 Pc  15 Sg
```
Jan. 1/Jup 20 Ar/Sat 25 Sg/Uran 28 Sg
Nep 8 Cp/Plut 12 Sc/N Node 27 Pc

```
        Sun    Merc   Venus  Mars
Feb. 1  11 Aq  28 Aq  20 Pc  16 Sg
     6  16 Aq  27 Aq  26 Pc  19 Sg
    11  21 Aq  22 Aq   2 Ar  22 Sg
    16  27 Aq  16 Aq   8 Ar  26 Sg
    21   2 Pc  13 Aq  13 Ar  29 Sg
    26   7 Pc  13 Aq  19 Ar   2 Cp
```
Feb. 1/Jup 23 Ar/Sat 29 Sg/Uran 29 Sg
Nep 9 Cp/Plut 13 Sc/N Node 26 Pc

```
        Sun    Merc   Venus  Mars
Mar. 1  11 Pc  15 Aq  24 Ar   5 Cp
     6  16 Pc  18 Aq   0 Tr   8 Cp
    11  21 Pc  23 Aq   5 Tr  12 Cp
    16  26 Pc  29 Aq  11 Tr  15 Cp
    21   1 Ar   6 Pc  16 Tr  19 Cp
    26   6 Ar  14 Pc  21 Tr  22 Cp
    31  11 Ar  22 Pc  26 Tr  25 Cp
```
Mar. 1/Jup 28 Ar/Sat 1 Cp/Uran 1 Cp
Nep 10 Cp/Plut 13 Sc/N Node 24 Pc

```
        Sun    Merc   Venus  Mars
Apr. 1  11 Ar  23 Pc  27 Tr  26 Cp
     6  16 Ar   2 Ar   2 Gm  29 Cp
    11  21 Ar  11 Ar   7 Gm   3 Aq
    16  26 Ar  21 Ar  11 Gm   6 Aq
    21   1 Tr   2 Tr  16 Gm   9 Aq
    26   6 Tr  12 Tr  19 Gm  13 Aq
```
Apr. 1/Jup 5 Tr/Sat 2 Cp/Uran 1 Cp
Nep 10 Cp/Plut 12 Sc/N Node 22 Pc

```
        Sun    Merc   Venus  Mars
May  1  11 Tr  23 Tr  23 Gm  16 Aq
     6  16 Tr   2 Gm  26 Gm  19 Aq
    11  21 Tr  10 Gm  28 Gm  23 Aq
    16  25 Tr  17 Gm   0 Ce  26 Aq
    21   0 Gm  22 Gm   0 Ce  29 Aq
    26   5 Gm  25 Gm   0 Ce   2 Pc
    31  10 Gm  27 Gm  29 Gm   5 Pc
```
May 1/Jup 12 Tr/Sat 2 Cp/Uran 1 Cp
Nep 10 Cp/Plut 11 Sc/N Node 21 Pc

```
         Sun    Merc   Venus  Mars
June 1  11 Gm  27 Gm  29 Gm   6 Pc
     6  16 Gm  26 Gm  26 Gm   9 Pc
    11  20 Gm  24 Gm  23 Gm  12 Pc
    16  25 Gm  21 Gm  20 Gm  15 Pc
    21   0 Ce  19 Gm  18 Gm  18 Pc
    26   5 Ce  18 Gm  15 Gm  21 Pc
```
June 1/Jup 20 Tr/Sat 1 Cp/Uran 30 Sg
Nep 10 Cp/Plut 10 Sc/N Node 19 Pc

```
         Sun    Merc   Venus  Mars
July 1   9 Ce  20 Gm  14 Gm  24 Pc
     6  14 Ce  23 Gm  14 Gm  26 Pc
    11  19 Ce  28 Gm  15 Gm  29 Pc
    16  24 Ce   5 Ce  16 Gm   1 Ar
    21  28 Ce  14 Ce  19 Gm   3 Ar
    26   3 Lo  24 Ce  21 Gm   5 Ar
    31   8 Lo   4 Lo  25 Gm   7 Ar
```
July 1/Jup 26 Tr/Sat 28 Sg/Uran 29 Sg
Nep 9 Cp/Plut 10 Sc/N Node 18 Pc

```
         Sun    Merc   Venus  Mars
Aug. 1   9 Lo   7 Lo  25 Gm   7 Ar
     6  14 Lo  17 Lo  29 Gm   9 Ar
    11  19 Lo  27 Lo   3 Ce  10 Ar
    16  23 Lo   6 Vr   8 Ce  11 Ar
    21  28 Lo  15 Vr  12 Ce  11 Ar
    26   3 Vr  23 Vr  17 Ce  11 Ar
    31   8 Vr   0 Lb  22 Ce  11 Ar
```
Aug. 1/Jup 2 Gm/Sat 27 Sg/Uran 28 Sg
Nep 8 Cp/Plut 10 Sc/N Node 16 Pc

1988

	Sun	Merc	Venus	Mars
Sept 1	9 Vr	2 Lb	23 Ce	11 Ar
6	14 Vr	8 Lb	28 Ce	11 Ar
11	18 Vr	15 Lb	4 Lo	10 Ar
16	23 Vr	20 Lb	9 Lo	9 Ar
21	28 Vr	24 Lb	15 Lo	7 Ar
26	3 Lb	27 Lb	20 Lo	6 Ar

Sept 1/Jup 5 Gm/Sat 26 Sg/Uran 27 Sg
Nep 8 Cp/Plut 10 Sc/N Node 14 Pc

	Sun	Merc	Venus	Mars
Oct. 1	8 Lb	27 Lb	26 Lo	4 Ar
6	13 Lb	24 Lb	2 Vr	3 Ar
11	18 Lb	18 Lb	7 Vr	2 Ar
16	23 Lb	13 Lb	13 Vr	1 Ar
21	28 Lb	12 Lb	19 Vr	0 Ar
26	3 Sc	14 Lb	25 Vr	0 Ar
31	8 Sc	20 Lb	1 Lb	0 Ar

Oct. 1/Jup 6 Gm/Sat 27 Sg/Uran 27 Sg
Nep 7 Cp/Plut 11 Sc/N Node 13 Pc

	Sun	Merc	Venus	Mars
Nov. 1	9 Sc	22 Lb	2 Lb	0 Ar
6	14 Sc	29 Lb	9 Lb	0 Ar
11	19 Sc	7 Sc	15 Lb	1 Ar
16	24 Sc	15 Sc	21 Lb	2 Ar
21	29 Sc	23 Sc	27 Lb	3 Ar
26	4 Sg	1 Sg	3 Sc	5 Ar

Nov. 1/Jup 4 Gm/Sat 29 Sg/Uran 28 Sg
Nep 8 Cp/Plut 12 Sc/N Node 11 Pc

	Sun	Merc	Venus	Mars
Dec. 1	9 Sg	9 Sg	9 Sc	7 Ar
6	14 Sg	17 Sg	15 Sc	8 Ar
11	19 Sg	25 Sg	22 Sc	10 Ar
16	24 Sg	2 Cp	28 Sc	13 Ar
21	29 Sg	10 Cp	4 Sg	15 Ar
26	4 Cp	18 Cp	10 Sg	17 Ar
31	10 Cp	26 Cp	17 Sg	20 Ar

Dec. 1/Jup 30 Tr/Sat 2 Cp/Uran 30 Sg
Nep 9 Cp/Plut 14 Sc/N Node 9 Pc

Moon's Positions

	1	4	7	10	13	16	19	22	25	28	31
Jan.	5 Gm	12 Ce	18 Lo	23 Vr	0 Sc	11 Sg	25 Cp	10 Pc	23 Ar	2 Gm	9 Ce
Feb.	21 Ce	27 Lo	2 Lb	9 Sc	19 Sg	3 Aq	18 Pc	2 Tr	11 Gm	18 Ce	
Mar.	12 Lo	17 Vr	24 Lb	2 Sg	13 Cp	26 Aq	11 Ar	24 Tr	2 Ce	8 Lo	14 Vr
Apr.	26 Vr	3 Sc	12 Sg	23 Cp	6 Pc	19 Ar	2 Gm	10 Ce	17 Lo	22 Vr	
May	29 Lb	8 Sg	20 Cp	2 Pc	14 Ar	26 Tr	6 Ce	13 Lo	18 Vr	25 Lb	4 Sg
June	18 Sg	0 Aq	13 Pc	25 Ar	5 Gm	14 Ce	21 Lo	26 Vr	3 Sc	12 Sg	
July	25 Cp	9 Pc	22 Ar	2 Gm	10 Ce	17 Lo	22 Vr	28 Lb	7 Sg	19 Cp	4 Pc
Aug.	19 Pc	2 Tr	12 Gm	20 Ce	26 Lo	1 Lb	7 Sc	15 Sg	27 Cp	13 Pc	27 Ar
Sept	12 Tr	22 Gm	29 Ce	5 Vr	10 Lb	16 Sc	25 Sg	6 Aq	21 Pc	6 Tr	
Oct.	18 Gm	26 Ce	1 Vr	7 Lb	13 Sc	21 Sg	2 Aq	15 Pc	29 Ar	12 Gm	22 Ce
Nov.	4 Lo	10 Vr	15 Lb	23 Sc	2 Cp	12 Aq	24 Pc	8 Tr	20 Gm	30 Ce	
Dec.	6 Vr	11 Lb	18 Sc	28 Sg	9 Aq	21 Pc	3 Tr	15 Gm	25 Ce	2 Vr	7 Lb

1989

		Sun	Merc	Venus	Mars
Jan.	1	11 Cp	27 Cp	18 Sg	20 Ar
	6	16 Cp	4 Aq	24 Sg	23 Ar
	11	21 Cp	10 Aq	0 Cp	25 Ar
	16	26 Cp	12 Aq	7 Cp	28 Ar
	21	1 Aq	10 Aq	13 Cp	1 Tr
	26	6 Aq	4 Aq	19 Cp	4 Tr
	31	11 Aq	28 Cp	25 Cp	7 Tr

Jan. 1/Jup 27 Tr/Sat 6 Cp/Uran 2 Cp
Nep 10 Cp/Plut 15 Sc/N Node 8 Pc

		Sun	Merc	Venus	Mars
Feb.	1	12 Aq	28 Cp	27 Cp	7 Tr
	6	17 Aq	26 Cp	3 Aq	10 Tr
	11	22 Aq	27 Cp	9 Aq	13 Tr
	16	27 Aq	1 Aq	15 Aq	16 Tr
	21	2 Pc	6 Aq	22 Aq	19 Tr
	26	7 Pc	12 Aq	28 Aq	22 Tr

Feb. 1/Jup 26 Tr/Sat 9 Cp/Uran 3 Cp
Nep 11 Cp/Plut 15 Sc/N Node 6 Pc

		Sun	Merc	Venus	Mars
Mar.	1	10 Pc	16 Aq	2 Pc	24 Tr
	6	15 Pc	23 Aq	8 Pc	27 Tr
	11	20 Pc	0 Pc	14 Pc	0 Gm
	16	25 Pc	8 Pc	20 Pc	3 Gm
	21	0 Ar	17 Pc	27 Pc	6 Gm
	26	5 Ar	26 Pc	3 Ar	9 Gm
	31	10 Ar	6 Ar	9 Ar	12 Gm

Mar. 1/Jup 29 Tr/Sat 12 Cp/Uran 5 Cp
Nep 12 Cp/Plut 15 Sc/N Node 5 Pc

		Sun	Merc	Venus	Mars
Apr.	1	11 Ar	8 Ar	10 Ar	13 Gm
	6	16 Ar	18 Ar	16 Ar	16 Gm
	11	21 Ar	28 Ar	23 Ar	19 Gm
	16	26 Ar	8 Tr	29 Ar	22 Gm
	21	1 Tr	18 Tr	5 Tr	25 Gm
	26	6 Tr	25 Tr	11 Tr	28 Gm

Apr. 1/Jup 3 Gm/Sat 14 Cp/Uran 5 Cp
Nep 12 Cp/Plut 15 Sc/N Node 3 Pc

		Sun	Merc	Venus	Mars
May	1	11 Tr	1 Gm	17 Tr	1 Ce
	6	15 Tr	5 Gm	24 Tr	4 Ce
	11	20 Tr	7 Gm	0 Gm	7 Ce
	16	25 Tr	6 Gm	6 Gm	10 Ce
	21	0 Gm	4 Gm	12 Gm	14 Ce
	26	5 Gm	2 Gm	18 Gm	17 Ce
	31	10 Gm	29 Tr	24 Gm	20 Ce

May 1/Jup 10 Gm/Sat 14 Cp/Uran 5 Cp
Nep 12 Cp/Plut 14 Sc/N Node 1 Pc

		Sun	Merc	Venus	Mars
June	1	10 Gm	29 Tr	25 Gm	20 Ce
	6	15 Gm	28 Tr	2 Ce	23 Ce
	11	20 Gm	29 Tr	8 Ce	27 Ce
	16	25 Gm	2 Gm	14 Ce	0 Lo
	21	0 Ce	7 Gm	20 Ce	3 Lo
	26	4 Ce	13 Gm	26 Ce	6 Lo

June 1/Jup 17 Gm/Sat 13 Cp/Uran 4 Cp
Nep 12 Cp/Plut 13 Sc/N Node 30 Aq

		Sun	Merc	Venus	Mars
July	1	9 Ce	21 Gm	2 Lo	9 Lo
	6	14 Ce	0 Ce	8 Lo	12 Lo
	11	19 Ce	10 Ce	14 Lo	15 Lo
	16	23 Ce	21 Ce	20 Lo	18 Lo
	21	28 Ce	1 Lo	26 Lo	21 Lo
	26	3 Lo	12 Lo	2 Vr	25 Lo
	31	8 Lo	21 Lo	8 Vr	28 Lo

July 1/Jup 23 Gm/Sat 11 Cp/Uran 3 Cp
Nep 11 Cp/Plut 13 Sc/N Node 28 Aq

		Sun	Merc	Venus	Mars
Aug.	1	9 Lo	23 Lo	10 Vr	28 Lo
	6	14 Lo	2 Vr	16 Vr	2 Vr
	11	18 Lo	10 Vr	22 Vr	5 Vr
	16	23 Lo	17 Vr	28 Vr	8 Vr
	21	28 Lo	24 Vr	3 Lb	11 Vr
	26	3 Vr	0 Lb	9 Lb	14 Vr
	31	8 Vr	5 Lb	15 Lb	17 Vr

Aug. 1/Jup 0 Ce/Sat 9 Cp/Uran 2 Cp
Nep 10 Cp/Plut 12 Sc/N Node 27 Aq

1989

```
           Sun    Merc    Venus   Mars                    Sun    Merc    Venus   Mars
Sept 1    9 Vr   6 Lb   16 Lb   18 Vr      Oct. 1    8 Lb   27 Vr   21 Sc    7 Lb
     6   13 Vr   9 Lb   22 Lb   21 Vr           6   13 Lb   26 Vr   27 Sc   11 Lb
    11   18 Vr  11 Lb   28 Lb   24 Vr          11   18 Lb    0 Lb    3 Sg   14 Lb
    16   23 Vr  10 Lb    4 Sc   28 Vr          16   23 Lb    6 Lb    8 Sg   17 Lb
    21   28 Vr   6 Lb   10 Sc    1 Lb          21   28 Lb   14 Lb   14 Sg   21 Lb
    26    3 Lb   1 Lb   16 Sc    4 Lb          26    3 Sc   22 Lb   19 Sg   24 Lb
                                               31    8 Sc    1 Sc   24 Sg   27 Lb
```

Sept 1/Jup 6 Ce/Sat 7 Cp/Uran 1 Cp   Oct. 1/Jup 10 Ce/Sat 8 Cp/Uran 2 Cp
Nep 10 Cp/Plut 13 Sc/N Node 25 Aq   Nep 10 Cp/Plut 14 Sc/N Node 23 Aq

```
           Sun    Merc    Venus   Mars                    Sun    Merc    Venus   Mars
Nov. 1    9 Sc   2 Sc   25 Sg   28 Lb      Dec. 1    9 Sg   20 Sg   24 Cp   18 Sc
     6   14 Sc  11 Sc    1 Cp    1 Sc           6   14 Sg   28 Sg   27 Cp   22 Sc
    11   19 Sc  19 Sc    6 Cp    5 Sc          11   19 Sg    5 Cp    0 Aq   25 Sc
    16   24 Sc  27 Sc   10 Cp    8 Sc          16   24 Sg   12 Cp    3 Aq   28 Sc
    21   29 Sc   4 Sg   15 Cp   11 Sc          21   29 Sg   19 Cp    5 Aq    2 Sg
    26    4 Sg  12 Sg   19 Cp   15 Sc          26    4 Cp   24 Cp    6 Aq    5 Sg
                                               31    9 Cp   26 Cp    6 Aq    9 Sg
```

Nov. 1/Jup 11 Ce/Sat 9 Cp/Uran 2 Cp   Dec. 1/Jup 9 Ce/Sat 12 Cp/Uran 4 Cp
Nep 10 Cp/Plut 15 Sc/N Node 22 Aq   Nep 11 Cp/Plut 16 Sc/N Node 20 Aq

Moon's Positions

```
         1        4        7       10       13       16       19       22       25       28       31
Jan.  19 Lb   26 Sc    6 Cp   19 Aq    2 Ar   14 Tr   25 Gm    3 Lo   10 Vr   15 Lb   21 Sc
Feb.   4 Sg   14 Cp   28 Aq   12 Ar   25 Tr    4 Ce   12 Lo   18 Vr   24 Lb   30 Sc
Mar.  12 Sg   22 Cp    6 Pc   21 Ar    4 Gm   14 Ce   21 Lo   27 Vr    2 Sc    9 Sg   17 Cp
Apr.   1 Aq   14 Pc   29 Ar   13 Gm   23 Ce    0 Vr    6 Lb   11 Sc   18 Sg   27 Cp
May    8 Pc   23 Ar    7 Gm   19 Ce   27 Lo    2 Lb    8 Sc   15 Sg   24 Cp    4 Pc   17 Ar
June   2 Tr   16 Gm   27 Ce    5 Vr   11 Lb   17 Sc   24 Sg    4 Aq   15 Pc   28 Ar
July  11 Gm   22 Ce    0 Vr    7 Lb   12 Sc   20 Sg   30 Cp   12 Pc   25 Ar    7 Gm   18 Ce
Aug.   1 Lo    9 Vr   15 Lb   20 Sc   28 Sg    8 Aq   21 Pc    5 Tr   17 Gm   27 Ce    5 Vr
Sept  17 Vr   23 Lb   29 Sc    6 Cp   16 Aq    0 Ar   15 Tr   28 Gm    7 Lo   14 Vr
Oct.  20 Lb   25 Sc    2 Cp   11 Aq   23 Pc    9 Tr   23 Gm    4 Lo   11 Vr   17 Lb   22 Sc
Nov.   4 Sg   11 Cp   20 Aq    2 Ar   17 Tr    2 Ce   13 Lo   20 Vr   25 Lb    1 Sg
Dec.   8 Cp   16 Aq   27 Pc   11 Tr   25 Gm    8 Lo   16 Vr   22 Lb   28 Sc    5 Cp   13 Aq
```

1990

	Sun	Merc	Venus	Mars
Jan. 1	10 Cp	26 Cp	6 Aq	10 Sg
6	15 Cp	22 Cp	5 Aq	13 Sg
11	20 Cp	16 Cp	3 Aq	17 Sg
16	26 Cp	11 Cp	0 Aq	20 Sg
21	1 Aq	10 Cp	27 Cp	24 Sg
26	6 Aq	12 Cp	25 Cp	27 Sg
31	11 Aq	16 Cp	22 Cp	1 Cp

Jan. 1/Jup 5 Ce/Sat 16 Cp/Uran 6 Cp
Nep 12 Cp/Plut 17 Sc/N Node 18 Aq

	Sun	Merc	Venus	Mars
Feb. 1	12 Aq	17 Cp	22 Cp	2 Cp
6	17 Aq	22 Cp	21 Cp	5 Cp
11	22 Aq	29 Cp	21 Cp	9 Cp
16	27 Aq	5 Aq	22 Cp	13 Cp
21	2 Pc	13 Aq	24 Cp	16 Cp
26	7 Pc	21 Aq	26 Cp	20 Cp

Feb. 1/Jup 2 Ce/Sat 19 Cp/Uran 8 Cp
Nep 13 Cp/Plut 18 Sc/N Node 17 Aq

	Sun	Merc	Venus	Mars
Mar. 1	10 Pc	25 Aq	28 Cp	22 Cp
6	15 Pc	4 Pc	2 Aq	26 Cp
11	20 Pc	13 Pc	5 Aq	0 Aq
16	25 Pc	22 Pc	10 Aq	3 Aq
21	0 Ar	2 Ar	14 Aq	7 Aq
26	5 Ar	12 Ar	19 Aq	11 Aq
31	10 Ar	22 Ar	24 Aq	14 Aq

Mar. 1/Jup 1 Ce/Sat 22 Cp/Uran 9 Cp
Nep 14 Cp/Plut 18 Sc/N Node 15 Aq

	Sun	Merc	Venus	Mars
Apr. 1	11 Ar	24 Ar	25 Aq	15 Aq
6	16 Ar	3 Tr	0 Pc	19 Aq
11	21 Ar	10 Tr	5 Pc	23 Aq
16	26 Ar	15 Tr	10 Pc	26 Aq
21	1 Tr	17 Tr	15 Pc	0 Pc
26	6 Tr	17 Tr	21 Pc	4 Pc

Apr. 1/Jup 3 Ce/Sat 24 Cp/Uran 10 Cp
Nep 15 Cp/Plut 17 Sc/N Node 14 Aq

	Sun	Merc	Venus	Mars
May 1	10 Tr	15 Tr	26 Pc	8 Pc
6	15 Tr	12 Tr	2 Ar	11 Pc
11	20 Tr	9 Tr	8 Ar	15 Pc
16	25 Tr	8 Tr	13 Ar	19 Pc
21	0 Gm	9 Tr	19 Ar	22 Pc
26	5 Gm	11 Tr	25 Ar	26 Pc
31	9 Gm	15 Tr	1 Tr	0 Ar

May 1/Jup 7 Ce/Sat 25 Cp/Uran 9 Cp
Nep 15 Cp/Plut 17 Sc/N Node 12 Aq

	Sun	Merc	Venus	Mars
June 1	10 Gm	16 Tr	2 Tr	1 Ar
6	15 Gm	22 Tr	8 Tr	4 Ar
11	20 Gm	28 Tr	14 Tr	8 Ar
16	25 Gm	7 Gm	19 Tr	11 Ar
21	29 Gm	16 Gm	25 Tr	15 Ar
26	4 Ce	26 Gm	1 Gm	19 Ar

June 1/Jup 13 Ce/Sat 25 Cp/Uran 9 Cp
Nep 14 Cp/Plut 16 Sc/N Node 10 Aq

	Sun	Merc	Venus	Mars
July 1	9 Ce	7 Ce	7 Gm	22 Ar
6	14 Ce	18 Ce	13 Gm	25 Ar
11	18 Ce	28 Ce	19 Gm	29 Ar
16	23 Ce	8 Lo	25 Gm	2 Tr
21	28 Ce	17 Lo	1 Ce	6 Tr
26	3 Lo	25 Lo	7 Ce	9 Tr
31	8 Lo	2 Vr	13 Ce	12 Tr

July 1/Jup 19 Ce/Sat 23 Cp/Uran 8 Cp
Nep 13 Cp/Plut 15 Sc/N Node 9 Aq

	Sun	Merc	Venus	Mars
Aug. 1	9 Lo	4 Vr	14 Ce	13 Tr
6	13 Lo	10 Vr	20 Ce	16 Tr
11	18 Lo	15 Vr	26 Ce	19 Tr
16	23 Lo	20 Vr	3 Lo	22 Tr
21	28 Lo	23 Vr	9 Lo	24 Tr
26	3 Vr	24 Vr	15 Lo	27 Tr
31	7 Vr	22 Vr	21 Lo	0 Gm

Aug. 1/Jup 26 Ce/Sat 21 Cp/Uran 6 Cp
Nep 13 Cp/Plut 15 Sc/N Node 7 Aq

1990

	Sun	Merc	Venus	Mars
Sept 1	8 Vr	22 Vr	22 Lo	0 Gm
6	13 Vr	17 Vr	28 Lo	3 Gm
11	18 Vr	13 Vr	5 Vr	5 Gm
16	23 Vr	10 Vr	11 Vr	7 Gm
21	28 Vr	11 Vr	17 Vr	9 Gm
26	3 Lb	15 Vr	23 Vr	10 Gm

Sept 1/Jup 3 Lo/Sat 19 Cp/Uran 6 Cp
Nep 12 Cp/Plut 15 Sc/N Node 6 Aq

	Sun	Merc	Venus	Mars
Oct. 1	8 Lb	22 Vr	29 Vr	12 Gm
6	12 Lb	0 Lb	6 Lb	13 Gm
11	17 Lb	9 Lb	12 Lb	14 Gm
16	22 Lb	18 Lb	18 Lb	14 Gm
21	27 Lb	27 Lb	24 Lb	15 Gm
26	2 Sc	5 Sc	1 Sc	14 Gm
31	7 Sc	13 Sc	7 Sc	14 Gm

Oct. 1/Jup 8 Lo/Sat 19 Cp/Uran 6 Cp
Nep 12 Cp/Plut 16 Sc/N Node 4 Aq

	Sun	Merc	Venus	Mars
Nov. 1	8 Sc	14 Sc	8 Sc	14 Gm
6	13 Sc	22 Sc	14 Sc	13 Gm
11	18 Sc	0 Sg	21 Sc	11 Gm
16	23 Sc	8 Sg	27 Sc	10 Gm
21	28 Sc	15 Sg	3 Sg	8 Gm
26	3 Sg	22 Sg	10 Sg	6 Gm

Nov. 1/Jup 12 Lo/Sat 20 Cp/Uran 7 Cp
Nep 12 Cp/Plut 17 Sc/N Node 2 Aq

	Sun	Merc	Venus	Mars
Dec. 1	9 Sg	29 Sg	16 Sg	4 Gm
6	14 Sg	5 Cp	22 Sg	2 Gm
11	19 Sg	9 Cp	28 Sg	1 Gm
16	24 Sg	10 Cp	5 Cp	0 Gm
21	29 Sg	6 Cp	11 Cp	29 Tr
26	4 Cp	0 Cp	17 Cp	28 Tr
31	9 Cp	25 Sg	23 Cp	28 Tr

Dec. 1/Jup 14 Lo/Sat 22 Cp/Uran 8 Cp
Nep 13 Cp/Plut 19 Sc/N Node 1 Aq

Moon's Positions

	1	4	7	10	13	16	19	22	25	28	31
Jan.	27 Aq	8 Ar	20 Tr	4 Ce	15 Lo	24 Vr	30 Lb	6 Sg	13 Cp	23 Aq	4 Ar
Feb.	18 Ar	1 Gm	13 Ce	23 Lo	1 Lb	8 Sc	13 Sg	21 Cp	1 Pc	14 Ar	
Mar.	29 Ar	12 Gm	23 Ce	2 Vr	10 Lb	16 Sc	21 Sg	29 Cp	9 Pc	23 Ar	8 Gm
Apr.	22 Gm	3 Lo	12 Vr	18 Lb	24 Sc	30 Sg	7 Aq	17 Pc	2 Tr	17 Gm	
May	30 Ce	9 Vr	15 Lb	21 Sc	27 Sg	3 Aq	12 Pc	25 Ar	11 Gm	25 Ce	5 Vr
June	18 Vr	24 Lb	30 Sc	6 Cp	13 Aq	22 Pc	4 Tr	19 Gm	3 Lo	14 Vr	
July	21 Lb	27 Sc	3 Cp	10 Aq	19 Pc	0 Tr	14 Gm	27 Ce	9 Vr	17 Lb	23 Sc
Aug.	5 Sg	11 Cp	19 Aq	29 Pc	11 Tr	24 Gm	6 Lo	17 Vr	25 Lb	1 Sg	7 Cp
Sept	19 Cp	28 Aq	9 Ar	22 Tr	5 Ce	16 Lo	25 Vr	3 Sc	9 Sg	15 Cp	
Oct.	22 Aq	4 Ar	18 Tr	1 Ce	13 Lo	22 Vr	29 Lb	5 Sg	11 Cp	17 Aq	27 Pc
Nov.	12 Ar	27 Tr	11 Ce	23 Lo	1 Lb	8 Sc	14 Sg	19 Cp	26 Aq	6 Ar	
Dec.	20 Tr	5 Ce	19 Lo	28 Vr	5 Sc	11 Sg	17 Cp	23 Aq	1 Ar	13 Tr	28 Gm